	Motorway with junction number			**Railway station**
	Primary route – dual/single carriageway		**D**	**Docklands Light Railway station**
	A road – dual/single carriageway			**Private railway station**
	B road – dual/single carriageway			**Bus, coach station**
	Minor road – dual/single carriageway			**Ambulance station**
	Other minor road – dual/single carriageway			**Coastguard station**
	Road under construction			**Fire station**
	Pedestrianised area			**Police station**
DY7	**Postcode boundaries**			**Accident and Emergency entrance to hospital**
	County and unitary authority boundaries		**H**	**Hospital**
	Railway			**Place of worship**
	Railway under construction			**Information Centre** (open all year)
	Tramway, miniature railway		**P**	**Parking**
	Rural track, private road or narrow road in urban area		**P&R**	**Park and Ride**
	Gate or obstruction to traffic (restrictions may not apply at all times or to all vehicles)		**PO**	**Post Office**
	Path, bridleway, byway open to all traffic, road used as a public path			**Camping site**
	The representation in this atlas of a road, track or path is no evidence of the existence right of way			**Caravan site**
				Golf course
	Adjoining page indicators			**Picnic site**
			Prim Sch	**Important buildings, schools, colleges, universities and hospitals**
			River Medway	**Water name**
				Stream
				River or canal – minor and major

Walsall

174
94

Allot Gdns	**Allotments**	Meml	**Memorial**	
Acad	**Academy**			
Cemy	**Cemetery**			
C Ctr	**Civic Centre**			
CH	**Club House**			
Coll	**College**			
Crem	**Crematorium**			
Ent	**Enterprise**			
Ex H	**Exhibition Hall**			
Ind Est	**Industrial Estate**			
Inst	**Institute**			
Ct	**Law Court**			
L Ctr	**Leisure Centre**	Trad Est	**Trading Estate**	*House*
LC	**Level Crossing**	Univ	**University**	
Liby	**Library**	Wks	**Works**	
Mkt	**Market**	YH	**Youth Hostel**	VILLA

Non-Roman antiquity

Roman antiquity

The dark grey border on the inside edge of some pages indicates that the mapping does not continue onto the adjacent page

■ The small numbers around the edges of the maps identify the 1 kilometre National Grid lines

The scale of the maps is 3.92 cm to 1 km
2½ inches to 1 mile 1: 25344

0	¼	½	¾	1 mile
0	250m	500m	750m	1 kilometre

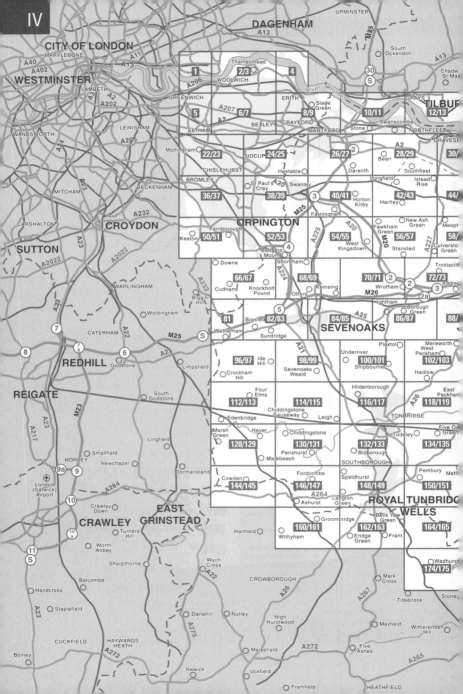

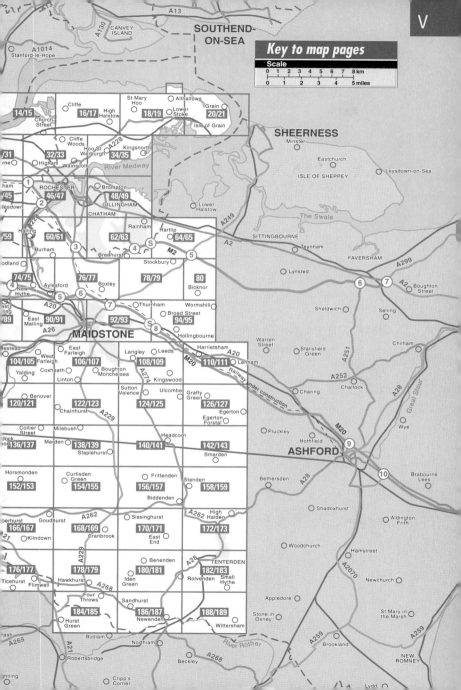

Route planning

Scale

| 0 | 1 | 2 | 3 | 4 | 5 | 6 | 7 | 8 km |
| 0 | | 1 | | 2 | | 3 | | 4 | 5 miles |

Major administrative and Postcode boundaries

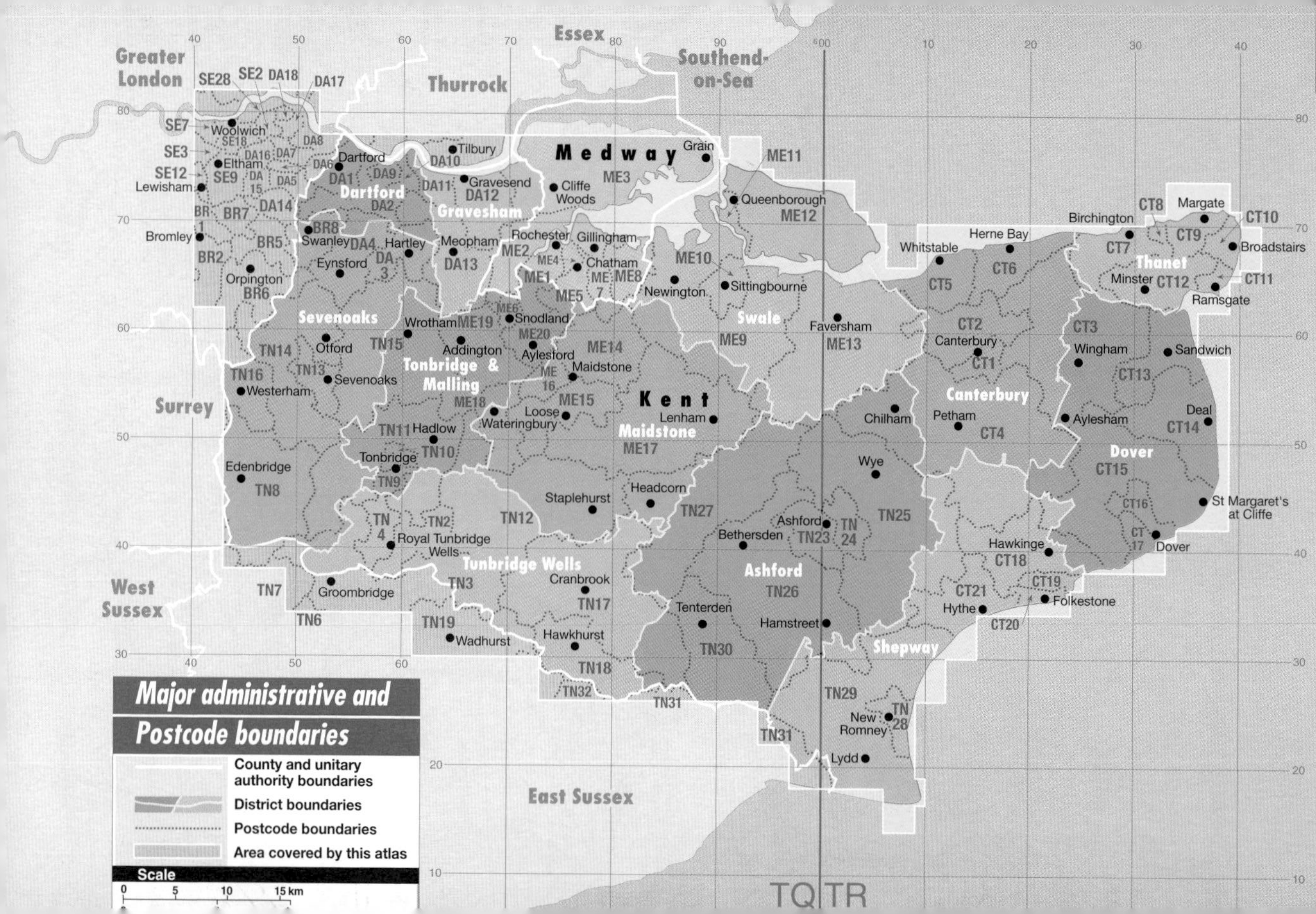

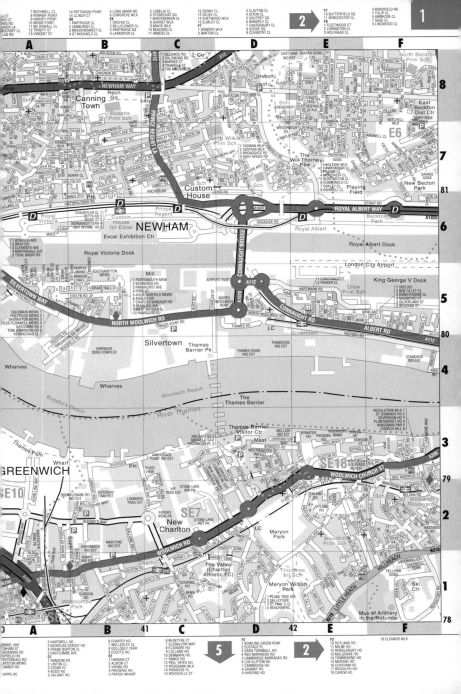

A2
1 PRESTON HO
2 LINDSAY HO
3 FRASER HO
4 PICKERING HO
5 GRINLING HO
6 WATERGATE HO
7 GLEBE HO
8 ELLISTON HO
9 SLATER CL
10 JIM BRADLEY CL
11 SIR MARTIN BOWES HO
12 CASTLE RD
13 BATHWAY
14 POLYTECHNIC ST

B1
1 BRANHAM HO
2 FORD HO
3 WILFORD HO
4 PARKER HO
5 WEAVER HO
6 TWISS HO
7 HEWETT HO

B2
1 CHURCHILL HO
2 GENERAL GORDON PL
3 CENTRAL CT
4 ASHLAR PL
5 BINGHAM POINT
6 TROY CT
7 EARDLEY POINT
8 ORMSBY POINT
9 HAVEN LODGE

B2
10 GREEN LAWNS
11 SCOTTS PASSAGE

C1
1 GLENMOUNT PATH
2 CLAYMILL HO
3 GEORGE AKASS HO

D1
1 BERT REILLY HO
2 EMMANUEL HO
3 HEAVITREE CL

E1
1 WILLOWFIELDS CL
2 FOX HOLLOW CL
3 GOLDSMID ST

F1
1 MARBLE HO
2 CRYSTAL HO
3 BERYL HO
4 GALENA HO
5 RUSHEYMEAD HO

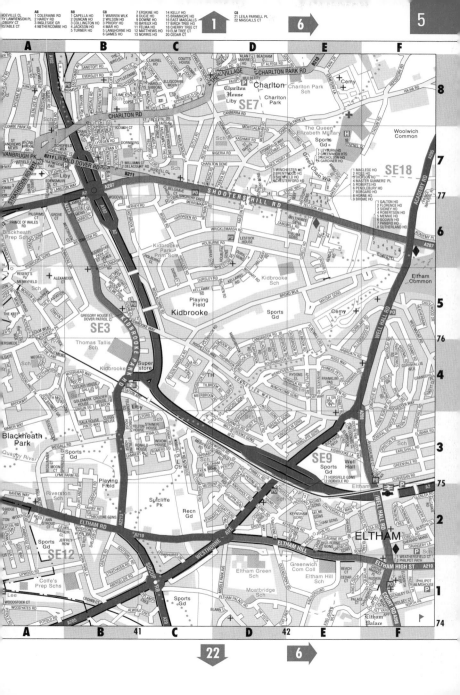

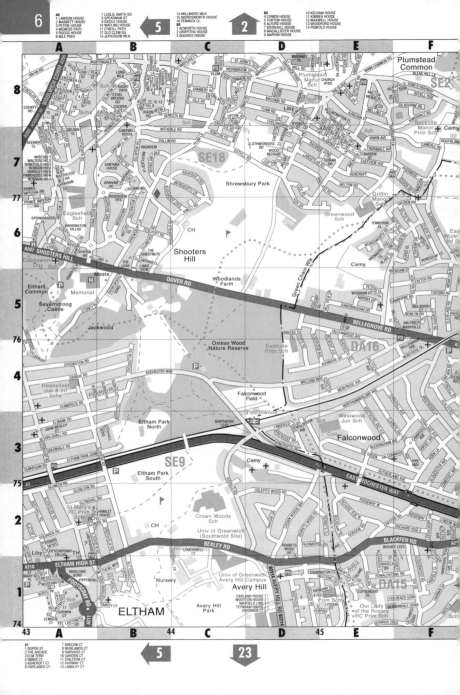

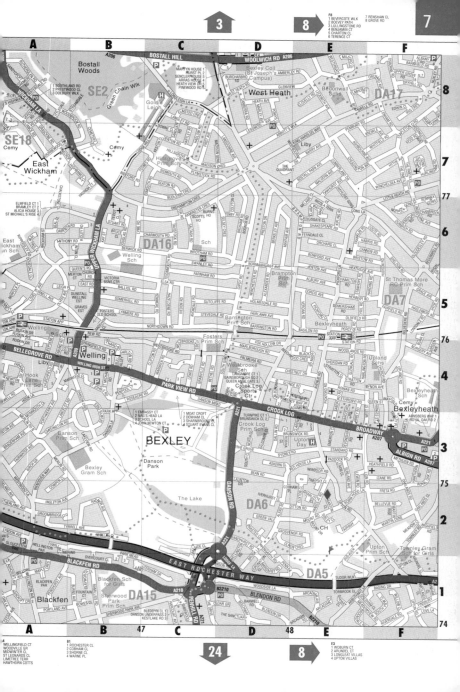

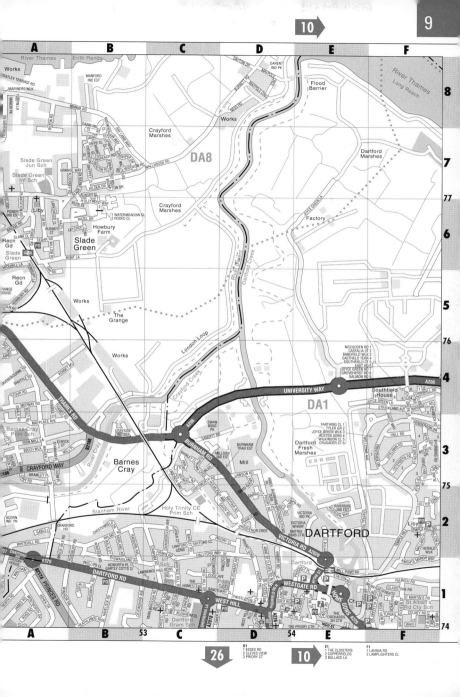

Purfleet

RM19

RM20

RM 20

Paper Mills

LONDON ROAD PURFLEET

A1090

LINDEN

HUTSON TERR

STONEHOUSE LA

STONEHOUSE CNR

A202

LONDON ROAD WEST THURROCK

EASTERN AVE

THE GLAD BSNS CTR

WATERSDALE IND PARK

THURROCK BSNS CTR Wks

Purfleet Thames Terminal

Wks

OLIVER CL

LC

Sewage Works

Jetties

River Thames
Long Reach

Jetties

Chy

Jetty

Littlebrook Power Sta

Dartford Tunnel

Tanks

Crossways

Pontoon

DA1

Littlebrook Nature Park

CANTERBURY WAY

Queen Elizabeth 2 Bridge

EDISONS PK

Freightliner Terminal

Cemy

A206

UNIVERSITY WAY

WODEHOUSE RD
WORDSWORTH WAY

A3
1 WILKINSON CL
2 MACMILLAN GDNS
3 NIGHTINGALE GR
4 PEPYS CL
5 BOXWOOD CT
6 RIVER VIEW

Tolls

CLIPPER BVD

CROSSWAYS BVD

CLARE CAUSEWAY

A2

CHAUCER WAY

Marsh St

Temple Hill

ANCHOR BVD

Crossways

ST MARY'S RD

CHARLES ST

Stone Crossing

BELL CL

Stone

DA2

DARTFORD

R3228

A2
1 KNIGHTS MANOR WAY
2 REDWOOD CT
3 BEECH CT
4 CHURCHILL PK
5 ASPEN CT

COTTON LA

ORCHARD TERR

LOWER CHURCH HILL 1
UPPER CHURCH HILL 2

A2
1 JACKSON CL
2 SUTHERLAND CL
3 RICHARDSON CL

UNICORN WLK

DA9

Archery House

BOW ARROW LA

Little Brook

Rifle & Pistol Ranges

TA Ctr

Horns Cross

Milestone Sch

Stone House

Stone Lodge Farm Park

LONDON RD

A226

Recn Gd

HEDGE PLACE RD

PLANTATION CL

BLUEWATER PARKWAY

New Town

COLYER RD

CARRINGTON RD

FULWICH RD

BOW ARROW LA

Bow Arrow

BEVIS CL

ALAMEIN RD

A226

A2

A206

8
77
7
6
77
6
5
76
4
3
75
2
1
74

A B C D E F

55 56 C 57

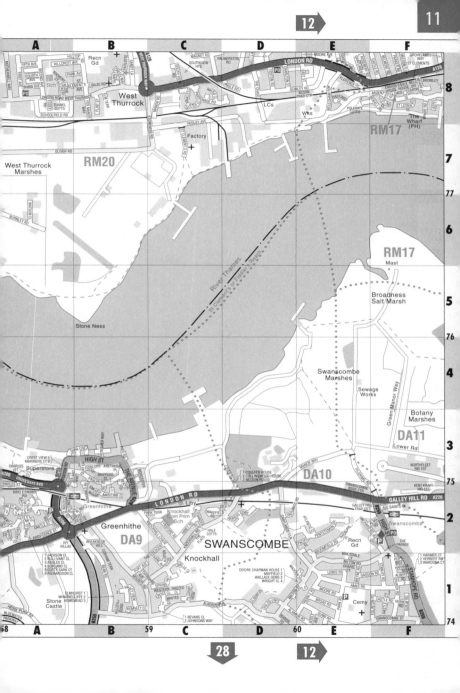

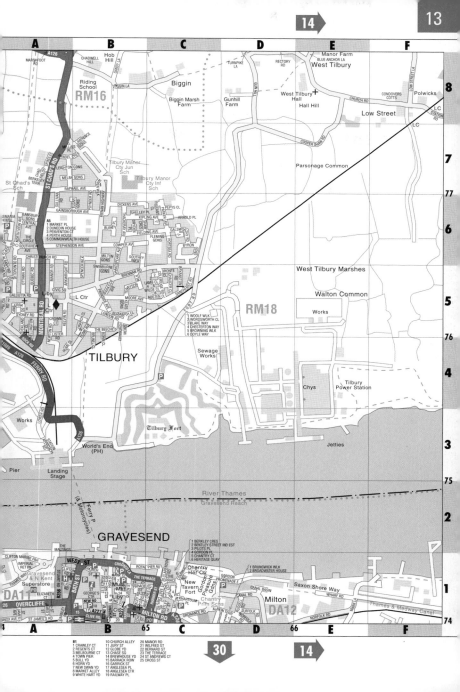

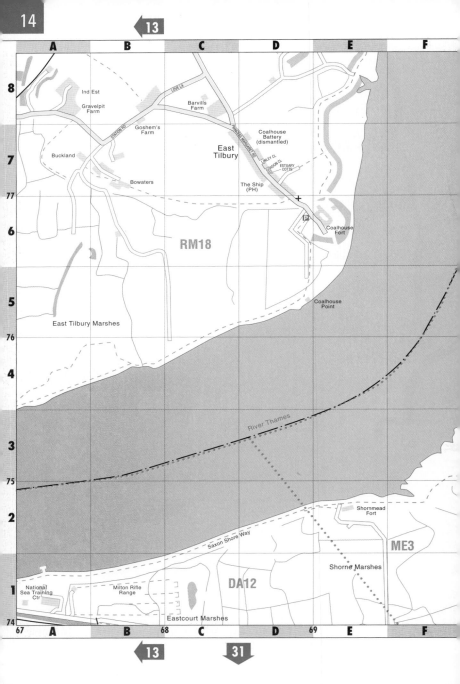

| | **A** | **B** | **C** | **D** | **E** | **F** |

8

Ind Est

Gravelpit
Farm

LOVE LA

Barvills
Farm

7

STATION RD

Goshem's
Farm

PRINCE MARGARET RD

Coalhouse
Battery
(dismantled)

East
Tilbury

Buckland

LINLEY CL

LONDON CL

ESTUARY
COTTS

Bowaters

77

The Ship
(PH)

+

RM18

P

Coalhouse
Fort

6

5

Coalhouse
Point

East Tilbury Marshes

76

4

River Thames

3

75

Saxon Shore Way

2

Shornmead
Fort

ME3

Shorne Marshes

DA12

1

National
Sea Training
Ctr

Milton Rifle
Range

Eastcourt Marshes

74

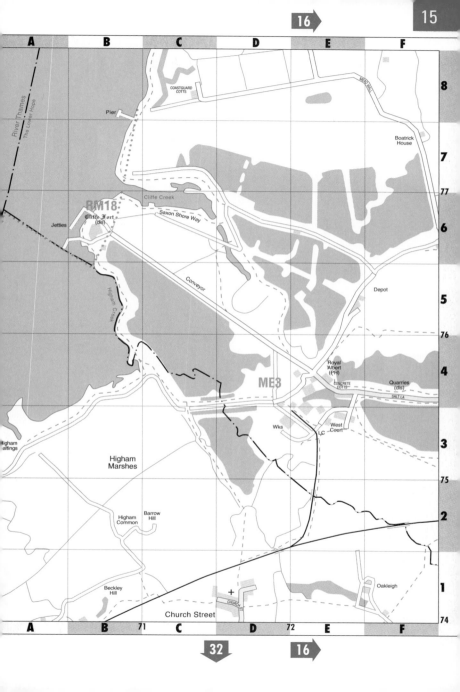

A B C D E F

8
7
77
6
5
76
4
75
3
2
1
74

River Thames
The Lower Hope

COASTGUARD COTTS

Pier

Boatrick House

MEAD WALL

Cliffe Creek

RM18

Cliffe Fort (dis)

Jetties

Saxon Shore Way

Conveyor

Higham Creek

Depot

Royal Albert (PH)

ME3

CONCRETE COTTS

Quarries (dis)

SALT LA

Wks

West Court

LC

Higham Saltings

Higham Marshes

Higham Common

Barrow Hill

75

Beckley Hill

Oakleigh

CHURCH ST

Church Street

71   72

15

A   B   C   D   E   F

8

7

77

6

Ryestreet
Common

Farthing Wall

BEAD WALL
PICKLE WAY
Ham Wall
Mast
Allen's
Hill

CHURCH
CL
NORTH RD
MINSKIN RD
RHAN LA
REED ST
THAMES
TERR

B2000

BUTTWAY LA

MISKIN COTTS
QUICKRELLS
ROOKERY CRES

COMMON LA

Rye Street
Farm

Manor
Farm

West
Street

SWINGATE AVE
QUICKRELLS
AVE
WADLANDS RD

ST HELEN'S RD

ROOKERY
LODGE

Saxon Shore Way

Marshga

Cliffe

DICKENS CL
CHANCERY RD

West Street
Farm

CHURCH ST

St Helens
CE Prim Sch

TURNER ST
HILLCROFT RD

ME3

Cooling
Castle
Farm

Cooling Castle

Horsesh
and Cas
Inn

MAIN RD

76

5

4

75

NEW RD

Higham RD

HIGHAM RD

NORWOOD CL

MORNING
CROSS COTTS

COOLING RD

Berry Court
Farm

Cooling

Mount
Pleasant

SALT LA

Redbarn

STATION RD

Newlands
Farm

WILL SUM RD

Gattons
Farm

Cooling Court
Farm

3

RECTORY RD

BUCKLAND RD

Buckland
Farm

The Rectory

SOUTH BANK

Alma
House

2

The
Grange

TOWN RD

B2000

Cooling
Street

New Barn
Farm

The
Grange

Perry Hill
Farm

PERRY HILL

Bell
Farm

COOLING RD

Spendiff
Farm

1

74

Mortimers
Farm

Rough
Shaw

73   A   B   74   C   D   75   E   F

A   B   C   D   E   F

Cooling
Marshes

Old Sea Wall

Decoy Fleet

The Mean

8

Swigshole

Buckland
Marshes

Buckland Fleet

7

Decoy
Farm

77

Whalebone
Marshes

6

Masts

Eastborough
Farm

Saxon Shore Way

Northward Hill

DECOY HILL RD

5

Bromhey
Farm

Northward Hill
Nature Reserve

Clinchstreet
Farm

Childs
Farm

MAIN RD

76

Buckhole
Farm

Eastborough
Bungalow

ME3

MARSH CRES
WOOD AVE
THAMES AVE
HARRISON DR
COT. RD
DRIFTWAY AVE
WILLOWBANK DR
DRAYTON CL
HARVEL CL
HOLMES CL
CARDINALS

4

LIPWELL HILL

COOLING RD

BUCKHOLE FARM RD

Dalham
Farm

High Halstow
Prim Sch

LINKS
CHR WAY
CHURCH
MAY WAY
CHRISTMAS LA

High
Halstow

LC

KNIGHT ST

St Margaret's
Ct

3

WYBOURNES LA

PH

HILL CRN RD
HILL CROWN

PO

75

Wybournes
Farm

2

Ducks
Court

NAR COURT RD

Solomon's
Farm

Lodge Hill
Wood

Wybornes
Wood

RATCLIFFE HIGHWAY

A228

1

74

A   B   77   C   D   78   E   F

34 ◀   18 ▶

A   B   C   D   E   F

8

7

77

6

5

76

4

3

75

2

1

74

Ramsgreen

Coombe House

May Land

SHAKESPEARE FARM RD

NIGHT FARM RD

Moat Farm

HALL RD

Noreland Cottage

Ross Farm

St Mary Hoo

HOOPERS LA

RATCLIFFE HIGHWAY

Newlands Farm

ME3

St Mary's

NEWLANDS FARM RD

Bell Wood

Walnut Tree Farm

CLINCH ST

Saxon Shore Way

Fenn Street

Fenn Bell Inn (PH)

COLUMBINE RD

Turkey Hall Farm

Malmaynes Hall Farm

MALMAYNES HALL RD

A

Jackson's Corner

THE STREET

Fenn Farm

Fisher's Wood

New Barn Farm

RATCLIFFE HIGHWAY

CHRISTMAS LA

Parbrook Cott

PASBROOK RD

Tudor Farm

A228

SHARNAL ST

ROPER'S GREEN LA

Sharnal Street

Cold Arbour

STOKE RD

North Street

North Street Farm

Tunbridge Hill

20

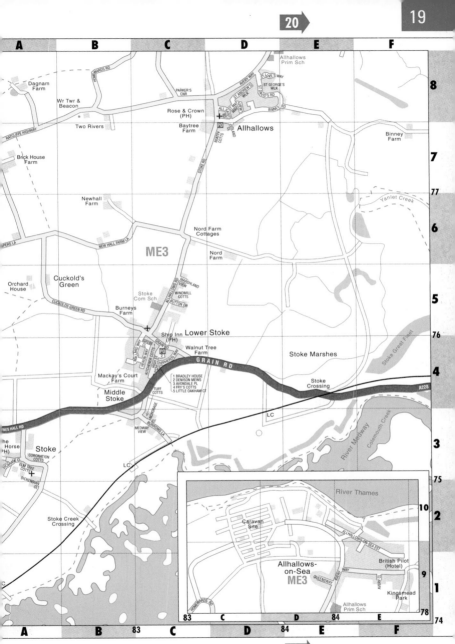

A B C D E F

8

Dagnam Farm

Wr Twr & Beacon

Two Rivers

RATCLIFFE HIGHWAY

HOWARDS RD

PARKER'S CNR

Rose & Crown (PH)

Baytree Farm

Allhallows Prim Sch

ST ANDREWS WAY

ST JAMES WAY

ST ANDREW DR

ST GEORGE'S WLK

ZY'S RD

BINNEY RD

Allhallows

Binney Farm

7

Brick House Farm

77

Newhall Farm

STOKE RD

Yantlet Creek

6

Nord Farm Cottages

NEW HALL FARM LA

PIPERS LA

ME3

Nord Farm

Cuckold's Green

Orchard House

Stoke Com Sch

MARSHLAND VIEW

WINDMILL COTTS

BUTTON DR

5

CUCKOLDS GREEN RD

Burneys Farm

Ship Inn (PH)

Lower Stoke

Walnut Tree Farm

Stoke Marshes

Stoke Great Fleet

76

GRAIN RD

Stoke Crossing

4

Mackay's Court Farm

1 BRADLEY HOUSE
2 DENISON MEWS
3 AVONDALE PL
4 FRY'S COTTS
5 LITTLE OAKHAM CT

TUFF COTTS

LC

A228

Middle Stoke

YNES HALL RD

MEDWAY VIEW

BIRCHMILL LA

Stoke Marshes

River Medway

Colemouth Creek

3

he Horse (PH)

Stoke

CORONATION COTTS

VICARAGE CL

ELM TREE COTTS

DICKENS RD

LC

River Thames

75

Caravan Site

Allhallows-on-Sea

ME3

British Pilot (Hotel)

ALLHALLOWS-ON-SEA RD

Stoke Creek Crossing

QUEENSWAY

AVERY CL

Kingsmead Park

10

2

9

1

Allhallows Prim Sch

DIAMONDS RD

78

74

A B C 83 C D 84 E F

19

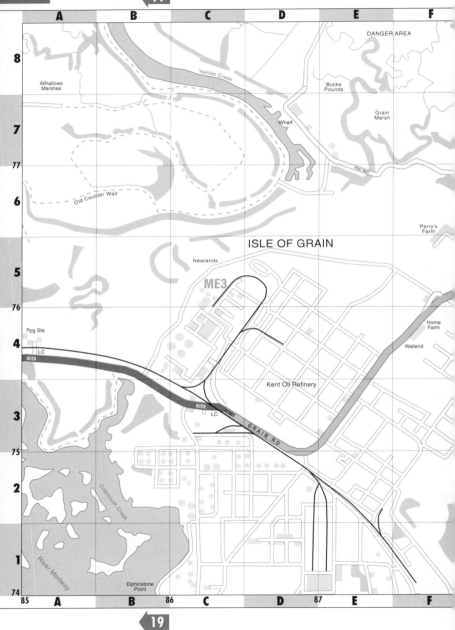

DANGER AREA

Allhallows
Marshes

Yantlet Creek

Bucks
Pounds

Grain
Marsh

Wharf

PEAT WAY

Old Counter Wall

Perry's
Farm

ISLE OF GRAIN

Newlands

ME3

Home
Farm

Ppg Sta

Wallend

LC

A228

Kent Oil Refinery

A228

LC

GRAIN RD

Colemouth Creek

River Medway

Elphinstone
Point

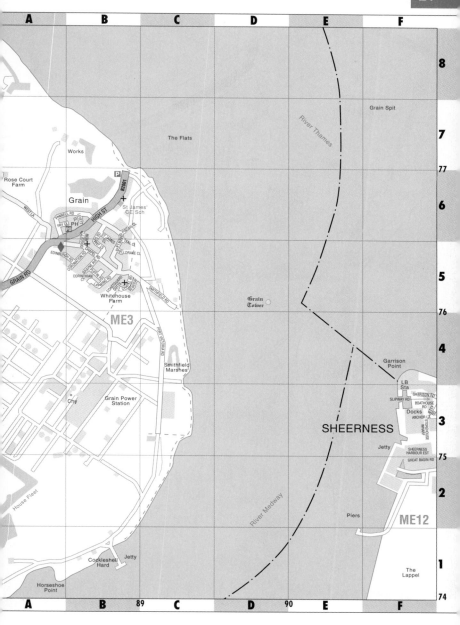

A B C D E F

8

Grain Spit

7

River Thames

77

Rose Court
Farm

Grain

Works

The Flats

6

St James'
C.E. Sch

HIGH ST

WILL LA

5

GRAIN RD

ME3

Grain
Tower

76

Whitehouse
Farm

Edinburgh

CORINTHIAN
CT

PORT VICTORIA RD

SMITHFIELD RD

Garrison
Point

4

Smithfield
Marshes

LB
Sta
GARRISON RD
SLIPWAY RD
BOATHOUSE
RD

Chy

Grain Power
Station

Docks
ANCHOR LA

SHEERNESS

STOREHOUSE WHARF

3

Jetty

75

SHEERNESS
HARBOUR EST

GREAT BASIN RD

House Fleet

River Medway

Piers

ME12

2

Cocklesshell
Hard

Jetty

The
Lappel

1

Horseshoe
Point

74

A B 89 C D 90 E F

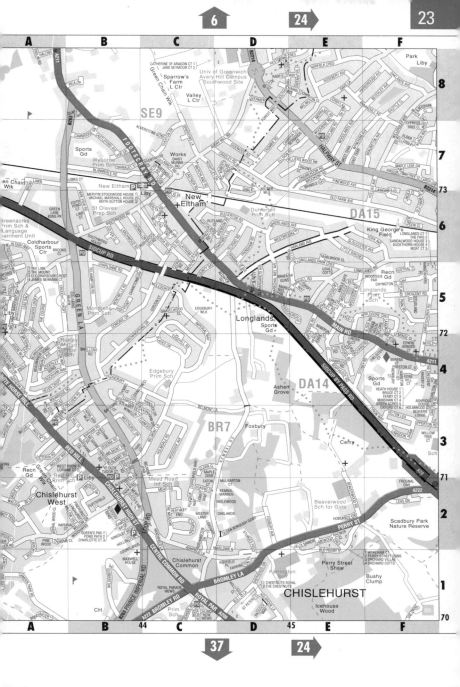

18

49

B6
1 SELWYN PL
2 LEIGH TERR
3 WOULDHAM TERR

37

C5
1 MOUNTFIELD WAY
2 HORTON TOWER
3 ELMSTONE TERR
4 TIDEBROOK CT
5 BELGRAVE CL
6 SANDWAY PATH

24

C5
7 HARBLEDOWN PL
8 BAPCHILD PL
9 ALKHAM TOWER

DA14

8

7

69

6

5

68

4

3

67

2

1

66

A   B   C   D   E   F

St Paul's Cray

BR7

Leesons Prim Sch

Poverest

Poverest Prim Sch

St Mary Cray

BR5

St Mary Cray

BR6

Priory Gdns Cemy

Liby

Ramsden

ORPINGTON

Derry Downs

Kevingtown

BR8

Pauls Cray Hill Park

BR8

Garnfield Bank

Hockenden Wood

The Warren

Sheepcote Farm

Walden Manor

Griff's Wood

Lone Barn Farm

D1
1 BREDGAR HOUSE
2 WITTERSHAM HOUSE
3 CHALLOCK HOUSE
4 HOLLINGBOURNE TOWER
5 THURNHAM HOUSE
6 PECKHAM HOUSE
7 STOCKBURY HOUSE
8 EASTLING HOUSE
9 NEWINGTON HOUSE

10 FAWKHAM HOUSE
11 HOUGHAM HOUSE
12 BEKESBOURNE TOWER
13 LENHAM HOUSE
14 LAMBERHURST CL
15 LODDEN CT
16 KENNETT CT
17 EDEN CT
18 CUCKMERE CT
19 DARENTH CT

20 MEDWAY CT
21 MEON CT
22 STOUR CT
23 RAVENSBOURNE CT
24 ROTHER CT
25 RYE FIELD
26 BOX TREE WLK

E6
1 WHITEOAK CT
2 KENNET CT
3 WHITE OAK SQ
4 ST ANDREW'S CT
5 RUXTON CT
6 BERKELEY CT

DA14

A28

B2173

MAIDSTONE RD

Birchwood
Corner
BIRCHWOOD TERR 1
JESSAMINE TERR 2

Nursery

Nursery

Hextable
Sch

COLLEGE RD

NEW BARN RD

SPRING VALE
CL

EGERTON AVE

MAIN RD

SQUIRES
FIELD

VEITCHIL
BARN

8

Burnt House
Farm

KIDDENS

PH

OAKWOOD
CT

Birchwood
Prim Sch

New Barn Park
Swanley New
Barn Railway

1 ACACIA WLK
3 HEATHFIELD TERR

ALDER WAY

THE BIRCHES

THE SPINNEY

P

ARCHER
WAY

HOCKENDEN LA

CHAPMAN'S LA

Hockenden

Hockenden
House

STAR LA

SHEPCOTE LA

GRANHAM RD

HEATHWOOD GDNS

DALE RD

LARCH
WLK

Sports
Ctr

JUNIPER
WLK

MAPLE CL

INGLEWOOD

White Oak

White Oak
Prim Sch

HEATH
CL

MORTON
CL

SWANLEY LA

69

LONDON RD

ST LUKES
COTTS

HART DYKE
CREST

CHURCH
VIEW

THE
SQUARE

Liby
Swanley
Sch

P
i

Swanley
CT

Civic
Ctr

Swanley
Sch

P
P

PARK ROAD
IND EST

SHERIDAN

B258

LONDON RD

B258

7

6

Bourne Wood

WATERTON
WOOD END DR

LYNDEN WAY

MORE
CL

HEWITT PL

DAMSON

GOLDSEL RD

STATION APP

WINTON
CT

BEVAN
PL

High Firs
Prim Sch

5

68

BR5

BR8

HEATHER
END

LAGOS WAY

AMEN COR

AZALEA DR

ERICA

OVERMEAD

HAZEL END

PUMP HILL

4

PETHAM COURT
COTTS

Petham
Court

Crouch
Farm

CROCKENHILL RD

Crockenhill
Prim Sch

The
Green

WOODLANDS
TERR

BRAMBLE CL

CRAY RD

GREEN COURT RD

BROADWAY 1
KINGSNORTH CT 2

MAIN RD

Recn
Gd

BIRCHES CROSS RD

SEVEN ACRES

PH

Cemy

Crockenhill

CHURCH FARM
CL

1 HORNETTS CL
2 SCHOOL COTTS
3 CHURCH COTTS

Gosenhill
Farm

LYNGFORD RD

WESTED FARM
COTTS

3

67

Bleak House
Farm

BARNES HILL

DALTONS RD

THE GREEN RD

HARVEST WAY

NEWPORTS

WOODMOUNT

Allot
Gdns

HIGHCROFT
HALL

Wested
Farm

BR5

DA4

M25

2

1

66

	A	B	C	D	E	F

DA13

Grubb Street

Ryecroft Farm

Ryecrofts Wood

8

GALS RD

WILSON LA

GREEN STREET GREEN RD

B260

Mile End Green

WHITEHILL RD

Whitehill

Railway under construction

B255

DA2

Pinden

Pinden End Farm

Longfield

B255

SOUTHDOWN RD

7

WEST SIDE

MAIN RD

Liby

69

RABBITS RD

ESSEX CL

PH

PO

KENT RD

ROWAN CL

CHEYNE WK

CAVENDISH

RUSSELL SQ

Longfield

Oakwood RD

DA4

Dene Bottom Farm

EATON SQ

THE ORCHARD

BRAMBLE CL

Axton Chase Sch

6

Dean Bottom

THE MEWS 1
ST. JAMES SQ 2
GROSVENOR SQ 3
BEDFORD SQ 4
ST. GEORGES SQ 5
SLOANE SQ 6

HOTTSFIELD

FAIRACRE PL

MERTON AVE

OXFIELD

VIEWPOINTS CT

TIMBLEDOWN

Churchdown Wood

QUAKERS

WELL FIELD

1 SILVERDALE
2 MERRYFIELDS
3 EVERGLADE CL
4 FORTUNA CL

LARKS FIELD

GRESHAM AVE

68

CANADA FARM RD

Beeches Farm

Hill Barn Farm

OLD DOWNS

WICKHAM WAY

GREEN WAY

Canada Farm

CASTLE HILL

Hartley Green

STACK RD

STACK LA

4

FAWKHAM RD

DA3

CULVEY CL

Our Lady of Hartley RC Prim Sch

Liby

BRAMBLEFIELD CL

Lane Oak Farm

BORDERS HILL

Hartley Cty Prim Sch

POUND ASH WAY

ASH RD

OVAL WAY

FAIRBY LA

CHANTRY AVE

Hartle

3

Nursery

Football Ground

Sports Club

Pennis Farm

YATES DI

67

VALLEY RD

MANOR LA

Pennis Wood

The Black Lion (PH)

2

THREE GATES RD

The Grove

Fawkham CE Prim Sch

Parkfield Wood

Fawkham Manor

CH

TN15

Chapel Wood

Mast

1

BLORE LA

OLIVER MILL 1
CHAPEL WOOD 2

CHAPEL WOOD RD

66

58	A	B	59	C	D	60	E	F

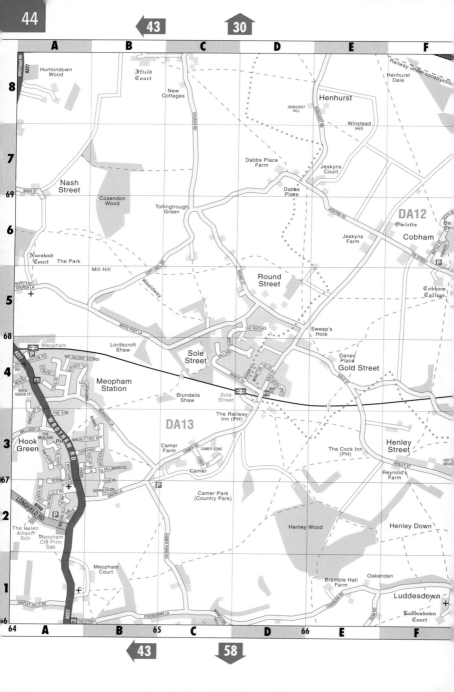

B7
1 NEWARK CT
2 AVELING CT
3 FRIARY PREC
4 GROVE CT

B8
1 ALEXANDER CT
2 EPPE CL
3 FLORENCE ST
4 ARCHWAY CT
5 ST MICHAEL'S CT

C8
1 BILL STREET RD
2 MAYFAIR
3 CHRISTIAN CT
4 PEMBERTON SQ
5 EVELYN RD

C1
1 BAKENHAM HO
2 LEEKE HO
3 TRANSOM HO
4 SPINNAKER CT

E4
1 BINGLEY RD
2 ST BARTHOLOMEW'S TERR
3 HOSPITAL LA
4 ST BARTHOLOMEW'S LA
5 MEDWAY HEIGHTS
6 HAMOND HILL
7 CRESSEY CT
8 LUMSDEN TERR
9 ORDNANCE TERR

F3
1 ORCHARD VILLAS
2 CLAREMONT WAY
3 MOUNT VIEW CT
4 SILVER HILL GDNS
5 CORONATION FLATS
6 RIVER VIEW CL
7 SAUNDERS ST

F4
1 CAMBRIDGE TERR
2 MEETING HOUSE LA
3 CLOVER ST
4 MILLWOOD CT
5 JAMES ST
6 COPPERFIELD HO
7 SPRINGFIELD HO
8 BERKELEY MOUNT
9 LANSDOWNE CT

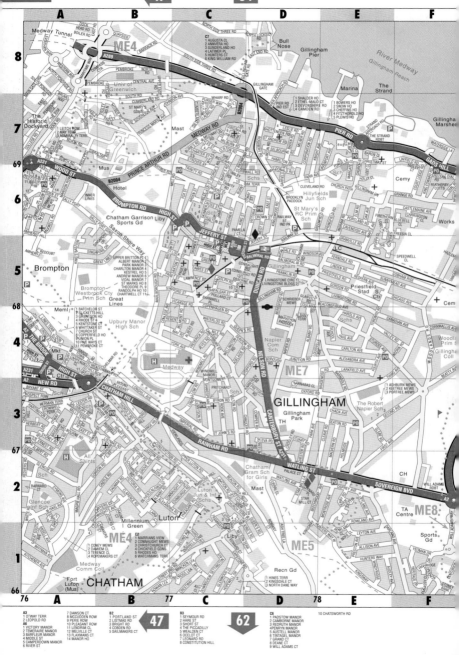

River Medway
Gillingham Reach

Nor Marsh

Copperhouse Marshes

Ferol
Peak

Cinque Port Marshes

Horrid
Hill

Walnut Tree
Farm

Saxon Shore Way

PH
B2004
GRANGE
RDBT
Grange
Grange Rd
BUTTERMERE CL
Grench
Manor
Allot
Gdns
Mill Hill

THE SPIERS
ME7
Lower
Twydall
LADDS
CNR

Sharp's
Green

Visitor Ctr

LOWER RAINHAM RD

Riverside
Country Park

Mariners
Farm

Bloors
Wharf

Cemy
Sports
Field
CORNWALLIS
RDBT
BREDGAR RD
Little London
Farm
MANOR
CT
1 BISHOPBOURNE GN
2 HEADCORN RD
Three Mariners
(PH)

Bloors
Place
B2004

BEECHINGS WAY
IND CTR
LITTLEBOURNE AVE

1 FORDWICH GN
2 BONNINGTON GN
3 SELLINGE GN

Pump
Farm

PUMP RD

Lower
Rainham

Featherby
Inf & Jun
Schs
HARBLEDOWN
MANOR

Liby
P

WOOTTON
GN

Twydall
Twydall
Schs
PIKEFIELDS
WOODCHURCH RD
BRENCHLEY RD
LEWIS AVE
CECIL AVE

ABSALOM
CT

Rainham
Mark
Gram Sch

Thames View
Inf & Jun
Schs

THE
WILLOWS

Prim
Sch
CHELMAR RD

ROMANY
NORFOLK
RD

ME8

Cozenton
Park

SOVEREIGN BVD
1 TATSFIELD CL
2 KESTON CT
HOATH WAY A278
A2

Liby
P

Rainham

The
Ice Bowl
SHERMAN
CL
GRANT CL
Superstore
LONDON RD
A2
DENBIGH RD
BIRLING AVE
HIGH ST A2
STATION RD

Works
BOSTON RD
HUDSON RD
Playing
Fields
P

F1
1 CREVEQUER CHAMBERS
2 RAINHAM SH CTR
3 GRESHAM CL
4 HARRISON CT
5 MAPLINS CL

A   80   B   C   D   81   E   F

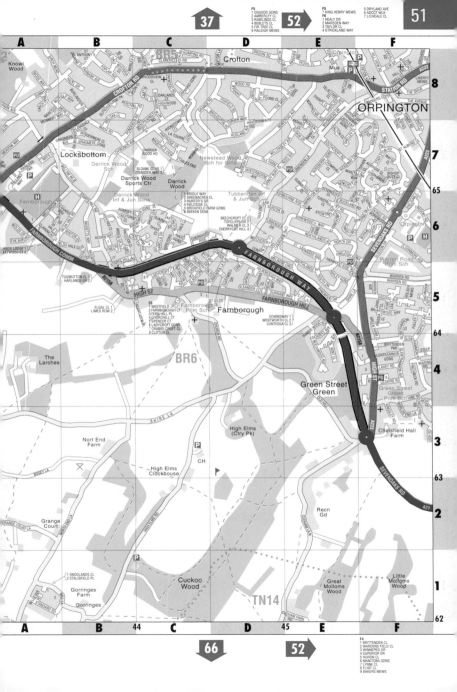

37   52

Map Labels

58

A B C D E F

8

L Ctr
Meopham
Com Prim
Sch
Liby
Lomer
Farm

A227
MEADFIELD RD
ARNOLD AVE
Meopham

Foxendown

OAKHEAD
BLENHEIM CL
WARMAN'S
BINNS
CHELSFIELD LA
HACKS LA

MILLERS WHARF
GROVNVILLE RD
The
Larches

Brimstone
Wood

Dene
Manor

Rid Ridge

KENT
TERR

7

A227

WELLINGTON
COTTS

Meopham
Green

WHITEHILL RD

Dunstan
Wood

Wood Hill
Farm

STEELE LA

CROCKERS DR

65

Dilmer
Wood

6

Waares Meadow
Farm

HORN'S OAK RD

Nutfield
Farm

CHANDLER

Merry
Hill

Purvil
Wood

Strawberry
Hill

Rochester
Forest

Coomb Hill
Farm

Priestwood

CHARITY FM RD

5

David
Street

PRIESTWOOD RD

Priestwood
Green

DEAN LA

Lenniker
Wood

PLUG LA

Ham
Farm

Great Buckland
Farm

LOCKYERS HILL

WEALDWAY

64

Haddocks
Wood

Eastfield
Farm

LUXON RD

Luxon Wood

4

HERON HILL LA

Dean
Mead

DA13

Lie
Wood

RISING HILL

+

3

LACEY LA

Beechen
Wood

Harvel House
Farm

ST FRANCIS RD

Harvel

HORNFIELD
COTTS
PH
HARVEL ST

Harvel Hill
Farm

Harvel Hike

LEYWOOD RD

Little Delmar
Farm

Boughurst Street
Farm

Holly
Hill

63

BUCK LA

SCHOOL LA

HARVEL HIKE

Upper
Harvel

WHITE HORSE LA

2

Ridge
Wood

BEECHENLEA DR

BEECHWOOD AVE

Sparrowhaugh
Farm

PARRIS RD

HARVEL HIKE

Poundgate

WEALDWAY

1

MEADOW LA

BEECHWOOD RD

HIGHVIEW

PARRIS RD

Swanswood
Farm

Daniel
Chambers

BULLS HORSE RD

North
Downs Wa

62

64 A B 65 C D 66 E F

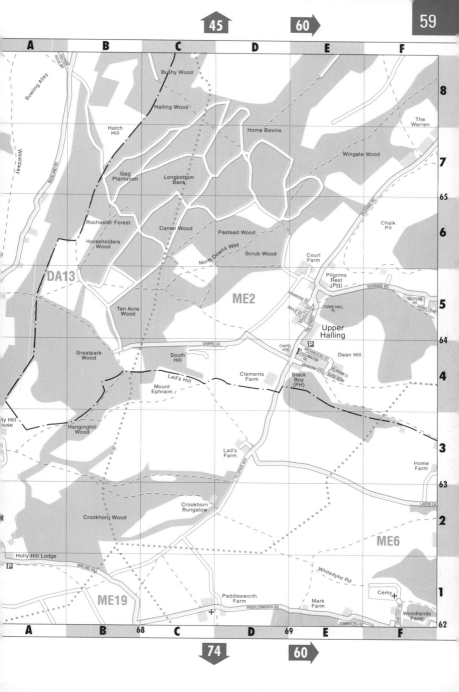

A B C D E F

8

Bowling Alley

Bushy Wood

Halling Wood

Hatch Hill

Home Bavins

The Warren

7

Wealdway

Wingate Wood

Gag Plantation

Longbottom Bank

65

Rochester Forest

Canon Wood

Pastead Wood

Chalk Pit

6

Horseholders Wood

North Downs Way

Scrub Wood

Court Farm

DA13

Ten Acre Wood

ME2

Pilgrims Rest (PH)

VICARAGE RD

REDFERN HO

HARE'S DENNE

5

PRIMROSE RD

BROWNDENS RD

Turks Hall PL

Upper Halling

GROVE RD

PADDLE CL

THE STREET

Greatpark Wood

South Hill

CHAPEL LA

CHAPEL HO

P

CHILLINGTON CL

MEADOW CRES

DEAN MDW

MEADOW CL

Dean Hill

64

Clements Farm

Black Boy (PH)

BARN MDW

4

Mount Ephraim

Lad's Hill

Hanginghill Wood

lly Hill ouse

Lad's Farm

Home Farm

3

Crookhorn Bungalow

63

LADDS LA

Crookhorn Wood

ME6

2

Holly Hill Lodge

P

BIRLING HILL

Whitedyke Rd

Cemy

Woodlands Farm

ME19

Paddlesworth Farm

PADDLESWORTH RD

Mark Farm

1

TOWNSEND RD

62

A B 68 C D 69 E F

A B C D E F

8 7 65 6 5 64 4 3 63 2 1 62

Nashenden Farm

HM Prison

Splewo

Medway Secure Training Ctr

ROCHESTER

ME1

Little Monk Wood

Well Wood

Gorse Wood

Upper Nashenden Farm

Monk Wood

Factories

Rochester Airport

Wks

The Thomas Aveling Sch
Warren Wood Cty/Prim Sch

KELLY HOUSE 1
HERO WLK 2
ASSOCIATION WLK 3
EXETER WLK 4

CITY WAY

HORSTED WAY

Fort Horsted

ME4

Mid Kent Coll of Higher & F Ed

CHATHAM

Horsted Farm

Superstore

Superstores

Hotel

Wks

Horsted Cty Jun & Inf Schs

Chatham Gram Sch for Boys

Chatham South Sch

Huntsman's Cnr

St Stephens Mews

Ridge Meadow Prim Sch

Girls Sch

Liby

Greenacre Sch

Bradfields Sch

Oaklands Cty Inf & Jun Sch

Weeds Grn

Bleakwood Rd

Syle Wood

Middle Hill

Middlehill Wood

Bridge Woods

ME5

Buckmore Park

Durham Hill Farm

The Robin Hood (PH)

Burham Common

North Downs Way

ME1

Sports Ctr

Lord Leas

Bridgewood Manor Hotel

Taddington Wood

Marston Dr

Kit Hill

Walderslade

Tunbury Cty Prim Sch

Hepplewhite Mews

Podkin Wood

Robin Hood La

The Upper Bell Inn (PH)

Bluebell Hill

Kent Centenary Walks

Warren Rd

Crem

Impton Wood

74 75

E4
1 LAVENDER CL
2 ASPEN WAY
3 HONEYSUCKLE CL
4 GENTIAN CL

F4
1 MALLOW WAY
2 JASMINE CL
3 HAREBELL CL
4 ROSEMARY CL
5 LINDEN HOUSE
6 OAK HOUSE

F5
1 SAFFRON WAY
2 WILLOW HO
3 PINE HO
4 ROWAN HO
5 HAWTHORN HO

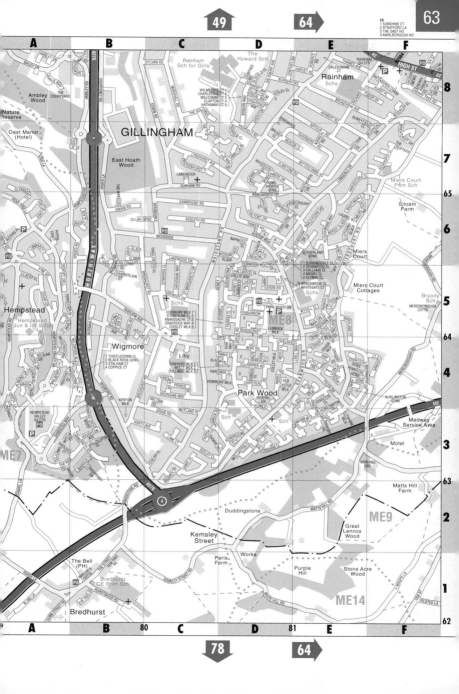

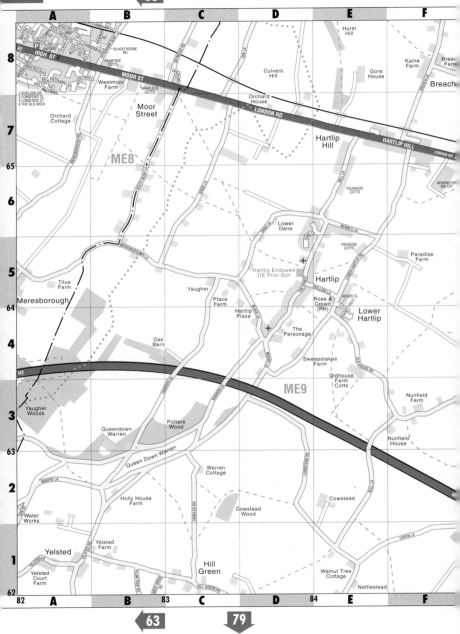
63

A B C D E F

8

1 SHELDEN DR
2 LONGFORD CL
3 LONGFORD CT
4 THE OLD ORCH

Blackthorne RD

PEARTREE COTTS

Westmoor Farm

WAKELEYS COTTS

Orchard House

Culvers Hill

Hurst Hill

Gore House

Kaine Farm

Breach Farm

Breach

Orchard Cottage

Moor Street

LONDON RD

Hartlip Hill

HARTLIP HILL

LONDON RD

7

ME8

65

FOURACRE COTTS

NEWINGTON IND EST

6

Lower Dane

PARADISE COTTS

Paradise Farm

MUNKS LA

Hartlip Endowed CE Prim Sch

Hartlip

5

Titus Farm

Meresborough

Yaugher

Place Farm

Hartlip Place

Rose & Crown (PH)

AUGER CL

Lower Hartlip

64

Oak Barn

The Parsonage

4

Sweepstakes Farm

Oldhouse Farm Cotts

ME9

Nunfield Farm

M2

Yaugher Woods

3

Queendown Warren

Potters Wood

Nunfield House

63

Queen Down Warren

Warren Cottage

MAGPIE LA

2

Holly House Farm

Cowstead Wood

Cowstead

Water Works

1

Yelsted

Yelsted Farm

Hill Green

Walnut Tree Cottage

Nettlestead

GREEN LA

Yelsted Court Farm

HILL GREEN RD

62

82 A B 83 C D 84 E F

51

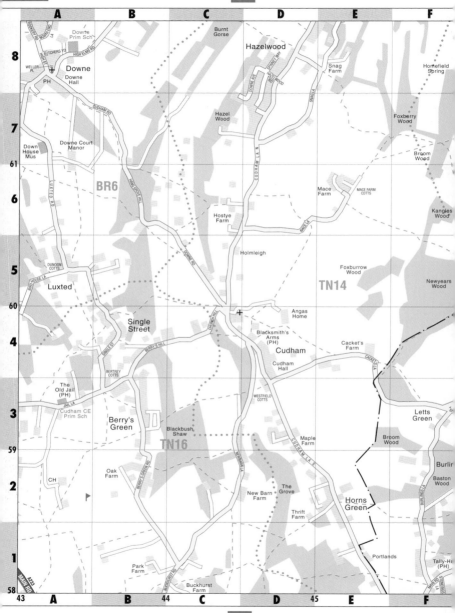

Downe Prim Sch

Burnt Gorse

Hazelwood

Snag Farm

Hornfield Spring

Downe

Downe Hall

Foxberry Wood

Down House Mus

Downe Court Manor

Hazel Wood

Broom Wood

BR6

Mace Farm

MACE FARM COTTS

Kangies Wood

Hostye Farm

Holmleigh

Foxburrow Wood

Luxted

Dunoon Cotts

TN14

Newyears Wood

Single Street

Angas Home

Blacksmith's Arms (PH)

Cacket's Farm

Berry's Hill

Cudham

Letts Green

Bertrey Cotts

Cudham Hall

The Old Jail (PH)

JAIL LA

Westfield Cotts

Broom Wood

Cudham CE Prim Sch

Berry's Green

Burlir

Blackbush Shaw

Maple Farm

Baston Wood

TN16

CH

Oak Farm

New Barn Farm

The Grove

Horns Green

Thrift Farm

Park Farm

Buckhurst Farm

Portlands

Tally-He (PH)

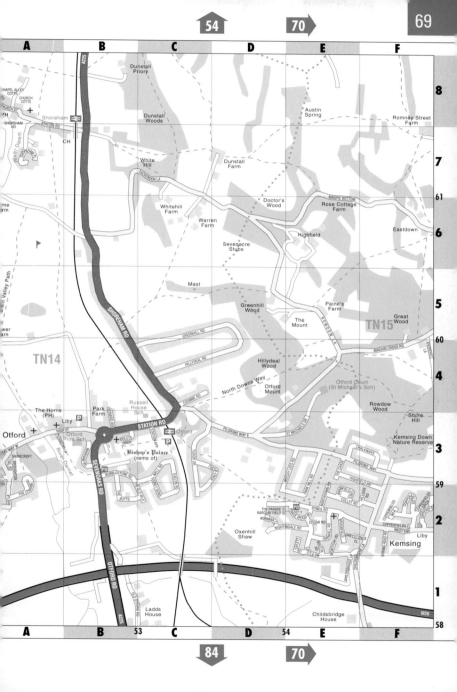

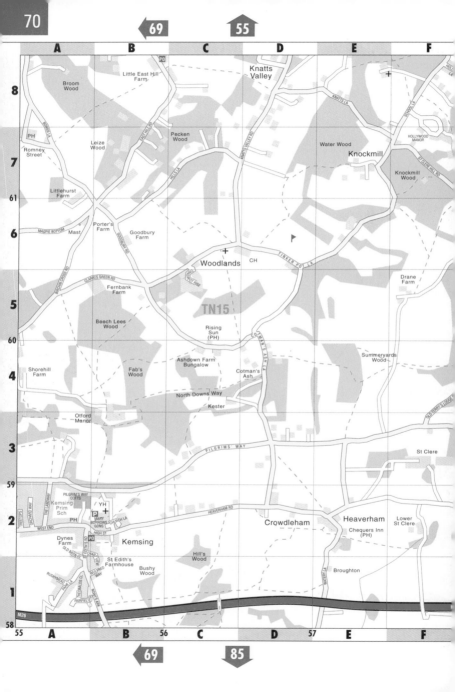

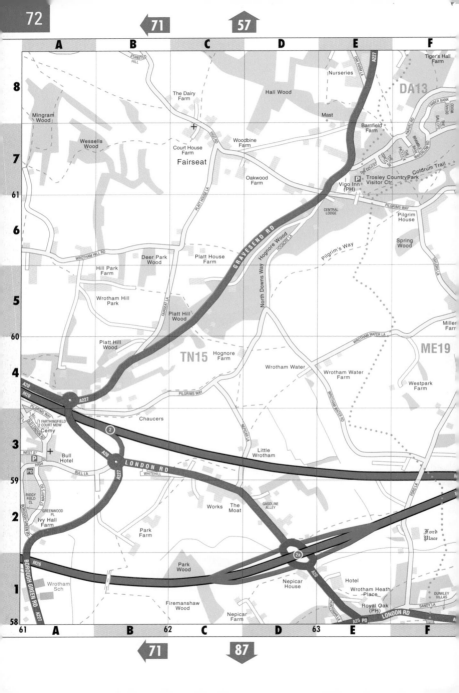

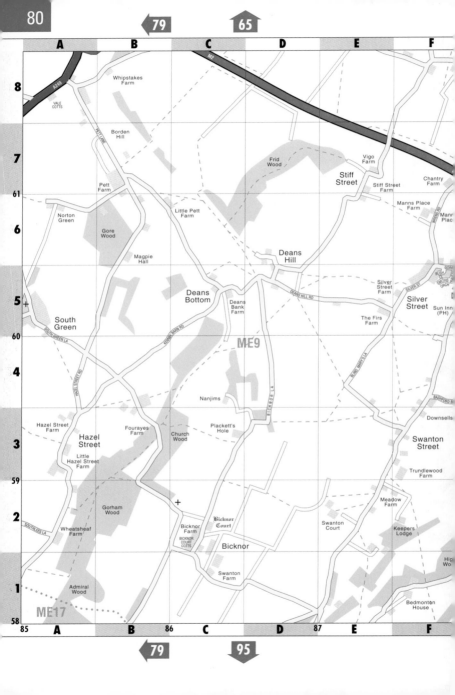

A B C D E F

Beaverstock Farm
Fox & Hounds (PH)
South Street

Withins Wood

Scott's Lodge

TN14 8

Shellem Wood

Cudham Frith

MAIN RD

Southwood

Bombers Farm

Buckhurst

Cudham Grange

GRAYS RD

SILVERSTED LA

Joeland's Wood

7

57

Hawley's Corner

Gray's Farm

SILVERSTED LA

Hogtrough Hill

6

North Downs Way

WESTERHAM HILL

Little Betsom's Farm

John Groom's Home
Pilgrim House

5

Betsom's Hill

THE AVENUE

The Hill Sch

56

Hill Park

Betsons Farm

TN16

Holywell Shaw

4

Gaysham Fm

Force Green

M25

3

Hartley Wood

LONDON RD

Charmans Farm

BEGGARS LA

55

Westerham Wood

A25

2

Churchill CE Prim Sch

Court Lodge

HARTLEY RD
OAK RD
LOUISE LA
MADAN RD

BLOOMFIELD TERR

ROSELANDS C

HORTONS WAY

D1
1 HORTONS WAY
2 MARKET WAY
3 MORETON RD
4 AUSTIN CT
5 ST MARY'S CT
6 DUNCANS COTTS
7 FULLERS HILL
8 WINTERTON CT
9 QUEBEC COTTS
10 QUEBEC SQ

Green Croft

CROYDON RD

Westerham

Library

A25

BRASTED RD

The Granary

Valence Sch

1

Squerryes Sand Pit

MARLBOROUGH CT
THE GRANGE

DELAGARDE RD
BARTLETT RD

Dunsdale House

54

A B C 44 D 45 E F

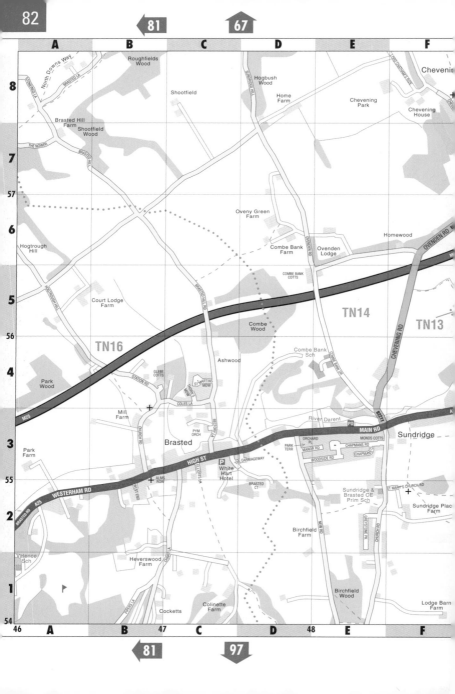

A **B** **C** **D** **E** **F**

Noah's Ark

Cockney's Wood

CHAUCER IND PK

Kemsing

HONEYPOT LA.

8

Penfield

CHURCH ST

Tanners Cross

Stonepitts

WATERY LA.

7

57

Seal

GARDEN TERR

Fullers Hill Farm

Broomsleigh

Chart Farm

Oldbury Hill

6

SWIFT'S CT

TN15

MAIDSTONE RD

GROVE RD

EXEDE RD

PILGRIMS WAY

Styants Bottom

Oldbury Wood

5

CH

The Grove

Larchwood Farm

Styants Wood

P

SEVENOAKS RD

A25

56

Chance Wood

Oak Bank Hall

Redhill Wood

Seal Chart

Crown Point Inn (PH)

Frankfield House

Fish Ponds Wood

4

SEAL HILL

Hanger Wood

Raspit Hill

3

Hall Place

Godden Green

The Padwell (PH)

CHURCH RD

St Lawrence CE Prim Sch

55

VAUXHALL LA

RN 15

Buck's Head (PH)

BUCK RD

Great Roger's Wood

STONE STREET RD

Stone Street

Rose & Crown (PH)

2

Stake Farm

Lord's Spring Wood

Diantshatch Wood

Sevenoaks Prep Sch

Rambles Wood

Lower Bitchet

THE LOCKS

Bitchet Green

SCABHARROW

CROSS LA

1

54

A **B** 56 **C** **D** 57 **E** **F**

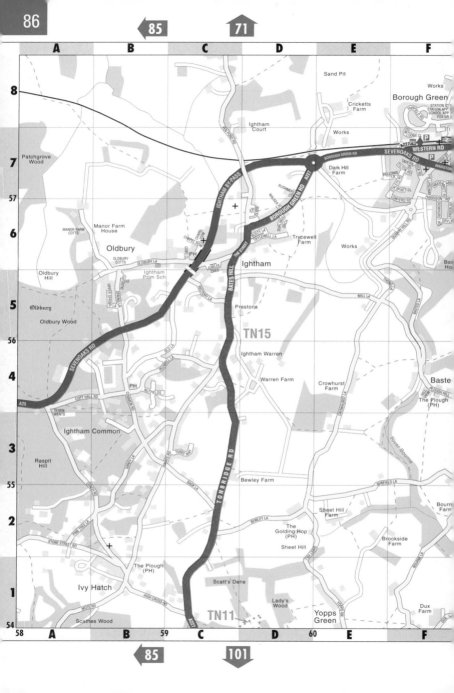

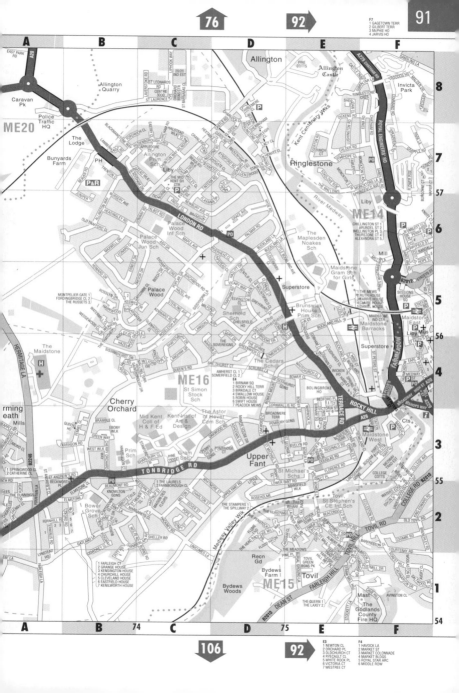

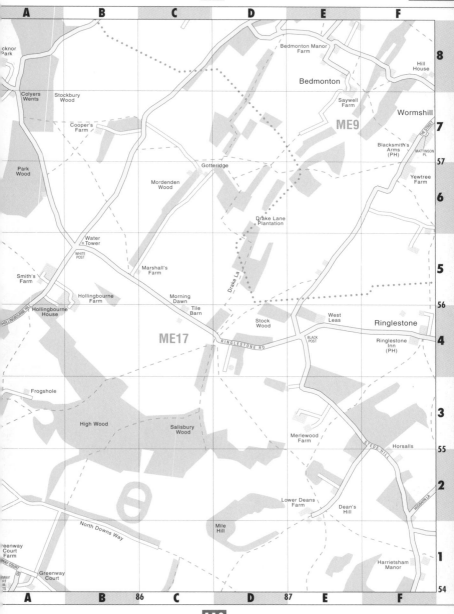

8

cknor
Park

Bedmonton Manor
Farm

Hill
House

Colyers
Wents

Stockbury
Wood

Bedmonton

Saywell
Farm

Wormshill

Cooper's
Farm

ME9

7

Blacksmith's
Arms
(PH)

MATTINSON
PL

THE STREET

57

Park
Wood

Gotteridge

Mordenden
Wood

Yewtree
Farm

6

Drake Lane
Plantation

Water
Tower

WHITE
POST

Marshall's
Farm

Drake La

5

Smith's
Farm

Morning
Dawn

56

Hollingbourne
Farm

Tile
Barn

Stock
Wood

West
Leas

Ringlestone

Hollingbourne
House

HOLLINGBOURNE RD

ME17

RINGLESTONE RD

BLACK
POST

Ringlestone
Inn
(PH)

4

Frogshole

High Wood

Salisbury
Wood

Merlewood
Farm

SYCE'S HILL

Horsalls

3

55

North Downs Way

Lower Deans
Farm

Dean's
Hill

HOGARTH LA

2

Mile
Hill

Harrietsham
Manor

1

Greenway
Court
Farm

Greenway
Court

WAY
RT
M
TS

HART COURT

54

81

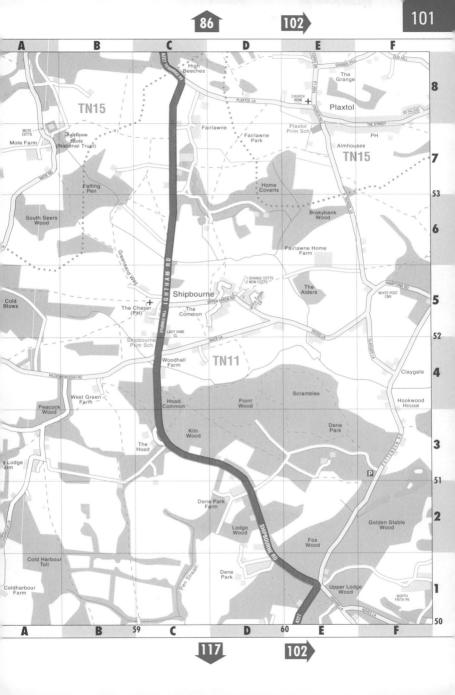

A B C D E F

8

TN15

High Beeches

GRANGE HILL

DUX HILL

The Grange

PLAXTOL LA

CHURCH ROW

Plaxtol

ST HILDAS

THE STREET

MOTE COTTS
Mote Farm

Ightham Mote
(National Trust)

Fairlawne

Fairlawne Park

Plaxtol Prim Sch

PH

TN15

7

MOTE RD

Fatting Pen

Home Coverts

Almhouses

53

South Seers Wood

Brakybank Wood

6

Greensand Way

Fairlawne Home Farm

Cold Blows

Shipbourne

1 GRANGE COTTS
2 NEW COTTS

The Alders

HAMPTONS RD

WHITE POST CNR

5

IGHTHAM RD

The Chaser (PH)

UPPER GREEN RD

The Common

REEDS LA

CLAYGATE LA

52

STUMBLE HILL

LADY VANE CL

BACK LA

TN11

Claygate

4

Shipbourne Prim Sch

Woodhall Farm

HILDENBOROUGH RD

West Green Farm

Scrambles

Hookwood House

Peacock Wood

Hoad Common

Point Wood

Dene Park

P

51

3

y Lodge arm

The Hoad

Kiln Wood

PHILPOTS RD

Cold Harbour Toll

Dene Park Farm

Lodge Wood

SHIPBOURNE RD

Fox Wood

Golden Stable Wood

2

Coldharbour Farm

Pen Stream

Dene Park

Upper Lodge Wood

NORTH FRITH PK.

1

A227

HIGH LA

A227

ASHES LA

50

A B C D E F

| A | B | C | D | E | F |

8

DUX HILL

Quarry Wood

BOURNE VALE

HYDERS FORGE

THE STREET

COUNCIL HOUSES

BROOK LA

Broadfield Farm

Plaxtol Spoute

TN15

SPINNERS WENTS

ALLEN LA

7

Allen's Farm

THE CREST

Wealdway

PECKHAM BUSH RD

SWANTON RD

Pecki Hu

OWL LA MY

Upper Farm

Rats Castle

ME1

53 +

ROUGHWAY LA

Crooked Chimneys

THE COBBS

GOVER HILL

Mills

BARTON COTTS

Roughway

Gover Hill

6

Dunk's Green

Greensand Way

Stickland's Wood

Adams Well

FE

The Kentish Rifleman (PH)

DUNK'S GREEN RD

The Artichoke Inn (PH)

5

Puttenden Manor Farm

Fish Farm

Hamptons

PILLAR BOX LA

PARK RD

Oxen Hoath

HAMPTONS RD

52

Hamptons Park

TN11

Vines Farm

4

River Bourne

Four Wents

OVENDEN RD

Oxen Hoath Park

Park Farm

Oxenhoath Mill Farm

Pear Tree Farm

3

Clearhedges Wood

Frith Wood

Mount Pleasant

Cricketers Cottage Farm

51

The Common

COMMON RD

2

Stallion's Green

HIGH HOUSE LA

Moat

CARPENTERS LA

PALMERS BROS

LONGMEAD RD

MAIDSTONE RD

Yewtree Wood

Hadlow

CEMETERY LA

The Harrow (PH)

1

North Frith Farm

Hope Farm

MILL VIEW

THE PADDOCK

MAGDALEN

GOLDINGS

HIGH ST

PARK VILLAS

ST JAMES CL

PRIAR CL

CHESFIELD CL

50 +

CHURCH ST

BROOKFIELDS

A26

61 | A | **62** | B | C | **63** | D | E | F

ME18

ME16

ME15

ME18

Teston

tle Court
ge Farm

Barham
Court

Barham
Mews

TONBRIDGE RD

TESTON HOUSE

P

River Medway

Court Lodge
Farm

Court Lodge

Barming
Bridge

St Helens
Cotts

Kettle
Corner

Lower Gallants
Farm

B2010

LOWER RD

HOPPERS
CNR

Gallants
Court

Wynngarth
Farm

West
Farleigh

MILL
COTTS

The Tickled Trout
(PH)

West Farleigh
Hall

Tutsham
Hall

Good Intent
(PH)

Farleigh
Green

Gallants
Farm

Marshall's
Cottages

SMITH'S HILL

EWELL LA

B2163

The
Thatched
House

Roses
Farm

Hospital Barn
Farm

Quarry Wood

Quarry
Farm

HEATH RD

Castle
Farm

North Folly
Farm

B2163

SMALL PROFITS

Henhurst
Wood

Shingle Barn
Farm

Fox
Pitt

The
White House
(PH)

YALDING HILL

Downs Farm

SHINGLE BARN LA

Greybury
Wood

Buston Manor

Greensand Way

Barn Hill

Hill Farm

BUSTON MANOR
FARM COTTS

Malice
Wood

North Park
Farm

Gennings
Farm

Broomfield

ALMSHOUSES

SALTER'S
CROSS

Cheveney
Farm

LUGHORSE LA

Obelisk
House

lding CE
rim Sch

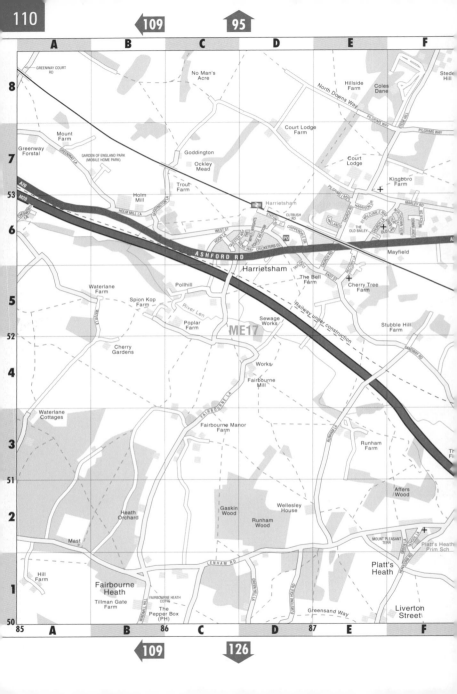

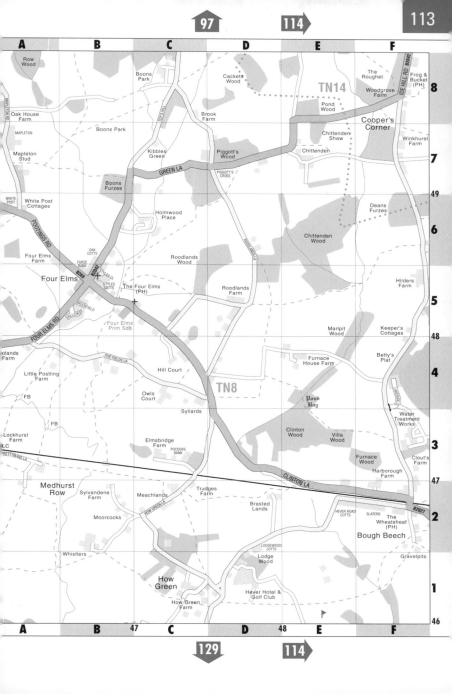

A **B** **C** **D** **E** **F**

8

Faulkners
Hill Farm

TN14

Bushes
Wood

Bushes
Plantation

Bushes
Farm

Winkhurst
Green

7

Nature
Reserve

Bough Beech Reservoir
Nature Centre

49

Bore Place

Deans
Wood

Field
Trail

6

Sharp's
Place

Batfold
Wood

Bough Beech Resr

Kilnhouse
Farm

The Old
Forge

Little
Sidcup

Hale
Farm

5

Bushy
Wood

48

Damper's
Wood

Hickens

Brownings
Cottage

Brownings
Farm

4

CH

TN8

Mountjoy
Farm

HALE OAK RD

Polebrook
Farm

3

Cole's
Farm

Birdfield
Plantation

Cha
Fa

Waterlake

Breeches
Wood

47

The
Horseshoes

Camp
Hill

Chiddingstone
Causeway

Waterlake
Cottage

Somerden

2

CHEQUERS HILL
COTTS THE ALDER

B2027

Jessop's
Farm

Baldocks

TN11

Trad
Est

PO

B20

Penshurs

1

River Eden

Ppg
Sta

Chested
Farm

Beckett's
Farm

Chested

46

Mill
Farm

Sandhole

49 **A** **B** **50** **C** **D** **51** **E** **F**

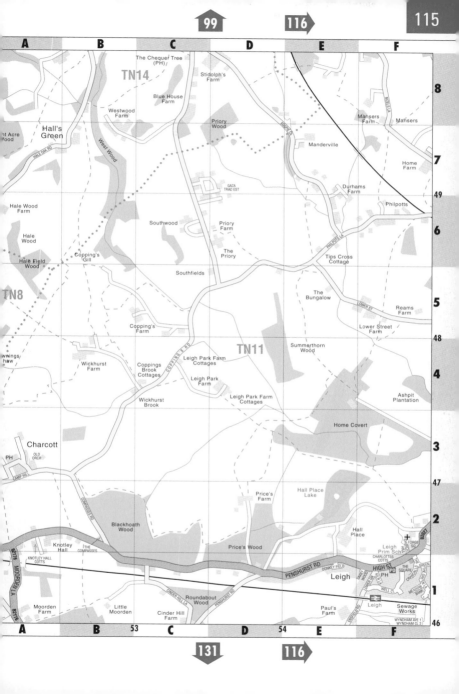

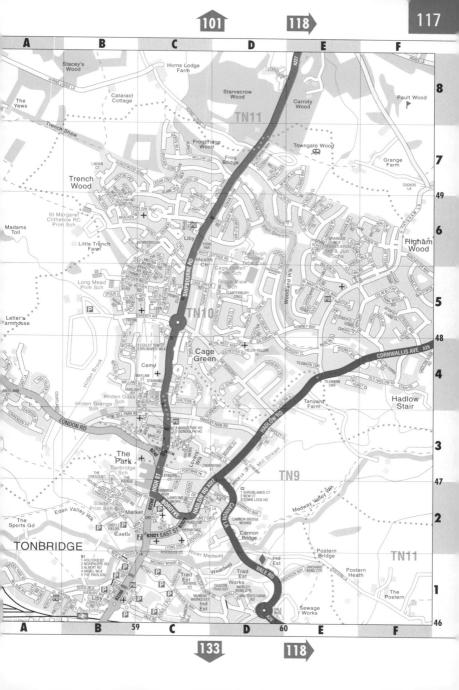

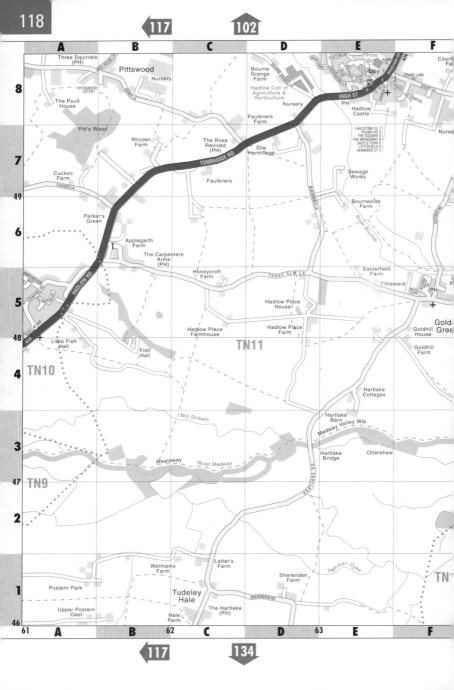

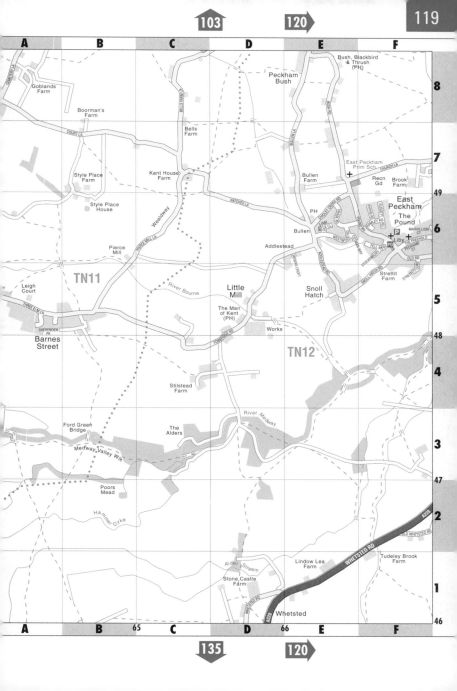

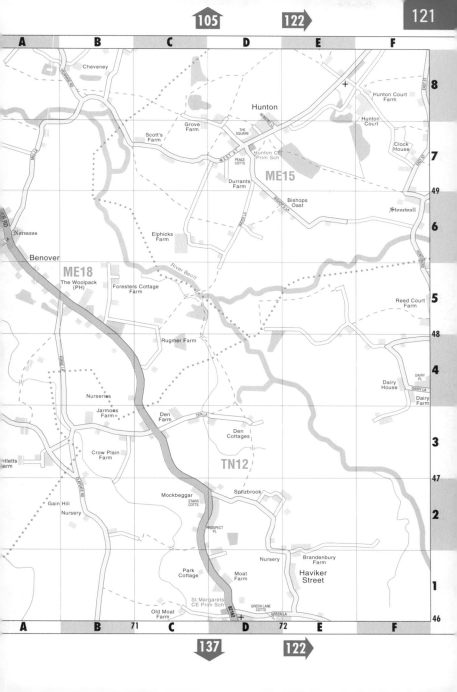

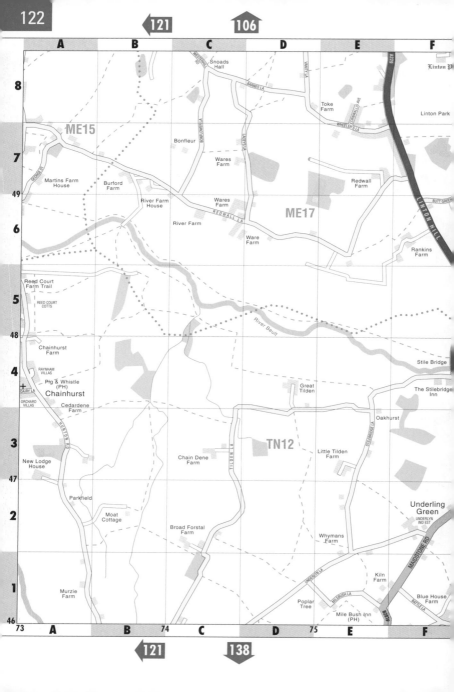

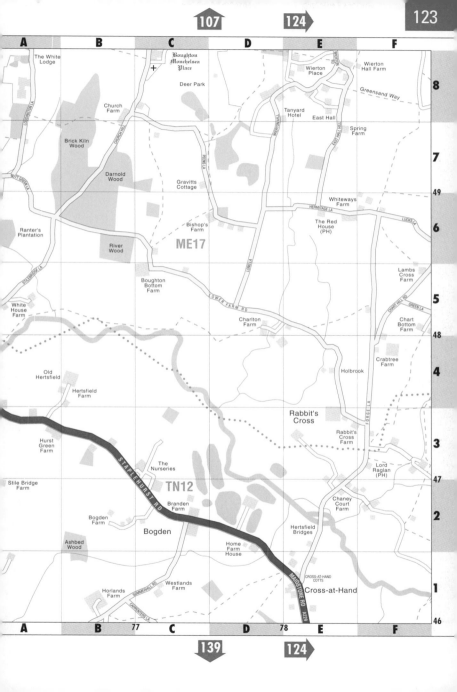

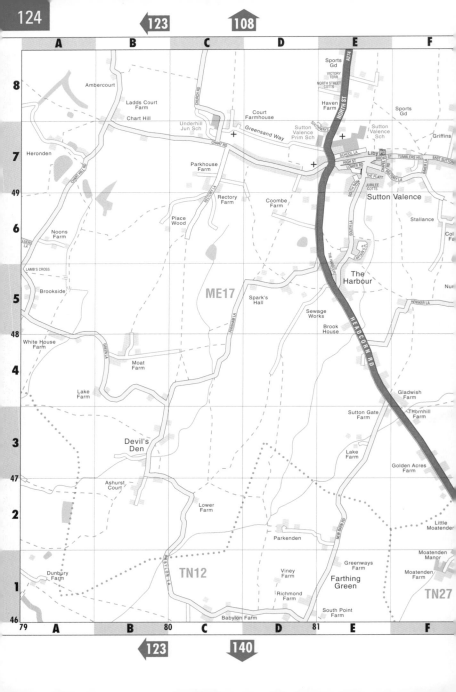

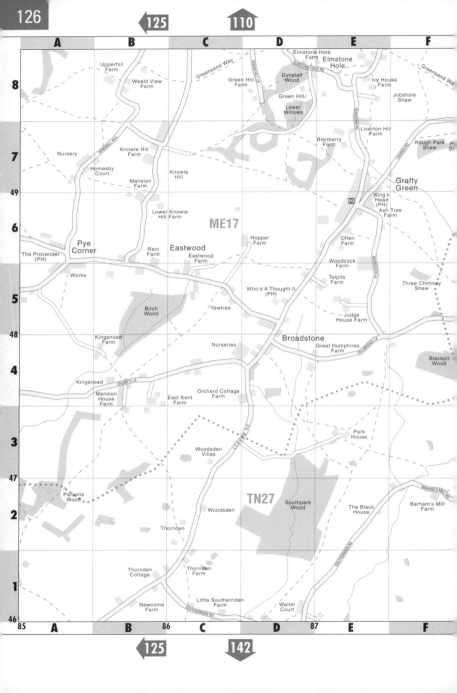

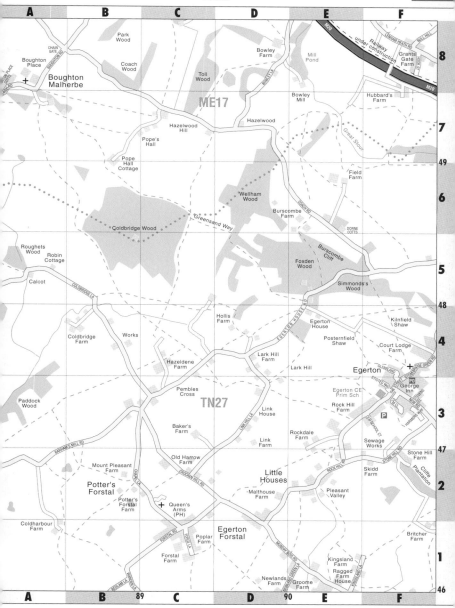

112

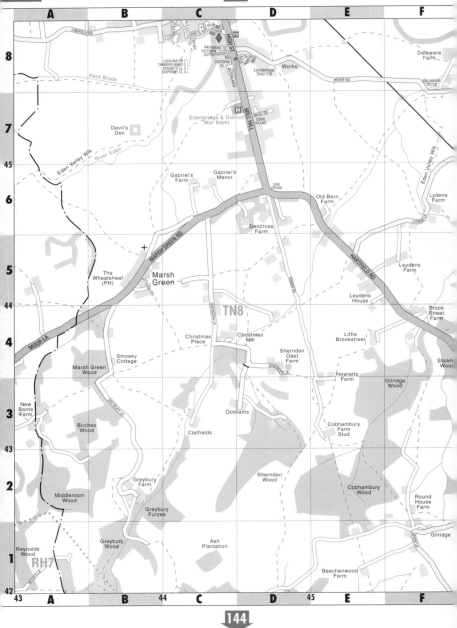

A   B   C   D   E   F

8

LINGFIELD RD

Kent Brook

Delaware
Farm

KATHERINE RD
VICTORIA
COTTS VICTORIA
RD
VICTORIA
CL

LUCILINA DR 1
TANNERS MEAD 2
DOGGETS CL 3
SIXPENNY CL 4

HIGH ST

ASHBY'S
CL

Works

EDENBRIDGE
TRAD CTR

HEVER RD

DELAWARE
COTTS

7

Devil's
Den

River Eden

Eden Valley Wlk

Edenbridge & District
War Meml

MILL HILL

MEAD RD
EDEN
VILLAS

45

Eden Valley Wlk

6

Gabriel's
Farm

Gabriel's
Manor

DEN
CROSS

Old Barn
Farm

Lydens
Farm

5

The Wheatsheaf
(PH)

Marsh
Green

MARSH GREEN RD

Dencross
Farm

ROMAN RD

HARTFIELD RD

Leydens
Farm

44

TN8

Leydens
House

Brook
Street
Farm

4

MOOR LA

Smoaky
Cottage

Christmas
Place

Christmas
Mill

Shernden
Oast
Farm

SIXPENNY LA

Howletts
Farm

Little
Brookstreet

Gilridge
Wood

Stickh
Wood

3

New
Barns
Farm

Marsh Green
Wood

Birches
Wood

JACKROW LA

Ockhams

Clatfields

Cobhambury
Farm
Stud

43

2

Middleroom
Wood

Greybury
Farm

Greybury
Furzes

Shernden
Wood

Cobhambury
Wood

Round
House
Farm

Gilridge

1

Reynolds
Wood

RH7

DUCKS LA

Greybury
Wood

Ash
Plantation

Beechenwood
Farm

42

43   A   B   44   C   D   45   E   F

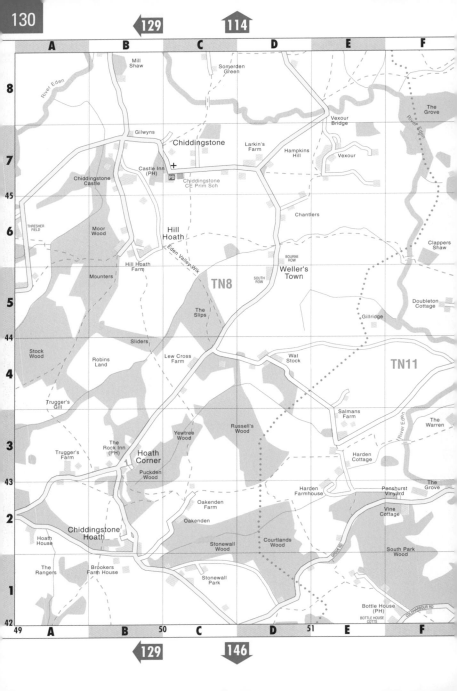

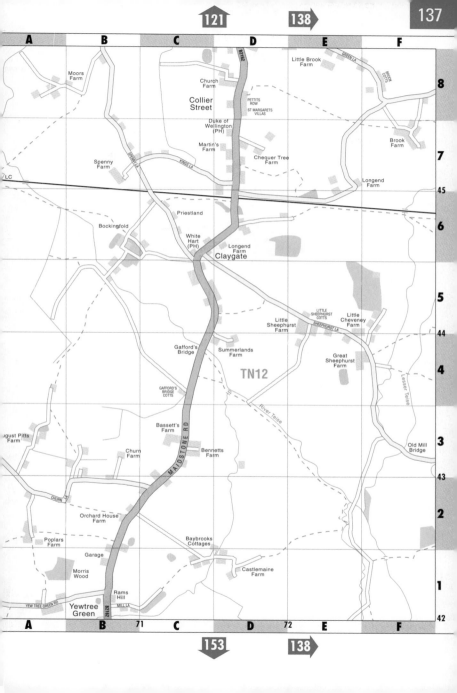

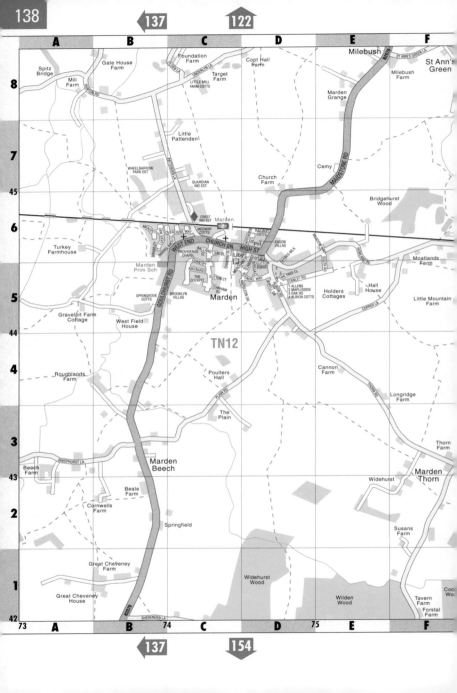

A   B   C   D   E   F

8

Little Crew Den

RUFFLES LA

GRAMMERHILL RD

Allingham Farm

CARPENTERS LA

Summer Hill

Sundridge Nurseries

Clapper Farm

Sweetlands Farm

MAIDSTONE RD

A229

7

Wanshurst Green

Newhaven Farm

45

Abbotsleigh

CLAPPER LA

6

Knowles Hill

Overbridge Farm

Duckhurst Farm

Newtown Cotts

Sewage Works

Staplehurst

LINDRIDGE LA

HONEYCREST IND PK

LODGE RD

DICKENS CT

STATION RD

5

Mountain Farmhouse

Lindridge

Limekiln Farm

Works

MARKET PARTH

Fisher's Farm

TN12

Fouracre

WARDEN RD

FURTHER FIELD

GREEN LA

WATKINS

FISHERS CL

1 BENDEN CL
2 WEAVERS CL
3 KNOWLES WLK

44

Baldwins Farm

MARLPIT

BARN MDW

BROOKS CL

CLUCKOLE'S CNR

HEADCORN RD

Hen & Duckhurst Farm

TOWN CL

ALEN SQ

3

MARIAN SQ

4

Staplehurst

HURST CL

CORNFORTH CL

Great Pagehurst Farm

POPE DR

DUTCH

BUTCHER

Aydhurst Farm

BOWER WLK

Staplehurst Sch

Liby

HIGH ST

3

Little Pagehurst

PAGEHURST RD

GYBBON

CHAPEL LA

LITTLE TREE CL

VINE CT

The Wild Duck (PH)

OWEN'S DR

P.O.

Dourne Farm

KIRKMAN CT

43

Park House

ANTILHURST

CHURCH GN

FRITTENDEN RD

2

The Laurels

FIVE OAK LA

Clarkes Farm

HANNAH WK

HALLIWANGS

GARDEN CL

CRANBROOK RD

A229

Saynden Farm

PRIESTLEY LA

Brattle Farm Mus

PINNOCK LA

Henhurst Farm

The Quarter

Iden Park

1

Ely Court

SOUTHENDEN RD

Gooseberry Wood

42

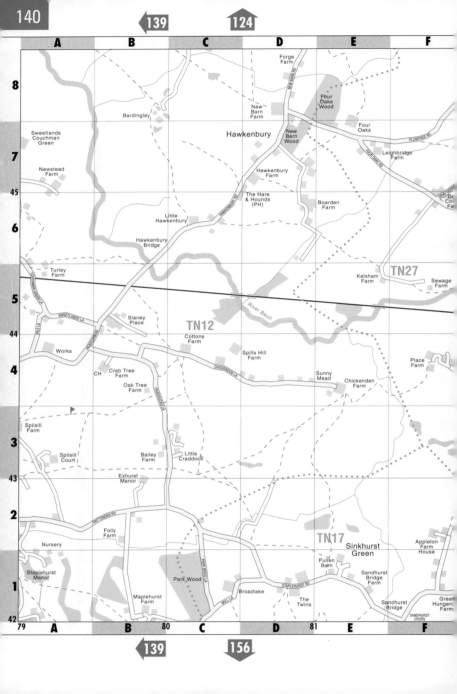

A B C D E F

8
7
45
6
5
44
4
3
43
2
1
42

Plumtree Green
Plumtrees Farm
Barradale Farm
Sunhill Farm

Pinkhorn Farm
Nursery
Nursery

MAIDSTONE RD
STONESTILE RD
PROVIDENCE PL
R OAKS RD

Little Peckham Farm

Little Tilden

Tattlebury
Tilden

Summerhill Farm
Black Mill Farm
Millbank

Headcorn Prim Sch

Hazelpits Farm

Hoggs Bridge

KETTLEBURY RD

LEDBURY RD

LENHAM RD

Sunnyside Farm

Witherden Farm

Woodside Farm

The Ringles (Nursery)

Vineyard

BLACK MILL LA
SUMMERHILL

MOAT RD

Stephen's Bridge

White Horse (PH)

Sewage Works

Kings Arms (PH)

HIGH ST
STATION RD
WHEELER ST

Chantry Farm

River Sherway

1 BLACK HORSE CT
2 TOLLGATE PL

Frank's Bridge

Little East End

CHURCH WLK
PO
FOREMAN CT
RUSHFORD CL

SMARDEN RD

Waterlane Farm

Kettle Bridge

Forstal Farm

Pell Bridge

River Beult

Headcorn
TN27

Headcorn

Wick Farm

WATER LA

New House Farm

Dairy
New Bridge

Headcorn Airfield

Brook Wood Farm

Bletchenden

Hammer Stream

BIDDENDEN RD

Brook Wood

Waterman Quarter

The Hall
Stanley House

TN17

Little Brookwood

Vine Farm

Curtis Farm

Tile Barn Farm

Little Hungerden

Coldharbour Farm

A274

A B 83 C D 84 E F

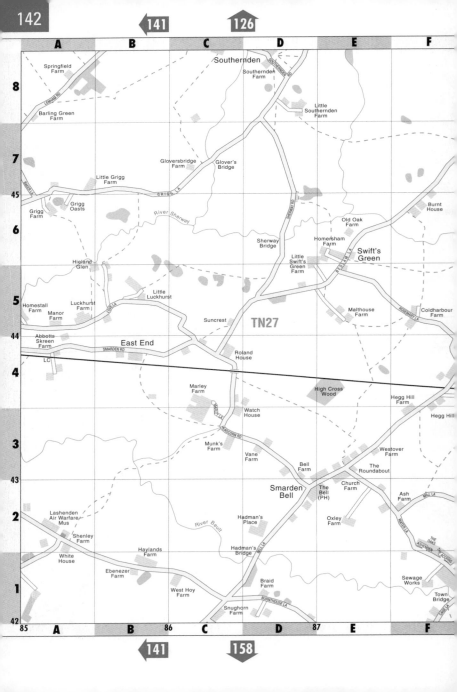

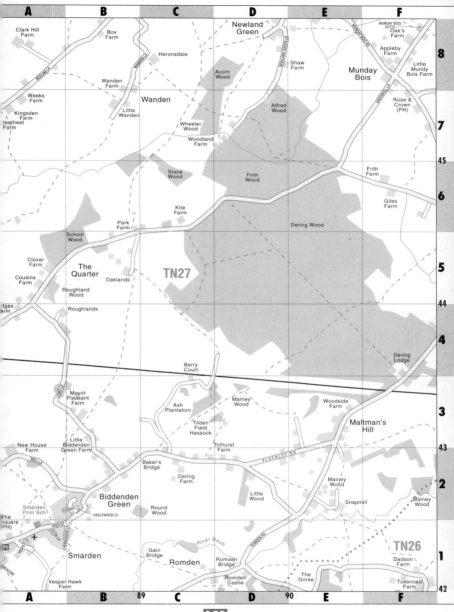

RH7

Dry Hill

Jules Wood

Ten Acre Wood

Willow Bed

Minepit Wood

Crippenden Manor

Ludwells Farm

Polefie

Beeches Farm

Leighton Manor

Old Furzefield Wood

Liveroxhill Wood

Ravenscroft Farm

Cloudhurst Gill

Woodlands Farm

Sussex Border Path

TN8

Clay's Wood

Marlpit Shaw

Waystrod Manor

Lower Stonehurst Farm

Basing & Smithers Farm

Drews Rough

Scarletts

Furnace Farm

Pondtail

Kent Water

GATWICK FARM COTTS

Scarletts Lake

Furnace Pond

Vanguard Way

Cleavers Farm

Mill Wood

Reading's Wood

Bank Farm

Roger's Town

Holtye Common

A264 HOLTYE RD

Steadleaze Wood

Cooper's Wood

COUNTESS OF THANET'S ALMSHOUSES

Holtye

High Meadows

Home Farm

RH19

Holtye Golf Club

Hammerwood

Brooklands

Hammerwood Park

Hammer Wood

Cansiron Wood

CANSIRON LA.

Wet Wood

Sewage Works

Little Cansiron Farm

The Grove COTTS

Water Wood

TN7

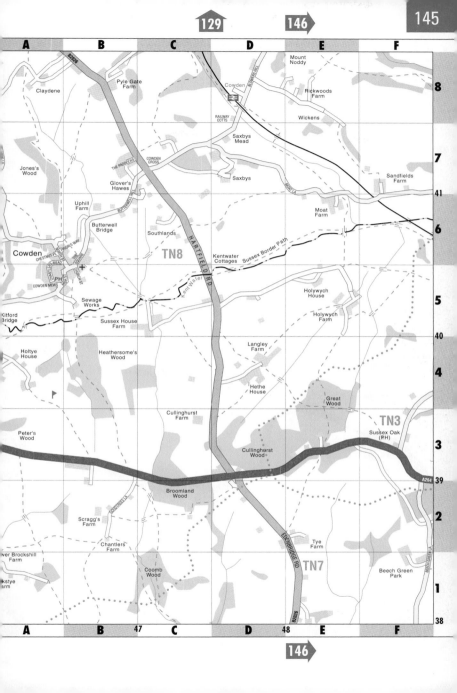

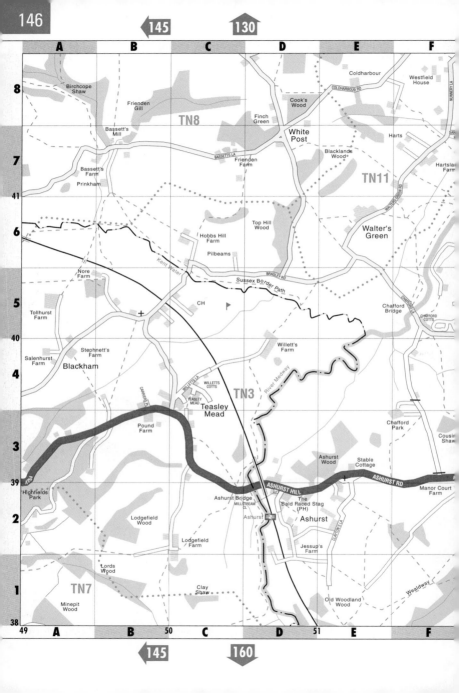

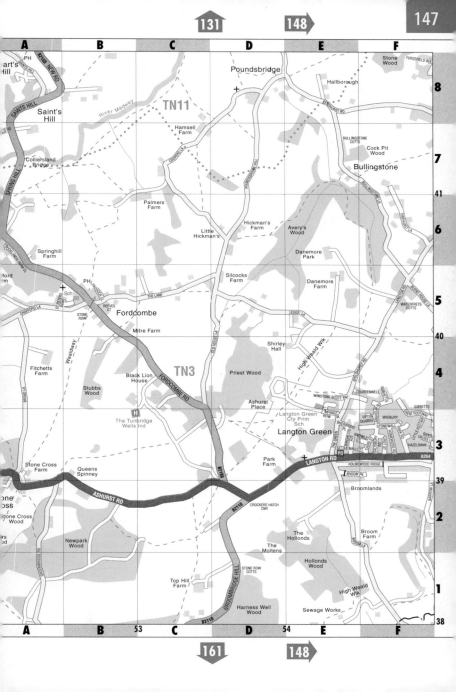

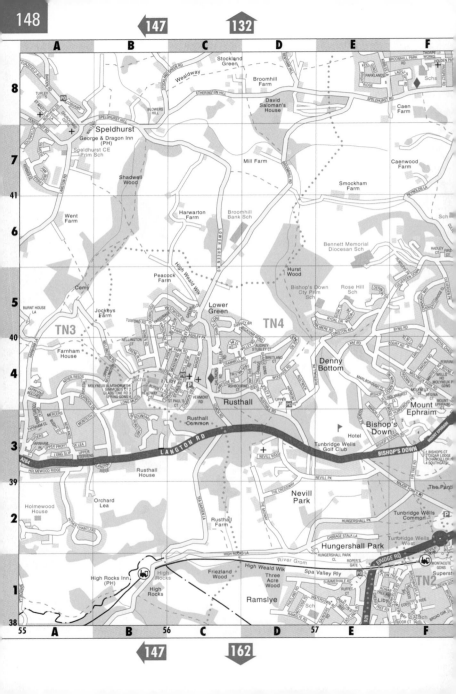

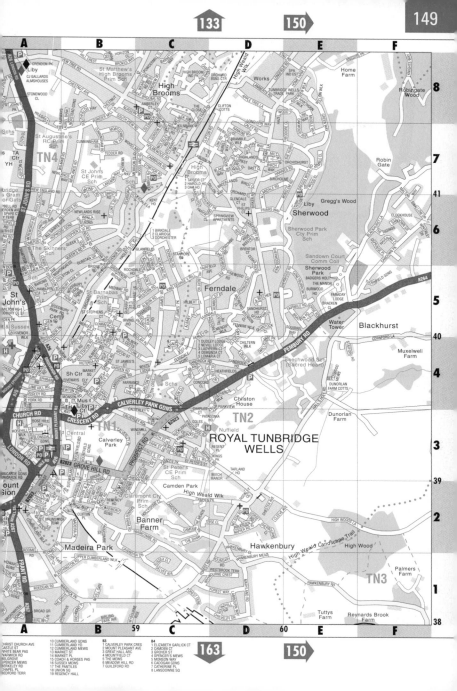

149
134

A   B   C   D   E   F

8

TN11

Sandhill Farm

Newbars Wood

Marshleyharbour Wood

Forest Wood

Lower Green

Pembury Cty Prim Sch

Snipe Wood

7

Pembury

Liby

Pembury CL

Romford

41

Priory Farm

Ridgewaite Way

Woodhill Pk

Greenleas

Henwood Green

6

Pembury Grange

Superstore

Sycamore Cotts

Pembury

Hubble's Farm

Stabledene Way

PO

Playing Field

Hastings Rd

The Coach House

Camden Ave

Chalket La

5

St George's Sch

Larkfield Hall

Chalket Farm

TN2

High Weald Landscape Trail

Pastheap Farm

Hastings Rd

40

Fletchers

Fletchers Farm

4

Mouseden

Little Bayhall Farm

Great Bayhall

Brickhurst Wood

TN12

3

Great Bayhall Farm

Gull Rough Wood

39

Little Bayhall

High Woods La

2

TN3

Old Dundle

Dodhurst

Dundale Rd

1

River Teise

Dundale Farm

Dundale Wood

Brown's Lodge

38

61   A   B   62   C   D   63   E   F

149
164

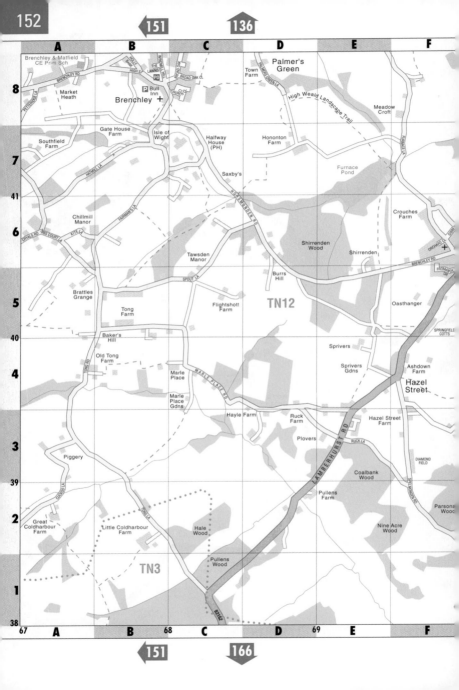

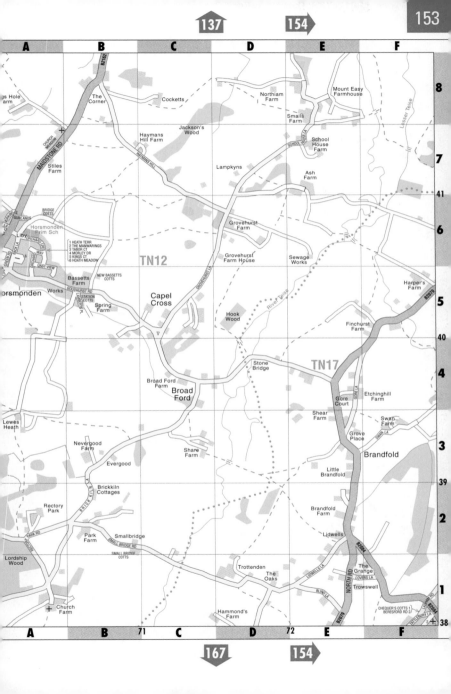

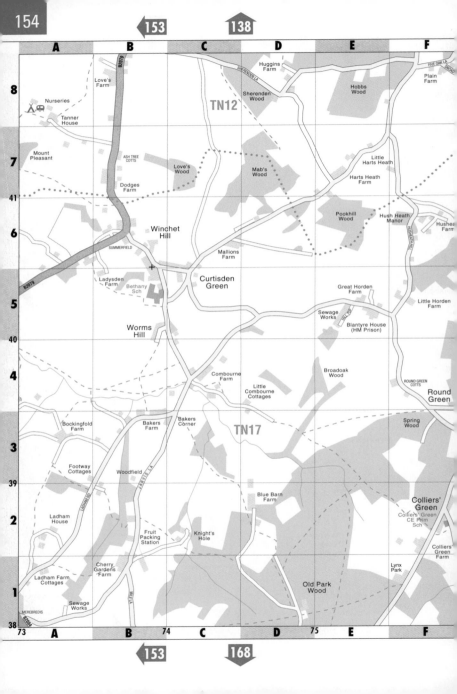

A **B** **C** **D** **E** **F**

Love's Farm

Huggins Farm

Plain Farm

8

Nurseries

Tanner House

Sherenden Wood

Hobbs Wood

TN12

Mount Pleasant

ASH TREE COTTS

Love's Wood

Mab's Wood

Little Harts Heath

7

Dodges Farm

Harts Heath Farm

41

Pookhill Wood

Hush Heath Manor

Hushes Farm

Winchet Hill

6

SUMMERFIELD

Mallions Farm

Curtisden Green

Great Horden Farm

Little Horden Farm

Ladysden Farm

Bethany Sch

5

Worms Hill

Sewage Works

Blantyre House (HM Prison)

40

Broadoak Wood

4

Combourne Farm

Little Combourne Cottages

ROUND GREEN COTTS

Round Green

Bockingfold Farm

Bakers Farm

Bakers Corner

TN17

Spring Wood

3

Footway Cottages

Woodfield

39

Blue Barn Farm

Colliers' Green

2

Ladham House

Colliers' Green CE Prim Sch

Fruit Packing Station

Knight's Hole

Colliers' Green Farm

Cherry Gardens Farm

Lynx Park

1

Ladham Farm Cottages

Old Park Wood

Sewage Works

MEREBREDIS

38

73 **A** **B** **74** **C** **D** **75** **E** **F**

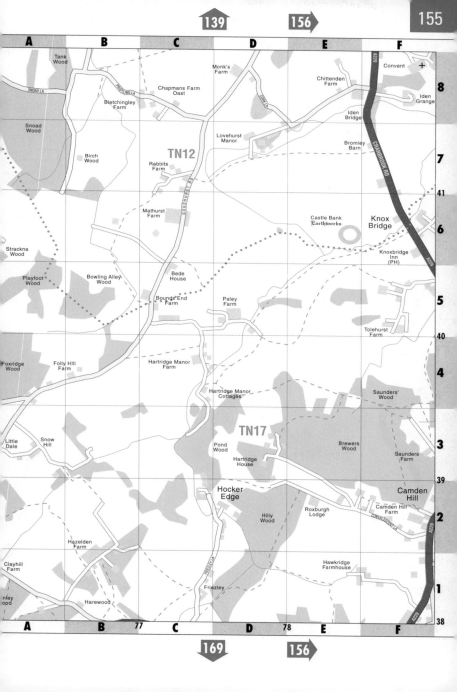

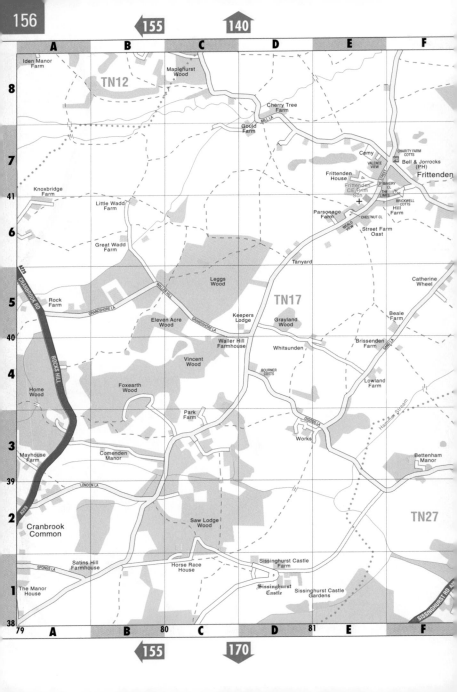

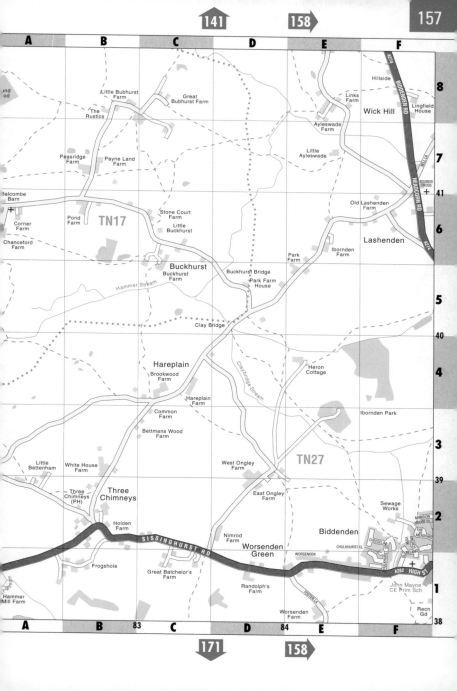

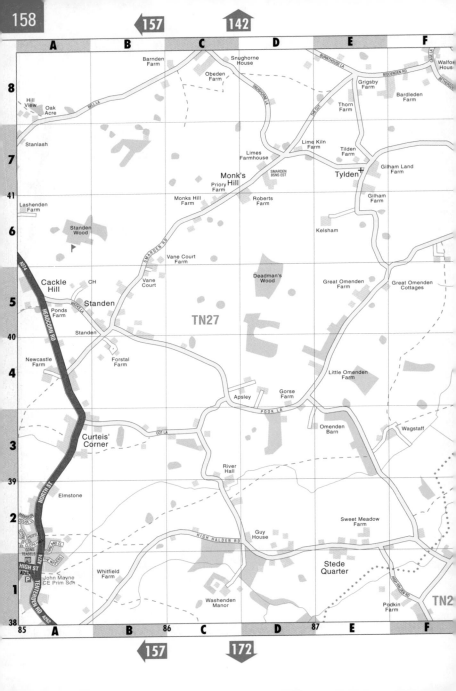

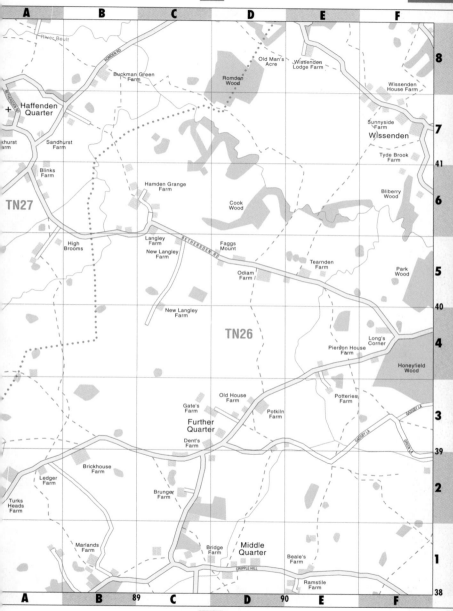

River Beult

ROMDEN RD

Buckman Green
Farm

Old Man's
Acre

Romden
Wood

Wissenden
Lodge Farm

Wissenden
House Farm

8

BETHERSDEN RD

Haffenden
Quarter

Sunnyside
Farm

Wissenden

7

Sandhurst
Farm

Tyde Brook
Farm

41

xhurst
arm

Blinks
Farm

Hamden Grange
Farm

Bliberry
Wood

6

TN27

Cook
Wood

High
Brooms

Langley
Farm

New Langley
Farm

BETHERSDEN RD

Faggs
Mount

Tearnden
Farm

Park
Wood

5

Odiam
Farm

New Langley
Farm

40

TN26

Long's
Corner

4

Pierson House
Farm

Honeyfield
Wood

Old House
Farm

Potteries
Farm

Gate's
Farm

Potkiln
Farm

3

Further
Quarter

GADDEN LA

Dent's
Farm

39

Brickhouse
Farm

Ledger
Farm

Brunger
Farm

2

Turks
Heads
Farm

Marlands
Farm

Bridge
Farm

Middle
Quarter

Beale's
Farm

1

CRIPPLE HILL

Ramstile
Farm

38

A B C D E F

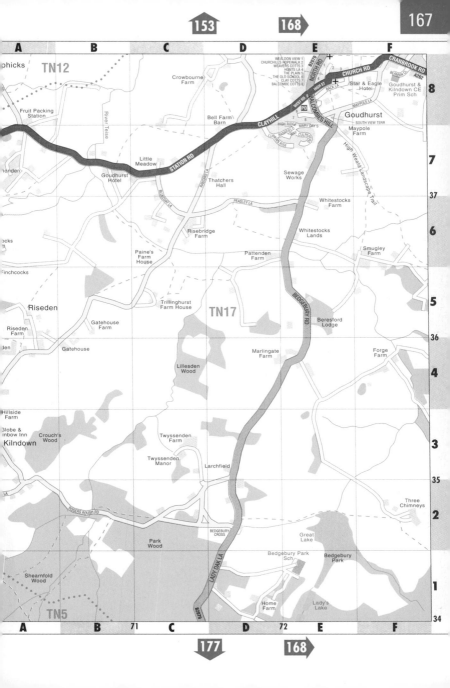

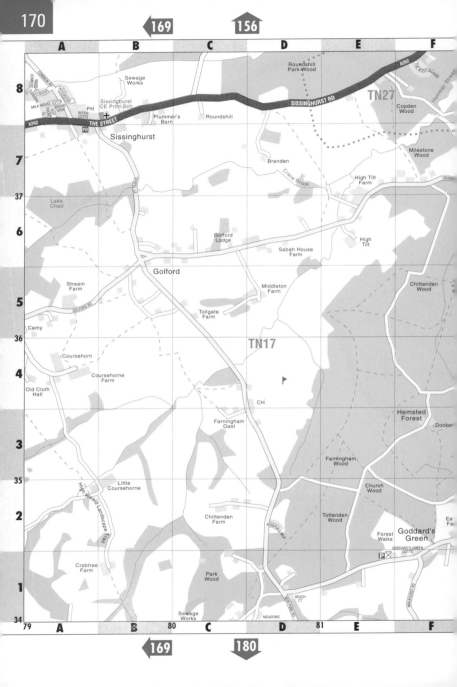

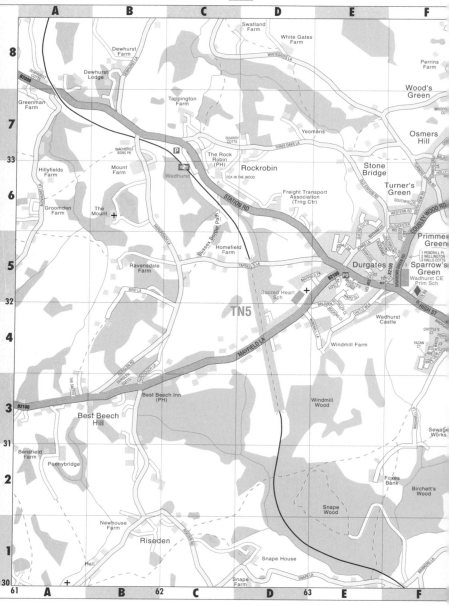

Swatland Farm

White Gates Farm

Dewhurst Farm

WHITEGATES LA

Perrins Farm

Dewhurst Lodge

Wood's Green

B2099

DEWHURST COTTS

Greenman Farm

WOODS CO

Tappington Farm

7

Yeomans

THREE OAKS LA

Osmers Hill

QUARRY COTTS

WADHURST BSNS PK

33

Hillfields Farm

P

Wadhurst

The Rock Robin (PH)

Rockrobin

Stone Bridge

Mount Farm

FOX IN THE WOOD

Turner's Green

6

SOUTHFIELD

WESTERN RD

Groomden Farm

The Mount

STATION RD

Freight Transport Association (Trng Ctr)

Primmer Green

1 PENDRILL PL
2 WELLINGTON
3 HALLS COTTS

Sussex Border Path

Homefield Farm

Sparrow's Green

Durgates

Wadhurst CE Prim Sch

5

Ravensdale Farm

TAPSELL'S LA

MAYFIELD PK

B2100

BIRD LA

Sacred Heart Sch

LITTLE

HIGH ST

32

TN5

Wadhurst Castle

MAYFIELD LA

Windmill Farm

CRITTLE'S

4

FAZAN CT

COURTHOPE AVE

THE SMITHS

FARNDEN COTTS

Windmill Wood

Best Beech Inn (PH)

3

B2100

Best Beech Hill

Sewage Works

31

Bensfield Farm

Pennybridge

Foxes Bank

2

Birchett's Wood

Snape Wood

Newhouse Farm

Riseden

1

DEER RD

Snape House

Hall

SNAPE LA

30

Snape Farm

BIRCHETTS LA

A   B   C   D   E   F

Newbury's

NEWBURY COTTS

NEWBURY LA

MONKS LA

WRANGDELL LA

The Colleens

B2100

Ladymeads Farm

NEWBRIDGE LA

8

Lower Cousley Wood

Gate House Farm

COUSLEY WOOD RD

PH

Cousley Wood

Pell Green

Great Butts

7

Little Butts Farm

33

BALACLAVA LA

Great Pell Oast

1 FAIR VIEW
2 DEEPDENE
3 THE LEAS
4 PELL CL
5 BIRCH KILN COTTS

Bewl Water

Bryant's Farm

6

Pell Bridge

Sussex Border Path

Newbarn

Wishdown

5

Vicarage Green

BLACKSMITHS LA

Little Pell Farm

Southfields

32

Foxhole

TN5

Little Whiligh

Chesson's Farm

4

Long Wood

WARD LA

1 THE SQUARE
2 KINGSLEY CT

Wadhurst

LOWER HIGH ST

GREAT DIX FIELD/PARK RD

FOSGILL LA

Whiligh

Birchett's Green

BIRCHETTS GREEN LA

Birchett's Green Farm

3

lands
omm
Coll

Stone Cross

Moseham

Whiligh

31

PRIMMERS LA

Darby's Farm

DARBY'S LA

Holbeam Wood

2

HIGH ST

Shover's Green House

STONEGATE RD

Cattle Breeding Ctr

B2099

1

Shover's Green

Upper Wallands Farm

Normanswood

Bugsey's Farm

Wallcrouch Farm

Valland Manor

CHURCHSETTLE LA

Wallcrouch

30

A   B   65   C   D   66   E   F

A   B   C   D   E   F

8

Brick Kiln
Cottages

TN17

Sugarloaf
Hill

Hedgingford
Wood

WHITELIMES

Louisa
Lodge

PARK LA

Foresters
Cottage

TN17

Tubslake

Frith
Wood

Badger's
Oak

Osborne's

HAWKHURST RD

A229

7

33

Louisa
Lake

Rose
Farm

6

Frith
Farm

Trenley
Farm

Yewtree
Farm

Limes
Grove
Farm

Tanyard
Farm

STATION
COTTS

LIMES GR

Gill's
Green

5

32

TN18

Siseley
Farm

Gill's
Green
Farm

CRANBROOK RD

PEASTENOAK RD

SOPER'S LA

4

Soper's Lane
Farm

SLIP MILL RD

WELLINGTON CTS

Trewint
Farm

Wellington
Arms
(PH)

3

31

Little
Pix Hall
Farm

Slip
Mill

SYDNEY TERR 1
CASTLE TERR 2
SANDROOK VILLAS 3

LIGHTFOOT
GN

SPRINGFIELD
IND EST

Lightfoot
Green

Elm Hill
Farm

CH

2

A268

Hawkhurst
Cottage

H

High
Street

HIGH ST

SLIP VILLAS

PHILPOTT'S
CROSS

Marlborough
House
Sch

Sch

A268

HIGHGATE HILL

Elm Hill
House

IDDENDEN
COTTS

NORTH HILL RD

F2
1 EDEN CT
2 DAINTONS COTTS
3 OAK TERR
4 NORMAN VILLAS
5 ARMITAGE PL
6 SCHOOL TERR
7 WESTERN AVE
8 HIGHGATE CT
9 NORTHGROVE RD
10 CRANE HOUSE GDNS
11 CRANE HOUSE
12 POST OFFICE RD

LORENDEN
PK

Seacox
Poultry Farm

1

Delmonden
Manor

DELMONDEN RD

Hurstwood
Cottage

Hensill
House

Cockshot

TN19

Sussex Border Path

30
73   A   B   74   C   D   75   E   F

8

7

33

TN17

6

5

32

TN18

4

3

31

2

1

30

Mill Crest Farm

Robin's Wood

Cranbrook Wood

School Farm

CRANBROOK RD

The Moat

B2086

Crit Hall

B2086

Tubslake Farm

Baretilt Farm

Attwater Farm

Netter's Hall Farm

Potter's Farm

ATTWATERS LA

Little Nineveh

NINEVEH LA

Forest Farm

POTTER'S LA

Four Wents

The Forest

Merry Mead Farm

Ellenden

Tilden Farm

Great Nineveh

White Chimney Wood

WATER LA

Paul's Farm

TN18

Woodsden Farm

Diprose

Beal's Green

Lower Ellenden Farm

Ockley

OCKLEY LA

Furnace Mill Farm

Park Farm

Hinxden Farm

HARTNOKES

Tongswood Home Farm

The Paper Mill

Duvals Farm

Gun Green

WHITE'S LA

Hinksden Bridge

Hawkhurst

St Ronan's Sch

Tongs Wood

CHURCH WLK

Fowler's Park House

DICKENS WAY

CONGHURST DR

Roughland Wood

RYE RD

WATER LA

Hotel

Pipsden

CONGS LA

Foxhole

Hawkhurst Place Farm

A268

Links Farm

Steven's Farm

8

Mount Pleasant Farm

Mount-Hall Farm

Colebarn Farm

Halden Place

Cott Farm

Mount Le Hoe

Stepneyford Bridge

Stumble Wood

7

Nine Acre Wood

STEPNEYFORD LA

Maplesden Farm

33

Beacon Wood

Greenlane Farm

HALDEN LA

Brick Kiln Wood

6

Hole Park

Rawlinson Farm

Windmill (dis)

Rawlinson Gill

Beacon Hill

TN17

Halden Lane Farm

5

Beacon Hall Farm

Sewage Works

32

RANTERS OAK

B E N E N D E N   R D

Chessenden

CATTELLO COTTS

A28

TENTERDEN RD

4

The Orchards

West Cross

Windmill Farm

TANYARD
The Bull Inn
B2086
REGENT ST
HIGH ST
Mus
Rolvenden

WIN FIELDS

Windmill (dis)

Mill House

SPARKESWOOD CL

OLD RECTORY

Sparkeswood

3

Dingleden Farm

Kemsdale House

HIGH

High Weald Landscape Trial

Rolvenden Prim Sch

SUMNER CL

PIES LA

HIGH ST
SUMMERY

OLD PARSONAGE

Pookwell Wood

The Wilderness

31

Elphees

MAYTHAM RD

2

Rowenden Vineyard

Toad Hall

Great Maytham

SANDHURST LA

Devenden

Merrington Place

Farnell Wood

HASTINGS RD

Cherrygarden Farm

Cornhill

1

Mallards

BLIND LA

A28

FROG'S LA

LITTLE JOB'S CROSS

30

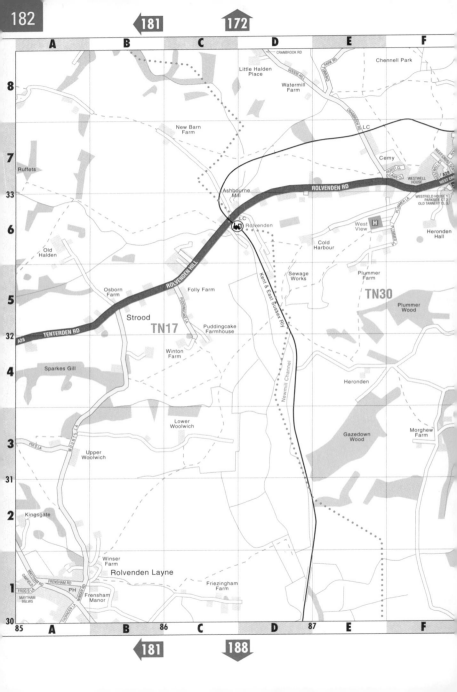

A7
1 PITTLESDEN PL
2 PARK VIEW TERR
3 STATION MEWS
4 ST MILDREDS CL
5 EASTWELL
6 SAYERS LA
7 THEATRE SQ
8 JACKSONS LA
9 BELLS LA
10 BURGESS ROW
11 MAYOR'S PL
12 CEDAR CT
13 BENNETTS MEWS
14 AUSTENS ORCH

DRURY RD 1
ST BENETS WAY 2
ST BENETS CT 3

WOODCHURCH RD
B2067

CH

Lower Knockwood Farm

Pearce Barn

Pigeon Hoo

St Benets Way
St Benets Ct

ASHFORD RD

MOUNT PLEASANT
CRAYTHORNE HO

TENTERDEN

EAST HILL
B2067

Kent & East Sussex Rwy

esden
Manor
Farm Ind
Est

LC

eden

TH

Mus

HIGH ST

Liby

SMALLHYTHE RD

Tenterden
CE Jun
Sch

L Ctr

Tenterden
Inf Sch

ORCHARD
VIEW

ELMFIELD

THE
BUNGALOWS

Huson
Farm

Belgar

Finchden
Manor

APPLEDORE RD

Maynards

Leigh Green
Ind Est

Leigh
Green

Gibbet Oak
Farm

ronden

GROVE
COTTS

Belcot Manor
Farm

Tilder Gill

Forstal
Farm

Haynes
Farm

TN30

Kench Hill

Settes Wood
Farm

Morghew

Ratsbury

The
Quarter

Broad
Tenterden

Pick Hill
Farm

PICKHILL
OAST

Finchbourne
Wood

SMALL HYTHE RD

Ashenden

Coneyboro'
Wood

Hongland

Summer
Hill

Liby

Old Gate
Cottage

Dumbourne

Great Hanging
Wood

Reading Sewer

Tenterden
Vineyard

Small Hythe

Spots
Farm

Great
Bulleigh

Bulleigh
Barn

B2082

Mus

8
33
7
6
5
32
4
31
3
2
1
30

A   B   89   C   D   90   E   F

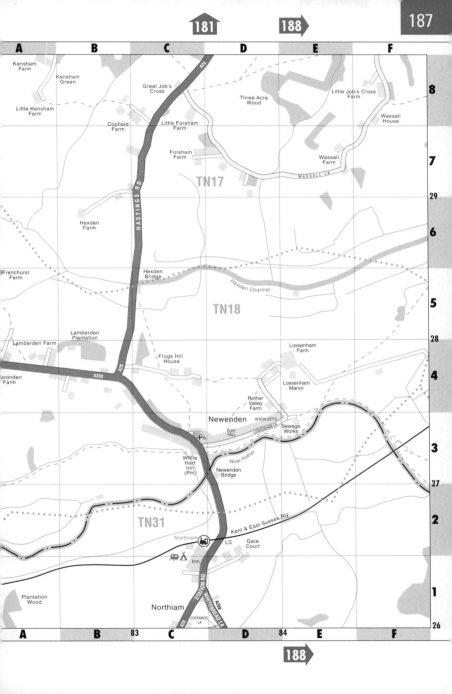

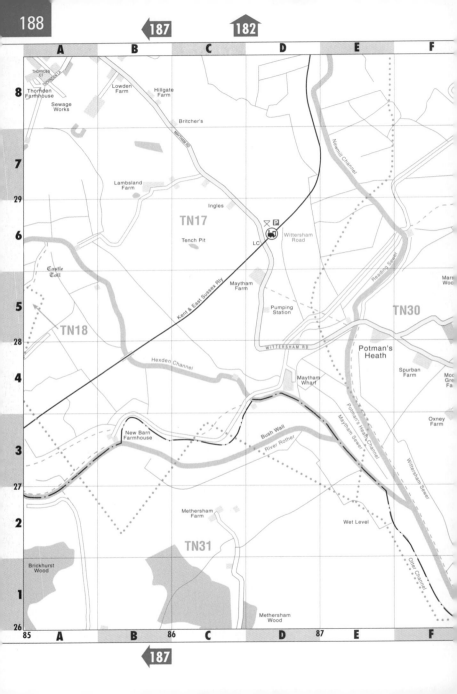

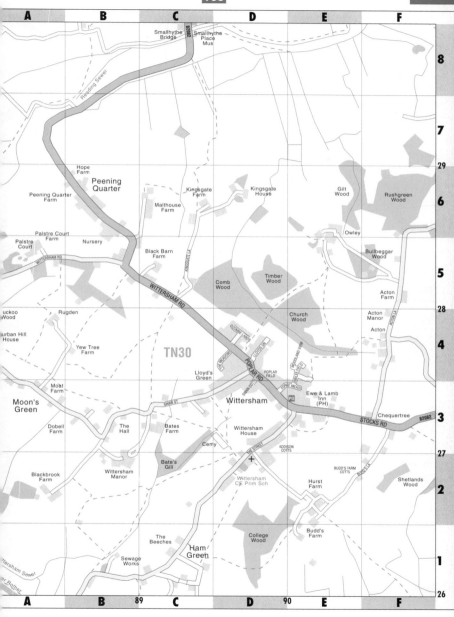

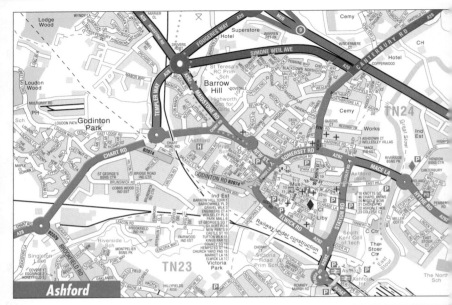

Ashford

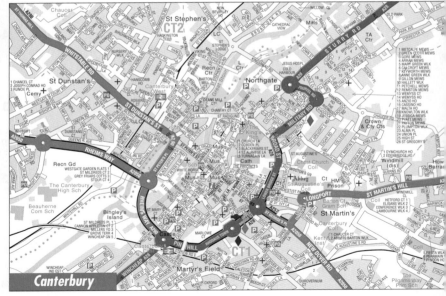

Canterbury

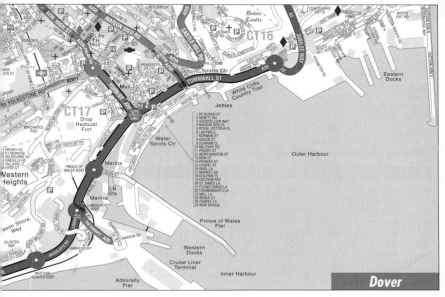

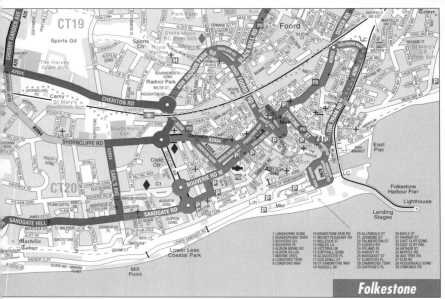

Dover

1 DE BURGH ST
2 HEWITT RD
3 GOODFELLOW WAY
4 MAISON DIEU PL
5 ROYAL VICTORIA PL
6 LADYWELL
7 NORMAN ST
8 SAXON ST
9 DURHAM CL
10 MILITARY RD
11 PRIORY ST
12 WORTHINGTON ST
13 NEW ST
14 PRINCES ST
15 CHAPEL PL
16 GAOL LA
17 MARKET SQ
18 DOLPHIN PAS
19 DOLPHIN PAS
20 ST JAMES LA
21 FLYING HORSE LA
22 FISHMONGER'S LA
23 MILL LA
24 BENCH ST
25 CHAPEL LA
26 NEW BRIDGE

Folkestone

1 LANGHORNE GDNS
2 SHAKESPEARE TERR
3 BOUVERIE SQ
4 BOUVERIE PL
5 ALBION MEWS RD
6 ALBION VILLAS
7 MARINE CRES
8 LONGFORD TERR
9 LONGFORD WAY
10 BRADSTONE NEW RD
11 MOUNT PLEASANT RD
12 BELLEVUE ST
13 INGLES LA
14 VICTORIA GR
15 COPTHALL GDNS
16 GLOUCESTER PL
17 GUILDHALL ST
18 ST EANSWYTHE WAY
19 RUSSELL RD
20 ALLENDALE ST
21 JESMOND ST
22 PALMERSTON ST
23 SUSSEX RD
24 RYLAND PL
25 HARVEY PL
26 MARGARET ST
27 ELMSTEAD PL
28 CAMBRIDGE TERR
29 SAFFRON'S PL
30 BAYLE ST
31 RADNOR ST
32 EAST CLIFF GDNS
33 EAST CLIFF PAS
34 ARTHUR ST
35 MYRTLE RD
36 ASH TREE RD
37 ELM RD
38 ROSSENDALE GDNS
39 ORMONDE RD

Church Rd **6** Beckenham BR2..........**53** C6

Place name	Location number	Locality, town or village	Postcode district	Page and grid square
May be abbreviated on the map	Present when a number indicates the place's position in a crowded area of mapping	Shown when more than one place has the same name	District for the indexed place	Page number and grid reference for the standard mapping

Public and commercial buildings are highlighted in magenta. **Places of interest** are highlighted in blue with a star*

Index of localities, towns and villages

Addington 73 C2
Allhallows 19 C7
Allhallows-on-Sea 19 D9
Ash 56 E5
Aylesford 75 D1
Badgers Mount 53 A1
Barking 8 F8
Barnes Street 119 A5
Basted 86 E4
Bean 28 B5
Bells Yew Green 163 A5
Beltring 120 B4
Benenden 180 D6
Benover 121 A7
Betsham 28 D3
Bexley 7 A2
Bidborough 132 C3
Biddenden 157 C2
Biddenden Green 143 A2
Birling 74 B5
Bitchet Green 85 D1
Bodiam 185 A3
Bogden 123 C1
Borough Green 86 D6
Bough Beech 113 F4
Boxley 77 C2
Brandfold 153 F3
Brasted 82 A2
Bredhurst 63 A1
Brenchley 152 A6
Broad Street 94 A6
Broadstone 126 D3
Bromley 36 A4
Burham 60 C1
Capel 134 F6
Chainhurst 122 A4
Chalk 31 A6
Chart Sutton 108 B1
Chartway Street 109 A8
Chatham 47 E4
Chattenden 33 F4
Chelsfield 52 D4
Chestnut Street 65 D4
Chiddingstone
  Causeway 114 F2
Chislehurst 37 A7
Cliffe 15 C8
Cliffe Woods 33 A8
Cobbarn 161 B2
Cobham 44 F6
Cold Harbour 65 F8

Coldblow 25 B7
Collier Street 137 E8
Colt's Hill 135 B4
Congelow 120 F8
Cooling 16 E4
Cowden 145 D8
Coxheath 106 A4
Cranbrook 169 B4
Cranbrook Common 156 A2
Crayford 8 D2
Crockenhill 39 C2
Crockham Hill 96 B1
Crouch 87 B3
Cudham 66 C4
Culverstone Green 57 F2
Cuxton 46 B2
Dartford 9 C3
Detling 78 A1
Ditton 75 A1
Downe 66 A8
East End 171 C2
East Farleigh 106 A7
East Malling 90 A6
East Peckham 119 F6
East Tilbury 14 B7
Eccles 75 F5
Edenbridge 112 A2
Egerton 127 E6
Eltham 5 A2
Erith 4 A1
Eynsford 54 B4
Farningham 40 D3
Farthing Street 50 E2
Fawkham Green 56 B7
Five Oak Green 135 B7
Flimwell 177 C3
Fordcombe 147 C4
Four Elms 113 A6
Frant 163 B4
Frittenden 156 D8
Gillingham 48 F4
Golden Green 118 F6
Goudhurst 167 A5
Grain 21 B5
Gravesend 13 A1
Grays 12 A8
Greenwich 1 D3
Groombridge 161 A6
Hadlow 102 D1
Hale Street 120 B7
Halling 60 A4

Halstead 67 F6
Harrietsham 110 B5
Hartley 42 E4
Hartlip 64 C3
Hawkhurst 179 A1
Hawley 26 E4
Hayes 36 A1
Headcorn 141 A4
Hever 129 B7
Hextable 25 E1
High Halden 173 E7
High Halstow 17 C4
Higham 32 B2
Hoo St Werburgh 34 C5
Horsmonden 153 A5
Horton Kirby 41 C4
Hunton 121 D6
Hurst Green 184 A3
Ide Hill 97 D6
Ightham 86 C5
Istead Rise 43 F7
Kemsing 70 A1
Kilndown 166 F3
Kings Hill 89 A1
Kingsnorth 35 C8
Kingswood 109 D2
Kit's Coty 76 C7
Knockmill 70 F8
Laddingford 120 E4
Lamberhurst 166 A5
Langley Heath 108 E3
Larkfield 75 A1
Lashenden 158 B8
Leeds 109 A7
Leigh 115 E1
Lenham 111 B7
Lewisham 22 A4
Leybourne 74 C2
Lidsing 62 F1
Longfield 42 D6
Lower Stoke 19 C3
Luddesdown 44 E8
Lunsford 74 F3
Maidstone 92 B4
Marden 138 B6
Marlpit Hill 112 B4
Matfield 151 C6
Meopham 58 A1
Meopham Station 44 A2
Mereworth 103 C7
Mill Street 89 C7

Nettlestead 104 B5
Nettlestead Green 104 C1
New Ash Green 56 E7
New Barn 43 A6
New Hythe 75 A4
New Street 57 D4
New Town 89 A8
Newbury's 175 B8
Newenden 187 C3
Newham 1 F5
Newington 65 A5
Northfleet 12 A2
Northiam 187 C1
Oad Street 65 F1
Offham 88 C7
Oldbury 86 B5
Orpington 38 A1
Otford 69 A2
Otham 108 B7
Otham Hole 108 A6
Paddock Wood 135 E6
Parkgate 172 C1
Pembury 150 E7
Penshurst 131 A3
Platt 87 C5
Platt's Heath 110 F1
Plaxtol 101 E6
Plaxtol Spoute 102 A8
Plumtree Green 141 F7
Potman's Heath 188 D4
Potter's Forstal 127 B2
Poundsbridge 147 C7
Pratling Street 76 B4
Pratt's Bottom 52 A1
Purfleet 10 C8
Pye Corner 126 B7
Rabbit's Cross 123 D5
Rainham 4 D8
Rochester 47 B3
Rolvenden 181 E4
Royal Tunbridge Wells . .149 B4
Ryarsh 73 F4
St Mary's Island 34 B1
St Paul's Cray 38 A6
Seabrook 186 B5
Seal 85 A7
Sevenoaks 84 A4
Sheerness 21 F3
Shipbourne 101 C5
Shoreham 68 F6
Shorne 31 D5

Sidcup 24 A3
Silver Street 80 F5
Sissinghurst 170 A8
Snodland 75 A6
Sole Street 44 B5
Speldhurst 148 B8
Stansted 56 E1
Staplehurst 139 C5
Stockbury 79 D8
Stone 10 E1
Sundridge 82 D3
Sutton at Hone 27 A2
Sutton Valence 124 C6
Swanley 39 B8
Swanscombe 11 A3
Tenterden 183 A6
Teston 105 A7
The Moor 184 E7
Thurnham 78 D1
Ticehurst 176 C1
Tilbury 13 A3
Tonbridge 117 A1
Trottiscliffe 73 A4
Turnden 169 B4
Tylden 158 F8
Ulcombe 125 D5
Underling Green 122 E3
Upper Halling 59 C4
Upper Upnor 33 D4
Vigo Village 73 A8
Wadhurst 175 F8
Wateringbury 104 C7
West Farleigh 105 B5
West Kingsdown 55 D5
West Malling 89 B8
West Peckham 103 A6
West Thurrock 11 A7
Westerham 81 B2
Whetsted 119 F1
Withyham 160 B5
Wittersham 189 C3
Woolwich 2 A8
Wormshill 95 F7
Wouldham 60 C3
Wrotham 71 C3
Wrotham Heath 73 D7
Yalding 104 E2
Yelsted 64 A1

A

aron Hill Rd E6 ....2 A8
bbess Cl E6 ....3 D1
bbeville Ho ME1 ....47 C4
bbey Brewery Ct ME19 ....89 C8
bbey Court Sch ME2 ....46 E8
bbey Cres DA17 ....4 B2
bbey Gate Cotts ME14 ....76 F2
bbey Gr SE2 ....3 B2
bbey Lodge SE12 ....22 B4
bbey Mount DA17 ....3 F1
bbey Pl DA1 ....9 D2
bbey Prim Sch SE2 ....3 C3
bbey Rd Bexley DA6,DA7 ....7 E3
Erith DA17 ....3 E3
Gillingham ME8 ....49 A2
Gravesend DA12 ....30 E7
Rochester ME2 ....46 F8
Swanscombe DA9 ....11 C2
bbey Terr SE2 ....3 C2
bbey Wood Rd
Kings Hill ME19 ....89 A5
Woolwich SE2 ....3 C3
bbey Wood Sta SE2 ....3 C3
bbey Wood Sta SE2 ....3 C3
bbeyhill Rd DA15 ....24 C6
bbots Cl BR5 ....37 C1
bbots Court Rd ME3 ....34 F5
bbots Field
Gravesend DA12 ....30 C2
Maidstone ME16 ....91 B2
bbotswood Cl [7] DA17 ....3 E3
bbott Rd TN15 ....86 F7
bbott's Wlk DA7 ....7 D7
bbotts Cl Rochester ME1 ....47 B3
Swanley BR8 ....40 A5
Woolwich SE28 ....3 C6
berdeen House [9]
ME15 ....107 E7
berford Gdns SE12 ....5 E6
bergeldie Rd SE12 ....5 B1
bery St SE18 ....2 E2
bigail Cres ME5 ....61 E5
bingdon Mews ME19 ....89 C8
bingdon Rd ME16 ....90 F2
bingdon Way BR6 ....52 B6
binger Cl BR1 ....36 C4
binger Dr ME5 ....62 D2
bsalom Ct ME8 ....49 C2
cacia Cl BR5 ....37 D4
cacia Ct SE12 ....4 B8
cacia Way DA15 ....23 F7
cacia Wlk BR8 ....39 D7
cademy Dr ME7 ....48 F1
cademy Pl SE18 ....6 A6
cademy Rd SE18 ....5 C7
cer Ave TN2 ....163 C8
chilles Rd ME5 ....62 C2
cland Cl SE18 ....6 D7
corn Cl Chislehurst BR7 ....23 B7
Five Oak Green TN12 ....135 B7
corn Gr ME20 ....90 D8
corn Ind Pk 9 A2
corn Pl ME15 ....107 E6
corn Rd Crayford DA1 ....8 F2
Gillingham ME7 ....48 F4
corn Trad Ctr RM20 ....11 E8
corn Way
Hurst Green TN19 ....184 A3
Orpington BR6 ....51 B6
corn Wharf Rd ME1 ....47 C6
corns The
Biddenden Green TN27 ....142 F1
Sevenoaks TN13 ....84 A4
cott Fields ME18 ....120 E8
cre Cl ME1 ....47 E1
cre Gr ME4 ....60 B4
cres Rise TN5 ....176 E1
cton La TN30 ....173 B4
cton Pl ME18 ....105 A1
cworth House [1] ME8 ....6 B8
cworth Pl DA1 ....9 C1
dam Cl ME17 ....106 D3
dams Cl TN30 ....173 B1
dams Sq DA6 ....7 E4
damson Rd E16 ....1 A7
dbert Dr ME15 ....106 B4
dcot Wlk [8] ME6 ....51 F6
dderley Gdns SE9 ....23 A4
ddington La ME19 ....73 B4
ddison Cl
East Malling ME19 ....74 F1
Orpington BR5 ....37 C3
ddison Cotts TN30 ....189 D3
ddison Dr SE12 ....5 B2
ddison Rd BR2 ....36 D4
ddlestead Rd TN12 ....119 E6
delaide Rd
Chislehurst BR7 ....23 B3
Gillingham ME7 ....48 C4
Tilbury RM18 ....12 F5
delaide The ME3 ....33 E3
den Terr [1] ME4 ....92 A7
disham Dr ME16 ....91 B7
dmaston Rd SE18 ....6 C8
dmers Way DA13 ....73 B8
dmiral Cl BR5 ....38 D5
dmiral Moore Dr [3]
ME20 ....75 F1

Admiral Seymour Rd SE9 ....5 F3
Admiral Way ME19 ....89 A1
Admiral's Wlk ME4 ....47 F7
Admirals Ct E6 ....2 B7
Admirals Wlk Chatham ME5 ....62 B3
Goddard's Green TN17 ....170 D2
Swanscombe DA9 ....11 B2
Tenterden TN30 ....173 C1
Admiralty Rd ME2 ....33 F1
Admiralty Terr
Upper Upnor ME2 ....48 A7
Upper Upnor ME2 ....33 F1
Afghan Rd ME4 ....47 E4
Agate Cl E16 ....1 D7
Agaton Rd SE9 ....23 C6
Agnes Cl E6 ....2 A6
Ainsdale Cl ME3 ....37 D1
Aintree Cl DA12 ....30 B5
Aintree House [1] ME15 ....107 F6
Aintree Rd ME5 ....62 C3
Airedale Cl DA2 ....27 C7
Airport Rdbt E16 ....1 D5
Aisher Rd SE28 ....3 C6
Aisher Way TN13 ....84 A1
Ajax Rd ME1 ....61 C8
Akehurst La TN13 ....84 C2
Alabama St SE18 ....6 E7
Alamein Ave ME5 ....62 A7
Alamein Gdns DA2 ....27 D8
Alan Cl DA1 ....9 C3
Alan Marre Ho SE7 ....5 C8
Alanbrooke DA12 ....30 C8
Alanthus Ct SE12 ....5 A1
Alban Cres DA4 ....41 A1
Albany Cl Sidcup DA5 ....24 D8
Tonbridge TN9 ....133 D7
Albany Hill TN2 ....149 C5
Albany Park Sta DA14 ....24 C6
Albany Rd Chatham ME4 ....48 B2
Chislehurst SE9 ....23 B3
Erith DA17 ....7 E8
Gillingham ME7 ....48 C4
Rochester ME1 ....47 C4
Sidcup DA5 ....24 C8
Tilbury RM18 ....13 A6
Albany St ME14 ....92 B5
Albany Terr Chatham ME4 ....47 E4
Chatham ME7 ....48 D4
Albatross Ave ME2 ....46 C6
Albatross Way ME2 ....46 C6
Albemarle Rd ME5 ....62 C2
Albert Cotts TN1 ....149 B4
Albert Manor ME7 ....48 B5
Albert Murry Cl DA12 ....30 C8
Albert Pl ME2 ....47 B7
Albert Rd Bromley BR2 ....36 D4
Chatham ME4 ....48 A3
Chislehurst SE9 ....22 E5
Dartford DA2 ....26 C5
Erith DA17 ....7 E8
Gillingham ME7 ....48 C4
Newham E16 ....1 F5
Orpington,Chelsfield BR6 ....52 A5
Orpington,St Mary Cray BR5 ....38 B3
Rochester ME1 ....47 C3
Sidcup DA5 ....25 B8
Swanscombe DA10 ....11 F1
Tonbridge TN9 ....117 B1
Albert Reed Gdns ME15 ....91 E2
Albert Reed Gdns ME14 ....91 F6
Albert Wlk E16 ....2 B4
Alberta Rd DA8 ....8 D8
Albion Cotts TN12 ....135 D5
Albion Cl [2] SE18 ....1 E2
Albion Ho E16 ....2 B5
Albion Pl Maidstone ME14 ....92 B4
Newington ME9 ....65 B6
Albion Rd Bexley DA6 ....8 A3
Chatham ME5 ....62 B2
Gravesend DA12 ....30 C8
Marden TN12 ....138 D5
Royal Tunbridge Wells TN1 ....149 C5
Albion Way ME1 ....112 C4
Albright Ind Est RM13 ....4 F8
Albury Ave DA7 ....7 D3
Albury Ct ME5 ....62 D2
Albyfield BR1 ....36 F6
Alchins Cotts ME17 ....106 E2
Alconbury DA6 ....8 B2
Aldeburgh St SE10 ....1 A1
Alder Cl TN4 ....133 D1
Alder La TN17 ....181 C1
Alder Rd DA14 ....23 F5
Alder Way BR8 ....39 D7
Aldermary Rd BR1 ....36 A6
Alderney Rd DA8 ....9 A7
Alders Cotts TN12 ....135 A5
Alders Meadow TN9 ....116 F2
Alders Rd TN11,TN12 ....134 C6
Alders The ME18 ....103 D7
Aldersgrove Ave SE9 ....22 D5
Aldershot Rd ME5 ....62 A7
Alderwood Prim Sch SE9 ....6 E1
Aldingham Ct ME16 ....91 E5
Aldington La ME14 ....93 D8
Aldington Rd
Adelaide The ME3 ....1 D1
Maidstone ME14 ....92 F4
Aldon Cl ME14 ....92 C6
Aldon Ct ME14 ....92 C6
Aldon La ME19 ....88 C8
Aldwick Cl SE9 ....23 D5
Alen Sq TN12 ....139 F4
Alers Rd DA6 ....7 D2

Alestan Beck Rd E16 ....1 D7
Alex Hughes Cl ME8 ....74 F6
Alexander Cl Hayes BR2 ....36 A1
Sidcup DA15 ....24 F8
Alexander Ct Greenwich SE3 ....5 B5
[1] Rochester ME2 ....47 B8
Alexander McLeod Inf Sch
SE2 ....3 B1
Alexander McLeod Jun Sch
SE2 ....3 B1
Alexander Rd Bexley DA7 ....7 D5
Chislehurst BR7 ....23 B3
Swanscombe DA9 ....11 C2
Alexandra Ave ME4 ....48 C4
Alexandra Cl DA8 ....39 E7
Alexandra Glen ME5 ....62 A1
Alexandra Hospl The ME5 ....91 D4
Alexandra Rd Chatham ME4 ....48 B2
Erith DA8 ....8 E7
Gravesend DA10 ....30 E8
Tilbury RM18 ....12 F5
Tonbridge TN9 ....133 B8
Alexandra St
Maidstone ME14 ....91 F6
Newham E16 ....1 A8
Alfan La DA2 ....25 D3
Alford House [6] SE18 ....6 B8
Alford Rd DA8 ....4 C1
Alfred Cl ME14 ....48 B2
Alfred Pl DA11 ....29 F7
Alfred Rd Erith DA17 ....3 F1
Gravesend DA11 ....30 B6
Hawley DA2 ....27 B5
Alfred St ME7 ....48 C8
Alfriston Gr ME19 ....89 C3
Alice Thompson Cl SE12 ....22 C6
Alicia House DA16 ....7 B6
Alison Cl E6 ....2 A7
Alkerden La DA9,DA10 ....11 C1
Alkham Rd ME14 ....92 C5
Alkham Tower ME8 ....38 C5
All Saints CE Prim Sch
ME15 ....92 A3
All Saints Cl SE18 ....11 F2
All Saints Hospl ME4 ....48 A2
All Saints Rd
Allhallows ME3 ....19 D8
Hawkhurst TN18 ....179 A1
Royal Tunbridge Wells TN4 ....149 A6
All Saints Rise TN4 ....149 A6
All Saints' CE Prim Sch
ME4 ....48 A3
All Saints' Rd DA11 ....29 F7
Allan Cl TN4 ....148 C8
Allandale Pl ME8 ....52 D7
Allandale Rd DA2 ....149 D7
Allard Cl BR5 ....38 C2
Allen Cl ME5 ....62 C6
Allen Rd BR2 ....36 A3
Allenby Rd ME15 ....107 A7
Allendale Cl DA2 ....27 D7
Allens TN12 ....138 D5
Allens La TN15,TN11 ....102 A7
Allenswood Rd ME9 ....5 F5
Allhallows Prim Sch ME3 ....19 D8
Allhallows Rd
Lower Stoke ME3 ....19 C5
Newham E6 ....2 A7
Allhallows-on-Sea Est
ME3 ....19 E10
Alliance Rd SE18 ....7 A7
Alliance Way TN12 ....135 F6
Allington Cl DA12 ....30 F7
Allington Dr Rochester ME2 ....46 E8
Tonbridge TN10 ....118 A5
Allington Prim Sch ME16 ....91 C7
Allington Rd
Gillingham ME8 ....49 A3
Orpington BR6 ....37 E1
Paddock Wood TN12 ....135 F7
Allington Way ME16 ....91 B6
Allison Ave ME7 ....48 C5
Allnutt Mill Cl ME15 ....91 E2
Allotment La ME14 ....84 C5
Allsworth Cl ME9 ....65 B6
Alma Pl Hadlow TN11 ....118 B8
Rochester ME2 ....47 A7
Alma Rd Eccles ME20 ....75 F6
New Town ME19 ....89 A8
Orpington BR5 ....38 C2
Sidcup DA14 ....24 A5
Swanscombe DA10 ....11 F2
Almon Pl ME1 ....47 D5
Almond Cl BR2 ....36 F3
Almond Dr BR8 ....39 D7
Almond Gr ME7 ....63 A4
Almond Rd DA2 ....27 C8
Almond Way BR2 ....37 A2
Almonds The ME14 ....93 A4
Alms Row TN16 ....82 B3
Almshouses
Penshurst TN11 ....131 C4
Yalding ME18 ....105 A1
Alnwick Ct [5] DA2 ....10 B1
Alnwick Rd Eltham SE12 ....22 B8
Newham E16 ....1 C8
Alonso Ho [4] ME4 ....35 D7
Alpha Cl ME1 ....47 D5
Alpine Bsns Ctr E6 ....2 C8
Alpine Copse [2] BR1 ....37 A7
Alpine Way E6 ....2 B8
Alsike Rd DA10 ....4 E1
Altash Way SE9 ....22 F5
Altbarn Ind Est ME5 ....77 C5
Alton Cl Bexley DA5 ....24 E7
Alton Ave ME17 ....97 A5
Alton Cl DA5 ....24 E7

Alton Cotts DA4 ....54 E8
Alverstone Gdns SE9 ....23 C7
Alwold Cres SE12 ....5 C1
Amanda Cl ME5 ....61 F3
Amar Ct SE18 ....2 F2
Amardeep Ct SE18 ....2 F1
Ambassador Gdns E6 ....1 F8
Amber La ME17 ....108 A1
Amber Way ME17 ....108 B1
Amberleaze Dr TN2 ....150 D6
Amberley Cl
[2] Orpington BR6 ....51 F5
Tonbridge TN9 ....133 A8
Amberley Ct Sidcup DA14 ....24 C3
Speldhurst TN4 ....149 C8
Amberley Rd SE2 ....7 D8
Amblecote Cl SE12 ....22 B5
Amblecote Mdw SE12 ....22 B5
Amblecote Rd SE12 ....22 B5
Ambleside Rd DA7 ....8 A5
Ambley Gn ME8 ....63 A8
Ambley Rd ME8 ....63 B8
Ambrook Rd DA17 ....4 A3
Ambrose Cl Crayford DA1 ....9 A3
[6] Newham E6 ....1 F8
Orpington BR6 ....51 F7
Ambrose Hill ME5 ....48 C2
Amels Hill ME9 ....79 F8
Ames Ave ME14 ....93 A4
Ames Rd DA10 ....11 E1
Amesbury Rd BR1 ....36 D6
Amethyst Ave ME5 ....61 F3
Amherst Cl Maidstone ME16 ....91 D4
Orpington BR5 ....38 A5
Amherst Cty Prim Sch
TN13 ....83 F4
Amherst Dr BR5 ....38 A5
Amherst Hill Chatham ME7 ....48 A6
Sevenoaks TN13 ....83 F4
Amherst Rd Rochester ME1 ....47 B3
Royal Tunbridge Wells TN4 ....149 A5
Sevenoaks TN13 ....84 A5
Amherst Redoubt ME4 ....48 A5
Amhurst Bank Rd
TN2,TN11,TN12 ....134 F4
Amhurst Wlk SE28 ....3 A5
Ames House ME15 ....106 F3
Ampleforth Rd SE2 ....3 C4
Amsbury Rd ME15,ME17 ....106 B2
Amshurst Villas ME15 ....106 A4
Ancaster St SE18 ....6 E7
Anchor & Hope La SE7 ....1 C2
Anchor Bay Ind Est DA8 ....8 F7
newham E16 ....1 C7
Anchor La ME12 ....21 F3
Anchor Rd ME1 ....47 C1
Anchorage Cl ME3 ....19 C5
Anchorage Flats TN12 ....136 A6
Anchorage Point Ind Est
SE7 ....1 C3
Ancona Rd SE18 ....2 D8
Andace Pk BR1 ....36 C8
Anderson Way DA17 ....4 B4
Andorra Ct BR1 ....36 C8
Andover Cl E6 ....1 C7
Andover Rd BR6 ....37 E1
Andover Wlk [12] ME15 ....107 F6
Andover Broughton Way
ME14 ....92 B4
Andrew Cl DA1 ....8 D2
Andrew Manor ME7 ....48 C6
Andrew Rd TN4 ....149 C8
Andrew Wells Ho [7] BR1 ....22 B1
Andrewes Gdns E6 ....1 C7
Andrews Cl
Royal Tunbridge Wells TN2 ....149 D5
St Paul's Grey BR5 ....38 B5
Andringham Lodge [8]
BR1 ....36 B8
Andwell Cl SE2 ....3 B1
Anerley Rd ME16 ....91 D7
Angel Cl ME19 ....89 F1
Angel La TN18 ....178 E1
Angel Row TN18 ....186 B5
Angel Terr TN18 ....186 B6
Angel Wlk [4] ME19 ....117 B1
Angelica Dr E6 ....2 B8
Angerstein Bsns Pk SE10 ....1 A2
Angle Rd RM20 ....11 D8
Anglesea Ave SE18 ....2 B2
Anglesea Ctr [8] DA11 ....13 B1
Anglesea Rd [7] DA11 ....13 B1
Anglesea Rd Orpington BR5 ....38 C3
Woolwich SE18 ....2 B2
Anglesey Ave ME15 ....107 A7
Anglesey Cl ME7 ....62 B7
Anglesey Rd SE18 ....2 C3
Angley Ct TN12 ....153 A5
Angley Rd TN17 ....169 C5
Angley Sch TN17 ....169 C5
Angley Wlk
Cranbrook TN17 ....169 D6
Cranbrook TN17 ....169 D6
Anglia Ctr The MN13 ....4 E8
Anglian Ind Est IG11 ....3 A8
Ankerdine Cres SE18 ....6 B6
Ann St SE18 ....2 D2
Ann Stroud Ct SE12 ....5 A2
Annandale Rd DA15 ....23 F8
Anne of Cleves Rd DA1 ....9 D1
Annesley Rd SE3 ....5 B6
Annetts Hall TN15 ....87 A8
Annex The BR8 ....40 B6
Annie Rd ME5 ....74 F6
Annvera Ho [2] ME7 ....48 C7
Ansell Ave ME4 ....48 A1
Anson Ave M18,ME19 ....88 F3
Anson Cl ME5 ....62 C6

Anson Rd ME19 ....88 E2
Anstridge Rd SE9 ....6 D1
Antelope Rd SE18 ....1 F3
Anthony Cl TN13 ....83 E7
Anthony Rd DA16 ....7 A6
Anthony Roper
Cty Prim Sch DA4 ....40 A8
Anthonys La BR8 ....26 B1
Anthonys Way ME2 ....47 E8
Aperfield Rd DA8 ....8 F8
Apollo Ave BR1 ....36 B8
Apollo House ME5 ....62 A6
Apollo Way
St Mary's Island ME4 ....34 C2
Woolwich SE18 ....2 D3
Apple Cl ME6 ....75 A6
Apple Ct TN12 ....135 F6
Apple Orch BR8 ....39 D5
Apple Tree Cl ME14 ....90 F2
Apple Tree La TN2 ....149 D8
Applecott Cl ME14 ....61 D7
Appleby Cl E6 ....1 A7
Applecross Cl ME1 ....47 B4
Appledore Ave DA7 ....8 C6
Appledore Cl BR2 ....36 A4
Appledore Cres DA14 ....23 F5
Appledore Ct ME16 ....91 C7
Appledore Rd
Gillingham ME8 ....49 A3
Tenterden TN30 ....183 E7
Appleforth Cl BR6 ....52 C6
Applegarth Dr DA1 ....26 F6
Applegarth House DA8 ....8 F5
Applegate TN17 ....169 C5
Applehaw Cl DA11 ....30 A3
Appleshaw Cl DA11 ....30 A3
Appleton Dr ME5 ....26 B5
Appletons TN11 ....118 E8
Appold St DA8 ....8 F8
Approach The ME1 ....51 F8
April Cl BR6 ....51 F5
Appledene DA12 ....30 D2
Apsley St TN4 ....148 D4
Aragon Cl BR2 ....36 F1
Arbroath Rd SE9 ....5 E4
Arbrook Cl BR5 ....38 A6
Arbury Rd BR1 ....22 E1
Arbuthnot La DA5 ....7 E1
Arcade The [2] SE9 ....6 A1
Arcadia Rd DA13 ....43 F8
Arcadian Ave DA5 ....7 E1
Arcadian Cl DA5 ....7 E1
Arcadian Rd DA5 ....7 E1
Archer Rd Chatham ME5 ....62 B6
Orpington BR5 ....38 A4
Archer Way BR8 ....40 A7
Archery Cl ME1 ....33 B7
Archery Rd SE9 ....26 D8
Archery House Hospl DA2 ....10 B1
Archery Rd SE9 ....6 A1
Archway Ct [8] ME2 ....47 B8
Arden Bsns Pk ME2 ....47 E8
Arden St ME7 ....48 C6
Ardenlee Dr ME14 ....92 B5
Arethusa Pl DA9 ....11 B3
Arethusa Rd ME1 ....61 C8
Argall Ho [3] SE18 ....2 B3
Argent St RM17 ....12 B7
Argles Cl DA1 ....11 A2
Argyle Cl ME1 ....61 E8
Argyle Rd Newham E16 ....1 B7
Royal Tunbridge Wells TN4 ....149 A5
Sevenoaks TN13 ....84 B2
Argyll Rd SE18 ....2 C3
Ariel Cl DA12 ....30 F4
Ariel Ct [5] DA17 ....4 A1
Arkwright Rd RM18 ....13 A5
Arlington Cl DA15 ....23 E8
Arlott Cl ME14 ....91 F6
Armada Ct ME4 ....47 E1
Armada Way Chatham ME4 ....2 C7
Newham E6 ....2 C7
Armitage Pl [3] TN18 ....178 F2
Armour Cl DA1 ....30 C8
Armstrong Cl
Badgers Mount TN14 ....68 B4
Bromley BR1 ....36 E6
Newham E6 ....1 F7
Armstrong Rd ME15 ....92 A1
Armytage Cl ME13 ....34 C4
Arne Cl ME5 ....62 B6
Arne Gr BR6 ....51 F7
Arnhem Dr ME5 ....61 F7
Arnold Ave DA13 ....58 B8
Arnold Cl ME7 ....48 F4
Arnold Rd DA11 ....30 D6
Arnolds La DA4 ....27 A7
Arnolds La DA4 ....27 A2
Arnott Cl SE28 ....3 C5
Arnsberg Way DA6,DA7 ....8 A2
Arran Cl DA8 ....8 A6
Arran Gn ME2 ....46 C7
Arran Rd SE6 ....22 F8
Arrandene House [3] BR5 ....38 B7
Arras Ho SE7 ....3 O1
Arras House 7 D8
Arsenal Rd SE9 ....5 F5
Artemis Cl DA12 ....30 E8
Arthur Gr SE18 ....2 C2
Arthur Rd Gillingham ME8 ....63 E7
Rochester ME1 ....47 D3

Arthur Ruxley Est DA14 ... 24 D2
Arthur St Erith DA8 ... 8 F7
  Gravesend DA11 ... 30 A8
  Grays RM17 ... 12 C8
Arthur St W DA11 ... 30 A8
Arthur Toft House **5**
  RM17 ... 12 B8
Artillery Ho SE18 ... 2 A1
Artillery Pl SE18 ... 2 A2
Artillery Row DA12 ... 30 C8
Artington Cl BR6 ... 51 C6
Artisan Cl E6 ... 2 A6
Arun Cl BR5 ... 38 C1
Arundel DA14 ... 24 A3
Arundel Cl Chatham ME5 ... 62 D1
  Sidcup DA5 ... 24 F1
  Tonbridge TN9 ... 133 A8
Arundel Cl **5** DA6 ... 7 E3
Arundel Dr BR6 ... 52 B5
  Royal Tunbridge Wells TN1 ... 149 B2
Arundel St ME14 ... 91 F6
Ascot Cl
  Borough Green TN15 ... 87 B7
  Chatham ME5 ... 62 C2
Ascot Ct DA15 ... 24 A4
Ascot House **2** ME15 ... 107 F6
Ascot Rd Gravesend DA2 ... 30 B5
  Orpington BR5 ... 37 F5
Ash Cl Aylesford ME20 ... 75 E1
  Chatham ME5 ... 48 D1
  Edenbridge TN8 ... 112 B1
  Gillingham ME8 ... 49 B3
  Orpington BR5 ... 37 D4
  Royal Tunbridge Wells TN2 ... 163 D7
  Sidcup DA14 ... 24 B5
  Swanley BR8 ... 39 D7
Ash Cres ME3 ... 32 C3
Ash Ct SE12 ... 22 A8
Ash Gr Lewisham SE12 ... 22 A7
  Maidstone ME15 ... 91 C6
Ash Keys DA13 ... 73 B8
Ash La TN15 ... 84 E6
Ash Platt Rd TN15 ... 84 E6
Ash Rd Dartford DA1 ... 26 D7
  Gravesend DA12 ... 30 C4
  Hartley DA3 ... 42 F3
  Hawley DA2 ... 26 F4
  New Ash Green DA3,TN15 ... 56 E7
  Orpington BR6 ... 51 F3
  Rochester ME2 ... 46 F6
  Westerham TN16 ... 81 E2
Ash Row BR2 ... 37 A3
Ash Tree Cl TN15 ... 55 F2
Ash Tree Cotts TN12 ... 154 B7
Ash Tree Dr TN15 ... 55 F2
Ash Tree La ME5 ... 48 D1
Ashbank Cotts ME17 ... 109 B7
Ashbee Cl ME6 ... 75 A7
Ashbourne Ave DA7 ... 7 F7
Ashbourne Cl TN15 ... 148 D4
Ashbourne Rise BR6 ... 51 E6
Ashburn Ct BR1 ... 22 A1
Ashburn Mews ME7 ... 48 E3
Ashburnham Cl TN13 ... 99 C8
Ashburnham Rd Erith DA8 ... 4 C2
  Maidstone ME14 ... 92 B8
  Tonbridge TN10 ... 117 C3
Ashburton Rd E16 ... 1 A7
Ashby Cl ME7 ... 60 A4
Ashby's Cl TN8 ... 128 D8
Ashbys Yd TN9 ... 117 C1
Ashcombe Dr TN8 ... 112 B4
Ashcroft Ave DA15 ... 7 A1
Ashcroft Cres DA15 ... 7 A1
Ashcroft Ho **3** Eltham SE9 ... 6 A1
Ashcroft Rd TN12 ... 136 A5
Ashdale Rd SE12 ... 22 B7
Ashden Wlk TN10 ... 117 C7
Ashdown Cl Coldblow DA5 ... 25 C8
  Maidstone ME15 ... 91 D3
  Royal Tunbridge Wells TN4 ... 148 F4
Ashen E6 ... 2 A7
Ashen Dr DA1 ... 25 A1
Ashen Grove Rd TN15 ... 55 B1
Ashenden TN27 ... 142 F2
Ashenden Cl ME4 ... 33 C2
Ashenden Wlk TN2 ... 149 E8
Asher Reeds TN3 ... 148 A8
Ashes La TN11 ... 118 B8
Ashfield La BR7 ... 23 C1
Ashfield Pl BR7 ... 23 D1
Ashford Dr ME17 ... 109 D3
Ashford Rd
  Durrant Green TN26,TN30 ... 173 A6
  Harrietsham ME17 ... 110 C6
  Maidstone ME14 ... 93 D3
  Maidstone,Grove
  Green ME14 ... 92 D4
  Tenterden TN30 ... 183 B8
Ashgrove Rd TN13 ... 99 B3
Ashlar Pl **5** SE18 ... 2 A2
Ashleigh Ct DA13 ... 57 F1
Ashleigh Commercial Est
SE18 ... 2 B1
Ashleigh Gdns TN27 ... 141 D6
Ashley Cl TN13 ... 83 E1
Ashley Gdns Orpington BR6 ... 51 E5
  Royal Tunbridge Wells TN4 ... 148 C5
Ashley House BR5 ... 38 A7
Ashley Park Cl TN14 ... 148 C5
Ashley Pk TN4 ... 148 C5
Ashley Rd Gillingham ME8 ... 49 C2
  Sevenoaks TN13 ... 84 B3

Ashley Rd continued
  Tonbridge TN11 ... 116 C5
Ashmead Cl ME5 ... 62 C3
Ashmead Gate ME1 ... 36 C8
Ashmore Gdns DA11 ... 29 D5
Ashmore Gr DA16 ... 6 C4
Ashridge Cres SE18 ... 6 C7
Ashridge House DA14 ... 23 F4
Ashton Way ME19 ... 89 C6
Ashtree Cl BR6 ... 51 B6
Ashurst Cl DA1 ... 8 A1
Ashurst Hill TN3 ... 146 D2
Ashurst Rd Maidstone ME14 ... 92 C5
  Royal Tunbridge Wells TN3 ... 147 B2
Ashurst Sta TN3 ... 146 D2
Ashwater Rd SE12 ... 22 A7
Ashwell Cl **6** E6 ... 1 E7
Ashwood Cl ME4 ... 33 C7
Ashwood Pl DA2 ... 28 B5
Askern Cl DA6 ... 7 D3
Askews Farm La
  RM17,RM20 ... 11 E8
Askham Lodge **10** SE12 ... 22 A8
Aspdin Rd DA11 ... 29 E5
Aspen Cl Orpington BR6 ... 52 A5
  Swanley BR8 ... 39 D8
Aspen Copse BR1 ... 36 F7
Aspen Ct DA12 ... 30 A2
Aspen Gn DA18 ... 3 F3
Aspen House **2** DA15 ... 24 A5
Aspen Way
  2 Tilbury RM18 ... 61 E4
  Royal Tunbridge Wells TN4 ... 133 C1
Aspian Dr ME17 ... 106 D3
Asquith Rd ME8 ... 63 C6
Association Wlk ME1 ... 61 C7
Aster Rd ME3 ... 34 E3
Astley ME17 ... 11 E8
Astley St ME14 ... 92 A4
Aston Cl Chatham ME5 ... 62 A2
  Sidcup DA14 ... 24 A5
Aston Ct E16 ... 1 C7
Astor of Hever Com Sch
The ME16 ... 91 C3
Astra Dr DA12 ... 30 F3
Astra Rd IG11 ... 3 A8
Athelstan Gn ME17 ... 94 C2
Athelstan Rd ME4 ... 47 F2
Athelstan Way BR5 ... 38 A8
Athol Cl DA13 ... 84 C5
Athol Rd DA8 ... 4 E1
Atkinson Cl BR6 ... 52 A5
Atkinson Rd E16 ... 1 C8
Atlanta Ct ME4 ... 47 D3
Atlantic Cl DA10 ... 11 C2
Atlas Gdns SE7 ... 1 C2
Atlas Rd DA1 ... 9 F4
Atterbury Cl TN16 ... 81 D1
Attfield Dr DA ... 10 A2
Attlee Rd SE28 ... 3 B6
Attwaters La TN18 ... 179 C6
Atwater Cl ME17 ... 111 D5
Auckland Cl RM18 ... 13 A5
Auckland House **10** ME15 ... 107 E1
Auckland Rd TN1 ... 149 C5
Auden Rd ME20 ... 75 A3
Audley Ave Gillingham ME7 ... 48 E1
  Tonbridge TN9 ... 116 F2
Audley Cl ME1 ... 91 B5
Audley Dr E16 ... 1 B4
Audley Rise TN9 ... 116 F1
Audley Wlk BR5 ... 38 C3
Audrey Sturley Ct TN4 ... 148 E4
Auger Cl ME5 ... 64 E5
Augusta Cl **4** ME7 ... 48 C7
Augustine Ho TN10 ... 117 C3
Augustine Rd
  2 Gravesend DA12 ... 30 C8
  St Paul's Cray BR5 ... 38 D6
Austell Manor **5** ME7 ... 48 C6
Austen Cl Swanscombe DA9 ... 11 C1
  Tilbury RM18 ... 13 C5
  Woolwich SE28 ... 2 C5
Austen Gdns DA1 ... 9 F3
Austen Rd DA8 ... 8 B7
Austen Way ME20 ... 74 F4
Austens Orch **4** TN30 ... 183 A7
Austin Ave BR2 ... 36 E4
Austin Cl ME5 ... 48 E2
Austin Ct **4** TN16 ... 81 D1
Austin Rd Gravesend DA11 ... 29 F7
  Orpington BR5 ... 38 A4
Austral Cl DA15 ... 23 F5
Autumn Glade ME5 ... 77 D8
Avalon Cl BR6 ... 52 D7
Avalon Rd BR5,BR6 ... 52 C8
Avard Gdns BR6 ... 51 C6
Avards Cl TN18 ... 184 E8
Avebury Ave TN9 ... 117 B1
Avebury Rd BR6 ... 51 D7
Aveley Cl DA8 ... 8 F8
Aveling Cl ME13 ... 34 D6
Aveling Ct **3** ME2 ... 47 B7
Avenons Rd **3** E16 ... 1 A8
Avenue Le Puy TN9 ... 117 C1
Avenue Rd Bexley DA7,DA6 ... 7 E4
  Erith DA8 ... 8 D7
  Sevenoaks TN13 ... 84 C3
Avenue The Aylesford ME20 ... 75 E1
  Borough Green TN15 ... 87 A8
  Bromley BR1 ... 36 C6
  Gravesend DA11 ... 30 A8
  Hill Park TN16 ... 81 A4
  Orpington BR6 ... 51 F8
  Orpington,Keston Mark BR2 ... 50 D7
  Sidcup DA5 ... 24 D8
  St Mary's Island ME4 ... 34 C2

Avenue The continued
  St Paul's Cray BR5 ... 24 B1
  Swanscombe DA9 ... 11 B2
  Tonbridge TN9 ... 117 B2
Averenches Rd ME14 ... 92 F5
Avery Cl
  Allhallows-on-Sea ME3 ... 19 E9
  Maidstone ME15 ... 91 F1
Avery Hill Rd SE9 ... 23 D7
Avery La ME15,ME17 ... 108 D6
Avery Way ME3 ... 19 D8
Aviemore Gdns ME14 ... 92 F4
Avington Cl ME15 ... 91 F1
Avocet Mews SE28 ... 2 D3
Avocet Wlk ME5 ... 62 D2
Avon Cl Gravesend DA12 ... 30 D6
  Tonbridge TN10 ... 117 C5
Avon Ct DA14 ... 24 B5
Avon St TN1 ... 149 C5
Avondale Mews BR1 ... 22 A2
Avondale Rd Bexley DA16 ... 7 C5
  Bromley BR1 ... 22 A2
  Chislehurst SE9 ... 22 E6
  Gillingham ME7 ... 48 C5
Avonmouth Rd DA1 ... 9 D2
Avonstowe Cl BR6 ... 51 C7
Awliscombe Rd DA16 ... 6 F5
Axford Ct ME8 ... 64 A8
Axminster Cres DA16 ... 7 C6
Axtaine Rd BR5 ... 38 D2
Axtane DA13 ... 28 F1
Axtane Cl DA4 ... 41 C8
Axton Chase Sch DA3 ... 42 F6
Aycliffe Cl BR1 ... 36 F5
Ayelands DA3 ... 56 E8
Ayelands La DA3 ... 56 E8
Aylesbury Rd BR2 ... 36 A6
Aylesford Cres ME8 ... 49 B4
Aylesford Prim Sch ME20 ... 75 E2
Aylesford Sta ME20 ... 75 D1
Aymscombe Angle BR6 ... 38 A2
Azalea Dr BR8 ... 39 E5

B

Babb's La TN17 ... 180 A6
Babbacombe Rd BR1 ... 22 B1
Babington House SE5 BR7 ... 22 F2
Babylon La RM17 ... 124 B1
Back La Godden Green TN15 ... 85 A2
  Goudhurst TN17 ... 167 E8
  Horsmonden TN12 ... 153 A6
  Ightham TN15 ... 86 C2
  Maidstone ME17 ... 107 E1
  Sevenoaks TN13,TN14 ... 83 C1
  Shipbourne TN11 ... 101 D4
  Sidcup DA5 ... 25 A8
Back Rd Sandhurst TN18,BR5 ... 186 B5
  Sidcup DA14 ... 24 A4
Back St ME17 ... 108 E6
Backfields ME1 ... 47 B4
Baden Powell Ho **5** DA17 ... 4 A3
Baden Powell Rd TN13 ... 83 E5
Baden Rd ME7 ... 48 D7
Bader Wlk DA9 ... 29 F5
Bader Cres ME5 ... 62 A7
Badgers Copse BR6 ... 51 F8
Badgers Croft SE9 ... 23 A5
Badgers Holt TN2 ... 149 E5
Badgers Rd TN14 ... 53 B1
Badgers Rise TN14 ... 53 A1
Badlow Cl DA8 ... 8 E7
Badminton Mews E16 ... 1 A5
Badsell Park Farm TN12 ... 135 C3
Badsell Rd TN12 ... 135 D6
Baffin Cl ME4 ... 47 F2
Bagshaw Ho **3** BR1 ... 36 A8
Bailey Dr ME7 ... 49 A1
Baird Ho **8** DA17 ... 4 A3
Bakenham Ho ME1 ... 47 C3
Baker Beall Rd DA7 ... 8 B4
Baker Hill Cl DA11 ... 29 F4
Baker La Headcorn TN27 ... 141 F7
  Sutton Valence ME17 ... 124 F7
Baker Rd SE18 ... 5 E8
Baker St Burham ME1 ... 60 F1
  Rochester ME1 ... 47 C3
Baker's Wlk ME1 ... 47 C6
Bakers Cross TN17 ... 169 D4
Bakers Mews **9** BR6 ... 51 F4
Bakery Cl TN17 ... 156 E7
Balaclava La TN5 ... 175 A6
Balcaskie Rd SE9 ... 5 F1
Balchen Rd SE3 ... 5 D5
Balcombe Cl DA6 ... 7 D3
Balcombe Cotts TN17 ... 167 E8
Balcombes Hill TN17 ... 167 E8
Baldock Rd TN5 ... 174 E4
Baldwyn's Pk DA5 ... 25 D6
Baldwyn's Rd DA5 ... 25 D6
Balfour Inf Sch ME1 ... 47 C1
Balfour Jun Sch ME1 ... 47 E2
Balfour Rd Bromley BR2 ... 36 D4
  Chatham ME4 ... 47 E2
Balgowan St SE18 ... 2 G1
Ball's Gn TN7 ... 160 B5
Ballamore Rd BR1 ... 22 A5
Ballard Bsns Pk ME2 ... 46 F5
Ballard Ind Est TN12 ... 138 C6
Ballard Ind Est ME5 ... 77 C8
Ballard Way TN12 ... 136 B7
Ballens Rd ME5 ... 62 C3

Balliol Rd DA16 ... 7 B5
Balls Cotts ME3 ... 33 F4
Balmer Cl ME8 ... 63 D7
Balmoral Ct SE12 ... 22 B4
Balmoral Gdns DA15 ... 24 F8
Balmoral House **10** ME15 ... 107 F5
Balmoral Rd
  Gillingham ME7 ... 48 D5
  Sutton at Hone DA4 ... 27 B1
Balmoral Trad Est E6 ... 2 C3
Balmoral Rd TN9 ... 133 B7
Baltimore Pl DA16 ... 6 F5
Banbury Villas DA3 ... 28 F1
Banchory Rd SE3 ... 5 B7
Bankside DA3 ... 42 F6
Bankside Chatham ME5 ... 62 B8
Bankside TN9 ... 133 B7
Bancroft Rd TN13 ... 71 F3
Bandfield Wlk DA1 ... 9 F4
Bangor Rd ME2 ... 46 D6
Bank Cotts ME17 ... 96 B3
Bank Hos DA2 ... 27 A3
Bank La TN11,TN15 ... 100 A3
Bank St Chatham ME4 ... 48 B3
  Cranbrook TN17 ... 169 C5
  Gravesend DA12 ... 13 B1
  Maidstone ME14 ... 92 A4
  Sevenoaks TN13 ... 84 C2
  Tonbridge TN9 ... 117 C2
Bankfield Ho TN17 ... 167 E7
Bankfields TN27 ... 141 C5
Banks La DA6 ... 7 F3
Banks Rd ME12 ... 21 E7
Bankside Chatham ME5 ... 62 B8
  Northfleet DA11 ... 12 C1
  Sevenoaks TN13 ... 83 E6
  Wadhurst TN5 ... 174 E5
Bankside Cl DA5 ... 25 D4
Banky Mdw ME16 ... 91 F5
Banner Farm Rd TN2 ... 149 B2
Banning St ME7 ... 47 B8
Bannister Gdns BR5 ... 38 C6
Bannister Rd ME14 ... 92 A7
Bannockburn Prim Sch
SE18 ... 2 F2
Bannockburn Rd SE18 ... 2 F2
Banstead Ct **3** BR1 ... 36 E6
Banwell Rd DA5 ... 7 D1
Bapchild Pl **10** BR5 ... 38 C5
Barbados Terr **2** ME14 ... 92 A7
Barberry Ave ME5 ... 61 E5
Barcham Ct ME15 ... 106 F5
Barchester Way TN10 ... 117 F6
Barclay Ave TN10 ... 118 A5
Barclay Field TN15 ... 69 E2
Barcombe Rd ME4 ... 38 A6
Bardell Terr ME1 ... 47 D5
Barden Ct ME14 ... 92 B5
Barden Park Rd TN9 ... 117 A1
Barden Rd
  Bidborough TN3 ... 131 F2
  Tonbridge TN9 ... 117 B2
Barden St SE18 ... 6 E7
Bardsley Cl TN12 ... 120 A7
Barfield DA4 ... 41 B8
Barfield Rd ME1 ... 37 A6
Barfleur Manor **3** ME7 ... 48 A6
Barfreston Cl ME15 ... 91 F2
Bargate Cl SE18 ... 2 F1
Barge House Rd E16 ... 2 B4
Bargrove Rd ME14 ... 92 C5
Barham Cl
  Chislehurst BR7 ... 23 B3
  Gravesend DA12 ... 30 F7
  Maidstone ME15 ... 107 E5
  Orpington BR2 ... 36 E1
Barham Ct BR2 ... 36 E1
Barham Mews ME18 ... 105 B8
Barham Rd
  Chislehurst BR7 ... 23 B3
  Dartford DA1 ... 27 A8
Barham's Mill Rd TN27 ... 127 B3
Baring Cl SE12 ... 22 A6
Baring Prim Sch SE12 ... 22 A8
Baring Rd SE12 ... 22 B6
Bark Hart Rd BR6 ... 38 B1
Barker Rd ME14 ... 91 F3
Barking Rd E16 ... 1 A8
Barkis Cl ME1 ... 61 D7
Barley Fields ME14 ... 92 E5
Barleycorn ME19 ... 74 E1
Barleymow Cl ME5 ... 62 C7
Barlow Cl ME8 ... 63 E6
Barlow Cl ME8 ... 63 E5
Barlow Way RM13,RM9 ... 4 E8
Barming Prim Sch ME16 ... 90 F2
Barming Rd ME18 ... 89 F2
Barming Sta ME16 ... 90 F6
Barn End Ctr DA2 ... 26 C5
Barn End Dr DA2 ... 26 C4
Barn End La DA2 ... 26 C4
Barn Hill ME15 ... 105 E2
Barn Mdw
  Stapleleurst TN12 ... 139 E4
  Upper Halling ME2 ... 59 E4
Barnaby Terr ME1 ... 47 C1
Barnard Ct Chislehurst BR7 ... 37 D8
  Woolwich SE18 ... 2 A1
Barnard Gn **6** ME14 ... 92 C5
  2 Dartford DA2 ... 10 B1
Barncroft Cl ME14 ... 92 D7
Barncroft Dr ME7 ... 49 A1
Barndale Ct DA12 ... 31 E3
Barned Ct ME16 ... 90 F2
Barnehurst Ave DA7,DA8 ... 8 C6
Barnehurst Cl DA8 ... 8 C6
Barnehurst Inf Sch DA7 ... 8 C6
Barnehurst Jun Sch DA8 ... 8 C6

Barnehurst Rd DA7 ... 8 C6
Barnehurst Sta DA7 ... 8 C6
Barnes Cray Prim Sch DA1 ... 9 A4
Barnes Cray Rd DA1 ... 9 A4
Barnes Ct E16 ... 1 C6
Barnes La ME17 ... 122 D6
Barnes Wlk TN12 ... 138 C2
Barnesdale Cres DA8 ... 38 A4
Barnet Dr BR2 ... 50 E6
Barnet Wood Rd BR2 ... 50 C6
Barnett Cl DA8 ... 4 F7
Barnetts Ct BR4 ... 133 C7
Barnetts Rd TN11 ... 116 A6
Barnetts Way TN4 ... 133 C6
Barney Cl SE7 ... 1 C2
Barnfield Chatham ME5 ... 62 B8
  Gravesend DA11 ... 30 A4
  Royal Tunbridge Wells TN2 ... 162 F1
  Tenterden TN30 ... 173 C2
Barnfield Cl Crockenhill BR8 ... 39 C8
  New Barn DA3 ... 43 D5
  Swanley BR8 ... 10 F7
Barnfield Cres ME15 ... 69 E7
Barnfield Gdns SE18 ... 6 B3
Barnfield Rd Erith DA17 ... 7 F7
  Sevenoaks TN13 ... 83 E6
  St Paul's Cray BR5 ... 38 D6
  Woolwich SE18 ... 6 B3
Barnhill Rd ME14 ... 92 A4
Barnhurst Rd ME14 ... 92 A6
Barnsole Inf Sch ME7 ... 48 E6
Barnsole Jun Sch ME7 ... 48 E6
Barnsole Rd ME7 ... 48 E5
Barnwell Pl ME7 ... 48 E6
Barnwell Rd DA1 ... 9 F4
Barnwood Cl ME1 ... 61 B8
Baron Cl Gillingham ME7 ... 48 E4
  Maidstone ME14 ... 92 F9
Barons Cl TN4 ... 149 A3
Barr Rd DA12 ... 30 F6
Barrack Cnr TN13 ... 84 C2
Barrack Rd ME4 ... 48 B8
Barrack Row
  Beckenham TN17 ... 180 D6
  13 Gravesend DA11 ... 13 C2
Barrel Arch Cl TN12 ... 138 C2
Barretts Green Cotts **5**
TN18 ... 179 A2
Barretts Rd
  Hawkhurst TN18 ... 179 A2
  Sevenoaks TN13 ... 83 E7
Barrie Dr ME20 ... 74 F4
Barrier Point Rd E16 ... 1 C5
Barrier Rd ME4 ... 47 F4
Barrington Cl ME5 ... 61 F5
Barrington Ct South DA7 ... 7 D5
Barrington Rd DA7 ... 7 D6
Barrington Villas SE18 ... 6 A6
Barrow La TN3 ... 147 F1
Barrowfields ME5 ... 62 D1
Barry Ave DA7 ... 7 E5
Barry Ct SE6 ... 51 C7
Barry Rd E6 ... 1 E7
Barth Rd SE18 ... 2 E2
Bartholomew Way BR8 ... 39 E6
Bartletts ME1 ... 62 C1
Bartlett Rd Gravesend DA11 ... 30 A7
  Westerham TN16 ... 81 C1
Barton Cl Bexley DA7 ... 7 E4
  Yalding ME18 ... 104 F1
Barton Cotts TN11 ... 102 A6
Barton Rd Maidstone ME15 ... 92 A2
  Rochester ME2 ... 47 A7
  Sidcup DA14 ... 24 D2
  Sutton at Hone DA4 ... 27 B1
Basden Cotts **2** TN18 ... 179 A2
Baseing Cl E6 ... 2 C4
Bashford Barn La ME9 ... 80 F7
Basi Cl ME2 ... 33 C1
Basil Terr ME15 ... 92 A1
Basildon Rd DA7 ... 2 F5
Basing Cl ME15 ... 92 B3
Basing Dr DA5 ... 7 F1
Basket Gdns SE9 ... 5 E2
Basmere Cl ME14 ... 92 C6
Bassant Rd SE18 ... 6 F8
Bassett's Forge TN5 ... 174 E5
Bassetts Cl BR6 ... 51 B6
Bassetts La TN8,TN11 ... 146 C7
Bassetts Way BR6 ... 51 B6
Basted La Basted TN15 ... 86 B6
  Crouch TN15 ... 87 B4
Baston Rd SE18,SE2 ... 3 A1
Baston Manor Rd BR2,BR4 ... 50 B6
Baston Rd BR2 ... 50 B8
Bat & Ball Cnr TN14 ... 84 C7
Bat & Ball Sta TN14 ... 84 C6
Batchelor St ME4 ... 48 A4
Batchelors TN2 ... 150 E8
Batchwood Gn BR5 ... 38 A6
Bates Cl ME20 ... 75 A3
Bath Hard ME1 ... 47 B4
Bath Rd DA1 ... 26 B8
Bath St DA11 ... 13 B1
Baths Rd BR1,BR2 ... 36 D5
Bathurst Cl TN12 ... 139 D3
Bathurst Rd ME14 ... 92 B6
Bathway SE18 ... 2 A2
Batt's Rd DA12 ... 45 A4
Batten Cl E6 ... 1 F8
Batten Ct DA8 ... 8 C8
Battle La TN12 ... 139 A8
Battle Rd DA8,DA17 ... 4 F2

attle St DA12 ....44 F6
attlefields TN15 ....71 F3
attlesmere Rd ME3 ....33 B8
augh Rd DA14 ....24 C3
axter Rd E16 ....4 A2
ay Cl ME3 ....34 E3
ay Manor La RM20 ....10 F8
ay The DA13 ....73 A8
ayard Cl DA7 ....8 B3
ayeux Ho 6 SE7 ....5 C8
ayfield Rd SE9 ....5 D3
ayhall Rd TN9 ....149 C3
ayham Abbey* TN3 ....165 B5
ayham Ct TN5 ....174 E6
ayham Rd Royal
  Tunbridge Wells TN2,TN3 ....163 C7
ayham Rd DA13 ....84 D4
ayley's Hill TN14 ....98 E3
ayliss Ave SE28 ....3 D6
ayly Rd DA1 ....10 A1
ayne Cl E6 ....1 F7
aynham Cl DA5 ....7 F1
ayswater Dr ME8 ....63 D8
aytree Rd Bromley BR1 ....36 D8
  Sidcup DA15 ....23 F7
aywell RM17 ....74 E2
azes Shaw DA3 ....56 F8
each Ct Eltham SE9 ....5 E1
  Goddard's Green TN17 ....170 D1
  Chatham CA SE7 ....5 D8
eacon Cl ME8 ....63 D7
eacon Dr DA2 ....28 B3
eacon Hill ME5 ....48 D2
eacon Hill La ME3 ....33 F4
eacon Oak Rd TN30 ....183 B8
eacon Rd Chatham ME5 ....48 E3
  Erith DA8 ....9 B7
  Lenham ME17 ....111 C5
eacon Rise TN13 ....84 A1
eacon Wlk TN14 ....98 F8
eacon Wlk TN30 ....173 B1
eacon Wood Ctry Pk*
  DA2 ....28 B4
eaconfields TN13 ....84 A1
eacons The ME12 ....106 C2
eacons Wlk 1B E6 ....1 E8
eaconsfield Ave ME7 ....48 E5
eaconsfield Cl SE3 ....5 A8
eaconsfield Par SE9 ....22 E4
eadon Rd BR2 ....36 A4
eagles Cl BR5 ....52 D8
eagles Wood Rd TN2 ....150 E7
eam Cl TN17 ....167 F8
eamish Rd ME3 ....38 C2
eams The ME15 ....92 F1
ean Hill Cotts DA2 ....26 E3
ean La DA2 ....28 B6
ean Rd Bexley DA6 ....7 D3
  Swanscombe DA9 ....28 A7
eanshaw SE9 ....23 A4
earsted Sta
  ME14 ....93 B5
earsted Green Bsns Ctr
  ME14 ....93 C4
earsted Rd ME14 ....92 E6
eaton Cl DA9 ....11 B2
eatrice Gdns DA11 ....29 E6
eatty Ave ME7 ....48 A4
eatty Cotts ME3 ....19 D7
eatty Rd ME1 ....61 D8
eaufighter Rd ME19 ....88 E3
eaufort E6 ....2 A8
eaufort Ave ME8 ....48 D6
eaufort Rd ME2 ....46 E8
eaufort Wlk ME15 ....107 E4
eaulieu Ave E16 ....1 B5
eaulieu Rd TN10 ....117 B4
eaulieu Rise ME1 ....47 D1
eaulieu Wlk ME14 ....91 C7
eaumanor Gdns SE9 ....23 A4
eaumont Dr DA11 ....29 F8
eaumont Rd
  Maidstone ME16 ....91 B2
  Northfleet DA11 ....29 E8
  Orpington BR5 ....37 D3
eaver Pk ME15 ....107 E8
eaver Rd ME15 ....91 B7
eaverbank Rd SE9 ....23 D7
eavers Lodge DA14 ....23 F3
eaverwood Rd BR7 ....23 E2
eaverwood Sch for Girls
  BR7 ....23 E2
ebbington Rd SE18 ....2 E2
eblets Cl BR6 ....51 F5
eckenham Dr ME16 ....91 D7
eckenham La 1B
  Tonbridge TN9 ....133 B8
eckets Field TN11 ....131 A3
eckett Cl BR5 ....52 A8
eckett DA17 ....3 F3
ecketts Cl BR6 ....51 F7
eckford Dr BR5 ....52 A8
eckley Cl DA12 ....31 B6
eckley Mews ME5 ....61 F5
eckman Cl TN14 ....68 C4
ecks Rd DA14 ....24 A5
ecksbourne CI ME14 ....92 A8
eckton Park Sta E6 ....1 F6
eckton Rd E16 ....1 A8

Beckton Spec Sch E16 ....1 D8
Beckton Sta E6 ....2 A8
Beckworth Pl ME16 ....91 B2
Becton Pl DA8 ....8 C6
Bedale Wlk DA2 ....27 B7
Beddington Gn BR5 ....37 F8
Beddington Rd BR5 ....37 F8
Beddow Way ME20 ....76 B3
Bedens Rd BR5 ....24 C3
Bedford Ave ME8 ....49 D1
Bedford Pl ME16 ....91 E4
Bedford Rd Dartford DA1 ....27 A8
  Northfleet DA11 ....29 F6
  Orpington BR6 ....38 A1
  Royal Tunbridge Wells TN4 ....133 A1
  Sidcup DA15 ....23 E5
Bedford Sq DA12 ....42 E6
Bedford Terr 9 TN1 ....149 A2
Bedgebury Cl
  Chatham ME1 ....61 D8
  Maidstone ME14 ....92 C6
Bedgebury Cross TN17 ....167 D2
Bedgebury Lower Sch
  TN18 ....184 F7
Bedgebury
  National Pinetum* TN17 ....177 E8
Bedgebury Park Sch
  TN17 ....167 E1
Bedgebury Rd Eltham SE9 ....5 D3
  Goudhurst TN17 ....167 E5
Bedivere Rd BR1 ....22 A5
Bedlam La TN12 ....142 E6
Bedonwell Inf Sch SE2 ....7 E8
Bedonwell Jun Sch SE2 ....7 E8
Bedonwell Rd Bexley DA7 ....7 E8
  Erith DA7,DA17 ....7 E8
Bedwell Rd DA17 ....4 A1
Bedwin Cl ME1 ....61 D7
Beeby Rd E16 ....1 B8
Beech Ave Sidcup DA15 ....24 A8
  Swanley BR8 ....39 E5
Beech Copse BR1 ....36 F7
Beech Ct Crayford DA1 ....10 A1
  Paddock Wood TN12 ....136 A7
Beech Dell BR2,BR6 ....50 F6
Beech Dr ME16 ....91 C5
Beech Gr ME3 ....32 C3
Beech Green La
  Cowden TN7 ....145 F1
  Withyham TN7 ....160 B7
Beech Haven Ct DA1 ....8 D2
Beech House 7 DA15 ....24 A8
Beech Hurst TN5 ....150 D7
Beech Hurst Cl ME15 ....92 B2
Beech La TN12 ....151 C4
Beech Manor TN2 ....149 D3
Beech Rd Dartford DA1 ....26 D7
  East Malling ME19 ....89 F7
  Hoo St Werburgh ME3 ....34 E3
  Kings Hill ME19 ....88 F2
  Newenden TN18 ....187 C3
  Orpington BR6 ....52 A3
  Rochester ME7 ....46 F6
  Sevenoaks TN13 ....84 B2
Beech St TN1 ....149 B4
Beech Wlk DA1 ....9 A3
Beecham Rd TN10 ....117 E6
Beechcroft BR7 ....23 A1
Beechcroft Ave DA7 ....8 D5
Beechcroft Cl BR6 ....51 D6
Beechcroft Rd BR6 ....51 D6
Beechen Bank Rd ME5 ....62 A1
Beechenlea La BR8 ....40 B6
Beeches Ct SE12 ....22 B5
Beeches Cl ME3 ....22 A2
Beeches The
  Aylesford ME20 ....75 E1
  Chatham ME5 ....48 F7
  Hextable BR8 ....25 F1
  Royal Tunbridge Wells TN2 ....149 D5
  Sole Street DA13 ....44 D5
  The Moor TN18 ....184 E7
  Tilbury RM18 ....13 B5
Beechfield Cotts 5 BR1 ....36 C7
Beechfield Rd Bromley BR1 ....36 C7
  Erith DA8 ....8 E7
Beechhill Rd SE9 ....6 A2
Beechin Wood La TN15 ....87 D5
Beeching Rd ME5 ....62 B3
Beechings Gn ME8 ....49 C3
Beechings Way ME8 ....49 C3
Beechings Way Ind Ctr
  ME8 ....49 B4
Beechlands Cl DA3 ....43 A4
Beechmont Rd TN13 ....99 B6
Beechmont Rise TN10 ....117 B6
Beechmore Dr ME5 ....61 D3
Beechmore Br ME5 ....62 A2
Beechway DA5 ....7 D7
Beechwood Ave
  Chatham ME5 ....48 D2
  Orpington BR6 ....51 E4
Beechwood Cres DA7 ....7 D4
Beechwood Dr
  Orpington BR6 ....50 D6
  Vigo Village DA13 ....58 A1
Beechwood Gdns DA13 ....58 A1
Beechwood Mews TN2 ....149 E4
Beechwood Rd ME19 ....90 F3
Beechwood Rise BR7 ....23 B4
Beechwood Sch
  (Sacred Heart) TN2 ....149 E4
Beechy Lees Rd TN14 ....69 E3
Beeken Dene BR6 ....51 C6
Beesfield La DA4 ....41 A1
Beeston Ct 1B 1 A6
Begbie Rd SE3 ....5 C5
Beggars La TN16 ....81 E3

Begonia Ave ME8 ....49 C2
Beke Rd ME8 ....63 D4
Bekesbourne Tower 12
  BR5 ....38 D1
Beladon Haw TN14 ....68 A8
Belfast Ho 1B ME15 ....107 E7
Belfield Rd TN12 ....150 D6
Belford Gr SE18 ....2 A2
Belgrave Cl 1B ME5 ....38 C5
Belgrave Ct SE7 ....5 C7
Belgrave Rd TN1 ....149 B4
Belgrave Rd ME8 ....75 F6
Belgrove 5 TN1 ....149 A2
Bell Cl DA9 ....10 F2
Bell Cres ME1 ....75 F8
Bell Farm Gdns ME16 ....90 F7
Bell Gdns BR5 ....38 C4
Bell Ho Erith DA8 ....3 D1
  Grays RM17 ....11 E8
Bell La Burham ME1 ....75 F8
  Chatham ME5 ....77 B7
  Larkfield ME20 ....75 B2
  Lashenden TN27 ....158 B8
  Maidstone ME14 ....93 A5
  Newnham TN27 ....171 C5
  Staplehurst TN12 ....139 E3
Bell Meadow ME15 ....107 E6
  Goudhurst TN17 ....153 F1
  Kit's Coty ME20 ....76 E7
  Northfleet DA11 ....29 E8
Bell Square Market Pl
  SE18 ....2 A2
Bell St ME1 ....75 F8
Bell Water Gate SE18 ....2 A3
Bell Way ME17 ....109 E2
Bell Wood Com Sch
  ME15 ....107 E5
Bell Wood Inf Sch ME15 ....107 E5
Bell's Cl TN30 ....183 A7
Bell's Farm La TN11 ....119 C8
Bells Farm Rd TN11,TN12 ....103 D1
Bells La ME3 ....183 A7
Bellwood Cl ME3 ....34 E6
Belmont Ave DA16 ....6 E4
Belmont Cl ME16 ....90 F2
Belmont Ct 4 ME15 ....92 B4
Belmont La BR7 ....23 C3
Belmont Par BR7 ....23 C3
Belmont Prim Sch DA7 ....8 C2
Belmont Rd Chislehurst BR7 ....23 B3
  Erith DA8 ....8 B8
  Gillingham ME7 ....48 C4
  Grays RM17 ....11 F8
  Harrow Ave ME9 ....65 F8
Belson Rd SE18 ....1 F2
Beltana Dr DA12 ....30 E4
Belton Rd DA14 ....24 A4
Beltring Sta TN12 ....120 B4
Beltring Hop Farm* TN12 ....120 B4
Beltring Rd Royal
  Tunbridge Wells TN4 ....149 A6
Beltwood Rd DA17 ....4 C3
Beluncle Villas ME3 ....35 C7
Belvedere Cl DA12 ....30 C7
Belvedere Ho 9
  ME15 ....107 F5
Belvedere Ind Est DA17 ....4 B3
Belvedere Link Bsns Pk
  DA17 ....4 B3
Belvedere Rd Bexley DA7 ....7 C5
  Erith SE28 ....3 D5
  Grays RM17 ....11 F8
Belvoir Cl SE9 ....22 E5
Ben Tillet Cl E16 ....1 C6
Benares Rd SE18 ....2 F2
Benden Cl TN12 ....139 F4
Bendmore Ave SE2 ....3 A2
Bendon Way ME8 ....63 D8
Benedict Cl 6 Erith DA17 ....3 E3
  Halling ME2 ....60 B4
  Orpington BR6 ....51 F8
Benenden CE Prim Sch
  TN17 ....180 D6
Benenden Gn ME8 ....63 D4
Benenden Hospl TN17 ....171 C3
Benenden Manor ME8 ....49 B3
Benenden Rd
  Benenden TN17 ....181 B4
  Cranbrook TN17 ....169 E1
  Fosten Green TN27 ....171 F5
Benenden Sch TN17 ....180 C8
Benhall Mill Rd TN2,TN3 ....163 D8
Benjamin Ct 4 DA17 ....7 F8
Benn Ho SE7 ....1 C1
Bennett Cl DA16 ....6 E5
Bennett House DA11 ....29 F5
Bennett Meml
  Diocesan Sch TN4 ....148 E6
Bennett Way DA2 ....27 C7
Bennetts Ave TN15 ....71 C7
Bennetts Copse BR7 ....22 E2
Bennetts Cotts ME7 ....78 A8

Bennetts Mews 6 TN30 ....183 A7
Benover Rd ME18 ....120 F7
Benson Rd RM17 ....12 C8
Bensted Cl ME15 ....121 D7
Bentfield Gdns SE9 ....22 D5
Bentham Hill TN3,TN4 ....132 D1
Bentham Rd SE28 ....3 C5
Bentley Cl Aylesford ME20 ....75 F1
  Chatham ME5 ....62 D2
  New Barn DA3 ....43 C7
Bentley Sta DA12 ....13 C1
Bentley Street Ind Est 13 C1
Bentley's Mdw TN15 ....84 F7
Bentii Cl ME16 ....90 F2
Berber Rd ME7 ....47 B8
Bercta Rd SE9 ....23 C6
Berengrave La ME8 ....49 F2
Berens Cl ME7 ....37 F3
Berens Rd BR5 ....38 D4
Berens Way BR5 ....37 F6
Beresford Ave ME1 ....47 E2
Beresford Ct TN17 ....166 F2
Beresford Dr BR1 ....36 E6
Beresford Rd
  Gillingham ME7 ....48 D4
  Goudhurst TN17 ....153 F1
  Kit's Coty ME20 ....76 E7
  Northfleet DA11 ....29 E8
Beresford Square Market Pl
  SE18 ....2 A2
Berger Cl BR5 ....37 E3
Bergland Pk ME2 ....47 D8
Bering Wlk E16 ....1 D7
Berkeley Ave DA7 ....7 A6
Berkeley Cl Chatham ME1 ....61 D8
  Orpington BR6 ....37 E2
  Pembury TN2 ....150 E7
Berkeley Cres DA1 ....26 E7
Berkeley Ct 3 ....39 E6
Berkeley Mount 4 ME4 ....47 F4
Berkeley Rd 7 TN1 ....149 A2
Berkeley Terr ME18 ....104 E8
Berkhampstead Rd 5 DA17 ....4 A1
Berkley Cres DA12 ....13 C1
Berkley Rd DA12 ....13 B1
Berkshire Cl ME5 ....62 C8
Bermuda Rd RM18 ....13 A5
Bernal Cl SE28 ....3 D6
Bernard Ashley Dr SE7 ....1 B1
Bernard St 22 DA13 ....13 B1
Bernards Ct DA15 ....23 E7
Bernersmede SE3 ....5 A4
Berry Rd ME3 ....34 E3
Berry's Green Rd TN16 ....66 B2
Berry's Hill TN16 ....66 B4
Berryfield Cl BR1 ....36 E7
Berryhill SE9 ....6 B2
Berryhill Gdns SE9 ....6 B2
Berrylands Hartley DA3 ....43 A3
  Orpington BR6 ....52 A6
Bert Reilly Ho 10 SE12 ....5 B1
Bertha Hollamby Rd DA14 ....24 C3
Bertrand Way SE28 ....3 B5
Bertrey Cotts TN16 ....66 B3
Berwick Cres DA15 ....6 E1
Berwick Cl DA2 ....10 B8
Berwick Rd Bexley DA16 ....7 B6
  Newham E16 ....1 C8
Berwick Way TN14 ....84 B7
Berwyn Gr ME15 ....107 A6
Beryl Ave E6 ....1 E8
Beryl Rd SE18 ....2 E1
Besant Ct 15 SE18 ....2 E6
Bessels Green Rd TN13 ....83 D3
Bessels Meadow TN13 ....83 D3
Bessels Way TN13 ....83 D4
Bessie Lansbury Cl E6 ....2 C4
Best St ME4 ....47 F4
Beta Rd ME3 ....35 D7
Betenson Ave TN13 ....83 F4
Betham Rd Betsham DA13 ....28 D3
  Erith DA8 ....8 F7
  Maidstone ME15 ....107 F6
  Swanscombe DA10 ....28 B5
Betterton Dr DA14 ....24 E6
Bettescombe Rd ME8 ....63 E7
Betts Rd E16 ....1 C6
Beult Mdw ME7 ....149 C4
Beult Rd DA1 ....9 F1
Bevan Pl BR8 ....39 F5
Bevan Rd SE2 ....3 B1
Bevans Cl DA9 ....11 C2
Bevercote Wlk 7 DA17 ....7 F8
Beveridge Ct 3 SE28 ....3 A6
Beverley Ave DA15 ....23 F8
Beverley Cl ME8 ....63 F8
Beverley Cres TN9 ....117 A6
Beverley Gdns ME8 ....63 F8
Beverley Rd Bexley DA7 ....7 A5
  Maidstone ME16 ....90 F2
Bevill Allen Cl 1 SE2 ....3 C1
Bevin Ho 2 ....148 C5

Bewl Water* 176 C6
Bewl Water Visitors Ctr*
  TN5 ....176 B8
Bewlbridge La
  Lamberhurst TN3,TN5 ....166 B1
  Wadhurst TN5 ....175 F8
Bewley La TN15 ....86 D2
Bexhill Dr RM17 ....11 F8
Bexley Cl DA1 ....8 E2
Bexley Coll Erith DA17 ....4 B1
Bexley Coll
  (St Joseph's Campus) SE2 ....7 D8
Bexley Gram Sch DA5 ....25 B7
Bexley High St DA5 ....25 B7
Bexley Hospl DA5 ....25 C6
Bexley La Crayford DA1 ....8 E2
  Sidcup DA14 ....24 C5
Bexley Rd Eltham SE9 ....6 C2
  Erith DA8 ....4 F1
  Erith,Northumberland
    Heath DA8 ....8 C8
Bexley Sta DA5 ....25 A8
Bexleyheath Sch DA7 ....7 F4
Bexleyheath Sta DA7 ....7 E6
Bexon La ME9 ....80 F5
Bickley Cres BR1 ....36 E5
Bickley Park Rd BR1 ....36 E6
Bickley Park Sch BR1 ....36 C6
Bickley Prim Sch BR1 ....36 E7
Bickley Rd 2 Bromley BR1 ....36 E6
  Tonbridge TN9 ....133 B8
Bickley Sta BR1 ....36 E6
Bickmore Way TN9 ....117 D3
Bicknor Court Cotts ME9 ....80 C2
Bicknor La ME9 ....80 D3
Bicknor Rd
  Maidstone ME15 ....107 F4
  Orpington BR6 ....37 F2
Bidborough CE Prim Sch
  TN3 ....132 E4
Biddenden Cl ME15 ....92 F3
Biddenden La TN12 ....141 E5
Biddenden Rd
  Durrant Green TN26,TN26 ....173 A6
  Headcorn TN27 ....141 E2
  Tenterden TN30 ....172 E6
  Tylden TN27 ....158 F8
Biddenden Vineyard*
  TN27 ....172 A5
Biddenden Way
  Eltham SE9 ....23 A4
  Istead Rise DA13 ....29 E1
Biddulph Ho 17 SE18 ....1 F2
Bideford Rd DA16 ....7 B7
Biggin La RM16 ....13 B8
Bignell Rd SE18 ....2 B1
Bilberry Cl ME14 ....92 E5
Bill Hamling Cl SE9 ....22 F6
Bill Street Rd ME2 ....33 C1
Billet Hill TN15 ....56 C6
Billings 42 F3
Bilsby Gr SE9 ....22 D4
Bilsington Cl ME5 ....62 B8
Bilton Rd DA8 ....9 A8
Binbury La ME14,ME9 ....79 A5
Bines The 136 A5
Bingham Point 8 SE18 ....2 B2
Bingham Rd ME2 ....33 C1
Bingley St ME5 ....74 F8
Bingley Cl 1 Chatham ME1 ....47 E4
  Newham E16 ....1 C7
Binland Gr ME5 ....61 D3
Binnacle Rd ME1 ....61 C8
Binney Rd ME3 ....19 D8
Binsey Wlk 2 SE2 ....3 C4
Birbetts Rd SE9 ....22 F6
Birch Cl Eynsford DA4 ....54 D7
  Martin 135 D1
  New Barn DA3 ....43 C7
  Royal Tunbridge Wells TN2 ....149 D7
  Sevenoaks TN13 ....83 B4
  Tonbridge TN11 ....116 D4
Birch Cres ME20 ....90 D8
Birch Dr Bexley DA6 ....7 A3
Birch Gr 22 C1
  Gillingham ME7 ....63 A4
Birch Kiln Cotts TN5 ....175 A6
Birch Mead BR6 ....51 A8
Birch Pl Sevenoaks TN13 ....84 A3
  Stone DA9 ....10 E1
Birch Row BR2 ....37 A2
Birch Tree Ho 18 SE12 ....5 B2
Birch Tree Way ME15 ....92 B3
Birch Wlk TN2 ....149 D7
Birchden Cotts TN3 ....161 C6
Birchdene Dr SE28 ....3 A5
Birches The Greenwich SE7 ....5 B8
  Swanley BR8 ....39 E6
  Tonbridge TN9 ....133 A6
Birchetts Ave 147 E3
Birchetts Green La TN5 ....175 A2
Birchfields 62 A3
Birchin Cross Rd TN15 ....70 A5
Birchington Cl Bexley DA7 ....8 B6
  Maidstone ME15 ....92 C5
  Orpington BR5 ....38 C1
Bircholme TN2 ....149 D7

Bircholt Rd ME15 107 F4
Birchway TN15 55 F2
Birchwood Ave
  Bidborough TN4 132 E3
  Sidcup DA14 24 C5
Birchwood Dr DA2 25 E4
Birchwood La TN14 67 F4
Birchwood Par DA2 25 E4
Birchwood Park Ave BR8 39 F6
Birchwood Prim Sch BR8 39 D8
Birchwood Rd
  Dartford DA2,BR8 25 D3
  Maidstone ME16 91 C5
  Orpington BR5 37 E5
Birchwood Terr BR8 39 C8
Bird House La BR6 66 A5
Bird in Hand St TN3 161 B8
Bird La TN5 174 B5
Bird-in-Hand La BR1 36 D7
Birdbrook Rd SE3 5 C4
Birdham Cl BR1 36 E4
Birkbeck Prim Sch DA14 24 B5
Birkbeck Rd DA14 24 A5
Birkdale TN1 149 B6
Birkdale Cl BR6 37 D2
Birkdale Ct 3 ME16 91 E4
Birkdale Rd SE2 3 A2
Birken Rd TN2 149 D6
Birkhall Cl ME5 62 A5
Birling Ave Gillingham ME8 49 E1
  Maidstone ME14 93 A4
Birling Cl ME14 93 A4
Birling Dr TN2 149 A1
Birling Hill DA13,ME19,ME6 59 B1
Birling Park Ave TN2 163 B8
Birling Pk ME19 74 C5
Birling Rd Erith DA8 8 E6
  Leybourne ME19 74 C3
  Royal Tunbridge Wells TN2 163 B8
  Ryarsh ME19 74 A5
  Snodland ME6 74 F7
Birnam Sq 1 ME16 91 E4
Birtrick Dr DA13 43 F4
Bishop Butt Cl BR6 51 F7
Bishop John Robinson CE Prim Sch SE28 3 C6
Bishop's Down TN4 148 F3
Bishop's Down Cty Prim Sch TN4 148 E5
Bishop's Down Park Rd TN4 148 F4
Bishop's Down Rd TN4 148 F3
Bishop's La ME15 121 D6
Bishopbourne Gn ME8 49 B4
Bishops Ave BR1 36 C6
Bishops Cl Eltham SE9 23 C6
  Nettlestead ME18 104 D6
Bishops Ct
  Royal Tunbridge Wells TN4 148 F3
  Stone DA9 10 E2
Bishops Gn BR1 36 C8
Bishops Mews TN9 133 C8
Bishops Oak Ride TN10 117 C6
Bishops Way ME15 91 F4
Bishops Wlk
  Chislehurst BR7 37 C8
  Rochester ME1 47 C5
Bishopsbourne Ho 2 BR1 22 B1
Black Eagle Cl TN16 96 C8
Black Horse Ct TN27 141 E5
Black Horse Mews TN15 87 A7
Black Horse Rd 14 DA14 24 A4
Black Mill La TN27 141 B6
Black Post ME17 95 E4
Black Rock Gdns ME7 63 B4
Blackberry Field BR5 38 A8
Blackberry Way TN12 136 B6
Blackbrook La BR1,BR2 37 A5
Blackdale Farm Cotts DA1 27 B6
Blackfen Par DA16 7 A1
Blackfen Rd DA15 7 B1
Blackfen Sch for Girls DA15 7 B1
Blackhall La TN15 84 E3
Blackheath Bluecoat CE Sec Sch SE3 5 B7
Blackheath High Sch SE3 5 A7
Blackheath High Sch GPDST (Jun Dept) SE3 5 A5
Blackheath Pk SE3 5 A5
Blackheath Prep Sch SE3 5 A6
Blackhurst La TN2 149 F6
Blacklands
  East Malling ME19 89 F8
  Mill Street ME19 89 F7
Blacklands Dr ME19 89 F8
Blacklands Jun Sch ME19 89 F7
Blackman Cl ME3 34 D7
Blackman's La TN11 118 D6
Blackmans Cl DA1 26 C7
Blackmanstone Way ME16 91 B7
Blackmead TN13 83 E6
Blackness La BR2 50 D2
Blacksmith Dr ME14 92 D5
Blacksmith's La TN5 175 A5
Blacksmiths Field TN32 185 C1
Blacksmiths La BR5 38 C4
Blacksole La TN15 71 F3
Blacksole Rd TN15 71 F3
Blackthorn Ave
  Chatham ME5 62 A3
  Royal Tunbridge Wells TN4 133 C1
Blackthorn Cl TN15 55 F2
Blackthorn Dr ME20 75 B2
Blackthorn Gr DA7 7 E4
Blackthorne Rd ME8 64 B8
Blackwater Cl RM13 4 E8
Bladindon Dr DA5 24 D8
Blair Cl DA15 6 E2
Blair Dr TN13 84 B4
Blake Cl DA16 6 E6
Blake Dr 3 ME20 74 F4
Blake Gdns DA1 9 F3
Blake Way
  Royal Tunbridge Wells TN2 149 D7
  Tilbury RM18 13 C5
Blakemore Way DA17 3 E3
Blakeney Cl ME14 93 B4
Blaker Ave ME1 47 E1
Blaker Ct SE7 5 C7
Blanchard Cl SE9 22 E5
Bland St SE9 5 D3
Blanmerle Rd SE9 23 B7
Blann Cl SE9 5 D1
Blatchford Cl ME19 74 F1
Blatchington Rd TN1 149 B1
Bleak Hill La SE18 6 F8
Bleakwood Rd ME5 61 F4
Blean Rd ME8 49 C2
Blean Sq ME14 92 C6
Bleddyn Cl DA15 7 C1
Bledlow Cl SE28 3 C6
Blendon Dr DA5 7 D1
Blendon Rd
  Maidstone ME14 92 C5
  Sidcup DA5 7 D1
Blendon Terr SE18 6 C8
Blenheim Ave ME4 47 E2
Blenheim Cl Dartford DA1 9 C1
  Maidstone ME15 92 F3
  Meopham DA13 58 B8
Blenheim Ct DA15 23 D5
Blenheim Dr DA16 6 F6
Blenheim Gr DA12 30 C8
Blenheim Inf Sch BR6 52 C8
Blenheim Jun Sch BR6 52 C8
Blenheim Rd
  Bromley BR1,BR2 36 E5
  Dartford DA1 9 C1
  Orpington BR5,BR6 52 C8
  Sidcup DA15 24 C7
Blenheim Way TN5 177 C3
Bletchington Ct 3 DA17 4 A2
Blewbury Ho 3 SE2 3 C4
Bligh Prim Inf Sch ME2 46 C7
Bligh Rd DA11 13 A1
Bligh Way ME2 46 D6
Bligh's Meadow Sh Prec TN13 84 C2
Bligh's Rd TN13 84 B2
Bligh's Wlk TN13 84 C2
Blind La Bredhurst ME7 63 A1
  Goudhurst TN17 153 E1
  Lidsing ME7 62 F1
Blind Mary's La ME9 80 E4
Bliss Way TN10 117 E5
Blithdale Rd SE2 3 A2
Blockhouse Rd 5 RM17 12 C8
Blockmakers Ct ME4 48 B1
Bloomfield Rd
  Bromley BR2 36 D4
  Woolwich SE18 2 B1
Bloomfield Terr TN16 81 E2
Bloomsbury Wlk 2 ME15 92 A4
Bloors La ME8 49 D1
Bloors Wharf Rd ME7 49 F4
Blowers Grove Wood ME7 63 B3
Blowers Hill Cowden TN8 145 D8
  Speldhurst TN3 148 B8
Bloxam Gdns SE9 5 E2
Blue Anchor La RM18 13 E8
Blue Boar La ME1 47 D5
Blue Chalet Ind Pk TN15 55 D4
Bluebell Cl Gillingham ME7 48 F6
  Orpington BR6 51 C8
Bluebell Wlk TN12 136 A5
Blueberry La TN14 67 C4
Bluebird Way SE28 2 D4
Bluecoat La TN17 167 C6
Bluett St ME14 92 A5
Bluewater Parkway DA9 27 F7
Blunden La ME18 105 A1
Blunts Rd SE9 6 A2
Blyth Rd SE28 3 C6
Blythe Ct SE12 22 A8
Blythe Hill BR5 38 A8
Blythe Rd ME15 92 B4
Boakes Meadow TN14 68 F8
Boarders La TN5 176 C3
Boarley Ct ME14 76 F1
Boarley La ME14 76 F2
Boathouse Rd ME12 21 F3
Bobbing Hill ME9 65 F5
Bocking Cl TN5 174 E4
Bockingford La ME15 106 F8
Bodiam Cl ME8 49 C3
Bodiam Ct ME16 91 F3
Bodiam Rd TN18, TN32 185 F3
Bodle Ave DA10 11 E1
Bodmin Cl BR5 38 C1
Bodsham Cres ME15 93 B3
Boevey Path 2 SE2 7 F8
Bogey La BR6 51 A3
Bognor Rd DA16 7 D6
Boiler Rd ME4 48 A8
Boley Hill ME1 47 C6
Boleyn Rd TN15 69 E2
Boleyn Way DA10 28 E8
Bolingbroke Ho ME16 91 E3
Bollon Ct 9 SE12 22 B5
Bolner Cl ME5 61 F2
Bombay House 1 ME15 107 E5
Bombers La TN16 81 D7
Bonar Pl BR7 22 E1
Bonaventure Ct DA12 30 F4
Bonchester Cl BR7 23 A1
Bond Cl TN14 67 D4
Bond Rd ME8 63 E5
Bond St RM17 12 C8
Bondfield Cl TN4 133 A1
Bondfield Ho SE18 6 A7
Bondfield Rd
  East Malling ME19 89 F8
  4 Newham E6 1 F8
Boneashe La TN15 87 D6
Boneta Rd SE18 1 F3
Bonflower La ME17 122 C7
Bonney Way BR8 39 E6
Bonnington Gn ME8 49 C3
Bonnington Rd ME14 92 C6
Bonnington Twr BR2 36 E3
Bookins Cl ME17 107 D5
Booth Cl SE28 3 B6
Booth Rd ME4 47 F2
Bootham Cl ME2 46 D5
Borden CE Prim Sch ME9 65 F3
Bordyke TN9 117 C2
Boreham Ave E16 1 A7
Boresisle TN30 173 B2
Borgard Ho SE18 5 E6
Borgard Rd SE18 1 F2
Borkwood Ct BR6 51 F6
Borkwood Pk BR6 51 F6
Borkwood Way BR6 51 E6
Borland Cl DA9 11 A2
Borough Green & Wrotham Sta TN15 86 F7
Borough Green Prim Sch TN15 87 A7
Borough Green Rd
  Borough Green TN15 86 E7
  Ightham TN15 86 D6
  Wrotham TN15 72 A1
Borough Rd ME7 48 D4
Borstal HM Prison & Youth Custody Ctr ME1 47 B1
Borstal Manor Com Sch ME1 46 F2
Borstal Mews ME1 47 A2
Borstal Rd ME1 47 B3
Borstal St ME1 47 A2
Bostall Hill SE2 3 B1
Bostall La SE2 3 B1
Bostall Manorway SE2 3 B2
Bostall Park Ave DA7 7 E7
Bostall Rd BR5 24 B1
Boston Gdns ME8 49 C1
Boston Rd ME5 62 C2
Bosville Ave TN13 84 A4
Bosville Dr TN13 84 A4
Bosville Rd TN13 84 A4
Boswell Cl BR5 38 C3
Boswell Ho BR2 36 D4
Bosworth Ho DA8 4 E1
Botany TN9 117 C1
Botany Bay La BR7 37 C7
Botha Rd E13 1 C8
Bothwell Cl 7 E16 1 A8
Botsom La TN15 55 D4
Bott Rd DA2 26 F4
Bottle House Cotts TN11 130 F1
Bottlescrew Hill ME17 107 B4
Boucher Dr DA11 29 F4
Bough Beech Reservoir Nature Ctr* TN14 114 A7
Boughton Cl ME8 49 B3
Boughton Ho BR1 22 E1
Boughton La ME15 107 B6
Boughton Monchelsea Cty Prim Sch ME17 107 B2
Boughton Par ME15 107 A7
Boughton Place Cotts ME17 127 A8
Boughton Rd
  Lenham ME17 111 B2
  Woolwich SE28 2 E3
Boultwood Rd E6 1 F7
Boundary Ho 3 DA11 29 F7
Boundary Rd Chatham ME4 47 E3
  Royal Tunbridge Wells TN2 149 D1
  Sidcup DA15 6 E2
Boundary St 2 DA8 8 F7
Boundary The TN3, TN4 148 B3
Bounds Cross TN27 157 F7
Bounds Oak Way TN4 132 E3
Bounds The ME20 75 E1
Bourdillon Ct SE9 22 E6
Bournbrook Rd SE3,SE9 5 D4
Bourne Cl TN9 117 D3
Bourne Ct ME1 47 D5
Bourne Ent Ctr TN15 87 A7
Bourne Grange La TN11 118 D8
Bourne Ind Pk DA1 8 E2
Bourne La Bodiam TN32 184 F1
  Plaxtol TN15 86 F1
  Tonbridge TN9 117 D3
Bourne Mead DA5 8 D2
Bourne Par DA5 25 B8
Bourne Pk TN11 118 F5
Bourne Rd
  Bexley DA1,DA5 8 D2
  Bromley BR2 36 D5
  Gravesend DA12 30 F6
  Sidcup DA5 25 B8
Bourne Row TN8 130 D6
Bourne Vale Hayes BR2 36 A2
  Plaxtol Spoute TN15 102 A8
Bourne Way Hayes BR2 50 A8
  Swanley BR8 39 C6
Bourner Cotts TN17 156 D4
Bourneside Terr ME17 94 D2
Bournewood Cl ME15 92 F1
Bournewood Rd
  Bexley SE18,SE2 7 A7
  Orpington BR5 38 C2
Bournville Ave ME4 47 F1
Bovarde Ave ME19 89 C3
Bow Arrow La DA2 10 B1
Bow Hill ME18 104 D5
Bow Rd ME18 104 E7
Bow Terr ME18 104 E7
Bowater Pl SE3 5 B7
Bowater Rd SE18 1 D3
Bowen Rd TN4 148 B4
Bower Cl ME16 91 E4
Bower Gr ME5 62 C1
Bower Grove Sch ME16 91 B2
Bower La Eynsford DA4 54 F6
  Maidstone ME16 91 E3
Bower Mount Rd ME16 91 D4
Bower Pl ME16 91 E3
Bower Rd BR8 26 A2
Bower St ME16 91 E4
Bower Terr ME16 91 E3
Bower Wlk TN12 139 E3
Bowers Ave DA11 29 F4
Bowers Ho ME7 48 E7
Bowers Rd TN14 68 F8
Bowers Wlk 1 E6 1 F7
Bowes Cl DA15 7 B1
Bowes Ct 24 DA2 10 B1
Bowes Rd ME2 47 B8
Bowes Wood DA3 56 F7
Bowesden La Shorne DA12 31 F1
  Shorne Ridgeway ME2 46 A8
Bowford Ave DA7 7 E6
Bowley La ME17 127 D8
Bowling Green Row 1 SE18 1 F2
Bowls Pl TN12 136 A7
Bowman Ave E16 1 A6
Bowman Cl ME5 62 C5
Bowmans Rd DA1 25 F8
Bowmead SE9 22 F6
Bown Cl RM18 13 B5
Bowness Rd DA7 8 B5
Bowyer Cl E6 1 F8
Bowzell Rd TN14 99 A2
Box Tree Wlk 26 BR5 38 D1
Boxgrove Prim Sch SE2 3 C3
Boxgrove Rd SE2 3 C3
Boxley Cl ME14 92 B8
Boxley Cotts DA4 41 C5
Boxley Rd Chatham ME5 62 B2
  Maidstone ME14 92 B7
Boxley St E16 1 B5
Boxmend Ind Est ME15 107 F3
Boxshall House 7 SE18 6 B8
Boy Court La TN27 125 F1
Boyard Rd SE18 2 B1
Boyces Hill ME9 65 D6
Boyle Ho 12 DA17 4 A3
Boyle Way TN12 120 B7
Boyne Pk TN4 148 F4
Boyton Court Rd ME17 125 A6
Brabourne Ave ME8 49 C3
Brabourne Cres DA7 7 F8
Bracken Cl Newham E6 1 F8
  Royal Tunbridge Wells TN2 149 E5
Bracken Hill ME5 62 A1
Bracken Lea ME5 48 C1
Bracken Rd TN2 149 E5
Bracken Wlk TN10 117 B6
Brackendene DA2,DA5 25 E4
Brackens The BR6 52 A5
Brackley Cl ME14 92 C5
Brackwood Cl ME8 63 D5
Bracondale Ave DA13 43 F8
Bracondale Rd SE2 3 A2
Bradbourne Ct TN13 84 B6
Bradbourne La ME20 75 B1
Bradbourne Park Rd TN13 84 A4
Bradbourne Rd
  Grays RM17 12 B8
  Sevenoaks TN13,TN14 84 B5
  Sidcup DA5 25 A8
Bradbourne Sch The TN13 84 A6
Bradbourne Vale Rd TN13,TN14 84 A5
Bradbury Ct
  3 Greenwich SE3 5 A7
  2 Northfleet DA11 29 F7
Braddick Cl ME15 107 B6
Bradenham Ave DA16 7 A3
Bradfield Rd E16 1 B4
Bradfields Ave ME5 61 F5
Bradfields Ave W ME5 61 F5
Bradfields Sch ME5 62 A6
Bradford Cl BR2 36 F1
Bradford St TN9 117 B1
Bradfords Cl ME4 34 C2
Bradley House ME3 19 C4
Bradley Rd Penshurst TN3 146 D5
  Upper Halling ME2 59 E5
Bradley Stone Rd E6 1 F8
Bradymead E6 2 B7
Braeburn Way ME19 89 C3
Braemar Ave DA7 8 C3
Braemar Gdns DA15 23 D5
Braes The ME3 32 C3
Braeside Ave TN13 83 F3
Braeside Cl TN13 83 F4
Braeside Cres DA7 8 C3
Braesyde Cl DA17 3 F2
Brake Ave ME5 61 E5
Brakefield Rd DA13 29 B1
Bramber Ct 9 DA2 10 B1
Bramble Ave DA2 28 C5
Bramble Bank DA13 72 F7
Bramble Cl Maidstone ME16 91 B3
Bramble Cl *continued*
  Tonbridge TN11 116 F4
Bramble Croft DA8 4 C2
Bramble La TN13 99 B7
Bramble Reed La TN12 151 B7
Bramble Wlk TN2 149 D7
Bramblebury Rd SE18 2 C1
Brambledown
  Chatham ME5 62 B8
  Hartley DA3 42 F5
Bramblefield Cl DA3 42 E6
Brambletree Cotts ME1 46 E2
Brambletree Cres ME1 46 F2
Bramdean Cres SE12 22 A7
Bramdean Gdns SE12 22 A7
Bramhope Ho 15 SE7 5 C8
Bramhope La SE7 5 B8
Bramley Cl Gillingham ME8 64 B8
  Istead Rise DA13 29 F1
  Orpington BR6 37 B1
  Swanley BR8 39 E5
Bramley Cres ME15 92 F3
Bramley Ct Bexley DA16 7 B6
  Marden TN12 138 B6
Bramley Dr TN17 169 D4
Bramley Gdns
  Coxheath ME17 106 C3
  Paddock Wood TN12 135 E7
Bramley Pl DA1 9 A3
Bramley Rd
  East Peckham TN12 119 F6
  Snodland ME6 75 A8
Bramley Rise ME2 46 E8
Bramley Way ME19 89 A2
Bramleys TN27 141 D5
Brampton Prim Sch DA7 7 D5
Brampton Rd DA7 7 E6
Bramshot Ave SE3,SE7 5 B8
Bramshott Cl ME16 91 C6
Branbridges Ind Est TN12 120 A5
Branbridges Rd TN12 120 B4
Brandon Rd DA1 27 A8
Brandon St DA11 30 B8
Brandreth Rd E6 1 F7
Brands Hatch Cotts DA3 56 A6
Brands Hatch Rd DA3 56 A7
Branham Ho 1 SE18 2 B1
Bransell Cl BR8 39 C3
Bransgore Cl ME8 63 D7
Branston Cres BR5 37 D1
Branstone Ct RM19 10 B8
Brantingham Cl TN9 132 F7
Branton Rd DA9 10 F1
Brantwood Ave DA8 8 C7
Brantwood Rd DA7 8 B4
Brantwood Way BR5 38 C6
Brasenose Rd ME7 48 E4
Brassey Dr ME20 90 D8
Brasted Cl Bexley DA6 7 D2
  Orpington BR6 52 A8
Brasted Ct Brasted TN16 82 D2
  Rochester ME2 33 A1
Brasted Hill TN14 82 A7
Brasted Hill Rd TN16 82 C5
Brasted La TN14 67 A1
Brasted Rd Erith DA8 8 E7
  Westerham TN16 81 E1
Brattle Farm Mus* TN12 139 D1
Brattle Wood TN13 99 C6
Braundton Ave DA15 23 F7
Braunstone Dr ME16 91 D7
Bray Dr E16 1 A6
Bray Gdns ME15 106 F5
Braywood Rd SE9 6 D3
Breach La ME9 64 F8
Breach Rd RM20 10 F8
Breakneck Hill DA9 11 B2
Breakspears Dr BR5 38 A8
Breaside Prep Sch BR1 36 D8
Breckonmead BR1 36 C7
Brecon Ct 7 SE9 6 A1
Bredgar Cl ME14 92 C5
Bredgar House 1 BR5 38 D1
Bredgar Rd ME8 49 B4
Bredhurst CE Prim Sch ME7 63 B1
Bredhurst Rd ME8 63 B4
Breedon Ave TN4 132 F1
Bremner Cl BR8 40 A5
Brenchley & Matfield CE Prim Sch TN12 152 A8
Brenchley Ave DA11 30 B3
Brenchley Cl Chatham ME1 47 D2
  Chislehurst BR7 37 A8
Brenchley Rd
  Gillingham ME8 49 B2
  HorsmondenZ TN12 152 F6
  Maidstone ME15 91 F2
  Matfield TN12 151 F8
  St Paul's Cray BR5 37 F7
Brenda Ct 4 DA14 24 A4
Brenda Terr DA10 28 E8
Brendon 16 DA14 24 A4
Brendon Ave ME5 62 A3
Brendon Cl Erith DA8 8 E6
  Royal Tunbridge Wells TN2 149 D5
Brendon Rd SE9 23 D6
Brenley Gdns SE9 5 D3
Brennan Rd RM18 13 B5
Brent Cl Chatham ME5 61 E5
  Dartford DA2 10 B1
  Sidcup DA5 24 E7
Brent La DA1 27 A7
Brent Prim Sch The DA2 27 C8
Brent Rd Newham E16 1 A8
  Woolwich SE18 6 B7
Brent The Dartford DA1 27 B8

rent The *continued*
Tonbridge TN10 ....117 C6
rent Way DA2 ....10 B1
rentfield Rd DA1 ....27 B8
rentlands Dr DA1 ....27 A7
rentor Ct TN2 ....149 D6
rentwood Cl SE9 ....23 C7
rentwood Ho SE18 ....5 D7
renzett Cl ME5 ....62 B5
renzett House ◨ BR5 ....38 C4
retland Ct TN4 ....148 D4
retland Rd TN4 ....148 D4
reton Rd ME1 ....47 C2
rett Wlk ME8 ....63 D4
rewer Rd ME3 ....33 B7
rewer St
  amberhurst TN3
  Maidstone ME14 ....92 A5
rewers Field DA2 ....26 C4
rewers Rd DA12 ....45 C8
rewery La TN13 ....84 C2
rewery Rd Orpington BR2 ....36 E1
  Woolwich SE18 ....2 D1
rewhouse Rd SE18 ....1 F2
rewhouse Yd ◨ DA12 ....13 B1
rian Cres TN4 ....149 B8
riar Cl Larkfield ME20 ....75 A2
  ◨ Marfpit Hill TN8 ....113 D6
riar Dale ME3 ....32 B4
riar Fields ME14 ....92 E5
riar Rd DA5 ....25 D5
riar Wlk TN10 ....117 C6
riars The TN15 ....55 D4
riars Way DA3 ....43 A4
riarswood Way BR6 ....51 F5
riary Ct DA14 ....24 B3
riary Gdns BR1 ....22 B3
rice Rd ME3 ....32 B3
rick Ct RM17 ....12 A8
rick Field View ME2 ....33 C1
rick Kiln La
  Chickenden TN12 ....153 B2
  dicombe ME17 ....125 D5
rickenden Rd TN17 ....169 D4
rickfield Cotts SE18 ....6 F8
rickfield Farm Gdns BR6 ....51 C6
rickfields Pembury TN2 ....150 E8
  West Malling ME19 ....74 B1
rickwell Cotts TN17 ....156 F6
rickworks Cl TN4 ....148 D4
ridewell La TN30 ....183 A7
ridge Bsns Pk TN12 ....135 C7
ridge Cl Dartford DA2 ....10 B1
  Tonbridge TN9 ....133 C8
ridge Cotts TN12 ....153 A6
  ◨ Grays RM17 ....12 88
ridge Ho Chatham ME1 ....47 B4
  Royal Tunbridge Wells TN4 ....149 B5
ridget Ho
  Bexley DA7 ....7 E5
  Erith DA8 ....8 F6
  Gillingham ME7 ....48 C7
  ◨ Grays RM17 ....12 C8
ridgelands Rd SE13 ....38 B3
  rochester ME1 ....47 C2
ridge St ME15 ....106 F5
ridgeland Rd E16 ....1 A6
ridgen Rd DA5 ....24 E8
ridge Par DA2 ....10 B2
ridgewater Ct BR7 ....37 E6
ridgewater Pl ME19 ....74 E2
ridle Way ME6 ....51 C6
rier Cl ME5 ....62 C8
right Cl DA2 ....3 D2
right Ct ◨ SE28 ....3 C5
right Rd ◨ ME4 ....48 B2
right Ridge TN4 ....148 E8
righlands DA11 ....29 F4
rigstock Rd DA17 ....4 B2
rimpsfield Cl SE2 ....3 B3
rimstone Cl BR6 ....52 C3
rimstone Hill DA13 ....58 D8
rindle Cl DA15 ....23 E7
rindle Way ME5 ....62 C1
rindle's Field TN9 ....133 A7
rindley Cl DA7 ....8 A4
rindley Way BR1 ....22 A3
rinkburn Cl SE2 ....3 A2
rinkers La TN5 ....175 A2
rinklow Cres SE18 ....6 B7
rinkwood Gdns TN9 ....133 D8
risbane House RM18 ....12 F6
risbane Rd ME4 ....48 A3
riset Prim Sch SE9 ....5 D3
riset Rd SE9 ....5 D3
rishing La ME15 ....107 E5
rishing La ME17 ....107 D4
rishing Rd ME15,ME17 ....107 F3
risley's Row TN5 ....60 F1
rissenden Cl ME2 ....34 A3
ristol Cl ME2 ....46 D5
ristol Rd DA12 ....30 D5
ristow Rd 7 E6
ritannia Bsns Pk ME20 ....90 E7
ritannia Cl ME4 ....60 A4
ritannia Dr DA12 ....30 F3
ritannia Village Sch E16 ....1 B5
rittain Cl SE19 ....22 E7
rittain Ho SE9 ....22 E7
rittains La TN13 ....83 F2
ritten Cl TN10 ....117 F6
rittenden Cl ◨ BR6 ....51 F2
rittenden Par BR6 ....51 F4
ritton St ME7 ....48 B5
rixham Rd DA16 ....7 D6
rixham St SE6 ....2 D4
road Bridge Cl SE3 ....5 A7

Broad Ditch Rd DA13 ....29 D1
Broad Gr TN2 ....149 A1
Broad La Dartford DA2 ....26 B4
  Royal Tunbridge Wells TN3 ....147 A4
Broad Lawn SE9 ....23 A7
Broad Oak Brenchley TN12 ....152 C8
  Groombridge TN3 ....161 C6
Broad Oak Cl
  Brenchley TN12 ....152 C8
  Royal Tunbridge Wells TN2 ....148 F1
  St Paul's Cray BR5 ....38 A5
Broad Rd DA10 ....11 E1
Broad St ME17 ....124 E7
Broad Street Hill ME17 ....94 D7
Broad View TN17 ....172 A8
Broad Wlk Eltham SE3,SE9 ....5 E5
  Orpington BR6 ....52 D7
  Sevenoaks TN13 ....99 E7
Broadcloth TN12 ....169 D3
Broadcroft TN2 ....162 F8
Broadcroft Rd BR5 ....37 D2
Broader La ME14 ....78 B2
Broadfield Rd ME15 ....107 A8
Broadgate Rd E16 ....1 D7
Broadheath Dr BR7 ....22 F3
Broadhoath TN15 ....85 E1
Broadlands Dr ME5 ....62 B4
Broadlands Rd BR1 ....22 B4
Broadmead TN2 ....162 F8
Broadmead Ave TN2 ....162 F8
Broadmere Terr ME16 ....91 D3
Broadoak ME19 ....74 E2
Broadoak Ave ME15 ....107 A8
Broadoak Cl DA4 ....27 A2
Broadoak Rd DA8 ....8 D7
Broadstone Parkway 75 A1
Broadview DA13 ....57 F6
Broadview Ave ME8 ....63 E8
Broadwater Down TN2 ....162 E8
Broadwater Down TN2 ....162 F8
Broadwater Down
  Cty Prim Sch TN2 ....148 F1
Broadwater Gdns BR6 ....51 C6
Broadwater House DA12 ....13 D1
Broadwater La TN2,TN4 ....148 F1
Broadwater Rd
  East Malling ME19 ....89 D6
  Woolwich SE28 ....2 D3
Broadwater Rise TN2 ....148 F1
Broadway Bexley DA6 ....7 F3
  Bexley DA6 ....8 A3
  Crockenhill BR8 ....39 C3
  Gillingham ME8 ....49 A3
  Grays RM17 ....12 B8
  Maidstone ME14 ....91 F4
  Tilbury RM18 ....12 F5
Broadway Sh Ctr ◨ DA6 ....8 A3
Broadway The
  Hadlow TN11 ....118 E8
  Lamberhurst TN3 ....166 B5
Broadwood DA11 ....30 B3
Broadwood Rd ME3 ....34 A4
Brock Rd E13 ....1 B8
Brockbank Cl ME5 ....62 A1
Brockdene Dr BR2 ....50 D6
Brockenhurst Ave ME15 ....92 C1
Brockenhurst Cl ME8 ....63 C7
Brockenhurst Ho ◨ TN1 ....2 A5
Brocklebank Rd SE7 ....1 B2
Brocklebank Rd Ind Est
  SE7 ....1 B2
Brockway TN15 ....87 A7
Brockwell Cl BR5 ....37 F4
Brockwood Gr SE2 ....9 D4
Broke Farm Dr BR6 ....52 C2
Brokes Way TN4 ....149 B8
Brome Ho SE18 ....6 B8
Brome Rd SE9 ....5 F4
Bromehead Way ME4 ....60 D2
Bromholm Rd SE2 ....3 B3
Bromley Cl Chatham ME5 ....62 B4
  Newington ME9 ....65 A5
Bromley Coll of Further
  & Higher Ed BR2 ....36 D3
Bromley Comm BR2 ....36 D3
Bromley General Hospl
  BR2 ....36 B5
Bromley High Sch for Girls
  BR1 ....36 D6
Bromley Ind Ctr BR1 ....36 D6
Bromley La BR7 ....23 D1
Bromley Manor Mans ◨
  BR2 ....36 A6
Bromley Mus* BR6 ....38 B2
Bromley North Sta BR1 ....36 A8
Bromley
  Public Golf Course BR2 ....36 E2
Bromley Rd BR7 ....37 B8
Bromley South Sta BR1 ....36 A6
Bromley Valley
  Gymnastics Ctr BR5 ....38 A7
Brompton Cl DA15 ....9 B7
Brompton Farm Rd ME2 ....33 A2
Brompton Hill ME4 ....47 F6
Brompton La ME2 ....47 A8
Brompton Rd ME7 ....48 B6
Brompton-Westbrook
  Prim Sch ME7 ....48 A5
Bronington Cl ME5 ....62 A5
Bronte Cl Erith DA8 ....8 B7
  Lunsford ME20 ....74 F3
  Tilbury RM18 ....13 C5
Bronte Gr DA1 ....9 F3
Bronte Sch DA11 ....30 A8
Bronte View DA12 ....30 C7

Bronze Age Way DA8,DA17 ....4 C3
Brook Cotts
  Collier Street TN12 ....137 F8
  East Farleigh ME15 ....106 C7
Brook Ct Lewisham SE12 ....22 C5
  ◨ Maidstone ME16 ....91 E3
Brook Dr TN4 ....148 D3
Brook Hill SE18 ....112 D3
Brook La Bexley DA5 ....7 D2
  Bromley BR1 ....22 A2
  Greenwich SE3 ....5 B5
  Plaxtol Spoute TN15 ....102 A8
  Snodland ME6 ....75 A6
  Tonbridge TN9 ....117 D2
Brook Rd Lunsford ME20 ....74 F4
  Northfleet DA11 ....29 E7
  Royal Tunbridge Wells TN2 ....148 F7
  Swanley BR8 ....39 D7
Brook St Erith DA8 ....8 B7
  Snodland ME6 ....75 B8
  Tonbridge TN9 ....133 A8
Brook The ME4 ....48 A4
Brook Vale DA8 ....8 B6
Brookbank ME14 ....92 A8
Brookdale Rd DA5 ....7 C1
Brookdene TN12 ....135 B7
Brookdene Rd SE18 ....2 F2
Brooke Dr DA12 ....31 B7
Brooke Rd DA15 ....23 E7
Brookes Pl ME9 ....65 B6
Brookfield Four Elms TN8 ....113 B5
  Kemsing TN15 ....69 E2
  Sandhurst TN18 ....186 B5
Brookfield Ave ME20 ....75 A4
Brookfield Cl TN4 ....133 A1
Brookfield Rd ME20 ....75 A2
Brookfield Jun Sch
  (Larkfield) ME20 ....75 A2
Brookfields TN11 ....102 E1
Brookhill Rd SE18 ....2 B1
Brookhurst Gdns TN4 ....132 E3
Brooklands Dartford DA1 ....26 E7
  Headcorn TN27 ....141 C6
  Royal Tunbridge Wells TN2 ....149 D7
Brooklands Ave DA15 ....23 D6
Brooklands Farm GT TN3 ....147 A6
Brooklands Prim Sch SE3 ....5 A4
Brooklands Rd ME20 ....75 A4
Brooklyn Paddock ME7 ....48 D6
Brooklyn Rd BR2 ....36 D4
Brooklyn Villas TN12 ....138 C5
Brookmead TN11 ....116 E4
Brookmead Ave BR1 ....36 F4
Brookmead Rd ME7 ....33 B7
Brookmead Way BR5 ....38 A3
Brooks Cl Eltham SE9 ....23 A6
  Staplehurst TN12 ....139 E4
Brooks Pl ME14 ....92 A4
Brookside
  Cranbrook TN17 ....169 D4
  Hoo St Werburgh ME3 ....34 E5
  Orpington BR6 ....37 F2
Brookside Rd DA13 ....29 F1
  Stockbury SE3 ....5 A4
Broom Ave BR5 ....38 B7
Broom Cl BR2 ....36 E3
Broom Hill Rd ME2 ....46 F8
Broom La TN3 ....147 E2
Broom Mead DA6 ....8 A2
Broom Pk TN3 ....147 E3
Broomcroft Rd ME8 ....49 F2
Broomfield House ME14 ....90 F3
Broomfield Rd Bexley DA6 ....8 A2
  Kingswood ME17 ....109 D4
  Sevenoaks TN13 ....83 F5
  Swanscombe DA10 ....11 E2
Broomfields DA3 ....42 E4
Broomhill Bank Sch TN3 ....148 C5
Broomhill Park Rd TN4 ....148 F8
Broomhill Rd Dartford DA1 ....9 B1
  Orpington BR6 ....38 A2
  Royal Tunbridge Wells TN3 ....148 D7
Broomhills DA13 ....28 E4
Broomleigh BR1 ....36 B5
Broomscroft Cotts ME18 ....89 C1
Broomshaw Rd ME6 ....90 F3
Broomwood Cl DA5 ....25 D6
Broomwood Rd BR5 ....38 A3
Brougham Ct ◨ DA2 ....10 B1
Broughton Rd
  Orpington BR6 ....51 D8
  Otford TN14 ....69 A3
Brow Cl BR5 ....38 D2
Brow Cres BR5 ....38 D2
Brown Rd DA12 ....30 E7
Brown St ME8 ....49 F2
Browndens Rd ME2 ....59 E4
Brownelow Copse ME5 ....62 B1
Brownhill Ct ME5 ....62 A4
Browning Cl Bexley DA16 ....6 E6
  ◨ Lunsford ME20 ....74 F4
Browning Rd DA1 ....9 F3
Browning Wlk RM18 ....13 C5
Brownings TN9 ....112 C4
Brownspring Dr SE9 ....23 B5
Broxbourne Rd BR6 ....37 F2
Bruce Cl DA16 ....7 B5
Bruce Ct DA15 ....23 F4
Bruce Gr BR6 ....38 A3
Bruces Wharf Rd RM17 ....12 A8
Brucks The ME18 ....104 E7
Brummel Cl DA7 ....8 C4
Brunel Cl RM18 ....13 B4
Brunel Way ME4 ....48 A7
Brungers Wlk TN10 ....117 B5
Brunswick Cl DA6 ....7 D3

Brunswick House Prim Sch
  ME16 ....91 E5
Brunswick Rd DA6 ....7 E3
Brunswick St E ME15 ....92 A3
Brunswick Terr TN1 ....149 A2
Brunswick Wlk ◨ DA12 ....30 D6
Brushwood Lodge ◨ DA17 ....4 A2
Bruton Cl BR7 ....22 F1
Bryanston Rd RM18 ....13 C5
Bryant Cl ME18 ....104 D6
Bryant Rd ME2 ....47 A7
Bryant St ME4 ....48 A3
Bryony St ME8 ....63 F5
Bubblestone Rd TN14 ....69 83
Buckden Cl SE12 ....5 A6
Buckham Thorns Rd TN16 ....81 C1
Buckhole Farm Rd ME23 ....17 C4
Buckhurst Ave TN13 ....84 C2
Buckhurst La
  High Halden TN26 ....174 A6
  Sevenoaks TN13 ....84 C2
Buckhurst Rd TN16 ....81 B7
Buckingham Ave DA16 ....6 E3
Buckingham Cl BR5 ....37 E2
Buckingham Dr BR7 ....23 C8
Buckingham Rd
  Gillingham ME7 ....48 D5
  Maidstone ME16 ....91 B6
  Royal Tunbridge Wells TN1 ....149 B2
Buckingham Row ME15 ....107 E7
Buckland Cl ME5 ....62 A2
Buckland Hill ME16 ....91 E5
Buckland La ME16 ....91 D6
Buckland Rd
  Cliffe Woods ME3 ....33 A8
  Luddesdown DA13 ....59 A7
  Maidstone ME16 ....91 E4
  Orpington BR6 ....51 E6
Buckler Gdns SE9 ....22 F5
Bucklers Cl TN2 ....149 C3
Buckles Ct SE2 ....3 D2
Buckley Cl DA1 ....8 F5
Bucks Cross Rd
  Chelsfield BR6 ....52 E5
  Northfleet DA11 ....29 D7
Buckthorn House DA15 ....23 F5
Buckwheat Ct SE2 ....3 D3
Budd Ho ◨ SE7 ....1 C1
Budd's Farm Cotts TN30 ....189 E2
Budd's La TN30 ....189 F2
Budgin's Hill BR6 ....67 C8
Budleigh Cres DA16 ....7 C6
Bugglesden Rd
  Biddenden TN27 ....172 D5
Bugsby's Way SE10,SE7 ....1 A1
Bull Alley DA16 ....7 B4
Bull Fields ME6 ....75 A8
Bull Hill Egerton ME17 ....127 F8
  Horton Kirby DA4 ....41 A5
Bull La Chislehurst BR7 ....23 D1
  Eccles ME20 ....75 F5
  Higham ME3 ....32 D7
  Stockbury ME9 ....79 E7
  Wrotham TN15 ....72 A3
Bull Lane Cotts TN3 ....165 C4
Bull Orch ME18 ....90 F2
Bull Rd ME19 ....74 C5
Bull Yd ◨ DA1 ....13 B1
Bullace La ◨ DA1 ....9 E1
Bullbanks Rd DA17 ....4 C2
Bulldog Rd ME5 ....62 B2
Bullen La TN12 ....119 E7
Buller Rd ME4 ....47 F2
Bullers Cl DA14 ....24 E3
Bullers Wood Dr BR7 ....22 F1
Bullers Wood Sch for Girls
  BR7 ....36 F8
Bullfinch Cl
  Paddock Wood TN12 ....136 A5
  Sevenoaks TN13 ....83 D5
Bullfinch Cnr TN13 ....83 E5
Bullfinch Dene TN13 ....83 D5
Bullfinch La TN13 ....83 E5
Bullingstone Cotts TN3 ....147 E7
Bullingstone La TN3 ....147 F7
Bullion Cl TN12 ....135 F6
Bullivant Cl DA9 ....11 C2
Bulls Pl TN2 ....150 D6
Bulrush Cl ME5 ....61 F3
Bumbles Cl ME1 ....61 D7
Bungalows The TN30 ....183 D7
Bunker's Hill Erith DA8 ....4 A2
  New Ash Green TN15 ....57 B4
Bunkers Hill DA14 ....24 F5
Bunny La TN3 ....162 E5
Bunters Hill Rd ME23 ....17 D2
Bunton St SE18 ....2 A3
Burberry La ME17 ....109 B5
Burch Rd DA11 ....12 F1
Burchwood Rd SE2 ....3 D3
Burdett Ave DA12 ....31 F4
Burdett Cl DA14 ....24 E3
Burdett Rd TN4 ....148 B4
Burdock Ho ◨ ME15 ....107 D7
Burford Rd BR1 ....36 E5
Burgate Cl DA1 ....8 F3
Burgess Hall Dr ME17 ....108 F6
Burgess Rd ME2 ....46 F7
Burgess Row ◨ DA1 ....183 A7
Burghclere Dr ME16 ....91 B2
Burghfield Rd DA13 ....29 F1
Burgonye Gr ME14 ....91 F7
Burham Ct Prim Sch ME1 ....75 F8
Burham Rd ME1 ....60 D8
Burial Ground La ME15 ....91 E1

Burleigh Ave DA15 ....6 F2
Burleigh Cl ME2 ....46 E8
Burleigh Rd DA11 ....76 F1
Burley Rd E16 ....1 C8
Burlings La TN14 ....66 F2
Burlington Cl ◨ Newham E6 ....1 E7
  Orpington BR6 ....51 B8
Burlington Gdns ME8 ....63 E4
Burlington Lodge BR7 ....22 F1
Burma Way ME5 ....61 F6
Burman Cl DA2 ....27 C8
Burmarsh Cl ME5 ....62 B5
Burnaby Rd DA11 ....12 E1
Burnell Ave DA16 ....7 A5
Burnett Rd DA8 ....9 D8
Burnham Cres DA1 ....9 C3
Burnham Rd Dartford DA1 ....9 C3
  Sidcup DA14 ....24 E6
Burnham Terr DA1 ....9 D2
Burnham Trad Est DA1 ....9 D2
Burnham Wlk ME8 ....63 E3
Burnley Rd RM20 ....11 A6
Burns Ave DA15 ....7 B1
Burns Cl Bexley DA16 ....6 F6
  Erith DA8 ....9 B7
Burns Cres TN9 ....133 A7
Burns Ho DA16 ....7 C6
Burns Pl RM18 ....13 B6
Burns Rd ME1 ....91 C2
Burnt Ash Hill SE12 ....22 A7
Burnt Ash La BR1,SE12 ....22 B3
Burnt Ash Prim Sch BR1 ....22 A3
Burnt Ash Rd SE12 ....22 A8
Burnt House La
  Dartford DA1 ....26 F5
  Hawley DA2 ....26 F4
  Royal Tunbridge Wells TN3 ....148 A5
Burnt Oak Terr TN18 ....186 C5
Burnt Oak Jun Mix Sch
  DA15 ....24 A7
Burnt Oak La DA15 ....7 A1
Burnt Oak Terr ME17 ....142 D1
Burntash Rd ME20 ....90 F8
Burntwood Rd TN13 ....99 88
Burntwood Rd TN13 ....99 B7
Burnwood Gr TN13 ....99 B7
Burr Bank Terr DA2 ....26 F4
Burr Cl DA7 ....7 F4
Burrage Gr SE18 ....2 C2
Burrage Pl SE18 ....2 B1
Burrage Rd SE18 ....2 C2
Burrard Rd E16 ....1 B7
Burrfield Dr BR5 ....38 D4
Burritt Mews 47 C3
Burrows La ME3 ....19 C3
Burrowswood Villas TN3 ....161 B7
Bursdon Cl DA15 ....23 F6
Burslem St TN2 ....149 E7
Bursted Wood Prim Sch
  ....8 B5
Burston Rd ME17 ....106 B2
Burt Rd E16 ....1 C5
Burton Cl ME3 ....33 C3
Burwash Ct BR5 ....38 C4
Burwash Rd SE18 ....2 D8
Burwood Ave BR2 ....50 B6
Burwood Ho ◨ TN2 ....149 E5
Burwood Sch BR6 ....52 D8
Busbridge Rd
  Bromley BR2 ....106 E6
  Snodland ME6 ....74 E7
Bush Cl ME9 ....80 F5
Bush Rd Cuxton ME2 ....46 B2
  East Peckham TN12 ....119 E8
Bush Row ME20 ....76 A3
Bushell Way BR7 ....23 A3
Bushey Ave BR5 ....37 D2
Bushey Ct DA8 ....9 A6
Bushey Ho SE9 ....22 C5
Bushey Lees DA15 ....6 F1
Bushfield Wlk DA10 ....28 E8
Bushmeadow Rd ME8 ....49 F2
Bushmoor Cres SE18 ....6 B6
Bushy Gill TN3 ....148 A3
Bushy Gr ME17 ....109 D4
Buston Manor Farm Cotts
  ME18 ....105 B2
Busty La TN15 ....86 D6
Butcher Cl TN12 ....139 E3
Butcher Wlk DA10 ....28 E8
Butcher's La ME19 ....88 D1
Butchers La TN15 ....56 D8
Butchers Rd E16 ....1 A7
Butchers Yd BR6 ....66 A8
Butler House ◨ RM17 ....12 B8
Butler's Cotts DA7 ....8 A5
Butler's Pl DA3 ....56 E7
Butt Green La ME17 ....123 A7
Butt Haw Cl ME3 ....34 E3
Buttercup Cl TN12 ....136 A5
Butterfield Sq ◨ E6 ....1 F7
Butterfly Ave DA1 ....26 E6
Butterfly La SE9 ....23 B8
Buttermere Cl ME7 ....49 A5
Buttermere Rd BR5 ....38 D5
Buttmarsh Cl SE18 ....2 B1
Button Dr ME3 ....19 C5
Button Ho ME3 ....33 A6
Button La ME15 ....93 B2
Button St BR8,DA4 ....40 C5
Butts The TN4 ....148 E8
Buttway La ME3 ....16 A6
Buxton Cl Chatham ME4 ....62 D1

Buxton Cl continued
Maidstone ME15 ....107 A8
Buxton Rd DA8 ....8 D7
Buzzard Creek Ind Est IG11 ..3 A8
Bychurch Pl 4 ME15 ......92 A3
Bycliffe Mews DA11 ....29 F8
Bycliffe Terr DA11 ....29 F8
Byland Cl SE2 ....3 B3
Byng Rd TN4 ....148 F5
Bynon Ave DA7 ....7 F4
Byrneside TN11 ....116 E4
Byron Cl SE28 ....3 C5
Byron Dr DA8 ....8 B7
Byron Gdns RM18 ....13 C6
Byron Prim Sch ME7 ....48 C3
Byron Rd Dartford DA1 ....10 B3
  Gillingham ME7 ....48 C3
  Maidstone ME14 ....92 B7
Bywater Ho SE18 ....1 E3

C

Cabbage Stalk La TN4 ...148 E2
Cable Cl DA8 ....4 C3
Cacket's La TN14 ....66 E4
Cade La TN13 ....99 C7
Cadlocks Hill TN14 ....52 F1
Cadnam Cl ME2 ....46 E8
Cadogan Ave DA2 ....27 D8
Cadogan Gdns 3 TN1 ...149 B4
Cadogan Rd SE18 ....2 C3
Cadwallon Rd SE9 ....23 C6
Caerleon Cl DA14 ....24 C3
Caernarvon Dr ME15 ......91 F1
Cage Green Prim Sch
  TN10 ....117 D5
Cage Green Rd TN10 .....117 C5
Cage La TN27 ....142 F1
Cagney Cl ME3 ....33 C3
Cairns Cl DA1 ....9 D2
Caistor Rd TN9 ....117 A1
Caithness Gdns DA15 ......6 F1
Calais Cotts DA3 ....56 A8
Calcott Wlk SE9 ....22 D4
Calcutta House 3 ME15 .107 E5
Calcutta Rd RM18 ....13 A5
Calder Rd ME14 ....91 E7
Calderwood DA12 ....31 D7
Calderwood St SE18 ....2 A2
Caldew Ave ME8 ....49 C1
Caldy Rd DA17 ....4 B3
Caledonian Ct ME8 ....63 E8
Calehill Cl ME14 ....92 C6
Caley Rd TN2 ....149 D7
Calfstock La DA4 ....40 F5
Caling Croft DA3 ....42 F1
Caliph Cl DA12 ....30 D5
Callams Cl ME8 ....63 D6
Callaways La ME9 ....65 B6
Callis Way ME8 ....63 D5
Calshot Ct 7 DA2 ....10 B1
Calverley Cl TN1 ....149 C3
Calverley Park Cres 1
  TN1 ....149 B3
Calverley Park Gdns TN1 .149 C4
Calverley Pk TN1 ....149 B3
Calverley Rd TN1 ....149 B4
Calverley St TN1 ....149 B4
Calvert Cl Erith DA17 ....4 B2
  Sidcup DA14 ....24 F2
  Calverton Prim Sch E16 ....1 D7
Calvin Cl BR5 ....38 D6
Calydon Rd SE7 ....1 B1
Cambert Way SE3 ....5 B3
Camberwell La TN14 ......97 F4
Camborne Manor 2 ME7 .48 C6
Camborne Rd Bexley DA16 ..6 F5
  Sidcup DA14 ....24 C5
Cambray Rd BR6 ....37 F2
Cambria Ave ME1 ....46 F2
Cambria Cl DA15 ....23 E7
Cambria Cres DA12 ....30 F4
Cambria Ho 2 DA8 ....8 E7
Cambrian Gr DA11 ....30 A8
Cambrian Rd TN4 ....149 C7
Cambridge Ave DA16 ....6 F3
Cambridge Barracks Rd
  SE18 ....1 F2
Cambridge Cres ME15 ...107 D7
  Gr SE12 ....5 A2
Cambridge Gdns TN2 .....149 B2
Cambridge Gn SE9 ....23 B7
Cambridge Ho
  3 Greenwich SE18 ....1 F2
  8 Maidstone ME15 ....107 D7
Cambridge Rd Bromley BR1 .22 A1
  Gillingham ME8 ....63 C6
  Rochester ME2 ....47 A8
  Sidcup DA14 ....23 E4
Cambridge Row SE18 ....2 B1
Cambridge St TN2 ....149 C3
Cambridge Terr 1 ME4 ....47 F4
Cambus Rd E16 ....5 A8
Camdale Rd SE18 ....6 E7
Camden Ave TN2 ....150 C6
Camden Cl Chatham ME5 ...62 B5
  Chislehurst BR7 ....37 C8
  Northfleet DA11 ....29 D7
Camden Cotts TN17 ....169 F8
Camden Ct 10 Erith DA17 ....4 A1
  Pembury TN2 ....150 D6
  2 Royal Tunbridge Wells
  TN1 ....149 B4
Camden Gr BR7 ....23 B2

Camden Hill TN2 ....149 B3
Camden Park Rd BR7 ......23 A1
Camden Pk TN2 ....2 F7
Camden Rd TN1 ....149 C2
Camden Rd Sta TN1 ....149 B4
  Royal Tunbridge Wells TN1 .149 B4
  Sevenoaks TN13 ....98 D5
  Sidcup DA5 ....24 F8
Camden St ME14 ....92 A5
Camden Terr TN17 ....169 F8
Camden Way BR7 ....23 A1
Camel Rd E16 ....1 D5
Camelia Cl ME8 ....63 D7
Camelot Cl SE28 ....2 D4
Camer Gdns DA13 ....44 C3
Camer Park (Ctry Pk)* 44 C2
Camer Park Rd DA13 ......44 C2
Camer Rd DA13 ....44 C3
Camer St DA13 ....44 C3
Cameron Cl Chatham ME5 .62 B8
  Dartford DA5 ....25 E5
Cameron Rd BR2 ....36 A4
Cameron Terr 12 SE12 ....22 B5
Camerons 4 TN18 ....179 A2
Camomile Dr ME14 ....91 F6
Camp Hill TN11 ....115 A3
Camp Hill Cotts TN11 ....114 F2
Camp Site The DA14 ....25 A1
Camp Way ME15 ....107 C6
Campbell Cl SE18 ....6 A6
Campbell Rd
  Gravesend DA11 ....29 F8
  Maidstone ME15 ....92 A3
  Royal Tunbridge Wells TN4 .149 A6
Camperdown Manor 5
  ME7 ....48 A6
Campfield Rd SE9 ....22 D8
Campion Cl Chatham ME5 .61 E3
  Newham E6 ....1 F6
  Northfleet DA11 ....29 E4
Campion Cres TN17 ....169 A2
Campion Ct 5 RM17 ....12 D8
Campion Pl SE28 ....3 B5
Campleshon Rd ME8 ....63 D5
Campus Way ME8 ....63 A8
Camrose Ave DA8 ....8 B8
Camrose St SE2 ....3 A2
Canada Farm Rd DA4 ......42 A6
Canada Rd DA8 ....9 B7
Canada Terr 3 ME14 ......92 A7
Canadian Ave ME7 ....48 F4
Canal Basin DA12 ....13 D1
Canal Rd Gravesend DA12 ..13 D1
  Higham ME3 ....32 C8
  Rochester ME2 ....47 C7
Canal Road Ind Pk 2 ....30 D8
Canberra Rd Erith DA7 .....7 D8
  Greenwich SE7 ....5 D8
Canberra Sq RM18 ....13 A5
Canbury Path BR5 ....38 A5
Canning St ME14 ....92 A6
Cannock Sch BR6 ....52 F5
Cannon Bridge Works
  TN9 ....117 D2
Cannon La TN9 ....117 D2
Cannon Pl SE7 ....1 E1
Cannon Rd DA7 ....7 F6
Canon Cl ME1 ....47 A2
Canon La ME18 ....89 C1
Canon Rd BR1 ....36 D6
Cansiron La TN7,TN8 ....144 E2
Canterbury Ave DA15 ......24 C6
  Canterbury Cl Dartford DA1 .27 A8
  7 Newham E6 ....1 F7
Canterbury Cres TN10 ....117 D5
Canterbury Ct 7 SE12 .....22 B5
Canterbury Ho Erith DA8 ...8 F7
  8 Maidstone ME15 ....107 D7
Canterbury Rd
  Gravesend DA12 ....30 C6
  Pembury TN2 ....150 E6
Canterbury St ME7 ....48 C4
  Canterbury Way RM16,DA1 .10 D5
Cantwell House SE18 ....6 B7
Cantwell Rd SE18 ....6 B7
Capel Cl Gillingham ME8 ...63 D4
  Orpington BR2 ....36 E1
Capel Pl DA2 ....26 C4
  Capel Prim Sch TN12 ....134 F7
Capelands DA3 ....57 A8
Capell Cl ME17 ....106 C3
Capella Ho 1 SE7 ....5 B8
Capetown House 1
  ME15 ....107 F5
Capital Ind Est DA17 ....4 B3
Capstan Cl DA2 ....10 C3
  Capstan Ctr RM17 ....12 E7
Capstone Farm Ctry Pk* 62 D5
Capstone Rd Chatham ME5 .48 D1
  Gillingham ME7 ....62 F6
  Lewisham BR1 ....22 D1
Captain's Cl ME17 ....124 E6
Captain's Wlk The TN15 ..87 C7
Capulet Mews E16 ....1 A5
Caraway Cl E13 ....1 B8
Cardens Rd ME3 ....33 B8
Cardiff St SE18 ....6 E7
Cardigan Rd ME23 ....17 F3
Cardinal Cl Chislehurst BR7 .37 D8
  Tonbridge TN9 ....133 D8
  Cardwell Prim Sch SE18 .....2 A2
Carew Ho 10 SE18 ....6 E7
Carey Ct DA6 ....8 B2
Caring La ME14,ME17 ......93 C1
Caring Rd ME15,ME17 .....93 C1
Carisbrooke Ave DA5 ....24 D7

Carisbrooke Ct
  20 Dartford DA2 ....10 B1
  25 Sidcup DA14 ....24 A4
Carisbrooke Dr ME16 ......91 D4
Carisbrooke Rd
  Bromley BR2 ....36 C5
  Rochester ME2 ....32 E1
Carl Ekman House DA11 ..29 D8
Carleton Pl DA4 ....41 C5
Carleton Rd DA1 ....27 A8
Carlisle Cl ME8 ....46 C5
Carlisle Rd DA1 ....10 A1
Carlton Ave Gillingham ME7 .48 E4
  Stone DA9 ....10 E1
Carlton Cres Chatham ME5 .62 D8
Carlton Gdns ME15 ....149 C4
Carlton Gn DA14 ....23 F4
Carlton Par BR5 ....38 B2
Carlton Rd Bexley DA16 ....7 B4
  Erith DA8 ....8 C8
  Royal Tunbridge Wells TN1 .149 C4
  Sidcup DA14 ....23 F3
Carlyle Ave BR1 ....36 D6
Carlyle Rd SE28 ....3 B5
Carman's Cl ME15,ME17 .106 F3
Carmelite Way DA3 ....42 F4
Carnation Cl ME19 ....75 A1
Carnation Cres ME19 ......74 F1
Carnation Rd ME2 ....46 D7
Carnation St SE2 ....3 B1
Carnbrook Rd SE3 ....5 D4
Carnecke Gdns SE9 ....5 E2
Caroline Cres ME16 ....91 D7
Carolyn Dr BR6 ....52 A7
Carpeaux Cl ME4 ....48 A4
Carpenters Cl ME1 ....47 E2
Carpenters Ct BR1 ....36 D7
Carpenters La
  Hadlow TN11 ....102 D2
  Staplehurst TN12 ....139 C8
Carpinus Cl ME5 ....62 B1
Carr Gr SE18 ....1 E2
Carrack Ho DA8 ....4 E1
Carriageway The TN16 ....82 D3
Carrick Dr TN13 ....84 B4
Carrie House ME16 ....91 E5
Carriers Pl TN13 ....146 B4
Carriers Rd TN17 ....169 D5
Carrill Way DA17 ....3 D3
Carrington Cl ME7 ....48 F6
Carrington Rd DA1 ....10 D1
Carroll Cl ME2 ....60 B4
Carroll Gdns ME20 ....74 F3
Carronade Pl SE28 ....2 D3
Carsington Gdns DA1 ......26 D6
Carson Rd E16 ....1 A8
Carston Cl SE12 ....5 A2
Carter's Hill TN15 ....100 B6
Carters Hill SE9 ....22 C7
Carters Hill Cl SE9 ....22 C7
Carters Hill La DA13 ....57 F2
Carters Row DA11 ....29 F6
Cartmel Rd DA7 ....8 A6
Cartmel Cl ME7 ....32 E4
Carton Rd ME3 ....32 B3
Carville Ave TN4 ....132 F1
Carvoran Way ME8 ....63 C5
Cary's Field TN13 ....83 E7
Cascade Cl BR5 ....38 C6
  Cascades L Ctr DA12 ....31 A4
Caspian Wlk E16 ....1 D7
Cassilda Rd SE2 ....3 A2
Casstine Cl BR8 ....25 F1
Castalia Ct DA1 ....9 F4
Castasterbridge Rd SE3 ....5 A4
Castle Ave 12 SE18 ....2 A2
  Castilion Prim Sch SE28 ....3 C7
Castilla Ho 8 BR1 ....22 B1
Castle Ave ME1 ....47 C4
Castle Dene ME14 ....91 F8
Castle Dr TN15 ....69 E2
Castle Farm Rd TN14 ......54 A3
Castle Fields TN9 ....117 B2
Castle Hill Hartley DA3 .....42 E4
  Rochester ME1 ....47 C6
  Thurnham ME14 ....78 D1
  Tonbridge TN11 ....133 F5
Castle Hill Ct ME1 ....47 C6
Castle Hurst TN32 ....185 B1
Castle La DA12 ....31 B6
Castle Rd Chatham ME4 ....48 B2
  Eynsford DA4 ....54 C5
  Grays RM17 ....11 F8
  Maidstone ME16 ....91 D7
  Royal Tunbridge Wells TN4 .149 A7
  Swanscombe DA10 ....11 F1
Castle St Bexley DA16 ....7 C5
  2 Royal Tunbridge Wells
  TN1 ....149 A2
  2 Royal Tunbridge
  Wells,Southborough TN4 ..132 F2
  Stone DA9 ....10 F1
  Swanscombe DA10 ....11 F1
  Tonbridge TN9 ....117 C2
  Upper Upnor ME2 ....33 E1
  Wouldham ME1 ....60 C4
Castle Terr Hadlow TN11 ..118 E8
  Hawkhurst TN18 ....178 F3
Castle View Bsns Ctr ME1 ..47 C6
Castle View Mews ME1 ....47 C6
Castle View Rd ME2 ....47 A7
Castle Way ME19 ....74 F2
Castle Wlk TN5 ....174 E4
Castlecombe Prim Sch
  SE9 ....22 E3
Castlecombe Rd SE9 ....22 E4
Castlefields DA13 ....43 F8
Castleford Ave SE9 ....23 B7

Castlemaine Ave ME7 ......48 F6
Castleton Ave DA7 ....8 D5
Castleton Rd SE9 ....22 D4
Castlewood Day Hospl
  SE18 ....6 A6
Castlewood Dr SE9 ....5 F5
Cates Ct TN12 ....120 A7
Cathcart Dr BR6 ....37 E1
Catherine Cl ME16 ....91 A3
Catherine of Aragon Ct
  DA1 ....23 D8
Catherine Pl 7 TN1 ....149 B4
Catherine St ME1 ....47 D3
Catkin Cl ME5 ....61 F1
Catlyn Cl ME19 ....90 A8
Catterick Rd ME5 ....62 D2
Catsstock Rd SE9 ....22 D7
Catts Pl TN12 ....136 C4
Causton Rd TN17 ....169 C5
Cave Hill ME15 ....91 F1
Cavell Cres DA1 ....10 B3
Cavendish Ave Bexley DA16 ..6 F4
  Erith DA8 ....8 C8
  Gillingham ME7 ....48 E6
  Sevenoaks TN13 ....84 A5
  Sidcup DA15 ....24 A8
Cavendish Cl TN10 ....117 D7
Cavendish Ct TN9 ....117 D3
Cavendish Dr TN2 ....149 B1
Cavendish Rd ME1 ....47 D3
Cavendish Sq DA3 ....42 D6
Cavendish Way ME15 ......93 B3
Caversham Cl ME8 ....49 F1
Caveside Cl BR7 ....37 A8
Caxton Cl Hartley DA3 ......42 F5
  Tenterden TN30 ....182 F7
Caxton La TN11 ....118 E8
Cayser Dr ME17 ....109 E2
Caysers Croft TN12 ....119 E6
Cazeneuve St ME1 ....47 C5
Cecil Ave Gillingham ME8 ..49 E3
  Rochester ME2 ....47 B8
Cecil Rd Gravesend DA11 ..29 E7
  Rochester ME1 ....47 C3
Cecil Road Prim Sch DA11 .29 F7
Cecil Way BR2 ....36 A1
Cedar Ave Gravesend DA12 .30 C4
  Sidcup DA15 ....24 A8
Cedar Cl Ditton ME20 ......90 D8
  Meopham Sta DA13 ....44 A3
  Orpington BR2 ....50 E7
  Swanley BR8 ....39 C7
Cedar Copse BR1 ....36 F7
Cedar Cres Orpington BR2 ..50 E7
  Tonbridge TN10 ....117 C7
Cedar Ct Eltham SE9 ....5 E1
  8 Greenwich SE7 ....5 C8
  Maidstone ME14 ....92 B5
  Royal Tunbridge Wells TN4 .149 A5
  12 Tenterden TN30 ....183 A7
  Maidstone ME15 ....90 E2
  Sutton at Hone DA4 ....41 B7
Cedar Gdns ME9 ....79 E8
  Cedar Gr Gillingham ME7 ....63 A5
  Sidcup DA5 ....7 D1
Cedar Ho 10 Newham E6 ...1 F7
Cedar Lodge TN4 ....148 F3
Cedar Mount SE9 ....22 D7
Cedar Pl 8 SE7 ....1 C1
  Cedar Rd Bromley BR1 ....36 C7
  Dartford DA1 ....26 D7
  Erith DA8 ....9 A6
  Hoo St Werburgh ME3 ......34 E3
  Rochester ME2 ....46 F6
Cedar Ridge TN2 ....149 D5
Cedar Terrace Rd TN13 ...84 B4
Cedarhurst Cotts 5 DA5 ..25 A8
Cedarhurst Dr SE9 ....5 C2
Cedarmore Ct BR7 ....37 C8
  Cedars Sch The
  Maidstone ME15 ....91 D4
  Rochester ME1 ....47 C4
Cedars The TN12 ....136 A7
Cedarwood House ME15 .106 B6
Cedric Rd SE9 ....23 C5
Celandine Dr SE28 ....3 B5
Celestine Cl ME5 ....62 A1
Cement Bsns Cotts RM17 .12 C8
Cement Industry
  Heritage Ctr* DA11 ....12 B2
Cemetery La Hadlow TN11 ..103 A1
  Woolwich SE7 ....1 B1
Cemetery Rd Bexley SE2 ....7 B7
  Halling ME2 ....60 A6
  Snodland ME6 ....59 F1
Centenary Ct DA4 ....41 A2
Central Ave Chatham ME4 ...48 B8
  Gravesend DA12 ....30 B5
  Tilbury RM18 ....13 A6
Central Bsns Pk ME2 ....47 E2
Central Ct 8 SE3 ....1 D2
Central Lodge TN15 ....72 E6
Central Par Rochester ME1 .47 D5
  Sidcup DA15 ....24 A5
Central Par Villas BR5 .....38 C7
Central Park Gdns ME4 ....47 D7
Central Rd Dartford DA1 .....9 E2
  New Hythe ME20 ....75 F4
  Rochester ME2 ....47 A7
Central St ME1 ....149 A3
Central Terr ME3 ....33 F6
Central Way SE28 ....3 B6
  Centre 2000 ME10 ....92 C1
Centre Common Rd BR7 ..23 C1
Centre Ct DA11 ....31 C8
Centre Rd DA3 ....56 E7
Centurion Way DA18 ....4 A3

Centurion Cl ME8 ....48 F1
Century Rd ME8 ....63 D6
Ceres Rd SE18 ....2 F1
Cerne Rd DA12 ....30 E6
Cervia Way DA12 ....30 F4
Chada Ave ME7 ....48 B7
Chadd Dr BR1 ....36 D7
Chadfields RM18 ....13 A6
Chadwell Hill RM17 ....13 A4
Chadwick Cl DA11 ....29 E6
Chadwick Cl 4 SE28 ....3 B6
Chadwick Way SE28 ....3 D6
Chadwin Rd E13 ....1 A8
Chaffey Ho 6 SE7 ....1 C1
Chaffinch Cl ME5 ....61 F2
Chaffinch Way TN12 ......136 A5
Chafford Cotts TN3 ....146 F2
Chafford La TN3 ....146 F2
Chain Gate ME17 ....127 A8
Chalcombe Rd SE2 ....3 B3
Chalet Cl DA5 ....25 D1
Chalfont Ct 3 DA17 ....4 A1
Chalfont Dr ME8 ....63 D7
Chalgrove Mews ME2 ....60 A6
Chalice Way DA9 ....10 F1
Chalk Ave TN30 ....173 B1
Chalk Ct RM17 ....12 A2
Chalk La TN17 ....168 E1
  Chalk Par Birk BR5 ....38 D5
  Chalk Pit Hill ME4 ....48 A6
  Chalk Rd Chalk DA12 ....31 A4
  Higham ME3 ....32 C7
  Newham E13 ....1 A8
Chalkenden Ave ME8 ....49 A4
Chalket La TN2 ....150 C7
Chalkpit Cotts DA12 ....31 E1
Chalkstone Cl DA16 ....7 A6
Chalkways TN14 ....66 A4
Chalky Bank DA11 ....30 A4
Chalky Rd ME9 ....79 C1
Challenge Cl DA12 ....30 F7
Challenger Cl TN12 ....136 A5
Challock Ho 3 Erith DA8 ....8 E7
  8 Orpington BR5 ....38 D1
Challock Wlk BR5 ....92 C4
Chamberlain Ave ME16 ....91 C6
Chamberlain Cl SE28 ....2 D2
Chamberlain Rd ME8 ....63 B8
Chancel Cl TN15 ....55 E2
Chancellor Ho TN4 ....148 F7
Chancellor Way TN13 ....84 A6
Chancelot Rd SE2 ....3 B2
Chancery Ct DA1 ....27 A8
Chancery La ME15 ....92 B2
Chanctonbury Cl SE9 ....23 C5
Chanctonbury Ct ME14 .....92 B5
  Chandler Ave E16 ....1 A8
Chandler's Hill DA13 ....58 C5
Chandler's Rd DA13 ....58 C5
Chandlers Dr DA8 ....4 E2
Chandlers Wharf ME1 ......47 B7
Chandos Rd TN1 ....149 B4
Chantel Alley Cotts TN14 ..69 A4
Chapel Cl Crayford DA1 .....8 F2
  Ryarsh ME19 ....73 F7
  West Thurrock RM20 ....11 B8
Chapel Cotts ME17 ....108 F7
Chapel Ct DA10 ....12 E1
Chapel Farm Rd SE9 ....23 A5
Chapel Field Cotts DA4 ....41 B8
  Grain ME3 ....21 B7
  Snodland ME6 ....60 A7
  Sutton Valence ME17 ......124 E7
Chapel Row TN15 ....86 C6
Chapel St East Malling ME19 .90 A4
  Ryarsh ME19 ....73 F7
Chapel View TN15 ....86 D4
  Chapel Wlk TN14 ....66 C8
Chapel Wood Rd DA3,TN15 .56 E8
Chaplin Cl ME3 ....33 CC
Chaplin Dr TN27 ....141 D8
Chapman Ave ME15 ....107 D7
Chapman Rd DA17 ....3 F3
Chapman Way
  East Malling ME19 ....89 F8
  Tenterden TN30 ....182 D7
Chapman's Hill DA13,TN15 .57 F4
Chapman's La
  Hockenden BR8 ....39 A4
  St Paul's Cray BR5,BR8 ....38 D2
Chapmans Cl TN14 ....82 E1
Chapmans End BR5 ....38 E2

Chapmans Rd TN14 ....82 E3
Chapter Rd ME2 ....46 F8
Chapter Sch ME2 ....60 C7
Chardwell Cl E16 ....1 F7
Charford Rd E16 ....1 A8
Charing Cl BR6 ....51 F6
Charing House 5 DA8 ....8 F7
Charing Rd ME8 ....49 E3
Charlot Way ME2 ....60 A5
Charity Farm Cotts TN17 ...156 F7
Charlbury Cl ME14 ....91 C3
Charldane Rd SE9 ....23 B5
Charlecote Ct ME14 ....63 D8
Charles Busby Ct 2 ME20 ..75 F1
Charles Cl Sidcup DA14 ......24 B4
Snodland ME6 ....75 A8
Charles Ct Erith DA8 ....51 D5
Royal Tunbridge Wells TN2 ..149 C3
Charles Dickens Ave ME3 ...32 C2
Charles Dickens Ctr (Mus)*
ME1 ....47 C5
Charles Dr ME2 ....46 B2
Charles Flewmell Mews
E16 ....1 A5
Charles Grinling Wlk SE18 ...2 A2
Charles Rd TN14 ....53 B1
Charles St Chatham ME4 .....47 E3
Grays RM17 ....12 C8
Maidstone ME16 ....91 E3
Newham E16 ....1 C5
Rochester ME2 ....47 A7
Royal Tunbridge Wells TN4 ..149 A8
Stone DA9 ....10 F2
Charles Winchup Rd E16 .....1 B5
Charlesfield SE9 ....22 C5
Charlesford Ave ME17 ....109 D3
Charlieville Rd DA8 ....8 C7
Charlock Cl Bexley DA6 ......91 D8
Chatham ME5 ....62 B6
Charlotte Ct BR7 ....23 B2
Charlotte Dr ME8 ....49 C1
Charlotte Park Ave BR1 .....36 E6
Charlotte Pl RM20 ....11 B8
Charlottes Cotts TN11 .....115 F1
Charlton Church La SE7 ......1 C1
Charlton Dene SE7 ....5 D7
Charlton La
Charlway Street ME7 ....125 C8
Greenwich SE7 ....1 D1
West Farleigh ME15 ....105 E6
Charlton Manor Prim Sch
SE7 ....48 B5
Charlton Manor Prim Sch
SE7 ....5 D7
Charlton Park La SE7 ....5 E8
Charlton Park Rd SE7 ....5 D8
Charlton Park Sch SE7 ....5 E8
Charlton Rd SE3,SE7 ....5 B8
Charlton St Grays RM20 .....11 D8
Maidstone ME16 ....91 C2
Charlton's Way TN4 ....148 E1
Charminster Rd SE9 ....22 D4
Charmouth Rd DA16 ....7 C6
Charnwood La BR6 ....52 B1
Charnwood Villas BR6 ....52 C1
Charne The TN14 ....69 A2
Charnock ME8 ....63 E8
Charnock DR6 ....51 C5
Charr Mnr ME17 ....108 B1
Chart Hill Rd ME17 ....124 A7
Chart PI ME8 ....63 E3
Chart Rd ME17 ....124 C7
Chart View TN15 ....70 B2
Charter Dr DA5 ....24 E8
Charter St Chatham ME4 .....47 E3
Gillingham ME7 ....48 C7
Charterhouse Dr TN13 ....84 A4
Charterhouse Rd BR6 ....52 A6
Charton Cl 5 DA17 ....7 B8
Chartway TN13 ....84 C3
Chartway St ME17 ....109 C1
Chartwell (National Trust)*
TN16 ....96 F4
Chartwell Bsns Ctr BR1 .....36 D6
Chartwell Cl Rochester ME2 ..33 B1
Sidcup SE9 ....23 D6
Chartwell Ct
Maidstone ME15 ....92 B3
Rochester ME4 ....47 E4
Chartwell Dr BR6 ....51 D5
Chase Sq 5 DA11 ....13 B1
Chase The Bexley DA7 ....8 B4
Bromley BR1 ....36 B6
Chatham ME4 ....47 D2
Gillingham ME8 ....49 A2
Kemsing TN15 ....69 E3
Pratt's Bottom BR6 ....52 A1
Trosbridge TN10 ....117 C5
West Thurrock RM20 ....11 D8
Chastilian Rd DA1 ....26 A8
Chatfield Way ME19 ....75 B1
Chatham Ave BR2 ....36 A2
Chatham GM ME4 ....47 F1
Chatham Gram Sch
for Boys ME4 ....61 E8
Chatham Gram Sch
for Girls ME5 ....48 C2
Chatham Hill ME4 ....48 B3
Chatham Hill Rd TN14 ....84 C6
Chatham Ho 10 SE18 ....1 F2
Chatham Rd
Kit's Coty ME20 ....76 D6
Maidstone ME14 ....76 E1
Maidstone,Sandling ME14 ....76 E4
Chatham Ski Ctr ME7 ....62 E6
Chatham South Sch ME4 .....61 F8
hatham St SE18 ....2 B3

Chatham Sta ME4 ....47 E4
Chatsworth Ave
Bromley BR1 ....22 B4
Sidcup DA15 ....24 A7
Chatsworth Dr ME2 ....33 B1
Chatsworth Ho 3 BR2 ....36 A5
Chatsworth Rd Cliffe DA15 ..24 A7
Chatsworth Rd
Dartford DA1 ....9 C3
19 Gillingham ME7 ....48 C6
Chattenden Barracks
Royal Sch of Military
Engineering ME3 ....33 F5
Chattenden Ct ME14 ....92 B6
Chattenden La ME3 ....33 F5
Chattenden Prim Sch ME3 ...33 F4
Chattenden Terr ME3 ....33 F4
Chatterton Rd BR2 ....36 D4
Chatwell Ct ME7 ....48 C5
Chaucer Cl
13 Maidstone ME15 ....107 E7
Rochester ME2 ....47 B8
Tilbury RM18 ....13 C5
Chaucer Gdns TN9 ....132 F7
Chaucer Ind Pk TN15 ....85 D8
Chaucer Pk DA1 ....26 F8
Chaucer Rd Bexley DA6 ......6 F4
Gillingham ME7 ....48 D3
Northfleet DA11 ....29 D5
Sidcup DA15 ....24 C7
Chaucer Way ME20 ....75 A3
Chaundrye Cl SE9 ....5 E1
Chauntler Cl E16 ....1 B6
Chauser Way DA1 ....10 A3
Chave Rd DA14,DA2 ....24 B1
Cheeselands TN27 ....157 F2
Cheffins Ho ME7 ....48 E7
Chegwell Dr ME5 ....62 B4
Chegworth La ME17 ....110 A6
Chegworth Rd ME17 ....109 F5
Cheldoc Rise ME4 ....34 C2
Chelmar Rd ME8 ....48 B4
Chelmsford Cl E6 ....1 F7
Chelmsford Ho ME15 ....107 E6
Chelmsford Rd ME2 ....46 B5
Chelsea Ct 8 BR1 ....36 E6
Chelsfield Hill BR6 ....52 C2
Chelsfield Ho ME15 ....91 D5
Chelsfield La
Badgers Mount BR6,TN14 ....53 B2
Chelsfield BR5,BR6 ....52 D7
Orpington BR5 ....38 D2
Chelsfield Lakes
Golf Course BR6 ....52 E3
Chelsfield Park Hospl BR6 ...52 F5
Chelsfield Prim Sch BR6 .....52 E5
Chelsfield Rd BR5 ....38 C3
Chelsfield Sta BR6 ....52 B5
Chelsiter Ct DA14 ....23 F4
Chelsworth Dr SE18 ....6 D8
Cheltenham Cl
Gravesend DA12 ....30 C3
Maidstone ME15 ....107 F6
Cheltenham Rd BR6 ....52 A2
Cheney Cl ME8 ....63 D5
Cheney's Cotts DA12 ....31 A2
Chenies Cl TN2 ....163 A8
Chenies The Dartford DA2 ...25 F7
Orpington BR6 ....37 E3
Chennell Park Rd TN30 ....172 E1
Chennells The TN26 ....173 C7
Chepstow House 3
ME15 ....107 F6
Chequer's Cotts TN13 ......153 F1
Chequers Cl Chatham ME5 ...77 A8
Istead Rise DA13 ....43 F7
St Paul's Cray BR5 ....38 A3
Chequers Ctr ME15 ....92 A4
Chequers Hill Cotts TN8 ...114 A2
Chequers La RM9 ....3 F8
Cherbourg Cres ME5 ....61 F7
Cherbury Cl SE28 ....3 D7
Cheriton Ave BR2 ....36 A4
Cheriton Ct 12 SE12 ....22 A8
Cheriton Dr SE18 ....6 D8
Cheriton Rd ME8 ....63 D8
Cherries Way ME16 ....91 A2
Cherries The ME16 ....91 A2
Cherry Amber Cl ME8 ....63 F8
Cherry Ave BR8 ....39 D5
Cherry Cl ME17 ....111 D6
Cherry Ct DA14 ....24 B5
Cherry Gr TN10 ....117 E5
Cherry Hill Ct ME9 ....65 B6
Cherry Orch Ditton ME20 ....90 C8
Greenwich SE7 ....5 C6
Newham E6 ....1 E7
Cherry Orch The TN11 ......102 E1
Cherry Orchard GF BR5 .....38 C4
Cherry Orchard Inf Sch SE7 ..5 C7
Cherry Orchard Rd BR2 .....50 E8
Cherry Orchard Way ME16 ...91 B3
Cherry Rd ME3 ....34 E3
Cherry Tree Cl RM17 ....12 C8
Cherry Tree Ct 7 SE7 ....5 C8
Cherry Tree La DA2 ....25 F5
Cherry Tree Rd
Gillingham ME8 ....63 F8
Royal Tunbridge Wells TN2 ..148 E1
Cherry Trees DA3 ....42 F4
Cherry View ME17 ....107 B3
Cherry Wlk BR2 ....36 A1
Cherrycot Hill BR6 ....51 D6
Cherrycot Rise BR6 ....51 C6
Cherrydown Rd DA14 ....24 D6
Cherryfields TN17 ....180 D6
Cherrywood Dr DA11 ....29 E5

Chervil Mews SE28 ....3 B5
Chervilles ME16 ....91 A2
Cherwell Cl TN10 ....117 B4
Chesfield Ct TN11 ....102 F1
Chesham Ave BR5 ....37 B3
Chesham Dr ME8 ....63 E6
Cheshire Rd
Maidstone,Shepway ME15 ...107 E7
Maidstone,Willington ME15 ...92 C7
Cheshunt Cl DA13 ....44 A3
Cheshunt Rd DA17 ....4 A1
Chessenden La TN27 ....143 A1
Chessington Ave DA7 ....7 F7
Chester Ave TN2 ....149 D2
Chester Cl ME2 ....46 D6
Chester Rd Gillingham ME7 ..48 D2
Sidcup DA15 ....23 E8
Chesterfield Ho SE18 ....6 D8
Chesterfield Dr Dartford DA1 .9 B2
Sevenoaks TN13 ....83 D5
Chesterford Ho SE18 ....2 D2
Chesterton Rd Cliffe ME3 ...16 B5
13 Lunsford ME20 ....74 F4
Chesterton Way RM18 ....13 C5
Chestfield Cl ME8 ....49 E2
Chestnut Ave Chatham ME5 ..61 F4
Hill Park TN16 ....81 A6
Speldhurst TN4 ....149 B8
Staplehurst TN12 ....139 F4
Stone DA9 ....27 F8
Chestnut Cl
Edenbridge TN8 ....112 B2
Frittenden TN17 ....156 E6
Kings Hill ME19 ....89 A2
Northfleet DA11 ....12 F1
Orpington BR6 ....52 A5
Royal Tunbridge Wells TN4 ..149 B8
Sidcup DA14 ....24 A6
Tenterden TN30 ....173 C1
Uckombe ME17 ....57 F5
Chestnut Dr Bexley DA7 ......7 E4
Coxheath ME17 ....106 B3
Kingswood ME17 ....109 D2
Chestnut Gr ME20 ....75 A8
Chestnut La Matfield TN12 ..135 D1
Sevenoaks TN13 ....84 B3
Vigo Village ME3 ....73 B8
Chestnut PI TN8 ....145 A5
Chestnut Rd Dartford DA1 ...26 D7
Rochester ME2 ....46 E6
Chestnut Rise SE18 ....2 E1
Chestnut St ME9 ....44 A5
Chestnut Wlk
Addington ME19 ....73 C3
Chislehurst BR7 ....23 D1
11 Erith DA17 ....4 A1
The Moor TN18 ....184 F8
Woolwich SE18 ....6 A5
Cheswick Cl DA1 ....8 E3
Chesworth Cl DA8 ....8 F5
Chetney Cl ME17 ....46 C7
Chetwood Wlk 7 E6 ....1 F8
Cheveney Wlk 8 BR2 ....36 A6
Chevening CE Prim Sch
TN13 ....83 B5
Chevening Cl ME5 ....62 A5
Chevening Cres DA7 ....62 A8
Chevening House BR6 ....38 A8
Chevening La TN14 ....67 E3
Chevening Rd
10 Greenwich SE10 ....1 A1
Sevenoaks TN13,TN14 ....83 B6
Sundridge TN14 ....82 F4
Chevenings The DA14 ....24 C5
Cheviot Cl Erith DA7 ....8 F5
Cheviot Rd DA11 ....12 D1
Chevron Cl E16 ....1 A7
Chevron House RM17 ....12 B7
Cheyne Cl BR2 ....50 E7
Cheyne Wlk Longfield DA3 ..42 D6
Meopham DA13 ....58 A8
Chicago Ave ME7 ....48 F5
Chichester Cl
Gillingham ME8 ....64 A8
Greenwich SE3 ....5 C6
Newham E6 ....1 E7
Chichester Ct TN13 ....25 A8
Chichester Dr TN13 ....23 F2
Chichester Rd Stone DA9 ...10 F1
Tonbridge TN9 ....133 A8
Chichester Rise DA12 ....30 D4
Chickenden La TN17 ....140 C4
Chickfield Gdns 4 ME5 ......48 C2
Chicks La TN17 ....167 A2
Chiddingstone Ave DA7 ......7 F7
Chiddingstone Castle*
TN8 ....130 B7
Chiddingstone
CE Prim Sch TN8 ....130 C7
Chiddingstone Cl ME15 ....107 F6
Chidley Cross Rd TN12 .....119 E6
Chieftain Cl ME7 ....49 A3
Chieveley Dr TN2 ....149 D1
Chieveley Rd DA7 ....8 B4
Chieveley Rd DA7 ....8 B3
Chiffinch Gdns DA11 ....29 E5
Childs Cres SE10 ....10 D1
Childs Way TN15 ....71 F3
Childsbridge La TN15 ....84 F7
Childsbridge Way TN15 ......84 F7

Childscroft Rd ME8 ....49 F2
Chilham Cl Chatham ME4 ....47 E3
Sidcup DA5 ....24 F8
Chilham Ho
10 Maidstone ME15 ....107 E8
Rochester ME2 ....33 C1
Chilham Rd Chislehurst SE9 ..22 E4
Gillingham ME8 ....49 A3
Maidstone ME16 ....91 C7
Chilham Way BR2 ....36 A4
Chillington Ct ME2 ....59 E4
Chillington St ME14 ....91 F6
Chilliwack Rd ME3 ....33 F5
Chilston Cl TN4 ....149 A5
Chilston Rd Lenham ME17 ..111 D5
Royal Tunbridge Wells TN4 ..149 A5
Chiltenhall TN8 ....112 A2
Chiltern Cl Erith DA7 ....8 E6
Maidstone ME15 ....92 F1
Chiltern Ct 5 ME15 ....6 A1
Chiltern Rd DA11 ....49 A8
Chiltern Way TN9 ....117 C4
Chilterns DA14 ....24 A3
Chilterns, The BR1 ....36 B7
Chiltern Dr ME3 ....49 E1
Chimes The ME1 ....47 C5
Chinbrook Cres
8 Lewisham SE12 ....22 B5
Chinbrook Rd SE12 ....22 B5
Chippendale Cl ME5 ....61 F1
Chippendale Dr ME17 ......110 D6
Chipperfield Rd BR5 ....38 A7
Chipstead Cl ME16 ....91 A3
Chipstead La TN13 ....83 D5
Chipstead Park TN13 ....83 C5
Chipstead Pk TN13 ....83 D5
Chipstead Place Gdns
TN13 ....83 D5
Chipstead Rd Erith DA8 ......8 E7
Gillingham ME8 ....63 D4
Chipstead Sq TN13 ....83 C5
Chislehurst & Sidcup
Gram Sch DA15 ....24 B6
Chislehurst Caves* BR7 .....37 A8
Chislehurst CE Prim Sch
BR7 ....23 C1
Chislehurst Cl ME15 ....107 F6
Chislehurst High St BR7 ....23 B2
Chislehurst Rd
Bromley BR1,BR7 ....36 E8
Orpington,Broom Hill BR6 ...38 A2
Orpington,Petts
Wood BR5,BR6 ....37 E4
Sidcup DA14 ....24 A3
Chislehurst Sta BR7 ....37 A7
Chislet Wlk ME8 ....63 D5
Chiswell Sq SE3 ....5 B5
Chorleywood Cres BR5 ......38 A7
Christ Church Ave Erith DA8 ..8 E8
1 Royal Tunbridge
Wells TN1 ....149 A2
Christ Church CE Sch SE13 ...6 A6
Christ Church Cres 2
DA12 ....30 C8
Christ Church Ct 8 DA12 ...30 C8
Christchurch Ct 8 ME5 ......62 B6
Christchurch House 11
ME15 ....107 E5
Christchurch Rd
Dartford DA1 ....9 C1
Sidcup DA14 ....23 F5
Tilbury RM18 ....13 D6
Christen Way ME15,ME17 ..107 F3
Christian Cl 3 ME2 ....47 C8
Christian Fields Ave DA12 ...30 C4
Christie Cl ME5 ....62 B6
Christie Dr 8 ME20 ....74 F4
Christie House DA6 ....8 B3
Christmas La ME23 ....53 B1
Christmas St ME7 ....133 F3
Christmas St ME7 ....48 E7
Christopher Cl DA15 ....6 F2
Chudleigh 7 DA14 ....24 B4
Chudleigh Cl ME17 ....157 F1
Chulkhurst Cl TN27 ....157 F1
Church Alley BR1 ....13 B1
Church Ave DA14 ....23 A1
Church Cl Brenchley TN12 ..152 C8
Cliffe ME3 ....16 B6
Mereworth ME18 ....103 D8
Church Cotts
Cranbrook TN17 ....169 D5
Crockenhill BR8 ....39 D2
Hoo St Werburgh ME3 ....34 A8
Ticehurst TN5 ....69 A8
Tonbridge TN10 ....117 B4
Wateringbury ME18 ....104 E1
Church Cres ME17 ....110 F6
Church Cl ME2 ....24 D5
Church Farm Cl
Crockenhill BR8 ....39 D3
Hoo St Werburgh ME3 ....34 A8
Church Field Dartford DA2 ...26 D6
Edenbridge TN8 ....112 D1
Sevenoaks TN13 ....83 F5
Snodland ME6 ....60 B1
Church Field Cotts TN15 ....84 F7
Church Fields ME19 ....89 B8
Church La
Hollingbourne ME17 ....94 E3
Marden TN12 ....138 C6
Rochester ME7 ....47 C8
Staplehurst TN12 ....139 E2
Church Manor Way
SE18,E3 ....3 A2
Church Meadow TN12 ......153 A7
Church Mews ME8 ....63 F8
Church Path
Gillingham ME7 ....48 E6
Northfleet DA11 ....12 C1
Stone DA9 ....10 F1
Church Rd Bexley DA7,DA6 ...7 F6
Bexley,Welling DA7 ....7 B5
Bitchet Green TN15 ....85 E3
Brasted TN16 ....82 B3
Bromley BR1,BR2 ....36 E8
Chart Sutton ME17 ....124 C8
Chelsfield BR6 ....52 D4
Crockenhill BR8 ....39 D2
Erith DA8 ....4 D1
Goudhurst TN17 ....167 F8
Grafty Green ME17 ....126 F7
Gravesend DA12,DA13 ....30 D1
Harrietsham ME17 ....110 E6
Hartley DA3 ....43 A2
Hextable BR8 ....44 C8
Hucking ME17 ....79 E1
Kildown TN17 ....166 F3
Lamberhurst TN3 ....166 C6
Maidstone,Shepway ME15 ...91 E2
Maidstone,Tovil ME15 ....91 E2
Offham ME18 ....88 D8
Orpington,Farnborough BR6 ..51 D5
Orpington, Keston BR2 ....50 D3
Paddock Wood TN12 ....136 B6
Royal Tunbridge Wells TN1 ..149 A3
Royal Tunbridge Wells,
Southborough TN4 ....132 C2
Ryarsh ME19 ....74 A3
Sandhurst TN18 ....185 F4
Seal TN15 ....84 F6
Sevenoaks Weald TN14 ......99 B3
Sidcup DA14 ....24 A4
Stone DA9 ....10 F2
Sundridge TN14 ....82 E2
Sutton at Hone DA4 ....27 A2
Swanley Village BR8 ....40 D8
Swanscombe DA10 ....11 F1
Tenterden TN30 ....173 B2
Tilbury RM18 ....12 F6
Tilbury, Low Street RM18 ....13 E8
Tonbridge TN11 ....116 D6
West Kingsdown TN15 ....55 E3
West Peckham ME18 ....103 A6
Church Row
Chislehurst BR7 ....37 C8
Plaxtol TN15 ....101 E8
Snodland ME6 ....75 A7
West Peckham ME18 ....103 B6
Church Row Mews BR7 ......23 C1
Church Sq ME17 ....111 D5
Church St Burham ME1 ....60 F1
Chatham ME4 ....47 E5
Cliffe ME3 ....16 B5
Cowden TN8 ....145 B3
Edenbridge TN8 ....112 D1
Gillingham ME7 ....48 E6
Gravesend DA11 ....13 B1
Grays RM17 ....12 C8
Hadlow TN11 ....118 E8
Higham ME3 ....32 D7
Hoo St Werburgh ME3 ....34 A8
Maidstone,
Boughton Monchelsea ME17 107 B2
Maidstone, Loose ME15 ....106 F5
Maidstone,Tovil ME15 ....91 D4
Newnham E16 ....2 B5
Northfleet DA11 ....29 A3
Rochester ME1 ....47 C4
Seal TN15 ....84 F6
Shoreham TN14 ....69 A8
Teston ME18 ....105 A6
Ticehurst TN5 ....176 D1
Tonbridge TN9 ....117 B8
Church Terr ME5 ....48 C2
Church View
Biddenden TN27 ....157 F2

Church View continued
Swanley BR8 .... 39 D6
Church Wlk Dartford DA2 .. 26 D5
East Malling ME19 .... 90 A7
Eynsford DA4 .... 54 E7
Gravesend DA12 .... 30 D2
Gravesend DA12 .... 30 A8
Hawkhurst TN18 .... 179 A1
Headcorn TN27 .... 141 C5
Churchbury Rd SE9 .... 22 D8
Churchfield ME19 .... 73 D3
Churchfield Rd DA16 .... 7 A4
Churchfield Sch SE2 .... 3 A2
Churchfields Terr ME1 ..... 47 B4
Churchill Ave ME5 .... 62 A7
Churchill Bsns Ctr TN16 .. 81 D1
Churchill CE Prim Sch
  TN16 .... 81 C2
Churchill Cl DA1 .... 27 B7
Churchill Cotts ME17 .... 108 F6
Churchill Ct 4 BR6 .... 51 C5
Churchill Ho
  Benenden TN17 .... 180 E6
  Maidstone ME16 .... 91 B2
  1 Woolwich SE18 .... 2 B2
Churchill Pk DA1 .... 10 A2
Churchill Rd
  Gravesend DA11 .... 29 F7
  Grays RM17 .... 12 D8
  Horton Kirby DA4 .... 41 C5
  Newham E16 .... 1 C7
Churchill Sq ME19 .... 89 A3
Churchill Way BR1 .... 36 A7
Churchills Ropewalk
  TN17 .... 167 E8
Churchsettle La TN5 .... 175 C1
Churchside DA13 .... 73 A8
Churchyard Cotts TN3 .. 148 A8
Churn La TN12 .... 137 A2
Chute Cl ME8 .... 63 D4
Chyngton Cl DA15 .... 23 F5
Cimba Wood DA12 .... 30 E4
Cinder Hill La TN11 ...... 115 C1
Cinderhill Wood TN12 .. 135 C2
Cinnabar Cl ME5 .... 62 A1
Circle The RM18 .... 13 A6
Circuit Rd SE28 .... 3 A4
Circular Way SE18 .... 6 A8
Cirrus Cres DA12 .... 30 E3
City Way ME1 .... 47 D2
Civic Sq RM18 .... 13 A5
Civic Way TN1 .... 149 A3
CJ Gallards Almshouses
  TN4 .... 149 A8
Clacket La TN16 .... 96 A8
Clacketts Farm ME19 ..... 74 B5
Claire House ME16 .... 91 E5
Clandon Cl BR1 .... 22 A2
Clandon Rd ME5 .... 62 D2
Clanricarde Gdns 1 TN1 149 A3
Clanricarde Rd 2 TN1 .. 149 A3
Claphatch La TN5 .... 176 A5
Clapper La TN12 .... 139 D6
Clapton Ct ME8 .... 63 D8
Clara Pl SE18 .... 2 A2
Clare Ave TN9 .... 116 F1
Clare Causeway DA9 .... 10 F3
Clare Cnr SE9 .... 23 B8
Clare Ct BR7 .... 36 F8
Clare La ME19 .... 89 E8
Clare Way Bexley DA7 ...... 7 E6
  Sevenoaks TN13 .... 99 C8
Claremont Cl Newham E16 .. 2 A5
  Orpington BR6 .... 51 A6
Claremont Cres DA4 .... 8 E3
Claremont Cty Prim Sch
  TN2 .... 149 B2
Claremont Gdns TN2 ..... 149 B2
Claremont Pl
  Benenden TN17 .... 180 C4
  1 Gravesend DA11 .... 30 B8
Claremont Rd Bromley BR1 36 F5
  Hextable BR8 .... 25 E1
  Maidstone ME14 .... 92 B5
  Royal Tunbridge Wells TN1 149 B2
Claremont St E16 .... 2 A4
Claremont Way 2 ME4 .... 47 F3
Clarence Ave
  Bromley BR1,BR2 .... 36 E5
  Newham E16 .... 1 C7
Clarence Cres DA14 .... 24 B5
Clarence Ct ME14 .... 92 E4
Clarence Pl DA12 .... 30 B7
Clarence Rd Bexley DA6 ... 7 E3
  Bromley BR1 .... 36 E6
  Chatham ME4 .... 48 B2
  Chislehurst BR7 .... 22 E6
  Grays RM17 .... 12 A8
  Royal Tunbridge Wells TN1 149 A3
  Sidcup DA14 .... 24 B5
Clarence Row
  Gravesend DA12 .... 30 B8
  Royal Tunbridge Wells TN1 149 A3
Clarendon Cl
  Maidstone ME14 .... 93 A4
  St Paul's Cray BR5 .... 38 A6
Clarendon Gdns
  Dartford DA2 .... 27 D8
  Rochester ME2 .... 33 A1
  Royal Tunbridge Wells TN1 149 A1
Clarendon Gn BR5 .... 38 A5
Clarendon Gr BR5 .... 38 A5
Clarendon Mews BR5 ...... 38 A6
Clarendon Path BR5 ...... 38 A5
Clarendon Pl Dartford DA2 25 E3

Clarendon Pl continued
  Maidstone ME14 .... 92 A4
  Sevenoaks TN13 .... 84 A2
Clarendon Rd
  Gravesend DA12 .... 13 C1
  Sevenoaks TN13 .... 84 A2
Clarendon Way
  Royal Tunbridge Wells TN2 149 A1
  St Paul's Cray BR5,BR7 ... 37 F6
Claret Ho TN13 .... 84 B3
Clareville Rd BR5 .... 51 C8
Clarewood Dr ME19 .... 89 E8
Claridge TN1 .... 149 B6
Claridge Ct ME7 .... 62 F4
Clark Cl DA8 .... 9 A6
Clark Mews ME20 .... 75 F1
Clarkbourne Dr RM17 .... 12 D8
Clarkes Green Rd TN15 ... 70 B5
Clarks La TN14 .... 67 F7
Claston Cl DA1 .... 8 E3
Clavadal Rd TN12 .... 136 A7
Clavell Cl ME8 .... 63 E4
Clay Cotts TN17 .... 167 E8
Clay Hill Rd TN3 .... 165 D6
Clay Wood Cl BR6 .... 37 E2
Claybridge Rd SE12 .... 22 C4
Claydon Mews ME8 .... 2 A1
Clayfarm Rd SE9 .... 23 C6
Claygate ME15 .... 92 D1
Claygate Cross TN15 ..... 87 A3
Claygate La TN11 .... 101 F4
Claygate Rd TN12 .... 121 B2
Clayhill TN17 .... 166 D7
Clayhill Cres SE9 .... 22 D4
Clayhill Ho 2 SE18 .... 2 C1
Clayton Cl 8 E6 .... 1 F7
Clayton Croft Rd DA2 .... 26 A6
Clayton's La TN3 .... 146 E2
Claytonville Terr DA17 .... 4 C4
Claywood La DA2 .... 28 D5
Clayworth Cl DA15 .... 7 B1
Cleanthus Cl SE18 .... 6 B6
Cleanthus Rd SE18 .... 6 B6
Clearway ME19 .... 73 A1
Clearways Bsns Est
  .... 55 E3
Cleave Ave BR6 .... 51 E4
Cleave Rd ME7 .... 48 E3
Cleavers TN17 .... 170 A8
Cleavers Cl TN17 .... 170 A8
Cleaveland ME18 .... 120 E5
Cleeve Ave TN2 .... 149 D2
Cleeve Ct ME19 .... 89 B3
Cleeve Park Gdns DA14 ... 24 B6
Cleeve Park Sch DA14 .... 24 C5
Clegg House SE3 .... 5 B3
Clematis Ave ME8 .... 63 B5
Clement Cl ME16 .... 91 D5
Clement St BR8,DA4 ...... 26 D2
Clenches Farm La TN13 .. 84 A1
Clenches Farm Rd TN13 .. 84 A1
Clendon Way SE18 .... 2 D2
Clerks Field TN27 .... 141 D5
Clermont ME7 .... 63 A4
Clevedale Rd DA14 .... 24 D5
Cleve Rd DA1 .... 24 D5
Clevedon Ho BR1 .... 22 E1
Cleveland TN1 .... 149 D4
Cleveland Ho
  Maidstone ME16 .... 91 B2
  Northfleet DA11 .... 12 D1
Cleveland Rd Bexley DA16 .. 6 F5
  Gillingham ME7 .... 48 D6
Clevely Cl SE7 .... 1 D2
Cleves View 2 DA11 .... 9 D1
Clewer Ho 8 SE2 .... 3 D4
Clewson Rise ME14 .... 92 B8
Cliff Hill ME17 .... 107 D4
Cliff Hill Rd ME17 .... 107 C4
Cliff Reach DA9 .... 10 F1
Cliffe Rd ME2 .... 33 A1
Cliffe Woods Prim Sch
  ME3 .... 33 C8
Clifford Ave BR7 .... 22 F2
Clifford Ho 6 ME14 .... 92 B4
Clifton Cl Maidstone ME14 92 B5
  1 Orpington BR6 .... 51 C5
  Rochester ME2 .... 46 F7
Clifton Cotts TN2 .... 149 D8
Clifton Gr DA11 .... 30 B8
Clifton Marine Par DA11 12 F1
Clifton Pl TN1 .... 149 B2
Clifton Rd Bexley DA16 ..... 7 A4
  Gillingham ME7 .... 48 C7
  Gravesend DA11 .... 13 A1
  Rochester ME2 .... 46 E8
  Sidcup DA14 .... 23 E4
Cliftonville Ct SE12 .... 22 A7
Clinch Cl 15 E16 .... 1 A8
Clinch St ME3 .... 18 A4
Clinton Ave Bexley DA16 ... 7 A3
  Rochester ME2 .... 46 E8
Clinton Cl ME17 .... 106 B3
Clinton La TN8 .... 113 E3
Clipper Bvd DA9 .... 10 F3
Clipper Bvd W DA9 .... 10 D4
Clipper Cl ME2 .... 47 E7
Clipper Cres DA12 .... 30 F4
Clipper Ct ME2 .... 47 E7
Clive Ave DA1 .... 8 F1
Clive Ho ME20 .... 90 F8
Clive Rd Erith DA17 .... 4 A2
  Gravesend DA11 .... 13 B1
  Rochester ME1 .... 47 C3
Cliveden Cl ME16 .... 91 C5
Clock Ho The DA15 .... 24 A7
Clock House La TN13 ...... 84 A1

Clock Tower Mews
  Snodland ME6 .... 60 A1
  Woolwich SE28 .... 3 B6
Clockhouse TN2 .... 149 F6
Cloisterham Rd ME1 ...... 61 D7
Cloisters Ave BR7 .... 36 F4
Cloisters Ct DA7 .... 8 B4
Cloisters The
  1 Dartford DA1 .... 9 E1
  Lenham ME17 .... 111 C5
Cloonmore Ave BR6 .... 51 F6
Close The Addington ME19 73 C2
  Birling ME19 .... 74 B5
  Borough Green TN15 .... 87 A8
  Bough Beech TN8 .... 114 A2
  Dartford DA2 .... 26 D5
  Groombridge TN3 .... 161 C6
  Ightham TN15 .... 86 D6
  New Barn DA3 .... 43 B7
  Orpington BR5 .... 37 E3
  Rochester ME1 .... 47 C4
  Royal Tunbridge Wells TN2 149 C8
  Sevenoaks TN13 .... 83 E3
  Sidcup DA14 .... 24 B3
  1 Sidcup,Old Bexley DA5 .. 25 A8
Cloth Hall Gdns TN27 .... 158 A2
Clothier Ho ME7 .... 48 B7
Clothworkers Rd SE18 ...... 6 D7
Cloudberry CI ME16 .... 91 D6
Cloudesley Cl ME1 .... 47 B1
Cloudesley Rd Bexley DA7 .. 7 F6
  Erith DA8 .... 8 E7
Clovelly Rd DA7 .... 7 E8
Clovelly Way BR6 .... 37 F3
Clover Bank View ME5 ..... 62 B6
Clover Ct 1 RM17 .... 12 D8
Clover Rd ME3 .... 34 E3
Clover St 3 ME4 .... 47 F4
Clover Terr 4 ME5 .... 107 D8
Clover Way TN12 .... 136 A5
Cloverdale Gdns DA15 ...... 6 F1
Clovers The DA1 .... 29 E4
Club Gardens Rd BR2 ..... 36 A2
Clyde Rd TN10 .... 117 C6
Clydesdale Ho DA18 .... 3 E1
Clydon Cl DA8 .... 8 F8
Coach & Horses Pas 15
  TN2 .... 149 A2
Coach Dr The DA13 .... 72 E7
Coach Rd
  Egerton ME17,TN27 ...... 127 E6
  Ightham TN15 .... 86 B2
  Royal Tunbridge Wells TN4 148 C3
Coal Ct RM17 .... 12 A8
Coalhouse Fort★ RM18 .. 14 E6
Coastguard Cotts
  Cliffe ME3 .... 15 C8
  Erith DA8 .... 21 B5
  Coates Hill Rd BR1 .... 37 A7
  Cob Dr DA12 .... 31 E3
  Cobb Cl ME2 .... 46 D8
  Cobbetts Way TN8 .... 112 C8
  Cobbett Cl ME19 .... 89 F8
  Cobbett Rd SE9 .... 5 E4
  Cobbett's Ride TN2 ...... 148 F1
  Cobblestones ME7 .... 62 F5
  Cobbs Cl
  Paddock Wood TN12 ...... 135 F6
  Wateringbury ME18 ...... 104 E7
  Cobbs The TN11 .... 102 E6
  Cobden Ct Bromley BR2 ... 36 C5
  3 Woolwich SE28 .... 3 C5
  Cobden Rd
  4 Gillingham ME4 .... 48 B2
  Orpington BR6 .... 51 D6
  Sevenoaks TN13 .... 84 C4
  Cobdown Cl ME20 .... 75 F2
  Cobfield ME17 .... 108 A1
  Cobham Ave DA14 .... 24 D2
  Cobham Cl Bromley BR2 .. 36 E2
  Maidstone ME16 .... 91 E4
  2 Rochester ME2 .... 46 F7
  2 Sidcup DA15 .... 7 B1
  Cobham Cty Prim Sch
  DA12 .... 45 A5
  Cobham Hall Sch DA12 ... 45 C6
  Cobham House 4 DA8 .... 8 F7
  Cobham Pl DA6 .... 7 D2
  Cobham Rise ME7 .... 48 F5
  Cobham St DA11 .... 30 B8
  Cobham Terr DA9 .... 11 C2
  Cobhambury Rd DA12 ..... 45 B4
  Cobhams TN3 .... 148 A8
  Cobland Rd SE12 .... 22 C4
  Cobs Cl TN15 .... 86 C6
  Cobsdene DA12 .... 30 E8
  Cobtree Cl ME5 .... 62 C8
  Cobtree Rd ME17 .... 106 C3
  Cobtree Wharf ME20 ...... 76 C2
  Cockerhurst Rd TN14 ...... 53 E2
  Cockmannings La BR5 ...... 38 B5
  Cockmannings Rd BR5 ..... 38 D2
  Cockmount La TN5 .... 174 F5
  Cockpit The TN12 .... 138 C5
  Cocksett Ave BR6 .... 51 E4
  Cocksure La DA14 .... 25 D4
  Codrington Cres DA12 ..... 30 D3
  Codrington Gdns DA12 ... 30 D3
  Cogate Rd TN12 .... 135 E6
  Colchester Ct ME5 .... 62 A2
  Cold Arbor Rd TN13 .... 83 D3
  Cold Blow Cres DA5 .... 25 D7
  Cold Harbour Rd ME19 .... 89 F6
  Coldblow La ME14 .... 79 A2
  Coldbridge La TN27 ...... 127 B5
  Coldharbour Crest SE9 .... 23 A5
  Coldharbour La
  Aylesford ME20 .... 76 A1

Coldharbour La continued
  Hucking ME14,ME9 .... 79 B1
  Rainham RM13 .... 4 F6
  Tonbridge TN11 .... 116 E7
Coldharbour Rd
  Benenden TN17 .... 180 B4
  Northfleet DA11 .... 29 F5
  Penshurst TN8,TN11 ...... 146 E8
Coldharbour Sports Ctr
  SE9 .... 23 A6
Coldred Rd ME15 .... 107 F4
Coldrum La ME19 .... 73 C6
Cole Cl SE28 .... 3 A5
Cole Terr ME17 .... 111 C4
Colebrook Ind Est TN2 .. 133 E1
Colebrook Rd TN4 .... 149 C8
Colebrooke Ct DA14 ...... 24 B4
Colegate Dr ME14 .... 93 C4
Coleman Rd DA17 .... 4 A2
Colemans Heath SE9 ...... 23 B5
Colepits Wood Rd SE9 .... 6 D2
Coleraine Rd 6 SE3 .... 5 A8
Colesgate Dr ME14 .... 93 C4
Coleridge Cl 4 ME20 .... 74 F4
Coleridge Rd Dartford DA1 . 10 B3
  Tilbury RM18 .... 13 C5
Coleridge Way BR6 .... 38 A3
Coles Ct TN2 .... 149 C3
Coles La TN16 .... 82 C4
Coleshall Cl ME15 .... 107 F6
Colets Orch TN14 .... 69 B3
Colewood Dr ME2 .... 46 B8
Coffe's Prep Sch SE12 ...... 5 B1
Colin Blythe Rd TN10 ... 117 F5
Colin Chapman Way DA3 .. 55 E6
Colin Cl DA2 .... 10 B1
Coll of Guidance Studies
  BR6 .... 37 F1
College Ave Gillingham ME7 48 B4
  Maidstone ME15 .... 91 F3
  Tonbridge TN9 .... 133 A7
College Cotts ME16 .... 91 F3
College Cl 5 ME15 .... 92 A3
College Dr TN2 .... 149 D4
College Gn BR1 .... 36 A8
College Rd Bromley BR1 ... 36 A8
  Chatham ME4 .... 48 A7
  Hextable BR8 .... 25 F3
  Maidstone ME15 .... 91 F2
  New Hythe ME20 .... 75 B7
  Northfleet DA11 .... 12 B2
College View SE9 .... 22 D7
College Yd ME1 .... 47 C6
Coller Cres DA2 .... 27 E8
Collet Rd TN15 .... 69 E2
Collet Wlk ME8 .... 63 D4
Collier Cl E6 .... 2 B6
Collier Street
  CE Prim Sch TN12 .... 121 C1
Colliers Wood BR2 .... 50 D5
Colliers' Green
  CE Prim Sch TN17 .... 154 F2
Collindale Ave Erith DA8 ... 8 B8
  Sidcup DA15 .... 24 A7
Collings Wlk ME8 .... 63 D4
Collington Cl DA11 .... 29 E8
Collington Ho 3 SE7 .... 5 C8
Collington Terr ME15 .... 107 E4
Collingwood House DA9 .. 11 D2
Collingwood Ind Ctr
  ME17 .... 109 A8
Collingwood Rd ME20 .... 76 C7
Collis St ME2 .... 47 A8
Collison Pl TN30 .... 183 D7
Colman House 8 ME14 .... 92 A4
Colman Rd E16 .... 1 C8
Colne Rd TN10 .... 117 B5
Colney Rd DA1 .... 9 F1
Colonade The 14 TN18 .. 179 A2
Colonel Stephens Way
  TN30 .... 173 B2
Colonel's Way TN4 .... 133 A3
Coltness Cres SE2 .... 3 B1
Colts Hill Pl TN12 .... 135 B5
Coltsfoot Ct RM17 .... 12 D8
Coltsfoot Dr ME14 .... 92 F4
Coltstead DA3 .... 56 E7
Columbia Wharf Rd RM17 12 A8
Columbine Ave E6 .... 1 E8
Columbine Cl
  East Malling ME19 .... 74 F1
  Rochester ME2 .... 46 E7
Columbine Rd
  East Malling ME19 .... 89 F8
  Rochester ME2 .... 46 E7
Columbus Sq DA8 .... 8 F8
Colveine Ct SE9 .... 22 D7
Colyer Cl SE9 .... 23 B6
Colyer Ho SE7 .... 1 C4
Colyer Rd DA11 .... 29 D6
Colyers Cl DA8 .... 8 E6
Colyers La DA8 .... 8 E6
Colyers Prim Sch DA7 ...... 8 D6
Colyers Wlk DA8 .... 8 E6
Colyton Cl DA16 .... 7 D6
Combe Bank Cotts TN14 .. 82 D6
Combe Bank Dr TN14 ...... 82 E4
Combe Bank Sch TN14 ... 82 D5
Combedale Rd SE10 .... 1 A1
Combeside SE18 .... 6 F7
Comfrey Cl ME14 .... 92 D4
Command Rd ME14 .... 91 F8
Commerce Way TN8 ...... 112 C3
Commercial Pl DA12 ...... 13 C1
Commercial Rd
  Paddock Wood TN12 ...... 135 F6
  Rochester ME2 .... 47 A7
  Royal Tunbridge Wells TN1 149 B5

Commercial Rd continued
  Tonbridge TN9 .... 133 C8
Commissioner's Rd ME7 .. 47 F7
Commodore Rd ME14 ..... 92 C5
Common La Cliffe ME3 .... 16 C6
  Dartford DA2 .... 26 B5
Common Rd Burham ME1 .. 61 B1
  Sidcup,Old Bexley DA5 ... 25 A8
  Wouldham ME3 .... 33 B5
  Hadlow TN11 .... 102 E2
  Ightham TN15 .... 86 B4
  Sissinghurst TN17 .... 170 A8
Common The ME1 .... 47 C6
Common View TN4 .... 148 C4
Common Wall ME3 .... 16 A6
Commonside BR2 .... 50 C6
Commonwealth House
  RM18 .... 13 A5
Commonwealth Way SE2 .. 3 C3
Commority Rd DA13 .... 73 B8
Comp La TN15 .... 87 E6
Compass Cl ME1 .... 47 C1
Compass Ctr ME4 .... 48 B8
Compasses Rd TN11 ..... 115 B2
Compasses The TN11 .... 115 B2
Compton Cl ME5 .... 62 D2
Compton Pl DA8 .... 8 F8
Concord Ave ME5 .... 61 E5
Concord Cl
  Paddock Wood TN12 ...... 135 E7
  Royal Tunbridge Wells TN2 149 C4
Concorde Dr E6 .... 1 E8
Concrete Cotts ME3 ...... 15 E4
Condover Cres SE18 .... 6 B7
Condovers Cotts RM18 ... 13 F8
Conduit Rd SE18 .... 6 B7
Coney Hall Par BR4 .... 50 A8
Coneyburrow Rd TN2 .... 149 E5
Conference Rd SE2 .... 3 C2
Conghurst La TN18 ...... 185 B6
Congleton Gr SE18 .... 6 C1
Congo Rd SE18 .... 2 D1
Congress Rd SE2 .... 3 C4
Congreve Rd SE9 .... 5 F4
Congreve Wlk 6 E16 .... 1 D8
Conifer Ave DA3 .... 42 E3
Conifer Cl BR6 .... 51 D6
Conifer Dr Chatham ME5 .. 62 A1
  Culverstone Green DA13 .. 57 F2
Conifer Way ME19 .... 89 C8
Coningsborough Ct 15 DA2 10 B1
Coniscliffe Cl BR7 .... 37 A8
Coniston Ave Bexley DA16 .. 6 E4
  Royal Tunbridge Wells TN4 148 B5
Coniston Cl Bexley DA7 ..... 8 C6
  Dartford DA1 .... 26 B7
  Erith DA8 .... 8 E7
  Gillingham ME7 .... 49 A6
Coniston Rd DA2 .... 27 D8
Connaught Br E16 .... 1 E5
Connaught Cl ME15 ...... 107 F4
Connaught Mews
  2 Chatham ME4 .... 48 C2
  Woolwich SE18 .... 2 A1
Connaught Rd
  Chatham ME4 .... 48 D5
  Gillingham ME7 .... 48 D5
  Newham,Silvertown E16 ... 1 D5
  Woolwich SE18 .... 2 B1
Connaught Way TN4 ..... 148 F5
Conquest Ind Est ME2 ... 47 A6
Conrad Cl ME4 .... 63 D4
Consort Cl ME14 .... 92 B5
Constable Ave E16 .... 1 C5
Constable Rd
  Northfleet DA11 .... 29 E5
  Tonbridge TN10 .... 117 C5
Constable St E16 .... 1 C8
Constitution Hill
  8 Chatham ME5 .... 48 B3
  Gravesend DA12 .... 30 C7
  Snodland ME6 .... 75 A8
Constitution Rd ME5 ...... 48 B2
Constitution Rise SE18 .... 6 A6
Constance St
  8 Gravesend DA11 .... 30 B7
  Newham E16 .... 1 E5
Contessa Cl BR6 .... 51 E5
Convalescent La TN17 ... 155 F2
Conway Cl ME2 .... 32 C1
Conway Ct BR5 .... 38 C2
Conway Gdns RM17 .... 12 B7
Conway Inf & Jun Sch SE18 2 E2
Conway Mews ME7 .... 48 A6
Conway Rd Maidstone ME16 91 C6
  Woolwich SE18 .... 2 E2
Conyer Rd TN15 .... 86 F6
Conyers Wlk ME8 .... 63 D4
Cooden Cl BR1 .... 22 B1
Cook Cl ME5 .... 62 C6
Cook Sq DA8 .... 8 F7
Cookham Dene Cl BR7 .... 37 D8
Cookham Hill ME1 .... 47 A2
Cookham Rd DA14,BR8 ... 39 A8
Cookhams The BR6 .... 51 D6
Cookhill Rd SE2 .... 3 B3
Cooks Wharf ME1 .... 47 E4
Cookson Gr DA8 .... 8 B8
Coolfin Rd E16 .... 1 A7
Cooling Castle★ ME3 ..... 16 E4
Cooling Common ME3 ..... 16 C6
Cooling Comm ME3 .... 33 DE
Cooling Rd Cliffe ME3 ...... 15 C6
  High Halstow ME23 .... 17 C2
  Rochester ME2 .... 33 B2
Cooling St ME3 .... 16 C5
Coomb Field TN8 .... 128 C8
Coombe Ave TN14 .... 84 B1
Coombe Cl Chatham ME5 .. 62 B3

Coombe Cl continued
Snodland ME6 . . . . .75 A7
Coombe Farm La ME4 . . . . . .18 E6
Coombe La TN30 . . . . .183 A7
Coombe Lands TN30 . . . . . .189 D4
Coombe Lea BR1 . . . . .36 E6
Coombe Lodge SE7 . . . . .5 C8
Coombe Rd
Gravesend DA12 . . . . .30 C6
Hoo St Werburgh ME3 . . . . .34 E5
Maidstone ME15 . . . . .91 F2
Otford TN14 . . . . .69 C4
Coomfield Dr DA2 . . . . .27 D4
Cooper Cl DA9 . . . . .10 F2
Cooper Ct SE18 . . . . .6 B8
Cooper Rd Chatham ME5 . . . .62 B3
Snodland ME6 . . . . .74 E6
Cooper Shaw Rd RM18 . . . . .13 E7
Cooper's Ct DA11 . . . . .29 F7
Coopers Cl DA4 . . . . .41 D8
Coopers Cotts DA2 . . . . .27 F4
Coopers La Lewisham SE12 . .22 B6
Poundsbridge TN11,TN3 . . . . .147 C7
Coopers Sch BR7 . . . . .37 C2
Coopers' Lane Prim Sch
SE12 . . . . .22 B6
Coote Rd DA7 . . . . .7 F6
Copenhagen Rd ME7 . . . . . . .48 C4
Copley Dene BR1 . . . . .36 D8
Copper Beech Cl
Gravesend DA12 . . . . .30 D8
⓻ Rochester ME5 . . . . .38 C4
Copper Beech View TN9 . .133 A8
Copper La TN12 . . . . .138 E5
Copper Tree Ct ME15 . . . . .107 A5
Copper Tree Wlk ME5 . . . . .62 C1
Copperfield Cl DA12 . . . . . . .31 A7
Copperfield Cres ME3 . . . . .32 C2
Copperfield Dr ME17 . . . . . . .31 A7
Copperfield Ho ⓻ ME4 . . . .47 F4
Copperfield Rd Erith SE28 . . .3 A7
Rochester ME1 . . . . .47 C2
Copperfield Way BR7 . . . . . .23 C2
Copperfields
⓻ Dartford DA1 . . . . .9 E1
Kemsing TN15 . . . . .69 F2
Copperfields Cl TN15 . . . . . .69 F2
Copperfields Orch TN15 . . .69 F2
Copperfields The ME1 . . . . . .47 B4
Copperfields Wlk TN15 . . . .69 F2
Coppergate ME7 . . . . .62 F5
Copperhouse La ME7 . . . . . . .49 B6
Copperhouse Rd ME2 . . . . . .46 C7
Copperpenny Dr ME7 . . . . . .63 B3
Coppers La TN12 . . . . .135 E1
Coppice Ct ME7 . . . . .63 B4
Coppice Rd ME5 . . . . .62 C2
Coppice The
Aylesford ME20 . . . . .75 E1
Bitchet Green TN15 . . . . .85 D1
Dartford DA5 . . . . .25 D5
Pembury TN2 . . . . .150 D7
Vigo Village DA13 . . . . .73 B8
Coppice View ME14 . . . . .92 E6
Copping's Rd TN11 . . . . .115 C4
Copse Bank TN15 . . . . .84 F7
Copse Rd TN11 . . . . .116 E4
Copse Side DA3 . . . . .42 A6
Copse The ME3 . . . . .34 E3
Copsehill ME19 . . . . .74 E2
Copsewood Cl DA15 . . . . .6 E1
Copsewood Way ME15 . . . . .93 A3
Copt Hall TN18 . . . . .187 D3
Copt Hall Rd Ightham TN15 . .86 A4
Sole Street DA13 . . . . .44 B5
Coptefield Dr DA17 . . . . .3 E3
Copthall Ave TN14 . . . . .179 A1
Copthorne Ave BR2 . . . . .50 F8
Coralline Wlk ⓸ SE2 . . . . . . .3 C4
Corbylands Rd DA15 . . . . . . .23 E7
Corbylands Rd DA15 . . . . . . .23 E8
Cordelia Cres ME1 . . . . .46 F7
Corelli Rd SE18,SE3 . . . . .5 E6
Corhaven House ⓷ DA4 . . . .8 E7
Corinthian Ct ME3 . . . . .21 B5
Corinthian Manorway DA8 . .4 D2
Corinthian Rd DA8 . . . . .4 D2
Cork House BR5 . . . . .38 B6
Cork La TN12 . . . . .155 D8
Cork St Ind Est ME20 . . . . . . .75 F6
Corkwell St ME4 . . . . .47 E3
Cormorant Cl ME2 . . . . .46 C7
Corn Mill Dr BR6 . . . . .38 A2
Cornel House ⓸ DA15 . . . . . .24 A5
Cornelia Pl DA8 . . . . .8 E8
Cornell Cl DA14 . . . . .24 F2
Corner Farm Rd TN12 . . . . .139 E4
Corner Gn SE3 . . . . .5 A5
Cornfield Way TN10 . . . . . . .117 D6
Cornfield TN18 . . . . .179 A1
Cornford Cl Hayes BR2 . . . . . .36 A4
Pembury TN2 . . . . .150 B6
Cornford La TN2 . . . . .150 B5
Cornford Pk TN2 . . . . .150 C6
Cornforth Cl TN12 . . . . .119 F4
Cornwall Ave DA16 . . . . .6 F4
Cornwall Cl ME15 . . . . .107 E7
Cornwall Cres ME1 . . . . .60 D4
Cornwall Dr BR5 . . . . .24 A1
Cornwall Rd Dartford DA1 . . . .9 F4
Gillingham ME7 . . . . .48 D6
Rochester ME1 . . . . .47 C3
Cornwallis Ave
Chatham ME5 . . . . .47 E1

Cornwallis Ave continued
Gillingham ME8 . . . . .49 A4
Linton ME17 . . . . .122 E8
Sidcup SE9 . . . . .23 D6
Tonbridge TN10 . . . . .117 F4
Cornwallis Cl DA8 . . . . .8 F8
Cornwallis Cotts ME17 . . . .106 E2
Cornwallis Rd
Maidstone ME16 . . . . .91 D4
Woolwich SE18 . . . . .2 B3
Cornwallis Rdbt ME8 . . . . . .49 A4
Cornwallis Sch The
ME15 .106 F2
Cornwallis Wlk SE9 . . . . .5 F4
Cornwell Ave DA12 . . . . .30 C5
Corona Rd SE12 . . . . .22 A8
Corona Terr ME6 . . . . .74 F6
Coronation Cl DA5 . . . . .7 E1
Coronation Cotts
Lower Stoke ME3 . . . . .19 A3
Ticehurst TN5 . . . . .176 F2
Coronation Ct DA8 . . . . .8 D7
Coronation Flats ⓺ ME4 . . .47 F3
Coronation Rd
Chatham ME5 . . . . .48 C2
Grain ME3 . . . . .21 B5
Corporation Rd ME7 . . . . .48 D7
Corporation St ME1 . . . . .47 C6
Corral Cl ME5 . . . . .62 A1
Corrall Almshouses ⓸
ME15 . . . . .92 A3
Corrance Gn ME15 . . . . .107 A8
Corrender Rd TN10 . . . . .117 A3
Corseley Rd TN3 . . . . .161 B5
Cory's Rd ME1 . . . . .47 D6
Cossack St ME1 . . . . .47 E4
Cossington Rd ME5 . . . . .62 B1
Costells Mdw TN16 . . . . .81 D1
Cot La TN27 . . . . .158 B3
Cotleigh Ave DA5 . . . . .24 D6
Cotman Way TN12 . . . . .119 E6
Cotman's Ash La TN15 . . . . .70 D4
Cotmandene Cres ME4 . . . . .38 A7
Coton Rd DA16 . . . . .7 A4
Cotswold Cl DA7 . . . . .8 E5
Cotswold Gdns ME15 . . . . . . .93 A2
Cotswold Rd DA11 . . . . .29 E5
Cotswold Rise BR6 . . . . .37 F3
Cottage Ave BR2 . . . . .36 E3
Cottage Field Cl DA14 . . . . . .24 C7
Cottage Rd ME4 . . . . .47 F6
Cottall Ave ME4 . . . . .47 E4
Cottenham Cl ME19 . . . . .89 F7
Cotton La DA9 . . . . .10 D2
Couchman Green La
TN12 .139 F7
Coulman St ME7 . . . . .48 D5
Coulter House DA9 . . . . .11 C2
Coulters Cl ME14 . . . . .92 D5
Coulton Ave DA11 . . . . .29 E7
Council Ave DA11 . . . . .12 C1
Council Cotts
Chiddingstone
Causeway TN11 . . . . .131 A8
Coxheath ME15 . . . . .106 A4
Key's Green TN12 . . . . .151 C4
Council Hos TN15 . . . . .102 A8
Countess of Thanet's
Almshouses ME4 . . . . .144 F3
County Gate SE9 . . . . .23 C5
County Gr ME19 . . . . .89 B8
County Rd ME7 . . . . .48 C6
County Rd Maidstone ME14 . .92 A5
Newham E6 . . . . .2 B8
Coupland Pl SE18 . . . . .2 C1
Course The SE9 . . . . .23 A5
Court Ave DA17 . . . . .4 A2
Court Broomes ME17 . . . . . .125 C8
Court Cres ME19 . . . . .89 E5
Court Dr ME16 . . . . .91 D4
Court Farm Rd SE9 . . . . .22 E5
Court La Dartling ME14 . . . . . .78 C5
Hadlow TN11 . . . . .119 B7
Court Lane Pl TN11 . . . . .118 F8
Court Lodge Shorne DA12 . . .31 E2
Court Lodge Cotts
East Farleigh ME15 . . . . .106 A7
Horton Kirby DA4 . . . . .41 C6
Court Lodge Rd ME7 . . . . . . .48 F6
Court Mdw Gillingham ME8 . .49 F1
Wrotham TN15 . . . . .71 F3
Court Mews DA11 . . . . .12 B1
Court Rd Burham ME1 . . . . . . .75 F8
Dartford DA2 . . . . .27 E3
Eltham SE9 . . . . .22 F1
Royal Tunbridge Wells TN4 . . .148 F4
Court Road
(Orpington By-Pass)
Chelsfield BR6,TN14 . . . . .52 D5
Orpington BR6 . . . . .38 B2
Court St BR1 . . . . .36 A7
Court Yd SE9 . . . . .5 F1
Courtaulds Cl SE28 . . . . .3 A5
Courtenay Rd ME15 . . . . .91 F2
Courteney Rd ME8 . . . . .63 B8
Courtenwell TN13 . . . . .147 E4
Courtfield Ave ME5 . . . . .62 B3
Courthope TN12 . . . . .138 C5
Courtlands Ave SE12 . . . . . . .5 B2
Courtland Gr SE28 . . . . .3 D6
Courtlands Chislehurst BR7 . .23 B2
Teston ME18 . . . . .105 A8
Tonbridge TN10 . . . . .117 A3
Courtlands Ave SE12 . . . . . . .5 B2
Courtlands Cl ME18 . . . . .105 A8
Courtlands Farm TN17 . . . . .169 A3
Courtleet Dr DA8 . . . . .8 B6

Courtwood Dr TN13 . . . . .84 A3
Courtyard Gdns TN15 . . . . . .71 F3
Courtyard The ME8 . . . . .63 A8
Cousley Wood Rd TN5 . . . . .175 C7
Couthurst Rd SE3 . . . . .5 B8
Coutts Ave DA12 . . . . .31 E4
Coutts Ho SE7 . . . . .5 C8
Covelees Wall E6 . . . . .2 A7
Coventry Cl ⓸ Newham E6 . . .1 F7
Rochester ME2 . . . . .46 D6
Coventry Rd TN10 . . . . .117 D5
Coverdale Ave ME15 . . . . . .107 D6
Coverdale Cl ME5 . . . . .62 B1
Covert The Chatham ME5 . . . .62 B1
Orpington BR6 . . . . .37 E3
Vigo Village DA13 . . . . .72 E7
Covet Wood Cl BR5 . . . . .37 F3
Covey Hall Rd ME6 . . . . .60 A1
Cow La TN8 . . . . .129 D1
Cow Leaze E6 . . . . .2 A7
Cowan Cl E6 . . . . .1 E8
Cowbeck Cl ME8 . . . . .63 D6
Cowden Cl TN18 . . . . .184 E8
Cowden Cross TN8 . . . . .145 C7
Cowden La TN18 . . . . .184 E7
Cowden Mews TN18 . . . . . . .145 A5
Cowden Rd
Maidstone ME14 . . . . .92 C5
Orpington BR6 . . . . .37 F2
Cowden Sta TN18 . . . . .145 D4
Cowdrey Cl
Maidstone ME16 . . . . .91 B2
Rochester ME1 . . . . .47 B2
Cowdrey Ct DA1 . . . . .26 B8
Cowdrey Way DA1 . . . . .11 A2
Cowen House ⓸ SE18 . . . . . . .6 A8
Cowley Ave DA9 . . . . .11 A2
Cowper Ave RM18 . . . . .13 A6
Cowper Ct Bexley DA16 . . . . . .7 A2
Bromley BR2 . . . . .36 D5
Cowper Rd Bromley BR2 . . . . .36 C5
Erith DA17 . . . . .4 A2
Gillingham ME7 . . . . .48 D3
Cowstead Rd ME9 . . . . .64 D2
Cox St ME14 . . . . .78 E6
Cox's Cl ME5 . . . . .74 F8
Coxheath Prim Sch
ME7 . . . . .106 C3
Coxmount Rd SE7 . . . . .1 D1
Coxwell Rd SE18 . . . . .2 D1
Cozenton Cl ME8 . . . . .49 E1
Crabbs Croft Cl ⓻ BR6 . . . . .51 C5
Crabtree Cl ME19 . . . . .89 A2
Crabtree Manorway N
. . . . .4 C5
Crabtree Manorway S DA17 .4 C3
Crabtree Rd ME8 . . . . .63 D8
Crabtree Rndbt ME14 . . . . . . .76 E2
Craddock Way ME8 . . . . .63 D5
Cradducks La TN12 . . . . .140 B4
Cradles Rd ME9 . . . . .64 C2
Cradley Rd SE9 . . . . .23 D7
Cragie Wlk ME8 . . . . .63 C8
Craig Ho Greenwich SE3 . . . . . .5 A4
Rochester ME1 . . . . .47 E1
Craigerne Rd SE3 . . . . .5 B7
Craigholm SE18 . . . . .6 A6
Craigton Rd SE9 . . . . .5 F3
Crales Ho SE18 . . . . .1 F3
Crampton's Rd TN14 . . . . . . .84 B7
Cramptons DA7 . . . . .7 D4
Cranborne Ave ME15 . . . . . . .92 C1
Cranbourne Ave ME15 . . . . .107 B8
Cranbrook CE Prim Sch
TN17 .169 D5
Cranbrook Cl
Gillingham ME8 . . . . .49 C3
Hayes BR2 . . . . .36 A3
Maidstone ME15 . . . . .107 F7
Cranbrook House ⓵ DA8 . . . .8 F7
Cranbrook Mus* TN17 . . . . .169 D5
Cranbrook Rd
Benenden TN17 . . . . .179 F8
Erith DA7 . . . . .7 F6
Fosten Green TN27 . . . . .171 C6
Gill's Green TN18 . . . . .178 F4
Goudhurst TN17 . . . . .168 A8
Knox Bridge TN12,TN17 . . . . .155 F7
Parkgate TN30 . . . . .172 C1
Tenterden TN30 . . . . .182 F7
Cranbrook Sch* TN17 . . . . . . .169 D6
Cranbrook Union Mill*
TN17 .169 D4
Crandalls TN17 . . . . .115 F1
Crane House ⓫ TN18 . . . . . .178 F2
Crane House Gdns ⓾
TN18 .178 F2
Crane La TN17 . . . . .169 D5
Cranford Cl ME18 . . . . .89 D1
Cranford Ho DA1 . . . . .9 A2
Cranford Rd Dartford DA1 . . .26 E7
Tonbridge TN10 . . . . .118 A5
Cranham Sq TN12 . . . . .135 C5
Cranleigh Cl Bexley DA5 . . . . .8 B1
Orpington BR6 . . . . .52 A7
Cranleigh Dr SE28 . . . . .3 B6
Cranleigh Gdns
Chatham ME4 . . . . .47 D3
Maidstone ME16 . . . . .91 C7
Cranley Par SE9 . . . . .22 E4
Cranley Rd SE9 . . . . .22 E4
Cranmer Cl ME15 . . . . .107 B8
Cranmer Rd TN13 . . . . .83 E4
Cranmere Ct ME2 . . . . .47 C8
Cranmore Rd BR7 . . . . .22 F3
Cranstone Cl ⓽ DA14 . . . . . .24 B4
Cranwell Rd TN4 . . . . .148 C4
Crathie Rd SE12 . . . . .5 B1
Craven Rd BR6 . . . . .52 D7

Crawfords BR8 . . . . .25 E1
Crawley Ct ⓵ DA11 . . . . .13 B1
Crawshay Cl TN13 . . . . .84 A4
Cray Ave BR5 . . . . .38 B4
Cray Bldgs DA14 . . . . .24 C2
Cray Cl DA1 . . . . .9 A3
Cray Rd Crockenhill BR8 . . . . .39 C3
Erith DA17 . . . . .8 A8
Sidcup DA14 . . . . .24 C2
Cray Valley Rd BR5 . . . . .38 B4
Craybrooke Rd DA14 . . . . . . .24 B4
Crayburne DA13 . . . . .28 F4
Craybury End SE9 . . . . .23 C6
Craydene Rd DA8 . . . . .8 F6
Crayfields Bsns Pk BR5 . . . . .38 C5
Crayfields Ind Pk BR5 . . . . . .38 C6
Crayford Cl ME14 . . . . .92 C6
Crayford Commercial Ctr
DA1 . . . . .8 E1
Crayford High St DA1 . . . . . . .8 E2
Crayford Ind Est DA1 . . . . . . .8 F2
Crayford L Ctr DA1 . . . . .8 E3
Crayford Rd DA1 . . . . .8 E1
Crayford Sta DA1 . . . . .8 E2
Crayford Way DA1 . . . . .9 A3
Craylands BR5 . . . . .38 C6
Craylands La DA10 . . . . .11 D2
Craylands Sq DA10 . . . . .11 D2
Crayleigh Terr DA14 . . . . .24 C2
Craymill Sq DA1 . . . . .8 F5
Crays Par The BR5 . . . . .38 C7
Crayside Ind Est DA1 . . . . .9 B3
Craythorne TN8 . . . . .183 B8
Craythorne Ho TN30 . . . . . . .183 B8
Creasey's Row TN14 . . . . .97 E5
Credenhall Dr BR2 . . . . .36 F1
Crediton Rd E16 . . . . .1 A7
Credo Way RM20 . . . . .11 B8
Creek The DA11 . . . . .12 B2
Creek Way RM13 . . . . .4 E8
Cremorne Rd DA11 . . . . .12 D8
Crescent Ave RM17 . . . . .12 D8
Crescent Cotts TN13 . . . . . . .83 E7
Crescent Ct ⓵ Grays RM17 . .12 D8
Sidcup DA15 . . . . .24 A5
Crescent Dr BR5 . . . . .37 C3
Crescent Gdns ME2 . . . . .47 C7
Crescent Rd Bromley BR1 . . .22 A1
Erith DA8 . . . . .8 F8
Royal Tunbridge Wells TN1 . .149 B3
Sidcup DA15 . . . . .23 F5
Woolwich SE18 . . . . .2 C1
Crescent The
Bidborough TN4 . . . . .132 E4
Borough Green TN15 . . . . .87 A8
Groombridge TN3 . . . . .161 C7
Longfield DA3 . . . . .42 E6
Maidstone ME14 . . . . .91 F8
Northfleet DA11 . . . . .29 F6
Sevenoaks TN13 . . . . .84 A4
Sidcup DA14 . . . . .23 F4
Sidcup DA15 . . . . .24 C8
Crescent Way
Chatham ME1 . . . . .61 D5
Orpington BR6 . . . . .51 E5
Cressey Ct ⓽ ME4 . . . . .47 E4
Cressingham Ct ⓵ DA17 . . . . .4 A1
Crest Ave RM17 . . . . .12 B7
Crest Cl TN14 . . . . .68 B8
Crest Ind Est TN12 . . . . .138 C5
Crest Rd ME1 . . . . .47 C1
Crest View DA9 . . . . .11 A3
Crest View Dr BR5 . . . . .37 C4
Crestway ME5 . . . . .62 B8
Crete Hall Rd DA11 . . . . .12 E1
Creton St SE18 . . . . .2 A3
Creve Coeur Cl ME14 . . . . . . .93 A5
Crevequer Chambers ⓵
ME8 . . . . .49 F1
Cricket Ground Rd BR7 . . . . .37 B8
Cricketers Cl
Bells Yew Green TN3 . . . . .164 A5
Erith DA8 . . . . .4 B1
Harrietsham ME17 . . . . .110 D6
Cricketers Dr DA13 . . . . .58 A7
Cripple Hill TN26 . . . . .159 D1
Cripple St ME15 . . . . .107 A4
Crisfield Ct TN30 . . . . .173 B2
Crismill La ME14,ME17 . . . . .93 F3
Crispe Cl ME8 . . . . .63 D4
Crispin Ct ME17 . . . . .106 C3
Crispin Rd ME2 . . . . .46 C7
Crispin Way ME19 . . . . .89 A3
Crittall's Cnr DA14 . . . . .24 A1
Crittenden Bglws ME15 . . . .106 A4
Crittenden Cotts ME15 . . . .106 A4
Crittenden Rd TN12 . . . . .135 D3
Critle's Ct TN5 . . . . .174 F4
Crocken Hill Rd TN12 . . . . . .150 F7
Crockenhill Cl ME15 . . . . . . .106 A4
Crockenhill La BR8,DA4 . . . . .40 C2
Crockenhill Prim Sch BR8 . .39 C3
Crockenhill Rd BR5,BR8 . . . .38 D4
Crockham Way SE9 . . . . .23 A4
Croft Cl Chatham ME5 . . . . . . .62 C1
Chislehurst BR7 . . . . .22 F3
Erith DA17 . . . . .7 F8
Tonbridge TN11 . . . . .117 F5
Croft Ct TN8 . . . . .112 C1
Croft Gdns ME17 . . . . .111 D4

Croft La TN8 . . . . .112 C1
Croft Rd Bromley BR1 . . . . . . .22 A2
Westerham TN16 . . . . .81 C1
Croft The Leybourne ME19 . . .74 E2
Swanley BR8 . . . . .39 C6
Croft Way Sevenoaks TN13 . .83 F2
Sidcup DA15 . . . . .23 E5
Crofters The ME8 . . . . .63 F7
Crofton Ave
Orpington BR5,BR6 . . . . .51 C8
Sidcup DA5 . . . . .24 D8
Crofton Inf Sch BR5 . . . . .37 D2
Crofton Jun Sch BR5 . . . . . . .37 D2
Crofton La BR5,BR6 . . . . .37 D2
Crofton Rd BR6 . . . . .51 B8
Crofton Rd SE18 . . . . .2 D1
Croftside SE9 . . . . .6 C2
Cromarty Cl ⓻ BR1 . . . . .36 C7
Crombie Rd DA15 . . . . .23 D7
Cromer Pl ⓹ BR6 . . . . .37 D1
Cromer Rd ME2 . . . . .47 B8
Cromer St TN9 . . . . .117 A1
Cromford Cl BR6 . . . . .51 E7
Cromlix Cl BR7 . . . . .37 B7
Crompton Gdns ME15 . . . . . . .92 B3
Cromwell Ave BR2 . . . . .36 B5
Cromwell Ct ME2 . . . . .36 B5
Cromwell Mews BR7 . . . . .37 A8
Cromwell Rd
Maidstone ME14 . . . . .92 B5
Royal Tunbridge Wells TN2 . . .149 C3
Cromwell Terr ME4 . . . . .48 A3
Cronin Cl ⓶ ME20 . . . . .74 F4
Crook Log DA6 . . . . .7 D3
Crook Log Prim Sch DA6 . . . . .7 D2
Crook Log Sports Ctr DA7 . . . .7 D4
Crooked La DA11,DA12 . . . . .13 B1
Crookston Rd SE9 . . . . .6 A4
Croombs Rd E16 . . . . .1 C8
Crosby House DA1 . . . . .9 A1
Crosier Cl SE3 . . . . .5 E6
Crosley Rd ME7 . . . . .48 D3
Cross Ct ⓻ SE28 . . . . .3 B6
Cross Dr ME17 . . . . .109 B1
Cross Keys Maidstone ME14 . .93 C4
Sevenoaks TN13 . . . . .99 A8
Cross La Sidcup DA5 . . . . .24 E8
Ticehurst TN5 . . . . .176 D2
Cross La E DA12 . . . . .30 B6
Cross La W DA11 . . . . .30 B6
Cross Lane Gdns TN5 . . . . . .176 D1
Cross Rd Dartford DA1 . . . . .9 C1
Hawley DA2 . . . . .26 F4
Northfleet DA11 . . . . .12 F1
Orpington, Keston Mark BR2 . .50 F8
Orpington, St Mary Cray BR5 . .38 B4
Sidcup DA14 . . . . .24 B4
Cross St Chatham ME4 . . . . . . .48 A4
Erith DA8 . . . . .8 E8
Gillingham ME7 . . . . .48 C6
⓶ Gravesend DA12 . . . . .13 B1
Maidstone ME14 . . . . .92 A6
Rochester ME2 . . . . .47 B8
Cross Way ME7 . . . . .47 C3
Cross-at-Hand Cotts
TN12 .123 E2
Crossbrook Rd SE3 . . . . .5 E4
Crossfield Cl ⓻ ME1 . . . . . . .47 B5
Crossways Chatham ME5 . . . .61 E6
Erith SE28 . . . . .3 D7
Orpington BR5 . . . . .37 D4
Crossway The
Chislehurst SE9 . . . . .22 D6
Royal Tunbridge Wells TN4 . . .148 C3
Crossways
Chart Sutton ME17 . . . . .108 B1
Dartford DA2 . . . . .10 D3
Hextable BR8 . . . . .25 F1
Crossways Bvd DA9 . . . . .10 E3
Crouch Croft SE9 . . . . .23 A5
Crouch House Cotts TN8 . .112 B2
Crouch House Rd TN8 . . . . .112 B2
Crouch La Crouch TN15 . . . . .87 B6
Linkhill TN18 . . . . .186 D6
Crow Cnr ME1 . . . . .47 C5
Crow Dr TN14 . . . . .68 C4
Crow Hill TN15 . . . . .87 A7
Crow Hill Rd TN15 . . . . .87 A7
Crow La ME1 . . . . .47 C5
Crowden Way SE28 . . . . .3 C6
Crowhurst La Basted TN15 . . .86 E4
West Kingsdown TN15 . . . . .56 B4
Crowhurst Oast TN12 . . . . . .103 D1
Crowhurst Rd TN15 . . . . .86 F6
Crowhurst Way BR5 . . . . .38 C4
Crown Acres TN12 . . . . .120 A6
Crown Cl ME2 . . . . .33 C1
Crown Dr Bromley BR2 . . . . . .36 E4
Cranbrook TN17 . . . . .169 C5
Eltham SE12 . . . . .5 B1
Crown Gn DA12 . . . . .31 E3
Crown Ho ME1 . . . . .47 B4
Crown La Bromley BR2 . . . . . .36 C4
Chislehurst BR7 . . . . .37 C8
Shorne DA12 . . . . .31 E4
Crown Lane Spur BR2 . . . . . .36 D3
Crown Rd Grays RM17 . . . . . .12 A8
Marlpit Hill TN8 . . . . .112 D4
Orpington BR6 . . . . .38 B2
Shoreham TN14 . . . . .69 A8
Crown St ME7 . . . . .48 D6
Crown Woods Sch SE9 . . . . . .6 C2
Crown Woods Way SE9 . . . . . .6 D2

Crownfields
Maidstone ME14 ....92 F4
Sevenoaks TN13 ....89 B2
Crowther Cl TN12 ....139 E4
Croxley Cl BR5 ....38 B7
Croxley Gn BR5 ....38 B8
Croyde Cl DA15 ....23 D8
Croydon Cl DA15 ....62 C4
Croydon Rd
Orpington BR2,BR4,BR6 ...50 C7
Westerham TN16 ....91 B2
Crozier House SE3 ....5 B4
Cruden Rd DA12 ....30 F6
Crump's La ME17 ....126 B4
Crumpsall St SE2 ....3 C3
Crundale 2 ME14 ....92 A5
Crundale Rd ME8 ....49 C3
Crundale Tower BR5 ....38 C1
Crundwell Rd TN4 ....132 F1
Crusader Cl ME8 ....63 B8
Crusader Ct DA1 ....9 F3
Crusoe Rd DA8 ....4 D1
Crutches La ME3 ....32 B1
Cryals Ct TN12 ....151 E5
Cryals Rd TN12 ....151 D5
Crystal Ho 8 SE18 ....2 F1
Cuckmere Ct 8 BR5 ....38 D1
Cuckold's Cnr ME3 ....3 C2
Cuckold's Cnr TN12 ....139 F4
Cuckolds Cnr DA3 ....57 B7
Cuckolds Green Rd ME3 ...19 B5
Cuckoo La
Lamberhurst TN12 ....152 A2
Tonbridge TN11 ....118 A7
Cuckoowood Ave ME14 ...76 F1
Cudham CE Prim Sch
TN16 ....66 A3
Cudham Cl ME14 ....92 C6
Cudham La N TN14 ....66 D2
Cudham La S TN14 ....66 D2
Cudham Park Rd TN14 .....51 E1
Cudham Rd BR6 ....66 B7
Cuff Cres SE9 ....5 D1
Cugley Rd DA2 ....27 C8
Culcroft DA3 ....42 F6
Culpeper Cl
Hollingbourne ME17 ....94 E2
Rochester ME2 ....47 E6
Culpeper Ct TN7 ....167 E7
Culpepper Rd
Coxheath ME17 ....106 B3
Gillingham ME8 ....63 D4
Culverden Ave TN4 ....149 A6
Culverden Down TN4 .....148 F5
Culverden Park Rd TN4 ..148 F5
Culverden Pk TN4 ....148 F5
Culverden Sq TN4 ....149 A5
Culverden St TN1 ....149 A4
Culverstone Green
Prim Sch 57 F3
Culverstone House BR5 ...38 B6
Culverton Cl 10 DA14 ......24 A4
Culvey Cl DA3 ....42 D6
Cumberland Ave
Bexley DA16 ....6 F3
Gravesend DA12 ....30 C8
Maidstone ME15 ....107 D8
Cumberland Comp Sch E16 ..1 A8
Cumberland Ct
Sevenoaks TN13 ....83 E7
Tonbridge TN10 ....117 A4
Cumberland Dr
Dartford DA1 ....26 F8
Erith DA7 ....7 E7
Cumberland Gdns 10
TN1 ....149 A2
Cumberland Mews 12
TN1 ....149 A2
Cumberland Rd
Gillingham ME4,ME7 ....48 B7
Gillingham ME7 ....48 C7
Newham E13 ....1 B8
Cumberland Wlk TN1 ......149 A2
Cumberland Yd 11 TN1 ....149 A2
Cumbrian Ave DA7 ....8 E5
Cundy Rd E16 ....1 C7
Cunningham Cl TN4 ....149 B7
Cunningham Cres ME5 ....62 A8
Cunningham Ho ME1 ....47 B4
Cunningham Rd TN4 ....149 B7
Cupola Cl BR1 ....22 B3
Curlew Cl SE28 ....3 D6
Curlew Cres ME5 ....44 C6
Curlews The DA12 ....30 D6
Curran Ave DA15 ....6 F2
Currie Rd TN4 ....149 A5
Curteis Rd TN30 ....173 B1
Curtis Way Chatham ME1 ..61 D7
7 Woolwich SE28 ....3 B6
Curtismill Cl BR5 ....38 B6
Curtismill Way BR5 ....38 B6
Curzon Cl BR6 ....51 D6
Curzon Ct SE9 ....23 C5
Curzon Dr ME17 ....112 C7
Curzon Rd Chatham ME4 ...47 F3
Maidstone ME14 ....92 A6
Custom House
for Excel Sta** E16 ....1 B6
Cut The ME27 ....158 E8
Cutbush & Corrall Cl 1
ME14 ....92 B4
Cutbush Almshouses
3 Maidstone ME14 ....92 A4
2 Maidstone ME15 ....92 A3
Cutbush Rd ME17 ....110 D6

Cutmore St DA11 ....30 B8
Cutter Ridge Rd DA13 .....45 A1
Cutty Sark Ct DA9 ....11 A2
Cuxton BR5 ....37 C4
Cuxton Cl DA6 ....7 E2
Cuxton Com Inf Sch ME2 ..46 B2
Cuxton Com Jun Sch ME2 ..46 B2
Cuxton Ind Est ME2 ....46 C1
Cuxton Rd
Maidstone ME15 ....107 F5
Rochester ME2 ....46 F5
Cuxton Sta SE2 ....46 C2
Cyclamen Rd BR8 ....39 D5
Cygnet Cl ME20 ....75 A2
Cygnet Gdns DA11 ....29 F6
Cygnet L Ctr DA11 ....29 E6
Cygnet Rd ME5 ....62 C2
Cypress Ave ME3 ....34 E3
Cypress Cl ME7 ....48 E6
Cypress Gr TN2 ....163 C8
Cypress Rd ME2 ....33 C1
Cypress Tree Cl DA15 .....23 F7
Cyprus Pl E6 ....2 A6
Cyprus Sta E6 ....2 A6
Cyril Lodge 8 DA14 ....24 A4
Cyril Rd Bexley DA7 ....7 E5
Orpington BR6 ....38 A2

D

D'arcy Pl BR2 ....36 A5
Dabbling Cl DA8 ....9 B7
Dabells TN17 ....169 D4
Daerwood Cl BR1 ....36 F1
Daffodil Rd ME2 ....46 F7
Dagmar Rd ME4 ....48 B2
Dagnam Gdns BR1 ....22 A5
Dagonet Rd BR1 ....22 A5
Dahlia Dr BR8 ....39 F7
Dahlia Rd SE2 ....3 B2
Dainton Cl 2 BR1 ....36 B8
Daintons Cotts 2 TN18 ..178 F2
Dairsie Ct 4 BR1 ....36 C7
Dairsie Rd SE9 ....6 A4
Dairy Cl 3 Lewisham BR1 ..22 A1
Woolwich SE18 ....2 D7
Dairy La Chainhurst TN12 .121 F4
Crockham Hill TN8 ....96 B1
Woolwich SE18 ....1 F7
Dairy Pl TN12 ....121 F4
Daisy Munns Ho SE9 ......23 C7
Dakota Gdns E6 ....1 E8
Dalberg Way SE2 ....3 D3
Dale Cl Crayford DA1 ....8 F1
Greenwich SE3 ....5 A4
Dale Cl BR1 ....36 D6
Dale End DA1 ....8 F1
Dale Rd Crayford DA1 ....8 F1
Northfleet DA13 ....29 A4
Rochester ME1 ....47 C3
Swanley BR8 ....39 C6
Dale St Chatham ME4 ....47 E2
Royal Tunbridge Wells TN1 ..149 B4
Dale The BR2 ....50 D6
Dale View DA8 ....8 F5
Dale Wk DA2 ....27 C7
Dale Wood Rd BR6 ....37 E1
Dalemain Mews E16 ....1 A5
Daleside BR6 ....52 A5
Daleside Cl BR6 ....52 A4
Dalison Ct ME2 ....60 A4
Dallin Rd Bexley DA6 ....7 D3
Woolwich SE18 ....6 B7
Dalmeny Rd DA8 ....8 B6
Dalton Cl BR6 ....51 E7
Dalton St ME7 ....48 C6
Daltons Rd BR5,BR8 ....53 C7
Damien Cl ME4 ....48 A2
Damigos Rd DA12 ....30 F7
Damon Cl DA14 ....24 B5
Damon Ct DA14 ....24 B5
Damson Cl BR8 ....39 D5
Damson Rd ME3 ....34 E3
Danaway Cotts ME9 ....65 C3
Dando Cres SE3 ....5 B4
Dandridge Cl SE10 ....1 A1
Dane Cl Chatham ME5 ....62 C2
Sidcup DA5 ....25 A8
Dane Ct ME17 ....64 F6
Dane La ME9 ....64 D6
Dane Rd TN14 ....68 F2
Danecourt Sch ME8 ....49 A2
Danefield Ct
Maidstone ME14 ....93 B4
Sevenoaks TN13 ....83 C4
Danehill Wlk DA14 ....24 A5
Danemore TN30 ....183 B8
Danes Cl DA11 ....29 C5
Danes Hill ME7 ....49 A6
Danescombe SE12 ....22 A7
Daniel Ho ME16 ....91 E5
Danns La ME18,ME19 ....89 A1
Dansington Rd DA16 ....7 A3
Danson Cres DA16 ....7 B4
Danson La DA16 ....7 B3
Danson Mead DA16 ....7 C4
Danson Rd Bexley DA6 ....7 A2
Sidcup DA5 ....7 D1
Danson Underpass DA5 ......7 C1
Danson Way ME8 ....49 D2
Danvers Rd TN9 ....133 B7
Darby Gdns ME3 ....32 B3
Darby La TN5 ....175 B2
Darent Cl TN13 ....83 C5

Darent Ind Pk DA8 ....9 D8
Darent Mead DA4 ....41 B8
Darent Valley Hospl DA2 ...27 E7
Darent Ave TN10 ....117 C5
Darenth Com Prim Sch
DA2 ....27 E2
Darenth Cotts TN14 ....68 F8
Darenth Ct 13 BR5 ....38 D1
Darenth Dr DA12 ....31 B7
Darenth Gdns TN16 ....81 D1
Darenth Hill DA2 ....27 C3
Darenth La TN13 ....83 E6
Darenth Park Ave DA2 ......27 D6
Darenth Rd Bexley DA16 .....7 A4
Dartford DA1 ....26 F7
Darenth Rd S DA2 ....27 B4
Darenth Rise ME5 ....62 B3
Darenth Way TN14 ....69 A8
Darenth Wood Rd DA2 ......27 E6
Dargate Cl ME16 ....91 D7
Dargets Rd ME5 ....62 A3
Darland Ave ME7 ....48 E1
Darland House SE9 ....6 D1
Darland La DA1 ....8 F4
Darman La TN12,ME18 .....120 D3
Darnets Field TN14 ....68 F2
Darnley Cl ME2 ....46 D6
Darnley Ho ME2 ....47 B3
Darnley Rd Gravesend DA11 .30 A8
1 Grays RM17 ....12 B8
Rochester ME2 ....46 E6
Darnley St DA11 ....30 B8
Darns Hill BR8 ....39 C2
Darrick Wood Ho BR6 ....51 C7
Darrick Wood Inf & Jun
Schs BR6 ....51 B6
Darrick Wood Rd BR6 ....51 C8
Darrick Wood Sch BR6 ......51 B6
Darrick Wood Sports Ctr
BR6 ....51 B7
Dart Cl ME2 ....46 F7
Dartford Borough Mus*
DA1 ....26 E8
Dartford Gram Sch DA1 ....11 C1
Dartford Gram Sch for Girls
DA1 ....26 C8
Dartford Hospl Specl Sch
DA3 ....43 A6
Dartford Rd Coldblow DA5 ..25 C7
Dartford DA1 ....26 F8
Farningham DA4 ....41 A5
Sevenoaks TN13 ....84 C3
Dartford Sta DA1 ....9 E1
Dartford Technology Coll
DA1 ....26 F6
Dartford Trad Est DA1 ......26 F6
Dartmouth Rd BR2 ....36 A2
Darwin Cl BR6 ....51 D5
Darwin Cl 4 Eltham SE9 .....6 A1
Rochester ME1 ....47 D5
Darwin Dr TN10 ....117 D6
Darwin Rd Bexley DA16 ......6 F4
Tilbury RM18 ....12 C6
Dashmonden Cl ME12 ....4 B4
Dashwood Cl DA6 ....8 A2
Dashwood Rd DA11 ....30 A6
Davall House 10 RM17 ......12 B8
Davenport Ave ME7 ....49 A6
Davenport Rd DA14 ....24 E6
David Coffer Ct ME4 ....48 A2
David Salomon's Ho* TN3 .148 D8
Davidson Tower BR1 ....22 B3
Davis Ave DA11 ....29 E7
Davis Cl TN13 ....84 C5
Davy's Pl DA12 ....30 E2
Dawbourne TN30 ....173 B3
Dawes Cl DA9 ....10 F2
Dawes St ME7 ....48 C5
Dawson Ave BR5 ....38 B7
Dawson Cl 8 SE18 ....2 C2
Dawson Ct 7 ME7 ....48 A6
Dawson Dr BR8 ....25 E1
Day Ho 2 ME14 ....92 F5
Days La DA15 ....23 E8
Days Lane Prim Sch DA15 ...6 F1
Dayton Dr DA8 ....9 D8
De Lapre Cl BR5 ....38 D2
De Luci Rd DA4 ....41 E2
De Lucy Prim Sch SE2 ....3 B4
De Lucy St SE2 ....3 B2
De Mere Cl ME8 ....63 D6
De Quincey Mews E16 ....1 A5
De Warren Ho DA11 ....12 D1
Deacon Cl ME2 ....46 E8
Deacon Est The ME20 ......76 A2
Deacon Trad Ctr ME17 ......94 A8
Deacon Trad Est TN12 .....117 D1
Deacons Leas BR6 ....51 D6
Deacons Leas ME9 ....51 D6
Deakin Leas TN9 ....133 B7
Deal Ho ME15 ....107 E8
Dean & Chapter Cotts
DA3 ....29 B2
Dean La DA13 ....58 C5
Dean Rd
Luddesdown DA13 ....58 E8
Rochester ME2 ....46 F8
Woolwich SE28 ....3 A6
Dean St ME15 ....106 C6
Deane Cl 3 ME4 ....48 C6
Deane Rd TN8 ....96 C2
Deangate Ridge
Sports Ground ME3 ....34 D8
Deans Cl 7 TN9 ....133 B8
Deans Hill Rd ME9 ....80 D5
Deansfield Cl ME8 ....49 C6
Deansfield Jun Sch SE9 ......6 A4
Deanwood Cl ME8 ....63 D6
Deanwood Dr ME8 ....63 E4

Deanwood
Prim Education Tech Sch
ME8 ....63 D3
Debrabant Cl DA8 ....38 D8
Decoy Hill Rd ME23 ....17 F6
Deepdene TN5 ....175 A6
Deepdene Rd DA16 ....7 A4
Deerhurst Cl DA3 ....43 C6
Deerhurst Gdns ME16 ....91 D4
Deerleap La TN14 ....67 E6
Defiance Wlk SE18 ....1 F3
Defiant Cl ME5 ....62 B6
Defoe Cl Chatham ME5 ......62 B6
Erith DA8 ....8 F6
Degema Rd BR7 ....23 B3
Deidre Chapman House
DA10 ....11 E1
Delacourt Rd SE3 ....5 B7
Delafield Rd SE7 ....1 C1
Delagarde Rd TN16 ....81 C1
Delamere Gdns 3 ME6 .....75 A8
Delamere Rd ME16 ....75 A8
Delaware Cotts TN8 ....128 F8
Delce Inf Sch ME1 ....47 D2
Delce Jun Sch ME1 ....47 C2
Delce Rd ME1 ....47 D4
Delisle Rd SE28 ....2 E4
Delius Dr TN10 ....117 F6
Dell The Dartford DA5 ....25 E7
Woolwich SE2 ....3 A1
Delme Cres SE3 ....5 B5
Delmonden Rd
Hawkhurst TN18 ....178 B1
The Moor TN18 ....184 C8
Delvan Cl SE18 ....6 A7
Delves Ave TN2 ....149 C1
Demelza House Hospice
ME9 ....65 F6
Den Cross TN8 ....128 D6
Den La TN12 ....121 A3
Denbigh Dr TN10 ....117 D6
Denberry Dr DA14 ....24 B5
Denbigh Ave ME8 ....49 D1
Denbigh Cl BR7 ....22 F2
Denbigh Rd TN4 ....149 C7
Denbridge Rd BR1,BR7 .....36 F7
Dene Ave DA15 ....24 B8
Dene Cl DA2 ....25 E4
Dene Dr New Barn DA3 .....43 B7
Orpington BR6 ....52 B7
Dene Holm Rd DA11 ....29 E5
Dene Lodge Cl TN15 ....86 F7
Dene Rd DA1 ....26 F8
Dene The TN3 ....84 B1
Dene Way TN3 ....148 A7
Denecourt BR5 ....38 C1
Denecroft DA3 ....44 B3
Denham Rd ME9 ....65 B7
Denham St 2 SE10 ....1 A1
Denison Mews ME1 ....19 C4
Deniston Ave DA5 ....24 E7
Denison Ho 10 SE18 ....1 E2
Denmark Rd BR1 ....36 B8
Denmark St E13 ....1 A1
Dennard Way BR6 ....51 A6
Dennettsland Rd TN8 ....96 C1
Dennington Ct TN4 ....133 A2
Dennis Cadman Ho 8
ME20 ....75 F1
Dennis Rd DA11 ....30 B5
Dennis Willocks Cl ME9 .....65 B6
Denny Cl 3 E6 ....1 E8
Denny Ct 13 DA2 ....10 B1
Densole Cl DA15 ....107 F6
Denton Cl ME15 ....107 E8
Denton Court Rd DA12 ......30 E8
Denton Rd Bexley DA16 ......7 C7
Dartford DA5 ....25 E8
Denton St DA12 ....30 E8
Denton Terr DA5 ....25 E8
Denver Cl BR6 ....37 E3
Denver Ind Est RM13 ....4 F8
Denver Rd DA1 ....26 A8
Depford Cl ME8 ....49 C1
Derby Rd Chatham ME5 .....48 E2
1 Grays RM17 ....12 B8
Maidstone ME15 ....107 C8
Derby Road Bridge ME15 ...107 C8
Derifall Cl E6 ....1 F8
Dering Way DA12 ....30 F7
Deringwood Dr ME15 ....92 F1
Dernier Rd TN10,TN9 ....117 C4
Derrick Gdns SE7 ....1 C3
Derry Downs BR5 ....38 C3
Derwent Cl DA1 ....26 B7
Derwent Cres DA7 ....8 A5
Derwent Dr Orpington BR5 ...37 D2
Royal Tunbridge Wells TN4 ..148 C5
Derwent House 8 ME15 ...107 E7
Derwent Lodge Sch TN1 ..149 B4
Derwent Rd TN10 ....117 C5
Derwent Way ME8 ....63 D8
Detling CE Prim Sch
ME14 ....78 A1
Detling Cl ME2 ....49 C2
Detling Hill ME14 ....78 B2
Detling Rd Bromley BR1 ....22 A3
Erith DA8 ....8 B7
Northfleet DA11 ....29 D7
Devalls Cl E6 ....2 A6
Devema Cl BR7 ....37 A8
Devenish Rd SE2 ....3 A4
Devon Cl Chatham ME5 ......62 C7
Gillingham ME8 ....49 F1
Devon Ct DA4 ....41 B8

Devon Rd Maidstone ME15 .107 C8
Sutton at Hone DA4 ....41 C8
Devonshire Ave DA1 ....26 F8
Devonshire Cl TN2 ....162 F8
Devonshire Rd Bexley DA6 ...7 F3
Cheslehurst SE9 ....22 E6
Gillingham ME7 ....48 D7
Gravesend DA12 ....30 B6
Newham E16 ....4 F1
Orpington BR6 ....38 A2
Devonshire Sq BR2 ....36 B5
Dewberry Cl ME4 ....34 B1
Dewberry Gdns E6 ....1 E8
Dewhurst Cotts TN5 ....174 A7
Dewhurst La TN5 ....174 B8
DeWinter Ho TN13 ....84 A3
Dewlands Ave DA2 ....28 B3
Dexter Ho 3 DA18 ....3 E3
Dhekelia Cl ME14 ....92 A7
Dial Cl Gillingham ME7 ....48 F6
Swanscombe DA9 ....11 D2
Dial Rd ME7 ....48 F6
Diameter Rd BR5 ....37 C3
Diamond Cotts TN12 ....135 B7
Diamond Field TN12 ....152 F3
Diana Cl DA8 ....8 E8
Dianne Ct SE12 ....22 A7
Dianthus Cl SE2 ....3 B1
Dibden La TN13,TN14 ....98 E8
Dibden Rd TN13 ....98 E8
Dickens Ave Dartford DA1 ..10 A3
Tilbury RM18 ....13 B6
Dickens Cl Erith DA8 ....8 B7
Hartley DA3 ....42 F4
Langley Heath ME17 ....108 A6
Dickens Ct Rochester ME2 ...47 D8
Staplehurst TN12 ....139 F5
Dickens Dr Chislehurst BR7 .23 C2
East Malling ME19 ....74 F1
Dickens Ho 3 DA17 ....4 A3
Maidstone ME14 ....91 E8
Rochester ME1 ....47 C2
Dickens Way TN18 ....179 A3
Dickensian Cl ME23 ....19 A2
Dickley La ME17 ....111 A6
Dickson Ho SE18 ....5 E6
Dickson Rd SE9 ....5 E4
Digdog La TN12,TN17 ......156 D3
Dignals Cl ME8 ....49 F2
Dilhorne Cl SE12 ....22 B5
Dillon Way TN2 ....149 D6
Dillywood Cotts ME3 ....32 E7
Dillywood La ME3 ....32 E7
Dimmock Cl TN12 ....136 B7
Dingleden La TN17 ....180 F2
Dippers Cl TN15 ....69 F2
Discovery Dr ME19 ....89 B3
Discovery Rd ME15 ....93 B2
Distingbury Rd TN11 ....134 C4
Disraeli Cl
Maidstone ME15 ....107 E5
Woolwich SE28 ....3 C5
Dittisham Rd SE9 ....22 E4
Ditton CE Jun Sch ME20 ....75 C1
Ditton Court Cl ME20 ....75 B1
Ditton Inf Sch ME20 ....75 B1
Ditton Pl ME20 ....75 B1
Ditton Rd DA6 ....7 E2
Dixon Cl Maidstone ME15 ...91 F2
4 Newham E6 ....1 F7
Dixon Ho SE2 ....3 C1
Dixwell Cl ME8 ....63 D5
Dobell Rd SE9 ....5 F2
Dobson Rd DA12 ....30 E3
Dock Approach Rd RM17 ...12 A8
Dock Head Rd
Chathenden ME4 ....34 A1
Gillingham ME4 ....48 A8
Dock Rd Chatham ME4 ....48 A8
Gillingham ME4 ....48 A8
Grays RM17 ....12 DB
Grays RM17 ....12 E5
Tilbury RM18 ....12 E5
Dockland E16 ....2 A5
Dockside Rd E16 ....1 D6
Doctor Hope's Rd TN17 ...169 D4
Dodd Rd TN10 ....117 C5
Doddington Ct ME16 ....91 E5
Doddington Rd ME8 ....49 D3
Doebury Wlk SE18 ....7 A8
Dog Cotts RH19 ....144 B3
Doggets Cl TN8 ....128 C8
Doggetts Row ME3 ....21 B6
Dogwood Cl Chatham ME5 ..62 D1
Northfleet DA11 ....29 D7
Dolphin Cl SE28 ....3 D4
Dolphin Dr ME8 ....63 E5
Dombey Cl Higham ME3 .....32 C3
Rochester ME1 ....47 C3
Domonic Dr SE9 ....23 B8
Donaldson Rd SE18 ....6 A6
Doncaster Cl 7 ME15 ......107 F6
Donet Cl ME8 ....63 C5
Dongola Rd ME2 ....47 B8
Donkey Field TN11 ....115 E1
Donkey La DA4 ....55 B8
Donnington Cl 1 DA16 ......10 B1
Donnington Rd TN13 ....83 D7
Doon Brae TN4 ....133 A2
Dorado Gdns BR6 ....52 D2
Doran Gr SE18 ....6 E7
Dorchester TN1 ....149 B6
Dorchester Ave DA5 ....24 E8
Dorchester Cl
Cliffe Woods ME3 ....33 B7
Dartford DA1 ....26 F7
St Paul's Cray BR5 ....38 B6
Dorchester Ct DA12 ....30 D5

Dorcis Ave DA7 .....7 E5
Doria Dr DA12 .....30 F5
Doric Ave TN4 .....132 F1
Doric Cl TN4 .....132 F1
Dorin Ct TN2 .....149 C3
Doris Ave DA8 .....8 C6
Dorking Rd TN1 .....149 C6
Dormers Dr DA13 .....44 B2
Dornberg Cl SE3 .....5 A7
Dornberg Rd SE3 .....5 A7
Dornden Dr TN3 .....148 A4
Dorden Gdns ME5 .....62 B2
Dorne Cotts TN27 .....127 E6
Dorney Rise BR5 .....37 F5
Dorothy Ave TN17 .....169 C4
Dorothy Evans Cl DA7 .....8 B3
Dorrit Way Chislehurst BR7 .....23 C2
  Rochester ME1 .....47 D2
Dorset Ave DA16 .....6 F3
Dorset Cotts TN7 .....160 B4
Dorset Cres DA12 .....30 E4
Dorset Rd Chislehurst SE9 .....22 E6
  Royal Tunbridge Wells TN2 .....149 D2
Dorset Road Inf Sch SE9 .....22 E6
Dorset Sq ME8 .....49 D1
Dorset St TN13 .....84 C2
Dorset Way ME15 .....107 C8
Dorton Coll TN15 .....84 F5
Dorton Dr TN15 .....84 F5
Dorton House
  (Royal London Society
  Sch for the Blind) TN15 .....84 F5
Dorville Rd SE13 .....5 A2
Dothill Rd SE18 .....6 C7
Dotterel Cl ME5 .....62 D2
Doubleton La TN11 .....131 A5
Douglas Siddons Ct RM17 .....12 C8
Douglas Almshouses
  ME17 .....111 D5
Douglas Bldgs TN12 .....139 E5
Douglas Rd Bexley DA16 .....7 B6
  Lenham ME12 .....111 D5
  Maidstone ME16 .....91 E3
  Newham E16 .....1 A8
  Tonbridge TN9 .....133 A8
Douro Stables TN4 .....149 A4
Doust Way ME1 .....47 D5
Dove App E6 .....1 E8
Dove Cl ME5 .....62 B6
Dove Rd TN10 .....117 C6
Dovedale Cl DA16 .....7 A5
Dovedale Rd DA2 .....27 C7
Doveney Cl BR5 .....38 D6
Dover Ho
  Maidstone ME15 .....107 E8
  Rochester ME2 .....33 C1
Dover Patrol SE3 .....5 C5
Dover Rd Northfleet DA11 .....29 D8
  Woolwich DA16 .....6 C5
Dover Rd E DA11 .....29 F7
Dover Road Prim Sch DA11
  .....29 E7
Dover St ME15 .....91 C2
Doves Cl BR2 .....36 E2
Dowding Way TN2 .....133 E1
Dowling Wlk DA11 .....29 E5
Dower House Cres TN4 .....132 E3
Dowgate Cl TN9 .....133 D7
Dowlerville Rd BR6 .....51 F4
Dowling Cl ME6 .....74 E7
Dowling Ho DA17 .....3 F3
Down Ave TN3 .....166 A4
Down House* BR6 .....66 A7
Down La TN3 .....163 B1
Down's Ct TN27 .....141 E5
Downage The DA11 .....30 A6
Downash Ct TN5 .....177 A3
Downash Ho TN5 .....177 A3
Downbank Ave DA7 .....8 D5
Downderry Way ME20 .....75 B1
Downe Ave TN14 .....66 D8
Downe Cl ME9 SE7 .....7 C7
Downe Prim Sch BR6 .....66 A8
Downe Rd
  Cudham BR6,TN14 .....66 C5
  Farthing Street BR2 .....50 E2
Downend SE18 .....2 B2
Downer Ct ME1 .....61 E8
Downham Way BR1 .....22 A4
Downings E6 .....2 A7
Downlands DA17 .....110 F6
Downleys Cl SE9 .....22 E6
Downman Rd SE9 .....5 E4
Downs Ave Chislehurst BR7 .....22 F1
  Dartford DA1 .....27 A8
Downs Cl ME14 .....92 B8
Downs Rd Istead Rise DA13 .....29 D3
  Maidstone ME14 .....92 B8
  Yalding ME18 .....105 A1
Downs The ME5 .....61 D1
Downs Valley DA3 .....42 E5
Downs View Durham ME1 .....60 F1
  West Malling ME19 .....89 B8
Downs View Cl ME6 .....52 C1
Downs View Rd ME14 .....92 B8
Downs Wood DA3 .....42 E5
Downside 47 A7
Downsview Chatham ME5 .....62 C8
  Trottiscliffe ME19 .....73 A5
Downsview Cl BR8 .....39 F6
Downsview Prim Sch ME4 .....48 A6
Downsview Rd TN13 .....83 F2
Downsway BR6 .....51 E5
Doyle Cl DA8 .....8 E6
Doyle Way ME18 .....113 C5
Drage Rd TN12 .....119 E6
Drake Cres SE28 .....3 C7

Drake Ct BR5 .....38 B3
Drake Hall E16 .....1 B5
Drake's Ave ME2 .....46 F8
Draper Cl DA17 .....3 F2
Draper Ct BR1 .....36 E5
Draper St TN4 .....132 F1
Drawbridge Cl ME15 .....107 E8
Drawell Cl SE18 .....2 E1
Dray Corner Rd TN27 .....140 F7
Dray Ct TN11 .....118 E8
Drays Cotts DA4 .....41 B5
Drayton Ave BR6 .....37 B1
Drayton Cl ME23 .....17 E4
Drayton Rd TN9 .....133 C8
Drew Prim Sch E16 .....1 E5
Drew Rd E16 .....1 E5
Drewery Dr ME8 .....63 C5
Driffield Gdns TN9 .....132 F7
Drift The BR2 .....50 D7
Drive The Chislehurst BR7 .....37 E8
  Erith DA8 .....8 B8
  Gravesend DA12 .....30 E4
  New Barn DA3 .....43 B6
  Orpington BR6 .....51 F8
  Royal Tunbridge Wells TN2 .....149 B1
  Sevenoaks TN13 .....84 B3
  Sidcup DA14 .....24 B4
  Sidcup DA5 .....24 D8
  St Paul's Cray BR7 .....37 F6
  Tonbridge TN9 .....133 B7
Drove Way The DA13 .....29 E1
Drudgeon Way DA2 .....28 B5
Drummond Cl DA8 .....8 F6
Drury Rd TN8 .....173 B1
Dry Bank Ct TN10 .....117 C4
Dry Bank Rd TN10 .....117 C4
Dry End Rd ME20 .....75 C5
Dry Hill Park Cres TN10 .....117 C3
Dry Hill Park Rd TN10 .....117 B3
Dry Hill Rd TN9 .....117 B3
Dryden Ho BR2 .....36 D4
Dryden Pl RM18 .....13 B6
Dryden Rd DA16 .....6 F6
Dryden Way BR6 .....38 A1
Dryhill La TN14 .....83 B3
Dryhill Rd DA17 .....7 F8
Dryland Ave BR6 .....51 F6
Dryland Rd
  Borough Green TN15 .....86 F6
  Snodland ME6 .....74 F8
Duchess Cl ME7 .....48 C6
Duchess Of Kent Dr ME5 .....62 B4
Duchess' Wlk TN15 .....84 E2
Ducie Ho SE7 .....5 C8
Ducketts Rd DA1 .....8 F2
Duddington Cl SE9 .....22 D4
Dudley Ho DA11 .....12 A8
Dudley Lodge TN2 .....149 C4
Dudley Rd TN1 .....149 A4
Dudsbury Rd DA1 .....9 B2
Dukes Meadow TN11 .....114 F2
Dukes Meadow Dr ME7 .....62 F6
Dukes Orch DA5 .....25 C7
Dukes Rd TN1 .....149 C5
Dukes Wlk ME15 .....92 A4
Dulverton Prim Sch SE9 .....23 D6
Dulverton Rd SE9 .....23 D6
Dumbreck Rd SE9 .....6 A4
Dunbar Ct BR2 .....36 A6
Dunblane Rd SE9 .....5 E5
Duncan Cl SE9 .....5 E4
Duncan Rd ME7 .....48 C5
Duncans Cotts TN16 .....81 D1
Duncroft SE18 .....6 E7
Dundale Rd TN12,TN3 .....151 A3
Dundonald Cl E6 .....1 E7
Dunedin Ho
  Maidstone ME15 .....107 E8
  Tilbury RM18 .....13 B5
Dunera Dr ME14 .....92 A7
Dunk's Green Rd TN11 .....102 A5
Dunkeld Ho ME15 .....107 E7
Dunkery Rd SE9 .....22 E5
Dunkin Rd DA1 .....10 A3
Dunkirk Cl DA12 .....30 C3
Dunkirk Dr ME5 .....61 C6
Dunkley Villas TN15 .....72 F1
Dunlop Ct TN18 .....179 A2
Dunlop Rd RM18 .....12 F6
Dunn Street Rd ME7 .....78 A8
Dunning's La ME1 .....47 C4
Dunnings The ME1 .....91 A2
Dunnock Rd E6 .....1 E7
Dunnose Ct RM19 .....10 B8
Dunoon Cotts BR6 .....66 A5
Dunorlan Farm Cotts
  TN2 .....149 E4
Dunstable Ct SE3 .....5 A7
Dunstall Welling Est DA16 .....7 B5
Dunstan Glade BR5 .....37 D3
Dunstan Gr TN4 .....149 B6
Dunstan Rd TN4 .....149 B6
Dunster Terr DA2 .....10 B1
Dunster Terr ME15 .....107 E8
Dunton Green
  Cty Prim Sch TN13 .....83 E7
Dunton Green Sta TN14 .....83 E7
Dunvegan Rd SE9 .....5 F3
Dunwich Rd DA7 .....7 F6
Dupree Rd SE7 .....1 B1
Durant Rd BR8 .....26 A2
Durban House ME12 .....107 E5
Durban Rd TN1 .....149 A4
Durham Rd Bromley BR2 .....36 A5
  Gillingham ME8 .....63 C7

Durham Rd continued
  Sidcup DA14 .....24 B3
Durham Rise SE18 .....2 D1
Duriun Way DA8 .....9 B7
Durley Gdns BR6 .....52 B7
Durlings Orch TN15 .....86 D6
Durndale La
  Northfleet DA11 .....29 E4
  Northfleet DA11 .....29 F5
Durrant Way
  Orpington BR6 .....51 D5
  Swanscombe DA10 .....28 E8
Durrell Gdns ME15 .....48 C1
Dursley Cl SE3 .....5 C5
Dursley Gdns SE3 .....5 C6
Dursley Rd SE3 .....5 C5
Duval Dr ME1 .....61 E8
Duvard's Pl ME9 .....65 F1
Dux Court Rd ME23 .....17 D2
Dux Hill TN15 .....101 F8
Dux La TN15 .....86 F1
Duxberry Cl BR2 .....36 E4
Duxford Ho SE2 .....3 D4
Dyke Dr BR5 .....38 C2
Dykewood Cl DA5 .....25 C5
Dylan Rd DA17 .....4 A3
Dymchurch Cl BR6 .....51 E6
Dyneley Rd SE12 .....22 C5
Dynes Rd TN15 .....69 E2
Dynevor Rd TN4 .....149 C2

E

Eagle Cl ME20 .....75 A2
Eagle Heights
  Bird of Prey Ctr* DA4 .....54 E8
Eagle House ME7 .....11 F8
Eagle Way DA11 .....12 A2
Eagles Rd DA9 .....11 B2
Eaglesfield Rd SE18 .....6 B6
Eaglesfield Sch SE18 .....6 A6
Eaglestone Cl TN15 .....87 A8
Ealdham Prim Sch SE9 .....5 C3
Ealdham Sq SE9 .....5 C3
Ealing Cl ME5 .....62 A1
Eardemont Cl DA1 .....8 F3
Eardley Point SE18 .....2 B2
Eardley Rd Erith DA17 .....4 A1
  Sevenoaks TN13 .....84 B3
Earl Cl ME5 .....62 B4
Earl Rd DA11 .....29 E6
Earl Rise SE18 .....2 D2
Earl St ME14 .....91 F4
Earl's Rd TN4 .....148 F4
Earlshall Rd SE9 .....6 A3
Eason Villas TN12 .....138 D6
East Beckton District Ctr
  E16 .....1 F8
East Borough Prim Sch
  ME14 .....92 B5
East Cliff Rd TN4 .....149 A4
East Crescent Rd DA12 .....13 C1
East Cross TN30 .....183 B7
East Ct ME5 .....62 A1
East Dr BR5 .....38 B3
East End Rd ME4,ME7 .....48 D8
East Farleigh Prim Sch
  .....106 B6
East Farleigh Sta ME16 .....106 B8
East Hall Hill ME17 .....123 F7
East Hall Rd BR5 .....38 F2
East Ham Ind Est E6 .....1 F8
East Ham Manor Way E6 .....2 A7
East Hill Dartford DA1 .....26 F8
  Sutton at Hone DA4 .....41 D7
  Tenterden TN30 .....183 B8
East Hill Dr DA1 .....26 F8
East Hill Rd TN15 .....70 B7
East Ho TN1 .....9 F4
East Holme SE4 .....54 D8
East Kent Ave DA11 .....12 C1
East La DA4 .....41 D7
East Malling Research Sta
  (Horticultural) ME19 .....90 A6
East Malling Sta ME19 .....90 A6
East Mascalls SE7 .....5 D8
East Milton Rd DA12 .....30 D6
East Park Rd ME20 .....91 A8
East Peckham Prim Sch
  TN12 .....119 F6
East Rd Bexley DA16 .....7 B5
  Chatham ME4 .....48 A7
  Gillingham ME7 .....48 C6
East Rochester Way
  Coldblow DA5 .....25 D8
  Sidcup DA5,DA15 .....7 C1
East Row ME1 .....47 C5
East St Addington ME19 .....73 D3
  Bexley DA7 .....8 A3
  Bromley BR1 .....36 A7
  Chatham ME4 .....48 A3
  Gillingham ME7 .....48 D6
  Grays RM20 .....11 E8
  Harrietsham ME17,TN27 .....125 C4
  Hunton ME15 .....121 F7
  Snodland ME6 .....75 B8
  Tonbridge TN9 .....117 C2
East Street W TN19 .....73 D3
East Sutton Park
  (HM Young Offender Inst
  & Prison) ME17 .....125 C4
East Sutton Rd
  Hearnden Green ME17,TN27 .....125 C4
  Sutton Valence ME17 .....125 A2
East Terr Gravesend DA12 .....13 C1
  Sidcup DA15 .....23 E7

East Thamesmead Bsns Pk
  DA18 .....3 F4
East Thurrock Rd RM17 .....12 C8
East Weald Dr TN30 .....173 B1
East Wickham Inf Sch DA16 .....6 F6
East Wickham Jun Sch
  .....7 A6
East Woodside DA5 .....24 E7
Eastbrook Rd SE3 .....5 B6
Eastbury Rd Newham E6 .....2 A8
  Orpington BR5 .....37 D3
Eastcombe Ave SE7 .....5 B8
Eastcote BR6 .....37 F1
Eastcote Prim Sch DA16 .....6 D4
Eastcott Cl ME15 .....48 C1
Eastcourt Gn ME8 .....49 B4
Eastcourt La
  Gillingham ME8 .....49 B3
  Gillingham,Lower
  Twydall ME7,ME8 .....49 C4
Easterfields ME19 .....90 C5
Eastern Ave RM20 .....10 F8
Eastern Rd ME7 .....48 F6
Eastern Way Erith SE28 .....3 D5
  Grays RM17 .....12 A8
Eastfield Gdns TN10 .....117 E5
Eastfield House ME16 .....91 B2
Eastfield Terr DA1 .....9 F4
Eastgate ME1 .....47 C5
Eastgate Cl SE28 .....3 D7
Eastgate Cl ME1 .....47 C5
Eastgate Rd TN30 .....183 C8
Eastgate Terr ME1 .....47 C5
Eastland Ct BR1 .....36 C7
Eastlands TN4 .....162 E8
Eastlands Rd TN4 .....148 E1
Eastleigh Rd DA7 .....8 C4
Eastling Cl ME8 .....49 D3
Eastling House BR5 .....38 D1
Eastmead Cl BR1 .....36 E7
Eastmoor Pl SE7 .....1 D3
Eastmoor St SE7 .....1 D3
Eastnor Rd SE9 .....23 C7
Eastry Cl ME16 .....91 C7
Eastry Rd DA8 .....8 A7
Eastview Ave SE18 .....6 E7
Eastville Rd BR2 .....36 A2
Eastwell TN30 .....183 A7
Eastwell Barn Mews
  TN30 .....183 A8
Eastwell Cl Maidstone ME14 .....92 C5
  Paddock Wood TN12 .....135 E6
Eastwood Meadows TN30 .....183 A8
Eaton Ct BR7 .....23 C2
Eaton Rd DA14 .....24 D6
Eaton Sq DA3 .....42 D6
Ebbsfleet Ind Est DA11 .....12 B2
Ebbsfleet Wlk DA11 .....12 B1
Ebdon Way SE3 .....5 B4
Ebony Wlk ME16 .....91 B5
Ebury Cl BR2 .....50 E7
Eccles Bsns Ctr ME20 .....75 F6
Eccleston Cl BR6 .....37 D1
Eccleston Rd ME15 .....91 F8
Echo Cl ME15 .....107 F6
Echo Ct DA12 .....30 C6
Eclipse Rd E13 .....1 B8
Edam Ct DA14 .....24 A5
Eddington Cl ME15 .....107 B6
Eden Ave ME5 .....62 A7
Eden Cl DA5 .....25 D4
Eden Ct
  Hawkhurst TN18 .....178 F2
  Orpington BR5 .....38 D1
Eden Farm La ME17 .....89 D8
Eden High School ME23 .....17 E4
  Royal Tunbridge Wells TN1 .....149 A2
Eden Valley Sch TN8 .....112 C2
Eden Villas TN8 .....128 D7
Edenbridge & District
  War Mem Hospl TN8 .....128 D7
Edenbridge Ct BR5 .....38 D5
Edenbridge
  Golf & Country Club TN8 .....112 A2
Edenbridge
  Information Ctr* TN8 .....112 C2
Edenbridge Prim Sch
  TN8 .....112 D1
Edenbridge Rd TN7 .....145 E1
Edenbridge Sta TN8 .....112 C3
Edenbridge Trad Ctr
  TN8 .....112 D2
Edendale Rd DA7 .....8 D5
Edenhurst TN13 .....84 A2
Edgar Cl BR8 .....39 F6
Edgar Rd ME19 .....69 E2
Edge Hill SE18 .....6 B8
Edge Hill Ct DA14 .....23 F4
Edgeborough Way BR1 .....36 D8
Edgebury Orpington BR7 .....23 B4
Edgebury Prim Sch BR7 .....23 C5
Edgebury Wlk BR7 .....23 C5
Edgefield Cl DA1 .....27 B7
Edgehill Gdns DA13 .....43 F8
Edgehill Rd BR7 .....23 C4
Edgeler Ct ME6 .....74 F7
Eger Pl ME5 .....92 A4
Edgewood Dr BR6 .....52 A5
Edgeworth Rd SE9 .....5 D3
Edgington Way DA14 .....24 D1
Edinburgh Ct DA8 .....9 B7
Edinburgh Mews RM18 .....13 B5

Edinburgh Rd
  Chatham ME4 .....48 C2
  Gillingham ME7 .....48 D5
  Grain ME3 .....21 B5
Edinburgh Sq ME15 .....107 C7
Edington Rd SE2 .....3 B3
Edisbury House ME8 .....63 D5
Edison Gr SE18 .....6 F7
Edison Rd Bexley DA16 .....6 F6
  Bromley BR2 .....36 A7
Edith Cl BR1 .....36 D6
Edith Pond Ct SE9 .....23 B6
Edith Rd BR6 .....52 C3
Ediva Rd DA13 .....44 A4
Edmund Cl Maidstone ME16 .....91 A3
  Meopham Sta DA13 .....44 A4
Edmund Hurst Dr E6 .....2 B8
Edmund Rd Bexley DA16 .....7 A4
  Orpington BR5 .....38 C3
Edmunds Ave BR5 .....38 D6
Edna Rd ME14 .....91 F8
Edward Cl Chatham ME5 .....48 C1
  Newham E16 .....1 A8
Edward Harvey Ct SE3 .....3 F1
Edward Rd Bromley BR1 .....22 C1
  Chislehurst BR7 .....23 B3
Edward St Chatham ME4 .....48 A3
  Rochester ME2 .....47 B7
  Royal Tunbridge Wells,
  Modest Corner TN4 .....148 F8
  Royal Tunbridge Wells,
  Rustall TN4 .....148 C3
Edward Tyler Rd SE12 .....22 C6
Edward Wlk ME19 .....89 F8
Edwards Rd DA17 .....4 A2
Edwards Ct SA4 .....54 E7
Edwards Gdns BR8 .....39 D5
Edwards Rd DA17 .....4 A2
Edwin Arnold Ct DA15 .....23 F4
Edwin Cl DA7 .....7 F8
Edwin Petty Pl DA2 .....27 C8
Edwin Rd Dartford DA2 .....26 C5
  Gillingham ME8 .....63 C8
Edwin St Gravesend DA12 .....30 B8
  Newham E16 .....1 A8
Edwina Pl ME9 .....65 C7
Egdean Wlk TN13 .....84 C4
Egerton Ave BR8 .....39 F8
Egerton CE Prim Sch
  TN27 .....127 F3
Egerton Cl DA1 .....26 B7
Egerton House Rd TN27 .....127 E4
Egerton Rd ME14 .....92 F1
Eggie La TN11,TN14 .....115 E7
Egham Rd E13 .....1 B8
Eglantine La DA4 .....41 B3
Eglinton Hill SE18 .....6 B7
Eglinton Inf Sch SE18 .....6 A8
Eglinton Jun Mix Sch SE18 .....6 A8
Eglinton Rd
  Swanscombe DA10 .....11 F1
  Woolwich SE18 .....6 A8
Egremont Rd ME15 .....92 F2
Egret Cl ME4 .....34 B2
Eileen Ct BR7 .....23 A3
Eisenhower Dr E6 .....1 E8
Elaine Ave ME2 .....46 C7
Elaine Prim Sch ME2 .....46 E6
Elbourne Trad Est DA17 .....4 B3
Elder Cl
  Hoo St Werburgh ME3 .....34 E3
  Kingswood ME17 .....109 D2
  Sidcup DA15 .....23 F7
Elder Ct SE18 .....63 B6
Elderslie Rd SE9 .....6 A1
Eldon St ME4 .....48 A4
Eldon Way TN12 .....135 F7
Eldred Dr BR5 .....52 D8
Eleanor Wlk SE18 .....1 F2
Elenmore Ct ME1 .....36 E5
Elford Cl SE3 .....5 C3
Elford Rd ME3 .....16 B5
Elgal Ct BR5 .....51 B5
Elgar Cl TN10 .....117 E6
Elgar Gdns RM18 .....13 B6
Elgin Gdns ME2 .....46 D5
Elham Cl Bromley BR1 .....22 D1
  Gillingham ME8 .....49 B3
Elibank Rd SE9 .....6 A3
Eling Ct ME15 .....107 A8
Eliot Rd DA1 .....10 B2
Elizabeth Cl RM18 .....13 B5
Elizabeth Ct Chatham ME5 .....62 A3
  Erith DA8 .....8 D7
  Gravesend DA11 .....13 A1
Elizabeth Garlick Ct
  ME14 .....149 B4

Elizabeth Garrett
  Anderson Ho DA14 .....4 A3
Elizabeth House ME14 .....92 A6
Elizabeth Huggins Cotts
  DA11 .....30 B6
Elizabeth Pl DA14 .....40 E3
Elizabeth Smith's Ct ME19 .....89 F7
Elizabeth Terr SE9 .....10 C2
Elizabeth Terr SE9 .....6 A3
Elizabeth Way BR5 .....38 C4
Ellen Cl BR1 .....36 D6
Ellen Wilkinson Prim Sch
  E6 .....1 E8
Ellen's Pl ME15 .....65 C6
Ellenborough Rd DA14 .....24 E3

Ellenswood Cl ME15 . . . . .93 A1
Ellerman Rd RM18 . . . . .12 F5
Ellerslie DA12 . . . . .30 D8
Ellesmere Ct SE12 . . . . .22 A7
Ellingham Leas ME15 . . . . . .107 C7
Elliott Rd ME2 . . . . .36 D5
Elliott St DA12 . . . . .30 D8
Elliotts La TN16 . . . . .23 C3
Ellis Cl Sidcup SE9 . . . . .23 C6
  Swanley BR8 . . . . .39 D5
Ellis Ct DA1 . . . . .27 B7
Ellis Ho 7 ME4 . . . . .92 B4
Ellis Way DA1 . . . . .26 F6
Elliscombe Mount SE7 . . . . .5 C8
Elliscombe Rd SE7 . . . . .5 C8
Ellison Rd DA15 . . . . .23 D7
Elliston Ho 8 SE18 . . . . .2 A2
Elm Ave Chatham ME4 . . . . .47 F3
  Chattenden ME3 . . . . .34 A4
Elm Cl Dartford DA1 . . . . .26 C7
  Egerton TN27 . . . . .127 F3
  Higham ME3 . . . . .32 A2
Elm Cotts BR8 . . . . .40 B8
Elm Court Ind Est ME7 . . . . . . .62 E3
Elm Cres ME19 . . . . .89 F8
Elm Dr BR8 . . . . .39 D5
Elm Gr Erith DA8 . . . . .8 D7
  Maidstone ME15 . . . . .92 B3
  Orpington BR6 . . . . .37 F1
  Tonbridge TN11 . . . . .116 F5
Elm La TN10 . . . . .117 C3
Elm Par DA14 . . . . .24 A4
Elm Rd Dartford DA1 . . . . .26 D7
  Erith DA8 . . . . .9 A6
  Gillingham ME7 . . . . .48 E6
  Gravesend DA12 . . . . .30 C5
  Grays RM17 . . . . .12 C8
  Hoo St Werburgh ME3 . . . . .34 E5
  Orpington BR6 . . . . .52 A3
  Royal Tunbridge Wells TN4 . . .132 F1
  Sidcup DA14 . . . . .24 A4
  Stone DA9 . . . . .10 E1
  Westerham TN16 . . . . .81 E2
Elm Terr 8 Eltham SE9 . . . . .6 A1
  West Thurrock RM20 . . . . .11 B8
Elm Tree Cotts ME3 . . . . .19 A3
Elm Tree Ct 15 SE8 . . . . .5 C8
Elm Tree Dr ME1 . . . . .47 A2
Elm Wlk Aylesford ME20 . . . . . .75 E1
  Orpington BR6 . . . . .50 F7
Elmbank Dr BR1 . . . . .36 D7
Elmbourne Dr DA17 . . . . .4 B2
Elmbrook Gdns SE9 . . . . .5 E3
Elmcroft Ave DA15 . . . . .7 A1
Elmcroft Rd BR6 . . . . .38 A2
Elmdene Rd SE18 . . . . .2 B1
Elmfield Gillingham ME8 . . . . . .49 A3
  Tenterden TN30 . . . . .183 B8
Elmfield Cl Gravesend DA11 . . . .30 B7
  Sevenoaks Weald TN14 . . . . . . .99 B2
Elmfield Ct Bexley DA16 . . . . . . .7 B6
  Coxheath ME17 . . . . .106 C3
  Tenterden TN30 . . . . .183 B8
Elmfield Pk BR1 . . . . .36 A6
Elmfield Rd BR1 . . . . .36 A6
Elmhurst Erith DA17 . . . . .7 F8
  Swanscombe DA9 . . . . .11 B1
Elmhurst Ave TN2 . . . . .150 D8
Elmhurst Gdns ME4 . . . . .47 E3
Elmhurst Rd SE9 . . . . .22 E5
Elmington Cl DA5 . . . . .8 B1
Elmlee Cl BR7 . . . . .22 F2
Elmley Cl 15 E6 . . . . .1 E8
Elmley St SE18 . . . . .2 C2
Elmshurst Gdns TN10 . . . . . . .117 C7
Elmslie Ct SE9 . . . . .6 A1
Elmstead Ave BR7 . . . . .22 F3
Elmstead Cl TN13 . . . . .83 E5
Elmstead Glade BR7 . . . . .22 F2
Elmstead La BR7 . . . . .22 F1
Elmstead Rd DA8 . . . . .8 F6
Elmstead Woods Sta BR7 . . . . .22 E2
Elmsted Cres DA16 . . . . .7 C8
Elmstone Cl ME16 . . . . .91 B2
Elmstone Hole Rd ME17 . . . . .126 D8
Elmstone La ME16 . . . . .91 B2
Elmstone Rd ME8 . . . . .63 D7
Elmstone Terr 11 BR5 . . . . .38 C5
Elmtree Cotts TN14 . . . . .67 D4
Elmwood Dr DA5 . . . . .24 E8
Elmwood Rd ME3 . . . . .33 F6
Elphick's Pl TN2 . . . . .163 B8
Elrick Cl DA8 . . . . .8 E8
Elsa Rd DA16 . . . . .7 C5
Elsinore Ho 6 SE18 . . . . .1 F3
Elstow Cl Eltham SE9 . . . . .5 F2
  Eltham SE9 . . . . .6 A2
Elstree Gdns DA17 . . . . .3 E2
Elswyn Ho 10 DA14 . . . . .24 A5
Eltham CE Prim Sch SE9 . . . . . .5 F2
Eltham Coll SE9 . . . . .22 D6
Eltham Green Rd SE9 . . . . .5 C3
Eltham Green Sch SE9 . . . . .5 D1
Eltham High St SE9 . . . . .5 E1
Eltham Hill SE9 . . . . .5 E2
Eltham Hill Sch SE9 . . . . .5 E1
Eltham Palace* SE9 . . . . .5 E1
Eltham Palace Rd SE9 . . . . .5 D1
Eltham Park Gdns SE9 . . . . .6 A3
Eltham Rd SE12,SE9 . . . . .5 B2
Eltham Sta SE9 . . . . .5 F2
Elvington Cl ME16 . . . . .91 D5
Elwick Ct DA1 . . . . .9 E1
Elwill Way DA13 . . . . .43 F8

Elwyn Gdns SE12 . . . . .22 A8
Ely Cl Erith DA8 . . . . .8 F5
  Gillingham ME8 . . . . .49 E2
Ely Ct TN1 . . . . .149 B4
Ely Gdns TN10 . . . . .117 D4
Elysian Ave BR5 . . . . .37 F3
Embassey Ct DA14 . . . . .24 B5
Embassy Ct ME7 . . . . .48 F1
Embassy Gdns DA16 . . . . .7 B4
Ember Cl BR5 . . . . .37 C2
Emblin Ct 12 DA14 . . . . .24 A4
Emerald Cl Chatham ME1 . . . . . .61 D7
  Newham E16 . . . . .1 F7
Emersons Ave BR8 . . . . .25 F1
Emerton Cl DA6 . . . . .7 E3
Emery Rd DA8 . . . . .8 C7
Emily Jackson Cl TN13 . . . . . . .84 B3
Emily Jackson Ho TN13 . . . . . . .84 B3
Emily Rd ME5 . . . . .62 B6
Emmanuel Ho 2 SE18 . . . . .2 D1
Emmett Hill La ME18 . . . . .120 F5
Emmetts Garden* TN14 . . . . . . .97 D5
Empress Dr BR7 . . . . .23 B2
Empress Rd DA12 . . . . .30 D8
Emsworth Gr ME14 . . . . .92 D6
Enderfield Ct BR7 . . . . .37 A8
Engineer Cl SE18 . . . . .6 A8
Englefield Cl BR5 . . . . .37 F5
Englefield Cres
  Cliffe Woods ME3 . . . . .33 B7
  Orpington BR5 . . . . .38 A5
Englefield Path BR5 . . . . .38 A5
English Martyrs'
  RC Prim Sch ME2 . . . . .47 B8
Ennerdale Rd DA7 . . . . .8 A6
Enright Rd SE18 . . . . .6 C8
Ensfield Rd Leigh TN11 . . . . . .115 C1
  Tonbridge TN11 . . . . .132 A6
Ensign House RM17 . . . . .11 F8
Enslin Rd SE9 . . . . .23 A8
Enterprise Bsns Est ME2 . . . . . .47 E7
Enterprise Cl ME2 . . . . .47 D8
Enterprise Ctr The ME5 . . . . . . .77 C8
Enterprise Rd ME15 . . . . .92 A1
Enterprise Way TN8 . . . . .112 C3
Epaul La ME1 . . . . .47 C6
Epoe Cl 2 ME2 . . . . .47 B8
Epsom Cl Bexley DA7 . . . . .8 B4
  Maidstone ME15 . . . . .107 F6
  New Town ME19 . . . . .89 B8
Epsom Rd SE28 . . . . .3 B5
Erica Ct BR8 . . . . .39 E5
Eridge Green Cl BR5 . . . . .38 C1
Eridge Rd TN2,TN4 . . . . .148 E1
Eridge Sta TN3 . . . . .161 E2
Erindale SE18 . . . . .6 D8
Erindale Terr SE18 . . . . .6 D8
Erith Cl ME14 . . . . .92 A8
Erith High St DA8 . . . . .4 E1
Erith Rd Bexley DA7 . . . . .8 B4
  Erith DA8,DA17 . . . . .4 B1
Erith Sch DA8 . . . . .8 E7
Erith Small Bsns Ctr DA8 . . . . . .8 F8
Erith Sta DA8 . . . . .4 E1
Ermington Rd SE9 . . . . .23 C6
Ernest Rd ME16 . . . . .91 B5
Ernest Rd ME4 . . . . .48 A3
Erskine Ho 7 SE7 . . . . .5 B8
Erskine Park Rd TN4 . . . . .148 C4
Erskine Rd DA13 . . . . .73 B8
Erwood Rd SE7 . . . . .1 E1
Escott Gdns SE9 . . . . .22 E4
Escreet Gr SE18 . . . . .2 A2
Eshcol Rd ME3 . . . . .35 C6
Esher Cl DA5 . . . . .24 E7
Eskdale Cl DA2 . . . . .27 C7
Eskdale Rd DA7 . . . . .8 A6
Essenden Rd DA17 . . . . .4 A1
Essex Cl TN2 . . . . .162 F8
Essex Rd 1 Dartford DA1 . . . . . . .9 D1
  Gravesend DA11 . . . . .30 A7
  Halling ME2 . . . . .60 A6
  Longfield DA3 . . . . .42 D7
  Maidstone ME15 . . . . .107 E6
  West Thurrock RM20 . . . . .11 A8
Essex St SE18 . . . . .2 C2
Estelle Ct ME1 . . . . .61 D7
Estridge Way TN10 . . . . .117 F5
Estuary Cotts RM18 . . . . .14 D7
Etfield Gr DA14 . . . . .24 B3
Ethel Brooks Ho SE18 . . . . .6 B8
Ethel Rd E16 . . . . .1 B7
Ethel Terr BR6 . . . . .52 C2
Ethel-Maud Ct ME7 . . . . .48 D7
Ethelbert Cl BR1 . . . . .36 A6
Ethelbert Rd Bromley BR1 . . . . .36 A6
  Erith DA8 . . . . .8 C7
  Rochester ME1 . . . . .47 C4
  St Paul's Cray BR5 . . . . .38 D6
Ethelbert Rd DA15 . . . . .24 B5
Etherington Hill TN3 . . . . .148 C8
Ethnam La TN18 . . . . .186 E4
Ethronvi Rd DA7 . . . . .7 E4
Eton Cl ME5 . . . . .61 F4
Eton Ct TN13 . . . . .84 B4
Eton Rd BR6 . . . . .52 B6
Eton Way DA1 . . . . .9 C3
Eugenie Mews BR7 . . . . .37 B8
Europa Trad Est DA8 . . . . .4 D1
Europe Rd SE18 . . . . .1 F3
Euroway ME20 . . . . .90 E8
Eustace Pl 2 SE18 . . . . .1 F2
Eva Rd ME7 . . . . .48 D3
Evans Cl SE9 . . . . .11 A2
Evans Ct SE9 . . . . .22 E6

Evelyn Cl ME2 . . . . .47 C8
Evelyn Denington Rd E6 . . . . .1 F8
Evelyn Ho 5 ME2 . . . . .47 C8
Evelyn Rd Maidstone ME16 . . . .91 E3
  Newham E16 . . . . .1 B5
  Otford TN14 . . . . .69 B2
Evenden House TN17 . . . . .169 D5
Evenden Rd DA13 . . . . .44 A2
Evenlode Ho 5 SE2 . . . . .3 C4
Everard Ave BR2 . . . . .36 A1
Everest Cl 11 DA11 . . . . .29 E5
Everest Ct SE9 . . . . .22 E6
Everest Dr ME3 . . . . .34 E4
Everest La ME2 . . . . .33 B1
Everest Mews ME3 . . . . .34 E4
Everest Pl BR8 . . . . .39 D5
Everest Rd SE9 . . . . .23 A8
Everett Wlk DA17 . . . . .3 F1
Everglade Cl DA3 . . . . .42 F5
Everglades The ME7 . . . . .62 F6
Evergreen Cl
  Gillingham ME7 . . . . .63 A5
  Higham ME3 . . . . .32 B3
  Leybourne ME19 . . . . .74 E2
Eversfield Cl SE12 . . . . .22 B6
Eversley Ave DA7,DA8 . . . . .8 E5
Eversley Cl ME16 . . . . .91 C6
Eversley Cross DA7 . . . . .8 E5
Eversley Rd SE7 . . . . .5 B8
Everard Rd DA12 . . . . .30 D6
Evry Rd DA14 . . . . .24 C2
Ewart Rd ME4 . . . . .47 E1
Ewehurst La TN3 . . . . .147 F6
Ewell Ave ME19 . . . . .89 A8
Ewell La ME15 . . . . .105 D5
Ewins Cl TN12 . . . . .136 A6
Exedown Rd TN15 . . . . .71 C4
Exeter Cl Newham E6 . . . . .1 F7
  Tonbridge TN10 . . . . .117 D4
Exeter Rd Bexley DA16 . . . . .6 F5
  Gravesend DA12 . . . . .30 D5
  Newham E16 . . . . .1 A8
Exeter Wlk ME1 . . . . .61 C7
Exford Gdns SE12 . . . . .22 B7
Exford Rd SE12 . . . . .22 B7
Exmouth Rd Bexley DA16 . . . . . . .7 C7
  Bromley BR2 . . . . .36 B6
  Gillingham ME7 . . . . .48 C7
  Grays RM17 . . . . .12 B8
Exton Cl ME5 . . . . .62 C2
Exton Gdns ME14 . . . . .92 F5
Eynhorne St ME17 . . . . .111 C6
Eynsford Castle* DA4 . . . . .54 E8
Eynsford Cl BR5 . . . . .37 C3
Eynsford Cres DA5 . . . . .24 D7
Eynsford Rd Crockenhill BR8 . . .39 D3
  Eynsford DA4 . . . . .40 F1
  Maidstone ME16 . . . . .91 D7
  Swanscombe DA9 . . . . .11 C2
Eynsford Rise DA4 . . . . .54 D6
Eynsham Dr SE2 . . . . .3 B3
Eynswood Dr DA14 . . . . .24 C3

F

F Ave SE18 . . . . .2 B3
Fackenden La TN14 . . . . .69 C7
Factory Rd Newham E16 . . . . . . .1 E5
  Northfleet DA11 . . . . .12 C1
Faesten Way DA5 . . . . .25 E5
Fagus Cl ME5 . . . . .62 B1
Fair Acres BR2 . . . . .36 A4
Fair View TN5 . . . . .175 A6
Fair View Com Inf Sch
  ME8 . . . . .63 C5
Fair View Com Jun Sch
  ME8 . . . . .63 C5
Faircare Pl DA3 . . . . .42 E6
Fairbank Ave BR6 . . . . .51 B8
Fairbourne Heath Cotts
  ME17 . . . . .110 B1
Fairbourne La ME17 . . . . .110 C4
Fairby La DA3 . . . . .42 E3
Fairby Rd SE12 . . . . .5 B2
Faircrouch La TN5 . . . . .174 B5
Fairfax Bsns Ctr ME15 . . . . . . .107 F4
Fairfax Rd TN13 . . . . .83 D5
Fairfax Gdns SE3 . . . . .5 C6
Fairfax Mews E16 . . . . .1 B5
Fairfax Rd RM18 . . . . .12 F6
Fairfield Ave TN2 . . . . .149 C5
Fairfield Cl Kemsing TN15 . . . . .70 A2
  Sidcup DA15 . . . . .6 F1
Fairfield Cres TN9 . . . . .133 C8
Fairfield Gr SE7 . . . . .5 D8
Fairfield Rd Bexley DA7 . . . . .7 F5
  Borough Green TN15 . . . . .86 F8
  Bromley BR1 . . . . .22 A1
  Orpington BR5 . . . . .37 D3
Fairfield Way TN11 . . . . .116 F5
Fairfields DA12 . . . . .30 E3
Fairford Ave DA7 . . . . .8 C5
Fairharn Ave ME7 . . . . .9 A1
Fairlawn Ave DA7 . . . . .7 D5
Fairlawn Cl ME18 . . . . .105 A8
Fairlawn Ct SE7 . . . . .5 C7
Fairlead Rd ME1 . . . . .47 D1
Fairlight Cl TN4 . . . . .133 A2
Fairlight Cross DA3 . . . . .43 C6
Fairlight Ct TN10 . . . . .117 B4

Farningham Wood
(Nature Reserve)*
  BR8,DA4 . . . . .40 C4
Farnol Rd DA1 . . . . .10 A3
Faro Cl BR1 . . . . .37 A7
Farraday Cl ME1 . . . . .61 D8
Farrance Ct TN1 . . . . .149 B4
Farrant Cl BR6 . . . . .52 A3
Farrier Ct Bromley BR1 . . . . .36 A6
  Maidstone ME14 . . . . .92 E5
Farriers Cl DA12 . . . . .30 F7
Farriers Ct ME8 . . . . .63 D5
Farrington Ave BR5 . . . . .38 B6
Farrington Pl BR7 . . . . .23 D1
Farrington Sch BR7 . . . . .23 D2
Fartherwell Ave ME19 . . . . .89 A8
Fartherwell Rd ME19 . . . . .89 A8
Farthing Cl DA1 . . . . .9 F4
Farthing Cnr ME9 . . . . .65 B1
Farthing Hill TN5 . . . . .176 E1
Farthing St BR6 . . . . .50 F2
Farthingfield TN15 . . . . .72 A3
Farthings Cotts ME14 . . . . .76 F1
Farwell Rd DA14 . . . . .24 C4
Farwig La BR1 . . . . .36 A8
Fashoda Rd BR2 . . . . .36 D5
Fauchon's Cl ME14 . . . . .92 F3
Fauchon's La ME14 . . . . .92 F3
Faversham Rd ME17 . . . . .111 E7
Fawkham Ave DA3 . . . . .42 E5
Fawkham CE Prim Sch
  DA3 . . . . .42 B1
Fawkham Green Rd DA3 . . . . . . .56 B7
Fawkham House 10 BR5 . . . . . .38 D1
Fawkham Manor Hospl
  DA3 . . . . .42 C1
Fawkham Rd Longfield DA3 . . . .42 D6
  West Kingsdown TN15 . . . . .56 A4
Fawley Cl ME14 . . . . .91 E7
Fay Cl ME1 . . . . .47 B3
Faygate Cres DA6 . . . . .8 A2
Fazan Ct TN5 . . . . .174 F4
Fearon St SE10 . . . . .1 A1
Featherby Cotts ME7 . . . . .48 F6
Featherby Inf Sch ME8 . . . . .49 A3
Featherby Jun Sch ME8 . . . . . . .49 A3
Featherby Rd
  Gillingham,Lower
  Twydall ME7 . . . . .49 A3
  Gillingham,Twydall ME8 . . . . . .49 A3
Federation Rd SE2 . . . . .3 C2
Feenan Highway RM18 . . . . . . .13 B6
Felderland Cl ME17 . . . . .107 E5
Felderland Dr ME17 . . . . .107 E5
Feldspar Cl ME5 . . . . .62 A1
Felhampton Rd SE9 . . . . .23 B5
Felix Manor BR7 . . . . .23 E2
Felixstowe Rd SE2 . . . . .3 B3
Fell Mead TN12 . . . . .119 F6
Fellowes Way TN12 . . . . .116 E5
Fellows Cl ME8 . . . . .63 B6
Felltram Way SE7 . . . . .1 A1
Felma Ho 9 SE18 . . . . .2 E1
Felspar Cl SE18 . . . . .2 F1
Felstead Rd BR6 . . . . .52 B8
Felsted Rd E16 . . . . .1 D7
Felton Cl BR5 . . . . .37 B3
Felton House SE3 . . . . .5 B3
Felton Rd ME15 . . . . .91 E1
Felton La ME14 . . . . .23 F3
Fen Gr DA15 . . . . .6 F1
Fen Mdw TN15 . . . . .71 C1
Fen Pond Rd TN15 . . . . .86 C7
Fendyke Rd DA17 . . . . .3 D3
Fenn Cl BR1 . . . . .22 A2
Fennel Cl ME16 . . . . .92 E4
Fennell Cl ME1 . . . . .47 A3
Fennell St SE18 . . . . .6 A8
Fenner Rd 16 ME9 . . . . .26 A2
Fenton Cl BR7 . . . . .22 F3
Fenwick Cl 18 SE18 . . . . .6 A8
Ferbies TN3 . . . . .148 A7
Ferbies Cl TN3 . . . . .148 A7
Ferby Cl DA15 . . . . .23 F4
Ferdinand Terr TN3 . . . . .161 C7
Ferguson Ave DA12 . . . . .30 C4
Fern Bank DA4 . . . . .54 E8
Fern Cl DA8 . . . . .9 B2
Fern Ct DA7 . . . . .8 A3
Fern Down DA13 . . . . .27 F3
Fern Hill Pl 3 BR6 . . . . .51 C5
Fernbank Cl ME5 . . . . .61 F2
Ferndale Bromley BR1 . . . . .36 C7
  Royal Tunbridge Wells TN2 . . .149 C5
  Sevenoaks TN13 . . . . .84 C5
Ferndale Cl Bexley DA7 . . . . .7 E6
  Royal Tunbridge Wells TN2 . . .149 C4
Ferndale Point TN2 . . . . .149 C4
Ferndale Rd Gillingham ME7 . . .48 E5
  Gravesend DA12 . . . . .30 B6
Ferndale St E6 . . . . .2 B7
Ferndale Way BR6 . . . . .51 D5
Ferndell Ave DA5 . . . . .25 D5
Ferndene DA3 . . . . .43 D6
Ferndown Ave BR6 . . . . .51 D8
Ferndown Cl ME7 . . . . .49 A5
Ferndown Rd SE9 . . . . .22 D8
Fernheath Way DA2 . . . . .25 D5
Fernhill Rd ME16 . . . . .91 A2
Fernhill St E16 . . . . .2 B5
Fernholt TN11 . . . . .117 D7
Fernhurst Cres TN4 . . . . .133 A2
Fernleigh Rise ME20 . . . . .75 B2
Ferns The Larkfield ME20 . . . . . .75 A3
  Platt TN15 . . . . .87 B8
  Royal Tunbridge Wells TN1 . . .149 C4
Fernside La TN13 . . . . .99 C6
Fernwood Cl BR1 . . . . .36 C7

Ferranti Cl SE18 .... 1 D3
Ferrier Cl ME5 .... 63 E4
Ferrier Point 8 E15 .... 1 A8
Ferringham TN4 .... 148 E4
Ferry La Rainham RM13 .... 4 E7
Wouldham ME1 .... 60 C4
Ferry Pl SE18 .... 2 A3
Ferry Rd Halling ME2 .... 60 B4
Tilbury RM18 .... 13 A4
Festival Ave DA3 .... 43 D6
Festival Cl Erith DA8 .... 8 F7
Sidcup DA5 .... 24 D7
Ffinch Cl ME20 .... 90 D8
Fiddlers Cl DA9 .... 11 B3
Field Cl Bromley BR1 .... 36 C7
Chatham ME5 .... 61 E6
Field Dr TN8 .... 112 D3
Field Rd DA13,TN15 .... 57 E6
Fieldfare Rd SE28 .... 3 C6
Fielding Ave ME14 .... 13 B6
Fielding Dr ME20 .... 75 A3
Fields La ME18 .... 104 E7
Fieldside Cl BR6 .... 51 C6
Fieldway BR5 .... 37 D3
Fieldways TN18 .... 179 C7
Fieldworks Rd ME7 .... 48 A7
Fiennes Way TN13 .... 99 C8
Fiesta Dr RM9 .... 4 C8
Fife Rd E16 .... 1 A8
Fifteenpenny Fields SE9 .... 6 A2
Fifth Ave RM20 .... 11 A8
Figtree Terr ME14 .... 92 A7
Filborough Way DA12 .... 31 B6
Filmer La TN14 .... 84 E6
Filston La TN14 .... 68 E5
Filston Rd DA8 .... 4 C1
Finch Cl ME14 .... 91 E7
Finchale Rd SE2 .... 3 A3
Finchcocks* TN17 .... 167 A5
Finchley Cl DA1 .... 10 A1
Finchley Rd RM17 .... 12 B8
Findlay Cl ME8 .... 63 D6
Englesham Cl BR5 .... 38 D1
Finglesham Ct ME15 .... 107 C8
Finsbury Way DA5 .... 7 F1
Fintonagh Dr ME14 .... 92 B6
Finucane Dr BR5 .... 38 C2
Fir Done BR6 .... 51 A7
Fir Tree Cl
5 Orpington BR6 .... 51 F5
Staplehurst TN12 .... 139 F3
Tonbridge TN11 .... 116 E5
Fir Tree Gr Bredhurst ME7 .... 63 B1
Chatham ME5 .... 62 D1
Fir Tree Rd TN4 .... 148 F3
Firbank Cl E16 .... 1 A8
Fircroft Way TN8 .... 112 C3
Firecrest Cl DA3 .... 43 B6
Firethorn Cl ME7 .... 48 E6
Firmin Ave ME17 .... 107 D5
Firmin Rd DA1 .... 9 C2
Firmingers Rd BR6 .... 53 C5
Firs Cl ME20 .... 75 E1
Firs Ct TN4 .... 148 F6
Firs The Coldblow DA5 .... 25 D7
Sidcup DA15 .... 23 F5
Firside Gr DA15 .... 23 F7
First Ave Bexley DA7 .... 7 C7
Chatham ME4 .... 48 C2
Gillingham ME7 .... 48 E5
Northfleet DA11 .... 29 E7
West Thurrock RM20 .... 11 A8
First La ME15 .... 93 E2
First St TN3 .... 147 F3
Fisher Rd ME5 .... 62 A7
Fisher St Maidstone ME14 .... 92 A6
Newham E16 .... 1 A8
Fisher's Gate Cotts TN7 .... 160 A1
Fisher's Way DA17 .... 4 A5
Fishermans Wlk SE28 .... 2 E4
Fishermen's Hill DA11 .... 12 B2
Fishers Cl TN12 .... 139 F5
Fishers Rd TN12 .... 139 F5
Fishguard Way E16 .... 2 B5
Fishponds Rd BR2 .... 50 D5
Fitzroy Ct DA1 .... 27 B7
Fitzthorold Ho ME7 .... 48 E7
Fitzwilliam Mews E16 .... 1 A5
Fitzwilliam Rd ME14 .... 92 F5
Five Acre Wood Sch
ME15 .... 107 B7
Five Bells La ME1 .... 47 C4
Five Elms Rd BR2 .... 50 C7
Five Fields La TN8 .... 113 B4
Five Oak Green Rd
Five Oak Green TN11,TN12 .... 134 D6
Tonbridge TN11 .... 133 F7
Five Oak La TN12 .... 139 B1
Five Ways Ct ME4 .... 48 A4
Five Wents BR8 .... 40 A7
Fiveash Rd DA11 .... 29 F8
Fiveways TN1 .... 149 A4
Fiveways L Ctr ME4 .... 48 A4
Flack Gdns ME3 .... 34 E5
Flamingo Cl ME5 .... 62 A7
Flamsteed Rd SE7 .... 1 E1
Flats The Gravesend DA12 .... 30 E8
Swanscombe DA9 .... 11 C2
Flaxman Ct Erith DA17 .... 4 A1
8 Gillingham ME7 .... 48 C6
Flaxman Dr ME16 .... 91 C6
Flaxmore Ct DA7 .... 8 B4
Flaxmore Pl TN4 .... 133 A2
Flaxton Rd SE18 .... 6 D8
Fleet Ave DA2 .... 27 C7
Fleet Dale Par DA2 .... 27 C7
Fleet Ho ME7 .... 29 B2
Fleet Rd Dartford DA2 .... 27 C7

Fleet Rd continued
Northfleet DA11 .... 29 C6
Rochester ME1 .... 47 D1
Fleetdown Inf Sch DA2 .... 27 C6
Fleetdown Jun Sch DA2 .... 27 C6
Fleetwood Cl E16 .... 1 D8
Fleetwood Ct 1 Newham E6 .... 1 F8
Orpington BR6 .... 51 A6
Fleming Gdns RM18 .... 13 C6
Fleming Ho SE2 .... 3 C1
Fleming Way Erith SE28 .... 3 D6
Tonbridge TN10 .... 117 E7
Fletcher Cl E6 .... 2 B6
Fletcher Rd TN12 .... 139 E3
Fletchers Cl BR2 .... 36 B5
Fletching Rd SE7 .... 5 D8
Flimwell Bird Pk* TN5 .... 177 E2
Flimwell Cl TN5 .... 177 D4
Flint Cl 8 BR6 .... 51 F4
Flint Down Cl BR5 .... 38 A8
Flint Gn ME5 .... 62 C3
Flint La ME17 .... 111 C8
Flint St RM20 .... 11 B8
Flintmill Cres SE3,SE9 .... 5 F5
Floats The TN13 .... 83 E6
Flood Hatch ME15 .... 91 D2
Flora St DA17 .... 3 F1
Florance La TN3 .... 161 B6
Florence Cl RM17,RM20 .... 11 E8
Florence Cotts TN12 .... 136 A2
Florence Farm
Mobile Home Pk TN15 .... 55 C4
Florence House SE18 .... 5 F6
Florence Rd
1 Bromley BR1 .... 36 A8
Erith DA18,SE2 .... 3 C2
Maidstone ME16 .... 91 E3
Florence St 1 ME42 .... 47 B8
Florin Dr ME1 .... 47 C2
Flower Rise ME14 .... 91 F7
Flowerfield TN14 .... 68 F2
Flowerhill Way DA13 .... 29 E1
Floyd Cl TN4 .... 149 A8
Floyd Rd SE7 .... 1 C1
Flume End ME15 .... 91 D2
Flyers Way The TN16 .... 81 D1
Foalhurst Cl TN10 .... 117 E4
Foley Cl DA1 .... 27 B7
Foley St ME14 .... 92 A5
Folkestone House 4
ME15 .... 107 F6
Fontwell Cl ME15 .... 107 F6
Fontwell Dr BR2 .... 37 A4
Foord Almshouses ME1 .... 47 B3
Foord Cl DA2 .... 27 E6
Foord Rd ME17 .... 111 C5
Foord St ME1 .... 47 B3
Footbury Hill Rd BR6 .... 38 A2
Foots Cray High St DA14 .... 24 D2
Foots Cray La DA14 .... 24 C7
Footscray Rd SE9 .... 23 C7
Force Green La TN16 .... 81 E4
Ford Ho 2 SE18 .... 2 B1
Ford La Trottiscliffe ME19 .... 73 B5
Wrotham Heath TN15,ME19 .... 72 F2
Ford Rd DA11 .... 12 B2
Fordcombe CE Prim Sch
TN3 .... 147 B5
Fordcombe Cl ME15 .... 107 F7
Fordcombe Rd
Fordcombe TN3 .... 147 C4
Penshurst TN11 .... 131 A3
Fordcroft Rd BR5 .... 38 B4
Forde Ave BR1 .... 36 C6
Fordingbridge Cl ME16 .... 91 B5
Fords Park Rd E16 .... 1 A7
Fordwich Cl
Maidstone ME16 .... 91 B7
Orpington BR6 .... 38 A1
Fordwich Dr ME2 .... 33 A2
Fordwich Gn ME8 .... 49 C3
Foreland St SE18 .... 2 D2
Foreman Ctr TN27 .... 141 C5
Foremans Barn Rd ME15 .... 105 F3
Forest Cl BR7 .... 37 A8
Forest Dene TN27 .... 149 C1
Forest Dr Chatham ME5 .... 61 F2
Orpington BR2 .... 50 B6
Forest Gr TN10 .... 117 C5
Forest Hill ME15 .... 91 F1
Forest Lawns ME7 .... 36 C8
Forest Rd Erith DA8 .... 9 A6
Paddock Wood TN12 .... 136 A6
Royal Tunbridge Wells TN2 .... 149 C1
Forest Ridge BR2 .... 50 D4
Forest Way Kings Hill ME19 .... 89 A3
Royal Tunbridge Wells TN2 .... 149 C1
Sidcup DA15 .... 23 D8
Forestdale Rd ME5 .... 77 E8
Foresters Cl ME5 .... 61 F2
Foresters Cres DA7 .... 8 B3
Forge Cl
Five Oak Green TN12 .... 135 B7
Hayes BR2 .... 36 A1
Penshurst TN11 .... 131 B4
Forge Cotts ME18 .... 104 C2
Forge Croft TN8 .... 112 D1
Forge La Benover ME18 .... 121 B4
Boxley ME14 .... 77 C2
Bredhurst ME7 .... 63 A1
East Farleigh ME15 .... 106 C7
Egerton Forstal TN27 .... 127 C1
Gillingham ME7 .... 48 E7
Gravesend DA12 .... 30 H1
Headcorn TN27 .... 141 D5
High Halstow ME23 .... 17 E3

Forge La continued
Higham ME3 .... 32 C3
Horton Kirby DA4 .... 41 C5
Leeds ME17 .... 108 F7
Rabbit's Cross ME17,TN12 .... 123 F3
Shorne DA12 .... 31 E3
West Kingsdown TN15 .... 56 A1
West Peckham ME18 .... 103 A6
Forge Lane City Inf Sch
ME7 .... 48 E6
Forge Meadow ME17 .... 110 D6
Forge Meadows TN27 .... 141 D5
Forge Meads TN30 .... 189 C3
Forge Pl DA12 .... 30 F7
Forge Rd Cobbarn TN1 .... 161 C2
Royal Tunbridge Wells TN4 .... 133 A1
Forge Sq TN11 .... 115 F2
Forge The TN12 .... 135 B7
Forge View TN15 .... 100 B5
Forge Way
Paddock Wood TN12 .... 136 A7
Shoreham TN14 .... 68 F8
Forgefield Cotts TN18 .... 186 A4
Forgefield Ct BR5 .... 38 C4
Formby Rd ME2 .... 60 A7
Formby Terr ME2 .... 60 A6
Forsham La ME17 .... 124 C5
Forson Cl TN30 .... 183 B8
Forstal Cl BR2 .... 36 A6
Forstal Cotts ME20 .... 76 B2
Forstal La ME17 .... 106 D4
Forstal Rd
Egerton Forstal TN27 .... 127 C1
Pratling Street ME20 .... 76 C2
Forstal The Cobbarn TN3 .... 161 F3
Hadlow TN11 .... 118 F8
Pembury TN2 .... 150 E8
Forstall TN3 .... 148 A4
Forstall The TN11 .... 116 A2
Forsters ME17 .... 108 E4
Forsyth Cl ME19 .... 75 A1
Fort Amherst Heritage Pk
& Caverns* ME4 .... 47 F5
Fort Luton (Mus)* ME4 .... 48 A1
Fort Pitt Gram Sch ME4 .... 47 E4
Fort Pitt Hill ME1,ME4 .... 47 E4
Fort Pitt St ME4 .... 47 E3
Fort Rd Badgers Mount TN14 .... 68 C4
Tilbury RM18 .... 13 C5
Fort St Newham E16 .... 1 B5
Rochester ME1 .... 47 C5
Fortis Cl E16 .... 1 C7
Fortrye Cl DA11 .... 29 E6
Fortuna Cl DA3 .... 42 F5
Fortune Wlk SE28 .... 2 D3
Forty Acre La E16 .... 1 A8
Forward Way ME1 .... 61 C6
Fossdene Prim Sch SE7 .... 1 B1
Fossdene Rd SE7 .... 1 B1
Fosse Bank Cl TN9 .... 133 A2
Fosse Bank New Sch
TN11 .... 116 E7
Fosse Rd TN9 .... 117 B2
Fossington Rd DA17 .... 3 D2
Fosten La TN27 .... 171 E7
Foster Clark Est ME15 .... 92 B2
Foster Clarke Dr ME17 .... 107 D5
Foster St ME15 .... 92 A3
Fosters Cl BR7 .... 22 F3
Fosters Old Sch DA16 .... 7 B5
Fosters Prim Sch DA16 .... 7 B5
Fostington Way ME5 .... 61 F1
Foulds Cl ME8 .... 63 B5
Founder Cl E6 .... 2 B7
Foundry Wharf ME1 .... 47 E4
Fountain Ct Eynsford DA4 .... 54 E8
Sidcup DA14 .... 7 B1
Fountain Ent Pk ME20 .... 90 A1
Fountain La ME16 .... 91 A2
Fountain Rd ME2 .... 32 E1
Fountain Wlk DA11 .... 12 F1
Four Elms Hill ME3 .... 33 E4
Four Elms Prim Sch TN8 .... 113 B5
Four Elms Rd TN8 .... 112 D4
Four Elms Rdbt ME3 .... 33 E3
Four Oaks Rd TN12,TN27 .... 140 E7
Four Wents
Langley Heath ME17 .... 108 E3
Maidstone ME17 .... 107 F2
Fouracre Cotts ME9 .... 64 E6
Fourth Ave Gillingham ME7 .... 48 E4
West Thurrock RM20 .... 11 A8
Fourwents Rd ME3 .... 34 D7
Fowey Cl ME1 .... 62 C5
Fowler Cl Gillingham ME8 .... 63 C3
Sidcup DA14 .... 24 C5
Fox Cl Newham E16 .... 1 A8
Orpington BR6 .... 52 A5
Fox Gr TN15 .... 86 F7
Fox Hollow Cl SE18 .... 2 E1
Fox Hollow Dr DA7 .... 7 D5
Fox House Rd DA17 .... 4 B1
Fox in the Wood TN5 .... 174 C6
Fox La BR2 .... 50 C5
Fox Manor Way RM20 .... 11 A8
Fox St ME7 .... 48 C6
Foxburrow Cl ME8 .... 63 D5
Foxbury DA3 .... 42 E6
Foxbury Cl Bromley BR1 .... 22 B2
Orpington BR6 .... 52 A5
Foxbury Dr BR6 .... 52 A4
Foxbury Rd BR1 .... 22 B2
Foxbury Wlk DA16 .... 116 C6
Foxcroft Rd SE18 .... 6 B6
Foxden Dr ME15 .... 92 F1

Foxdown La DA13 .... 44 B1
Foxes Dale SE3 .... 5 A4
Foxfield Prim Sch SE18 .... 2 C2
Foxfield Rd BR6 .... 51 D8
Foxglove Cl 1 TN8 .... 112 D3
Foxglove Cres ME5 .... 61 E4
Foxglove Rise ME14 .... 91 E7
Foxgloves The TN12 .... 136 B5
Foxhole La
Four Throws TN18 .... 179 E1
Matfield TN12 .... 151 C8
Wadhurst TN5 .... 175 B4
Foxhole Rd SE9 .... 5 E2
Foxhome Cl BR7 .... 23 A2
Foxtail Cl ME4 .... 34 B2
Foxton Rd E16 .... 2 A4
Foxton Rd RM20 .... 11 D8
Foxwood Gr
Northfleet DA11 .... 29 E7
Pratt's Bottom BR6 .... 52 C1
Foxwood Rd DA2 .... 28 B5
Foxwood Way DA3 .... 43 D7
Framley Rd TN12 .... 117 F5
Framlingham Cres SE9 .... 22 F4
Frances St SE18 .... 1 F2
Francis Ave DA7 .... 8 A4
Francis Dr ME5 .... 62 A2
Francis La ME15 .... 107 F5
Francis Rd Dartford DA1 .... 9 D2
St Paul's Cray BR5 .... 38 D6
Tonbridge TN11 .... 116 D6
Frank Burton Cl 4 SE7 .... 1 B1
Frank Woolley Rd TN10 .... 117 F5
Frank's Hollow Rd TN3 .... 132 C2
Frankapps Cl ME9 .... 65 B6
Frankfield Rise TN2 .... 149 A1
Franklin Dr ME14 .... 92 D4
Franklin Pas SE9 .... 5 E4
Franklin Rd Bexley DA7 .... 7 E6
Gillingham ME7 .... 48 D5
Gravesend DA12 .... 30 D3
Franklins Cotts ME15 .... 106 C5
Franks Ct ME8 .... 49 B2
Franks La DA4 .... 41 B4
Frankswood Ave BR5 .... 37 C4
Frant Cotts ME17 .... 163 B4
Frant Field TN8 .... 112 C1
Frant Rd TN2,TN3 .... 163 A7
Frant Sta TN3 .... 163 F5
Fraser Cl Coldblow DA5 .... 25 C7
3 Newham E6 .... 1 E7
Fraser Ho 3 SE18 .... 2 A2
Fraser Rd DA8 .... 4 D1
Frederick Andrews Ct
RM17 .... 12 D8
Frederick Ho 4 SE18 .... 1 E3
Frederick Pl SE18 .... 2 B1
Frederick Rd ME7 .... 48 C4
Freehold The
East Peckham TN12 .... 119 F6
Hawkhurst TN18 .... 178 F2
Freeland Way SE28 .... 9 A6
Freelands Gr BR1 .... 36 B8
Freelands Rd Bromley BR1 .... 36 B8
Snodland ME6 .... 74 F8
Freeman Gdns ME4 .... 47 F2
Freeman Rd DA12 .... 30 E5
Freeman Way ME15 .... 107 E7
Freemasons Rd E16 .... 1 B7
Freewind CE Gillingham ME7 .... 48 C6
Orpington BR6 .... 51 F5
Freight La TN17 .... 169 C3
Fremantle House RM18 .... 12 F6
Fremantle Rd DA17 .... 4 A2
Fremlin Cl TN4 .... 148 B4
Fremlins Rd ME14 .... 93 C4
Frensham Rd
Rolvenden TN17 .... 182 A1
Sidcup SE9 .... 23 D6
Frensham Wlk ME5 .... 61 F1
Freshland Rd ME16 .... 91 B4
Freshwater Rd ME5 .... 62 B7
Freta Rd DA6 .... 7 F2
Frewing Cl BR7 .... 23 A3
Friar Rd BR5 .... 38 A4
Friars Ave ME5 .... 61 F2
Friars Mews SE9 .... 6 A2
Friars The* ME20 .... 75 E2
Friars Way TN2 .... 149 D6
Friars Wlk SE2 .... 3 D1
Friary Pl 3 ME2 .... 47 B7
Friary Prec ME2 .... 47 B7
Friday Rd DA8 .... 4 D1
Friday St ME17 .... 125 B6
Friezland Rd TN4 .... 148 D1
Friezley La TN17 .... 155 C1
Frimley Ct DA14 .... 24 C3
Frindsbury Hill ME2 .... 33 C1
Frindsbury Rd ME2 .... 47 B8
Frinstead Gr BR5 .... 38 D5
Frinsted Cl ME16 .... 91 F2
Friston Way ME1 .... 61 D8
Friswell Pl 1 DA6 .... 8 A3
Frittenden CE Prim Sch
TN17 .... 156 E6
Frittenden Rd
Rochester ME2 .... 33 D2
Staplehurst TN12 .... 140 B2
Frobisher Gdns ME1 .... 47 C2
Frobisher Way
Gravesend DA12 .... 30 D3

Frobisher Way continued
Swanscombe DA9 .... 11 B3
Frog La Rainham RM9 .... 4 D8
Royal Tunbridge Wells TN1 .... 149 A2
West Malling ME19 .... 89 C8
Frog's La TN17 .... 181 E1
Froghole La TN8,TN16 .... 96 D2
Frogmore Wlk ME17 .... 111 C5
Frognal Ave DA14 .... 24 A2
Frognal Cnr BR7 .... 22 F2
Frognal Pl DA14 .... 24 A3
Frogs Hole La TN17,TN27 .... 171 E3
Froissart Rd SE9 .... 5 E2
Fromandez Dr TN12 .... 152 F5
Frome Ct TN10 .... 117 B5
Front Cotts TN5 .... 176 E1
Frost Cres ME5 .... 62 A7
Froyle Cl ME16 .... 91 C6
Fruitfields TN5 .... 177 C3
Fry Cl ME3 .... 21 A6
Fry's Cotts ME3 .... 19 C4
Frythe Cres TN17 .... 169 D4
Frythe Cres TN17 .... 169 D4
Frythe Way TN17 .... 169 D4
Frythe Wlk TN17 .... 169 D4
Fuchsia St SE2 .... 3 B1
Fuggles Cl TN12 .... 135 E6
Fuggles Ct TN17 .... 180 D6
Fulbert Dr ME14 .... 92 F5
Fuller Cl Orpington BR6 .... 51 F5
Wadhurst TN5 .... 174 E5
Fullers Cl ME14 .... 93 A4
Fullers Hill 7 TN16 .... 81 D1
Fulmar Rd ME2 .... 46 D6
Fulmer Rd E16 .... 1 D8
Fulthorp Rd SE3 .... 5 A5
Fulwich Rd DA1 .... 9 F1
Furfield Cl ME17 .... 107 E5
Furnace Ave TN3 .... 166 A3
Furnace La
Hook Green TN3 .... 165 E4
Horsmonden TN12 .... 152 F7
Furner Cl DA1 .... 8 F4
Furness Sch BR8 .... 25 F2
Furnival Ct TN2 .... 163 A1
Furrell's Rd ME1 .... 47 D5
Further Field TN12 .... 139 E5
Furze Bank TN3 .... 113 B5
Furzefield Ave TN3 .... 148 A8
Furzefield Cl BR7 .... 23 B2
Furzefield Rd SE3 .... 5 B7
Furzehill Sq BR5 .... 38 B5
Fyfe Way BR1 .... 36 A7

G

Gable Cl DA1 .... 9 A2
Gables Cl ME4 .... 22 A7
Gables The 2 Bromley BR1 .... 22 B1
New Barn DA3 .... 43 C6
Gabriel Gdns DA12 .... 30 D3
Gabriel Spring Road (East)
DA3 .... 55 F8
Gabriel's Hill ME15 .... 92 A4
Gabrielspring Rd DA3 .... 55 D8
Gads Hill ME7 .... 48 F6
Gads Hill Sch ME3 .... 32 C2
Gadsby La TN26 .... 159 F3
Gadwall Cl E16 .... 1 B7
Gadwall Way SE28 .... 2 D4
Gifford's Bridge Cotts
TN12 .... 137 C4
Gagetown Terr 1 ME14 .... 91 F7
Gainsborough Ave
Dartford DA1 .... 9 C2
Tilbury RM18 .... 13 B6
Gainsborough Cl ME8 .... 63 D6
Gainsborough Ct 3 BR2 .... 36 C5
Gainsborough Dr
Maidstone ME16 .... 91 B4
Northfleet DA11 .... 29 D5
Gainsborough Gdns
TN10 .... 117 E5
Gainsborough Ho ME1 .... 47 D5
Gainsborough Sq DA7 .... 7 D4
Gaitskell Rd SE9 .... 23 C7
Galahad Ave ME2 .... 46 E6
Galahad Rd BR1 .... 22 A4
Galena Cl ME5 .... 62 A1
Galena Ho 8 SE18 .... 2 F1
Gallants La ME15 .... 105 F6
Galleon Bvd DA2 .... 10 D3
Galleon Cl Chatham ME1 .... 61 C8
Erith DA8 .... 4 D2
Galley Hill Rd DA11,DA10 .... 11 F2
Galley Hill Trad Est 1 ME19 .... 11 E2
Gallions Mount Prim Sch
.... 2 F1
Gallions Rd E16 .... 1 F6
Gallions Reach Sta E6 .... 2 B6
Gallions View Rd SE28 .... 2 E4
Gallon Cl SE7 .... 1 C2
Gallop The TN2 .... 72 F7
Gallosson Rd SE18 .... 2 E2
Gallus Sq SE3 .... 5 B4
Galsworthy Cl SE28 .... 3 B5
Galsworthy Cres SE3 .... 5 C6
Galsworthy Rd RM18 .... 13 C6
Galton House SE18 .... 5 C5
Games Ho 6 SE7 .... 5 C8
Gamma Rd ME3 .... 35 C8
Gandy's La ME17 .... 107 C2
Garden Ave DA7 .... 8 A4
Garden Cl Ide Hill TN16 .... 97 C3

Garden Cl continued
Lewisham SE12 . . . . .22 B5
Maidstone ME15 . . . . .107 E7
Staplehurst TN12 . . . . .139 F1
Garden Cotts Leigh TN11 . .116 A2
St Paul's Cray BR5 . . . . .38 C7
Garden Ct 10 SE9 . . . . .6 A1
Garden La BR1 . . . . .22 B2
Garden of England Pk
(Mobile Home Pk)
ME17 . . . . .110 B7
Garden Pl DA2 . . . . .26 D5
Garden Rd Bromley BR1 . . . .22 B2
Royal Tunbridge Wells TN1 . .149 B4
Sevenoaks TN13 . . . . .84 D5
Tonbridge TN9 . . . . .117 D2
Garden Row DA11 . . . . .29 F5
Garden St Gillingham ME7 . .48 A6
Royal Tunbridge Wells TN1 . .149 B4
Garden Terr TN15 . . . . .85 A6
Garden Way ME19 . . . . .88 F2
Gardenia ME2 . . . . .33 B2
Gardens The ME17 . . . . .106 C3
Gardiner Cl BR5 . . . . .38 C7
Gardiner Ho SE18 . . . . .5 E7
Gardiner St ME7 . . . . .48 C6
Gardyne Mews 12 TN9 . . . .133 B8
Gareth Gr BR1 . . . . .22 A4
Garfield Rd ME7 . . . . .48 D6
Gargany Wlk SE28 . . . . .3 D6
Garibaldi St SE18 . . . . .2 E2
Garland Rd SE18 . . . . .6 D7
Garlands TN11 . . . . .116 D8
Garlinge Rd TN4 . . . . .133 A1
Garner Dr ME19 . . . . .75 A1
Garnet Wlk 6 E6 . . . . .1 E8
Garnet Cl SE9 . . . . .5 F4
Garrard Cl Bexley DA7 . . . . . .8 A4
Chislehurst BR7 . . . . .23 B3
Garrick Dr SE28 . . . . .2 D3
Garrick St 16 DA11 . . . . .13 B1
Garrington Cl ME14 . . . . .92 C6
Garrison Cl SE18 . . . . .6 A7
Garrison Rd ME12 . . . . .21 F3
Garrolds Cl BR8 . . . . .39 D7
Garrow DA3 . . . . .43 B6
Garside Cl SE28 . . . . .2 D3
Garth Rd TN13 . . . . .99 C7
Gartly Cotts 9 C1
Garvary Rd E16 . . . . .1 B7
Garvock Dr TN13 . . . . .84 A1
Gas House Rd ME14 . . . . . . .47 C6
Gascoyne Cl ME15 . . . . .93 B2
Gascoyne Dr DA1 . . . . .9 F5
Gascoine Alley TN15 . . . . . . .72 D2
Gasson Rd SE10 . . . . .11 E1
Gassons Rd ME6 . . . . .74 E8
Gatcombe Cl Chatham ME5 . .62 A5
Maidstone ME16 . . . . .91 B5
Gatcombe Rd E16 . . . . .1 A5
Gate Farm Rd TN3,TN11 . . .132 C4
Gateacre Ct 14 DA14 . . . . . .24 B4
Gatefield Cotts TN17 . . . . .181 F4
Gatehouse
The .132 C4
Gatekeeper Chase ME8 . . . . .63 F8
Gates Green Rd BR2,BR4 . . .50 A6
Gateway Par DA12 . . . . .30 F4
Gatland La ME16 . . . . .91 B2
Gatling Rd SE18,SE2 . . . . . . .6 F7
Gaton Rd SE2 . . . . .3 C3
Gattons Way DA14 . . . . .24 F4
Gatwick Farm Cotts
RM19 . . . . .144 A4
Gatwick Rd DA12 . . . . .30 B6
Gault Cl ME15 . . . . .93 A2
Gautrey Sq 8 E6 . . . . .1 F7
Gavestone Cres SE12 . . . . . .22 B8
Gavestone Rd SE12 . . . . . . .22 B8
Gavin Ho SE18 . . . . .1 F3
Gayhurst Rd E8 . . . . .63 D6
Gaylor Rd RM18 . . . . .12 F6
Gaza Trad Est TN11 . . . . . . .115 D7
Gazelle Glade DA12 . . . . . . .30 F3
Gean Cl TN4 . . . . .149 F1
Geddes Pl 5 DA6 . . . . .8 A3
Gedge's Hill TN12 . . . . .135 F3
Geffery's St SE9 . . . . .22 E5
General Gordon Pl 2 SE18 . .2 B2
Genesta Glade DA12 . . . . . . .31 A3
Genesta Rd SE18 . . . . .6 C8
Geneva Ave ME8 . . . . .49 A2
Gentian Cl 4 Chatham ME5 . .61 E4
Maidstone ME14 . . . . .92 E5
George Akass Ho SE18 . . . . . .2 C1
George Crooks House 7
RM17 . . . . .12 B8
George La Hayes BR2 . . . . . .36 B1
Leeds ME17 . . . . .108 F3
Rochester ME1 . . . . .47 C6
George Marsham House
ME15 . . . . .106 F3
George St
Chainhurst ME15 . . . . .122 A7
Grays RM17 . . . . .12 A8
Maidstone ME14 . . . . .92 A3
Royal Tunbridge Wells TN2 . .149 B3
Staplehurst TN12 . . . . .139 E6
Tonbridge TN9 . . . . .133 B8
Wadhurst TN5 . . . . .174 F5
George Summers Cl ME2 . . .47 E8
Georges Cl BR5 . . . . .38 C5
Georgian Ct DA1 . . . . .26 B1
Georgian Dr ME17 . . . . .106 D3
Georgian Way ME8 . . . . .63 C4

Geraint Rd BR1 . . . . .22 A4
Gerald Ave ME4 . . . . .47 F2
Gerald Rd DA12 . . . . .30 E8
Gerda Rd SE9 . . . . .23 C6
Gerdview Dr DA2 . . . . .26 C4
Gerrard Ave ME1 . . . . .61 E8
Gertrude Rd DA17 . . . . .4 A2
Gibbet La TN12 . . . . .152 F6
Gibbetts TN3 . . . . .147 F3
Gibbs Hill Headcorn TN27 . .141 E5
Nettlestead ME18 . . . . .104 B5
Gibraltar Ave ME7 . . . . .48 B7
Gibraltar Hill ME4 . . . . .47 F4
Gibraltar La ME14 . . . . .91 F8
Gibson Cl DA11 . . . . .29 F5
Gibson Dr ME19 . . . . .88 F4
Gidd's Pond Cotts ME14 . . .92 E6
Giddyhorn La ME16 . . . . .91 C5
Gideon Cl DA17 . . . . .4 B2
Gifford Cl ME8 . . . . .49 C3
Giggs Hill BR5 . . . . .38 A8
Gighill Rd ME20 . . . . .74 F4
Gilbert Cl Eltham SE18 . . . . . .5 F6
Gillingham ME7 . . . . .63 A5
Swanscombe DA10 . . . . .11 D1
Gilbert Rd Bromley BR1 . . . .22 A1
Erith DA17 . . . . .4 A3
Gilbert Terr 2 ME14 . . . . . . .91 F7
Gilbourne Rd SE18 . . . . .6 F8
Gilchrist Cotts TN14 . . . . . . .99 C2
Gildenhill Rd BR8 . . . . .26 C1
Gildersome St SE18 . . . . .6 A8
Gill Ave Newham E16 . . . . . . .1 A7
Gill Cl DA11 . . . . .29 F5
Gill Ct SE18 . . . . .2 C2
Gill The TN2 . . . . .150 E8
Gill's Rd
Green Street Green DA2 . . . .28 B1
Horton Kirby DA4 . . . . .41 F8
Gillan Ct 5 SE12 . . . . .22 B5
Gilletts La ME19 . . . . .90 A6
Gillies Ct DA14 . . . . .23 E4
Gillies Rd TN15 . . . . .58 E5
Gillingham Coll The ME7 . . .48 F4
Gillingham Gate Rd ME7 . . .48 C8
Gillingham Gate Rd ME7 . . .48 C8
Gillingham Gn ME7 . . . . .48 E6
Gillingham Rd ME7 . . . . .48 D5
Gillingham Sta ME7 . . . . . . .48 D5
Gilmans Rd BR5 . . . . .38 B1
Gilroy Way BR5 . . . . .38 B6
Gimble Way TN2 . . . . .134 D1
Gingerbead La TN18 . . . . . .177 F2
Ginsbury Cl ME2 . . . . .47 E6
Gipps Cross La TN3 . . . . . . .147 F3
Gipsy La RM17 . . . . .12 C8
Gipsy Rd DA16 . . . . .7 D5
Giralda Cl E16 . . . . .1 D8
Glade Bsns Ctr The RM20 . .10 F8
Glade The Bromley BR1 . . . .36 D7
Chatham ME5 . . . . .62 A2
Greenwich SE7 . . . . .5 C7
Sevenoaks TN13 . . . . .84 B4
Glades The DA12 . . . . .30 D7
Gladeside Rd ME7 . . . . .63 B2
Gladeswood Rd DA17 . . . . . . .4 B2
Gladstone Rd Chatham ME4 .47 E2
Dartford DA1 . . . . .9 F1
Maidstone ME14 . . . . .92 B6
Orpington BR6 . . . . .51 C5
Royal Tunbridge Wells TN4 . .148 B4
Tonbridge TN9 . . . . .117 B1
Gladwell Rd BR1 . . . . .22 A2
Gladwyn Ct ME8 . . . . .63 D4
Glamford Rd ME2 . . . . .46 D5
Glamis Ct ME5 . . . . .62 A5
Glanfield Ct TN1 . . . . .149 C5
Glanville Rd Bromley BR2 . . .36 B6
Gillingham ME7 . . . . .48 D5
Rochester ME2 . . . . .47 A8
Glasbrook Rd SE9 . . . . .22 D8
Glasgow Ho 8 ME15 . . . . . .107 E7
Glass Yd SE18 . . . . .2 A3
Glassenbury Rd TN17 . . . . .168 E4
Glassmill La BR2 . . . . .36 A7
Glastonbury Ct BR5 . . . . . . .38 C1
Gleaming Wood Dr ME5 . . . .77 D8
Gleaners Cl ME14 . . . . .92 E4
Gleanings Mews ME1 . . . . . .47 C5
Glebe Cl TN27 . . . . .143 B2
Glebe Cotts TN16 . . . . .96 A1
Glebe Ct 7 SE18 . . . . .111 E5
Glebe Ho 7 SE18 . . . . .2 A2
Glebe House Dr BR2 . . . . . . .36 B1
Glebe La Maidstone ME16 . . .91 A1
Sevenoaks TN13 . . . . .84 B3
Glebe Meadow ME18 . . . . . .104 E7
Glebe Pl DA4 . . . . .41 C5
Glebe Rd Bromley BR1 . . . . . .36 A8
Gillingham ME7 . . . . .48 E6
Staplehurst TN12 . . . . .139 E6
Sevenoaks Weald TN14 . . . . .99 B3
Glebe The Bidborough TN3 .132 D3
Chislehurst BR7 . . . . .37 C8
Cuxton ME2 . . . . .46 C2
Pembury TN2 . . . . .150 D8
Penshurst TN11 . . . . .131 A3
Glebe Way DA8 . . . . .8 E8
Glebefield The TN13 . . . . . . .83 F4
Glebeland TN27 . . . . .127 F4
Glebelands
Bidborough TN3 . . . . .132 D3
Biddenden TN27 . . . . .157 F1
Crayford DA1 . . . . .8 F3
Penshurst TN11 . . . . .131 A3
Gleeson Dr BR6 . . . . .51 F6
Glen Ct Lewisham SE12 . . . .22 A8

Glen Ct continued
Sidcup DA14 . . . . .24 A4
Glen Dunlop House The
TN13 . . . . .84 C5
Glen Ho 6 E16 . . . . .2 A5
Glen View DA12 . . . . .30 C7
Glen View DA11 . . . . .36 D7
Glenavon Way 7 SE18 . . . . . .1 E2
Glencairn Cl E16 . . . . .6 B4
Glencairne Cl E16 . . . . .1 D8
Glencoe Inf Sch ME4 . . . . . . .48 A2
Glencoe Jun Sch ME4 . . . . . .48 A2
Glencoe Rd ME4 . . . . .48 A2
Glendale ME7 . . . . .39 F4
Glendale Cl SE9 . . . . .6 A4
Glendale La TN2 . . . . .149 D6
Glendale Rd Erith DA8 . . . . . .4 C2
Northfleet DA11 . . . . .29 E5
Glendale Way SE28 . . . . .3 C6
Glendower Cres BR6 . . . . . . .38 A3
Glendown Rd SE2 . . . . .3 A1
Gleneagles Cl BR6 . . . . .37 D1
Gleneagles Ct ME5 . . . . .61 F2
Gleneagles Dr ME15 . . . . . . .92 A1
Gleneagles Gn 1 BR6 . . . . . .37 D1
Gleneagles Rd SE9 . . . . .6 B3
Glengall Rd DA7 . . . . .7 E4
Glenhead Cl SE9 . . . . .6 B4
Glenlyon Rd SE9 . . . . .6 A2
Glenmore Pk TN2 . . . . .162 F8
Glenmore Rd DA16 . . . . .6 F6
Glenmount Path 1 SE18 . . . .2 C1
Glenrosa Gdns DA12 . . . . . . .31 A4
Glenrose Cl ME4 . . . . .34 D3
Glenshiel Rd SE9 . . . . .6 A2
Glentrammon Ave BR6 . . . . .51 F4
Glentrammon Cl BR6 . . . . . . .51 F5
Glentrammon Gdns BR6 . . . .51 F4
Glentrammon Rd BR6 . . . . . .51 F4
Glenure Rd SE9 . . . . .6 A2
Glenview SE2 . . . . .7 D8
Glenwood Cl Chatham ME5 . .48 C1
Gillingham ME7 . . . . .63 A7
Maidstone ME16 . . . . .91 C5
Tenterden TN30 . . . . .173 B3
Glimpsing Grn DA18 . . . . .3 E3
Glimpsing Gn DA18 . . . . .3 E3
Glistening Glade ME8 . . . . . .63 E6
Gload Cres BR5 . . . . .52 D8
Globe La ME4 . . . . .47 F5
Globe Wharf SE16 . . . . .1 B8
Gloucester Ave Bexley DA16 . .6 F3
Sidcup DA15 . . . . .23 E6
Gloucester Cl ME8 . . . . .64 A8
Gloucester Cres DA12 . . . . . .12 F5
Gloucester Par 8 DA15 . . . . .7 A1
Gloucester Rd
Dartford DA1 . . . . .26 D8
Erith DA17 . . . . .4 C2
Gravesend DA12 . . . . .30 C4
Maidstone ME15 . . . . .107 D8
Wadhurst TN5 . . . . .174 F6
Glover Cl SE2 . . . . .3 C2
Glovers Mill ME4 . . . . .47 D3
Gloxinia Rd DA13 . . . . .29 B2
Glyn Davies Cl TN13 . . . . . . .83 E7
Glyn Dr DA14 . . . . .24 B4
Glynde Rd DA7 . . . . .7 E4
Glyndebourne Pk BR6 . . . . . .51 B8
Glyndon Rd SE18 . . . . .2 D2
Glynne Cl ME8 . . . . .63 D6
Goad Ave ME5 . . . . .62 B3
Goddard's Green Cotts
TN17 . . . . .170 F1
Goddards St TN17 . . . . .169 B4
Godden Rd ME6 . . . . .74 F8
Goddings Dr ME1 . . . . .47 A3
Goddington Chase BR6 . . . . .52 B6
Goddington Rd BR6 . . . . .52 C7
Goddington La
Harrietsham ME17 . . . . .110 B6
Orpington BR6 . . . . .52 A7
Goddington Rd ME7 . . . . . . .48 B8
Godfrey ME2 . . . . .32 F1
Godfrey Evans Cl TN10 . . . .117 F5
Godfrey Hill SE18 . . . . .1 F2
Godfrey Ho 1 SE18 . . . . .2 A2
Godfrey Rd SE18 . . . . .1 F2
Godson Rd SE2 . . . . .3 C4
Godwin House SE18 . . . . . . .36 C6
Godwin Rd BR2 . . . . .36 C6
Gold St DA12,DA13 . . . . .44 E4
Goldace RM17 . . . . .11 F8
Goldcrest Cl Newham E16 . . .1 D8
Woolwich SE28 . . . . .3 C6
Golden Plover Cl DA14 . . . . .12 F6
Golden Sq TN30 . . . . .183 B8
Golden Wood Cl ME5 . . . . . . .77 D8
Goldfinch Cl Larkfield ME20 . .75 A1
Orpington BR6 . . . . .52 A5
Goldie Leigh Hospl SE2 . . . . .7 C8
Golding Cl ME20 . . . . .75 C1
Golding Gdns TN12 . . . . . . .120 A6
Golding Rd TN13 . . . . .84 C5
Goldings TN12 . . . . .135 E5
Goldings St E1 . . . . .1 B8
Goldings The ME8 . . . . .63 D8
Goldmark House SE3 . . . . . . .5 B4
Goldsel Rd BR8 . . . . .39 E5

Goldsmid Rd TN9 . . . . .133 C8
Goldsmith St 8 SE18 . . . . . . .2 E1
Goldsmith RM17 . . . . .11 F8
Goldsmith Cl DA7 . . . . .8 B4
Goldsmith Dr ME8 . . . . .63 E5
Goldsmith Rd ME8 . . . . .63 E5
Goldstone Wlk ME5 . . . . .62 A1
Goldsworth Dr ME2 . . . . .33 A1
Goldthorne Cl ME14 . . . . . . .92 C5
Goldthorne Cl ME14 . . . . . . .92 C5
Goldwing Cl E16 . . . . .1 A7
Golf Links Ave DA11 . . . . . . .30 B3
Golf Rd BR1 . . . . .37 A6
Golford Rd TN17 . . . . .169 F4
Gollogly Terr 8 SE7 . . . . .1 C1
Gooch Cl ME16 . . . . .91 D8
Goodall Cl ME8 . . . . .63 E5
Goodbury Rd TN15 . . . . .70 B6
Gooding Ho SE7 . . . . .1 C1
Goodley Stock Rd
TN8,TN16 . . . . .96 B6
Goodmead Rd BR6 . . . . .38 A1
Goods Hill TN30 . . . . .182 D8
Goods Station Rd TN1 . . . . .149 B4
Goodtrees La TN8 . . . . .145 B2
Goodwin Cl ME14 . . . . .112 B2
Goodwin Dr
Maidstone ME14 . . . . .92 B8
Sidcup DA14 . . . . .24 D6
Goodwin Rd ME3 . . . . .33 B7
Goodwins The TN2 . . . . .148 F1
Goodwood Cres DA12 . . . . . .30 C2
Goodworth Rd TN15 . . . . . . .71 F3
Goosander Way SE28 . . . . . . .2 D3
Goose Cl ME5 . . . . .62 A5
Goose Green Cl BR5 . . . . . . .38 A7
Goose Sq 5 E6 . . . . .1 F7
Gooseneck La TN27 . . . . . . .141 C5
Gordon Cl KM18 . . . . .14 D7
Gordon Ct ME17 . . . . .111 F8
Gordon Rd SE12 . . . . .22 A8
Gordon Pl DA12 . . . . .13 C1
Gordon Prim Sch SE9 . . . . . . .5 F3
Gordon Promenade E
DA12 . . . . .13 D1
Gordon Rd Chatham ME4 . . .48 B2
Dartford DA1 . . . . .26 D8
Erith DA17 . . . . .4 C2
Gillingham ME7 . . . . .48 E6
Gillingham,Brompton ME4 . . .48 A7
Hoo St Werburgh ME3 . . . . . .34 D5
Northfleet DA11 . . . . .29 E8
Rochester ME1 . . . . .47 A8
Royal Tunbridge Wells TN2 . .149 C2
Sevenoaks TN13 . . . . .84 B2
Sidcup DA15 . . . . .6 F1
Gordon Terr ME1 . . . . .47 C4
Gordon Way BR1 . . . . .36 A8
Gore Cl ME17 . . . . .107 C7
Gore Court Rd ME15 . . . . . .107 F5
Gore Farm Cotts DA2 . . . . . .27 C5
Gore Green Rd ME3 . . . . .32 E7
Gore La TN17 . . . . .153 E4
Gore Rd Dartford DA2 . . . . . .27 C5
Silver Street ME9 . . . . .80 F5
Gorham Cl ME4 . . . . .74 F7
Gorham Dr Maidstone ME15 . .93 A1
Tonbridge TN9 . . . . .133 E8
Gorman Rd SE18 . . . . .1 F2
Gorringe Ave DA4 . . . . .41 F2
Gorse Ave ME5 . . . . .61 F5
Gorse La TN14 . . . . .68 F2
Gorse Cres ME20 . . . . .90 D8
Gorse Rd Orpington BR5 . . . .53 A8
Rochester ME2 . . . . .33 A1
Gorse Wood Rd
Hartley DA3 . . . . .43 A5
New Barn DA3 . . . . .43 A6
Goss Hill BR8,DA2 . . . . .26 C2
Gossage Rd SE18 . . . . .2 D2
Gosshill Rd BR7 . . . . .37 A6
Gossington Cl BR7 . . . . .23 B4
Gothic Cl DA1 . . . . .26 D5
Goudhurst & Kilndown
CE Prim Sch TN17 . . . . . . .167 F8
Goudhurst Cl ME16 . . . . .91 E4
Goudhurst Rd
Cranbrook TN17 . . . . .169 D8
Gillingham ME8 . . . . .49 B3
Horsmonden TN12 . . . . .153 B5
Knox Bridge TN12,TN17 . . . .155 C6
Gouge Ave DA11 . . . . .29 E7
Gould Rd ME5 . . . . .62 A3
Goudhurst Rd TN12 . . . . . . .138 B5
Gourock Rd SE9 . . . . .6 A2
Gover Hill TN11,ME18 . . . . .102 E6
Grace Ave Bexley DA7 . . . . . .7 F5
Maidstone ME16 . . . . .91 D6
Grace Cl SE9 . . . . .22 D5
Gracious La TN13 . . . . .99 B5
Gracious Lane End TN14 . . .98 F5
Grafton Ave ME1 . . . . .61 B8
Graham Ct 11 BR1 . . . . .22 B1
Graham House SE18 . . . . .6 B7
Graham Rd DA7 . . . . .8 A3
Grain Rd Gillingham ME8 . . . .63 C3
Grain ME3 . . . . .21 B4
Grainey Field ME9 . . . . .64 E4
Grain View ME3 . . . . .117 E6
Grain Sch for Girls
Wilmington The DA2 . . . . . . .26 B5
Grampian Cl Orpington BR6 . .37 F3

Grampian Cl continued
Royal Tunbridge Wells TN2 . .149 D5
Grampian Way ME15 . . . . . . .93 A1
Granada House 8 ME15 . . . .92 A4
Granada St 9 ME15 . . . . .92 A4
Granary TN12 . . . . .136 B6
Grampian Cl Gillingham ME8 . .49 F1
Maidstone ME14 . . . . .92 E5
Granby Ho 8 SE18 . . . . .1 F2
Granby Rd Eltham SE9 . . . . . . .5 F4
Northfleet DA11 . . . . .30 D6
Woolwich SE18 . . . . .2 B3
Grand Ct 7 ME7 . . . . .48 C6
Grand Depot Rd SE18 . . . . . . .2 A1
Grandshore La TN17 . . . . . .181 B6
Grandsire Gdns ME3 . . . . . . .34 E3
Grange Cl Edenbridge TN8 . .112 C1
Leybourne ME19 . . . . .74 C2
Sidcup DA15 . . . . .24 A5
Westerham TN16 . . . . .81 C1
Grange Cotts TN11 . . . . .101 D5
Grange Cres
6 Dartford DA2 . . . . .10 B1
Erith SE28 . . . . .3 C7
Westerham TN16 . . . . .173 A3
Grange Dr Chislehurst BR7 . .22 F2
Pratt's Bottom BR6 . . . . .52 C2
Grange Gdns TN4 . . . . .148 D4
Grange Hill Chatham ME5 . . .48 B3
Plaxtol TN15 . . . . .101 E8
Grange Ho Erith DA8 . . . . .9 A5
Gravesend DA11 . . . . .30 A8
Maidstone ME16 . . . . .91 A2
Grange La Hartley DA3 . . . . . .43 B2
Maidstone ME14 . . . . .77 A1
Grange Park Coll ME19 . . . . .74 B3
Grange Rd Gillingham ME7 . . .49 A6
Gravesend DA11 . . . . .30 A8
Grays RM17 . . . . .12 B8
Orpington BR6 . . . . .51 C8
Platt TN15 . . . . .87 C7
Rochester ME1 . . . . .47 B7
Royal Tunbridge Wells TN4 . .148 D5
Sevenoaks TN13 . . . . .99 A8
Tenterden TN30 . . . . .172 F3
Grange Rd Gillingham ME7 . .49 A6
Grange The
East Malling ME19 . . . . .90 A7
Sutton at Hone DA4 . . . . . . .41 D8
West Kingsdown TN15 . . . . . .55 F2
Westerham TN16 . . . . .81 C1
Grange Way Erith DA8 . . . . . . .9 B7
Hartley DA3 . . . . .42 F3
Rochester ME1 . . . . .47 C3
Grangehill Pl SE9 . . . . .5 F4
Grangehill Rd SE9 . . . . .5 F4
Grangeways Cl DA11 . . . . . . .29 F4
Grangewood DA5 . . . . .24 F7
Granite St SE18 . . . . .2 F1
Grant Cl ME7 . . . . .49 B1
Grant Dr ME15 . . . . .107 D6
Grant Rd ME3 . . . . .33 C3
Grant's Cotts ME17 . . . . . . .111 B5
Granton Rd DA14 . . . . .24 C2
Granville Ct Erith SE2 . . . . . . .3 D1
Sevenoaks TN13 . . . . .84 A3
Granville Mews DA14 . . . . . .24 A4
Granville Rd Bexley DA7 . . . . .7 C4
Gillingham ME7 . . . . .48 E5
Gravesend DA11 . . . . .29 F7
Maidstone ME14 . . . . .92 A6
Royal Tunbridge Wells TN1 . .149 A3
Sevenoaks TN13 . . . . .84 A3
Sidcup DA14 . . . . .24 B4
Westerham TN16 . . . . .81 C1
Granville Sch The TN13 . . . . .84 C1
Grapple Rd ME14 . . . . .92 A7
Grasdene Rd SE18,SE2 . . . . . .7 A6
Grasmere Ave ME8 . . . . .64 B8
Grasmere Gdns BR6 . . . . . . .51 B7
Grasmere Gr ME2 . . . . .33 C2
Grasmere Rd Bexley DA7 . . . .8 C6
Orpington BR6 . . . . .51 B7
Grassington Rd DA14 . . . . . .24 A4
Grasslands ME17 . . . . .108 E4
Grassmere ME19 . . . . .74 F2
Grassy Glade ME7 . . . . .63 B6
Gravel La TN13 . . . . .99 B8
Gravel Hill 8 B2
Gravel Hill Cl DA6 . . . . .8 B4
Gravel Hill Prim Sch DA6 . . . .8 A4
Gravel Pit Way BR6 . . . . .38 A1
Gravel Rd Orpington BR2 . . . .50 D8
Sutton at Hone DA4 . . . . . . .27 B1
Gravel Wlk ME1 . . . . .47 C5
Gravelly Bottom Rd
ME17 . . . . .109 B2
Gravelly Ways TN12 . . . . . . .124 D4
Gravelwood Cl BR7 . . . . .23 C5
Graveney Cl ME3 . . . . .33 C7
Graveney Rd ME15 . . . . .107 F7
Graves Est DA16 . . . . .7 B6
Gravesend & North Kent
Hospl DA11 . . . . .13 A1
Gravesend Gram Sch
DA12 . . . . .30 D8
Gravesend Gram Sch
for Girls DA11 . . . . .13 C1
Gravesend Rd
Higham ME2,ME3,DA12 . . . .32 C2
Rochester ME2 . . . . .46 F8
Shorne DA12 . . . . .31 D5
Vigo Village TN15 . . . . .72 D8
Gravesham Com Hospl
Gravesham Ctr 12 DA12 . . . .30 B8
Gravesham Mus 4 DA11 . . .13 B1
Gray Ho SE17 . . . . .3 D1
Grayland Cl BR1 . . . . .36 D8

Graylands RM17 ....11 E8
Graylings The ME1 ....47 B3
Grayne Ave ME3 ....21 B5
Grays Farm Prim Sch BR5 ...38 B8
Grays Farm
  Production Village BR5 ....38 B8
Grays Farm Rd BR5 ....38 B8
Grays Rd TN1 ....81 D7
Grays Sh Ctr RM17 ....12 A8
Grays Sta RM17 ....12 A8
Grazeley Cl DA6 ....8 C2
Great Basin Rd ME12 ....21 F2
Great Bounds Dr TN4 ....132 E3
Great Brooms Rd TN4 ....149 C8
Great Courtlands TN3 ....148 A3
Great Elms TN11 ....102 E1
Great Elms Rd BR2 ....36 C5
Great Footway TN3 ....147 F3
Great Hall Arc 3 TN1 ....149 B3
Great Harry Dr SE9 ....23 A5
Great Ivy Mill Cotts ME15 ..106 F7
Great Lines ME7 ....48 B5
Great Maytham* TN17 ....181 F2
Great Oak ME3 ....184 A3
Great Queen St DA1 ....9 F3
Great South Ave ME4 ....48 A1
Great Thrift BR5 ....37 C5
Greatness La TN14 ....84 C6
Greatness Rd TN13,TN14 .....84 C6
Greatwood BR7 ....23 A1
Grebe Apartments 13
  ME15 ....107 E5
Grebe Cl ME3 ....19 C4
Grebe Ct ME20 ....74 F1
Grecian Rd TN1 ....149 B2
Grecian St ME14 ....92 A6
Green Acres DA14 ....23 F4
Green Bank Cl ME3 ....43 A5
Green Cl ME1 ....47 D2
Green Court Rd BR8 ....39 D3
Green Farm Cl BR6 ....51 F5
Green Farm La DA12 ....31 E5
Green Gdns BR6 ....51 F5
Green Hedges TN30 ....183 B8
Green Hill Maidstone ME15 ..93 B1
  Woolwich SE18 ....1 E6
Green Hill La ME17 ....110 D1
Green La
  Biddenden Green TN27 .....143 A1
  Cliffe ME3 ....16 B6
  Collier Street TN12 ....137 E8
  Devil's Den ME17 ....74 E4
  East End TN17 ....171 C2
  Eltham BR7,SE9 ....23 B5
  Four Elms TN8 ....113 C7
  Grain ME3 ....21 B5
  Langley Heath ME17 ....108 E3
  Maidstone ME17 ....107 C3
  Meopham Sta DA13 ....44 B2
  Paddock Wood TN12 ....46 A5
  Platt's Heath ME17 ....110 F2
  Stockbury ME9 ....64 F1
  Trottiscliffe ME19 ....73 A5
  Westerham TN16 ....159 F3
Green La The TN11 ....115 F1
Green Lands DA12 ....44 D4
Green Lane Bsns Pk SE27 ...23 A6
Green Lane Cotts
  Langley Heath ME17 ....121 D1
Green Lanes 11 SE18 ....8 B2
Green Pl DA1 ....8 E2
Green Rd TN12 ....153 A6
Green Sands ME5 ....77 C8
Green Sq TN5 ....174 F5
Green Wlk ME17 ....48 C5
Green Street Green
  Prim Sch BR6 ....51 F4
Green Street Green Rd
  DA1,DA2 ....27 D4
Green The
  Bexley,Bexley Heath DA7 .....8 A6
  Bexley,Falconwood DA16 ......6 E3
  Dartford DA2 ....27 D6
  East Farleigh ME15 ....106 B7
  Frant TN3 ....163 B3
  Hayes BR2 ....36 A2
  Leigh TN11 ....115 F1
  Lewisham BR1 ....22 A1
  Royal Tunbridge Wells TN2 .147 E3
  Sevenoaks TN13 ....84 D5
  Sidcup DA14 ....24 A4
  St Paul's Cray BR5 ....24 B1
  Westerham TN16 ....81 D1
Green Vale DA6 ....7 D2
Green View Ave TN11 ....116 C7
Green Way Bromley BR2 ....36 E3
  Eltham SE9 ....22 E6
  Hartley DA3 ....42 E4
  Maidstone ME16 ....91 D8
  Royal Tunbridge Wells TN2 ..149 E8
Green Wlk DA1 ....8 F3
Green's Cotts ME15 ....106 A6
Greenacre DA1 ....26 D6
Greenacre Cl Chatham ME5 ...62 A5
  Swanley BR8 ....39 E5
Greenacres ME5 ....61 F5
Greenacres SE9 ....6 A1
Greenacres Cl BR6 ....51 F6
Greenacres Prim Sch &
  Language Impairment
  Unit SE9 ....23 A6
Greenbank ME5 ....62 B8
Greenbank Lodge 2 BR7 ....37 A8
Greenbanks DA1 ....26 E6
Greenbay Rd SE7 ....5 D7
Greenborough Cl ME15 ....107 E6
Greencourt Rd BR5 ....37 E4

Greencroft Cl E6 ....1 D8
Greendale Wlk 4 DA11 ....29 E5
Greenfield TN8 ....112 D1
Greenfield Cl Eccles ME20 ....76 A6
  Royal Tunbridge Wells TN4 .148 C5
Greenfield Cotts ME14 ....77 A1
Greenfield Dr BR1 ....36 C7
Greenfield Gdns BR5 ....37 D2
Greenfield Rd Dartford DA2 ..25 D3
  Gillingham ME7 ....48 D6
Greenfields ME15 ....107 E8
Greenfields Cl ME3 ....33 D3
Greenfinches
  Gillingham ME7 ....62 F6
  New Barn DA3 ....43 B6
Greenfrith Dr TN10 ....117 B6
Greenhaven Dr SE28 ....3 B7
Greenhill DA12 ....139 E5
Greenhill Cts SE18 ....1 F1
Greenhill La TN27 ....143 F7
Greenhill Rd
  Northfleet DA11 ....29 F6
  Otford TN14 ....69 C5
Greenhill Terr SE18 ....1 F1
Greenhithe Cl DA15 ....23 E8
Greenhithe Sta DA9 ....11 A2
Greenholm Rd SE9 ....6 B2
Greening St SE2 ....3 C7
Greenlands TN5 ....174 F5
Greenlaw St SE18 ....2 A3
Greenleas TN12 ....150 C6
Greenleigh Ave BR5 ....38 B5
Greenlees ME14 ....92 A6
Greensand Rd ME15 ....93 A2
Greenshields Ind Est E16 .....1 A5
Greenside
  High Halden TN26 ....173 E7
  Maidstone ME15 ....92 B3
  Sidcup DA14 ....24 E7
  Swanley BR8 ....39 D7
Greenside Prim Sch SE16 ....16 D8
Greentrees Ave ME14 ....117 F5
Greenvale Gdns ME8 ....49 B2
Greenvale Rd SE9 ....6 A3
Greenview Cres TN11 ....116 E4
Greenway Wlk ME8 ....49 A4
Greenway Chatham ME5 ....61 D6
  Chislehurst BR7 ....23 B3
  Cranbrook TN17 ....169 B4
Greenway Court
  Farm Cotts ME17 ....95 A1
Greenway Court Rd ME17 .....95 A1
Greenway La ME17 ....110 A7
Greenway The BR5 ....38 B3
Greenways Maidstone ME14 ..92 F1
  New Barn DA3 ....43 B6
Greenways The TN2 ....135 F5
Greenwich Cl Chatham ME5 ..62 B4
  Maidstone ME16 ....91 D4
Greenwich Com Coll SE9 ......5 E1
Greenwich Cres E6 ....1 E8
Greenwich Hts SE7 ....5 E7
Greenwood Cl
  Orpington BR5 ....37 E3
  Sidcup DA15 ....24 A6
Greenwood House 8
  RM17 ....12 B8
Greenwood Pl TN15 ....83 F2
Greenwood Rd DA5 ....25 D4
Greenwood Way TN13 ....83 F2
Greggs Mews SE3 ....5 A7
Gregor Mews SE3 ....5 A7
Gregory Cl ME8 ....63 E4
Gregory Cres SE9 ....22 D8
Gregory House SE3 ....5 B5
Grenada Rd SE7 ....5 C8
Grenadier Cl ME15 ....92 F2
Grenadier St E16 ....2 A5
Grenville Cl DA13 ....58 A8
Gresham Ave TN10 ....42 F4
Gresham Cl
  8 Gillingham ME8 ....49 F1
  Sidcup DA15 ....7 F1
Gresham Rd
  Coxheath ME17 ....106 D3
  Newham E16 ....1 E7
Greshams Way TN8 ....112 A2
Gresswell Cl DA14 ....24 A5
Grey Wethers ME14 ....76 E4
Greybury La TN8 ....128 B3
Greyfriars Cl ME16 ....91 D5
Greyhound Way DA1 ....26 A1
Greys Park Cl BR2 ....50 D5
Greystone Pk TN14 ....82 E2
Greystones ME15 ....93 A2
Greystones Rd ME15 ....93 A2
Grieveson Ho ME14 ....92 B4
Grieves Rd DA11 ....29 F5
Griffin Manor Way SE18 ....2 D3
Griffin Manor Way SE28 ......2 D3
Griffin Rd SE18 ....2 D2
Griffin Way SE28 ....2 E3
Griffiths House 2 ME16 ....6 B8
Grigg La TN27 ....142 C7
Grigg's Cross BR5 ....38 D3
Griggs Way TN15 ....87 A7
Grimsby Gr E16 ....2 A4
Grinling Ho 10 SE18 ....2 A2
Grizedale Cl ME1 ....61 D8
Gromenfield TN3 ....161 C7
Groom Cl BR2 ....36 B5
Groombridge Cl DA16 ....7 A3

Groombridge Hill TN3 ....147 D1
Groombridge Pl* TN3 ....161 C8
Groombridge Place Gdns*
  TN3 ....161 C8
Groombridge Rd TN3 ....147 A1
Groombridge Sq 13
  ME15 ....107 F6
Groombridge Sta* TN3 ....161 C7
Grosmont Rd SE18 ....2 F1
Grosvenor Ave ME4 ....47 E3
Grosvenor Bridge TN1 ....149 B5
Grosvenor Cres DA11 ....9 D2
Grosvenor House 5
  ME15 ....107 F5
Grosvenor Pk TN1 ....149 A4
Grosvenor Rd Bexley DA6 ....7 E2
  Erith DA17 ....8 B8
  Gillingham ME7 ....49 A1
  Orpington BR5 ....37 E3
  Royal Tunbridge Wells TN1 .149 A4
Grosvenor Wlk TN1 ....149 A4
Grove Ave TN1 ....149 A2
Grove Cl BR2 ....50 A8
Grove CtSho TN6 ....183 B6
Grove Ct Greenwich SE3 ....5 B6
  4 Rochester ME2 ....47 B7
Grove Green La ME14 ....92 F5
Grove Green Rd ME14 ....92 E5
Grove Hill BR6 ....51 F5
Grove Hill Rd ME14 ....149 B3
Grove Market Pl SE9 ....5 F1
Grove Park Rd SE9 ....22 C6
Grove Park Sta SE12 ....22 B5
Grove Rd Bexley DA7 ....8 B2
  Chatham ME4 ....48 B2
  5 Erith DA17 ....7 F8
  Gillingham ME7 ....49 A6
  Maidstone ME15 ....107 C7
  Northfleet DA11 ....12 B2
  Penshurst TN11,TN8 ....130 C2
  Rochester ME2 ....47 A8
  Seal TN15 ....85 A3
  Sevenoaks TN13,TN14 ....84 C6
  Upper Halling ME2 ....59 E5
Grove The Bexley DA6 ....7 D3
  Gravesend DA12 ....30 B8
  Maidstone ME14 ....93 A3
  Pembury TN2 ....150 D8
  Sidcup DA14 ....24 E4
  Swanley BR8 ....39 F6
  Swanscombe DA10 ....11 F2
  West Kingsdown TN15 ....55 F1
Grove Vale BR7 ....23 A2
Grove Wood Cotts TN1 ....100 A1
Grovebury Cl DA8 ....8 D8
Grovebury Ct DA8 ....8 E7
Grovebury Rd SE2 ....3 B4
Groveherst Rd DA1 ....9 F4
Groveland La TN12 ....153 C5
Grovelands ME17 ....111 E5
Grovelands Rd BR5 ....24 A1
Grovelands Way RM17 ....11 F8
Grover St 3 TN1 ....149 B4
Groves The TN6 ....74 F7
Grovewood Cl ME14 ....74 E2
Grovewood Dr ME14 ....92 E4
Guardian Ct ME8 ....49 C1
Guardian Ind Est TN12 ....138 C7
Guestwick TN10 ....117 F5
Guibal Rd SE12 ....22 B7
Guild Rd Erith DA8 ....8 F8
  Greenwich SE7 ....5 D8
Guildhall Gdns ME2 ....46 C6
Guildhall Mus* ME1 ....47 C6
4 Royal Tunbridge Wells
  TN1 ....149 B3
Gulland Ho 6 ME14 ....92 B4
Gulands ME17 ....108 E4
Gulliver Rd DA15 ....23 E6
Gumley Rd RM20 ....11 E8
Gumping Rd BR5,BR6 ....51 C8
Gun Hill RM18 ....13 C8
Gun La Gillingham ME7 ....62 E3
  Rochester ME2 ....47 B7
Gundulph Ho TN10 ....117 C3
Gundulph Rd Bromley BR2 ....36 C6
  Chatham ME1 ....47 E4
Gundulph Sq ME1 ....47 E5
Gunfleet Cl DA12 ....30 E8
Gunlands TN12 ....153 A6
Gunn Rd DA10 ....11 F1
Gunner La SE18 ....2 A1
Gunning St SE18 ....2 E2
Gunnis Cl ME8 ....49 B2
Gurdon Rd SE7 ....1 B1
Guston Rd ME14 ....92 D4
Guy Barnett Gr SE3 ....5 A4
Gwillim Cl DA15 ....7 A2
Gwynn Rd DA11 ....29 C6
Gybbon Rise TN12 ....139 E3
Gybbon Rd TN17 ....181 F3
Gypsy Way ME23 ....17 E3

Ha-Ha Rd SE18 ....5 F8
Hackney Rd ME16 ....91 C2
Hadden Rd SE28 ....2 E3
Haddon Gr DA15 ....24 A8
Haddon Rd BR5 ....38 C4
Hadleigh Ct ME7 ....63 A3
Hadleigh Wlk 11 E6 ....1 E7
Hadley Cl DA17 ....58 B8
Hadley Ct TN4 ....148 F6

Hadley Gdns ME17 ....94 E2
Hadley House BR5 ....37 F7
Hadley Rd DA17 ....3 F2
Hadlow Coll
  Nature Reserve* SE12 ....22 C7
Hadlow Coll of Agriculture
  & Horticulture
  TN11 ....118 D8
Hadlow Ct TN9 ....117 C2
Hadlow Pk TN11 ....102 E1
Hadlow Prim Sch TN11 ....118 E8
Hadlow Rd Bexley DA16 ....7 C7
  Maidstone ME14 ....92 C5
  Sidcup DA14 ....24 A4
  Tonbridge TN9 ....117 C1
  Tonbridge,Higham Wood
    TN10,TN11 ....118 A5
Hadlow Stair Rd TN10 ....117 A5
Hadlow Way DA13 ....29 C1
Haffenden La TN12 ....138 D6
Haffenden Rd TN30 ....173 B1
Haig Ave Chatham ME1 ....47 D1
  Chatham,Luton ME4 ....48 A2
  Gillingham ME7 ....48 E4
Haig Ct BR7 ....23 B3
Haig Gdns DA12 ....30 C8
Haig Villas ME3 ....34 A5
Hailey Rd DA18 ....4 A4
Hailey Rd Bsns Pk DA18 ......4 A4
Haimes Ho Chatham ME4 ......52 A6
Hailstone Cl TN11 ....118 E8
Haimo Prim Sch SE9 ....5 D2
Haimo Rd SE9 ....5 D2
Hainault St SE9 ....23 B7
Halcot Ave DA6 ....8 C2
Haldane Gdns ME14 ....21 A7
Haldane Rd SE28 ....3 C6
Halden Cl ME15 ....107 F6
Halden La TN17 ....181 F6
Hale Cl BR6 ....51 C6
Hale Dr ME14 ....92 C7
Hale Ct TN12 ....120 A7
Hale End SE9 ....7 F8
Hale Oak Rd
  Hall's Green TN8,TN14 ....114 E4
  Sevenoaks Weald TN14 ....99 B1
Hale Rd ME3 ....33 C7
Hales St ME14 ....120 A7
Hales Cl TN30 ....183 B8
Hales Ct TN12 ....120 A7
Hales Rd SE18 ....183 B8
Haleys Pl ME1 ....76 A8
Half Moon La TN11 ....116 D6
Half Moon Way ME23 ....17 F3
Halfpence La DA12 ....45 E3
Halfpenny Cl ME16 ....91 A2
Halfway St DA15 ....23 E7
Halifax Cl ME5 ....62 B3
Halifield Dr DA17 ....3 E8
Hall Hill TN15 ....85 C4
Hall Pl* SE9 ....8 C1
Hall Place Cres DA1,DA5 ......8 D2
Hall Rd Aylesford ME20 ....75 F2
  Chatham ME5 ....62 C3
  Dartford DA1 ....9 A3
  High Halstow ME3 ....18 C6
  Northfleet DA11 ....29 C5
  Northfleet,Wombwell
    Park DA11 ....29 D6
  Wouldham ME1 ....60 C3
Hall The SE3 ....5 A4
Hall's Grove Rd TN2 ....22 D6
Hall's Hole Rd TN2 ....149 E4
Hallam Cl BR7 ....22 F3
Hallford Way DA1 ....9 C2
Hallgate SE3 ....5 A4
Halling Prim Sch ME2 ....60 B3
Halling Sta ME2 ....60 A5
Halls Cotts TN5 ....174 F5
Hallsfield Rd ME5 ....61 D2
Hallsville Prim Sch E16 ....1 A7
Hallwards ME12 ....139 E2
Hallwood Cl ME8 ....63 D5
Hallwood House ME5 ....62 C2
Hallywell Cres E6 ....1 F8
Halons Rd SE9 ....6 B1
Halsbrook Rd SE3 ....5 D4
Halstead La TN14 ....67 E5
Halstead Place Sch TN14 .....67 E6
Halstead Prim Sch TN14 ......67 E8
Halstead Rd DA8 ....8 E6
Halstow Cl ME15 ....107 B6
Halstow Prim Sch SE10 ....1 A1
Halstow Rd SE10,SE3 ....1 A2
Halt Robin La DA17 ....4 B2
Halt Robin Rd DA17 ....4 B2
Ham La Gillingham ME7 ....62 E3
Ham Hill Rd ME7 ....63 A3
Ham River Hill ME3 ....33 A6
Ham Shades Cl 5 DA15 ......24 A5
Hamble Rd TN10 ....117 C6
Hambledon Cl ME16 ....91 B3
Hambledown Rd DA15 ....23 D8
Hambro Ave BR2 ....50 A1
Hamelin Rd ME7 ....62 F8
Hamilton Ct DA11 ....149 A5

Hamilton Ho
  Coxheath ME17 ....106 C3
  Royal Tunbridge Wells TN4 ..133 A2
Hamilton Rd Bexley DA7 ....7 E5
  Gillingham ME7 ....48 D6
  Sidcup DA15 ....24 A4
Hamilton Wlk DA8 ....8 F7
Hamlea Cl SE12 ....5 A1
Hamlet Ho Eltham SE9 ....6 A2
5 Erith DA8 ....8 E7

Hamlin Rd TN13 ....83 E6
Hamlyn Ct TN13 ....83 E6
Hammelton Rd BR1 ....36 A8
Hammerwood Pk* RH19 ......144 C2
Hammond Way 2 SE28 ....3 B6
Hammond Rd ME18 ....179 A2
Hammonds Sp ME6 ....75 A8
Hamond Hill 6 ME4 ....47 F3
Hampden Way ME19 ....88 F3
Hampshire Dr ME15 ....107 C8
Hampshire Pk ME15 ....107 C8
Hampson Way ME14 ....93 A4
Hampstead Cl SE28 ....3 B5
Hampstead La ME14 ....104 C1
Hampton Cl ME5 ....62 A5
Hampton Cts TN14 ....67 F4
Hampton Cres DA12 ....30 E6
Hampton House DA7 ....8 B5
Hampton Rd ME14 ....92 C6
Hamptons Rd TN11 ....102 B5
Hamwick Gn ME5 ....62 C1
Hanameel St E16 ....1 B6
Hanbury Cl ME18 ....106 E7
Hanbury Wlk DA5 ....25 E5
Hancock Cl ME3 ....33 B1
Handel Cres RM18 ....13 A7
Handel Wlk TN10 ....117 C6
Hands Wlk E16 ....1 A7
Hanes Dene ME2 ....59 F5
Hang Grove Hill BR6 ....66 B6
Hangmans Cnr BR7 ....37 B8
Hanley Ct TN13 ....84 B4
Hanmer Way TN12 ....139 E2
Hanover Ave E16 ....1 A5
Hanover Cl ME14 ....92 B5
Hanover Dr Chislehurst BR7 ..23 C4
  Gillingham ME8 ....63 C3
Hanover Gn ME20 ....74 F3
Hanover Pl DA3 ....56 F8
Hanover Rd
  Coxheath ME17 ....106 C3
  Royal Tunbridge Wells TN1 ..149 A4
Hanover Way DA7 ....7 D4
Hansol Rd DA6 ....7 E2
Hansom Terr 1 BR1 ....36 B8
Hanway ME8 ....49 A2
Harbex Cl DA5 ....25 B8
Harbledown Manor ME8 ....49 B3
Harbledown Pl 7 BR5 ....38 C5
Harborough Ave DA15 ....23 F8
Harbour Cl 8 DA2 ....10 B1
Harbour The ME7 ....124 E5
Harbourland Cl ME14 ....92 B8
Harbourne La TN26,TN30 .....173 E5
Harbourne Rd ME14 ....92 C8
Harcourt Gdns ME8 ....63 E4
Harcourt Rd DA6,DA7 ....7 E4
Harden Ct 1 SE18 ....1 E2
Harden Rd DA11 ....29 F6
Hardie Cl ME9 ....74 F1
Harding Ho 9 SE18 ....1 F2
Hardinge Ave TN4 ....132 E3
Hardinge Cl ME8 ....5 D3
Hardinge St SE18 ....2 C3
Hardman Rd SE7 ....1 B1
Hardres Terr BR5 ....52 D8
Hards Town ME4 ....48 A4
Hardwick Cres 2 DA2 ....10 B1
Hardwick Cl DA8 ....8 D8
Hardwick Rd TN11 ....116 E6
Hardy Ave Newham E16 ....1 A5
  Northfleet DA11 ....29 E6
Hardy Cl ME20 ....75 F1
Hardy Gr DA1 ....10 A3
Hardy Rd SE3 ....1 A3
Hardy St ME14 ....92 A6
Hare St 2 Chatham ME4 ....48 B3
  1 Woolwich SE18 ....2 A3
Harebell Cl
  3 Chatham ME5 ....62 F4
  Maidstone ME14 ....92 F5
Harebell Dr E6 ....1 F8
Haredale Cl ME1 ....61 D7
Harefield Rd DA14 ....24 D5
Harenc Sch DA14 ....24 D5
Harescroft TN2 ....162 F7
Harewood Lincoln Ho
  DA11 ....12 D3
Harfst Way BR8 ....39 C8
Hargate Cl TN2 ....162 F8
Hargood Rd SE3 ....5 C5
Harland Ave DA15 ....23 E6
Harland Rd SE12 ....22 A7
Harland Way TN4 ....132 F4
Harlech Cl ME2 ....46 C6
Harlequin Ho 1 DA18 ....3 E3
Harley Gdns BR6 ....51 E6
Harleyford BR1 ....36 C8
Harmer Ct SE9 ....6 A1
Harmer Rd
  Royal Tunbridge Wells TN4 ..133 A2
  Swanscombe DA10 ....11 F1
Harmer St DA12 ....13 C1
Harmer St DA11 ....127 F3
Harmony St TN4 ....148 D4
Harness Rd SE28 ....3 A4
Harold Ave Erith DA17 ....3 F1
  Gillingham ME7 ....48 E4

Harold Gibbons Ct SE7 . . . . .5 C8
Harold Ho TN2 . . . . .149 C7
Harold Rd Cuxton ME2 . . . .46 C3
  Hawley DA2 . . . . .24 F4
Harp Farm Rd ME14 . . . . .77 C6
Harper Rd E6 . . . . .1 F7
Harpie La ME14 . . . . .77 F1
Harpswood ME17 . . . . .94 F1
Harptree Dr ME5 . . . . .61 F5
Harraden Rd SE3 . . . . .5 C6
Harrier Mews SE28 . . . . . .2 D4
Harrier Way E6 . . . . .1 F8
Harries Cl TN2 . . . . .149 E7
Harrietsham Sta ME17 . . .110 D6
Harriet Dr ME1 . . . . .47 B3
Harrington Rd 4 BR1 . . . .36 A8
Harrington Way SE18 . . . . .1 D3
Harris Cl DA11 . . . . .29 F5
Harris Ho ME2 . . . . .60 B4
Harris Rd DA7 . . . . .7 F6
Harrison Ct 8 ME9 . . . . . . .5 F5
Harrison Dr
  Harrietsham ME17 . . . .110 E6
  High Halstow ME23 . . . .17 E4
Harrison Rd TN15 . . . . . . .86 F7
Harrison Way TN13 . . . . . .84 A5
Harrogate Ct 6 SE12 . . . .22 A8
Harrow Cl TN8 . . . . .112 D3
Harrow Ct Chatham ME5 . .62 C4
  Stockbury ME9 . . . . .79 D8
Harrow Gdns BR6 . . . . . . .52 B6
Harrow Manor Way SE2 . . .3 C3
Harrow Rd Gillingham ME7 .62 F6
  Halstead TN14 . . . . .67 E4
Harrow Way ME14 . . . . . . .92 E5
Harrowby Gdns DA11 . . . .29 E6
Hart Dyke Cres BR8 . . . . .39 D6
Hart Dyke Rd
  Orpington BR5 . . . . .38 C1
  Swanley BR8 . . . . .39 D6
Hart Shaw DA3 . . . . .49 F8
Hart St ME16 . . . . .91 F3
Hart Street Bsns Ctr ME16 . .91 F3
Hartfield Cl TN1 . . . . .117 E5
Hartfield Cres BR4 . . . . . .50 A7
Hartfield Pl DA11 . . . . . . .29 D8
Hartfield Rd Hayes BR4 . .50 A6
  Hever TN8 . . . . .129 A4
Hartford Rd DA5 . . . . .8 A1
Hartford Wlk 3 DA17 . . . . .4 A1
Harting Rd SE9 . . . . .22 E5
Hartington Rd E16 . . . . . .51 C5
Hartington Rd E16 . . . . . . .1 B7
Hartington St ME4 . . . . . . .48 A3
Hartlake Rd TN11 . . . . . . .118 D3
Hartlands Cl DA5 . . . . .7 F1
Hartlepool Ct E16 . . . . .2 B4
Hartley Bottom Rd DA3 . . .43 C2
Hartley Cl Bromley BR1 . . .36 F7
  Maidstone ME15 . . . . . .107 F6
Hartley Court Gdns TN17 .169 A3
Hartley Cty Prim Sch DA3 . .42 E3
Hartley Hill DA3 . . . . .43 A1
Hartley Rd Bexley DA16 . . .7 C7
  Hartley TN17 . . . . .169 A3
  Longfield DA3 . . . . .42 E7
  Westerham TN16 . . . . . .81 D2
Hartlip Endowed
  CE Prim Sch ME9 . . . . . .64 D5
Hartlip Hill ME9 . . . . .64 F7
Hartmann Rd E16 . . . . .1 E5
Hartnokes TN18 . . . . .179 A2
Hartnup St ME16 . . . . .91 F2
Harton Cl BR1 . . . . .36 D8
Hartpiece Cl ME8 . . . . .49 F2
Hartshill Rd DA11 . . . . . . .29 F6
Hartslands Rd TN13 . . . . . .84 C4
Hartslock Dr DA18,SE2 . . .3 D4
Hartsmead Rd SE9 . . . . . .22 E6
Hartville Rd SE18 . . . . .2 E2
Hartwell Ho 2 SE7 . . . . . . .1 B1
Harty Ave ME8 . . . . .63 B3
Harvard Ct 6 SE9 . . . . .6 A1
Harvel Ave ME2 . . . . .46 F7
Harvel Ct BR5,BR7 . . . . . .38 A6
Harvel Cres SE2 . . . . .3 D1
Harvel La DA13 . . . . .58 B2
Harvel Rd DA13 . . . . .73 A8
Harvel St DA13 . . . . .58 C3
Harvest Bank Rd BR4 . . . .50 A7
Harvest Rd TN10 . . . . . . .117 D6
Harvest Ridge ME19 . . . . .74 D2
Harvest Way BR8 . . . . .39 D2
Harvesters Cl ME8 . . . . . . .63 E7
Harvesters Way ME14 . . . .92 D4
Harvey Gdns SE7 . . . . .1 C1
Harvey Point 4 E16 . . . . . .1 A8
Harvey Rd ME8 . . . . .63 E8
Harvill Rd DA14 . . . . .24 E3
Harwood Ave BR1 . . . . . . .36 B7
Harwood Ct 3 ME17 . . . . .12 C8
Haslemere Est ME15 . . . .107 F5
Haslemere Rd DA7 . . . . . . .8 A5
Hasler Cl SE28 . . . . .3 C6
Hasletts Cl TN1 . . . . .149 B6
Haslewood Cl TN27 . . . .143 B8
Hassenden Rd SE3 . . . . . . .5 B7
Hassock Wood BR2 . . . . .50 E6
Hassop Wlk SE9 . . . . .22 E4
Haste Hill Cl ME17 . . . . .107 B3
Haste Hill Rd ME17 . . . . .107 B3
Hasted Cl DA9 . . . . .11 C1
Hasted Rd Greenwich SE7 . .1 D1
  Newington ME9 . . . . .65 B7
Hasteds ME17 . . . . .94 D2

Hastings Cl RM17 . . . . .11 E8
Hastings Ho SE18 . . . . .1 F2
Hastings Rd
  Kipping's Cross TN2 . .150 F5
  Maidstone ME15 . . . . . . .92 B3
  Newenden TN17,TN18 . .187 C6
  Orpington BR2 . . . . .50 E8
  Pembury TN2 . . . . .150 D6
  The Moor TN18 . . . . . .184 F6
Hastings St SE18 . . . . .2 C3
Hatch Rd ME17 . . . . .111 C5
Hatches La TN11,TN12 . . .119 D6
Hatfield Cl SE3 . . . . .5 A7
Hatfield Rd ME2 . . . . .47 A8
Hatham Green La TN15 . . .56 D1
Hathaway Cl BR2 . . . . .36 F1
Hathaway Ct
  Gillingham ME8 . . . . .63 D8
  Rochester ME1 . . . . .47 B5
Hatherall Rd ME14 . . . . . . .92 B6
Hatherley Cres DA14 . . . .24 A6
Hatherley Rd DA14 . . . . . .24 A5
Hathern Gdns SE9 . . . . . . .23 A4
Hatmill La TN12 . . . . .152 A7
Hattersfield Cl DA17 . . . . .3 F2
Hatton Cl Northfleet DA11 . .29 E5
  Woolwich SE18 . . . . .6 D7
Hatton Ct BR7 . . . . .22 F1
Hatton Rd ME5 . . . . .62 C3
Havant Wlk ME15 . . . . . .107 F6
Havelock Rd Bromley BR2 . .36 B5
  Dartford DA1 . . . . .9 B1
  Erith DA17 . . . . .3 F2
  Gravesend DA11 . . . . . . .29 F7
  Tonbridge TN9 . . . . . . .117 B2
Haven Cl Chislehurst SE9 . .23 B5
  Istead Rise DA13 . . . . . . .43 F8
  Rochester ME1 . . . . .47 C2
  Sidcup DA14 . . . . .24 A2
  Swanley BR8 . . . . .39 F7
Haven Hill TN15 . . . . .57 A3
Haven Lodge 9 SE18 . . . . .2 B2
Haven St ME3 . . . . .33 C5
Haven Way ME4 . . . . .44 F8
Havengore Ave DA12 . . . .30 E8
Havering Ct TN2 . . . . . . .149 F6
Haverstock Ct 2 BR5 . . . .38 B7
Haverthwaite Rd BR6 . . . .51 D7
Havisham Cl ME1 . . . . .47 D2
Havisham Rd DA12 . . . . . .31 A7
Havock La 1 ME14 . . . . . . .91 F4
Hawbeck Rd ME8 . . . . .63 C3
Hawden Cl TN11 . . . . .116 C4
Hawden La TN11 . . . . .116 F4
Hawden Rd TN9 . . . . .117 B2
Hawes Rd BR1 . . . . .36 B8
Hawfield Bank BR6 . . . . . . .52 D7
Hawkenbury Cl TN2 . . . .149 D2
Hawkenbury Mead TN2 . .149 D1
Hawkenbury Rd
  Hawkenbury TN2 . . . . . .140 C6
  Royal Tunbridge Wells
  TN2 . . . . .149 E1
Hawkenbury Rise ME2 . . .33 B2
Hawkes Cl RM17 . . . . .12 B8
Hawkes Pl TN13 . . . . .99 A8
Hawkes Rd ME20 . . . . .75 F5
Hawkhurst CE Prim Sch
  Hawkhurst TN18 . . . . . .178 F2
  The Moor TN18 . . . . . .184 F8
Hawkhurst Cottage Hospl
  TN18 . . . . .178 D2
Hawkhurst Rd
  Flimwell TN5,TN18 . . . .177 E2
  Gillingham ME8 . . . . . . .49 B3
  Hartley TN17,TN18 . . . .178 F7
Hawkinge Wlk BR5 . . . . . .38 B6
Hawkins Ave DA12 . . . . . .30 C4
Hawkins Cl ME7 . . . . .48 A6
Hawksmoor Cl
  2 Newham E6 . . . . .1 E7
  Woolwich SE18 . . . . .2 F1
Hawksmoor Prim Sch SE28 . .3 B6
Hawkwell Cotts TN2 . . . .134 F2
Hawkwood ME16 . . . . .91 B5
Hawkwood Cl ME1 . . . . . .47 D5
Hawkwood La BR7 . . . . . . .37 C8
Hawley Cl ME16 . . . . .91 E4
Hawley Rd DA1,DA2,DA4 . .27 A4
Hawley Terr DA2 . . . . .27 A4
Hawley Vale DA2 . . . . . . .27 A4
Hawser Rd ME1 . . . . .47 C1
Hawstead La BR6 . . . . . . .52 F5
Hawthorn Cl
  Edenbridge TN8 . . . . . .112 C2
  6 Gillingham ME7 . . . . .30 C4
  Orpington BR5 . . . . .37 D3
Hawthorn Cotts 6 DA16 . .7 A4
Hawthorn House 6 ME5 . .61 F5
Hawthorn La TN13 . . . . . . .83 F5
Hawthorn Pl DA8 . . . . .4 C1
Hawthorn Rd Bexley DA6 . .7 F3
  Dartford DA1 . . . . .26 D7
  Rochester ME2 . . . . .46 E6
  Tenterden TN15 . . . . .6 F2
Hawthorn Wlk
  Royal Tunbridge Wells TN2 . .149 E8
  Tonbridge TN10 . . . . . .117 C7
Hawthorne Cl BR2 . . . . . .50 A8
Hawthornedene Rd BR2 . .50 A8
Hawthorne Ave ME8 . . . . .49 C2
Hawthorne Cl BR1 . . . . . .36 F5
Hawthorne Rd ME5 . . . . . .61 F1
  Hartley DA3 . . . . .42 F5
Hawthorns The ME20 . . . .75 E1
Haxted Rd BR1 . . . . .36 A6
Hay's Mead DA13 . . . . .44 F3

Hayday Rd E16 . . . . .1 A8
Haydens Cl BR5 . . . . .38 C3
Haydens Mews TN9 . . . . .117 C3
Haydens The TN9 . . . . . . .117 C3
Hayes Cl Hayes BR2 . . . . .50 A8
  Higham ME3 . . . . .32 C3
  West Thurrock RM20 . .11 C8
Hayes Gdn BR2 . . . . .36 A1
Hayes La Hayes BR2 . . . . .36 A4
  Stockbury ME9 . . . . .79 F6
Hayes Prim Sch BR2 . . . .36 B1
Hayes Rd Hayes BR2 . . . .36 A5
  Stone DA9 . . . . .10 F2
Hayes Sch BR2 . . . . .50 B8
Hayes St BR2 . . . . .36 B1
Hayes Terr DA12 . . . . .31 B6
Hayes Wlk ME19 . . . . .89 A2
Hayes Wood Ave BR2 . . .36 B1
Hayesbrook Sch TN9 . . .133 A8
Haysden La TN11,TN3 . .132 B5
Haysford Park Dr BR2 . . .36 A4
Hayfield ME19 . . . . .74 E2
Hayfield Rd BR5 . . . . .38 A4
Hayfields ME5 . . . . .62 D2
Haygate Ho ME1 . . . . .47 C4
Hayle Mill Cotts ME15 . .106 F8
Hayle Mill Rd ME15 . . . .106 F8
Hayle Rd ME15 . . . . .92 A3
Hayley Cl ME2 . . . . .46 C2
Hayman Wlk ME20 . . . . . .75 F6
Haymans Hill TN12 . . . .153 C7
Haymen St ME4 . . . . .47 E3
Hayne Rd DA11 . . . . .29 F5
Hayrick Cl ME14 . . . . .92 E5
Hays Rd ME6 . . . . .74 F6
Haysden Ctry Pk* TN11 . .132 D8
Haywain Cl Maidstone ME14 . .136 A5
  Paddock Wood TN12 . .136 A7
Hayward Ave ME7 . . . . . . .47 B8
Hayward Cl DA1 . . . . .8 D2
Hayward Dr DA1 . . . . .26 F6
Hayward's Ho ME1 . . . . . .47 C6
Haywood Dr BR2 . . . . .36 D5
Haywood Rd BR6 . . . . . . .51 E5
Hazel Ave
  Hoo St Werburgh ME3 . .34 E3
  Maidstone ME16 . . . . . . .91 C5
Hazel Cotts TN14 . . . . . . .68 A6
Hazel Dr DA8 . . . . .9 B6
Hazel End BR8 . . . . .39 E4
Hazel Gr Chatham ME5 . .62 B6
  Orpington BR6 . . . . .51 B8
Hazel Rd Dartford DA1 . .26 D6
  Erith DA8 . . . . .9 A6
Hazel Shaw TN10 . . . . . .117 D7
Hazel Street Rd ME9 . . . .80 D6
Hazel Wlk BR2 . . . . .37 A3
Hazelbank HB3 . . . . .147 F3
Hazelden Cl TN15 . . . . . . .56 A2
Hazeldene Rd DA16 . . . . . .7 C5
Hazelmere 8 DA14 . . . . .24 A4
Hazelmere Rd BR5 . . . . . .37 D5
Hazelmere Way BR2 . . . .36 A3
Hazels The ME8 . . . . .63 B5
Hazelwood Cl TN9 . . . . .133 B8
Hazelwood Cotts TN5 . .176 D1
Hazelwood Dr ME16 . . . .91 B4
Hazelwood Rd TN14 . . . .66 D8
Hazlemere Dr ME7 . . . . .49 A5
Hazlitt Cl 4 SE28 . . . . .3 C5
Hazlitt Dr ME16 . . . . .91 C5
Head Race The ME15 . . . .91 D2
Headcorn Prim Sch
  TN27 . . . . .141 C5
Headcorn Rd
  Biddenden Green TN27 . .142 C3
  Bromley BR1 . . . . .22 A3
  Gillingham ME8 . . . . .49 B4
  Lashenden TN27 . . . . . .158 E3
  Platt's Heath ME17 . . . .140 F1
  Staplehurst TN12 . . . . .140 B4
  Sutton Valence ME17 . .124 E4
  Ulcombe ME17 . . . . . . .125 F5
Headcorn Sta TN27 . . . .141 D4
Headingley Rd ME16 . . . .91 B6
Headley Cl TN8 . . . . .112 C2
Headley House 5 BR5 . . .38 A7
Headway Ct TN4 . . . . . . .148 B4
Heald Gr 1 BR6 . . . . .51 F6
Heansill La TN18 . . . . . .184 E8
Hearns Rd BR5 . . . . .38 C5
Heartenoak Rd TN18 . . .179 B3
Heath Ave DA7 . . . . .7 B8
Heath Cl Orpington BR5 . .38 C3
  Swanley BR8 . . . . .39 F7
Heath Cl TN12 . . . . .152 F6
Heath Gdns DA1 . . . . .26 C7
Heath House ME5 . . . . . . .23 F4
Heath La Dartford DA1 . .26 D7
  Dartford,Dartford
  Heath DA1,DA2 . . . . . . .26 B7
Heath Park Dr BR1 . . . . .36 A6
Heath Rd Coldblow DA5 . .25 C7
  Coxheath ME17 . . . . . .106 C3
  Crayford DA1 . . . . .8 E1
  Langley Heath ME17 . .108 E4
  Maidstone ME5 . . . . .63 D8
  Royal Tunbridge Wells TN2 . .148 F7
Heath Side DA5 . . . . .24 F8
Heath Terr TN11 . . . . . . .153 A6
Heath The TN9 . . . . .99 F5
Heath View Dr SE2 . . . . . . .7 D8
Heath Villas SE2 . . . . .2 E1
Heath Way DA7,DA8 . . . . .8 D6

Heathcote Ave DA1 . . . . . .26 B8
Heathclose Rd DA1 . . . . . .26 B7
Heathcote Ct ME20 . . . . .75 F2
Heathdene Dr DA17 . . . . . .4 B2
Heathend ME8 . . . . .25 E7
Heather Bank TN12 . . . .136 B6
Heather Cl Chatham ME5 . .61 E3
  Maidstone ME14 . . . . . .2 A7
Heather Dr Dartford DA1 . .26 A8
  Maidstone ME15 . . . . . .92 B2
  Tenterden TN30 . . . . . .173 B3
Heather End BR8 . . . . .39 E5
Heather Rd SE12 . . . . . . .22 A7
Heather Wlk TN10 . . . . .117 B6
Heatherbank
  Chislehurst BR7 . . . . .37 A7
  Eltham SE9 . . . . .23 A5
Heatherbank Cl DA1 . . . . .9 F1
Heatherside Rd DA14 . . .24 C5
Heatherwood Ct ME17 . .108 E4
Heathfield Chislehurst BR7 . .23 C2
  Langley Heath ME17 . .108 E4
Heathfield Ave Chatham ME5 . .62 B7
  Maidstone ME14 . . . . . .92 B7
Heathfield Cl Chatham ME5 . .62 B7
  Swanley BR8 . . . . .39 D7
Heathfield Ct ME14 . . . . .92 B7
Heathfield La BR7 . . . . . .23 C2
Heathfield Rd Bexley DA6 . .7 F3
  Maidstone ME14 . . . . . .92 B7
  Orpington BR6 . . . . .51 D5
  Sevenoaks TN13 . . . . . . .83 F5
Heathfield Terr Bexley SE18 . .6 F8
  Swanley BR8 . . . . .39 D7
Heathfields TN2 . . . . . . .149 D4
Heathlands Rise DA1 . . . . .9 B1
Heathlee Rd DA1 . . . . .8 E1
Heathley End 8 BR7 . . . .23 C2
Heathorn St ME14 . . . . . .92 B5
Heathside Ave Bexley DA7 . .7 E5
  Coxheath ME17 . . . . . .106 C4
Heathview TN18 . . . . . . .132 F2
Heathview Ave DA1 . . . . .8 D8
Heathview Cres DA1 . . . .26 B7
Heathway SE3 . . . . .5 A7
Heathwood Gdns
  Swanley BR8 . . . . .39 C7
  Woolwich SE7 . . . . .1 E7
Heathwood Wlk DA5 . . . .25 E7
Heaverham Rd TN15 . . . .70 C2
Heavitree Cl 3 SE18 . . . . .2 D1
Heavitree Rd SE18 . . . . . .2 D1
Hector St SE18 . . . . .2 E1
Hectorage Rd TN9 . . . . .133 D8
Hedge Place Rd DA9 . . . .11 A1
Hedgerow The ME14 . . . .92 E5
Hedgerows The DA11 . . .29 F6
Hedges The ME14 . . . . . .92 E5
Hedley Ave RM20 . . . . . . .11 C8
Hedley St ME14 . . . . .92 A5
Heights The SE7 . . . . .1 C1
Helen Allison Sch The
  DA13 . . . . .44 A2
Helen Cl DA1 . . . . .26 B8
Helen Cl 3 DA14 . . . . .24 B4
Helen Keller Cl TN10 . .117 D4
Helen St 5 SE18 . . . . .2 B2
Heligan Cl BR6 . . . . .51 F6
Hellyar St ME1 . . . . .47 C4
Helverswood TN4 . . . . . . .53 A2
Hemmings Cl DA14 . . . . .24 B6
Hempstead Inf Sch ME7 . .63 A5
Hempstead Jun Sch ME7 . .63 A5
Hempstead La ME7 . . . . .63 A4
Hempstead Rd
  Gillingham, Hempstead ME7 . .63 A6
  Gillingham, Hempstead ME7 . .63 B6
Hempstead Valley Dr ME7 . .63 A4
Hempstead Valley Sh Ctr
  ME7 . . . . .63 A3
Hemsted Forest
  Forest Walks* TN17 . .170 E2
Hemsted Rd DA8 . . . . .8 E7
Henbane Cl ME17 . . . . . .92 E5
Henderson Dr DA1 . . . . .10 A3
Hendley Dr TN17 . . . . . .169 C5
Hendry Ho ME3 . . . . .33 F6
Hendy Rd ME6 . . . . .75 B8
Henfield Cl DA5 . . . . .8 A1
Hengist Rd Eltham SE12 . .22 A8
  Erith DA8 . . . . .8 E8
Hengrove Ct DA5 . . . . .24 E7
Henham Gdns TN12 . . . .120 A6
Henhurst Hill DA12 . . . . .44 D8
Henhurst Rd
  Gravesend DA13 . . . . . .30 E1
  Henhurst DA12 . . . . . . .44 B7
Heniker La ME17 . . . . . .125 A4
Henley Bsns Pk ME2 . . . .47 C7
Henley Cl Chatham ME5 . .61 E2
  Gillingham ME8 . . . . . . .63 D8
  Royal Tunbridge Wells TN2 . .149 E8
Henley Ct DA5 . . . . .24 F8
Henley Deane DA11 . . . .29 F4
Henley Fields
  Maidstone ME16 . . . . . .92 E6
  Tenterden TN30 . . . . . .173 A2
Henley Meadows TN30 . .173 A2
Henley Rd Newham E16 . .1 C5
  Paddock Wood TN12 . .136 A7
Henley St DA13 . . . . .44 F3
Henley View TN30 . . . . .173 A2
Henniker Cotts TN17 . . .169 A3
Henry Addington Cl E6 . .1 F8
Henry Cooper Way SE9 . .22 D4
Henry St Bromley BR1 . . .36 B8
  Chatham ME4 . . . . .48 A3
  5 Grays RM17 . . . . .12 C8

Henson Cl BR6 . . . . .51 B8
Henville Rd DA1 . . . . .26 B7
Henwick Prim Sch SE9 . . .5 E4
Henwick Rd SE9 . . . . .5 E4
Henwood Green Rd
  TN12,TN2 . . . . .150 E6
Henwoods Cres TN2 . . . .150 E6
Henwoods Mount TN2 . .150 E6
Herald Wlk 2 DA1 . . . . . . .9 F2
Herbert Pl SE18 . . . . .6 B8
Herbert Rd Bexley DA7 . . .7 E5
  Bromley BR2 . . . . .36 C4
  Chatham ME4 . . . . .48 A1
  Gillingham ME8 . . . . .63 E7
  Hextable BR8 . . . . .26 B2
  Swanscombe DA10 . . . . .11 F3
  Woolwich SE18 . . . . .6 B8
Herdsdown ME3 . . . . .34 D8
Hereford Cl ME8 . . . . .49 D2
Hereford Rd ME15 . . . . .107 D2
Heritage Dr ME7 . . . . .48 F3
Heritage Hill BR2 . . . . . . .50 C5
Heritage Quay DA12 . . . .13 C1
Heritage Rd ME5 . . . . . . .62 A4
Heritage The BR6 . . . . . . .38 A2
Herman Terr ME4 . . . . . . .48 A1
Hermitage Ct
  Maidstone ME16 . . . . . . .91 A3
  Tonbridge TN9 . . . . . . .117 C2
Hermitage La Detling ME14 . .78 B6
  Maidstone ME16,ME20 . .90 F4
  Rabbit's Cross ME17 . .123 D6
Hermitage Rd ME3 . . . . . .32 E6
Hern The TN15 . . . . .87 C5
Herne Rd ME8 . . . . .49 C2
Heron Apartments 3
  ME15 . . . . .107 F5
Heron Cl TN12 . . . . .112 C7
Heron Cotts TN18 . . . . .187 D6
Heron Cres DA14 . . . . . . .23 E4
Heron Cres DA14 . . . . . . .36 C5
Heron Hill DA17 . . . . .4 A1
Heron Hill La DA3 . . . . . . .58 A6
Heron Rd ME20 . . . . .74 F5
Heron Way Chatham ME5 . .62 B2
  Lower Stoke ME3 . . . . . .19 C4
Heron Wlk BR8 . . . . .39 E7
Herongate Rd BR8 . . . . . .25 F5
Herons Way TN2 . . . . . . .150 E8
Herringham Rd SE7 . . . . . .1 C1
Herts Cres ME15 . . . . . .106 F3
Hertsfield Ave ME2 . . . . .33 A2
Hervey Rd SE3 . . . . .5 B6
Hesketh Ave 3 SE3 . . . . .5 A4
Heskett Pk TN2 . . . . . . .150 E6
Hever Ave TN15 . . . . .55 E4
Hever CE Prim Sch TN8 . .128 F5
Hever Castle* TN8 . . . . .129 D5
Hever Court Rd DA12 . . .30 D2
Hever Croft Eltham SE9 . .23 A4
  Rochester ME2 . . . . .46 F5
Hever Gdns Bromley BR1 . .37 A2
  Maidstone ME16 . . . . . . .91 E1
Hever Ho ME2 . . . . .22 C1
Hever Hotel & Golf Club
  TN8 . . . . .113 D1
Hever Rd Hever TN8 . . . .129 B2
  Four Elms TN8 . . . . . . .129 C5
  Stevenson TN15 . . . . . . .55 E4
Hever Sta TN8 . . . . .129 B6
Hever Wood Rd TN15 . . .55 E4
Heversham Rd DA7 . . . . . .8 A4
Hewett Ho 7 SE7 . . . . . . .2 E2
Hewett Pl BR8 . . . . .39 D7
Hewitt Cl Gillingham ME7 . .48 F6
Hextable Cl 1 BR1 . . . . . .21 F1
Hextable Inf Sch BR8 . . . .25 F1
Hextable Jun Sch BR8 . . .25 F1
Hextable Sch BR8 . . . . . . .39 F6
Hibbs Cl BR8 . . . . .39 D1
Hibernia Dr DA12 . . . . . . .30 F7
Hibernia Point 11 SE2 . . . .3 D4
Hicklin Cl SE7 . . . . .1 D1
Hickman Cl E16 . . . . .1 D8
Hickory Dell ME7 . . . . .63 A5
Hide Rd . . . . .2 A
Higgins' La ME4 . . . . .47 F3
High Banks
  Maidstone ME15 . . . . . .106 F3
  Rochester ME1 . . . . .47 D1
High Beeches
  Orpington BR6 . . . . .52 A
  Royal Tunbridge Wells TN2 . .149 D2
  Sidcup DA14 . . . . .24 E2
High Broom Ind Pk TN2 . .149 C7
High Brooms Rd TN4 . . .149 C5
High Brooms Sta TN4 . . .149 C5
High Croft Cotts ME9 . . .80 A
High Cross Rd TN15 . . . . .86 B
High Dewar Rd ME8 . . . . .64 A
High Elms BR6 . . . . .52 A
High Elms (Ctry Pk)* BR6 . .51 F4
High Elms Rd BR6 . . . . . .51 C
High Firs Rd BR8 . . . . .39 F
High Firs Prim Sch BR8 . .39 F
High Halden CE Prim Sch
  TN26 . . . . .173 E
High Halden Rd
  TN26,TN27 . . . . .158 C

High Halstow Prim Sch
ME23 . . . . .17 E3
High Hilden Cl TN10 . . . . .117 A4
High House La TN4 . . . . . . .102 C2
High Meads Rd E16 . . . . .1 D7
High Oak Hill ME9 . . . . .65 D8
High Point SE9 . . . . .23 B5
High Rd DA2 . . . . .26 C5
High Ridge TN17 . . . . .167 E8
High Rocks* TN3 . . . . .148 B1
High Rocks Halt* TN3 . . . . .148 B1
High Rocks La TN3, TN4 . . .148 C1
High St Aylesford ME20 . . . . .75 F3
  Bean DA2 . . . . .28 B5
  Bidborough TN3 . . . . .132 C3
  Biddenden TN27 . . . . .157 F1
  Biddenden Green TN27 . . .143 A1
  Borough Green TN15 . . . . . .86 F7
  Brasted TN14,TN16 . . . . . . .82 C3
  Brenchley TN12 . . . . .152 B8
  Bromley BR1 . . . . .36 A7
  Chatham ME4 . . . . .48 A4
  Cowden TN8 . . . . .145 B5
  Cranbrook TN17 . . . . .169 C4
  Dartford DA1 . . . . .9 E1
  Downe BR6 . . . . .66 A8
  East Malling ME19 . . . . .90 A6
  Edenbridge TN8 . . . . .112 C1
  Eynsford DA4 . . . . .54 E8
  Farningham DA4 . . . . .40 F2
  Flimwell TN5 . . . . .177 C3
  Frant TN3 . . . . .163 C4
  Gillingham ME7 . . . . .48 C5
  Gillingham,Brompton ME7 . .48 A6
  Goudhurst TN17 . . . . .167 E8
  Grain ME3 . . . . .21 B6
  Gravesend DA11 . . . . .13 B1
  2 Grays RM17 . . . . .12 A8
  Hadlow TN11 . . . . .118 E8
  Halling ME2 . . . . .60 A4
  Hawkhurst TN18 . . . . .178 E2
  Headcorn TN27 . . . . .141 C5
  Kemsing TN15 . . . . .70 B2
  Lamberhurst TN3 . . . . .166 B5
  Leigh TN11 . . . . .115 F1
  Lenham ME17 . . . . .111 D5
  Lower Stoke ME3 . . . . .19 C4
  Maidstone ME14 . . . . .91 F4
  Marden TN12 . . . . .138 D6
  Newington ME9 . . . . .65 C6
  Northfleet DA11 . . . . .12 C1
  Orpington BR6 . . . . .38 A1
  Orpington,Farnborough BR6 .51 C5
  Orpington,Green Street Green
  BR6 . . . . .51 F4
  Orpington,St Mary Cray BR5 .38 C4
  Otford TN14 . . . . .69 A3
  Pembury TN2 . . . . .150 C6
  Penshurst TN11 . . . . .131 B4
  Rainham ME8 . . . . .63 F8
  Rochester ME1 . . . . .47 C6
  Rochester, Strood ME2 . . . . .47 B7
  Rolvenden TN17 . . . . .181 E4
  Royal Tunbridge Wells TN1 .149 A2
  Seal TN15 . . . . .84 F6
  Sevenoaks TN13 . . . . .84 C2
  Sevenoaks,Chipstead TN13 . .83 C5
  Shoreham TN14 . . . . .53 F1
  Sidcup DA14 . . . . .24 A4
  Snodland ME6 . . . . .75 A8
  Staplehurst TN12 . . . . .139 F3
  Sutton Valence ME17 . . . . .124 E7
  Swanley BR8 . . . . .39 F5
  Swanscombe DA10 . . . . .11 F3
  Swanscombe,Greenhithe DA9 .11 B3
  Tenterden TN30 . . . . .183 A7
  Ticehurst TN5 . . . . .176 C1
  Tonbridge TN9 . . . . .117 C2
  Upper Upnor ME2 . . . . .33 F1
  Wadhurst TN5 . . . . .174 F4
  West Malling ME19 . . . . .89 C8
  Westerham TN16 . . . . .96 C8
  Wouldham ME1 . . . . .60 C5
  Wrotham TN15 . . . . .72 A3
  Yalding ME18 . . . . .104 F1
High Tor Cl BR1 . . . . .22 B1
High View ME1 . . . . .32 C4
High Woods La TN2 . . . . . . .150 B3
Higham Cl ME15 . . . . .91 E2
Higham Gdns TN10 . . . . . . .117 F5
Higham La TN10,TN11 . . . . .117 F6
Higham Rd Chart ME3 . . . . . .32 C5
Higham Rd Cliffe ME3 . . . . . .16 A4
  Rochester ME3 . . . . .33 C3
Higham Sch TN10 . . . . .117 E6
Higham Sta 32 D6
Higham View ME14 . . . . .79 A8
Highbanks Cl DA16 . . . . .7 B7
Highberry ME19 . . . . .74 E2
Highbrook Rd SE3 . . . . .5 D4
Highbury La TN30 . . . . .183 A7
Highcombe SE7 . . . . .5 B8
Highcombe Cl SE9 . . . . .22 E7
Highcroft Gn ME15 . . . . . . .107 F4
Highcroft Hall BR8 . . . . .39 D1
Highcross Rd DA13 . . . . .44 C6
Highdown Cotts TN17 . . . . .166 F3
Highfield Ave Erith DA8 . . . . .8 B8
  Orpington BR6 . . . . .51 F5
Highfield Cl Gillingham ME8 .63 D7
  Hawkhurst TN18 . . . . .179 A1
  Pembury TN2 . . . . .150 D6
Highfield Cotts DA2 . . . . .26 B2
Highfield Ct DA1 . . . . .26 D8
  Marlpit Hill TN8 . . . . .112 C4
  Bromley BR1 . . . . .36 F5
  Dartford DA1 . . . . .26 D8
  Gillingham ME8 . . . . .63 D7

Highfield Rd continued
  Kemsing TN14 . . . . .69 F3
  Royal Tunbridge Wells TN4 .149 C2
  St Paul's Cray BR7 . . . . .37 F6
Highfield Rd N DA1 . . . . .9 D1
Highfield Rd S DA1 . . . . .26 D7
Highfields Rd TN8 . . . . .112 C4
Highgate Ct 8 TN18 . . . . . . .178 F2
Highgate Hill TN18 . . . . . . .178 F1
Highgrove TN2 . . . . .163 A8
Highgrove Ct BR7 . . . . .36 E8
Highgrove Rd ME5 . . . . .62 A5
Highland Rd
  Badgers Mount TN14 . . . . . .68 C4
  Bexley DA6 . . . . .8 A3
  Maidstone ME15 . . . . .107 E6
Highlands Dartford DA1 . . . . .26 C8
  Royal Tunbridge Wells TN2 .149 D7
Highlands Hill BR8 . . . . .40 D5
Highlands Pk TN15 . . . . .84 E6
Highlands Rd BR5 . . . . .38 C2
Highmead SE18 . . . . .6 F7
Highridge ME7 . . . . .48 F1
Highridge Cl ME14 . . . . .92 F5
Highstead Cres DA8 . . . . .8 E7
Highview Vigo Village DA13 . .73 B8
  Woolwich SE18 . . . . .6 E8
Highview Cl ME15 . . . . .107 A8
Highview Dr ME5 . . . . .61 D5
Highview Rd DA14 . . . . .24 B4
Highway Prim Sch The
  . . . . .52 C5
Highway The BR6 . . . . .52 C5
Highwood Cl BR6 . . . . .51 C8
Highwood Dr BR6 . . . . .51 C8
Highwoods Cl ME3 . . . . .32 C3
Hilary Cl DA8 . . . . .8 C6
Hilary Gdns ME1 . . . . .46 F1
Hilbert Cl TN2 . . . . .149 C5
Hilborough Way BR6 . . . . . . .51 D5
Hilda May Ave BR6 . . . . .39 E7
Hilda Rd ME4 . . . . .48 A3
Hilda Vale Cl BR6 . . . . .51 A6
Hilda Vale Rd BR6 . . . . .51 B6
Hilden Ave TN11 . . . . .116 A7
Hilden Dr DA8 . . . . .9 B7
Hilden Grange Sch TN10 . . .117 B3
Hilden Oaks Sch TN10 . . . . .117 B3
Hilden Park Rd TN11 . . . . . .116 F4
Hildenborough
  CE Prim Sch TN11 . . . . . . .116 D6
Hildenborough Cres ME4 . .91 C7
Hildenborough Rd
  Leigh TN11 . . . . .116 A3
  Shipbourne TN11,TN15 . . .100 E4
Hildenborough Sta TN11 . .116 B6
Hilders Cl TN8 . . . . .112 B4
Hilders La TN8 . . . . .112 A4
Hill Brow Bromley BR1 . . . . .36 D8
  Crayford DA1 . . . . .8 F1
  Maidstone ME14 . . . . .93 A5
Hill Chase ME5 . . . . .61 E3
Hill Cl Chislehurst BR7 . . . . .23 B3
  Istead Rise DA13 . . . . .29 E1
Hill Cres Coldblow DA5 . . . . .25 C7
  Lenham ME17 . . . . .111 D5
Hill Crest
  Royal Tunbridge Wells TN4 .149 B8
  Sevenoaks TN13 . . . . .84 A5
  Sidcup DA15 . . . . .24 B8
Hill Ct ME8 . . . . .33 F4
Hill End Orpington BR6 . . . . .51 F8
  Woolwich SE18 . . . . .6 B8
Hill Farm Cl ME23 . . . . .17 E3
Hill Green Rd ME9 . . . . .79 D8
Hill House Rd DA2 . . . . .27 C8
Hill Rd Dartford DA2 . . . . . . .26 E6
  Rochester ME1 . . . . .47 A2
  Wouldham ME1 . . . . .60 F5
Hill Rise DA2 . . . . .27 E3
Hill Sch The TN16 . . . . .81 B4
Hill Shaw DA3 . . . . .42 F3
Hill St TN1 . . . . .149 B5
Hill The Cranbrook TN17 . . .169 D4
  Northfleet DA11 . . . . .12 C1
Hill Top TN17 . . . . .154 E5
Hill Top Cotts ME2 . . . . .47 A8
Hill View Basted TN15 . . . . . .86 F4
  Borough Green TN15 . . . . . .87 A7
Hill View Cl TN15 . . . . .87 A7
Hill View Dr DA16 . . . . .6 E5
Hill View Rd New Barn DA3 . .43 B6
  Orpington BR6 . . . . .51 F8
  Royal Tunbridge Wells TN4 .148 C4
  Tonbridge TN11 . . . . .116 F5
Hill View Way ME5 . . . . .61 E5
Hill's Terr ME4 . . . . .48 A7
Hillary Ave DA11 . . . . .29 E5
Hillary Ct SE9 . . . . .22 E6
Hillary Rd ME14 . . . . .92 A7
Hillbert Rd TN1 . . . . .149 E5
Hillborough Ave TN13 . . . . . .84 D5
Hillborough Gr ME5 . . . . .62 A3
Hillbrow DA1 . . . . .25 D4
Hillbury Gdns TN15 . . . . . . .176 D1
Hillcrest TN8 . . . . .112 B1
Hillcrest Ave ME20 . . . . .75 A1
Hillcrest Dr Cuxton ME2 . . . .46 C2
  Royal Tunbridge Wells TN2 .149 D7
  Stone DA9 . . . . .11 B1
Hillcrest Rd Bromley BR1 . . . .22 A4
  Chatham ME4 . . . . .48 B3
  Dartford DA1 . . . . .25 F8
  Marlpit Hill TN8 . . . . .112 C4
  Orpington BR6 . . . . .52 A8
Hillcroft Rd E6 . . . . .2 B8
Hillden Shaw ME15 . . . . .107 A8

Hilldown Lodge BR6 . . . . . . .52 B8
Hilldrop Rd BR1 . . . . .22 B2
Hillfield Rd TN13 . . . . .83 E7
Hillfield Villas TN26 . . . . . . .173 F8
Hillgarth TN4 . . . . .149 A8
Hillingdon Ave TN13 . . . . . . .84 D6
Hillingdon Rd Bexley DA7 . . . .8 C4
  Gravesend DA11 . . . . .30 A5
Hillingdon Rise TN13 . . . . . . .84 D5
Hillreach SE18 . . . . .1 F1
Hills La TN15 . . . . .70 C7
Hillsgrove Cl DA16 . . . . .7 C7
Hillsgrove Prim Sch DA16 . . . .7 C7
Hillshaw Cres ME2 . . . . .46 D5
Hillside Dartford DA2 . . . . . . .27 E3
  Erith DA17 . . . . .4 A3
  Farningham DA4 . . . . .40 F2
  Rochester ME1 . . . . .47 A2
  Tonbridge TN9 . . . . .133 A7
Hillside Ave
  Gravesend DA12 . . . . .30 D6
  Rochester ME2 . . . . .47 B8
Hillside Cotts TN5 . . . . .175 B8
Hillside Ct
  8 Rochester ME2 . . . . .47 A7
  Swanley BR8 . . . . .40 A5
  Wateringbury ME18 . . . . . .104 E7
Hillside Dr DA12 . . . . .30 D6
Hillside La BR2 . . . . .50 A8
Hillside Rd Chatham ME4 . . . .48 A4
  Crayford DA1 . . . . .9 A1
  Kemsing TN15 . . . . .69 F2
  Sevenoaks TN13 . . . . .84 D4
Hillside Terr DA12 . . . . .30 B7
Hillside The BR6 . . . . .52 B2
Hillsley Ct 13 DA14 . . . . .24 A4
Hilltop Tonbridge TN9 . . . . .133 B7
  West Farleigh ME15 . . . . . .105 D3
Hilltop Prim Sch ME7 . . . . . .48 F5
Hilltop Rd Rochester ME2 . . .33 C1
  West Thurrock RM20 . . . . . .11 B8
Hillview Cres BR6 . . . . .37 F1
Hillview Ho DA12 . . . . .30 C7
Hillview Rd BR7 . . . . .23 D3
Hillview Sch for Girls
  TN9 . . . . .133 D8
Hillydeal Rd TN14 . . . . .69 C4
Hillyfield Cl ME2 . . . . .32 F1
Hillyfields Jun Sch ME7 . . . .48 E6
Hilton Rd ME3 . . . . .33 B7
Hind Cres DA8 . . . . .8 D7
Hine The DA11 . . . . .12 B1
Hoath Cl ME8 . . . . .63 B7
Hoath La ME8 . . . . .63 B7
Hoath Meadow TN12 . . . . . .153 A6
Hoath Way ME7,ME8 . . . . . . .63 B5
Hobart Rd RM18 . . . . .13 A6
Hoblands End BR7 . . . . .23 E2
Hockenden La BR8 . . . . .39 B7
Hockers Cl ME14 . . . . .93 A8
Hockers La ME14 . . . . .93 A8
Hoddesdon Rd DA17 . . . . .4 A1
Hodgkins Cl SE28 . . . . .3 D6
Hodgson Cres BR5 . . . . .60 A1
Hodsoll Ct BR5 . . . . .38 A6
Hodsoll St TN15 . . . . .57 D1
Hodson Cres BR5 . . . . .38 D3
Hog Hill ME14 . . . . .93 B5
Hog La DA11 . . . . .29 D5
Hogarth Cl E16 . . . . .1 D8
Hogbarn La ME17 . . . . .95 F2
Hoghole La TN3 . . . . .165 F2
Hognore La TN15 . . . . .72 D6
Hogs Orch BR8 . . . . .40 B8
Hogtrough Hill TN16 . . . . . . .82 A5
Holaden Ct TN8 . . . . .112 C1
Holbeach Gdns DA15 . . . . .6 F1
Holborn La ME4 . . . . .47 F5
Holborn Rd E13 . . . . .1 B8
Holborough Rd ME6 . . . . .60 A1
Holborough House BR7 . . . . .37 D8
Holbrook La BR7 . . . . .23 D1
Holbrook Way BR2 . . . . .36 F4
Holburne Cl SE3 . . . . .5 C6
Holburne Gdns SE3 . . . . .5 D6
Holburne Rd SE3 . . . . .5 C6
Holcombe TN16 . . . . .81 D1
Holcombe Rd
  Chatham ME4 . . . . .47 F2
  Rochester ME1 . . . . .47 C3
Holcote Ct DA17 . . . . .3 E1
Holden Cnr TN4 . . . . .132 F1
Holden Park Rd TN4 . . . . . .148 F8
Holden Rd TN4 . . . . .132 F1
Holder Cl ME15 . . . . .107 C6
Holding St ME8 . . . . .49 F1
Hole La DA8 . . . . .112 A6
Holford St 1 TN9 . . . . .133 C8
Holgate St SE7 . . . . .1 D3
Holland Ho ME1 . . . . .47 D5
Holland Rd Chatham ME5 . . . .61 F4
  Maidstone ME14 . . . . .92 B5
Hollands Cl DA12 . . . . .30 F6
Hollies Ave DA15 . . . . .23 F7

Hollies The
  Gravesend DA12 . . . . .30 D2
  New Barn DA3 . . . . .43 C6
  Sidcup DA15 . . . . .24 A8
Holligrave Rd BR1 . . . . .36 A8
Hollin Cl TN4 . . . . .148 F4
Hollingbourne Ave DA7 . . . . . .7 F6
Hollingbourne Hill ME17 . . .94 F4
Hollingbourne Prim Sch
  ME17 . . . . .94 E2
Hollingbourne Rd ME16 . . . .90 C2
Hollingbourne Sta ME17 . . .94 C2
Hollingbourne Tower 4
  BR5 . . . . .38 D1
Hollington Rd ME14 . . . . .23 B2
Hollingworth Rd
  Maidstone ME15 . . . . .107 F5
  Orpington BR5,BR6 . . . . . . .37 B2
Hollingworth Way TN16 . . . .81 D1
Hollow La Hartlip ME9 . . . . . .64 F5
Hollow Rd ME2 . . . . .74 F6
Hollow Trees Dr TN11 . . . . .116 A1
Holly Bank TN12 . . . . .152 B8
Holly Bush La TN13 . . . . .84 C3
Holly Cl Chatham ME5 . . . . . .62 C8
  Gillingham ME7 . . . . .48 E6
Holly Cotts TN8 . . . . .112 B2
Holly Ct 1 DA14 . . . . .24 B4
Holly Farm Rd ME15 . . . . . .108 C6
Holly Hill La TN11 . . . . .58 F3
Holly Hill Rd DA8,DA17 . . . . . .4 B1
Holly Rd Dartford DA1 . . . . . .26 D7
  Orpington BR6 . . . . .52 A3
  Rochester,Strood ME2 . . . . .46 E5
  Rochester,Wainscott ME2 . .33 D7
Holly Tree Cl ME17 . . . . .109 F2
Hollybrake Cl BR7 . . . . .23 D1
Hollybush Cl ME5 . . . . .61 F1
Hollybush Ct TN13 . . . . .84 C3
Hollybush La BR6 . . . . .53 C4
Hollybush Rd DA12 . . . . .30 C6
Hollycroft ME2 . . . . .46 C2
Hollydale Dr BR2 . . . . .50 F7
Hollydene Rd TN5 . . . . .174 F6
Hollyshaw Cl TN2 . . . . .149 C2
Hollytree Ave BR8 . . . . .39 E7
Hollytree Dr ME3 . . . . .32 B3
Hollytree Par DA14 . . . . .24 C5
Hollywood La
  Knockmill TN15 . . . . .70 F8
  Rochester ME2 . . . . .33 A4
Hollywood Manor TN15 . . . .70 F7
Hollywood Way DA8 . . . . .9 B6
Holm Ct SE12 . . . . .22 B5
Holm Mill La ME17 . . . . .110 B6
Holm Wlk SE3 . . . . .5 A5
Holmbury Manor 2 DA14 . .24 A4
Holmbury Pk BR7 . . . . .22 E1
Holmcroft Way BR2 . . . . .36 F4
Holmdale Rd 23 C3
Holmdene Ct 5 BR1 . . . . . . .36 C6
Holmes Cl ME23 . . . . .17 E3
Holmes Ct ME19 . . . . .73 F4
Holmesdale
  Maidstone ME15 . . . . .106 F3
  Wadhurst TN5 . . . . .174 E5
Holmesdale Com Sch ME6 . .74 F7
Holmesdale Hill DA4 . . . . . . .41 D8
Holmesdale Rd Bexley DA7 . . .7 D5
  Sevenoaks TN13 . . . . .84 D4
  Sutton at Hone DA4 . . . . . . .41 D8
Holmesdale Sch
  (Farm Annex) ME6 . . . . . . .74 F6
Holmewood Ho TN3 . . . . . . .148 A2
Holmewood Rd TN4 . . . . . .149 C2
Holmewood Ridge TN3 . . . .147 F3
Holmhurst Cl TN4 . . . . .148 F4
Holmhurst Rd DA17 . . . . .4 B1
Holmleigh Ave DA1 . . . . .9 B2
Holmoaks Gillingham ME8 . .49 E2
  Maidstone ME14 . . . . .92 C5
Holmsdale Gr DA1,DA7 . . . . . .8 B4
Holmside Dr 48 E3
Holmwood Cl BR6 . . . . .52 C1
Holmwood Ct DA14 . . . . .23 F3
Holstein Way 8 DA18 . . . . . . .3 E3
Holt Cl SE28 . . . . .3 C6
Holt Rd E16 . . . . .1 F5
Holt Wood Ave ME19 . . . . . . .90 E8
Holtwood Cl ME8 . . . . .63 D6
Holtye Cres ME15 . . . . .92 B2
Holtye Golf Club TN8 . . . . . .144 A6
Holtye Rd RH19 . . . . .144 A3
Holwood Park
  Ave BR2,BR6 . . . . .50 F6
Holy Family RC Prim Sch
  Eltham SE3 . . . . .5 C3
  Maidstone ME15 . . . . .107 F4
Holy Innocents
  RC Prim Sch BR6 . . . . .51 F7
Holy Trinity CE Prim Sch
  Dartford DA1 . . . . .9 F1
  Gravesend DA12 . . . . .30 C8
Holy Trinity Coll
  & Prep Sch BR1 . . . . .36 C8
Holy Trinity Lamberley
  CE Prim Sch DA15 . . . . . . .24 A7
Holyhead Cl 11 E6 . . . . .1 F8
Holyoake Terr TN13 . . . . .84 A3
Holyrood Mews E16 . . . . .1 A5
Holywell Cl SE3 . . . . .5 A8
Home Ave Gravesend DA12 . .30 F5
Home Farm Cotts ME5 . . . . . .38 D8
Home Farm Ct TN3 . . . . .163 C4
Home Farm La TN11,TN2 . . .133 F1
Home Gdns DA1 . . . . .9 E1
Home Hill BR8 . . . . .25 F1
Home Lea BR6 . . . . .51 F5

Home Mead Cl 6 DA12 . . . .30 B8
Homedean Rd TN13 . . . . . . .83 C4
Homefarm Est ME20 . . . . . . .75 F1
Homefield Cl
  St Paul's Cray BR5 . . . . .38 B5
  Swanley BR8 . . . . .39 F6
Homefield Rd Bromley BR1 .36 C8
  Sevenoaks TN13 . . . . .83 E5
Homefield Rise BR6 . . . . .38 A1
Homemead
  7 Gravesend DA12 . . . . . . .30 B8
  Swanscombe DA9 . . . . .11 B1
Homemead Rd BR2 . . . . .36 F4
Homer Cl DA7 . . . . .8 C6
Homesdale Rd
  Bromley BR1,BR2 . . . . .36 C6
  Orpington BR5 . . . . .37 E2
Homestead Rd
  Marlpit Hill TN8 . . . . .112 B5
  Orpington BR6 . . . . .52 B4
Homestead The
  Crayford DA1 . . . . .8 E2
  Dartford DA1 . . . . .9 C1
  Groombridge TN3 . . . . .161 C7
Homevale Cotts TN14 . . . . . .67 E4
Homewards Rd ME3 . . . . . . .19 B8
Homewood Cotts DA12 . . . . .31 E1
Homewood Cres BR7 . . . . . .23 E2
Homewood Rd
  Royal Tunbridge Wells TN3 .147 F3
  Tenterden TN30 . . . . .173 B1
Homewood Sch
  & Sixth Form Ctr TN30 . . .173 B1
Homoeopathic Hospl TN1 . .149 A3
Honey Bee Glade ME8 . . . . . .63 E6
Honeybourne Way BR5 . . . . .37 D2
Honeycrest Ind Pk TN12 . . . .139 E5
Honeycrock Hill ME9 . . . . . . .79 F8
Honeyden Rd DA14 . . . . .24 E2
Honeypot Cl ME2 . . . . .47 B8
Honeysuckle Cl 4 SE12 . . . .22 A8
Honiton Rd DA16 . . . . .6 F5
Honor Oak Rd ME17 . . . . . . .111 C4
Hoo Comm ME3 . . . . .34 A4
Hoo Rd ME2,ME3 . . . . .33 B3
Hoo St Werburgh Mid Sch
  ME3 . . . . .34 C5
Hoo St Werburgh Prim Sch
  ME3 . . . . .34 D5
Hood Ave SE3 . . . . .38 B4
Hook Cl ME5 . . . . .61 E5
Hook Farm Rd BR2 . . . . .36 D4
Hook Green Ct DA13 . . . . . . .44 A4
Hook Green La DA2 . . . . .25 F5
Hook Green Rd DA13 . . . . . . .28 F1
Hook Hill TN5 . . . . .176 A6
Hook La Bexley DA16 . . . . .7 A4
  Harrietsham ME17 . . . . . . .111 F4
Hook Lane Prim Sch DA16 . . .7 A4
Hook Rd ME6 . . . . .74 F8
Hook St ME17 . . . . .127 F8
Hookfields DA11 . . . . .29 E5
Hookstead TN26 . . . . .173 C7
Hookwood Cotts TN14 . . . . .67 C8
Hookwood Rd BR6,TN14 . . . .67 C7
Hookwood Rd E16 . . . . .1 A7
Hooper's Pl ME1 . . . . .47 C4
Hooper's Rd ME1 . . . . .47 C4
Hoopers La ME3 . . . . .18 F5
Hoopers Yd TN15 . . . . .84 C1
Hop Pocket Cl TN17 . . . . . . .170 F8
Hop Pocket La TN12 . . . . . .135 F7
Hope Ave TN12 . . . . .102 E1
Hope Cl SE12 . . . . .22 B5
Hope Cotts DA12 . . . . .28 B6
Hope Rd E16 . . . . .1 B8
Hope St Chatham ME4 . . . . . .48 A3
  Maidstone ME14 . . . . .91 F6
Hope Terr ME3 . . . . .32 D7
Hopedale Rd SE7 . . . . .5 B8
Hopes Gr TN26 . . . . .173 D7
Hopewell Dr Chatham ME5 . .62 C8
  Gravesend DA12 . . . . .30 F3
Hopgarden Cl 12 TN8 . . . . .112 D3
Hopgarden La TN11 . . . . .99 A8
Hopgarden Oast ME18 . . . .104 F1
Hopgarden Rd TN10 . . . . . . .117 C6
Hoppers Cnr ME15 . . . . . . .105 D7
Hoppers Cnr BR2 . . . . .36 A1
Hopton Rd SE18 . . . . .2 C2
Hopwood Gdns TN4 . . . . . .148 F4
Horizon Cl TN4 . . . . .149 B6
Horley Cl DA6 . . . . .8 A2
Horley Rd SE9 . . . . .22 E4
Horn La SE10 . . . . .1 A2
Horn Link Way SE10 . . . . .1 A2
Horn Park Cl SE12 . . . . .5 B2
Horn Park La SE12 . . . . .5 B1
Horn Park Prim Sch SE12 . . . .22 B8
Horn Yd 6 DA11 . . . . .13 B1
Horn's Oak Rd DA13 . . . . . . .58 B6
Hornbeam Ave
  Chatham ME5 . . . . .62 B2
  Royal Tunbridge Wells TN4 .133 D1

Hornbeam Cl
Larkfield ME20 75 B2
Paddock Wood TN12 135 F5
Hornbeam House 6 DA15 24 A5
Hornbeam La DA7 8 C5
Hornbeam Way BR2 37 A3
Hornbeams DA13 73 B8
Horncastle Cl SE12 22 A8
Horncastle Rd SE12 22 A8
Horne Ho SE18 5 E6
Hornetts Cl BR8 39 D2
Hornfair Rd SE7 5 D7
Hornfield Cotts DA13 58 C3
Horning Cl SE9 22 E4
Horns La ME18 88 D1
Horns Lodge La TN11 117 A8
Horns Rd TN18 184 D8
Horsa Rd Eltham SE12 22 C8
Erith DA8 8 C7
Horse Leaze E6 2 A7
Horse Wash La ME1 47 C6
Horsecroft Cl BR6 38 B1
Horsegrove Ave TN5 176 F1
Horsell Rd BR5 38 B8
Horseshoe Cl
Gillingham ME7 62 F5
Maidstone ME14 92 E5
Horseshoes La ME17 108 E4
Horsfeld Gdns SE9 5 E2
Horsfeld Rd SE9 5 D2
Horsfield Cl DA2 27 C8
Horsham Rd DA6 8 A2
Horsley Ho SE18 6 A7
Horsley Rd Bromley BR1 36 B8
Rochester ME1 47 B4
Horsmonden Cl BR6 37 F2
Horsmonden Prim Sch
TN12 153 A6
Horsmonden Rd TN12 152 D6
Horsted Ave ME4 47 E1
Horsted Cty Inf Sch ME4 61 D5
Horsted Cty Jun Sch ME5 61 D5
Horsted Way ME1 61 D7
Horton Downs ME15 92 F1
Horton Kirby CE Prim Sch
DA4 41 C6
Horton Pl TN16 81 D1
Horton Rd DA4 41 C6
Horton Tower 2 BR5 38 C5
Horton Way DA4 40 F2
Hortons Cl TN17 180 D7
Hortons Way 1 TN16 81 D1
Horwood Cl ME1 61 B8
Hoselands View DA3 42 E5
Hoser Ave SE12 22 A6
Hosey Common La TN16 96 F5
Hosey Common Rd
TN8,TN16 96 D5
Hosey Hill TN16 96 E8
Hoskin's Cl E16 1 C7
Hospital La 3 ME1 47 E4
Hospital Rd
Hollingbourne ME17 109 E8
Sevenoaks TN13 84 C6
Hostler Cl ME2 60 B4
Hotel Rd ME8 49 A2
Hotham Cl
Sutton at Hone DA4 27 B1
Swanley Village BR8 40 B8
Hothfield Rd ME8 49 F1
Hottsfield DA3 42 E6
Hougham House 11 BR5 38 D1
Houghton Ave ME7 63 B3
Houselands Rd TN9 117 B2
Hove Cl RM17 12 A8
Hovendens TN17 170 A8
Hoveton Rd SE28 3 C7
How Green La TN8 113 C2
Howard Ave Rochester ME1 47 D3
Sidcup DA5 24 C8
Howard Dr ME16 91 B5
Howard Gdns TN2 149 A1
Howard Rd Bromley BR1 22 A1
Dartford DA1 10 A1
East Malling ME19 89 F8
Howard Sch The ME8 63 D8
Howarth Rd SE2 3 A2
Howbury La DA8 9 A5
Howbury Rd DA1,DA8 9 A5
Howbury Wlk ME8 63 D4
Howden Cl SE28 3 D6
Howells Cl TN15 55 E4
Howes Cotts TN18 184 F8
Howick Cl ME20 90 F8
Howick Mans SE18 1 E3
Howland Rd TN12 138 E6
Howlsmere Cl ME2 60 B3
Hubbard's Hill TN13,TN14 99 B4
Hubbard's La ME15 107 A3
Hubble Dr ME15 107 E7
Huckleberry Cl ME5 62 B3
Hudson Cl ME8 49 C1
Hudson Pl SE18 2 C1
Hudson Rd DA7 7 F6
Hugh Christie Tech Coll
The TN10 117 D6
Hughes Dr ME2 33 D2
Hulkes La ME1 47 E4
Hulsewood Cl DA2 26 B5
Hulsons Ct 1 TN18 179 A2
Humber Cres ME2 46 F7
Humber Rd Dartford DA1 9 D2
Greenwich SE3 5 A8
Humboldt Ct TN2 149 D5
Hume Ave RM18 13 B5
Hume Cl RM18 13 A4
Humphreys TN12 151 F6
Hundred of Hoo
Comp Sch The ME3 34 C5
Hungershall Park Cl TN4 148 E1
Hungershall Pk TN4 148 E2
Hunsdon Dr TN13 84 B4
Hunstanton Cl ME8 63 E3
Hunt Rd Northfleet DA11 29 F5
Tonbridge TN10 117 E6
Hunt St
Nettlestead ME15,ME18 104 F5
West Farleigh ME15 105 B5
Hunter's Gr BR6 51 C6
Hunters Cl DA5 25 E5
Hunters Ct 5 ME7 48 C7
Hunters Lodge 10 DA15 24 A5
Hunters Way
Gillingham ME7 48 E1
Royal Tunbridge Wells TN2 148 F1
Hunters Way W ME5 48 E1
Hunters Wlk TN14 67 E5
Huntersfield Cl ME5 62 C1
Huntingdon Wlk 2 ME15 107 E7
Huntingfield Rd DA13 44 A2
Huntington Cl TN17 169 D4
Huntington Rd ME17 106 B3
Huntley Ave DA11 12 C1
Huntley Mill Rd TN5 176 E3
Huntleys Pk TN4 148 F5
Hunton CE Prim Sch
ME15 121 D7
Hunton Hill ME15 105 F1
Hunton House 4 BR5 38 C4
Hunton Rd TN12 122 A3
Hunts Cl SE3 5 A5
Hunts Farm Cl TN15 87 A7
Hunts La TN17 167 E8
Hunts Mede Cl BR7 22 F1
Huntsman La
Maidstone ME14 92 B4
Wrotham Heath TN15 72 E1
Huntsman's Cnr ME4 61 E8
Huntsmans Cl ME1 47 E1
Huntsmoor House BR5 38 B5
Hurlfield DA2 26 C5
Hurlingham Rd DA7 7 F7
Huron Cl 5 BR6 51 F6
Hurricane Rd ME19 88 F3
Hurst Cl Chatham ME5 61 E6
Staplehurst TN12 139 F4
Tenterden TN30 182 F7
Hurst Ct Newham E6 1 D8
Sidcup DA15 24 A6
Hurst Farm Rd TN14 99 B3
Hurst Green CE Sch
TN19 184 A2
Hurst Hill ME5 61 E2
Hurst Ho SE2 3 D1
Hurst La Erith SE2 3 D1
Sevenoaks Weald TN14 99 B2
Hurst Pl Erith SE2 7 D8
Gillingham ME8 63 F8
Woolwich SE2 3 C1
Hurst Prim Sch DA5 24 D7
Hurst Rd Erith DA8 8 C7
Sidcup DA5 24 D7
Hurst Springs DA5 24 E7
Hurst The Crouch TN11 102 D7
Plaxtol Spoute TN15 87 C1
Royal Tunbridge Wells TN2 149 E7
Hurst Way Maidstone ME16 90 F2
Sevenoaks TN13 99 C8
Hurstbourne Cotts DA5 25 B8
Hurstfield BR2 36 A4
Hurstings The ME15 91 D2
Hurstmere Foundation Sch
DA15 24 C7
Hurstwood ME5 61 E4
Hurstwood Ave
Erith DA7,DA8 8 E6
Sidcup DA5 24 E7
Hurstwood Dr BR1 36 F6
Hurstwood La TN4 148 F3
Hurstwood Pk TN4 148 F3
Hurstwood Rd
Bredhurst ME7 63 B1
Detling ME14 78 B7
Husheath Hill TN17 154 F6
Hussar Ho ME1 47 C3
Husseywell Cres BR2 36 A1
Hutchings Rd SE28 3 A5
Hutsford Cl ME8 63 D5
Hutson Terr RM19 10 D8
Huxley Ct ME1 47 D4
Huxley Ho SE2 3 D1
Huxley Rd DA16 6 F4
Hyacinth Rd ME2 46 E6
Hybrid Cl ME1 47 D1
Hyde Dr BR5 38 B5
Hyde Rd Bexley DA7 7 F5
Maidstone ME16 91 D6
Hyde's Orch TN27 141 E5
Hyders Forge TN15 102 A8
Hylton St SE18 2 F2
Hyperion Dr ME2 32 F1
Hythe Ave DA7 7 F7
Hythe Cl Orpington BR5 38 C5
Royal Tunbridge Wells TN4 133 A1
Hythe St DA1 9 E1

I

Ice Bowl The* ME8 49 A1
Ickleton Rd SE9 22 E4
Icough Ct SE3 5 B7
Iddenden Cotts TN18 178 D2
Ide Hill CE Prim Sch TN14 97 F4
Ide Hill Rd TN14 97 F2
Iden Cres TN12 139 F2
Iden Rd ME2 33 C1
Idenwood Cl ME8 63 D6
Idleigh Court Rd DA3,DA13 57 C8
Ifield Cl ME15 107 F7
Ifield Cotts DA12 31 C2
Ifield Sch The DA12 30 C3
Ifield Way DA12 30 D2
Ightham By-Pass TN15 86 C7
Ightham Cotts DA2 28 B6
Ightham Mote * TN15 101 A7
Ightham Prim Sch TN15 86 B6
Ightham Rd Erith DA8 8 A7
Shipbourne TN11,TN15 101 C5
Ilkley Rd E16 1 C8
Illustrious Cl ME5 62 A6
Imber Ct 4 SE9 6 A1
Impala Gdns TN4 149 B6
Imperial Bsns Pk DA11 12 F1
Imperial Ct BR7 23 B2
Imperial Dr DA12 30 F3
Imperial Pl BR7 37 A8
Imperial Rd ME7 48 C3
Imperial Ret Pk DA11 13 A1
Imperial Way BR7 23 C5
Impton La ME5 62 A1
Inca Dr SE9 23 B8
Indus Rd SE7 5 C7
Ingle Rd ME4 47 F2
Ingleby Way BR7 23 A3
Ingleden Park Rd TN30 173 C1
Ingledew Rd SE18 2 D1
Ingleside Gr 3 SE3 5 A8
Ingleton Ave DA16 7 A2
Inglewood Chislehurst BR7 23 D2
Swanley BR8 39 E7
Inglewood Copse BR1 36 F7
Inglewood Rd DA7 8 D3
Ingoldsby Rd DA12 30 F7
Ingram Rd Dartford DA1 26 E7
Gillingham ME7 48 E6
Ingress Gdns DA9,DA10 11 D2
Ingress Terr DA13 28 E4
Inigo Jones Rd SE7 5 E7
Inner Lines ME7 48 A6
Institute Rd ME4 48 A4
Instone Rd DA1 26 D8
Inverary Pl SE18 6 D8
Inverine Rd SE7 1 B1
Invermore Pl SE18 2 C2
Inverness House 7
ME15 107 E7
Invicta Cl BR7 23 A3
Invicta Gram Sch ME14 92 C4
Invicta Inf Sch SE3 5 A7
Invicta Par 3 DA14 24 B4
Invicta Rd Dartford DA2 10 B1
Greenwich SE3 5 A8
Invicta Villas ME14 93 C4
Iona Cl ME5 62 D1
Iona Rd ME15 107 A7
Ireland Cl E6 1 F8
Irene Rd BR6 37 F2
Iris Ave DA5 7 E1
Iris Cl ME5 77 A8
Iris Cres DA7 7 F8
Iron Mill La DA1 8 F3
Iron Mill Pl DA1 8 F3
Ironside Cl ME5 62 A8
Ironstones TN3 148 B3
Irvine Rd ME3 32 B3
Irvine Way BR6 37 F2
Irving Ho TN1 149 B5
Irving Way BR8 39 D7
Irving Wlk DA10 28 E8
Irwin Ave SE18 6 E7
Isabella Dr BR6 51 C6
Isla Rd SE18 6 C8
Island Way East ME4 34 C1
Island Way West ME4 34 B2
Islehurst Cl BR7 37 A8
Islingham Farm Rd ME3 33 D4
Ismays Rd TN15 86 C3
Istead Rise DA13 29 F1
Istead Rise Prim Sch
DA13 43 E8
Ivedon Rd DA16 7 C5
Ivens Way ME17 110 D6
Iverhurst Cl DA6 7 D2
Iversgate Cl ME8 49 F2
Ives Rd TN9 116 F1
Ivor Gr SE9 23 B7
Ivor Ho DA14 24 C3
Ivorydown BR1 22 A4
Ivy Bower Cl DA9 11 B2
Ivy Cl Dartford DA1 27 A8
Gravesend DA12 30 D5
Kingswood ME17 109 D2
Ivy House La TN13,TN14 68 E2
Ivy La TN14 67 E3
Ivy Mews ME17 109 E2
Ivy Pl ME1 47 A2
Ivy Rd E16 1 A7
Ivy St ME8 63 F8
Ivy Villas DA9 11 A2
Ivybridge Ct 1 BR7 37 A8
Izane Rd DA6 7 F3

J

Jack Lobley Prim
Sch RM18 12 F6
Jackass La BR2 50 C4
Jacklin Cl ME5 61 F2
Jackson Ave ME1 61 E8
Jackson Cl Gillingham ME8 49 C1
Stone DA9 11 A2
Jackson Ho 4 SE7 5 B8
Jackson Rd BR2 50 F8
Jackson St SE18 6 A8
Jackson Way TN17 171 C3
Jacksons La 8 TN30 183 A7
Jacob Ho 5 DA18 3 D4
Jacob's La ME3 35 B6
Jade Cl E16 1 D7
Jade Hill ME2 60 A6
Jaffray Rd BR2 36 D5
Jaggard Way TN12 139 E3
Jagger Cl DA2 27 C8
Jago Cl SE18 6 C8
Jail La TN16 66 A3
Jamaica Terr ME14 92 A7
James Cl TN11 102 F1
James Newman Ct SE9 23 A5
James Rd Cuxton ME2 46 C2
Dartford DA1 26 A8
James St 5 Chatham ME4 47 F4
Gillingham ME7 48 C6
Maidstone ME14 92 A5
Rochester ME1 47 C4
James Watt Way DA8 8 F8
James Whatman Way
ME14 91 F5
Jane Seymour Ct DA15 23 D8
Janet Ct 4 DA7 8 A3
Janson Ct 11 DA14 24 B4
Japonica Cl ME5 62 C2
Jaquets Ct DA5 25 A6
Jarrah Cotts RM19 10 D8
Jarrett Ave ME2 33 C2
Jarvis Ho 4 ME14 91 F7
Jarvis La TN17 154 B3
Jarvis Pl TN30 173 B3
Jashada Ho SE18 2 A1
Jasmine Cl 2 Chatham ME5 61 F4
East Malling ME19 89 F8
Orpington BR6 51 B8
Jasmine Cotts TN3 161 C7
Jasmine Ct SE12 5 A1
Jasmine Rd ME19 89 F8
Jason Wlk SE9 23 A4
Jasper Ave ME1 47 D2
Jasper Rd E16 1 D7
Javelin Rd ME19 88 F3
Jay Gdns BR7 22 F4
Jefferson Dr ME8 49 C1
Jefferson Wlk 13 SE18 6 A8
Jeffery St ME7 48 C6
Jeffrey Cl TN12 139 E4
Jeffrey Ct DA8 8 C7
Jeffrey Row SE12 5 B2
Jeffrey St ME14 92 A5
Jeken Rd SE9 5 C3
Jellicoe Ave DA12 30 C5
Jellicoe Ave W DA12 30 C5
Jenkins Dr ME15 107 E5
Jenkins' Dale ME4 47 F3
Jenner Ho 4 DA17 4 A3
Jenner Rd ME1 47 C4
Jenner Way ME20 75 F6
Jennifer Ct ME3 34 F5
Jenningtree Rd DA8 9 B7
Jenningtree Way DA17 4 C4
Jenton Ave DA7 7 E5
Jerome Rd ME20 74 F4
Jersey Dr BR5 37 D3
Jersey Rd Newham E16 1 C8
Rochester ME2 47 A8
Jeskyns Rd DA12 44 E6
Jessamine Pl DA2 27 C8
Jessamine Terr BR8 39 C8
Jessett Cl DA8 4 D2
Jessup Cl SE18 2 C2
Jetty Rd Kingsnorth ME3 35 D7
Sheerness ME12 21 F3
Jetty Wlk 3 RM17 12 A8
Jevington Way SE12 22 B7
Jewell Gr TN12 138 D5
Jeyes Rd ME7 48 C4
Jezreels Rd ME7 48 D3
Jim Bradley Cl 10 SE18 2 A2
Jiniwin Rd ME1 61 D7
Joan Cres SE9 22 D8
Jockey La TN17 169 D5
Johannesburg House
ME15 107 F5
John Hunt Ct SE9 22 E6
John Mayne CE Prim Sch
TN27 157 F1
John Newton Ct DA16 7 B4
John Spare Ct TN4 149 A6
John St Grays RM17 12 C8
Maidstone ME14 92 A6
Rochester ME1 47 C4
Royal Tunbridge Wells TN4 149 A5
John Wesley Ct SE9 6 A3
John Wilson St SE18 2 A2
John's Rd DA13 43 F4
Johns Cl DA3 42 F4
Johnson Ave ME7 48 C7
Johnson Cl DA11 29 D5
Johnson Rd BR2 36 D4
Johnsons Ave TN14 53 B1
Johnsons Way DA9 11 C1
Joiners Ct ME4 48 B2
Jonas Dr TN5 174 E5
Jonas La TN5 174 E5
Jordan Cl ME15 107 E5
Josling Cl RM17 11 F8
Joy Rd DA12 30 C7
Joy Wood ME17 107 D5
Joyce Cl TN17 169 C5
Joyce Dawson Way SE28 3 A6
Joyce Green Ho DA1 9 F4
Joyce Green La Dartford DA1 9 E6
Dartford,Temple Hill DA1 9 F4
Joyce Green Wlk DA1 9 F3
Joyce Page Cl SE7 5 D8
Joyden's Wood Rd DA5 25 E5
Joydens Wood Inf Sch
DA5 25 E4
Joydens Wood Jun Sch
DA2 25 E4
Jubilee Cl DA9 11 C1
Jubilee Cnr ME17 125 E3
Jubilee Cotts
Sevenoaks TN14 84 B7
Sutton Valence ME17 124 E7
Jubilee Cres
Gravesend DA12 30 E6
Ightham TN15 86 C6
Jubilee Ct DA1 26 D8
Jubilee Ctry Pk *R2 37 B5
Jubilee Field TN30 189 E4
Jubilee Prim Sch SE28 3 C6
Jubilee Rd Chelsfield BR6 53 A4
West Thurrock RM20 11 B8
Jubilee Rise TN15 84 F6
Jubilee Terr ME7 48 C6
Jubilee Way DA14 24 A6
Judd Rd TN9 133 B7
Judd Sch The TN9 133 A8
Judeth Gdns DA12 30 E3
Judkins Cl ME5 62 C6
Juglans Rd BR6 38 A1
Julia Garfield Mews E16 1 B5
Julian Ct 3 DA14 24 A4
Julian Rd BR6 52 A4
Julians Cl TN13 99 A8
Julians Way TN13 99 A8
Junction Rd
Bodiam TN18, TN32 185 A1
Dartford DA1 9 D1
Gillingham ME7 48 D4
Juniper Cl Chatham ME5 62 A4
Maidstone ME16 91 B6
Royal Tunbridge Wells TN4 133 D1
Juniper La E6 1 E8
Juniper Wlk BR8 39 D
Jury St 11 DA11 13 B1
Jutland Cl ME3 19 D
Jutland Ho SE18 1 E

K

Kale Rd DA18 3 E4
Kashgar Rd SE18 2 F2
Kashmir Rd SE7 5 D
Katherine Ct ME5 62 B
Katherine Gdns SE9 5 D3
Katherine Rd TN8 128 C8
Kay St DA16 7 B6
Keary Rd DA10 28 F8
Keating Cl ME1 47 A1
Keats Ave E16 1 B5
Keats Gdns RM18 13 B5
Keats House DA1 8 E
Keats Rd Bexley DA16 6 F6
Erith DA17 4 C
Lunsford ME20 74 F
Kechill Gdns BR2 36 A
Kedleston Dr BR5 37 F4
Keeble Cl SE18 6 B8
Keedonwood Rd BR1 22 A
Keefe Cl ME5 61 D
Keel Gdns TN4 148 E
Keeley Mews ME7 48 E
Keeling Rd SE9 5 D
Keemor Cl SE18 6 A
Keep The SE3 5 A5
Keightley Dr SE9 23 C
Keir Hardy Ho 7 DA17 4 A
Keith Ave DA4 27 B
Keith Sutton House SE9 23 C
Kelbrook Rd SE3 5 E
Kelchers La TN11 118 F5
Kelham House 10 SE18 6 B
Kellaway Rd Chatham ME5 62 A
Greenwich SE3 5 D5
Kellner Rd SE28 2 F
Kelly Dr ME7 48 C
Kelly Ho 14 SE7 5 C
Kelly House ME1 61 C
Kelsall Cl SE3 5 B
Kelsey Rd BR5 38 B
Kelso Dr DA12 30 F
Kelvin Cl TN10 117 D
Kelvin Ho 3 DA17 4 A
Kelvin Par BR6 37 E
Kelvin Rd Bexley DA16 7 A
Tilbury RM18 13 A
Kemble Cl TN2 149 E
Kemble Dr BR2 50 E
Kemnal Rd BR7 23 D
Kemnal Tech Coll BR5 24 B
Kemnal Warren BR7 23 D
Kemp Cl ME5 61 E
Kempley Ct 2 RM17 12 D
Kempt St SE18 6 A
Kempton Cl Chatham ME5 62 C
Erith DA8 8 C
Kemsing Cl DA5 24 E
Kemsing Prim Sch TN15 70 A
Kemsing Rd Greenwich SE10 1 A
Wrotham TN15 71 C
Kemsing Sta TN15 85 D
Kemsley Cl Northfleet DA11 29 F
Swanscombe DA9 11 B
Kemsley Street Rd ME7 63 C
Kemsway Ct BR5 38 B

encot Cl DA18 . . . . .3 F4
endal Dr TN9 . . . . .117 C2
endal Pk TN4 . . . . .148 E5
endal Way ME8 . . . . .63 D8
endall Ct DA15 . . . . .24 A5
Kendall Lodge **10** BR1 . . .36 B8
Kendall Pl **1** ME1 . . . . .107 D8
endall Rd SE3 . . . . .5 B6
endon Bsns Pk ME2 . . . . .47 D8
enla Wlk DA12 . . . . .30 F5
enilworth Ct DA12 . . . . . .10 B1
enilworth Dr ME8 . . . . . .63 D6
enilworth Gdns
  Gillingham ME8 . . . . . . .63 D7
  Woolwich SE18 . . . . .6 B5
enilworth House ME16 . . .91 B2
enilworth Rd BR5 . . . . . .37 C3
enley Cl Sidcup DA5 . . . . .25 A8
  St Paul's Cray BR7 . . . . .37 E6
enley House **6** BR5 . . . .38 B7
enmere Rd DA16 . . . . . . .7 C5
ennacraig Cl E16 . . . . . . .1 A5
ennard Cl ME1 . . . . .46 F2
ennard St E16 . . . . .1 F5
ennedy Cl BR5 . . . . .37 D1
ennedy Gdns TN13 . . . . .84 D5
ennedy House TN12 . . . .180 E6
ennel Barn Rd ME9 . . . . .80 C5
ennet Ct **2** BR8 . . . . . .39 E6
ennet Rd Crayford DA1 . . .9 A4
  Tonbridge TN10 . . . . . .117 C5
ennett Ct **3** BR5 . . . . .38 D1
ennington Cl
  Gillingham ME8 . . . . . . .89 B4
  Maidstone ME15 . . . . . .107 F7
ensington Ct **4** RM17 . . .12 C8
ensington House ME16 . . .91 A2
ent & East Sussex
  Steam Rly* TN17 . . . . .188 C5
ent & Sussex Hospl
  TN4 . . . . .149 A4
ent Ave Bexley DA16 . . . . .6 F2
enthouse ME16 . . . . .92 C1
ent Cl Chatham ME1 . . . . .61 C8
  Orpington BR6 . . . . .51 E4
  Paddock Wood TN12 . . .136 A6
ent Coll TN2 . . . . .134 D3
ent County Optholmic
  & Aural Hospl ME14 . . .91 E6
ent County Show Gd
  ME14 . . . . .78 C3
ent Hatch Rd RH8,TN8 . . .96 B4
ent Ho TN1 . . . . .149 C6
ent House **10** TN18 . . .179 A2
ent Inst of Art & Design
  Chatham ME1 . . . . .47 F4
  Maidstone ME16 . . . . . .91 C3
ent Kraft Ind Est DA11 . . .11 F7
ent Music Sch TN9 . . . . .133 B8
ent Rd Dartford DA1 . . . . .9 E1
  Gravesend DA11 . . . . . . .30 A7
  Grays RM17 . . . . .12 C8
  Halling ME2 . . . . .60 A6
  Longfield DA3 . . . . .42 D7
  Orpington BR5 . . . . .38 B3
  Royal Tunbridge Wells TN4 .149 A6
  Snodland ME6 . . . . .75 A6
ent St SE18 . . . . .2 E2
ent Terr Higham ME3 . . . .32 D7
  Meopham DA13 . . . . . . .58 A7
entish Gdns TN2 . . . . . .162 E8
entish Rd DA17 . . . . .4 A2
entish Way BR1,BR2 . . . .36 A6
entlea Rd SE18 . . . . .2 E4
entmere Rd SE18 . . . . . . .2 E2
entstone Ct ME4 . . . . . . .48 A4
enward Ct TN11 . . . . . . .101 D7
enward Rd Eltham SE9 . . . .5 D2
  Maidstone ME16 . . . . . . .91 C5
alding ME18 . . . . .104 E2
enwood Ave
  Chatham ME5 . . . . .62 A4
  New Barn DA3 . . . . .43 C6
enwyn Rd DA1 . . . . .9 D2
enya Rd SE7 . . . . .5 D8
enya Terr **1** ME14 . . . .92 A7
enyon Wlk ME8 . . . . . . .63 B3
erry Cl E16 . . . . .1 A6
ersey Gdns SE9 . . . . . . .22 E4
esteven Cl ME7 . . . . . . .60 B5
estlake Rd DA5 . . . . .7 C1
eston Ave ME2 . . . . .33 B1
eston CE Prim Sch ME2 . . .50 D5
eston Ct DA16 . . . . .7 C7
eston Ct Gillingham ME8 . .49 A2
idcup DA5 . . . . .24 B8
eston Gdns BR2 . . . . . . .50 C6
eston Park Cl BR2 . . . . . .50 F7
estrel Ave E6 . . . . .1 E8
estrel Cl TN8 . . . . .112 D3
estrel Ho **4** ME7 . . . . .48 B6
estrel Rd ME5 . . . . .62 C2
eswick Cl TN9 . . . . .117 C2
eswick Dr ME16 . . . . . . .91 B5
eswick Rd Bexley DA7 . . . .8 A4
  Orpington BR6 . . . . .38 A2
etridge La ME18 . . . . . . .89 D2
ettle La ME15 . . . . .105 E6
ettlewell Ct BR8 . . . . . . .39 F7
evington Cl BR5 . . . . . . .37 E5
evington Dr BR7 . . . . . . .37 F5
evington Prim Sch BR5 . . .38 D4
evlands ME14 . . . . .92 C6
eycol Hill ME9 . . . . .65 F5
eycol Hospl ME9 . . . . . . .65 E6
eyes Ave ME4 . . . . .47 F2
eyes Gdns TN9 . . . . . . .132 F7
eyes Rd DA1 . . . . .10 A3

Keynes Ct **9** SE28 . . . . . .3 B6
Keynsham Gdns SE9 . . . . .5 E2
Keynsham Rd SE9 . . . . . . .5 E2
Keyworth Ct TN12 . . . . . .135 F6
Khalsa Ave DA12 . . . . . . .30 C8
Khartoum Pl DA12 . . . . . .13 C1
Khartoum Rd Chatham ME4 .47 F6
Gillingham ME7 . . . . .48 A6
Khyber Rd ME4,ME7 . . . . .48 A7
Kibbles La TN4 . . . . .148 E8
Kidbrooke Gdns SE3 . . . . .5 A6
Kidbrooke Gr SE3 . . . . . . .5 B6
Kidbrooke La SE9 . . . . . . .5 E3
Kidbrooke Park Cl SE3 . . . .5 B6
Kidbrooke Park Prim Sch
  SE3 . . . . .5 C6
Kidbrooke Park Rd
  SE12,SE3 . . . . .5 B4
Kidbrooke Sta SE3 . . . . . .5 D5
Kidbrooke Sta SE3 . . . . . .5 B4
Kidbrooke Way SE3 . . . . . .5 B5
Kidd Pl SE7 . . . . .1 E1
Kiddens BR8 . . . . .40 A1
Kilburn Ho **6** ME14 . . . .92 A5
Kibbles La TN4 . . . . .1 A8
Killewarren Way BR5 . . . .38 C3
Killick Cl TN13 . . . . .83 F6
Killick Rd ME3 . . . . .34 D5
Killicks Cotts ME18 . . . . .120 F8
Kiln Barn Rd ME19,ME20 . .90 C7
Kiln Field TN30 . . . . . . .183 C7
Kiln La TN11 . . . . .115 F1
Kiln Way TN12 . . . . .136 A5
Kilnbank TN12 . . . . .149 C7
Kilnbridge Cl ME15 . . . . .106 B7
Kilndown DA12 . . . . .30 E6
Kilndown Cl ME16 . . . . . .91 C7
Kilnfields BR6 . . . . .53 A4
Kilnwood TN14 . . . . .67 F6
Kimbell Pl SE3 . . . . .5 C3
Kimber House **11** SE18 . . .6 B8
Kimberley Dr DA14 . . . . .24 D6
Kimberley Rd ME7 . . . . . .48 D3
Kimberly Cl DA12 . . . . . . .3 F2
Kimmeridge Gdns SE9 . . .22 E4
Kimmeridge Rd SE9 . . . . .22 E4
Kincaid Rd ME7 . . . . .37 A8
Kincraig Dr TN13 . . . . . . .84 B4
Kinder Cl SE28 . . . . .3 C6
King & Queen Cl SE9 . . . .22 E4
King Arthur's Dr ME2 . . . .33 A1
King Edward Ave DA1 . . . . .9 D1
King Edward Rd
  Chatham ME4 . . . . .47 F2
  Gillingham ME7 . . . . . . .48 F6
  Maidstone ME15 . . . . . .91 F2
  Rochester ME1 . . . . .47 C5
  Stone DA9 . . . . .11 A2
King George Ave E16 . . . . .1 D7
King George Rd ME5 . . . . .61 E4
King George V Hill TN1 . . .149 C5
Kingswood Ave
  Gillingham ME7
  Meml Houses ME8 . . . . . .49 C2
Kit's Coty ME20 . . . . .7 E7
King Henry Mews **7** BR6 . .51 F5
King Hill ME19 . . . . .89 A5
King John's Wlk SE9 . . . . .5 E1
King St Chatham ME4 . . . .48 A4
  Gillingham ME7 . . . . . . .48 C6
  Gravesend DA12 . . . . . . .13 B1
  Maidstone ME14 . . . . . . .92 A4
  Rochester ME1 . . . . .47 C4
  West Malling ME19 . . . . .89 B3
King William Rd **6** ME7 . .48 C7
King's Bastion ME7 . . . . . .48 A5
King's Cotts ME18 . . . . . .104 D6
King's Highway SE18,SE2 . .6 F8
King's Orch Eltham SE9 . . .5 E1
  Rochester ME1 . . . . .47 C5
King's Rd Chatham ME5 . . .48 D1
  Tonbridge TN9 . . . . . . .133 D7
King's Sch ME1 . . . . .47 C5
King's Standing Ind Est
  TN2 . . . . .133 F2

Kings Row continued
  Maidstone ME15 . . . . . . .92 A1
Kings Standing Way TN2 . .133 F1
Kings Toll Rd TN2 . . . . . .151 A6
Kings Wlk RM17 . . . . . . .12 C8
Kingsand Rd SE12 . . . . . .22 A6
Kingsdale Ct Chatham ME5 .48 C1
  Swanscombe DA10 . . . . . .11 E1
Kingsdale Rd SE18 . . . . . .6 F8
Kingsdown Cl
  Gillingham ME7 . . . . . . .63 B4
  Gravesend DA12 . . . . . . .30 F7
  Maidstone ME16 . . . . . . .91 E4
Kingsdown Way BR2 . . . . .36 A3
Kingsfield Ho SE9 . . . . . .22 D5
Kingsford Cotts TN17 . . . .180 D6
Kingsford Rd E6 . . . . .1 F8
Kingsgate Cl Bexley DA7 . . .7 E6
  Maidstone ME16 . . . . . . .91 E4
  St Paul's Cray BR5 . . . . .38 C6
Kingsgate La SE9 . . . . . .189 C5
Kingsground SE9 . . . . . . .5 E1
Kingsholm Gdns SE9 . . . . .5 E3
Kingshurst Rd SE12 . . . . .22 A8
Kingsingfield Cl TN15 . . . .55 E3
Kingsingfield Rd TN15 . . .55 E2
Kingsland Gr TN27 . . . . .141 D5
Kingsland La TN27 . . . . .127 E1
Kingsley Ave DA1 . . . . . . .10 A2
Kingsley Ct Bexley DA6 . . . .8 A3
  Wadhurst TN5 . . . . .175 A4
Kingsley Mews BR7 . . . . . .3 C5
Kingsley Rd
  Maidstone ME15 . . . . . . .92 A3
  Orpington BR6 . . . . .51 F3
Kingsley Wood Dr SE9 . . .22 F5
Kingsman Par SE18 . . . . . .1 F3
Kingsman St SE18 . . . . . . .1 F2
Kingsmead Cl DA15 . . . . .24 A5
Kingsmere BR7 . . . . .36 E8
Kingsnorth Rd ME8 . . . . .39 C3
Kingsnorth Rd ME8 . . . . .49 C4
Kingsnorth Rd ME8 . . . . .49 C4
Kingston Cres ME5 . . . . . .62 C4
Kingston Ct DA11 . . . . . . .12 B1
Kingston Dr ME15 . . . . . .107 A8
Kingsway Chatham ME5 . . .48 D1
  Gillingham ME7 . . . . . . .48 E5
  Orpington BR5 . . . . .37 D4
Kingswear Gdns ME2 . . . .47 C2
Kingswood Ave
  Chatham ME4 . . . . .47 F2
  Erith DA17 . . . . .4 A2
  Swanley BR8 . . . . .39 F6
Kingswood Cl Dartford DA1 .9 F1
  Orpington BR5 . . . . .37 D2
  Royal Tunbridge Wells TN2 .149 C3
Kingswood Prim Sch
  ME7 . . . . .109 E2
Kingswood Rd
  Gillingham ME7 . . . . . . .48 D6
  Royal Tunbridge Wells TN2 .149 C3
  Sevenoaks TN13 . . . . . . .83 E7
Kingsworth CE ME15 . . . .34 E5
Kinlet Rd SE18 . . . . .6 C6
Kinnell Ct **5** DA14 . . . . .24 B4
Kinnings Row TN11 . . . . .117 C2
Kinross Ct TN13 . . . . . . .62 B7
Kinveachy Gdns SE7 . . . . .1 E1
Kipling Ave RM18 . . . . . .13 C6
Kipling Dr ME20 . . . . .7 F4
Kipling Rd Bexley DA7 . . . .7 E6
  Dartford DA1 . . . . .10 B2
Kippington Cl TN13 . . . . .83 F3
Kippington Dr SE9 . . . . . .22 D7
Kippington Rd TN13 . . . . .84 A2
Kirby Cl TN17 . . . . .169 D4
Kirby Rd Chattenden ME3 . .33 F5
  Dartford DA2 . . . . .27 D8
Kirk La SE18 . . . . .2 C1
Kirkcourt TN3 . . . . .84 A4
Kirkdale ME15 . . . . .106 F5
Kirkdale Cl ME15 . . . . . . .62 D1
Kirkdale Cotts ME15 . . . .106 F5
Kirkdale Rd
  Maidstone ME15 . . . . . . .106 F6
  Royal Tunbridge Wells TN1 .149 B4
Kirkham Rd E6 . . . . .1 E7
Kirkham St SE18 . . . . .6 E8
Kirkins Cl TN12 . . . . . . .153 A6
Kirkland Cl DA15 . . . . . . .6 E1
Kirkman Ct TN12 . . . . . .139 E3
Kirkside Rd SE3 . . . . .5 A8
Kit Hill Ave ME5 . . . . . . .61 E3
Kit's Coty House* ME20 . . .76 C6
Kitchener Ave
  Chatham ME4 . . . . .48 A1
  Gravesend DA12 . . . . . . .30 C5
Kitchener Cotts ME3 . . . . .19 C4
Kitchener Rd
  Chattenden ME3 . . . . . . .33 F4
  Rochester ME7 . . . . .47 A8
Kite La TN12 . . . . .153 A6
Knatts La TN15 . . . . .70 E8
Knatts Valley Rd TN15 . . .55 D2
Knave Wood Rd TN15 . . . .69 E2
Knaves Acre TN27 . . . . . .141 D5
Knavesacre Ct ME18 . . . . .63 D5
Knee Hill SE2 . . . . .3 C3
Knee Hill Cres SE2 . . . . . .3 C2
Knight Ave ME7 . . . . .48 D7
Knight Rd Rochester ME2 . .47 A6
  Tonbridge TN10 . . . . . . .117 C5
Knight's Ct DA8 . . . . .8 F7
Knight's Ridge TN2 . . . . .150 D7

Knight's Way TN27 . . . . .141 D6
Knighton Rd TN14 . . . . . .68 F2
Knightrider Ct ME15 . . . . .92 A3
Knightrider St **1** ME15 . .92 A3
Knights Cl
  Hoo St Werburgh ME3 . . .34 E5
  Pembury TN2 . . . . .150 D7
Knights Croft DA3 . . . . . .56 F7
Knights Manor Way DA1 . . .9 F2
Knights Rd Rochester ME2 . .47 A6
  Royal Tunbridge Wells TN2 .133 F1
Knights Rd
  Hoo St Werburgh ME3 . . .34 D5
  Newham E16 . . . . .1 A4
Knights Ridge BR6 . . . . . .52 B5
Knights Way TN2,TN11 . . .149 B7
Knightsbridge Cl TN4 . . . .148 E5
Knightsbridge Mews BR7 . .22 F1
Knock Mill La TN15 . . . . .71 A5
Knockhall Chase DA9 . . . .11 C2
Knockhall Com Prim Sch
  DA9 . . . . .11 C2
Knockhall Rd DA9 . . . . . .11 C2
Knockholt CE Prim Sch
  TN14 . . . . .67 B2
Knockholt Rd Eltham SE9 . .5 E2
  Halstead TN14 . . . . .67 F6
Knockholt Sta TN14 . . . . .52 E2
Knockhurst Ct TN30 . . . .173 C1
Knockwood Rd TN30 . . . .173 C1
Knole* TN15 . . . . .84 D1
Knole Cl TN14 . . . . .99 B2
Knole Gate DA15 . . . . . . .23 E5
Knole La TN13,TN15 . . . . .84 C1
Knole Rd Chatham ME5 . . .62 C3
  Dartford DA1 . . . . .26 B8
  Sevenoaks TN13 . . . . . . .84 C1
Knole The Eltham SE9 . . . .23 A4
  Istead Rise DA13 . . . . . .29 E1
Knole Way TN13 . . . . . . .84 C2
Knoll Cl BR6 . . . . .51 F8
Knoll Rd Sidcup DA14 . . . .24 B4
  Sidcup,Old Bexley DA5 . . .8 A1
Knoll Rise BR6 . . . . .37 F1
Knoll Wlk Cotts TN11 . . . .115 A2
Knotley Hall Cotts TN11 . . .115 A2
Knott Ct ME14 . . . . .91 F6
Knotts Pl TN13 . . . . .84 A3
Knowle Ave DA7 . . . . .7 F7
Knowle Cl TN3 . . . . .147 F8
Knowle Cotts TN3 . . . . . .163 E1
Knowle La TN12 . . . . . . .136 C3
Knowle Lodge BR7 . . . . . .22 F2
Knowle Rd Maidstone ME14 .92 B6
  Orpington BR2 . . . . .50 D8
  Paddock Wood TN12 . . . .136 D3
  Wouldham ME1 . . . . . . .60 D4
Knowles Gdns TN27 . . . . .141 D5
Knowles Wlk TN12 . . . . . .139 F4
Knowlton Gdns ME16 . . . .91 E2
Knowlton Gn BR2 . . . . . . .36 A4
Knowsley Way TN11 . . . . .116 D6
Knox Ct TN15 . . . . .84 F6
Kydbrook Cl BR5 . . . . . . .37 C2
Kyetop Wlk ME8 . . . . . . .63 D5
Kynaston Rd Bromley BR1 . .22 A3
  Orpington BR5 . . . . .38 B2

L
La Tourne Gdns BR6 . . . . .51 C7
Labour-In-Vain Rd TN15 . . .71 E5
Laburnham Pl SE9 . . . . . . .6 A2
Laburnum Ave
  Dartford DA1 . . . . .26 D7
  Swanley BR8 . . . . .39 D6
Laburnum Dr TN12 . . . . . .149 C7
Laburnum Gr ME20 . . . . . .75 A2
Laburnum Gr DA11 . . . . . .29 D8
Laburnum Rd ME2 . . . . . .46 E5
Laburnum Way BR2 . . . . .37 B2
Lacebark Cl DA15 . . . . . . .23 F8
Lacey Cl ME17 . . . . .108 E4
Laceys La ME17 . . . . . . .122 C7
Lacknut Cotts DA13 . . . . .57 E2
Lacy Cl ME16 . . . . .91 D7
Ladbrooke Cres DA14 . . . .24 D5
Ladbrooke Ho **7** ME14 . . .92 A5
Laddingford Farm Ind Est
  ME18 . . . . .120 D4
Laddingford St Mary's
  CE Prim Sch ME18 . . . . .120 E4
Ladds Cnr ME7 . . . . .49 B5
Ladds La ME6 . . . . .60 A2
Ladds Way BR8 . . . . .39 D5
Ladyfields Chatham ME5 . . .62 D2
  Northfleet DA11 . . . . . . .29 F4
Ladyfields Cl ME14 . . . . . .76 F5
Ladysmith Rd SE9 . . . . . . .6 B2
Ladywell House **2** BR5 . .38 B7
Ladywood Ave BR6 . . . . . .37 E4
Ladywood Rd Cuxton ME2 . .46 B2
  Dartford DA2 . . . . .27 E3
Lagonda Way DA1 . . . . . . .9 F3
Lagoon Rd BR5 . . . . .38 B4
Lake Ave BR1 . . . . .22 A2

Lake Dr ME3 . . . . .32 C6
Lake Rd Ditton ME20 . . . . .90 E8
  Royal Tunbridge Wells TN4 .148 E4
Lake View Rd TN13 . . . . . .84 A4
Lakedale Rd SE18 . . . . . . .2 E1
Lakelands
  Harrietsham ME17 . . . . .110 E6
  Maidstone ME15 . . . . . .107 A7
Lakeman Way TN4 . . . . . .149 B7
Laker Rd ME1 . . . . .61 C6
Lakes Rd BR2 . . . . .50 C5
Lakeside
  Royal Tunbridge Wells TN2 .149 E6
  Snodland ME6 . . . . .74 F6
Lakeside Ave SE28 . . . . . .3 A5
Lakeside Cl
  Bough Beech TN8 . . . . . .113 F4
  Sidcup DA5,DA15 . . . . . .7 D2
Lakeside Dr BR2 . . . . . . .50 E7
Lakeside Pk ME2 . . . . . . .47 E7
Lakeswood Rd BR5 . . . . . .37 C3
Lakeview Cl ME6 . . . . . . .75 A6
Lakeview Rd DA16 . . . . . . .7 B3
Lakewood Dr ME8 . . . . . .63 C6
Lamb Cl RM18 . . . . .13 C5
Lamb's Cross ME17 . . . . .129 A5
Lambard House **8** ME14 . .92 A5
Lambarde Ave SE9 . . . . . .23 A4
Lambarde Dr TN13 . . . . . .84 A4
Lambarde Rd TN13 . . . . . .84 A5
Lambardes DA3 . . . . .56 F7
Lamberhurst CE Prim Sch
  TN3 . . . . .166 B6
Lamberhurst Ct **4** BR5 . .38 D1
Lamberhurst Gn 49 B3
Lamberhurst Rd
  Horsmonden TN12,TN3 . .152 E3
  Maidstone ME16 . . . . . . .91 B7
Lamberhurst Vineyard*
  TN3 . . . . .144 D1
Lambersart Cl TN4 . . . . . .133 D1
Lambert Ct DA8 . . . . .8 C8
Lambert Mews **4** ME6 . . .75 A8
Lambert Rd E16 . . . . .1 B7
Lambert's Yd TN9 . . . . . . .117 B1
Lamberts Pl TN12 . . . . . . .153 B5
Lamberts Rd TN2 . . . . . . .149 D8
Lambes CE ME8 . . . . .63 C3
Lambeth Cl ME5 . . . . .62 B4
Lambeth Rd DA17 . . . . . . .4 A2
Lamborne Way BR1 . . . . .89 A2
Lambourn Way
  Chatham ME5 . . . . .62 C2
  Royal Tunbridge Wells TN2 .149 D1
Lambourne Pl SE3 . . . . . . .5 B6
Lambourne Rd ME15 . . . . .92 F2
Lambscroft Ave SE9 . . . . .22 D5
Lambsfrith Gr ME7 . . . . . .63 B3
Lamorbey Cl DA15 . . . . . .23 F6
Lamorna Ave DA12 . . . . . .30 D6
Lamorna Cl BR6 . . . . .38 A2
Lampington Row TN3 . . . .147 E3
Lamplighters Cl
  2 Dartford DA1 . . . . . . .9 F1
  Gillingham ME7 . . . . . . .62 F5
Lamport Cl SE18 . . . . .1 F2
Lamson Rd RM13 . . . . . . .4 F8
Lancashire Rd ME15 . . . . .107 E7
Lancaster Ct
  Gillingham ME8 . . . . . . .63 C7
  Gravesend DA12 . . . . . . .30 C5
Lancaster Way ME11 . . . . .88 F3
Lance Croft DA3 . . . . .56 F8
Lancelot Ave ME2 . . . . . . .47 A6
Lancelot Cl ME2 . . . . .46 E6
Lancelot Ct BR6 . . . . .52 B8
Lancelot Rd DA16 . . . . . . .7 A4
Lancer Ho ME1 . . . . .47 C3
Lancers Cl DA13 . . . . .44 A2
Lancet La ME15 . . . . . . .107 A6
Lancey Cl SE7 . . . . .1 E2
Lancing Rd BR6 . . . . .52 B8
Land Way ME3 . . . . .32 D5
Landale Gdns DA1 . . . . . .26 C8
Landor Ct ME7 . . . . .63 A3
Landseer Ave DA11 . . . . . .29 D5
Landseer Cl TN10 . . . . . .117 E6
Landstead Rd SE18 . . . . . .6 D7
Landway TN15 . . . . .84 F7
Landway The
  Borough Green TN15 . . . .86 F7
  Kemsing TN15 . . . . .70 A2
  Maidstone ME14 . . . . . . .93 A4
  St Paul's Cray BR5 . . . . .38 C6
Lane Ave DA9 . . . . .11 C1
Lane End DA2 . . . . .8 B4
Lane The Forcedome TN3 . .147 C5
  Greenwich SE3 . . . . .5 A4
Lanes Ave DA11 . . . . .30 A5
Laneside BR7 . . . . .23 C3
Langafel CE Prim Sch
  DA3 . . . . .43 A6
Langafel Cl DA3 . . . . .42 E7
Langbrook Rd SE3 . . . . . . .5 D4
Langdale Cl Gillingham ME8 .49 D1
  Orpington BR6 . . . . .51 C7
Langdale Cres DA7 . . . . . .8 A6
Langdale Rise ME16 . . . . .91 C5
Langdale Wlk **5** DA11 . . .29 E5
Langdon Rd Bromley BR2 . .36 B6
Langdon Shaw DA14 . . . . .23 F3
Langford Pl DA14 . . . . . . .24 A5

Langham Gr ME16 .....91 C4
Langholm Rd TN3 .....147 F3
Langhorne Ho 5 SE7 .....5 C8
Langlands Dr DA2 .....27 E3
Langley Ct 1 SE9 .....6 A1
Langley Gdns
　2 Bromley BR2 .....36 C5
　Orpington BR5 .....37 B3
Langley Ho 4 BR1 .....22 B1
Langley Rd DA16 .....7 C8
Langmore Ct DA7 .....7 D4
Langton Cl ME14 .....92 C5
Langton Green
　Cty Prim Sch TN3 .....147 E4
Langton Rd Royal
　Tunbridge Wells TN3, TN4 .....148 C3
　Speldhurst TN3 .....148 A7
Langton Ridge TN3 .....148 B3
Langton Way SE3 .....5 B7
Langworth Ct DA2 .....26 D5
Lankester Parker Rd 61 C6
Lannoy Rd SE9 .....23 C7
Lanridge Rd SE2 .....3 E3
Lansbury Cres DA1 .....10 A2
Lansbury Ct 4 SE28 .....3 B6
Lansbury Gdns RM18 .....13 A6
Lawn Cl Bromley BR1 .....22 B1
Lansdown Pl DA11 .....29 F7
Lansdown Rd Sidcup DA14 .....24 B5
　Tilbury RM18 .....12 F5
Lansdowne Ave Bexley DA7 .....7 D7
　Maidstone ME15 .....107 C6
　Orpington BR6 .....37 B1
Lansdowne Ct 4 ME4 .....47 F4
Lansdowne Cty Prim Sch
　RM18 .....12 F5
Lansdowne La SE7 .....1 D1
Lansdowne Mews SE7 .....1 D1
Lansdowne Rd
　Bromley BR1 .....22 B1
　Chatham ME4 .....47 E2
　Royal Tunbridge Wells TN1 .....149 B4
　Sevenoaks TN13 .....84 D5
　Tonbridge TN9 .....117 B2
Lansdowne Sq
　Northfleet DA11 .....12 F1
　4 Royal Tunbridge Wells
　TN1 .....149 B4
Lapins La ME19 .....74 F1
Lapis Cl DA12 .....31 B7
Lapwing Cl DA8 .....9 B7
Lapwing Rd ME3 .....21 B5
Lapwings SE3 .....43 B6
Lapwings The DA12 .....30 D6
Lapworth Cl BR6 .....52 C8
Larch Cl ME20 .....75 B2
Larch Cres
　Hoo St Werburgh ME3 .....34 E3
　Maidstone ME16 .....117 C6
Larch Dene BR6 .....51 A8
Larch Rd
　Paddock Wood TN12 .....135 F6
　Sidcup DA15 .....23 F7
Larch Rd DA1 .....26 D7
Larch Way BR2 .....37 A2
Larch Wlk BR8 .....39 D7
Larch Wood Cl ME5 .....62 D1
Larchcroft ME5 .....62 A4
Larches The ME3 .....32 C3
Larchwood Rd SE9 .....23 B6
Larkfield TN12 .....135 A7
Larkfield Ave ME7 .....48 F6
Larkfield Cl Hayes BR2 .....50 A8
　Larkfield ME20 .....75 A1
Larkfield Rd Larkfield ME20 .....75 B1
　Sevenoaks TN13 .....83 C4
　Sidcup DA14 .....23 F4
Larkfield Trad Est ME20 .....75 B5
Larkin Cl ME3 .....29 E5
Larkin Cl ME3 .....33 B2
Larking Dr ME16 .....91 D7
Larks Field DA3 .....42 F5
Larkspur Cl
　East Malling ME19 .....75 A1
　4 Newham E6 .....1 E8
　Orpington BR6 .....52 C7
Larkspur Lodge DA14 .....24 B5
Larkspur Rd Chatham ME5 .....61 E4
　East Malling ME19 .....74 F1
Larkstore Pk TN12 .....139 E5
Larkswood Cl DA8 .....9 A6
Larkwell La DA3 .....42 F5
Larne Rd DA8 .....8 E7
Laser Quay ME2 .....47 D6
Lashenden
　Air Warfare Mus* TN27 .....142 A2
Lassa Rd SE9 .....5 F2
Latham Cl Dartford DA2 .....27 E6
　Newham E6 .....1 E7
Latham Rd DA6 .....8 A2
Latimer Pl 4 ME2 .....48 C7
Latona Dr DA12 .....30 F3
Latymers TN11 .....131 B4
Launcelot Prim Sch ME1 .....22 A4
Launcelot Rd BR1 .....22 A4
Launder Way ME15 .....91 E2
Launton Dr DA6 .....7 D3
Laura Dr ME8 .....26 A1
Laura Pl ME1 .....47 A2
Laurel Ave DA12 .....30 C6
Laurel Bank
　Royal Tunbridge Wells TN4 .....149 B8
　Wadhurst TN5 .....175 A4
Laurel Cl Dartford DA1 .....26 C7
　Sidcup DA14 .....24 A5

Laurel Gr ME17 .....109 D2
Laurel Ho 5 SE1 .....5 C8
Laurel Rd Gillingham ME7 .....48 C7
　Royal Tunbridge Wells TN2 .....149 D7
Laurel Way TN2 .....149 D7
Laurel Wlk ME8 .....63 E6
Laurels The
　1 Bromley, Widmore BR1 .....36 B8
　Dartford DA2 .....26 C5
　Maidstone ME16 .....91 C2
　New Barn DA3 .....43 A6
Laurie Gray Ave ME5 .....61 D1
Lavenda Cl ME7 .....63 A4
Lavender Cl Bromley BR2 .....36 E3
　1 Chatham ME5 .....61 E4
　Swanley BR8 .....39 D6
Lavender Gdns TN5 .....176 E1
Lavender Hill Swanley BR8 .....39 D6
　Tonbridge TN9 .....133 C8
Lavender Ho 8 ME15 .....107 D8
Lavender Rd ME7 .....89 F8
Lavender Sq 8 TN18 .....179 A2
Lavenders Rd ME19 .....89 C6
Lavernock Rd DA7 .....8 A5
Laverstoke Rd ME16 .....91 C8
Lavidge Rd SE9 .....22 F6
Lavinia Rd DA1 .....9 F1
Lavisham Ho BR1 .....22 B3
Lawford Gdns DA1 .....22 B1
Lawn Cl Bromley BR1 .....22 B1
　Chatham ME4 .....48 B2
　Swanley BR8 .....39 C7
　Tenterden TN30 .....182 F7
Lawn Pk TN13 .....99 B8
Lawn Rd Gillingham ME7 .....48 C5
　Northfleet DA11 .....12 C1
　Tonbridge TN9 .....133 B8
Lawns Cres RM17 .....12 D8
Lawns The Brenchley TN12 .....152 B8
　Hadlow ME18 .....104 B4
Lawrence Sq DA11 .....29 F5
Lawrence Cl ME15 .....107 A7
Lawrence Ct ME2 .....45 A5
Lawrence Gdns RM18 .....13 B7
Lawrence Hill Gdns DA1 .....9 C1
Lawrence Hill Rd DA1 .....9 C1
Lawrence Rd Erith DA8 .....8 B7
　Hayes BR4 .....50 A6
　Tonbridge TN10 .....117 C6
Lawrence St ME7 .....48 C5
Lawson Cl E16 .....1 C8
Lawson Gdns DA1 .....9 D3
Lawson House 1 SE18 .....6 A8
Lawson Rd DA1 .....9 D3
Lawsons Mews TN9 .....117 C2
Laxey Rd BR6 .....51 F4
Laxey The ME15 .....91 E1
Laxton Cl ME15 .....92 F3
Laxton Dr ME17 .....108 A1
Laxton Gdns TN12 .....135 E7
Layfield Ho 8 SE10 .....1 A1
Layfield Rd ME7 .....48 F7
Layhams Rd BR2 .....50 A3
Laymarsh Cl DA17 .....3 F3
Layzell Wlk SE9 .....22 E5
Le May Ave SE12 .....22 B5
Le Temple Rd ME12 .....136 B6
Lea Ct ME4 .....47 E1
Lea Rd TN13 .....99 C8
Lea Vale DA1 .....8 D8
Leafield La DA14 .....24 F5
Leafy Glade ME8 .....63 B6
Leafy Gr BR2 .....50 C5
Leafy La DA13 .....58 A3
Leafy Oak Rd SE12 .....22 C3
Lealands Ave TN11 .....116 A1
Lealands Cl TN3 .....161 C6
Leaman Cl ME23 .....17 E4
Leamington Ave
　Bromley BR1 .....22 C3
　Orpington BR6 .....51 E6
Leamington Cl BR1 .....22 C3
Leamouth Rd E6 .....1 E8
Leander Dr DA12 .....30 F4
Leander Rd ME1 .....61 C2
Learoyd Gdns E6 .....2 A6
Leas Dale SE9 .....23 A5
Leas Gn BR7 .....23 F2
Leas The Wadhurst TN5 .....175 A6
　Woolwich SE18 .....6 D6
Leather Cl TN8 .....128 C8
Leatherbottle Gn DA18 .....3 F3
Leaves Green Rd BR2 .....50 D1
Lebrun Sq SE3 .....5 B4
Leckwith Ave DA7 .....7 E8
Leclair House SE3 .....5 B4
Leconfield Cl TN9 .....132 F7
Leda Rd SE18 .....1 F3
Lee Gn BR5 .....38 A4
Lee Green Rd ME3 .....33 B6
Lee Rd ME6 .....75 A8
Lee Sta SE12 .....5 F1
Leechcroft Ave Sidcup DA15 .....6 F1
　Swanley BR8 .....39 F6
Leeds & Broomfield
　CE Prim Sch ME17 .....109 A7
Leeds Castle* ME17 .....109 D7
Leeds Cl BR6 .....52 D8
Leeds Ho ME2 .....33 C1
Leeds Rd ME17 .....108 E3
Leeds Sq ME8 .....49 B3
Leeke Ho 3 ME1 .....47 C5
Lees Rd ME18 .....120 E7
Leesons Hill BR5,BR7 .....38 A6
Leesons Prim Sch BR5 .....38 B6
Leesons Way BR5 .....37 F7
Leet Cl ME1 .....47 E6
Leeward Rd ME1 .....47 C1

Leewood Cl SE12 .....5 A1
Leewood Pl BR8 .....39 D5
Legatt Rd SE9 .....5 D2
Legge La ME19 .....74 D6
Leggs' La TN3 .....147 E5
Leghorn Rd SE18 .....2 D1
Leicester Dr TN2 .....162 F8
Leicester Rd
　Maidstone ME15 .....107 D7
　Tilbury RM18 .....12 F5
Leigh Ave ME15 .....107 B6
Leigh City Tech Coll The
　DA1 .....9 B6
Leigh Green Ind Est
　TN30 .....183 E6
Leigh Sta TN11 .....115 F1
Leigh Pl DA16 .....7 A5
Leigh Prim Sch TN11 .....115 F1
Leigh Rd Gravesend DA11 .....30 B6
　Rochester ME3 .....33 C3
　Tonbridge TN11 .....116 D3
Leigh Terr
　2 St Paul's Cray BR5 .....38 B6
　Teston ME18 .....90 A1
Leighton Cl TN4 .....149 A7
Leighton Gdns RM18 .....13 A7
Leila Parnell Pl 2 SE7 .....5 C8
Leitch Row ME7 .....48 A7
Leith Hill BR5 .....38 A8
Leith Hill Gn BR5 .....38 A8
Leith Park Rd DA12 .....30 B7
Lemonwell Ct SE9 .....6 A2
Lemonwell Dr SE9 .....6 A2
Len Clifton Ho 4 SE18 .....1 F2
Len Valley Wlk ME15 .....92 F1
Lenderyou Cl DA1 .....26 E8
Lendon Rd TN15 .....86 F6
Lenham Cl 1 ME7 .....48 A6
Leneda Dr TN2 .....162 E8
Leney Rd ME18 .....104 E7
Lenfield Ave ME14 .....92 B4
Lenham Cl TN2 .....162 E8
Lenham Heath Rd ME17 .....111 C2
Lenham Ho Lenham ME17 .....111 E5
　13 Orpington BR5 .....38 D1
Lenham Rd
　Broadstone TN27,ME17 .....126 D3
　Erith DA7 .....7 F4
　Fairbourne Heath ME17 .....110 C1
　Headcorn TN27 .....141 E6
Lenham Way ME8 .....49 A3
Lennard Rd Orpington BR2 .....36 F1
　Sevenoaks TN13 .....83 E7
Lennox Ave DA11 .....13 A1
Lennox Ho 3 DA17 .....4 A3
Lennox Rd DA11 .....29 E8
Lennox Rd E DA11 .....30 A8
Lenor Cl DA6 .....7 E3
Lensbury Way SE2 .....3 C4
Lenside Dr ME15 .....93 A2
Lenton St SE18 .....2 D2
Leonard Ave Otford TN14 .....69 B3
　Swanscombe DA10 .....28 E8
Leonard Cl ME14 .....91 B6
Leonard Ct DA14 .....24 B5
Leonard Judge Ho DA2 .....27 E3
Leonard Pl BR2 .....50 E7
Leonard Rd
　3 Chatham ME4 .....48 B3
　Gillingham ME7 .....48 B3
Leonard Robbins Path 3
　SE28 .....3 B6
Leonard St E16 .....1 E5
Leopold Rd 2 ME4 .....48 A3
Lesley Cl Istead Rise DA13 .....43 F8
　Sidcup DA14 .....25 B8
　Swanley BR8 .....39 E6
Lesley Pl ME16 .....91 E4
Lesley Tew Ct TN10 .....117 C5
Leslie Cres TN30 .....173 B2
Leslie Rd Gillingham ME7 .....48 D7
　Newham E16 .....1 B7
Leslie Smith Sq 7 SE18 .....6 A8
Lesnes Abbey
　(remains of)* SE2 .....3 C2
Lesney Park Prim Sch DA8 .....8 D8
Lesney Park Rd DA8 .....8 D8
Lesney Pk DA8 .....8 D8
Lessness Ave DA7 .....7 D8
Lessness Heath Prim Sch
　DA7 .....4 A1
Lessness Pk DA17 .....4 A1
Lessness Rd 12 DA17 .....4 A1
Lested La ME17 .....108 B2
Lester Rd ME4 .....48 A3
Lestock House SE3 .....5 D6
Letchworth Ave ME4 .....47 F1
Letchworth Cl BR2 .....36 A4
Letchworth Dr BR2 .....36 A4
Letter Box La TN13 .....99 C6
Leverholme Gdns SE9 .....23 A4
Levett Cl ME3 .....21 B6
Levetts La TN32 .....185 D1
Leviathan Way ME4 .....34 A1
Lewd La TN27 .....143 A3
Lewes Cl RM17 .....12 A8
Lewes Rd BR1 .....36 D7
Lewin Rd DA6 .....7 E3
Lewing Cl BR6 .....51 E7
Lewis Ave ME8 .....49 B2
Lewis Court Dr ME17 .....107 C3
Lewis Cl DA11 .....29 F8
Lewis King Ho 8 BR1 .....22 B1
Lewis Rd Bexley DA16 .....7 C4
　Istead Rise DA13 .....43 F8
　Sidcup DA14 .....24 C5

Lewis Rd continued
　Swanscombe DA10 .....11 E1
Leybank TN11 .....116 F4
Leybourne Cl Chatham ME5 .....62 A2
　Hayes BR2 .....36 A3
Leybourne Dell TN17 .....180 E6
Leybourne Rd ME2 .....46 F8
Leybourne Way BR2 .....74 F4
Leybourne, St Peter &
　St Paul CE Prim Sch ME2 .....74 E2
Leybridge Ct SE12 .....5 A2
Leyburn Ct TN11 .....117 C3
Leyburn Ho SE18 .....5 E7
Leycroft Gdns DA8 .....9 B6
Leydenhatch La BR8 .....39 D8
Leyes Rd E16 .....1 E8
Leyhill Cl BR8 .....39 E4
Leyland Rd SE12 .....5 A2
Leysdown Ave DA7 .....8 C3
Leysdown Rd SE9 .....22 F6
Leyton Ave ME7 .....48 E1
Leyton Cross DA2 .....26 A6
Leyton Cross Rd DA2 .....25 F5
Leywood Rd DA13 .....58 D3
Lezayre Rd BR6 .....51 F4
Liberty Mews BR6 .....51 F8
Libya Terr 6 ME14 .....92 A7
Lichdale Cl 7 BR6 .....51 F6
Lichfield Cl ME8 .....49 D2
Lichfield Ho 16 ME15 .....107 E7
Liddon Rd BR1 .....36 D6
Lidsing Rd ME14 .....77 E6
Lidwells La TN17 .....153 E1
Lieth Park Rd DA12 .....30 C7
Liffler Rd SE18 .....2 E1
Lightfoot Gn TN18 .....178 E3
Lila Pl BR8 .....39 F5
Lilac Cres ME2 .....46 E6
Lilac Gdns BR8 .....39 D6
Lilac Pl DA13 .....44 B2
Lilac Rd ME2 .....46 E5
Liburne Gdns SE9 .....5 E2
Liburne Rd SE9 .....5 E2
Lilian Barker Cl SE12 .....5 A2
Lilk Hill ME14 .....93 C3
Lillechurch Rd ME3 .....32 F7
Lillesden Cotts TN18 .....184 E7
Lillieburn ME19 .....74 D2
Limavady Ho SE18 .....2 A2
Lime Ave DA11 .....29 D8
Lime Cl Bromley BR1 .....36 E5
　Frant TN3 .....163 B3
　Marden TN12 .....138 C6
Lime Ct Eltham SE9 .....5 E4
Lime Cres ME19 .....90 A7
Lime Gr Eltham SE9 .....23 B6
　Gillingham ME8 .....63 C3
Lime Gr Orpington BR6 .....51 B8
　Sidcup DA15 .....6 F1
Lime Hill Rd TN1 .....149 A4
Lime Kiln Dr SE7 .....5 B8
Lime Pit La TN13,TN14 .....68 C2
Lime Rd BR8 .....39 D6
Lime Row SE28 .....3 B6
Lime Tree Ave DA9 .....28 A7
Lime Tree Cl TN9 .....117 C2
Lime Tree Wlk TN13 .....84 B2
Lime Trees TN13 .....139 E4
Limepits Cross ME9 .....65 F3
Limes Cl TN30 .....183 C8
Limes Gr TN18 .....178 F5
Limes Row BR6 .....51 B5
Limes The Edenbridge TN8 .....112 C1
　Frittenden TN17 .....156 E6
　Lenham ME17 .....111 D5
　Orpington BR2 .....50 E8
Limetree Cl ME5 .....62 A1
Limetree Terr
　Lenham ME17 .....111 E6
　5 ME15 .....107 A4
Linwood Rd E8 .....8 C7
Linchmere Rd 7 SE12 .....22 A8
Linclon Cl ME2 .....46 C8
Lincoln Cl ME2 .....46 D6
Lincoln Ct ME2 .....22 C5
Lincoln Green Rd BR5 .....37 F4
Lincoln Rd Erith DA8 .....8 F5
　Maidstone ME15 .....107 D8
　Sidcup DA14 .....24 B3
Lincolnshire Terr DA2 .....27 D4
Lincon Rd ME7 .....48 D7
Linden Ave DA1 .....26 C7
Linden Chase Rd TN13 .....84 B5
Linden Cl Orpington BR6 .....52 A5
　Paddock Wood TN12 .....136 A6
　Purfleet RM19 .....10 C8
　Royal Tunbridge Wells TN4 .....149 A7
Linden Ct Sidcup DA14 .....23 E4
　Tonbridge TN10 .....117 B7
Linden Gdns TN2 .....148 F1
Linden House 5 ME5 .....61 F4
Linden Park Rd TN2 .....149 A2
Linden Rd ME17 .....106 C4
　Gillingham ME7 .....48 E5
Linden Sq TN13 .....83 E5
Lindenfield BR7 .....37 B1
Lindisfarne Cl DA12 .....30 E6
Lindisfarne Gdns ME16 .....91 E3
Lindridge La TN12 .....139 C5
Lindsay Ho 2 SE27 .....22 B8
Lindsey Ho 3 ME15 .....107 E7
Lindwood Cl 2 E6 .....1 F8
Lineacre Cl ME8 .....63 D6
Lines Terr ME4 .....48 A4
Ling Rd Erith DA8 .....8 E8
　Newham E16 .....1 A8
Lingey Cl DA15 .....23 F6

Lingfield Ave DA2 .....27 F1
Lingfield Cres SE9 .....6 C1
Lingfield Rd
　Borough Green TN15 .....87 ...
　Edenbridge TN8 .....128 ...
　Gravesend DA12 .....30 ...
Lingley Dr ME2 .....33 ...
Lingwood DA7 .....8 ...
Link Field BR2 .....36 ...
Link Hill La TN27 .....127 ...
Link The Eltham SE9 .....23 ...
　New Ash Green DA3 .....56 ...
Link Way Bromley BR2 .....36 ...
　Royal Tunbridge Wells TN2 .....149 ...
Linkden Cotts TN18 .....186 ...
Links Ct SE9 .....23 ...
Links The Addington ME19 .....74 ...
　Chatham ME5 .....62 ...
Links View Dartford DA1 .....26 ...
　Woolwich SE18 .....1 ...
Linkway ME20 .....75 ...
Linley Cl RM18 .....14 ...
Linnet Ave TN12 .....136 ...
Linnet Cl SE28 .....3 ...
Linslade Rd BR6 .....52 ...
Linsted Ct SE9 .....6 ...
Linton Cl Bexley DA16 .....7 ...
　2 Greenwich SE7 .....1 ...
Linton Dann Cl ME3 .....34 ...
Linton Gore ME17 .....106 ...
Linton Hill TN12 .....122 ...
Linton Mead Prim Sch
　SE28 .....3 ...
Linton Rd ME15 .....106 ...
Lintorn Symonds Rd ME3 .....33 ...
Linwood Ave ME2 .....46 ...
Lion & Bexley DA6 .....7 ...
Lionel Gdns SE9 .....5 ...
Lionel Oxley House 5
　ME7 .....12 ...
Lionel Rd Eltham SE9 .....133 ...
Lions Cl SE9 .....22 ...
Liphook Way ME16 .....91 ...
Lipscombe Rd TN2 .....149 ...
Lipton Cl SE28 .....3 ...
Liptraps La TN2 .....149 ...
Lipwell Hill ME23 .....17 ...
Lisbarell Cl BR7 .....23 ...
Liskeard Gdns SE3 .....5 ...
Lisle Cl DA12 .....31 ...
Lismore Cl ME15 .....107 ...
Lister Cl ME19 .....89 ...
Lister Ho SE3 .....5 ...
Lister Rd RM18 .....13 ...
Lister Wlk SE28 .....3 ...
Listmas Rd ME4 .....48 ...
Little Alley TN8 .....128 ...
Little Bayham Cotts TN3 .....164 ...
Little Birches DA15 .....23 ...
Little Boundes Cl TN4 .....132 ...
Little Brook Hospl DA2 .....10 ...
Little Browns La TN8 .....112 ...
Little Buckland Ave ME16 .....91 ...
Little Ct ME16 .....91 ...
Little Field TN12 .....139 ...
Little Footway TN3 .....147 ...
Little Heath SE7 .....1 ...
Little Heath Rd DA7 .....7 ...
Little Hill TN30 .....173 ...
Little Iridge Farm Cotts
　TN19 .....184 ...
Little ooh's Cross TN17 .....181 ...
Little John Ave ME5 .....61 ...
Little Julians Hill TN13 .....99 ...
Little Kit's Coty House*
　ME20 .....76 ...
Little Mallett TN13 .....147 ...
Little Market Row ME19 .....74 ...
Little Mill Farm Cotts
　TN12 .....138 ...
Little Mount Sion TN1 .....149 ...
Little Oakham Ct ME3 .....19 ...
Little Orch ME17 .....106 ...
Little Oxley ME19 .....74 ...
Little Pk TN5 .....174 ...
Little Queen St DA1 .....26 ...
Little Redlands BR1 .....36 ...
Little Robhurst TN26 .....171 ...
Little Sheephurst Cotts
　TN12 .....137 ...
Little Thrift BR5 .....37 ...
Little Wood TN13 .....84 ...
Little Wood Cl BR5 .....24 ...
Littlebourne Ave ME8 .....49 ...
Littlebourne Rd ME14 .....92 ...
Littlebrook Manor Way
　DA1 .....10 ...
Littlecombe SE7 .....1 ...
Littlecote Cl SE7 ......
Littlecroft Rd TN13 .....84 ...
Littlecroft Eltham SE9 .....6 ...
Littledale Dartford DA2 .....27 ...
　Woolwich SE2 .....3 ...
Littlejohn Rd BR5 .....38 ...
Littlejohn Rd ME17 .....38 ...
Littlemede SE9 .....23 ...
Littlemore Rd SE2 .....3 ...
Livesey St ME18 .....104 ...
Livingstone Bldgs ME7 .....48 ...
Livingstone Circ ME7 .....48 ...
Livingstone Gdns DA12 .....30 ...
Livingstone Hospl DA1 .....26 ...
Livingstone Rd
　Gillingham ME7 .....48 ...
　Gravesend DA12 .....30 ...

Livingstone Wlk 6 ME15 ..107 F5
Lizban St SE3 ....5 B7
Llanover Rd SE18 ....6 A7
Lloyds Gn TN30 ....189 D4
Loaland Bsns Ctr ME2 ..47 C8
Loam Ct DA1 ....26 E7
Loampits Cl TN9 ....117 D3
Lobelia Cl Gillingham ME7 ..48 E6
 6 Newham E6 ....1 E5
Locarno Ave ME4 ....49 A2
Lochat Rd ME3 ....33 E6
Lochmere Cl DA8 ....8 B8
Lock La ME14 ....76 D1
Lock St ME7 ....48 C5
Lock's Yd TN13 ....84 C2
Lockesley Dr BR5 ....38 A3
Lockham Farm Ave
 ME17 ....107 D5
Lockington Cl TN9 ....132 F7
Lockington Gr ME1 ....47 C5
Lockside TN9 ....117 C2
Locksley Cl ME5 ....61 E2
Lockswood ME16 ....91 D7
Lockyer Rd ME19 ....10 C8
Lockyers Hill DA13 ....58 F5
Lodden Ct 18 BR5 ....38 D1
Loddington La ME17 ....123 A8
Loder Cl ME17 ....111 B5
Lodge Ave DA1 ....9 C1
Lodge La Cl Orpington BR6 ..38 B1
 Wateringbury ME18 ..104 D8
Lodge Cres BR6 ....38 B1
Lodge Gdns ME17 ....125 F6
Lodge Hill DA16 ....7 B7
Lodge Hill La ME3 ....33 F7
Lodge La Cobham DA12 ..45 B5
 Sidcup DA5 ....7 D1
 Westerham TN16 ....96 C8
Lodge Rd Bromley BR1 ..22 C1
 Maidstone ME14 ....92 D5
 Staplehurst TN12 ....139 E5
 Tonbridge TN9 ....117 B2
Lodgewood Cotts TN8 ..113 D2
Logs Hill BR1,BR7 ....36 E8
Logs Hill Cl BR7 ....36 E8
Lolland Ho 9 SE18 ....1 E2
Lomaria Ct TN2 ....149 C4
Lomas La TN18 ....186 F5
Lombard St DA4 ....41 C5
Lombard Trad Est SE7 ..1 B2
Lombard Wall SE7 ....1 B2
Lombardy Cl ME7 ....63 A6
Lombardy Dr ME14 ....92 C5
London City Airport E16 ..1 E5
London Ind Pk The E6 ..2 A8
London La Bromley BR1 ..22 A1
 Cranbrook Common TN17 ..156 A2
London Rd Aylesford ME20 ..73 D2
 Badgers Mount TN14 ..68 C6
 Bidborough TN4 ....132 F3
 Bromley BR1 ....36 A8
 Chelsfield TN14 ....69 E2
 Crayford DA1 ....8 D2
 Ditton ME20 ....75 C1
 Farningham BR8,DA4 ..40 D3
 Filmwell TN5 ....177 D3
 Gillingham ME8 ....49 C1
 Grays RM17,RM20 ....11 E8
 Halstead TN14 ....67 E4
 Hartlip ME8,ME9 ....64 D7
 Hildenborough
  TN11,TN13,TN15 ....116 B7
 Hurst Green TN19 ....184 A3
 Maidstone ME16 ....91 C6
 Newington ME9 ....65 A6
 Northfleet DA11 ....12 E1
 Otford TN13 ....68 D1
 Rochester ME2 ....47 A7
 Royal Tunbridge Wells TN4 ..149 A8
 Royal Tunbridge Wells,
  Mount Sion TN1 ....149 A3
 Sevenoaks TN13 ....84 B2
 Sevenoaks,Dunton Green
  TN13 ....83 E7
 Swanley BR8 ....39 E6
 Swanley,White Oak BR8 ..39 D7
 Swanscombe DA9 ....11 C2
 Tilbury RM18 ....13 B5
 Tonbridge TN10,TN11 ..117 B3
 West Kingsdown TN15 ..56 A1
 Wrotham TN15 ....72 B3
 Wrotham Heath TN15,ME19 ..72 F1
London Rd E ME20 ....90 F8
London Road Purfleet
 RM19 ....10 C8
London Road
 West Thurrock RM20 ..11 A8
Londonderry Rd SE18 ....3 A8
Londonderry Rd 19 ME15 ..107 C7
Londonderry Par DA1 ....8 D2
Lonewood Way TN11 ....102 F2
Long Acre BR6 ....52 D8
Long Barn Rd TN14 ....99 B2
Long Catlis Rd ME8 ....63 D4
Long La Bexley DA7 ....7 E6
 Rabbit's Cross ME17 ..123 D5
Long Mark Rd 6 E16 ....1 D8
Long Mead Prim Sch
 TN10 ....117 B5
Long Mead Way TN10 ..117 B4
Long Meads TN3,TN4 ..148 B4
Long Mill La Crouch TN15 ..87 B3
 Platt TN15 ....87 C7
Long Rede La ME16 ....90 F3
Long Slip TN3 ....148 A3
Long Wlk SE18 ....6 B8
Longbury Cl BR5 ....38 B6
Longbury Dr BR5 ....38 B6

Longcroft SE9 ....23 A5
Longdon Wood BR2 ....50 E6
Longfellow Rd ME7 ....48 C3
Longfield TN30 ....183 A6
Longfield Ave
 High Halstow ME23 ....17 E4
 New Barn DA3,DA13 ....43 D7
Longfield Pl ME15 ....107 C8
Longfield Rd
 Meopham Sta DA3,DA13 ..43 E3
 Royal Tonbridge
  Wells TN1,TN2,TN11 ..133 E1
Longfield Sta DA3 ....42 E6
Longfields Dr ME4 ....93 A5
Longford Cl ME8 ....64 A8
Longford Ct ME8 ....64 A8
Longham Copse ME15 ....92 F1
Longhill Ave ME5 ....48 B3
Longhurst Dr ME5 ....61 F2
Longlands Ct DA15 ....23 F5
Longlands Park Cres
 DA15 ....23 E6
Longlands Prim Sch DA15 ..23 E5
Longlands Rd DA15 ....23 F5
Longleat Villas 8 ME8 ....7 E3
Longleigh La SE2,DA7 ....3 E2
Longley Rd Gillingham ME8 ..49 F1
 Rochester ME1 ....47 C4
Longmarsh View DA4 ....41 B8
Longmead ME7 ....37 A7
Longmead Dr DA14 ....24 D6
Longmeadow TN13 ....83 D6
Longmeadow Rd DA15 ..23 E7
Longparish DA15 ....107 F6
Longreach Rd DA8 ....9 B7
Longshaw Rd ME15 ....107 F5
Longspring Wood TN13 ..99 A6
Longten's Cotts DA12 ....31 E6
Longtown Ct 15 DA2 ....10 B1
Longview Way TN2 ....149 D7
Longwalk DA13 ....43 E8
Longwood ME5 ....62 B1
Longworth Cl SE28 ....3 D7
Lonsdale Cres DA2 ....27 C7
Lonsdale Dr ME8 ....63 E7
Lonsdale Gdns TN1 ....149 A3
Lonsdale Rd DA7 ....7 F5
Loop Rd BR7 ....23 C2
Loose Inf & Jun Schs
 ME15 ....107 A6
Loose Rd ME15 ....107 A7
Loraine Ct BR7 ....23 B3
Lord Chatham's Ride
 TN14 ....95 A1
Lord Roberts Terr SE18 ..2 A1
Lord Romney's Hill ME14 ..92 F3
Lord St Gravesend DA12 ..30 C8
 Newham E16 ....1 E5
Lord Warwick St SE18 ....1 F3
Lords Wood Cl ME5 ....62 B2
Lords Wood La ME5 ....62 B3
Lordswood Cl DA2 ....27 C8
Lordswood Ind Est ME5 ..77 C8
Lordswood Inf Sch ME5 ..62 B3
Lordswood Jun Sch ME5 ..62 B3
Lorenden Pk TN18 ....178 F1
Lorimar Bsns Ctr RM13 ..4 E8
Lorton Cl DA12 ....30 E6
Lossenham La TN18 ....187 D3
Louisville Ave ME4 ....48 D4
Louvain Rd DA9 ....27 E8
Lovage App E6 ....1 E8
Love La East End TN27 ..142 B5
 East Tilbury RM18 ....14 C8
 Rochester ME1 ....47 C5
 Sidcup DA5 ....24 F1
 Wateringbury ME18 ..104 D7
 Woolwich SE18 ....2 B2
Lovel Ave DA16 ....7 A5
Lovelace Ave BR2 ....37 A3
Lovelace Ct Gillingham ME8 ..3 D6
 West Kingsdown TN15 ..55 E4
Lovelace Gn SE9 ....5 F4
Lover's La DA9,DA10 ....11 D3
Lovers La TN17 ....153 F1
Lovibonds Ave BR6 ....51 B7
Low Cl DA9 ....11 A2
Low Meadow ME2 ....60 B5
Low Street La MN18 ....13 F8
Lowe Ave E16 ....1 A8
Lower Bell La ME20 ....75 B2
Lower Bloors La ME8 ....49 E3
Lower Boxley Rd 10 ME14 ..92 A5
Lower Camden BR7 ....36 F8
Lower Church Rd ME8 ....10 E2
Lower Croft BR8 ....39 F5
Lower East Rd ME4 ....48 B8
Lower Fant Rd ME16 ....91 D2
Lower Fant Rd ME17 ..123 D5
Lower Gn TN11 ....115 F1
Lower Gravel Rd BR2 ....36 F1
Lower Green Rd
 Pembury TN2 ....150 D7
 Royal Tonbridge Wells
  TN3,TN4 ....148 C6
Lower Hartlip Rd ME9 ..64 E5
Lower Haysden La
 TN11,TN9 ....132 D8
Lower Hazelhurst TN5 ..176 A4
Lower High St TN5 ....175 A4
Lower Higham Rd DA12 ..31 B7
Lower Park Rd DA7 ....4 A2
Lower Platts TN5 ....176 F1
Lower Rainham Rd ME7 ..48 E2
Lower Range Rd DA12 ..30 E8
Lower Rd Erith DA8 ....4 D2
 Erith,Belvedere DA17 ....4 B3

Lower Rd continued
 Hextable BR8 ....26 B1
 Higham DA12,ME3 ....32 B6
 Maidstone ME15 ....92 B3
 Northfleet DA11 ....12 A3
 Orpington BR5 ....38 B3
 Sutton Valence ME17 ..124 E7
 Tilbury RM18 ....13 A3
 West Farleigh ME15 ..105 C7
Lower Rochester Rd ME3 ..32 E6
Lower St Leeds ME17 ..109 A7
 Tonbridge TN1 ....115 F5
Lower Station Rd DA1 ....8 E1
Lower Stone St ME15 ....92 A3
Lower Tovil ME15 ....91 E2
Lower Twydall La
 ME7,ME8 ....49 C4
Lower Warren Rd ME20 ..76 E6
Lower Woodlands Rd
 ME7 ....49 A6
Lowfield St DA1 ....26 E8
Lownds Ct DA1 ....36 A7
Lowry Cl DA8 ....4 D2
Lowry The 4 TN9 ....133 B8
Loxwood Cl BR5,BR6 ....52 D8
Lubbock Cl ME15 ....107 E5
Lubbock Ct BR7 ....22 F1
Lubbock Rd BR7 ....22 F1
Lucas Rd ME6 ....74 E7
Lucerne Ct 18 DA18 ....3 E3
Lucerne Rd BR6 ....37 F1
Lucerne St ME14 ....92 A5
Lucilina Dr TN8 ....128 C8
Lucknow Rd TN12 ....136 A8
Lucknow St SE18 ....6 E7
Lucks Hill ME19 ....89 D8
Lucks La
 Paddock Wood TN12 ..136 B8
 Rabbit's Cross ME17 ..123 F6
Lucks Way TN12 ....138 B6
Luddenham Cl ME14 ..92 C6
Luddesdon Rd DA8 ....8 A7
Luddesdown House 5
 BR5 ....38 A6
Luddesdown Rd DA13 ..45 A2
Ludham Cl SE28 ....3 C7
Ludlow Cl BR2 ....36 A6
Luffield Rd SE2 ....3 B3
Luffman Rd SE12 ....22 B5
Lughorse La ME15,ME18 ..105 C1
Lullingstone Ave BR8 ....39 F6
Lullingstone Castle* DA4 ..54 B5
Lullingstone Cl
 Gillingham ME7 ....63 B3
 St Paul's Cray BR5 ....24 B1
Lullingstone Cres BR5 ..24 B1
Lullingstone La DA4 ....54 C8
Lullingstone Pk* DA4 ..53 F6
Lullingstone Pk Visitor Ctr*
 DA4 ....53 E6
Lullingstone Rd
 8 Erith DA17 ....7 F8
 Maidstone ME16 ....91 C7
Lullingstone Roman Villa
 (rems of)* DA4 ....54 B7
Lulworth Rd Bexley DA16 ..6 F5
 Chislehurst SE9 ....23 A6
Lumley Cl DA17 ....4 A1
Lumsden Terr 8 ME4 ..47 A4
Lunedale Rd DA2 ....27 C7
Lunsford Bsns Ctr
 ME20 ....74 F2
Lunsford La ME20 ....74 F2
Lunsford Prim Sch ME20 ..75 A2
Lupton Cl SE12 ....22 B4
Lurkins Rise TN17 ....167 D7
Lushington Rd ME14 ....91 E7
Lusted Rd TN13 ....83 E7
Luton High St ME5 ....48 C2
Luton Inf Sch ME5 ....48 C2
Luton Jun Sch ME5 ....48 C2
Luton Rd Chatham ME4,ME5 ..48 B2
 Sidcup DA14 ....24 C5
Luxfield Rd SE9 ....22 E7
Luxon Rd DA13 ....58 C8
Luxted Rd BR6 ....66 A6
Lyall Way ME8 ....63 E4
Lych Gate Rd BR6 ....38 A1
Lychfield Dr ME2 ....47 A8
Lydd Cl DA14 ....23 E5
Lydd Rd Chatham ME5 ..62 B5
 Erith DA7 ....7 F7
Lydden Ct SE9 ....23 C6
Lydens La TN8 ....128 F6
Lydford Ct 10 DA2 ....10 B1
Lydia Cotts 3 DA11 ....30 B8
Lydia Rd DA8 ....4 D8
Lydstep Rd DA7 ....23 A4
Lyford St SE18 ....1 E2
Lyle Cl ME2 ....47 B8
Lyle Ct ME15 ....91 C5
Lyle Pk TN13 ....99 A3
Lyme Farm Rd SE12 ....5 A3
Lyme Rd DA16 ....7 B6
Lyminge Cl Gillingham ME8 ..49 C2
 Sidcup DA14 ....23 F4
Lymington Cl 2 E6 ....1 F8
Lymington Ct ME15 ....107 F4
Lyndean Ind Est SE2 ....3 C3
Lynden La TN5 ....176 A1
Lynden Way BR8 ....39 D6
Lyndhurst Dr TN13 ....83 E3
Lyndhurst Rd Bexley DA7 ..8 B4

Lyndhurst Rd continued
 Maidstone ME15 ....107 C8
Lyndhurst Way DA13 ..43 F8
Lyndon Ave DA15 ....6 F2
Lyndon Rd DA17 ....4 A2
Lynette Ave ME2 ....33 A1
Lyngs Cl ME18 ....120 F8
Lynmead Cl TN8 ....112 B4
Lynmere Rd DA16 ....7 B5
Lymouth Rise BR5 ....38 B5
Lynne Cl 7 BR6 ....51 F4
Lynors Ave ME2 ....33 A1
Lynstead Cl BR1 ....36 C7
Lynstead House ME16 ..91 A1
Lynsted Cl DA6 ....8 B2
Lynsted Gdns SE9 ....5 D4
Lynsted Rd ME8 ....49 B3
Lynton Ave BR5 ....38 B5
Lynton Dr ME5 ....62 B3
Lynton Rd DA11 ....30 A7
Lynton Rd S DA11 ....30 A7
Lynton Way TN10 ....161 C6
Lynwood DA13 ....37 E1
Lyons Cres TN9 ....117 C2
Lyoth Rd BR5 ....51 C8
Lysander Rd ME19 ....88 F3
Lysander Way BR6 ....51 C7
Lytchet Rd BR1 ....22 B1
Lytham Ct SE28 ....3 E7
Lytton Strachy Path 8
 SE28 ....3 B6
Lyveden Rd SE3 ....5 B7

M
Mabbett House 2 SE18 ..6 A8
Mabel Cotts DA1 ....43 A6
Mabel Rd BR8 ....26 A2
Mablendon Rd TN9 ....133 A8
Macalister House 8 SE18 ..6 B8
Macaulay Cl ME20 ....75 A4
Macaulay Way 2 SE28 ....3 B5
Macbean St SE18 ....2 B3
Macdonald Ct TN12 ....136 A6
Macdonald Rd ME7 ..48 D6
Mace Ct ME17 ....12 E8
Mace Farm Cotts TN14 ..66 E6
Mace Gateway E16 ....1 A6
Mace La TN14 ....66 D6
Macgregor Rd E16 ....1 C8
Mackenders Cl ME20 ..76 A6
Mackenders Gn ME20 ..76 A6
Mackenders La ME20 ..76 A6
Mackenzie Way DA12 ..30 D2
Macleod Ho SE18 ....5 E6
Macmillan Gdns 2 DA1 ..10 A3
Macoma Rd SE18 ....6 D8
Macoma Terr SE18 ....6 D8
Mada Rd BR6 ....51 B7
Madan Rd TN16 ....81 E2
Madden Ave ME5 ....61 E5
Madden Cl DA10 ....11 E1
Maddocks Cl DA14 ....24 E3
Madeira Pk TN1 ....149 A2
Madginford Cl ME15 ....93 A2
Madginford Park Inf Sch
 ME15 ....93 A2
Madginford Park Jun Sch
 ME15 ....93 A2
Madginford Rd ME15 ..92 F2
Madison Cres DA7 ....7 C7
Madison Gdns DA7 ....7 C7
Madison Way TN13 ....83 F4
Madras House 2 ME15 ..107 E5
Mafeking Rd ME5 ....61 F3
Magdalen Cl ME7 ....65 A8
Magdelan Gr BR6 ....52 B6
Magnet Rd RM20 ....11 C8
Magnolia Ave ME8 ....63 B5
Magnolia Cl TN9 ....133 C7
Magpie Bottom TN15 ..69 C6
Magpie Cl ME20 ....75 A1
Magpie Gn 3 TN8 ....112 D3
Magpie Hall Cl BR2 ....36 E3
Magpie Hall La BR2 ....36 F3
Magpie Hall Rd ME4 ..48 A2
Magpie La ME14,ME17 ..63 F1
Magwitch Cl ME1 ....47 B4
Maida Rd Chatham ME4 ..48 B2
 Erith DA17 ....4 A3
Maida Vale Rd DA1 ....9 A2
Maiden Erlegh Ave DA5 ..24 E7
Maiden La DA1 ....9 A3
Maidstone Barracks Sta
 ME15 ....91 E5
Maidstone East Sta ME14 ..91 F5
Maidstone Gram Sch
 ME15 ....92 B2
Maidstone Gram Sch
 for Girls ME16 ....91 E5
Maidstone Hospl The
 ME16 ....91 A4
Maidstone Ind Ctr ME14 ..91 F5
Maidstone Ind Est ME14 ..91 F6
Maidstone Mus
 & Bentlif Art Gallery* ME14 91 F5
Maidstone Rd
 Chatham ME4 ....47 F2
 Chatham,Walderslade ME5 ..61 D4
 Chestnut Street ME9 ....65 D4
 Colt's Hill TN12,TN2 ..135 B4
 Five Wents ME17 ....108 E2
 Gillingham ME8 ....63 C6
 Gillingham,Bredhurst
  ME7,ME8 ....63 C1
 Goose Green ME18,TN11 ..103 C3
 Grays RM17 ....12 A8

Maidstone Rd continued
 Headcorn TN27 ....141 B7
 Horsmonden TN12 ....137 C3
 Lenham ME17 ....111 D5
 Matfield TN12 ....151 C6
 Nettlestead Green ME18 ..104 C3
 Oldbury TN15 ....85 C5
 Pembury TN2 ....134 E1
 Platt TN15 ....87 C7
 Rochester ME1 ....47 C3
 Sevenoaks TN13 ....83 E5
 Sidcup DA14 ....24 F1
 Staplehurst TN12 ....139 E7
 Swanley DA14,BR8 ....39 B8
 Underling Green TN12 ..122 F2
Maidstone West Sta ME16 ..91 E3
Mailyns The ME8 ....63 D7
Main Gate Rd ME4 ....47 F7
Main Rd Chattenden ME3 ..33 F4
 Cooling ME3 ....16 F4
 Crockenhill BR8 ....39 D3
 Cudham TN16 ....81 A7
 Farningham DA4 ....40 F3
 Halstead TN14 ....67 C3
 Hextable BR8 ....39 F8
 Hoo St Werburgh ME3 ..34 C5
 Kingsnorth ME3 ....35 D7
 Longfield ME3 ....62 B7
 Margil Hall TN8 ....112 B6
 Sidcup DA14,DA15 ....23 E5
 St Paul's Cray BR5 ....38 C7
 Sundridge TN14 ....82 E3
 Sutton at Hone DA4 ....41 A5
Main Road Gorse Hill DA4 ..55 D7
Mainridge Rd BR7 ....23 A4
Maison Des Fleurs ME16 ..91 C2
Majendie Rd SE18 ....2 D1
Major York's Rd TN4 ..148 F2
Malden Dr ME4 ....92 A8
Mall The 6 Bexley DA6 ..8 A3
 Bromley BR1 ....36 A6
Mallard Apartments 14
 ME15 ....107 E5
Mallard Cl DA1 ....9 F2
Mallard Path SE28 ....2 D3
Mallard Way
 Lower Stoke ME3 ....19 C4
 Marjpit Hill TN8 ....112 C3
Mallard Wlk Larkfield ME20 ..74 F2
 Sidcup DA14 ....24 C2
Mallards Way ME15 ....93 A1
Malling Ct ME19 ....89 F7
Malling Rd
 Kings Hill ME18,ME19 ..88 F2
 Lunsford ME6,ME20 ..74 F5
 Snodland ME6 ....75 A7
 Teston ME18 ....90 A1
Malling Sch The ME19 ..89 F7
Malling Terr ME16 ....91 C4
Mallingdene Cl ME13 ..33 B8
Mallings Dr ME14 ....93 C4
Mallings La ME14 ....93 C4
Mallow Cl DA11 ....29 E4
Mallow Ct RM17 ....12 D8
Mallow Way 1 ME5 ....61 A4
Mallows The ME14 ....91 F7
Mallys Pl DA4 ....41 C8
Malmaines Hall Rd ME3 ..18 D3
Malory Sch BR1 ....22 A4
Malt House La TN30 ....183 A7
Malt Mews ME1 ....47 C5
Malt Shovel Cotts DA4 ..54 D7
Malta Ave ME5 ....62 A7
Malta Rd E10 ....1 A8
Malta Terr 3 ME14 ....92 A7
Maltby Cl BR6 ....38 A1
Malthouse Cl ME17 ....111 D5
Malthouse Hill ME15 ..106 F4
Malthouse Rd TN14 ....56 F2
Malthus Path 7 SE28 ....3 C5
Maltings Cl TN11 ....118 E8
Maltings Ent Ctr The DA12 ..30 F7
Maltings The
 Gillingham ME8 ....64 A8
 Gravesend DA11 ....13 A1
 Maidstone,Grove Green
  ME14 ....92 E5
 Maidstone,The Quarries
  ME17 ....107 B4
 Orpington BR6 ....37 F1
Malton Mews SE18 ....6 E8
Malton St SE18 ....6 E8
Malus Cl ME5 ....62 B1
Malvern Ave DA7 ....7 E7
Malvern Rd DA11 ....12 D1
Malvern Rd Gillingham ME7 ..48 E3
 Orpington BR6 ....52 B6
Malvins Rd DA11 ....30 C6
Malyons Rd BR8 ....25 F1
Manchester Cl ME5 ....62 C6
Manchester Rd SE18 ....93 A5
Mandela Rd E16 ....1 A7
Mandeville Cl 1 ME14 ..92 A5
Mandeville Ct 4 SE3 ....5 A6
Mangold Way 14 DA18 ....3 E3
Mangravet Ave ME15 ..107 C7
Manitoba Gdns 6 BR6 ..51 F4
Mann Sq Sch TN9 ....133 D7
Manning St 3 SE28 ....3 B5
Manning Rd BR5 ....38 D4
Manningham Ho ME19 ....90 A6

Mannock Rd DA1 ....9 F4
Manor Cl Chalk DA12 ....31 B6
  Crayford DA1 ....8 E3
  Dartford DA2 ....26 A5
  Erith SE28 ....3 C7
  Maidstone ME14 ....93 B3
  Royal Tunbridge Wells TN4 ..148 E3
Manor Cotts
  Lamberhurst TN3 ....166 B5
  Langley Heath ME17 .....108 C5
Manor Ct Gillingham ME7 ...29 F4
  Maidstone ME14 ....93 B3
  Sole Street DA13 ....44 D4
Manor Dr DA3 ....43 A3
Manor Farm Cotts TN15 ....86 A6
Manor Field DA3 ....43 A3
Manor Forstal DA3 ....56 F7
Manor Gdns ME5 ....61 F4
Manor Gr TN10 ....117 C3
Manor Ho 10 Chatham ME7 ..48 A6
  Chislehurst BR7 ....37 D7
Manor House Dr ME16 ......91 D3
Manor House Gdns TN8 ...112 C1
Manor La
  Fawkham Green DA3 ....42 C2
  Hartley DA3 ....43 A3
  Rochester ME1 ....46 F3
Manor Park Ctry Pk* ME19 ..89 B7
Manor Pk Chislehurst BR7 ...37 D8
  Erith DA8 ....9 A8
  Royal Tunbridge Wells TN4 .148 E3
Manor Pl Bromley BR1 ......36 E8
  Chislehurst BR7 ....37 D7
Manor Rd Chatham ME4 ....47 F4
  Crayford DA1 ....8 E3
  Edenbridge TN8 ....112 B1
  Erith DA8 ....9 B8
  80 Gravesend DA12 ....13 B1
  Grays RM17 ....12 C8
  New Barn DA3 ....43 C4
  Royal Tunbridge Wells,
  Modest Corner TN4 ......132 E1
  Royal Tunbridge Wells,
  Rustall TN4 ....148 C4
  Sidcup DA15 ....24 A5
  Sidcup,Old Bexley DA5 ...25 B7
  Sole Street DA13 ....44 D4
  Sundridge TN14 ....82 D3
  Swanscombe DA10 ....28 E8
  Tilbury RM18 ....13 A5
  West Thurrock RM20 ......11 C8
Manor Rise ME14 ....93 B3
Manor St ME7 ....48 A6
Manor The TN2 ....149 C5
Manor Way Bexley DA7 ......8 D4
  Bromley BR2 ....36 E3
  Grays RM17 ....12 E7
  Grays RM17 ....12 D7
  Greenwich SE3 ....5 A3
  Northfleet DA11 ....29 E5
  Orpington BR5 ....37 C5
  Sidcup DA5 ....25 A7
  Swanscombe DA10 ....11 E3
Manor Way Bsns Ctr RM9 ....4 D8
Manorbrook SE3 ....5 A3
Manordene Rd SE28 ....3 D7
Manorfields Cl BR7 ....37 F6
Manorside Cl SE2 ....3 D2
Manse Ct DA14 ....24 C2
Manse Par BR8 ....40 A5
Manse Way BR8 ....40 A5
Mansel Dr ME1 ....47 A2
Mansergh Cl SE18 ....5 E7
Mansfield Cl BR5 ....38 D2
Mansfield Rd BR8 ....25 F2
Mansfield Wlk ME16 ....91 E2
Mansion House Cl TN27 ....158 A2
Mansion Row ME7 ....48 A6
Manthorpe Rd SE18 ....2 C1
Manton Rd SE2 ....3 A2
Manwarings The TN12 .....153 A6
Manwood St E16 ....1 F5
Maple Ave Gillingham ME7 ..48 C6
  Maidstone ME16 ....91 C6
Maple Cl Larkfield ME20 ....75 A2
  Orpington BR5 ....37 D4
  Royal Tunbridge Wells TN2 .149 A1
  Swanley BR8 ....39 E7
Maple Cres DA15 ....7 A1
Maple Ct Newham ME6 ......2 A8
  Sidcup DA14 ....24 B3
  Stone DA9 ....27 E8
Maple Leaf Dr DA15 ....22 F7
Maple Rd Dartford DA1 .....26 C7
  Gravesend DA12 ....30 C4
  Grays RM17 ....12 C8
  Hoo St Werburgh ME3 ....34 E4
  Rochester ME2 ....46 F6
Maplecroft Cl E6 ....1 E7
Mapledene BR7 ....23 C3
Maples The DA3 ....43 B6
Maplescombe La DA4 ....55 B6
Maplesden TN12 ....138 D5
Maplesden Cl ME16 ....90 F3
Maplesden Noakes Sch
  The ME16 ....91 E6
Mapleton TN8 ....113 A7
Mapleton Cl BR2 ....36 A3
Mapleton Rd TN8,TN16 .....96 E3
Maplin Ho 5 SE18 ....3 D4
Maplin Rd E16 ....1 B7
Maplins Cl 4 ME8 ....49 F1
Mar Ho 4 SE7 ....5 C8
Mara Ct ME4 ....47 F1

Maran Way DA18 ....3 D3
Marathon Paddock ME7 .....48 D4
Marble Ho 1 SE18 ....2 F1
Marbrook Ct SE12 ....22 C5
Marcellina Way BR6 ....51 F7
Marcet Rd DA1 ....9 G1
Marconi Ho SE2 ....3 C1
Marconi Rd DA11 ....29 D5
Marconi Way ME1 ....61 D7
Marcus Rd DA1 ....26 A8
Marden Ave BR2 ....36 A3
Marden Cres DA5 ....8 C2
Marden Prim Sch TN12 ....138 B5
Marden Rd Rochester ME1 ..33 C1
  Staplehurst TN12 ....139 C5
Marden Sta TN12 ....138 C6
Marechal Niel Ave DA15 ....23 D5
Marechal Niel Par DA15 ....23 D5
Margaret Gardner Dr SE9 ..22 F6
Margaret Rd DA5 ....7 D1
Margate Cl ME1 ....48 E6
Margetts La ME1 ....60 D1
Margetts Pl ME2 ....34 A3
Marian Sq TN12 ....139 F4
Marian Cl 1 BR7 ....36 A6
Marina Dr Bexley DA16 ......6 E5
  Dartford DA1 ....27 A7
  Northfleet DA11 ....12 F1
Marine Dr
  Hoo St Werburgh ME3 ....34 E3
  Woolwich SE18 ....1 F2
Marine View ME4 ....34 B1
Mariners Cl DA9 ....11 B3
Mariners The ME1 ....47 B4
Mariners Wlk DA8 ....8 F8
Marion Cl ME5 ....62 A2
Marion Cres
  Maidstone ME15 ....107 B8
  Orpington BR5 ....38 A4
Maritime Cl Rochester ME2 .47 D8
  Swanscombe DA9 ....11 A2
Maritime Ind Est SE7 ....1 B2
Maritime Way ME4 ....48 A8
Marjorie McClure Sch
  ....37 C8
Mark Cl Bexley DA7 ....7 E6
  Orpington BR2 ....50 E6
Mark La DA12 ....13 E1
Mark Way BR8 ....40 A4
Market Alley 8 DA11 ....13 B1
Market Bldgs 4 ME14 ......91 F4
Market Colonnade 3
  ME14 ....91 F4
Market Meadow BR5 ....38 C5
Market Par 5 DA14 ....24 B4
Market Pl 2 Bexley DA6 .....8 A3
  Dartford DA1 ....26 E8
  1 Royal Tunbridge
  Wells TN2 ....149 A2
  1 Tilbury RM18 ....13 A5
Market Sq Bromley BR1 ....36 A7
  Westerham TN16 ....81 D7
Market St Dartford DA1 .....26 E8
  2 Maidstone ME14 ....91 F4
  1 Royal Tunbridge
  Wells TN2 ....149 A2
  Staplehurst TN12 ....139 F5
  Woolwich SE18 ....1 E2
Market Way 2 TN16 ....81 D1
Marks Sq DA11 ....29 F4
Marlborough Cl
  Orpington BR6 ....37 F3
  Royal Tunbridge Wells TN4 .148 E4
Marlborough Cres TN13 ....83 E3
Marlborough Ct TN16 ......81 C1
Marlborough Ho 4 ME18 ...63 F8
Marlborough House Sch
  TN18 ....178 E2
Marlborough La SE7 ....5 C7
Marlborough Par ME16 .....90 F2
Marlborough Park Ave
  DA15 ....24 A7
Marlborough Rd Bexley DA7 .7 D4
  Bromley BR2 ....36 C5
  Dartford DA1 ....27 C8
  Gillingham ME7 ....48 B5
  Woolwich SE18 ....2 C2
Marle Place Gdns* TN12 ...152 C4
Marle Place Rd TN12 ......152 C4
Marler House DA8 ....8 F5
Marley Ave DA7 ....7 D8
Marley La TN27 ....142 C3
Marley Rd
  Harrietsham ME17 ....110 F6
  Hoo St Werburgh ME3 ....34 D6
Marley Way ME1 ....47 C2
Marlfield TN12 ....139 E4
Marlhurst TN8 ....112 D4
Marlin Ct 10 DA14 ....24 A4
Marling Way DA12 ....30 E3
Marlings Cl BR7 ....37 E5
Marlings Park Ave BR7 .....37 F6
Marlow Copse ME5 ....61 F1
Marlow Ct 3 TN13 ....84 B4
Marlowe Cl BR7 ....23 D2
Marlowe Gdns SE9 ....6 A1
Marlowes The DA1 ....9 B2
Marlowes The ME20 ....8 D3
Marlpit Cl TN8 ....112 C4
Marlpit Cotts ME17 ....107 E2
Marlpit Gdns TN5 ....176 E1
Marlpit The TN5 ....174 E5
Marlwood Cl DA15 ....23 E6
Marmadon Rd SE18 ....2 F3
Marne Ave DA16 ....7 A4

Marquis Dr ME7 ....63 B3
Marrabon Cl DA15 ....24 A7
Marram Ct ME1 ....12 E8
Marrians View 1 ME5 ......48 C2
Marriott Rd DA1 ....27 A8
Marsden Way 2 BR6 ....51 F6
Marsh Cres ME3 ....17 E4
Marsh Green Rd TN8 ....128 C5
Marsh La ME3 ....16 B6
Marsh Quarter La TN18 ...186 C3
Marsh Rd ME2 ....60 B5
Marsh St Dartford DA1 .....10 A5
  Rochester ME7 ....47 B7
Marsh Way
  New Hythe ME20 ....75 A4
  Rainham RM9 ....4 D8
Marshall Gdns TN11 ......102 E1
Marshall Path 10 SE28 .....3 B6
Marshall Rd 3 ME8 ....63 C8
Marshalls Gr SE18 ....1 E2
Marshalls Land TN30 .....173 A3
Marsham BR7 ....23 B3
Marsham Cres ME17 ....108 B1
Marsham St ME14 ....92 A4
Marsham Way ME2 ....60 A5
Marshbrook Cl SE3 ....5 D4
Marshland View ME3 ....9 C7
Marston Cl ME5 ....61 E3
Marston Ct DA14 ....23 F4
Marston Dr ME14 ....92 C5
Marston House RM17 ......12 A8
Marston Wlk ME5 ....61 E3
Martens Ave DA7 ....8 B3
Martens Cl DA7 ....8 C3
Martham Cl SE28 ....3 D6
Martin Bowes Rd SE9 ......22 E4
Martin Ct ME7 ....63 A3
Martin Dene DA6 ....7 F2
Martin Dr DA2 ....10 C1
Martin Hardie Way SE18 ..117 E5
Martin Ho BR2 ....37 F2
Martin House DA11 ....29 F6
Martin Rd Dartford DA1 ....26 C5
  Rochester ME2 ....47 B8
Martin Rise DA6 ....7 F2
Martin Sq ME20 ....75 A2
Martin St SE28 ....2 E5
Martin's Shaw TN13 ....83 C5
Martindale Ave Newham E16 ..1 A6
Martins Cl Higham ME3 ....32 D6
  St Paul's Cray BR5 ....38 D6
  Tenterden TN30 ....183 C8
Martyn House SE2 ....7 B8
Marvels Cl SE12 ....22 B6
Marvels La SE12 ....22 B6
Marvels Lane Prim Sch
  SE12 ....22 C4
Marvillion Ct TN12 ....119 F6
Marvin House 9 SE18 ....6 B8
Marwell TN16 ....81 B1
Marwood Cl DA16 ....7 B4
Mary Burrows Gdns TN15 .70 B2
Mary Day's TN17 ....167 E7
Mary Lawrenson Pl 2 SE3 ...5 A7
Mary Macarthur Ho 8
  DA17 ....4 A3
Mary Magdalene Ho 8
  ME16 ....133 B8
Marybank SE18 ....1 E1
Maryfield Cl ME5 ....25 E5
Maryland Ct ME6 ....63 E5
Maryland Rd TN2 ....149 D1
Maryon Ct BR5 ....38 B5
Maryon Gr SE7 ....1 E8
Maryon Rd SE7,SE18 ....1 E2
Maryville DA16 ....7 A4
Mascall's Court La TN12 ...136 B4
Mascall's Court Rd TN12 ..136 A4
Mascalls Ct 2 SE7 ....5 C8
Mascalls Pk TN12 ....135 F5
Mascalls Rd SE7 ....5 C8
Mascalls Sec Sch TN12 ....136 A4
Masefield Dr ME8 ....49 F4
Masefield Dr ME3 ....33 B8
Masefield Rd Dartford DA1 .10 B2
  Lunsford ME20 ....74 F4
  Northfleet DA11 ....29 D6
Masefield View BR6 ....51 C7
Masefield Way TN9 ....132 F7
Masham Ho 6 DA18 ....3 D4
Mason Cl Bexley DA7 ....8 B4
  Newham E16 ....1 A6
Masons Hill Bromley BR2 ..36 B5
  Woolwich SE18 ....2 B2
Master Gunners' Pl SE18 ...5 E6
Masters La ME19 ....74 B5
Masthead Cl DA2 ....10 C3
Matchless Dr SE18 ....6 A7
Matfield Cl BR2 ....36 A4
Matfield Cres ME14 ....92 C5
Matfield Rd DA17 ....8 A8
Matilda Cl ME8 ....49 E2
Matrix Bsns Ctr DA1 ....9 E2
Matterdale Gdns ME16 .....90 F3
Matthews Ho 12 SE7 ....5 C8
Matthews La TN11,ME18 ..102 F4
Mattinson PI ME9 ....95 F7
Matts Hill Rd ME9 ....78 C4
Maud Cashmore Way SE18 ..1 F3
Maude Rd BR8 ....26 A2
Maudslay Rd SE9 ....6 B5
Maundene Sch ME5 ....62 B5
Maunders Cl DA7 ....8 B4
Mavelstone Cl BR1 ....36 E8

Mavelstone Rd BR1 ....36 E8
Mavis Wlk 9 E6 ....1 E8
Maxey Rd SE18 ....2 C2
Maxim Rd Crayford DA1 .....8 E2
  Erith DA8 ....4 E2
Maximfeldt Rd DA8 ....4 E1
Maximilian Dr ME2 ....60 B4
Maxton Cl ME14 ....92 F5
Maxwell Dr ME16 ....91 B6
Maxwell Gdns BR6 ....51 F7
Maxwell Ho Chislehurst BR7 .23 B1
  10 Woolwich SE18 ....2 B2
Maxwell Rd Bexley DA16 .....7 B4
  Gillingham ME7 ....29 F7
  Orpington BR5 ....38 A4
May Avenue 11 DA11 ....29 F7
May Ct ME17 ....12 E8
May Pl DA12 ....44 D4
May Rd Gillingham ME7 ....48 C4
  Hawley DA2 ....26 F4
  Rochester ME1 ....47 C3
May St Cuxton ME2 ....46 B2
  Snodland ME6 ....75 B8
May Terr 2 ME7 ....48 A7
May Wynne Ho E16 ....1 B7
Maybury Ave DA2 ....25 F8
Maybury Cl BR5 ....37 B4
Maycotts La TN12 ....135 D1
Mayday Gdns SE3 ....5 E5
Mayerne Rd SE9 ....5 D2
Mayes Cl BR8 ....40 A5
Mayeswood Rd SE12 ....22 C4
Mayfair 2 ME2 ....47 C8
Mayfair Ave Bexley DA7 ....7 D6
  Maidstone ME15 ....107 A8
Mayfair Rd DA1 ....9 D2
Mayfield Bexley DA7 ....7 F3
  Sevenoaks TN13 ....83 E7
  Swanscombe DA10 ....11 E1
Mayfield Ct SE16 ....37 F2
Mayfield Cl Chatham ME5 ..62 A1
  Gillingham ME8 ....49 E2
Mayfield Ct DA14 ....24 B3
Mayfield La TN5 ....174 C4
Mayfield Pk TN5 ....174 E5
Mayfield Rd Bromley BR1 ...36 E4
  Erith DA17 ....4 C2
  Northfleet DA11 ....29 F8
  Royal Tunbridge Wells TN4 ..148 E4
  Maidstone ME15 ....24 C2
Mayfield Villas DA14 ....24 D2
Mayflower Ho ME1 ....47 B4
Mayfly Cl BR5 ....38 D5
Mayford Rd ME5 ....62 D2
Mayhill Rd SE7 ....5 B8
Maylam Ct TN10 ....117 C4
Maylands Dr DA14 ....24 D5
Maynard Cl DA8 ....8 F7
Maynard Rd ME5 ....48 D2
Maynard Pl ME5 ....48 D2
Maynards TN12 ....138 C5
Mayor's Pl 11 TN30 ....183 A7
Mayors La DA2 ....26 C3
Mayplace Ave DA1 ....9 F4
Mayplace Cl DA7 ....8 B4
Mayplace La Woolwich SE18 ..6 B7
  Woolwich SE18 ....2 B2
Mayplace Prim Sch DA7 .....8 C3
Mayplace Rd E DA7 ....8 C4
Mayplace Rd W DA7 ....8 A3
Maypole Gdns BR6 ....53 A4
Maypole Cress DA8 ....8 F6
Maypole La TN17 ....167 F8
Maypole Prim Sch DA5 .....25 E6
Maypole Rd Chelsfield BR6 ..52 F4
  Gravesend DA12 ....30 F7
Mayson Mews 10 SE10 ......1 A1
Maytham Bglws TN17 .....182 A1
Maytham Rd TN17 ....188 C7
Mayweed Ave ME5 ....61 E4
Mc Call Cres SE7 ....1 E1
Mc Dowall Cl 11 E16 ....1 A8
Mc Kenzie Rd ME5 ....62 A3
McAlpine Cres ME15 ....106 F3
McAuley Cl SE9 ....6 B1
McCabe Ct ME1 ....139 E2
McCudden Rd DA1 ....9 F4
McCudden Row ME7 ....48 A6
McDermott Rd TN15 ....86 F7
McIntyre Ct 6 ME16 ....91 F6
McKenzie Cl ME20 ....90 F8
McKillop Way DA14 ....24 C1
McLeod Rd SE2 ....3 B2
McMichael Way TN19 .....184 A3
Mcmillan Cl DA12 ....30 C4
McPhie Ho 8 ME14 ....91 F7
Mead Cl BR8 ....40 A4
Mead Cres DA1 ....26 C8
Mead Gn ME5 ....62 C3
Mead Rd Chislehurst BR7 ...23 C2
  Dartford DA1 ....26 D8
  Edenbridge TN8 ....128 D7
  Gravesend DA11 ....30 B6
Mead Road Inf Sch BR7 ....23 C2
Mead The Leybourne ME19 ..74 E2
  New Ash Green DA3 ....56 F8
Mead Wall ME3 ....15 F8
Mead Way Bromley BR2 ....36 A4
Meades Cl TN12 ....138 B6
Meadfield Rd ME15 ....105 F7
Meadow Bank Leigh TN11 ..13 F1
  West Malling ME19 ....89 C8
Meadow Bank Rd DA14 .....24 D3
Meadow Cl Erith DA8 ....4 D2
  Chislehurst BR7 ....23 C5
  Sevenoaks TN13 ....84 A4
  Upper Halling ME2 ....59 E4

Meadow Cres ME2 ....59 E4
Meadow Croft BR1 ....36 F6
Meadow Hill Rd 6 TN1 ....149 B3
Meadow La
  Marlpit Hill TN8 ....112 B4
  Vigo Village DA13 ....58 A1
Meadow Rd
  Gravesend DA11 ....30 A6
  Groombridge TN3 ....161 C7
  Northfleet DA11 ....12 B1
  Royal Tunbridge Wells,
  Rustall TN4 ....148 C4
  Royal Tunbridge Wells, St
  Johns TN1 ....149 A4
  Royal Tunbridge
  Wells,Southborough TN4 ..132 F1
  Tonbridge TN9 ....133 B8
Meadow The
  Chislehurst BR7 ....23 C2
  Pembury TN2 ....150 E8
Meadow View DA15 ....24 B8
Meadow View Cotts
  Hurst Green TN19 ....184 A3
  Laddingford ME18 ....120 E5
Meadow View Rd ME17 ...107 B3
Meadow Way Dartford DA2 .27 C8
  Marden TN12 ....138 E6
  Orpington BR6 ....51 A7
Meadow Wlk Dartford DA2 .26 C4
  Maidstone ME15 ....92 B3
  Snodland ME6 ....74 F7
Meadowbank Rd ME4 ......48 A4
Meadowdown ME15 ....92 B3
Meadowdown Cl ME7 ......63 A4
Meadowlands TN15 ....84 F7
Meadows Sch (Barnados)
  TN4 ....132 F2
Meadows The
  Biddenden TN27 ....157 F2
  Halstead TN14 ....67 H6
  Maidstone ME15 ....91 E2
  Orpington BR6 ....52 C4
  Wittersham TN30 ....189 D4
Meadowside Dartford DA1 ..26 C7
  Eltham SE3,SE9 ....5 C3
Meadowside Cotts TN5 ....176 F1
Meadowsweet Cl 11 E16 ....1 D8
Meadowview BR5 ....34 B2
Meadowview Rd DA6 ....7 F3
Meads The Hartley TN17 ..149 C2
  Royal Tunbridge Wells TN2 .149 C2
Meadside Wlk ME5 ....61 F6
Meadway Halstead TN14 ...116 E5
  Tonbridge TN11 ....116 E5
Meadway The
  Orpington BR6 ....52 B4
  Sevenoaks TN13 ....83 F5
Meath Cl BR5 ....38 B4
Medbury Rd DA12 ....30 F7
Medbury Rd DA12 ....30 F7
Mede Ho BR1 ....22 F1
Medebourne Cl SE3 ....5 A4
Medhurst Cres DA12 ....30 F6
Medhurst Gdns DA12 ......30 F6
Medick Ct RM17 ....8 E7
Medina House 6 DA8 ....8 E7
Medina Rd Ditton ME20 ....75 C1
  Tonbridge TN10 ....117 C6
Medlar Gr ME7 ....63 A4
Medlar Ho 2 DA15 ....24 A5
Medlar Rd RM17 ....12 E8
Medlars The
  Maidstone ME14 ....92 D6
  Meopham Sta DA13 ....44 A3
Medway Ave
  High Halstow ME23 ....17 E4
  Yalding ME18 ....104 F1
Medway Com Coll ME4 .....48 A1
Medway Cotts
  Iden Green TN17 ....180 D3
  Marden TN12 ....138 C6
Medway Ct 2 BR5 ....38 D1
Medway Ent Ctr ME2 ....47 D8
Medway Gdns ME4 ....47 F7
Medway Heritage Ctr* ME4 ..47 F7
Medway Hospl ME7 ....48 B4
Medway Hts 6 ME4 ....47 F7
Medway Meadows TN12 ..120 A6
Medway Rd Crayford DA1 ....8 F2
  Gillingham ME7 ....48 C7
  Royal Tunbridge Wells TN1 ..149 B5
Medway St Chatham ME4 ..47 F5
  Maidstone ME14 ....91 F3
Medway Trad Est ME16 .....91 F3
Medway View
  Barnes Street TN11 ....119 A5
  Lower Stoke ME3 ....19 C3
Medway Villas ME15 ......107 A8
Medway Wharf Rd TN9 ....117 C1
Meerbrook Rd SE3 ....5 C4
Meeson's La RM17 ....11 F8
Meeting House La 2 ME4 ..47 F6
Megrims Hill TN18 ....186 A6
Meirs Court Rd ME8 ....63 E6
Melanda Cl BR7 ....22 F3
Melanie Cl DA7 ....7 E6
Melbourne Cl Erith DA8 .....8 F7
Melbourne Ct ME19 ....37 E2
Melbourne Ho
  3 Gravesend DA11 ....13 B1
  Tilbury RM18 ....12 E6
Melbourne Rd
  Chatham ME4 ....48 A3
  Tilbury RM18 ....12 E6
Melbury Cl BR7 ....22 F2

Meldrum Cl BR5 ....38 C3
Melford Dr ME16 ....91 C4
Melliker La DA13 ....44 A3
Melling St SE18 ....6 E8
Mellish Ind Est SE18 .....1 D3
Mells Cres SE9 ....22 F4
Melody Cl ME8 ....63 C4
Melrose Ave ME19 ....89 C3
Melrose Cl Lewisham SE12 ..22 B7
Sevenoaks TN13 ....107 A7
Melrose Cres BR6 ....51 D5
Melthorpe Gdns SE3 ....5 E6
Melville Ct ME4 ....47 F6
Melville Rd Maidstone ME15 ..92 A3
Sidcup DA14 ....24 C6
Memess Path 4 SE18 .....6 A8
Memorial Hospl SE18 ....6 A5
Mendip Rd DA7 ....8 E6
Mendip Wlk TN2 ....149 D5
Mennie House SE18 ....5 F6
Meon Ct 2 BR5 ....38 D1
Meopham Com Prim Sch
DA13 ....58 A8
Meopham Cty Prim Sch
DA13 ....44 A2
Meopham Sta DA13 ....44 A4
Mera Dr DA7 ....8 A3
Merbury Rd SE28 ....2 E4
Merbury St SE18 ....2 B3
Mercer Dr ME17 ....110 F6
Mercer St TN1 ....149 B5
Mercer Way ME17 ....110 F5
Mercers Hawkhurst TN18 ..179 A1
Royal Tunbridge Wells TN3 ..148 A3
Mercers Cl TN12 ....135 E6
Mercers Pl ME19 ....89 A2
Merchant Pl TN12 ....138 C5
Merchland Rd SE9 ....23 C7
Mercury Cl ME1 ....47 A3
Mere Cl BR6 ....51 F8
Meresborough Cotts ME8 ..63 F5
Meresborough La
ME8,ME9 ....64 B5
Meresborough Rd ME8 ....64 A7
Mereside BR6 ....51 A8
Merewood Cl 1 BR1 ....37 A7
Merewood Ct DA5 ....8 C5
Mereworth Cl ME8 ....49 A3
Mereworth Cty Prim Sch
ME18 ....103 C8
Mereworth Dr SE18 ....6 C7
Mereworth Ho ME2 ....33 C1
Mereworth Rd
Mereworth ME18 ....103 C2
Royal Tunbridge Wells TN2 ..149 A6
Merganser Gdns SE28 ....2 D3
Meridian Cl BR1 ....22 D1
Meridian Pk ME2 ....47 E6
Meridian Trad Est SE7 .....1 D7
Meridian Trad Est SE7 ....5 D7
Merifield Rd SE9 ....5 C3
Merino Pl DA15 ....7 A2
Merivale Gr ME5 ....62 B4
Merlewood TN13 ....84 B4
Merlewood Dr BR7 ....36 F8
Merlin Ave ME20 ....74 F2
Merlin Cl TN10 ....117 E4
Merlin Gdns BR1 ....22 A5
Merlin Rd DA16 ....7 A3
Merlin Rd N DA16 ....7 A3
Mermaid Cl ME2 ....62 A6
Mermerus Gdns DA12 ....30 F4
Merrals Wood Rd ME2 ....46 D5
Merrilees Rd DA15 ....23 E8
Merriman Rd SE3 ....5 C6
Merriments La
TN18,TN19 ....184 D5
Merrion Cl TN4 ....149 B7
Merrion Way TN4 ....149 B7
Merry Boys Rd ME3 ....33 B8
Merrydown Way BR7 ....36 F8
Merryfields SE3 ....5 A5
Merryfield Cl 5 TN9 .....133 B8
Merryfield Ho SE9 ....22 C5
Merryfields Longfield DA3 ..42 F6
Rochester ME2 ....33 A1
Merryweather Cl DA1 .....9 F3
Mersey Rd TN10 ....117 B5
Merton Ave DA3 ....42 F5
Merton Ct ME5 ....62 C5
Merton Court Sch 24 C4
Merton Cl DA16 ....7 B5
Merton Gdns BR5 ....37 B4
Merton Rd ME15 ....92 F2
Mervyn Ave SE9 ....23 C6

Michael Tetley Hall
(Nursery Trng Coll, Dr
Barnardo's Home) TN2 ..149 D6
Michaels La DA3,TN5 .....56 C8
Michele Cotts ME3 ....32 C6
Micklam Cl BR5 ....38 A7
Micklam Rd BR5 ....38 A7
Mid Comp Cotts TN15 ....87 E6
Mid Kent Bsns Ctr H & F Ed ME6 ..75 B7
Chatham ME1
Maidstone,Cherry Orchard
ME16 ....91 C3
Mid Kent Coll of Higher
& F Ed ME1,ME4 .....61 E6
Mid Kent Sh Ctr The ME16 ..91 C7
Middle Field TN2 ....150 E8
Middle Garth TN17 ....169 D4
Middle La TN15 ....84 F6
Middle Mill Rd ME19 .....89 E3
Middle Park Ave SE9 ....22 E8
Middle Park Inf & Jun Sch
SE9 ....22 D8
Middle Row 6 ME1 ....164 A5
Middle St 4 ME7 ....48 A6
Middle Wlk TN2 ....149 E8
Middlefields ME8 ....49 A3
Middleham Ct 2 DA1 .....10 B1
Middlesex Rd ME15 ....107 D7
Middleton Ave DA14 .....24 C3
Middleton Cl DA16 ....63 E4
Middleton Cl 3 BR1 ....22 B1
Middlings Rise TN13 .....83 F1
Middlings The TN13 ....83 F2
Middlings Wood TN13 ....84 A2
Midfield Ave Bexley DA7 ..8 C4
Hextable BR8 ....26 B2
Midfield Prim Sch BR5 ....24 A1
Midfield Way BR5 ....38 B8
Midhurst Cl DA11 ....92 A3
Midhurst Hill DA6 ....8 A3
Midley Cl DA16 ....91 C7
Midsummer Ct SE12 ....5 A3
Midsummer Rd ME6 ....74 E8
Midway The TN4 ....148 D2
Midwinter Cl 8 DA16 .....7 A4
Miers Court Prim Sch
ME8 ....63 F7
Mierscourt Cl ME8 ....64 A8
Mierscourt Rd ME8 ....63 A5
Mike Spring Ct DA12 .....30 F4
Milburn Rd ME7 ....48 C7
Mildmay Pl TN14 ....68 F8
Mildred Cl DA1 ....10 A1
Mildred Rd DA8 ....4 E8
Mile La TN17 ....168 B8
Mile Oak Rd TN12 ....136 C3
Mile Stone Rd DA1 ....10 B1
Milebush La TN12 ....122 E1
Miles Dr SE28 ....2 D5
Miles Pl ME1 ....47 D3
Milestone Sch DA14 ....10 B1
Milford Cl SE2 ....7 E8
Maidstone ME16 ....90 E1
Military Rd ME4 ....47 F5
Milk House Cotts TN17 ..170 A8
Milk St Bromley BR1 ....22 B2
Newham E16 ....2 B5
Mill Bank TN27 ....141 C4
Mill Brook Rd BR5 ....38 C5
Mill Cl Lenham ME17 .....111 C4
Rochester ME2 ....33 B1
Mill Cotts ME15 ....105 B6
Mill Cres TN9 ....117 C2
Mill Ct Sutton at Hone DA4 ..41 C7
4 Woolwich SE28 ....2 D6
Mill Hall Bsns Est The
ME6 ....75 D2
Mill Hall Rd ME20 ....75 C2
Mill Hill TN8 ....128 D7
Mill Hill La DA12 ....31 D3
Mill House Cl DA4 ....40 F2
Mill La Benover ME18 .....121 A7
Biddenden Green TN27 ..143 A2
Chatham,Bluebell Hill ME5 ..61 D1
Chatham,Luton ME5 ....48 C1
Coxheath ME17 ....106 D4
Eynsford DA4 ....40 E1
Farthing Street BR6 ....51 B1
Frittenden TN17 ....156 D8
Hartlip ME9 ....64 E6
Hildenborough TN11,TN15 ..100 C2
Horsmonden TN12 ....137 B1
Ightham TN15 ....86 D5
Maidstone ME14 ....91 F6
Sevenoaks TN14 ....84 A6
Shoreham TN14 ....53 F1
Sissinghurst TN17 ....169 F8
Snodland ME6 ....75 B8
Tenterden TN30 ....173 B1
Tonbridge TN9 ....117 C2
Wateringbury ME18 ....104 D7
West Thurrock RM20 ....11 D8
Westerham TN16 ....96 C8
Woolwich SE18 ....2 A1
Mill Pl Chislehurst BR7 ..37 C5
Crayford DA1 ....9 A3
Mill Pond Cl DA14 ....84 D6
Mill Pond Rd DA1 ....9 E1
Mill Rd Erith DA8 ....8 F7
Gillingham ME7 ....48 C6
Hawley DA2 ....26 F4
Newham E16 ....1 A8
Northfleet DA11 ....29 E8
Rochester ME2 ....47 B8
Sevenoaks TN13 ....83 C8
Mill Row DA5 ....25 B8

Mill St
Benenden TN17,TN18 ....180 C3
Maidstone ME15 ....91 F4
Maidstone, Loose Hill ME15 ..106 F5
Mill Street ME19 ....89 F7
Snodland ME6 ....75 B8
Westerham TN16 ....96 D8
Mill Stone Cl DA4 ....41 C7
Mill Stream Pl TN9 ....117 D3
Mill Vale BR2 ....36 A7
Mill View TN11 ....102 D1
Mill Wlk ME16 ....91 A3
Millais Pl RM18 ....13 A7
Millbank Way SE12 ....5 A2
Millbro BR8 ....40 B8
Millbrook ME19 ....74 D1
Millbrook Ave SE9 ....22 F5
Millbrook Cl DA16 ....6 D3
Millbrook Rd ME15 ....91 F1
Millcroft Rd ME5 ....61 E4
Millenium Cl E16 ....1 B8
Miller Cl DA7 ....8 A8
Miller Rd DA12 ....31 A6
Miller Way ME2 ....33 D2
Millers Cotts TN11 ....134 C6
Millers Wharf ME15 ....91 F2
Millers Wlk DA13 ....58 A7
Millfield High Halden TN26 ..173 D7
New Ash Green DA3 ....56 E8
Millfield Dr DA11 ....29 F6
Millfield La DA3 ....56 E8
Millfield Rd TN15 ....55 D4
Millfields ME5 ....62 D2
Millfields Cl BR5 ....38 B5
Millfields Cotts BR5 ....38 B5
Millfordhope Rd ME2 ....46 F7
Millhall ME20 ....75 E2
Millhouse La ME19 ....73 D3
Milling St ME15 ....91 F2
Millpond Cl ME2 ....47 B8
Millpond La TN30 ....172 D2
Mills Cres TN15 ....84 A6
Mills Rd ME20 ....90 E7
Mills Terr ME4 ....48 A3
Millside Ind Est TN7 ....9 D3
Millstock Terr ME15 ....91 E2
Millstone Mews DA4 ....41 C8
Millstream Cl TN3 ....146 D2
Millward Wlk 14 SE18 ....6 A8
Millwood Ct 4 ME4 ....47 F4
Millwood Ho SE28 ....2 D3
Millwood Rd BR5 ....38 C6
Milne Gdns SE9 ....5 E2
Milne Ho 11 SE18 ....6 A8
Milner Rd ME7 ....48 D7
Milner Wlk SE9 ....23 D7
Milroy Ave DA11 ....29 F6
Milstead Cl ME14 ....92 C5
Milsted Rd ME8 ....49 C3
Milton Ave
Badgers Mount TN14 ....53 B1
Cliffe Woods ME3 ....33 B8
Gravesend DA12 ....30 C7
Milton Ct DA12 ....30 C6
Milton Dr TN2 ....149 D7
Milton Gdns ME9 ....65 B6
Tonbridge TN9 ....132 F7
Milton Hall Rd DA12 ....30 D7
Milton House DA11 ....13 C1
Milton Lodge 9 DA14 ....24 A4
Milton Pl DA12 ....13 C1
Milton Rd Bexley DA16 ..6 E4
Erith DA17 ....4 A2
Gillingham ME7 ....48 C3
Gravesend DA12 ....30 D8
Sevenoaks TN13 ....83 E6
Swanscombe DA10 ....11 E1
Milton Rd Bsns Pk 4
DA12 ....30 C8
Milton St Maidstone ME16 ..91 C7
Swanscombe DA10 ....11 D1
Milverton Way SE9 ....23 A4
Mimosa Cl BR6 ....52 C8
Mincers Cl ME5 ....62 C2
Mineral St SE18 ....2 E2
Minerva Cl DA14 ....23 E4
Minerva Rd ME2 ....47 A8
Ministry Way SE9 ....22 F6
Minshaw Ct DA14 ....23 D1
Minster Rd Bromley BR2 ..22 B1
Gillingham ME8 ....49 C3
Mint Bsns Pk E16 ....1 A8
Minters Orch TN15 ....87 B7
Miranda Ho 8 DA17 ....4 A1
Mirfield St SE7 ....1 D1
Miriam Ct DA14 ....24 B4
Miriam Rd SE18 ....2 F1
Mirror Path SE9 ....22 C5
Miskin Cotts ME3 ....16 B6
Miskin Rd Dartford DA1 ..26 D8
Hoo St Werburgh ME3 ....34 E5
Miskin Way DA12 ....30 D2
Mitchell Ave Chatham ME4 ..47 F2
Northfleet DA11 ....29 C6
Mitchell Cl Dartford DA1 ..26 E6
Erith DA17 ....4 C2
Lenham ME17 ....111 C5
Woolwich SE2 ....3 C2
Mitchell Rd Kings Hill ME19 ..88 F2
Orpington BR6 ....51 F6
Mitchell Way 2 BR1 .....36 A8
Mitchell Wlk Newham E16 ..1 B8
Swanscombe DA10 ....28 E8
Mitchem Cl TN15 ....55 E8
Mitre Ct 5 Erith DA17 .....4 A2
Tonbridge TN9 ....117 C2
Mitre Rd ME4 ....47 F4
Moat Cl Orpington BR6 ..51 F4
Sevenoaks TN13 ....83 D5

Moat Croft DA16 ....7 C4
Moat Ct Eltham SE9 ....5 F1
Sidcup DA15 ....23 F5
Moat Farm TN2 ....163 A7
Moat Farm Rd ME3 ....18 D6
Moat La Cowden TN8 ....145 E7
Erith DA8 ....9 A6
Moat Rd TN27 ....141 B5
Moatbridge Sch SE9 .....5 D1
Mockbegar La
TN17,TN27 ....171 C4
Model Farm Cl SE9 ....22 E5
Modest Cnr TN4 ....132 E1
Moira Rd SE9 ....5 F3
Molash Rd BR5 ....38 D5
Molehill Copse Prim Sch
ME15 ....107 D7
Moles Mead TN8 ....112 C2
Molescroft SE9 ....23 C5
Molescroft Way TN9 ....132 F7
Mollison Rise DA12 ....30 E3
Molyneux Almshouses
TN4 ....148 B3
Molyneux Ct TN4 ....148 B3
Molyneux Park Gdns TN4 ..148 F4
Molyneux Park Rd TN4 ..148 F4
Monarch Cl Chatham ME5 ..62 A6
Hayes BR4 ....50 A6
Tilbury RM18 ....13 B5
Monarch Dr E16 ....1 D8
Monarch Ho 8 DA17 .....4 A3
Monckton's Ave ME14 ....91 F7
Monckton's Dr ME14 ....91 F7
Monckton's La ME14 ....91 F7
Moncrieff Cl 4 E16 ....1 E7
Moncrif Cl ME14 ....93 B4
Monds Cotts TN14 ....82 E3
Monica James House 12
DA14 ....24 A5
Monk Dr E16 ....1 A6
Monk St SE18 ....2 A2
Monkdown ME15 ....93 A1
Monkmead Villas DA3 ....43 D4
Monks Cl SE2 ....3 D2
Monks Orch DA1 ....26 D6
Monks Way BR5 ....37 D1
Monks Orch Northfleet DA13 ..29 A2
6 Tonbridge TN9 ....133 B8
Monkton Ho Bexley DA16 ..6 F5
Borough Green TN15 .....86 F7
Monkwood Cl ME1 ....61 B8
Monmouth Cl Bexley DA16 ..7 A3
Gillingham ME8 ....49 D2
Mons Way BR2 ....36 E3
Monson Rd TN1 ....149 A4
Monson Way 5 TN1 .....149 B4
Mont St Aignan Way TN8 ..128 C8
Montacute Gdns TN4 ....148 F2
Montacute Rd TN2 ....149 A1
Montague Cl 10 DA15 ..24 A5
Montague Pl DA8 ....39 F5
Montague Terr 1 BR2 ....36 A5
Montbelle Prim Sch SE9 ..23 B5
Montbelle Rd SE9 ....23 B5
Montcalm Cl BR2 ....36 A3
Montcalm Cl BR2 ....36 A3
Monteith Ct TN1 ....148 A3
Monterey Cl DA5 ....25 C6
Montfort Ho ME7 ....89 A2
Montfort Rd Chatham ME5 ..61 F2
Kemsing TN15 ....69 E2
Rochester ME2 ....47 B8
Montgomery Ave ME5 ..62 A7
Montgomery Cl DA15 ....6 F1
Montgomery Rd
Gillingham ME7 ....48 C3
Royal Tunbridge Wells TN4 ..148 A3
Sutton at Hone DA4 ....41 D8
Montpelier Ave DA5 .....24 D8
Montpelier Gate ME16 ..91 B5
Montreal Rd
Sevenoaks TN13 ....83 E4
Tilbury RM18 ....13 A5
Montrose Ave Bexley DA16 ..6 E4
Chatham ME5 ....48 E6
Sidcup DA15 ....24 A8
Montrose Cl DA16 ....6 E4
Monypenny TN17 ....181 F3
Monypenny Cl TN11 ....118 D8
Moon Ct SE12 ....5 A3
Moon's La TN7 ....128 A1
Moonstone Dr ME5 ....62 B2
Moor Hill TN18 ....184 F8
Moor La TN8 ....128 A4
Moor Park Cl ME8 ....64 A8
Moor Rd The TN14 ....84 F7
Moor St ME8 ....64 B8
Moor The TN18 ....184 F8
Moorcroft Gdns BR2 ....36 E4
Moordale Ho TN11 ....115 A1
Moordown SE18 ....6 B6
Moore Ave Grays RM20 ..11 B8
Tilbury RM18 ....13 B5
Moore Cl DA2 ....27 D6
Moore Rd DA10 ....11 E1
Moore St ME2 ....47 A8
Moorfield Rd BR6 ....38 A1
Moorhouse Rd RH8,TN16 ..96 A6
Moorings The E16 ....1 C8
Moorland Rd BR1 ....36 A8
Moreland Ho ME8 ....49 B6
Morello Cl DA8 ....39 D5
Moreland Rd
Lamberhurst TN3 ....166 B5
Rochester ME2 ....33 A1
Morley Bsns Ctr TN9 ....117 D2
Morley Cl BR6 ....51 B8
Morley Dr TN12 ....153 A6
Morley Rd Chislehurst BR7 ..37 C8
Tonbridge TN9 ....117 D1
Mormer Rd TN12 ....99 D2
Morne Cotts TN14 ....68 F8
Morning Cross Cotts ME8 ..16 B4
Mornington Ave BR1 ....36 D6
Mornington Cres DA15 ..25 D7
Morris Cl East Malling ME19 ..74 F1
Orpington BR6 ....51 E7
Morris Gdns DA1 ....10 A2
Morry La ME17 ....125 D7
Morstan Gdns SE9 ....22 F4
Mortgramit Sq SE18 ....2 A3
Mortimer Rd Erith DA8 ....8 D8
Orpington BR6 ....38 A1
Mortimers Ave ME3 ....33 A8
Mortlake Rd E16 ....1 B7
Morton Cl
Maidstone ME15 ....107 D6
Swanley BR8 ....39 E7
Morvale Cl DA17 ....3 F2
Mosbank ME5 ....62 A3
Mossdown Cl DA17 ....4 A2
Mosslea Rd Bromley BR2 ..36 C4
Orpington BR6 ....51 C7
Mossy Glade ME8 ....63 E6
Mostyn Rd ME14 ....92 C4
Motel Way ME2 ....36 E3
Mosyer Dr BR5 ....52 D8
Mote Ave ME15 ....92 B3
Mote Cotts TN15 ....101 A7
Mote Hall Villas ME14 ....93 C4
Mote Park ME15 ....92 D2
Mote Rd
Ivy Hatch TN15,TN11 ....101 A7
Maidstone ME15 ....92 A3
Mote The DA14 ....56 F8
Motherwell Way RM20 ..11 A8
Mottingham Ct SE9 ....22 F7
Mottingham Gdns SE9 ..22 D7
Mottingham La
SE12,SE9 ....22 C8
Lewisham SE12,SE9 ....22 C8
Mottingham Prim Sch
SE9 ....22 F5
Mottingham Rd SE9 .....22 F5
Mottingham Sta SE9 ....22 F7
Mottisfont Rd SE2 ....3 B2
Mouat Ct ME5 ....62 A3
Moultain Hill BR8 ....40 A5
Mound The SE9 ....23 A5
Mount Ave ME18 ....105 A1
Mount Cl Bromley BR1 ..36 E8
Sevenoaks TN13 ....83 F4
Mount Culver Ave DA14 ..24 D2
Mount Dr Bexley DA6 .....7 E2
Maidstone ME14 ....93 B4
Mount Edgcumbe Rd
TN4 ....149 A3
Mount Ephraim TN4 ....149 A4
Mount Ephraim Ct TN4 ..148 F4
Mount Ephraim Rd TN1 ..149 A4
Mount Harry Rd TN13 ....84 B4
Mount La Hartlip ME9 ....64 D4
Maidstone ME14 ....93 B4
Mount Lodge ME1 ....47 B2
Mount Pleasant
Aylesford ME20 ....76 A3
Gillingham ME8 ....48 B3
Hook Green TN3 ....165 C6
Ide Hill TN14 ....97 F4
Paddock Wood TN12 ....135 F7
Tenterden TN30 ....183 C8
The Moor TN18 ....184 F8
Tonbridge TN11 ....116 D6
Wadhurst TN5 ....174 E5
Mount Pleasant Ave 2
TN1 ....149 B3
Mount Pleasant Ct TN1 ..149 B3
Mount Pleasant La TN3 ..93 A5
Mount Pleasant La TN13 ..166 A6
Mount Pleasant Rd
Dartford DA1 ....9 F1
Royal Tunbridge Wells TN1 ..149 A3
Sevenoaks Weald TN14 ..99 B2

Mount Pleasant Terr
ME17 . . . . .110 E2
Mount Pleasant Wlk DA5 . . . .8 C2
Mount Rd Bexley DA6 . . . . .7 F4
Chatham ME4 . . . . .47 F3
Crayford DA1 . . . . .8 F1
Rochester ME1 . . . . .47 B2
Mount Sion TN1 . . . . .149 A2
Mount The DA6 . . . . .8 B2
Mount View Ct **3** ME4 . . . .47 F3
Mountain Cl TN15 . . . . .71 F5
Mountbatten Ave
Chatham ME5 . . . . .62 A7
Higham ME3 . . . . .32 C4
Mountbatten Cl SE18 . . . . . . .6 E8
Mountfield TN15 . . . . .87 A7
Mountfield Cl DA13 . . . . .57 F2
Mountfield Gdns TN1 . . . . .149 B3
Mountfield Gdns TN1 . . . . .149 B3
Mountfield Pk TN9 . . . . .133 C8
Mountfield Rd TN1 . . . . .149 B3
Mountfield Way **1** BR5 . . .38 C5
Mounthurst Rd BR2 . . . . .36 A2
Mountjoy Cl SE2 . . . . .3 B4
Mounts Hill TN17 . . . . .180 E7
Mounts La TN17 . . . . .182 A3
Mounts Rd DA9 . . . . .11 B3
Mountsfield Cl ME16 . . . . . . .91 D5
Mountview Rd BR6 . . . . .38 A2
Moyle Cl ME8 . . . . .63 D4
Mozart Ct ME4 . . . . .47 E3
Muir Rd ME15 . . . . .91 A2
Muir St E16 . . . . .1 E5
Mulbarton Ct BR7 . . . . .23 D2
Mulberry Cl Gillingham ME7 .63 A4
Greenwich SE7 . . . . .5 D8
Meopham Sta DA13 . . . . .44 B3
Royal Tunbridge Wells TN4 . . .133 D1
Mulberry Ct Bexley DA16 . . . .6 F5
Maidstone ME14 . . . . .92 B5
Mulberry Rd ME2 . . . . .29 E4
Mulberry Way DA17 . . . . .4 C4
Mulgrave **15** SE18 . . . . .1 F2
Mulgrave Prim Sch SE18 . . . .2 A2
Mulgrave Rd SE18 . . . . .2 A2
Mullein Cl **3** RM17 . . . . . . .12 D8
Mullender Ct DA12 . . . . .31 A7
Muller Ho SE18 . . . . .2 A1
Multon Rd TN15 . . . . .55 E6
Munday Bois Cotts TN27 . .143 F8
Munday Bois Rd TN27 . . . .127 E1
Munday Rd E16 . . . . .1 A7
Munday Works Est TN9 . . .117 C1
Mundella Ct DA10 . . . . .28 E8
Mungeam Ho ME1 . . . . .47 C4
Mungo Park Rd DA12 . . . . . .30 D3
Mungo Park Way BR5 . . . . . .38 D2
Munn's La ME9 . . . . .64 E6
Munnery Way BR6 . . . . .51 B6
Munnings Ho E16 . . . . .1 E5
Murchison Ave DA5 . . . . .24 E7
Murrain Dr ME15 . . . . .93 A1
Murray Ave BR1 . . . . .36 B7
Murray Bsns Ctr BR5 . . . . . . .38 B6
Murray Ho **15** SE18 . . . . .1 F2
Murray Rd Rochester ME2 . . .47 C8
St Paul's Cray BR5 . . . . .38 B6
Murray Sq E16 . . . . .1 B7
Murton-Neale Cl **3**
TN18 . . . . .179 A2
Mus of Artillery
in the Rotunda* SE18 . . . . . .1 F1
Muscovy Ho DA18 . . . . .3 E4
Museum of Kent Rural Life*
ME14 .76 D1
Museum St ME14 . . . . .91 F4
Musket La
Hollingbourne ME17 . . . . .94 B2
Hollingbourne ME17 . . . . .94 A2
Mussenden La DA3,DA4 . . . .41 E3
Mustang Rd ME19 . . . . .88 F3
Mycenae Rd SE3 . . . . .5 A8
Mynn Cres ME14 . . . . .93 A4
Myra St SE2 . . . . .3 A2
Myrtle Alley SE18 . . . . .2 A3
Myrtle Cl DA8 . . . . .8 E6
Myrtle Cres ME5 . . . . .61 F5
Myrtle Pl DA2 . . . . .27 D8
Myrtle Rd DA1 . . . . .26 D6
Myrtledene Rd SE2 . . . . .3 A1

N

Nadine St SE7 . . . . .1 C1
Nag's Head La Bexley DA16 . .7 B4
Chatham ME1 . . . . .47 D4
Nagpur House **4** ME15 . .107 E5
Nairn Ct RM18 . . . . .12 F5
Nansen Rd SE12 . . . . .30 D4
Napier Com Sch ME4 . . . . . .48 D7
Napier Ct
2 Lewisham SE12 . . . . .22 B5
Maidstone ME14 . . . . .91 F7
Napier Rd Bromley BR2 . . . .36 B5
Erith DA17 . . . . .3 F2
Gillingham ME7 . . . . .48 D4
Northfleet DA11 . . . . .12 A8
Royal Tunbridge Wells TN2 . .149 D2
Napoleon Cl ME18 . . . . .138 D5
Napoleon Wlk ME17 . . . . . .111 C5
Napwood Cl ME8 . . . . .63 D6
Nares Rd ME8 . . . . .63 D4
Narrow Boat Cl SE28 . . . . . . .2 D4
Narrow Way BR2 . . . . .36 E3

Naseby Ct DA14 . . . . .23 F4
Nash Bank DA13 . . . . .43 F7
Nash Cl ME5 . . . . .62 C2
Nash Cotts **2** DA14 . . . . . .24 A5
Nash Croft DA11 . . . . .29 E4
Nash Gn BR1 . . . . .22 A2
Nash La BR2 . . . . .50 A4
Nash St DA13 . . . . .44 A7
Nashenden Farm La ME1 . . .61 A8
Nashenden La ME1 . . . . .46 F1
Nassau Path **8** SE28 . . . . . .3 C5
Natal Rd ME4 . . . . .48 A3
Nathan Way SE28,SE18 . . . . . .2 E3
Naylor's Cotts ME7 . . . . .63 B1
Neal Rd TN15 . . . . .55 E5
Neale St ME4 . . . . .48 A2
Neatscourt Rd E6 . . . . .1 D8
Neills Rd TN3 . . . . .165 D2
Nellington Ct TN4 . . . . .148 B4
Nellington Rd TN3,TN4 . . .148 B4
Nelson Ave TN9 . . . . .117 A1
Nelson Ho
8 Maidstone ME15 . . . . . .107 F5
Swanscombe DA9 . . . . .11 D2
Nelson Mandela Rd SE3 . . . .5 C4
Nelson Pl DA14 . . . . .24 A4
Nelson Rd Bromley BR2 . . . .36 C5
Dartford DA1 . . . . .9 C1
Erith DA17 . . . . .3 F1
Gillingham ME7 . . . . .29 F6
Northfleet DA11 . . . . .12 A8
Royal Tunbridge Wells TN2 . .149 D2
11 Sidcup DA14 . . . . .24 A4
Wouldham ME1 . . . . .60 C5
Nelson Terr ME5 . . . . .48 C1
Nepicar Farm* TN15 . . . . . . .72 D1
Nepicar La TN15 . . . . .72 D3
Neptune Bsns Pk ME2 . . . . .47 E7
Neptune Ho ME2 . . . . .47 E7
Neptune Way ME7 . . . . .47 E6
Neptune Wlk DA8 . . . . .4 D2
Nesbit Rd SE9 . . . . .5 D3
Nesbitt House DA14 . . . . . . .24 A4
Ness Rd DA8 . . . . .9 D8
Nestor Ct ME18 . . . . .105 A8
Nethercombe Ho **4** SE3 . . .5 A8
Nethewode Ct DA17 . . . . .4 A3
Netley Cl ME14 . . . . .92 D6
Nettlestead La ME18 . . . . .104 A6
Nevill Ct TN11 . . . . .74 C1
Nevill Gate TN2 . . . . .149 B1
Nevill Lodge TN2 . . . . .149 C4
Nevill Pk TN4 . . . . .148 E3
Nevill Pl ME6 . . . . .75 A7
Nevill Ridge TN4 . . . . .148 D3
Nevill St TN2 . . . . .149 A2
Nevill Terr TN2 . . . . .148 F2
Neville Cl Maidstone ME14 . .92 B8
Sidcup DA15 . . . . .23 F4
Neville Rd ME4 . . . . .47 E2
New Acres Rd SE28 . . . . .2 F4
New Ash Green Prim Sch
DA3 . . . . .56 F8
New Barn Pk BR8 . . . . .39 E8
New Barn Rd
Hawkenbury ME17,TN12 . . .124 E2
Northfleet Green DA13 . . . . . .29 C3
Swanley BR8 . . . . .39 F8
New Barn St E13 . . . . .1 A7
New Barns Rd ME14 . . . . . . .92 A8
New Bassetts Cotts TN12 . .153 B5
New Cotts Bean DA2 . . . . . . .28 B5
Shipbourne TN11 . . . . .101 D5
New Ct SE12 . . . . .30 E3
New Covenant Pl ME1 . . . . . .47 D4
New Cut TN9 . . . . .117 C2
New Cut Chatham ME4 . . . . .47 F4
East Farleigh ME15 . . . . .106 C7
New Cut Rd ME14 . . . . .92 D5
New Delhi House **5**
ME15 . . . . .107 E5
New Eltham Sta SE9 . . . . . . .23 C7
New England Rd TN4 . . . . . .149 A7
New Farm Ave BR2 . . . . .36 A5
New Hall Farm La ME3 . . . . .19 B6
New House La DA11 . . . . .30 A6
New Hythe La ME20 . . . . .75 B3
New Hythe Sta ME20 . . . . . . .75 C4
New Inn Cotts ME15 . . . . . .106 C2
New Lydenburg
Commercial Est SE7 . . . . .1 C3
New Lydenburg St SE7 . . . . . .1 C3
New Mill Rd BR5 . . . . .38 B7
New Pond Rd TN17 . . . . . . .180 D6
New Pound La ME18 . . . . . . .88 C1
New Rd Bexley DA16 . . . . .7 B5
Burham ME1 . . . . .60 F1
Chatham ME1 . . . . .47 D4
Chatham ME4 . . . . .47 F4
Cliffe ME3 . . . . .16 A4
Cranbrook TN17 . . . . .169 B4
Ditton ME20 . . . . .75 C1
East Malling ME19 . . . . .90 A8
Egerton TN27 . . . . .127 F3
Erith DA8 . . . . .3 D1
Fordcombe TN11 . . . . .131 A1
Gravesend DA11 . . . . .13 B1
Grays RM17 . . . . .12 A8
Grays RM17 . . . . .12 B8
Headcorn TN27 . . . . .141 D5
Hextable BR8 . . . . .26 A1
Langley Heath ME17 . . . . . . .108 C5
Meopham Sta DA13 . . . . .43 F4
Paddock Wood TN12 . . . . . .136 A6
Sundridge TN14 . . . . .82 E2
Sutton at Hone DA4 . . . . .41 D7

New Rd continued
Swanley BR8 . . . . .39 F6
New Road Ave ME4 . . . . .47 E4
New Road Cry Prim Sch
ME4 . . . . .48 A3
New Road Hill BR2,BR6 . . . .50 F7
New Sch at West Heath The
. . . . .99 B6
New St Chatham ME4 . . . . . .47 E3
New Street TN15 . . . . .57 D4
Westerham TN16 . . . . .96 C8
New Stairs ME4 . . . . .47 F4
New Street Hill BR1 . . . . .22 C3
New Street Rd DA3,TN15 . . .57 C6
New Swan Yd **7** DA12 . . . .13 B1
New Tavern Fort* DA12 . . . . .13 C1
New Villas ME15 . . . . .106 C7
New Wharf Rd TN9 . . . . .117 B1
New Wlk TN15 . . . . .71 F3
New Years La BR6,TN14 . . . .67 A5
Newark Cl **11** ME2 . . . . .47 B7
Newark Knok E6 . . . . .2 A7
Newark Yd ME2 . . . . .47 B7
Newbarn La TN14,TN16 . . . .66 C2
Newbery Rd DA8 . . . . .9 C6
Newborough Ct TN10 . . . . .117 C6
Newbury Ave ME15 . . . . .91 C6
Newbury Cl DA11 . . . . .33 B8
Newbury La TN5 . . . . .175 C8
Newbury Rd BR2 . . . . .36 A6
Newchurch Rd ME15 . . . . . . .92 A1
Newcomen Rd TN4 . . . . .149 A5
Newenden Cl ME14 . . . . .92 D6
Newenden Rd ME2 . . . . .33 C2
Newham Coll of FE
(Royal Docks Campus) E16 . .2 C5
Newham La ME4 . . . . .48 B3
Newham Way E13 . . . . .1 B8
Newhaven Gdns SE9 . . . . .5 D3
Newhaven La **4** E16 . . . . . . .1 A8
Newhouse Terr TN8 . . . . . . .112 C3
Newick Cl DA5 . . . . .8 B1
Newing Gn BR1 . . . . .22 D1
Newington Cbr Prim Sch
ME9 . . . . .65 B7
Newington TN15 . . . . .176 E1
Newington Ent Ctr ME9 . . . .65 C8
Newington House **9** BR5 . .38 D1
Newington Ind Est ME9 . . . .64 F6
Newington Rd BR6 . . . . .52 A4
Newington Wlk ME14 . . . . . .92 C6
Newitt Rd ME3 . . . . .34 E5
Newland Green La TN27 . . .143 D8
Newland St E16 . . . . .1 F5
Newlands TN3 . . . . .148 A3
Newlands Cl **8** SE9 . . . . . . .6 A1
Newlands Farm Rd ME14 . . .18 B4
Newlands La DA13 . . . . .57 F1
Newlands Rd TN4 . . . . .149 B7
Newlands Rise TN4 . . . . .149 A6
Newlands Way ME14 . . . . . .149 B7
Newling Cl E6 . . . . .1 F7
Newlyn Cl BR6 . . . . .52 A6
Newlyn Dr **11** ME14 . . . . . . .92 A4
Newlyn Dr TN3 . . . . .139 F5
Newlyn Ho DA16 . . . . .6 F5
Newman Ho BR1 . . . . .6 A7
Newman Rd BR1,DA11 . . . . .36 A8
Newman Rd DA11 . . . . .29 F6
Newmarket Gn SE9 . . . . .22 D8
Newnham Cl ME8 . . . . .49 C2
Newnham Lodge DA17 . . . . . .4 A1
Newnhams Cl BR1 . . . . .36 F6
Newports BR8 . . . . .39 D2
Newstead Ave BR6 . . . . .51 E8
Newstead Wood Sch
for Girls BR6 . . . . .51 D7
Newton Abbot Rd DA11 . . . .29 F6
Newton Ave TN10 . . . . .117 E7
Newton Cl Chatham ME5 . . .62 C2
1 Maidstone ME16 . . . . . . .91 E3
Newton Ct **4** BR1 . . . . .36 A6
Newton Gdns TN12 . . . . . . .135 F7
Newton Ho SE2 . . . . .3 C1
Newton Rd Bexley DA16 . . . . .7 A4
Royal Tunbridge Wells TN1 . .149 B4
Tilbury RM18 . . . . .12 E5
Newton Terr BR2 . . . . .36 D3
Newton Willows TN4 . . . . . .161 C7
Newton's Ct DA9 . . . . .10 D3
Newtown Cotts TN12 . . . . . .139 E6
Nicholas Cl ME19 . . . . .91 A3
Nicholas Ct ME1 . . . . .47 B3
Nicholas Stacey Ho **3** SE7 . .1 B1
Nickelby Cl SE28 . . . . .3 C7
Nickleby Cl SE28 . . . . .3 C7
Nickleby Dr ME1 . . . . .47 C2
Nickleby Rd DA12 . . . . .31 A7
Nicola Terr DA7 . . . . .7 E6
Nicolson Rd BR5 . . . . .38 D2
Nicolson Way TN13 . . . . .84 D5
Nigeria Rd SE7 . . . . .5 D7
Nightingale Cl
Gillingham ME8 . . . . .63 E6
Larkfield ME20 . . . . .74 F2
Northfleet DA11 . . . . .29 E4
Nightingale Cnr BR5 . . . . . . .38 D5
Nightingale Ct ME2 . . . . .46 C6
Nightingale Gr **8** DA1 . . . .10 A3
Nightingale Ho SE18 . . . . .2 A1
Nightingale La
Bromley BR1 . . . . .36 D7
Goathurst Common TN14 . . .98 B5
Nightingale Pl SE18 . . . . .6 A8

Nightingale Prim Sch SE18 . .2 B1
Nightingale Rd
Kemsing TN15 . . . . .69 E2
Orpington BR5 . . . . .37 C3
Nightingale Vale SE18 . . . . . .6 A8
Nightingale Way Newham E6 .1 E8
Swanley BR8 . . . . .39 E6
Nightingales The
Royal Tunbridge Wells TN14 .149 A5
Sissinghurst TN27 . . . . .170 F8
Nile Path **8** SE18 . . . . .6 A8
Nile Rd ME7 . . . . .48 C4
Nimrod Ho E16 . . . . .1 B8
Nine Acres Rd ME2 . . . . .46 B3
Nine Acres Sch SE18 . . . . . . .2 D1
Nine Elms Gr DA11 . . . . .30 A8
Nineveh La TN17,TN18 . . . .179 E6
Ninhams Wood BR6 . . . . . . .51 A6
Nita Ct SE12 . . . . .22 A7
Nithdale Rd SE18 . . . . .6 C7
Niven Cl ME3 . . . . .33 C3
Nizels La TN11 . . . . .115 F8
No 1 St SE18 . . . . .2 B3
No 2 St SE18 . . . . .2 B3
Noah's Ark TN15 . . . . .70 B1
Noble Tree Cross TN11 . . . .116 B6
Noble Tree Rd TN11 . . . . . . .116 B6
Noel Terr **15** DA14 . . . . .24 B4
Nook The ME18 . . . . .104 F2
Norah La ME3 . . . . .32 B3
Nordenfelt Rd DA8 . . . . .4 C2
Nore Cl ME7 . . . . .48 E1
Norfield Rd DA2 . . . . .25 D3
Norfolk Cl Chatham ME5 . . .62 C3
Dartford DA1 . . . . .10 A1
Gillingham ME8 . . . . .49 D2
Norfolk Cres DA15 . . . . .23 E8
Norfolk Gdns DA7 . . . . .7 F6
Norfolk Pl DA16 . . . . .7 A5
Norfolk Rd Gravesend DA12 .30 D8
Maidstone ME15 . . . . .107 C8
Royal Tunbridge Wells TN1 . .149 B2
Tonbridge TN9 . . . . .117 A1
Norham Ct **21** DA2 . . . . . . .10 B1
Norlands Cres BR7 . . . . .37 B8
Norman Cl Gillingham ME8 . .63 B5
Kemsing TN15 . . . . .69 D2
Maidstone ME14 . . . . .92 C8
Orpington BR6 . . . . .51 C7
Rochester ME2 . . . . .46 F4
Norman Ct TN8 . . . . .112 B2
Norman Par DA14 . . . . .24 B5
Norman Rd Dartford DA1 . . .26 E7
Erith DA17 . . . . .4 B3
Erith DA17 . . . . .4 B5
New Town ME19 . . . . .89 B8
Royal Tunbridge Wells TN1 . .149 B5
Snodland ME6 . . . . .75 A6
Norman Rise TN17 . . . . .169 D4
Norman St ME14 . . . . .92 A5
Norman Villas **4** TN18 . . .178 F2
Normandy Prim Sch DA7 . . . .7 E6
Normandy Terr E16 . . . . .1 B7
Normandy Way DA8 . . . . .8 E6
Normanhurst Ave DA7 . . . . . .7 D6
Normanhurst Rd
Borough Green TN15 . . . . . . .87 A7
St Paul's Cray BR5 . . . . .38 B7
Normans Cl DA11 . . . . .30 A8
Norreys Rd ME8 . . . . .63 E7
Norrington Rd ME15 . . . . . .107 B6
Norris Ho **8** SE7 . . . . .1 C1
Norris Way DA1 . . . . .8 F3
Norstead Gdns TN4 . . . . . . .149 B7
Norsted La BR6 . . . . .67 B8
North Ash Rd DA3 . . . . .56 F7
North Bank Cl ME1 . . . . .46 F5
North Beckton Prim Sch
. . . . .1 F8
North Borough Jun Sch
ME14 . . . . .92 A6
North Cl DA6 . . . . .7 D3
North Cray Cotts DA14 . . . .24 E2
North Cray Rd DA14 . . . . . . .24 E4
North Cres ME17 . . . . .106 D4
North Ct **5** Bromley BR1 . .36 B8
Maidstone ME15 . . . . .92 A1
North Dane Way ME5 . . . . . .62 C4
North Down TN12 . . . . .139 E4
North Downs Bsns Pk
TN13 . . . . .83 F7
North Downs Terr TN19 . . . .73 A5
North Dr BR6 . . . . .51 E6
North End La DA6 . . . . .51 B2
North End Trad Est DA8 . . . . .8 E8
North Farm La TN2 . . . . .133 E2
North Farm Rd TN2 . . . . . . .149 C8
North Folly Rd ME15 . . . . . .105 F3
North Frith Pk TN11 . . . . . . .101 F1
North Glade The DA5 . . . . . . .24 F7
North Hill Rd TN18 . . . . .178 C1
North Kent Ave ME2 . . . . . . .12 C1
North Lockside Rd ME4 . . . .48 D8
North Meadow ME1 . . . . . . .88 D7
North Pk SE9 . . . . .6 A1
North Pole La BR2 . . . . .50 A4
North Pole Rd ME16,ME18 . .90 C2
North Pondside Rd ME4 . . . .48 B8
North Rd Bromley BR1 . . . . . .36 B8
Chatham ME4 . . . . .48 A8
Cliffe ME3 . . . . .16 B6
Dartford DA1 . . . . .9 A4
Gillingham ME4,ME7 . . . . . . .48 A7
Goudhurst TN17 . . . . .153 E1
Woolwich SE18 . . . . .2 E2
North Riding DA3 . . . . .43 D6
North Side Three Rd ME4 . .48 C8

North St Bexley DA7 . . . . .8 A3
Biddenden TN27 . . . . .158 A2
Bromley BR1 . . . . .36 A8
Cowden TN8 . . . . .145 A6
Dartford DA1 . . . . .26 D8
Gravesend DA12 . . . . .30 B8
Headcorn TN27 . . . . .141 C5
Maidstone ME16 . . . . .90 F2
Rochester ME1 . . . . .47 B2
Royal Tunbridge Wells TN2 . .149 C3
Sutton Valence ME17 . . . . . .124 E8
North Terr SE18 . . . . .2 E2
North View ME15 . . . . .92 B1
North View Ave RM18 . . . . . .13 A6
North View Cotts ME15 . . .106 C7
North View Rd TN13,TN14 . .84 C6
North Way ME14 . . . . .92 B7
North West Kent Coll
. . . . .30 F7
North Woolwich
Old Sta Mus* E16 . . . . .2 A4
North Woolwich Rdbt E16 . .1 D5
North Woolwich Sta E16 . . . .2 A4
Northall Rd DA7 . . . . .8 C5
Northbourne BR2 . . . . .36 A2
Northbourne Rd ME9 . . . . . .49 B4
Northcote Rd
Gravesend DA11 . . . . .29 F7
Rochester ME2 . . . . .47 A7
Sidcup DA14 . . . . .23 E4
2 Tonbridge TN9 . . . . .117 B1
Northcourt Prim Sch
DA12 . . . . .30 E7
Northdown ME9 . . . . .79 D8
Northdown Cl
Maidstone ME14 . . . . .92 B7
Paddock Wood TN12 . . . . . .135 F6
Northdown Rd Bexley DA16 . .7 C5
Kemsing TN15 . . . . .69 E2
Longfield DA3 . . . . .42 E7
Northdown View ME17 . . . .110 F6
Northend Prim Sch DA8 . . . . .8 F6
Northend Rd DA8 . . . . .8 F6
Northfield DA3 . . . . .42 F6
Northfield Ave BR5 . . . . .38 C3
Northfield Cl BR1,BR7 . . . . . .36 E8
Northfields Maidstone ME16 .90 F2
Speldhurst TN3 . . . . .148 A8
Northfleet Cl ME14 . . . . .92 C5
Northfleet Ind Est DA11 . . . .11 F3
Northfleet Sch for Boys
DA11 . . . . .29 D7
Northfleet Sch for Girls
DA11 . . . . .29 D7
Northfleet Sta DA11 . . . . . . .12 B8
Northgate ME1 . . . . .47 C6
Northgrove Rd **9** TN18 . .178 F2
Northiam Sta TN31 . . . . .187 C2
Northlands Ave BR6 . . . . .51 E6
Northlands Cotts TN12 . . . .185 C1
Northleigh Cl ME15 . . . . . . .107 A6
Northolme Rise BR6 . . . . .51 E8
Northover BR1 . . . . .22 A4
Northpoint Bsns Est ME2 . .47 D8
Northridge Rd DA12 . . . . . . .30 C5
Northside Rd BR1 . . . . .36 A8
Northumberland Ave
Bexley DA16 . . . . .6 E4
Gillingham ME8 . . . . .49 E1
Northumberland Cl DA8 . . . . .8 F6
Northumberland Ct
ME15 .107 D7
Northumberland Gdns
BR1 . . . . .37 A5
Northumberland Heath
Prim Sch DA8 . . . . .8 C7
Northumberland Rd
Istead Rise DA13 . . . . .29 F1
Maidstone ME15 . . . . .107 D8
Newham E6 . . . . .1 F7
Northumberland Way DA8 . . .8 D6
Northview BR8 . . . . .39 E7
Northward Hill
Nature Reserve* ME23 . . . .17 E5
Northwood Ave ME23 . . . . . .17 E4
Northwood Pl DA18 . . . . .3 F3
Northwood Prim Sch DA18 . .3 F3
Norton Cres TN10 . . . . .117 B7
Norton Gr ME5 . . . . .61 E3
Norton Rd
Five Wents ME17 . . . . .108 D1
Royal Tunbridge Wells TN4 . .133 A1
Nortons La TN30 . . . . .172 E5
Nortons Way TN12 . . . . .135 B7
Norvic House DA8 . . . . .8 F7
Norway Terr **8** ME14 . . . . . .92 A7
Norwich Ave TN10 . . . . .117 D5
Norwich Cl ME2 . . . . .46 D6
Norwich Pl **7** DA6 . . . . .8 A3
Norwood Cl ME3 . . . . .16 B4
Norwood Cl DA1 . . . . .10 A3
Norwood La DA13 . . . . .44 B3
Notre Dame RC Prim Sch
. . . . .6 B8
Nottidge Rd TN4 . . . . .148 D1
Nottingham Ave
Maidstone ME15 . . . . .107 D7
Newham E16 . . . . .1 C7
Nottingham Wlk ME2 . . . . . .46 C6
Novar Cl BR6 . . . . .37 F2
Novar Rd SE9 . . . . .23 C7
Nower The TN14,TN16 . . . . .81 F8
Nuffield Hospl TN2 . . . . . . .149 C3
Nugent Ind Pk BR5 . . . . .38 C5

unnery La TN11 ...146 F8
unnington Cl SE9 ...22 E5
ursery Ave Bexley DA7 ...7 F4
Maidstone ME16 ...91 B6
Maidstone,Bearsted ME14 ...93 B3
ursery Cl Dartford DA2 ...27 C8
limwell TN5 ...177 B3
Orpington BR6 ...38 A2
Sevenoaks TN13 ...84 C5
Swanley BR8 ...29 C1
onbridge TN10 ...117 E4
ursery Gdns
Marden TN27 ...23 B2
Hoo St Werburgh ME3 ...34 E5
ursery Pl TN13 ...83 D4
ursery Rd Ditton ME20 ...75 C1
Sillingham ME8 ...63 D8
Meopham Sta DA13 ...144 A8
Paddock Wood TN12 ...135 F8
Royal Tunbridge Wells TN4 ...149 B8
ursery The Erith DA8 ...8 F7
urstead Ave DA3 ...43 D6
urstead Church La DA13 ...44 A5
urstead La DA3,DA13 ...43 D5
urstead Rd ME9 ...80 B4
ut Tree Cl BR6 ...52 D7
utfield Cl ME5 ...62 B8
utfield Way ME5 ...51 B8
utfields TN15 ...86 B4
uthatch La ME17 ...107 D7
uthatch Gdns SE28 ...2 D4
utley Cl BR8 ...39 F8
utmead Cl ME5 ...25 C7
uttall Ct BR5 ...38 B6
utwood Cl ME14 ...92 E4
uxley Rd DA17 ...4 A1
W Kent Coll DA1 ...26 D8
yanza St SE18 ...6 D8

O

O'Neill Path [11] SE18 ...6 A8
ak Apple St SE12 ...22 A7
ak Ave Gillingham ME7 ...48 E6
Sevenoaks TN13 ...99 B7
ak Cl Crayford DA1 ...8 D3
Hoo St Werburgh ME3 ...34 E3
ak Cotts TN6 ...113 B6
ak Ct BR1 ...36 F7
ak Dr Higham ME3 ...32 B4
Larkfield ME20 ...75 B2
ak End Cl TN4 ...133 A2
ak Farm La TN15 ...57 E1
ak Farm Gdns TN27 ...141 D6
ak Hill Rd TN13 ...84 A2
ak Ho RD [3] Chatham ME5 ...64 C4
Marden TN12 ...138 D5
Royal Tunbridge Wells TN2 ...149 C7
[5] Sidcup DA15 ...24 A5
ak La Gillingham ME8 ...64 D4
Headcorn TN27 ...141 D5
Sevenoaks TN13 ...99 A8
ak Lodge TN13 ...84 A3
ak La Lodge TN16 ...81 D2
ak Rd Erith,
Northumberland Heath DA8 ...8 C7
Erith,Slade Green DA8 ...9 A5
Five Oak Green TN12 ...135 B7
Gravesend DA12 ...30 C4
Grays RM17 ...12 A8
Hoo St Werburgh ME3 ...34 E3
Orpington BR6 ...52 A3
Rochester ME2 ...46 E6
Royal Tunbridge Wells TN2 ...149 D7
Stone DA9 ...10 E1
Westerham TN16 ...81 D2
ak Terr [3] TN18 ...178 F2
Oak Tree Ave
Maidstone ME15 ...107 C7
Stone DA9 ...27 F8
Oak Tree Cl Marden TN12 ...138 D5
Royal Tunbridge Wells TN1 ...149 A1
Oak Tree Gdns BR1 ...22 B3
Oak Trees Com Sch
BR7 ...107 C7
ak View TN8 ...112 B2
Oakapple La ME14 ...91 A3
Oakbrook Cl BR1 ...22 B2
Oakcroft [5] SE12 ...22 B5
Oakdale La TN8 ...96 C2
Oakdale Rd SE12 ...148 F4
Oakdene Ave
Chislehurst BR7 ...23 A3
Erith DA8 ...8 C8
Oakdene Rd Orpington BR5 ...38 A3
Sevenoaks TN13 ...84 A5
Oakenden Rd DA13 ...44 E1
Oakenham Ho [1] SE2 ...3 D4
Oakes Cl E6 ...1 F7
Oakfield Hawkhurst TN18 ...178 F2
Rolvenden TN17 ...182 A1
Oakfield Cotts TN17 ...180 D4
Oakfield Court Rd TN12 ...149 C3
Oakfield Inf Sch DA1 ...26 D6
Oakfield Jun Sch DA1 ...26 D6
Oakfield La
Marlpit Hill TN8 ...112 B5
Matfield TN12 ...151 D8
Oakfields TN13 ...84 B1
Oakham Dr BR2 ...36 A5
Oakhill House BR5 ...38 A8

Oakhill Rd BR6 ...51 F8
Oakhouse Rd DA6 ...8 A2
Oakhurst Ave DA7 ...7 E4
Oakhurst Cl ME5 ...61 F3
Oakhurst Gdns DA7 ...7 E7
Oakhurst Pl BR7 ...36 F8
Oakland Cl ME5 ...61 F3
Oakland Villas TN3 ...161 B7
Oaklands Chislehurst BR7 ...23 D2
Cranbrook TN17 ...169 D4
Oaklands Ave DA15 ...23 F8
Oaklands Cl Bexley DA6 ...7 F2
Orpington BR5 ...37 E3
West Kingsdown TN15 ...55 E4
Oaklands Cty Inf & Jun Sch
ME5 ...61 F4
Oaklands Rd Bexley DA6 ...7 F2
Dartford DA2 ...27 C7
Groombridge TN3 ...161 B6
Hawkhurst TN18 ...179 A1
Northfleet DA11 ...29 F4
Oaklands Way TN11 ...116 F4
Oaklea Rd TN12 ...135 F6
Oakleigh Cl Chatham ME5 ...61 E2
Orpington BR6 ...52 A8
Oakleigh Gdns BR6 ...51 E6
Oakleigh Park Ave BR7 ...37 A8
Oakley Cl [7] Newham E6 ...1 E7
West Thurrock RM20 ...11 C8
Oakley Ct DA1 ...27 B7
Oakley Dr Orpington BR2 ...50 E7
Sidcup SE9 ...23 D7
Oakley Lodge SE12 ...22 A8
Oakley Pk DA5 ...24 C8
Oakley Rd BR2 ...50 E8
Oakmead Meopham DA13 ...58 A8
Tonbridge TN10 ...117 C6
Oakmead Ave BR2 ...36 A3
Oakmere Rd SE2 ...7 A8
Oakmont Pl BR6 ...37 D1
Oaks Bsns Village The
ME5 ...62 C1
Oaks Dene ME5 ...61 F1
Oaks Forstal TN18 ...186 C5
Oaks Rd TN30 ...183 B8
Oaks Ave Aylesford ME20 ...75 E1
Biddenden Green TN27 ...142 F2
Swanley BR8 ...39 E7
Woolwich SE18 ...2 C1
Oakum Ct ME4 ...48 B2
Oakway Cl ME4 ...7 E1
Oakways SE9 ...6 B1
Oakwood Ave BR2 ...36 B6
Oakwood Cl
Chislehurst BR7 ...23 A2
Dartford DA1 ...27 B7
Oakwood Ct
Maidstone ME16 ...91 D3
Swanley BR8 ...39 C7
Oakwood Dr Bexley DA7 ...8 C3
Sevenoaks TN13 ...84 B4
Oakwood Gdns BR6 ...51 C8
Oakwood Park Gram Sch
ME16 ...91 C3
Oakwood Rd
Maidstone ME16 ...91 D3
Orpington BR6 ...51 C8
Oakwood Rise
Longfield DA3 ...42 E6
Royal Tunbridge Wells TN2 ...149 E7
Oasis The [6] BR5 ...36 C7
Oast Cl TN2 ...149 D7
Oast Ho The [3] ME8 ...63 F8
Oast House Way BR5 ...38 B5
Oast La TN10 ...117 A4
Oast View TN12 ...153 A6
Oast Way DA12 ...42 E3
Oastfield Ct TN15 ...84 C2
Oasts The ME14 ...93 B8
Oastview ME8 ...64 A8
Oatfield Cl TN17 ...169 C5
Oatfield Dr TN17 ...169 C5
Oatfield Rd BR6 ...37 F1
Occupation La SE18 ...6 B6
Ocelot Ct [3] ME4 ...48 B3
Ockham Dr BR5 ...24 A1
Ockley La TN18 ...179 A3
Ockley Rd TN18 ...179 A2
Octavia Cl ME5 ...61 F2
Octavia Way [3] SE28 ...3 B6
Odeon Ct [1] E16 ...1 A8
Odeon Par SE9 ...5 E3
Odiham Dr ME16 ...91 C7
Offen's Dr TN12 ...139 E3
Offenham Rd SE9 ...22 F4
Offham Prim Sch ME19 ...88 D8
Offham Rd ME19 ...89 A7
Officers' Rd ME4 ...48 B8
Officers Terr ME4 ...47 F7
Ogilby St SE18 ...1 F2
Okehampton Cres DA16 ...7 C6
Okemore Gdns BR5 ...38 C5
Old Ashford Rd ME17 ...111 E5
Old Bailey The ME17 ...110 E6
Old Barn Cl Gillingham ME7 ...62 F5
Kemsing TN15 ...70 A2
Tonbridge TN9 ...132 F8
Old Barn Rd ME19 ...74 E2
Old Barn Way [7] DA7 ...8 D4
Old Bexley Bsns Pk DA5 ...25 F8
Old Bexley CE Prim Sch
DA5 ...24 F7
Old Bexley La DA5 ...25 E6
Old Carriageway The
Gillingham ME7 ...62 F4
Sevenoaks TN13 ...83 C5

Old Castle Wlk ME8 ...63 D4
Old Chapel Rd BR8 ...39 C2
Old Chatham Rd
Kit's Coty ME20 ...76 D6
Maidstone ME14 ...76 F1
Old Church La ME18 ...103 E4
Old Church Rd
Burham ME1 ...60 C1
Matfield TN2 ...134 D2
Mereworth ME18,TN12 ...103 D5
Pembury TN2 ...150 D8
Old Coach La [3] SE18 ...6 A8
Old Coach Rd TN15 ...71 E5
Old Court Ho TN13 ...84 C2
Old Ctyd The BR1 ...36 B8
Old Dartford Rd DA4 ...40 F3
Old Dover Rd SE3 ...5 B7
Old Downs DA3 ...42 E4
Old Dr ME15 ...106 F6
Old Farm Ave DA15 ...23 E6
Old Farm Gdns BR8 ...39 F6
Old Farm Rd E DA15 ...24 A6
Old Farm Rd W DA15 ...23 F6
Old Forge La ME9 ...79 F3
Old Forge Way DA14 ...24 B4
Old Garden The TN13 ...83 D4
Old Gardens Cl TN2 ...163 B8
Old Hadlow Rd TN10 ...117 F4
Old Ham La ME17 ...111 A4
Old Hill Chislehurst BR7 ...37 A8
Orpington BR6 ...51 C4
Old Ho The BR7 ...37 D8
Old Homesdale Rd BR2 ...36 C5
Old House La TN3 ...147 D4
Old House Rd ME9 ...64 C4
Old Kent Rd TN13 ...136 A6
Old La TN15 ...86 C4
Old Lain ME17 ...110 F6
Old London Rd
Badgers Mount TN14 ...53 A1
Tonbridge TN10 ...117 C3
Wrotham TN15 ...71 F4
Old Loose Hill ME15 ...106 F4
Old Maidstone Rd DA14 ...24 F1
Old Manor Dr DA12 ...30 C7
Old Manor Way Bexley DA7 ...8 D5
Chislehurst BR7 ...22 F3
Old Mill Cl DA4 ...40 G1
Old Mill La ME20 ...75 F6
Old Mill Rd Maidstone ME17 ...93 F1
Woolwich SE18 ...6 D8
Old Oast Bsns Ctr The
ME20 ...76 A1
Old Orch Sandhurst TN18 ...186 B5
TN11 ...115 A3
Old Orch The ME8 ...64 A8
Old Orchard La ME19 ...74 B1
Old Otford Rd TN14 ...69 B1
Old Park Rd SE2 ...3 A1
Old Parsonage Ct ME19 ...89 C7
Old Pattens La ME1 ...47 D2
Old Perry St
Chislehurst BR7 ...23 E1
Northfleet DA11 ...29 E6
Old Polhill TN14 ...68 D4
Old Rd Chatham ME4 ...47 F4
Crayford DA1,DA7 ...8 D3
East Peckham TN12 ...120 A6
Wateringbury ME18 ...104 C7
Old Rd E DA12 ...30 D7
Old Rd W DA11 ...30 A7
Old Regent Dr TN17 ...181 E3
Old Riding School The
TN3 ...161 B2
Old School Cl ME17 ...111 D4
Old School Ct
Chattenden ME3 ...33 F4
Egerton TN27 ...127 F3
Old School House The
TN3 ...112 C1
Old School La ME19 ...73 F4
Old School The
Goudhurst TN17 ...167 E8
Maidstone ME16 ...91 D6
Old Soar Manor* TN15 ...87 B1
Old Soar Rd TN15 ...87 C1
Old Station Rd TN5 ...174 E6
Old Tannery Cl TN30 ...182 F7
Old Terry's Lodge Rd
TN15 ...71 A4
Old Timber Top Cottages The
TN13 ...84 C4
Old Tovil Rd ME15 ...92 A2
Old Trafford Cl ME16 ...91 B6
Old Tree La ME17 ...107 D3
Old Wardsdown TN5 ...177 B3
Old Watling St Cuxton ME2 ...46 B8
Gravesend DA11 ...30 A3
Old Weavers Cotts TN17 ...180 E8
Old Whetsted Rd TN12 ...120 A2
Old Yews The DA3 ...43 B6
Oldborough Manor
Com Sch ME15 ...107 A7
Oldbury Cl Oldbury TN15 ...86 B5
Orpington BR5 ...38 C5
Oldbury Cotts TN15 ...86 B6
Oldbury La TN15 ...86 B6
Oldchurch Cl BR8 ...39 E3
Oldfield Cl Bromley BR1 ...36 E3
Gillingham ME8 ...63 D8
Maidstone ME15 ...92 E1
Oldfield Rd Bexley DA7 ...7 E5
Bromley BR1 ...36 E3
Oleander Cl BR6 ...51 D5
Olive Rd DA1 ...26 D7
Oliver Cl Chatham ME4 ...48 B2

Oliver Cl continued
West Thurrock RM20 ...10 F7
Oliver Cres DA4 ...40 G1
Oliver Ct SE18 ...2 C2
Oliver Gdns E6 ...1 E8
Oliver Rd Staplehurst TN12 ...139 E4
Swanley BR8 ...39 D6
West Thurrock RM20 ...11 A7
Oliver Twist Cl ME1 ...47 B4
Olivers Cotts ME14 ...93 C4
Olivers Mill DA3 ...56 E8
Olivine Cl ME5 ...77 A8
Olliffe Cl ME5 ...61 F2
Olron Cres DA6 ...7 E2
Olven Rd SE18 ...6 C8
Olyffe Ave DA16 ...7 A5
Onslow Cres BR7 ...37 B8
Onslow Dr DA14 ...24 D6
Onslow Rd ME1 ...47 D3
Opal Cl [1] E16 ...1 D7
Opal Gn ME5 ...62 B2
Openshaw Rd SE2 ...3 B2
Orache Dr ME14 ...92 E5
Orange Court La BR6 ...51 A2
Orange Terr ME1 ...47 D5
Orangery La SE9 ...5 F1
Orbit Cl ME5 ...77 A8
Orbital One DA1 ...27 B6
Orchard Ave
Aylesford ME20 ...75 E1
Dartford DA1 ...26 B7
Erith DA17 ...7 F8
Gravesend DA11 ...30 B3
Rochester ME2 ...32 F1
Orchard Bank ME17 ...108 B1
Orchard Bsns Ctr
Maidstone ME16 ...91 C8
Paddock Wood TN12 ...136 A8
Royal Tunbridge Wells TN2 ...149 D8
Tonbridge TN9 ...117 C1
Orchard Cl Bexley DA7 ...7 F6
Coxheath ME17 ...106 C3
Edenbridge TN8 ...112 B2
Horsmonden TN12 ...152 F6
Langley Heath ME17 ...108 E4
New Barn DA3 ...43 B7
Royal Tunbridge Wells TN2 ...149 D6
Sevenoaks TN14 ...84 C7
Orchard Cotts
Chislehurst BR7 ...23 E2
East Farleigh ME16 ...106 A8
Orchard Cres TN12 ...153 A6
Orchard Ct TN17 ...180 D6
Orchard Dr
Edenbridge TN8 ...112 B2
Maidstone ME14 ...92 E4
Meopham Sta DA13 ...43 F8
Newington ME9 ...65 A5
Tonbridge TN10 ...117 E5
Orchard Glade TN27 ...141 E5
Orchard Gn Bromley BR1 ...36 C8
Orpington BR6 ...51 E8
Orchard Gr Larkfield ME20 ...75 B2
Orpington BR6 ...37 F1
Royal Tunbridge Wells TN2 ...149 B5
Orchard Hill DA1 ...26 B7
Orchard House DA8 ...8 F6
Orchard Ind Est TN12 ...107 F3
Orchard PI
[2] Maidstone ME16 ...91 E3
St Paul's Cray BR5 ...38 C6
Sundridge TN14 ...82 D3
Orchard Rd Bexley DA16 ...7 B4
Bromley BR1 ...36 C8
East Peckham TN12 ...120 A6
Erith DA17 ...4 A2
Northfleet DA11 ...29 C6
Orpington BR5 ...51 B5
Otford TN14 ...68 F3
Pratt's Bottom BR6 ...52 B5
Sevenoaks TN13 ...83 E5
Sidcup DA14 ...23 E4
Swanscombe DA10 ...11 E2
Tenterden TN30 ...173 A3
Orchard Rise TN8 ...161 B7
Orchard Rise E DA15 ...6 E2
Orchard Rise W DA15 ...6 E2
Orchard St Dartford DA1 ...9 E1
Gillingham ME8 ...63 E8
Maidstone ME15 ...92 A3
Orchard Terr DA9 ...10 E2
Orchard The
Maidstone ME14 ...93 B4
Sevenoaks TN13 ...83 E6
Swanley BR8 ...39 E7
Orchard View TN30 ...183 C8
Orchard Villas
Chainhurst TN12 ...122 A4
Mereworth ME18 ...23 E2
[1] Rochester ME4 ...47 F3
Sidcup DA14 ...24 C2
Orchard Way Dartford DA2 ...26 D5
Horsmonden TN12 ...153 A6
Kemsing TN15 ...70 A2
Snodland ME6 ...74 F1
Turnden TN17 ...169 B4
Orchardlea DA13 ...28 F3
Orchards Sh Ctr The DA1 ...9 E1
Orchid Cl [1] Newham E6 ...1 E8
Rochester ME2 ...46 D6
Orchidhurst TN2 ...149 D7
Ordnance Rd
Gravesend DA12 ...13 C1
Woolwich SE18 ...6 A6
Ordnance St ME4 ...47 E3
Ordnance Terr [3] ME4 ...47 E3
Oregon Sq BR6 ...37 D1
Orford Ct [7] DA2 ...27 B8

Oriental Rd E16 ...1 D5
Oriole Way Larkfield ME20 ...74 F2
Woolwich SE28 ...3 B6
Orion Rd ME1 ...61 C7
Orissa Rd SE18 ...2 E1
Orlestone Gdns BR6 ...52 E5
Orlick Rd DA12 ...31 B7
Ormesby Cl SE28 ...3 D6
Ormiston Rd SE10 ...1 A1
Ormonde Ave BR6 ...51 C8
Ormsby Gn ME8 ...63 E3
Ormsby Point [8] SE18 ...2 B2
Orpines The TN18 ...104 F7
Orpington By-Pass TN14 ...53 A2
Orpington Coll
of Further Education
BR6 ...38 A1
Orpington Hospl BR6 ...51 F6
Orpington Rd BR7 ...37 E6
Orpington Sta BR6 ...51 E8
Orpington Trad Est BR5 ...38 C5
Orwell Cl Lunsford ME20 ...74 F3
Rainham RM9 ...4 D8
Orwell Spike ME19 ...89 A5
Osberton Rd SE12 ...5 A2
Osborne Rd Erith DA17 ...7 F8
Gillingham ME7 ...48 C5
Osbourne Rd DA2 ...10 B1
Osgood Ave BR6 ...51 F5
Osgood Gdns [1] BR6 ...51 F5
Osmers Hill TN5 ...174 F7
Osmunda Ct TN2 ...149 C4
Osney Ho [4] SE2 ...3 D6
Osney Way DA12 ...30 F6
Osprey Ave ME5 ...48 E2
Osprey Cl E6 ...1 E8
Osprey Wlk ME20 ...74 F1
Ospringe Ct SE9 ...6 E3
Ospringe Pl TN2 ...149 F6
Osterberg Rd DA1 ...9 F3
Osterley Ct BR5 ...38 A8
Ostlers Ct [2] ME4 ...75 A8
Otford Cl Bromley BR1 ...37 A6
Sidcup DA5 ...8 B1
Otford Court
(St Michael's Sch) TN14 ...69 E4
Otford La TN14 ...68 B6
Otford Prim Sch TN14 ...69 B3
Otford Rd TN14 ...84 B2
Otford Sta TN14 ...69 C3
Otham La ME15 ...93 C2
Otham St Maidstone ME15 ...93 C2
Otham ME15 ...108 B7
Otley Rd E16 ...1 C8
Otlinge Rd BR5 ...38 D5
Ottawa Rd ME18 ...13 A5
Otterbourne Pl ME15 ...92 E1
Otterden Ct BR5 ...38 B8
Otterham Quay La ME8 ...64 B8
Otteridge Rd ME14 ...93 A3
Otters Cl BR5 ...38 D5
Ottershaw House BR5 ...38 B8
Otway St Chatham ME4 ...48 A3
Gillingham ME7 ...48 D6
Otway Terr [1] ME4 ...48 A3
Our Lady of Grace
RC Jun Mix Sch SE7 ...5 B8
Our Lady of Hartley
RC Prim Sch DA3 ...42 F4
Our Lady of the Rosary
RC Prim Sch DA15 ...6 E1
Our Lady's RC Prim Sch
DA1 ...9 D1
Oval The New Barn DA3 ...43 C6
Sidcup DA15 ...24 A8
Ovenden Rd
Sevenoaks TN14 ...82 F6
Sundridge TN14 ...82 D6
Over Minnis DA3 ...56 F7
Overcliffe DA11 ...13 A1
Overcourt Cl DA15 ...7 B1
Overdale TN14 ...99 B2
Overmead Eltham DA15 ...23 D8
Swanley BR8 ...39 E4
Overton Rd SE2 ...3 D3
Overy Liberty DA1 ...26 D8
Overy St DA1 ...9 E1
Owen Cl East Malling ME19 ...89 F8
Woolwich SE28 ...3 C5
Owenite St SE2 ...3 B2
Owens Way ME7 ...49 A8
Owl House Gdns* TN3 ...165 E7
Owletts* DA12 ...44 F6
Owletts DA11 ...107 D8
Ox La TN30 ...173 B2
Ox Lea TN3 ...161 A8
Oxenden Wood Rd BR6 ...52 C4
Oxenhill Rd TN15 ...69 E2
Oxenhoath Rd TN11 ...102 D4
Oxfield TN8 ...112 D1
Oxford Cl DA11 ...30 F6
Oxford Cl DA14 ...23 F4
Oxford Mews DA5 ...25 A7
Oxford Rd Gillingham ME7 ...48 D3
Maidstone ME15 ...108 D1
Sidcup DA14 ...24 B3
Oxhawth Cres BR2 ...37 B3
Oxleas E6 ...2 B7
Oxleas Cl DA16 ...6 D5
Oxleas Wood
Nature Reserve* SE18 ...6 C4
Oxley Shaw La ME19 ...74 E2
Oyster Catchers Cl E16 ...1 B7
Ozolins Way E16 ...1 A7

P

Pacific Cl DA10 ....11 E2
Packer PI ME5 ....62 A8
Packham CI BR6 ....52 C7
Packham Rd DA11 ....29 F5
Packhorse Rd TN13 ....83 C4
Packmores Rd SE9 ....6 E2
Pad's Hill ME15 ....92 A4
Paddlesworth Rd ME6 ....59 D1
Paddock Cl
   Fordcombe TN3 ....147 B5
   Greenwich SE3 ....5 A5
   Orpington BR6 ....51 B6
   Platt TN15 ....87 C6
   Sutton at Hone DA4 ....41 C8
Paddock Rd DA6 ....7 E3
Paddock The Chatham ME4 ....47 F4
   Hadlow TN11 ....102 E1
   Pembury TN2 ....150 C6
   Vigo Village DA13 ....72 F7
   Westerham TN16 ....81 C1
Paddock Way BR7 ....23 D1
Paddock Wood Prim Sch
   TN12 ....136 A6
Paddock Wood Sta TN12 ...136 A7
Paddocks Cl BR5 ....52 D8
Paddocks The
   Cowden TN8 ....145 B7
   Gillingham ME7 ....63 A5
   Sevenoaks TN13 ....84 D3
Padsole La ME15 ....92 A4
Padstow Manor [1] ME7 ...48 C6
Page Cl DA2 ....28 C5
Page Cres DA8 ....6 F7
Page Heath La BR1 ....36 D6
Page Heath Villas BR1 ...36 D6
Pageant Cl RM18 ....13 C6
Pagehurst Rd TN12 ....139 B3
Paget Gdns BR7 ....37 B8
Paget Rise SE18 ....6 A7
Paget Row ME7 ....48 C5
Paget St ME7 ....48 C5
Paget Terr SE18 ....6 B8
Pagitt St ME4 ....47 E3
Paiges Farm Cl TN14 ....99 C2
Painters Ash La DA11 ....29 D5
Painters Ash Prim Sch
   DA11 ....29 D5
Palace Ave ME15 ....92 A4
Palace Ct [5] Bromley BR1 ...36 B8
   Chatham ME5 ....48 D2
   Eltham SE9 ....5 F1
Palace Gr BR1 ....36 B8
Palace Rd Bromley BR1 ...36 B8
   Lewisham SE12 ....5 A8
Palace View Bromley BR1 ...36 B6
   Lewisham SE12 ....22 A6
Palace Wood Inf Sch
   ME16 ....91 C6
Palace Wood Jun Sch
   ME16 ....91 C6
Palewell Cl BR5 ....38 B7
Pallant Way BR6 ....51 A7
Pallet Way SE18 ....5 A6
Palm Ave DA14 ....24 D2
Palmar Cres DA7 ....8 A5
Palmar Rd Bexley DA7 ....8 A5
   Maidstone ME16 ....91 D6
Palmarsh Cl BR5 ....38 D5
Palmeira Rd DA7 ....7 D4
Palmer Ave DA12 ....30 D4
Palmers Brook TN11 ....102 F2
Palmers Green La TN12 ...136 D1
Palmerston Ave SE18 ....6 C8
Palmerston Rd
   Chatham ME4 ....47 F1
   Grays RM20 ....11 D8
Pamela Ct ME7 ....48 D5
Panbro House SE18 ....5 F6
Panfield Rd SE28 ....3 A3
Pankhurst Ave E16 ....1 B5
Pankhurst Ho SE18 ....6 A7
Pankhurst Rd ME14 ....34 D6
Pannell Rd ME3 ....21 A6
Panters The Bromley BR1 ...25 F1
Pantiles The
   Erith DA7 ....7 F7
   [17] Royal Tunbridge
      Wells[*] TN2 ....149 A2
Panton Cl ME5 ....62 C4
Pantyles The TN14 ....98 B5
Papillons Wlk SE3 ....5 A5
Papion Gr ME5 ....61 E2
Papyrus Rd ME20 ....75 B4
Parade The Crayford DA1 ...8 F2
   Gravesend DA12 ....30 C6
   Kemsing TN15 ....69 E2
   Meopham Sta DA13 ....44 A2
   Rochester ME2 ....47 B4
   Stapleford TN13 ....139 F3
   Swanscombe DA10 ....11 F2
Paradise Cotts ME9 ....64 E5
Paradise PI [4] SE18 ....1 E2
Paragon Cl E16 ....1 A7
Paragon The SE3 ....5 A5
Parbrook Rd SE3 ....18 B2
Parham Rd ME4 ....47 F2
Parish CE Prim Sch BR1 ...22 A1
Parish Gate Dr DA15 ....6 E1

Parish Wharf [5] SE18 ....1 E2
Park App DA16 ....7 B3
Park Ave Bromley BR1 ....22 A2
   Edenbridge TN8 ....112 B2
   Gillingham ME7 ....48 D3
   Gravesend DA12 ....30 C7
   Maidstone, Penenden ME17 ...106 E2
   Maidstone, Penenden
      Heath ME14 ....92 B6
   Northfleet DA11 ....29 E6
   Orpington,Goddington BR6 ...52 B7
   Orpington,Locksbottom BR6 ...51 A8
   Tonbridge TN11 ....116 F5
   West Thurrock RM20 ....11 B8
Park Barn Rd ME17 ....109 C5
Park Corner Rd DA13 ....28 F4
Park Cotts [8] TN18 ....179 A2
Park Cres Chatham ME4 ...61 F8
   Erith DA8 ....8 D8
Park Crescent Rd DA8 ....8 D8
Park Dr Longfield DA3 ....42 E6
   Woolwich SE7 ....5 E8
Park Farm Houses ME20 ...90 B8
Park Farm Rd Bromley BR1 ...36 D8
   Ryarsh ME19 ....73 F6
Park Gdns DA8 ....4 D2
Park Gr Barley DA7 ....8 C3
   Bromley BR1 ....36 B8
Park Hill Bromley BR1 ....36 F5
   Meopham Sta DA13 ....43 F5
Park Hill Rd TN14 ....69 E2
Park Ho Maidstone ME14 ...92 B6
   Sevenoaks TN13 ....84 C5
   Sidcup DA14 ....24 A3
Park House Gdns TN14 ...133 A2
Park La
   Gill's Green TN17,TN18 ...178 D7
   Godden Green TN15 ....85 A4
   Kemsing TN15 ....70 A1
   Maidstone, Cock
      Stone ME17 ....107 D2
   Maidstone, Ringlestone ME14 ...91 F7
   Sevenoaks TN13 ....84 C3
   Swanley Village BR8 ....40 C7
Park Manor ME7 ....48 B5
Park Mead DA15 ....7 B1
Park Mews BR7 ....23 B2
Park PI [9] Bromley BR1 ...36 B8
   Gravesend DA12 ....30 C8
   Hever TN8 ....129 D4
   Sevenoaks TN13 ....83 D4
Park Rd Addington ME19 ...73 C3
   Bromley BR1 ....36 B8
   Chislehurst BR7 ....23 B2
   Dartford DA1 ....27 A8
   Dunk's Green TN11 ....102 C5
   Gravesend DA11 ....30 C8
   Leybourne ME19 ....74 D3
   Marden Thorn TN12 ....139 A4
   Mereworth ME18 ....103 F5
   Orpington BR5 ....38 C4
   Royal Tunbridge Wells TN4 ...149 B5
   Royal Tunbridge Wells,
      Southborough TN4 ....133 A2
   Swanley BR8 ....39 F5
   Swanscombe DA10 ....11 E1
Park Road Ind Est BR8 ...39 F6
Park St TN2 ....149 C3
Park Terr Sundridge TN14 ...82 D3
   Swanscombe DA10 ....11 B2
Park The DA14 ....24 A3
Park View
   Culverstone Green TN15 ...57 C2
   Sevenoaks TN13 ....84 C3
Park View Cl
   Lewisham SE12 ....22 C5
   Maidstone ME15 ....92 E1
Park View Ct
   Lewisham SE12 ....22 C5
   Maidstone ME15 ....92 E1
Park View Rd Bexley DA16 ...7 C4
   Eltham SE9 ....23 B6
Park View Terr [2] TN30 ...183 A7
Park Villas TN11 ....102 F1
Park Way Coxheath ME17 ...106 D3
   Dartford DA5 ....25 E5
   Maidstone ME15 ....92 E1
Park Way Prim Sch ME15 ...92 E1
Park Wood Gn ME8 ....63 D5
Park Wood La TN12 ....140 C1
Park Wood Par ME15 ....107 F5
Park Wood Trad Est
   ME15 ....107 F4
Parkdale Rd SE18 ....2 E1
Parker Ave RM18 ....13 C6
Parker Cl Gillingham ME8 ...63 E5
   Newham E16 ....1 E5
Parker Ho [4] SE18 ....2 B1
Parker St E16 ....1 E5
Parker's Cnr ME3 ....19 C8
Parkfield Hartley DA3 ....42 E5
   Sevenoaks TN13 ....84 F4
Parkfield Rd ME8 ....49 F1
Parkfield Way ME8 ....36 F4
Parkfields ME2 ....46 C7
Parkgate Cotts BR6 ....53 C6
Parkgate Rd BR6 ....53 C6
Parkhill Rd
   Sidcup, Longlands DA15 ...23 E5
   Sidcup, Old Bexley DA5 ...24 E8
Parkhurst Gdns [3] DA5 ...25 A8
Parkhurst Rd DA5 ....25 A8
Parkland Cl TN11 ....99 D6
Parklands TN4 ....148 E8
Parkside Cliffe Woods ME3 ...33 B7
   Halstead TN14 ....67 F6
   Sidcup DA14 ....24 B6
Parkside Ave Bromley BR1 ...36 E5
   Crayford DA1,DA7 ....8 E5

Parkside Ave continued
   Tilbury RM18 ....13 B5
Parkside Cross DA7 ....8 E5
Parkside Ct [1] TN30 ....182 F7
Parkside Lodge DA17 ....4 C1
Parkside Par DA8 ....8 C7
Parkside Rd DA17 ....4 C2
Parkview TN7 ....149 D4
Parkway Erith DA18 ....3 E3
Parkway north DA18 ....3 E3
   Tonbridge TN10 ....117 D5
Parkway Prim Sch DA18 ...3 E3
Parkwood Cl TN2 ....149 C2
Parkwood Hall Sch BR8 ...40 B6
Parkwood Inf Sch ME8 ...63 E5
Parkwood Jun Sch ME8 ...63 E5
Parkwood Rd DA5 ....24 F8
Paroma Rd DA17 ....4 A3
Parr Ave ME7 ....48 D6
Parrock Ave DA12 ....30 C7
Parrock Rd DA12 ....30 C7
Parrock St DA12 ....30 B8
Parrock The DA12 ....30 C7
Parrs Head Mews ME7 ...47 C6
Parry Ave E6 ....1 F7
Parry PI SE18 ....2 B2
Parson's Croft TN13 ....129 C5
Parsonage Cl TN4 ....148 B5
Parsonage La
   Cold Harbour ME9 ....65 F8
   Lamberhurst TN3 ....166 B6
   Rochester ME2 ....47 C8
   Sidcup DA14 ....24 F4
   Sutton at Hone DA4 ....27 B2
Parsonage Manorway
   ....8 A8
Parsonage Rd
   Royal Tunbridge Wells TN4 ...148 B5
   West Thurrock RM20 ....11 C8
Parsons La Dartford DA2 ...26 B5
   Stansted TN15 ....56 E1
Partridge Ave ME7 ....74 F3
Partridge Cl [1] E16 ....1 E8
Partridge Dr Orpington BR6 ...51 C7
   St Mary's Island ME4 ....34 B1
Partridge Gn SE9 ....23 A5
Partridge Rd DA14 ....23 E4
Partridge Sq [3] E6 ....1 E8
Pasley Rd ME4,ME7 ....48 B7
Pasley Rd E ME7 ....48 B7
Pasley Rd W ME7 ....48 A7
Pasley Sq ME7 ....5 F1
Passfield Ho SE18 ....2 D2
Passfield Path [18] SE28 ...3 B6
Paston Ceres SE12 ....22 B8
Patagonia Ho TN2 ....149 C3
Patch The TN13 ....83 A5
Patience Cotts TN14 ....99 B2
Patricia Ct Bexley SE2 ....7 B7
   Chislehurst BR7 ....37 D8
Patrixbourne Ave ME8 ...49 C2
Pattenden Gdns TN12 ....120 A7
Pattenden La TN12 ....138 C7
Pattens Gdns ME1 ....47 E2
Pattens La ME1 ....47 E1
Pattens PI ME1 ....47 D2
Pattersons Cl DA2 ....27 D7
Patterson Ct DA1 ....10 A2
Pattison Point [14] E16 ...1 A8
Pattison Wlk SE18 ....2 C1
Paulinus Cl BR5 ....38 C6
Pavement The TN30 ....173 B3
Pavilion Gdns TN13 ....84 C3
Pavilion L Ctr The BR1 ...36 A7
Pavilion La ME18 ....104 A8
Pavilion The [8] TN9 ....117 B1
Paxton Cl SE12 ....22 C5
Paxton Rd BR1 ....22 A1
Payne's La ME15 ....107 B7
Paynes Cotts TN13 ....128 E2
Peace Cotts ME15 ....121 D7
Peace St SE18 ....6 A8
Peach Croft DA11 ....29 E4
Peach Hall TN10 ....117 C6
Peacock Mews [7] ME16 ...91 E4
Peacock Rise ME5 ....62 A4
Peacock St DA12 ....30 C8
Peal Cl ME3 ....34 E5
Pear Tree Ave ME20 ....75 D1
Pear Tree Cl Bexley DA8 ...8 D6
   Cranbrook ME17 ....169 D3
   Swanley BR8 ....39 D7
Pear Tree La
   Gillingham ME7 ....62 E7
   Maidstone ME15 ....107 B6
Pear Tree PI ME13 ....32 B3
Pear Tree Row ME17 ....108 B5
Pear Tree Way ME9 ....65 A5
Pearesswood Rd DA8 ....8 F6
Pearl Ct E16 ....2 A7
Pearse PI TN3 ....166 B5
Pearson Way DA1 ....26 F6
Pearson's Green Rd
   TN12 ....136 F3
Pearson's Green Rd
   TN12 ....136 D5
Peartree Cotts ME8 ....64 B8
Peartree La DA12,ME3 ...32 A2
Pease Hill TN15 ....54 F4
Peasley La TN17 ....167 D6
Peat Way ME3 ....20 E6
Peckham Cl DA15 ....23 E5
Peckham Ct ME2 ....47 C8
Peckham Ct TN12 ....119 F6
Peckham House [6] BR5 ...38 D1
Peckham Hurst Rd TN11 ...102 E7

Peel Rd BR6 ....51 C5
Peel St ME14 ....92 A6
Peel Yates Ho [12] SE18 ...1 E2
Pegasus Ct ME17 ....123 C7
Pegasus Ct DA12 ....30 C5
Peggotty Cl ME3 ....32 B3
Pegley Gdns SE12 ....22 A6
Pegwell St SE18 ....6 E7
Pelham Cotts DA5 ....25 B7
Pelham Prim Sch DA7 ....8 A4
Pelham Rd Bexley DA7 ....8 A4
   Gravesend DA11 ....30 A8
Pelham Terr Barr DA11 ...29 F8
Pelican Cl ME2 ....46 C6
Pelican St ME18 ....104 E7
Pell Cl TN5 ....175 A6
Pellipar Gdns SE18 ....1 F1
Pellipar Rd SE18 ....1 F1
Pells La TN15 ....71 A7
Pemberton Gdns BR8 ....39 E7
Pemberton Rd [4] ME2 ...47 C8
Pemble Cl TN12 ....135 A7
Pembroke ME4 ....48 B8
Pembroke Cl DA8 ....4 D2
Pembroke Ct ME14 ....48 A4
Pembroke Gdns ME8 ....63 E4
Pembroke Par DA8 ....4 C1
Pembroke PI DA11 ....41 B8
Pembroke Rd Bromley BR1 ...36 D7
   Coxheath ME17 ....106 C3
   Erith DA8 ....4 D1
   Newham E6 ....1 F7
   Sevenoaks TN13 ....84 B2
   Tonbridge TN9 ....117 A1
Pembroke Rise ME4 ....48 A7
Pembury Cl TN2 ....150 D7
Pembury Cres DA14 ....24 E6
Pembury Cty Prim Sch
   TN2 ....150 D8
Pembury Gdns ME16 ....91 D3
Pembury Gr TN9 ....133 C8
Pembury Grange TN2 ....150 A6
Pembury Hall Rd
   TN11,TN2 ....134 C3
Pembury Hospl TN2 ....150 B7
Pembury Rd Erith DA7 ....7 E8
   Pembury TN11 ....134 A2
   Royal Tunbridge Wells TN2 ...149 F4
   Tonbridge TN11,TN9 ....133 D7
Pembury Vineyard* TN2 ...134 F1
Pembury Walks
   TN11,TN9 ....134 C2
Pemdevon Rd ME7 ....49 E2
Pen Way TN10 ....117 E5
Pencroft Dr DA1 ....26 C8
Penda Rd DA8 ....8 B7
Pendennis Rd
   Orpington BR6 ....52 C8
   Sevenoaks TN13 ....84 B4
Penderel Mews TN30 ...183 B8
Pendlebury Ho SE18 ....5 G6
Pendragon Rd BR1,SE12 ...22 A5
Pendragon Sec Sch BR1 ...22 A5
Pendrell St TN5 ....174 F5
Penenden DA3 ....56 F8
Penenden Ct ME14 ....92 B7
Penenden Heath Rd ME14 ...92 C7
Penenden St ME14 ....92 A6
Penfold Cl Chatham ME5 ...62 B7
   Maidstone ME15 ....107 E5
Penfold Hill ME17 ....108 B8
Penfold House [14] SE18 ...1 E2
Penfold La DA5 ....24 D7
Penfold Way ME15 ....106 F6
Penfolds Cl TN10 ....117 C5
Penford Gdns SE9 ....5 D4
Pengarth Rd DA5 ....7 D1
Penguin Cl ME2 ....46 D6
Penhale Cl BR6 ....52 A8
Penhall Rd SE7 ....1 D2
Penhill Rd DA5 ....24 C8
Penhurst Cl ME14 ....92 F5
Penlee Cl TN8 ....112 C2
Penmon Rd SE2 ....3 A1
Penn Gdns BR7 ....37 B7
Penn La DA5 ....7 E1
Penn Yd TN2 ....150 C6
Pennant Rd ME1 ....61 C7
Pennell Cl DA1 ....26 D8
Pennine Way Erith DA2 ...8 E6
   Maidstone ME15 ....93 A1
Pennington Cl DA11 ....29 E5
Pennine Wlk TN2 ....149 D5
Pennington Manor [1]
   TN4 ....132 F2
Pennington PI TN4 ....133 B1
Pennington Rd TN4 ....133 A2
Pennington Way SE12 ...22 B6
Penny Cress Gdns ME1 ...91 C3
Pennyfields TN17 ....169 D4
Pennyroyal Ave E6 ....2 A7
Penpool La DA16 ....7 C5
Penn Manor [4] ME7 ...48 C6
Penshurst Ave DA15 ....7 A1

Penshurst CE Prim Sch
   TN11 ....131 A4
Penshurst Cl
   Gillingham ME8 ....49 E2
   New Barn DA3 ....43 D7
   West Kingsdown TN15 ....55 E4
Penshurst Enterprise Ctr
   TN11 ....131 B4
Penshurst Place* TN11 ...131 B4
Penshurst Rd Bexley DA7 ...7 F4
   Penshurst TN3,TN11 ....131 A5

Penshurst Rd continued
   Poundsbridge TN11,TN3 ...147 E1
Penshurst Sta TN11 ...114 F1
Penshurst Vineyard* TN11 ...130 F5
Penshurst Way BR5 ....38 C6
Penstocks The ME15 ....91 D2
Pensular Park Rd SE7 ....1 A1
Penton Ho [3] SE2 ....3 D4
Pentstemon Dr DA10 ....11 E2
Penventon Cl [3] RM18 ...13 A5
Pepingstraw Cl ME19 ....88 D2
Pepper Cl E6 ....1 F6
Pepper Hill DA11 ....29 E6
Pepper Hill La DA11 ....29 E6
Pepy's Way ME7 ....46 F1
Pepys Cl [4] Dartford DA1 ...10 A1
   Northfleet DA11 ....29 D7
   Tilbury RM18 ....13 E6
Pepys Cres E16 ....1 A7
Pepys Rise BR6 ....37 F2
Perch La TN3 ....151 D5
Percival Rd BR6 ....51 B8
Percy Rd DA7 ....7 E5
Percy St [3] RM17 ....12 C8
Percy Terr TN4 ....149 A6
Peregrine Cl DA16 ....6 F7
Peregrine Dr ME19 ....89 A2
Peridot St E6 ....1 E8
Perie Row [9] ME7 ....48 A6
Perimeter Rd ME20 ....75 C3
Periton Rd SE9 ....22 F7
Perkins Cl DA9 ....11 D2
Perpins Rd SE9 ....23 D6
Perran Cl DA3 ....42 F5
Perry Gr DA1 ....10 A3
Perry Hall Cl BR6 ....38 A2
Perry Hall Prim Sch BR6 ...37 F3
Perry Hall Rd BR6 ....38 A2
Perry Hill ME15 ....107 B6
Perry Ho DA14 ....24 A3
Perry Rd St Chatham ME4 ...47 E3
   Chislehurst BR7 ....23 E2
   Crayford DA1 ....8 E4
   Maidstone ME14 ....91 F6
   Northfleet DA11 ....29 F7
Perry Street Gdns BR7 ...23 E2
Perryfield St ME14 ....91 F6
Perrys La BR6,TN14 ....67 C6
Perth House [4] RM18 ...13 A5
Pescot Ave DA3 ....43 B6
Pested Bars Rd ME17 ....107 D5
Peter St [3] DA12 ....30 B8
Peterborough Gdns ME2 ...46 C6
Petersfield TN2 ....150 E7
Petersham Dr BR5 ....38 A7
Petersham Gdns BR5 ....37 F7
Peterstone Rd SE2 ....3 B4
Petham Court Cotts BR8 ...39 F4
Petham Gn ME8 ....49 C2
Petlands ME17 ....107 D5
Petrie House [3] SE18 ....6 A8
Pett Lane ME9 ....80 B7
Pett St SE18 ....1 D1
Petten Cl BR5 ....38 D1
Petten Gr BR5 ....38 D1
Petteridge La TN12 ....137 D8
Pettits Row TN12 ....137 C8
Pettman Cres SE28,SE18 ...2 D3
Petts Wood Rd BR5 ....37 C4
Petts Wood Sta BR5 ....37 C4
Petworth Rd DA6 ....8 A2
Peverel E6 ....2 A2
Peverel Dr ME14 ....93 A5
Peverel Gn ME8 ....63 D4
Peverill Ct [18] DA2 ....10 B1
Pheasant Cl E16 ....1 A6
Pheasant La ME15 ....107 B8
Pheasant Rd ME4 ....48 C2
Phelps Cl TN15 ....55 E4
Philimore Cl SE18 ....2 E1
Philipot Almshouse SE9 ...5 F1
Philipot Path SE9 ....5 E1
Philippa Gdns SE9 ....5 D2
Phillip Ave BR8 ....39 D5
Phillips Cl DA1 ....9 B1
Phillips Ct ME8 ....49 B2
Philpots La TN11 ....115 E6
Philpott's Cross TN18 ....178 E2
Phineas Pett Rd SE9 ....5 E1
Phipps Ho [4] SE7 ....1 B1
Phoenix Cotts ME18 ....104 D6
Phoenix Dr Orpington BR2 ...50 D7
   Wateringbury ME18 ....104 E7
Phoenix Ind Est ME2 ....47 B7
Phoenix Pk ME15 ....107 F4
Phoenix PI DA1 ....26 D8
Phoenix Yard Cotts ME18 ...89 F1
Picardy Manorway DA17 ...4 B3
Picardy Rd DA17 ....4 A2
Picardy St DA17 ....4 A1
Piccadilly The [4] ME5 ...48 B3
Pickering Ct [5] DA2 ....10 B1
Pickering Ho [20] DA2 ...10 B1
Pickering St ME15 ....107 B6
Pickford Cl DA7 ....7 E4
Pickford La DA7 ....7 E4
Pickford Rd DA7 ....7 E5
Pickforde La TN5 ....176 D1
Pickhill Oast TN30 ....183 B4
Pickhurst La BR2 ....36 A1
Pickle's Way ME3 ....16 A6
Pickmoss La TN14 ....69 E3
Pickwick Cres ME1 ....47 D3
Pickwick Ct SE9 ....22 F7
Pickwick Gdns DA11 ....29 D5
Pickwick House DA11 ...29 D5

ickwick Way BR7 ...... .23 C2
iedmont Rd SE12 .... .8 D1
ier Approach Rd ME7 ....48 D7
ier Par **3** E16 .... .2 A5
ier Pl ME2 .... .34 A3
ier Rd Erith DA8 .... .8 F8
  Gillingham ME7 ....54 F7
  Newham E16 .... .2 A4
  Northfleet DA11 .... .12 F1
  Swanscombe DA9 .... .11 B3
ier Rd Ind Est ME7 ....48 D7
ier Way SE28 .... .3 D2
ierce Mill La TN11 ....119 C6
iermont Pl BR1 .... .36 E7
igdown La TN8 ....129 D4
iggott's Cross TN8 ......113 D7
iggott's Rd DA13 .... .45 B2
ike Cl BR1 .... .22 B3
ikefields ME8 .... .49 C2
ikefish La TN12,ME18 ...120 F2
ikey La ME19 .... .89 C6
ike La TN12 ....140 A5
ilgrim's Way Cotts TN15 . .70 A2
ilgrims Ct Dartford DA1 ...10 A2
  Greenwich SE3 .... .5 A6
ilgrims Lakes ME17 .....110 E6
ilgrims Rd
  Upper Halling ME2 .... .59 F6
  Wouldham ME1 .... .60 E5
ilgrims View
  Maidstone,Sandling ME14 . .76 E3
  Swanscombe DA9 .... .11 C1
ilgrims Way Boxley ME14 ..77 E3
  Broad Street ME14,ME17 ..94 D6
  Cuxton ME2 .... .46 C3
  Dartford DA1 .... .27 B8
  Detling ME14 .... .78 B1
  Eccles ME20 .... .76 B6
  Hollingbourne ME17 ..... .94 F3
  Lenham ME17 ....111 B7
  Otford TN14 .... .68 E3
ilgrims Way
  ME2,ME6,ME19 .... .59 D3
  Wigo Village ME19 ...... .73 B7
  Wrotham TN15 .... .72 A3
  Wrotham TN15 .... .72 C4
ilgrims Way E TN14 ..... .69 D3
ilgrims Way W
  Otford TN13,TN14 .... .68 D3
  Otford TN14 .... .68 F3
ilgrims' Rd DA10 .... .11 E3
ilkington Rd BR6 .... .51 C8
illar Box La TN11 ....102 D5
illar Box Rd TN15 .... .85 E5
ilot Rd ME1 .... .61 C8
ilots Pl DA12 .... .13 C1
imp's Court Cotts ME15 ..106 E6
imp's Court Farm Ctr
  ME15 ....106 E6
impernel Cl ME14 .... .93 B4
impernel Way ME5 ...... .61 E4
inchbeck Rd BR6 .... .51 F4
incott Rd DA6 .... .8 A3
incroft Wood DA3 .... .43 C6
ine Ave DA12 .... .30 D7
ine Cl Larkfield ME20 .... .75 A2
  Swanley BR8 ....39 F5
ine Glade BR6 .... .50 F6
ine Gr Edenbridge TN8 ...112 B2
  Gillingham ME7 .... .63 A5
  Maidstone ME14 .... .92 B6
ine Ho **3** ME4 .... .47 F4
ine House **3** ME5 .... .61 F5
ine Lodge ME16 .... .91 C3
ine Pl ME15 .... .91 E1
ine Rd ME2 .... .46 F6
ine Ridge TN10 ....117 B6
ine Rise DA13 .... .44 A3
ine Tree La TN15 .... .86 A2
ine View TN15 .... .87 C7
inecrest Gdns BR6 ...... .51 B6
inecroft DA16 .... .7 A7
inecroft Wood DA3 ..... .43 C6
inehurst Chislehurst BR7 ..23 B2
  Sevenoaks TN14 .... .84 E6
inehurst Wlk **4** BR6 ..... .37 D1
ineneedle La TN13 ...... .84 B4
ine Rd BR1 .... .36 E7
inesfield La ME19 .... .73 B6
inewood BR7 .... .23 A2
inewood Ave
  Sevenoaks TN13 .... .84 D6
  Sidcup DA15,23 .... .23 A6
inewood Cl Orpington BR6 .37 D1
  Paddock Wood TN12 ....135 F6
inewood Ct TN4 ....133 A1
inewood Dr Chatham ME5 ..77 D8
  Orpington BR6 .... .51 E5
inewood Gdns TN4 .....133 A1
inewood Dr Bromley BR2 ..36 A5
  Erith SE2 .... .7 D8
  Royal Tunbridge Wells TN2 .149 D5
inkham TN12 ....120 A5
inkham Gdns TN12 .....120 A6
inks Hill BR8 .... .39 E4
innacle Hill DA7 .... .8 A3
innacle Hill N DA7 .... .8 B3
innacles The ME4 .... .34 C1
innell Rd SE9 .... .5 D3
innock La TN12 .... .29 C4
innock's Ave DA11 ..... .30 B7
intail Cl Grain ME3 ...... .21 B6
  Newham E6 .... .1 E8
intails The ME4 .... .34 B1
Pinto Way SE3 .... .5 B3
Pinton Hill TN5 ....176 B3

Pioneer Way BR8 .... .39 E6
Piper's Green Rd TN16 .... .97 B7
Pipers Cl TN5 ....175 A4
Pipers La TN16 .... .97 A8
Pippenhall SE9 .... .6 B1
Pippin Cl ME17 ....106 B2
Pippin Croft ME7 .... .63 A6
Pippin Rd TN12 ....119 F6
Pippin Way ME17 .... .89 A2
Pippins The DA13 .... .44 A3
Pirbright Cl ME5 .... .62 D2
Pirie St E16 .... .1 B5
Pirrip Cl DA12 .... .30 F6
Pit La TN8 ....112 C4
Pitfield DA3 .... .42 F5
Pitfield Cres SE28 .... .3 A5
Pitfield Dr DA13 .... .57 F7
Pitfold Rd SE12 .... .5 A1
Pitt Rd Langley Heath ME17 ..109 A2
  Maidstone ME16 .... .91 B1
  Orpington BR6 .... .51 C6
Pittlesden TN30 ....183 A7
Pittlesden Pl **1** TN30 .....183 A7
Pittsmead Ave BR2 ...... .36 A2
Pittswood Cotts TN11 ...118 A8
Pix's La TN17 ....182 A3
Pixot Hill TN12 .... .136 B2
Pizien Well Rd ME18 ....104 B7
Place Farm Ave BR6 ..... .37 D1
Place La ME9 .... .64 D4
Plain Rd TN12 ....138 C4
Plain The TN17 ....167 E8
Plains Ave ME15 .... .92 C1
Plaistow Gr BR1 .... .22 B1
Plaistow La BR1 .... .36 C8
Plaistow Sq ME14 ...... .92 C6
Plane Ave DA11 .... .29 D8
Plane Tree Ho SE7 ...... .1 C1
Plane Wlk TN10 .... .117 C7
Plantagenet Ho SE18 .... .1 F3
Plantation Cl DA9 .... .10 F1
Plantation Dr BR5 ...... .38 D1
Plantation La ME14 ..... .93 A3
Plantation Rd Erith DA8 ..9 A6
  Gillingham ME7 .... .49 A6
  Hextable BR8 .... .26 A2
Plantation The SE3 ...... .5 A5
Plat The TN8 ....112 D1
Platt CE Prim Sch TN15 ..87 C7
Platt Comm TN15 .... .87 C7
Platt House La TN15 ..... .72 C6
Platt Ind Est TN15 ...... .86 C5
Platt The Front TN2 .....163 B1
  Sutton Valence ME17 ...124 E7
Platt's Heath Prim Sch
  ME17 ....110 F2
Platters The ME8 .... .49 D2
Plaxdale Green Rd TN15 ..71 D7
Plaxtol Cl BR1 .... .36 C8
Plaxtol CE Prim Sch TN15 ..101 C7
Plaxtol Rd DA8 .... .65 B6
Playstool Rd ME9 .... .65 A6
Pleasance Rd BR5 .... .38 B6
Pleasant Ave ME7 .... .48 A6
Pleasant View DA8 ...... .4 E1
Pleasant View PH .... .51 C5
Pleasaunce Ct SE9 ...... .5 F3
Pleasure House Rd 125 A8
Plewis Ho ME7 .... .48 F4
Plomley Cl ME8 .... .63 D4
Plough Cotts ME17 .....108 E2
Plough Hill TN15 .... .86 F4
Plough Wents Rd ME17 ..108 B2
Ploughmans Wlk TN8 ...112 C3
Ploughmans Way
  Chatham ME5 .... .62 A1
  Gillingham ME8 .... .63 E6
Plover Cl Chatham ME5 .. .62 C1
  Marlpit Hill TN8 ....112 C3
Plover Rd ME20 .... .74 F2
Plowenders Cl ME19 ....73 D2
Pluckley Cl ME8 .... .49 C3
Pluckley Rd TN27 ....143 E8
Plug La DA13 .... .58 D5
Plum La SE18 .... .6 C7
Plum Tree Cotts TN18 ...184 E8
Plum Tree Rd ME9 ...... .79 B8
Plumcroft Prim Sch SE18 ..6 C8
Plumey Feather Cotts
  TN3 ....160 E3
Plummer La ME19 ...... .182 F6
Plummers Croft TN13 ... .83 E6
Plumpton Wlk **4** ME15 ..107 F6
Plumstead Common Rd
  SE18 .... .6 D8
Plumstead High St SE18,SE2 ..2 E1
Plumstead Manor Sch
  SE18 .... .6 D8
Plumstead Rd SE18 ..... .2 C2
Plumtree Gr ME7 .... .63 A6
Plumtree Rd TN27 ......140 F7
Plumtrees ME16 .... .91 A2
Plumtree Rd TN13 ...... .84 C3
Plymouth Ho TN13 ..... .84 C3
Plymouth Rd Bromley BR1 ..36 B8
  Newham E16 .... .1 A8
Plympton Cl **8** DA12 .... .3 E3
Plymstock Rd DA16 ..... .7 C7
Pocock La ME17 .... .62 C5
Pochard Cl ME4 .... .34 B1
Pococks Bank TN8 .....113 C3
Podkin Wood ME5 ...... .76 F8
Pointer Cl SE28 .... .3 D7
Pointer Sch The SE3 ..... .5 B5
Polebrook Rd SE3 .... .5 C4

Polegate Cotts RM17 .... .11 E8
Polesden Rd TN2 ....149 D2
Polhill TN13,TN14 ......175 A4
Polhill Dr ME5 .... .61 F2
Police Station Rd ME15 ..89 C8
Pollard Cl E16 .... .1 A6
Pollard Ct ME7 .... .48 C5
Pollard Wlk DA14 ...... .24 C2
Polley Cl TN2 ....150 D7
Pollyhaugh DA4 .... .54 E7
Polperro Cl BR6 .... .37 F3
Polthorne Gr SE18 ...... .2 D1
Polytechnic St **14** SE18 .. .2 A2
Pond Cl SE3 .... .5 A5
Pond Farm Rd
  Hucking ME17 .... .79 D1
  Oad Street ME9 .... .65 F5
Pond La TN15 .... .85 E2
Pond Path BR7 .... .23 B2
Pondfield La DA12 ...... .31 E1
Pondfield Rd BR6 .... .51 B7
Pondwood Rise BR6 .... .37 E2
Pontefract Rd BR1 ...... .22 A3
Pontoise Cl TN13 .... .83 F5
Pook La TN27 ....158 D3
Poona Rd TN1 ....149 B2
Pootings Rd TN8 ....128 E7
Pope Dr TN12 ....139 E4
Pope House La TN30 ....173 B4
Pope Rd BR2 .... .36 C4
Pope St SE16 .... .91 C2
Pope Street SE9 .... .22 F7
Popes Cotts TN17 ......168 C4
Popes Wood ME14 ..... .92 F6
Poplar Ave Gravesend DA12 ..30 C4
  Orpington BR6 .... .51 B8
Poplar Cl ME3 .... .34 E3
Poplar Gr ME16 .... .189 D4
Poplar Gr ME16 .... .91 C5
Poplar Mount DA17 .... .7 C4
Poplar Pl SE28 .... .3 A2
Poplar Rd Rochester ME2 ..46 E5
  Wittersham TN30 ....189 D4
Poplar Wlk DA13 .... .44 A3
Poplars Cl DA3 .... .43 C6
Poplars The DA12 ...... .30 E8
Poplicans Rd ME2 ...... .46 B3
Poppy Cl Gillingham ME7 ..48 A4
  Maidstone ME16 .... .91 D3
Popular Cl ME7 .... .46 F5
Porchester Cl
  Hartley DA3 .... .42 F5
  Maidstone ME15 ....107 A6
Porcupine Cl SE9 .... .22 E6
Porrington Cl BR7 ...... .37 A8
Port Ave DA9 .... .11 A1
Port Cl Chatham ME5 .... .62 B3
Port Victoria Rd ME3 .... .21 C8
Porter Cl RM20 .... .11 C8
Porter Rd E6 .... .1 F7
Porters Cl TN12 ....151 F6
Porters Wlk ME1 .... .47 C5
Porters Wood TN12 ....151 E6
Porteus Cl DA1 .... .26 D6
Porthkerry Ave DA16 ... .7 A3
Portland Ave
  Gravesend DA12 .... .30 B6
  Sidcup DA15 .... .24 A4
Portland Cres SE9 .... .22 E6
Portland Pl **1** ME6 ...... .75 A8
Portland Rd Bromley BR1 ..22 C3
  Chislehurst SE9 .... .22 F5
  Gillingham ME7 .... .48 E6
  Northfleet DA11 .... .12 D1
  Woulcham ME1 .... .60 C4
Portland St **1** ME4 ...... .48 B2
Portland Villas DA12 .... .30 B7
Portman Cl Bexley DA7 .. .7 E4
  Dartford DA5 .... .25 E7
Portman Pk TN9 ....117 C3
Portobello Par TN15 .... .56 A2
Portree Mews ME7 ..... .48 E3
Portsdown DA14 .... .91 B2
Portsea Rd RM18 ....13 C6
Portsmans Cotts ME19 ..89 B5
Portsmouth Cl ME2 .....46 D6
Portway Rd ME3 .... .33 B7
Portway Gdns SE18 ..... .5 D7
Post Barn Rd ME4 ...... .47 F2
Post Office Rd **12** TN18 ..178 F2
Postern La TN9,TN11 ...117 C1
Postley Commercial Ctr
  ME15 .... .92 A2
Postley Rd ME15 .... .92 A1
Postmill Dr ME15 .... .91 F1
Potash La TN15 .... .87 C6
Potter's La TN14 .... .82 A4
Pottery Rd Coldblow DA5 ..25 C6
  Hoo St Werburgh ME3 .. .34 D5
Potyn Ho ME1 .... .47 C4
Poulters Wood BR2 .... .50 D5
Pound Bank Cl TN15 .... .55 F2
Pound Cl BR6 .... .51 D8
Pound Court Dr BR6 .... .51 D8
Pound Green Ct **4** DA5 ..25 A8
Pound Ho TN11 ....118 E8
Pound La Halstead TN14 ..66 E4
  Sevenoaks TN13 .... .84 C3
Pound Park Rd SE7 ..... .1 D2
Pound Pl SE9 .... .6 A1
Pound Rd TN12 ....119 F6
Poundfield Rd TN18 .....186 B5

Poundsbridge Hill
  TN11,TN3 ....147 D7
Poundsbridge La TN11 ...131 D2
Pounsley Rd TN13 ...... .83 E6
Pout Rd ME5 .... .74 F7
Poverest Prim Sch BR5 .. .38 A4
Poverest Rd BR5 .... .38 A4
Povey Ave ME7 .... .33 C2
Powder Mill La
  Dartford DA1 .... .26 F6
  Leigh TN11 ....116 B1
  Royal Tunbridge Wells TN4 ..149 B8
  Tonbridge TN11 ....116 E2
Powdermill Cl TN4 ......149 C8
Powell Ave DA2 .... .27 E6
Powell Cl ME20 .... .76 A3
Powell Rd DA1 .... .9 C8
Power-nd Iest DA8 ...... .9 A4
Powerscroft Rd DA14 ....24 C2
Powis St SE18 .... .2 A3
Pownall Rd ME2 .... .33 C1
Powster Rd BR1 .... .22 B3
Powys Cl DA7 .... .7 D8
Poynder Rd RM18 ...... .13 B6
Poynings Cl BR6 .... .52 C8
Poyntell Cres BR7 ...... .37 D8
Poyntell Rd TN12 ....139 F4
Pragnell Rd SE12 .... .22 B6
Prall's La TN12 ....135 E2
Pratling St ME20 .... .76 C4
Pratt's Bottom Prim Sch
  TN14 .... .67 C8
Premier Par ME20 ...... .75 E1
Prentiss Cl SE17 .... .7 A2
Prescott Ave BR5 ...... .37 B3
Presentation Ho **9** DA12 ..30 B8
Prestburg Sq SE9 ...... .22 F4
Preston Ave ME7 .... .48 E1
Preston Ct DA14 .... .24 B5
Preston Dr DA7 .... .7 C6
Preston Hall Hospl ME20 ..75 F1
Preston Ho **1** SE18 ...... .2 A2
Preston Rd Northfleet DA11 ..29 E7
  Tonbridge TN9 ....117 A1
Prestons Rd BR2 .... .50 A8
Prestwood Cl SE18 ..... .7 A7
Pretoria Ho **4** Erith DA8 ..8 E7
  3 Maidstone ME15 .....107 E5
Pretoria Rd Chatham ME4 ..47 F2
  Gillingham ME7 .... .48 E4
Prettymans La TN8 .....112 F4
Pridmore Rd ME6 .... .74 F8
Priest's Wlk DA12 ...... .31 A6
Priestdale Ct ME4 ...... .47 F4
Priestfield Rd ME7 ...... .48 E5
Priestfield Stad
  (Gillingham FC) ME7 ... .48 E5
Priestfields ME1 .... .47 B3
Priestlands Park Rd DA15 ..23 F5
Priestley Dr Lunsford ME20 ..74 F4
  Tonbridge TN10 ....117 E7
Priestwood Rd DA13 ... .58 C5
Primrose Ave ME8 ...... .63 B5
Primrose Cl ME14 ...... .61 E7
Primrose Dr ME20 ...... .75 D1
Primrose Ho **10** ME15 ...107 E7
Primrose La ME19 ...... .89 B5
Primrose Terr DA12 .... .30 C7
Primrose Wlk ME12 ....136 A5
Prince Arthur Rd ME7 .. .48 B6
Prince Charles Ave
  Chatham ME5 .... .62 B4
  Sutton at Hone DA4 .... .41 D7
Prince Charles Ho DA4 .. .41 E7
Prince Consort Dr BR7 .. .37 D8
Prince Henry Rd SE7 ... .5 F3
Prince Imperial Rd
  Chislehurst BR7 .... .23 B1
  Woolwich SE18 .... .6 A6
Prince John Rd SE9 ..... .5 E2
Prince Of Wales Rd
  Greenwich SE3 .... .5 A6
  Newham E16 .... .1 C7
Prince Regent La E16 ... .1 C7
Prince Regent Sta E16 .. .1 C6
Prince Rupert Rd SE9 ... .5 F3
Prince's Plain BR2 ..... .36 E2
Prince's Plain Prim Sch
  BR2 .... .36 E2
Prince's St Rochester ME1 ..47 C5
  Royal Tunbridge Wells TN1 ..149 C3
Princes Ave Chatham ME5 ..62 B5
  Dartford DA1 .... .27 B8
  Orpington BR5 .... .37 E4
Princes Cl DA14 .... .24 D5
Princes Rd
  Dartford DA1,DA2 ...... .26 D7
  Gravesend DA12 .... .30 C5
  Hextable BR8 .... .26 A2
Princes St Bexley DA7 .. .7 F4
  Gravesend DA11 .... .13 B1
  Maidstone ME14 .... .92 A5
Princes View DA1 ...... .27 A7
Princess Alice Way SE28 ..2 D4
Princess Margaret Rd
  RM18 .... .14 D7
Princess Mary Ave ME4 ..48 B7
Princess Par BR6 .... .51 A7
Prinys Dr ME8 .... .63 C4
Priolo Rd SE7 .... .1 C1
Prior's Way TN8 ....145 A6
Priorsdean Cl ME16 .... .90 E1
Priorsford Ave BR5 ..... .38 B5
Priory Ave BR5 .... .37 E4
Priory Cl Bromley BR7 .. .36 F8
  Dartford DA1 .... .9 C1
  East Farleigh ME15 .....106 B8
Priory Ct **3** Dartford DA1 ..9 D1

Priory Ct *continued*
  Gillingham ME8 .... .49 A2
Priory Ctr The DA1 ..... .26 E8
Priory Dr SE2 .... .3 D1
Priory Fields DA4 ...... .54 F8
Priory Gate **1** ME14 .... .92 A5
Priory Gdns Dartford DA1 ..9 D2
  Orpington* BR6 .... .38 B2
Priory Gr Aylesford ME20 ..75 D1
  Tonbridge TN9 ....133 B8
Priory Hill DA1 .... .9 D1
Priory Ho **3** SE7 .... .5 C8
Priory La DA4 .... .40 F1
Priory Leas SE9 .... .22 E7
Priory Mews DA2 .... .27 C8
Priory Pl DA1 .... .9 D1
Priory Rd Dartford DA1 .. .9 D1
  Gillingham ME8 .... .49 A2
  Maidstone ME15 .... .92 A3
  Rochester ME7 .... .47 A6
  Tonbridge TN9 ....133 C8
Priory Sch The BR5 ..... .38 C1
Priory St TN9 ....133 B8
Priory Way TN30 ....183 C7
Priory Wlk TN9 ....133 B8
Pristling La TN12 ....155 B8
Pritchard Ct ME7 .... .48 A7
  Progress Est The ME15 ..108 A4
Prospect Ave ME2 ...... .47 B8
Prospect Cl DA17 .... .4 A2
Prospect Cotts
  Lamberhurst TN3 ....166 A3
  Pratt's Bottom BR6 .... .52 C2
Prospect Gr DA12 ...... .30 D8
Prospect Pk TN4 ....132 F1
Prospect Pl Bromley BR2 ..36 B6
  Collier Street TN12 .....121 C2
  Dartford DA1 .... .9 E1
  Gravesend DA12 .... .30 D8
  Grays RM17 .... .12 A8
  Maidstone ME16 .... .91 E3
Prospect Rd
  Royal Tunbridge Wells TN2 ..149 C3
  Royal Tunbridge
  Wells,Southborough TN4 ..132 F1
  Sevenoaks TN13 .... .84 C4
Prospect Row
  Chatham ME4 .... .48 A3
  Gillingham ME7 .... .48 A6
Prospect Vale SE18 ..... .1 E2
Prospero Ho **2** DA17 ... .4 A1
Provender Way ME14 ...92 E5
Providence Chapel TN12 ..138 C6
Providence Cotts
  Groombridge TN3 ....161 C7
  Higham ME3 .... .32 B2
Providence La ME1 ..... .47 C5
Providence Pl TN27 ....141 A7
Providence St DA9 ..... .11 B2
Prudhoe Ct DA2 .... .10 B1
Pudding La Maidstone ME14 ..91 F4
  Seal TN15 .... .84 F6
Pudding Rd ME8 .... .63 F8
Puddingcake La TN17 ...182 C5
Puddledock La
  Hextable BR8,DA2 ...... .25 F2
  Ide Hill TN16 .... .97 A3
Puffin Rd ME3 .... .21 B5
Pullington Cotts TN17 ...180 L6
Pullman Mews SE12 ... .22 B5
Pullman Pl SE9 .... .5 E2
Pump Cl ME19 .... .74 D1
Pump La ME7,ME8 ..... .49 D3
Punch Croft DA3 .... .56 E7
Purbeck Rd ME4 .... .47 E2
Purcell Ave ME10 ......117 F6
Purfleet By-Pass RM19 ..10 D8
Purland Rd SE28,SE18 .. .2 F4
Purneys Rd SE9 .... .5 D3
Purrett Rd SE18 .... .2 F1
Purser Way ME7 .... .48 C2
Putlands L Ctr TN12 ....136 A5
Puttenden Rd TN11 ....101 F3
Pym Orch TN16 .... .82 C3
Pynham Ct SE9 .... .3 B3
Pyrus Cl ME5 .... .77 A8

Q

Quadrant The DA7 ...... .7 D7
Quaggy Wlk SE3 .... .5 A3
Quaker Cl TN13 ....174 B4
Quaker Dr TN17 ....169 D6
Quaker La TN17 ....169 D6
Quaker's Hall La TN13 .. .84 C5
Quakers Cl DA3 .... .42 E6
Quantock Cl DA12 .....149 D5
Quantock Rd DA1 ...... .8 C4
Quarries The ME17 ..... .107 C4
Quarry Cotts TN9 ....133 A7
Quarry Cotts TN15 .....174 D7
Quarry Hill TN15 .... .84 D4
Quarry Hill Par **3** TN9 ..133 B8
Quarry Hill Rd
  Borough Green TN15 ... .86 F6
  Tonbridge TN9 ....133 B8
Quarry Rd Maidstone ME15 ..92 A2
  Royal Tunbridge Wells TN1 ..149 B3
Quarry Rise TN15 ......133 A7
Quarry Sq ME14 .... .91 F5
Quarry Wood Ind Est
  ME20 .... .90 E8
Quay La ME4 .... .11 B3
Quayside ME4 .... .48 B8

Quebec Ave TN16 ....81 D1
Quebec Cotts **9** TN16 ....81 D1
Quebec Rd RM18 ....13 A5
Quebec Sq **10** TN16 ....81 D1
Queen Anne Ave RM2 ....36 A6
Queen Anne Gate DA7 ....7 D4
Queen Anne Rd ME11 ....92 B4
Queen Borough Gdns BR7 ....23 D2
Queen Elizabeth
  Military Hospl The SE18 ....5 E7
Queen Elizabeth Sq
  ME15 ....107 D6
Queen Mary's Hospl DA14 .....24 A2
Queen Mother Ct The
  ME1 ....47 B4
Queen St Bexley DA7 ....7 F4
  Chatham ME4 ....48 A4
  Erith DA8 ....8 E8
Queen's Ave
  Maidstone ME16 ....91 D5
  Snodland ME6 ....75 A8
Queen's Dr TN14 ....84 C7
Queen's Farm Rd DA12 ....31 E7
Queen's Gdns TN4 ....149 B6
Queen's Mews **15** TN18 ...179 A2
Queen's Pas BR7 ....23 B2
Queen's Rd Bexley DA16 ....7 B5
  Bromley BR1 ....36 A7
  Chatham ME1 ....48 D1
  Chislehurst BR7 ....23 B2
  Gillingham ME7 ....48 C4
  Hawkhurst TN18 ....179 A2
  Maidstone ME16 ....91 C4
  Royal Tunbridge Wells TN4 ..149 B6
  Snodland ME6 ....75 A8
Queendown Ave ME8 ....63 D5
Queens Cotts TN5 ....174 E6
Queens Ct Edenbridge TN8 ....112 D1
  11 Hawkhurst TN18 ......179 A2
  1 Sidcup DA14 ....24 A4
Queens Gate Gdns BR7 ....27 D8
Queens Gdns DA2 ....27 B7
Queens Ho ME16 ....91 B3
Queens Rd Erith DA8 ....8 E8
  Gravesend DA12 ....30 C5
Queens Way ME14 ....79 B1
Queenscroft Rd SE9 ....5 D1
Queensland Ho **2** E16 ......2 A5
Queensway
  Allhallows-on-Sea ME3 ......19 D9
  Orpington BR6 ....50 A6
  Orpington BR5 ....37 C3
Queenswood Rd
  Kit's Coty ME20 ....76 D7
  Sidcup DA15 ....24 A5
Quern The ME15 ....91 E1
Quernmore Cl BR1 ....22 A2
Quernmore Rd BR1 ....22 A2
Quested Way ME17 ....110 C6
Quickrells Ave ME3 ....16 B5
Quickthorn Cres ME5 ....61 E5
Quiet Nook BR2 ....50 D7
Quilter Gdns BR5 ....38 C1
Quilter Rd BR5 ....38 D1
Quilter St SE18 ....2 F1
Quincewood Gdns TN10 ......117 E7
Quinion Cl ME5 ....49 B5
Quinnell St ME8 ....49 E1
Quixote Cres ME2 ....33 B1

R

Rabbits Rd DA4 ....41 E7
Rablus Pl DA4 ....40 F3
Racefield Cl DA12 ....31 E1
Rackham Cl DA16 ....7 B5
Radfield Way DA15 ....23 D8
Radland Rd E16 ....1 A7
Radleigh Gdns ME1 ....47 E1
Radley Ho **15** SE2 ....3 D4
Radnor Ave DA16 ....7 B2
Radnor Cl BR7 ....23 E2
Radnor Cres SE18 ....7 A7
Raeburn Ave DA1 ....9 B2
Raeburn Cl TN10 ....117 E6
Raeburn Pl DA10 ....11 E2
Raeburn Rd DA15 ....13 E6
Rafford Way BR1 ....36 B6
Raggatt Pl ME15 ....92 B2
Ragge Way TN15 ....84 F7
Ragstone Rd BR7 ....37 A8
Raglan Ct SE12 ....5 A2
Raglan Prim Sch BR2 ....36 C5
Raglan Rd Bromley BR2 ....36 C5
  Erith DA17 ....3 F2
  Woolwich SE18 ....2 B1
Ragstone Ct ME20 ....90 C8
Ragstone Rd ME15 ....93 A2
Railway App TN9 ....133 B8
Railway Cotts
  Cowden TN8 ....145 D8
  Marden TN12 ....138 D6
Railway Pl Erith DA17 ....4 A1
  19 Gravesend DA12 ......13 B1
Railway Sidings The DA13 .....44 B4
Railway St Chatham ME4 ......47 F4
  Gillingham ME7 ....48 D2
  Northfleet DA11 ....12 A2
Railway St Ind Pk ME7 ....48 D6
Railway Terr TN16 ....81 D1

Rainham Cl
  Maidstone ME15 ....92 A1
  Sidcup SE9 ....6 E1
Rainham Mark Gram Sch
  ME8 ....49 D2
Rainham Rd ME5 ....48 C3
Rainham Sch for Girls
  ME8 ....63 C8
Rainham Sh Ctr ME8 ....63 F8
Rainham Sta ME8 ....49 F1
Rainton Rd SE7 ....1 A1
Raleigh Mews **6** BR6 ....51 F5
Ramac Ind Est SE7 ....1 B1
Ramac Way SE7 ....1 B1
Ramillies Cl ME5 ....62 A6
Ramillies Rd DA15 ....7 B1
Rammell Mews TN17 ....169 D4
Rampion Cl ME14 ....92 E5
Ramsden Jun & Inf Sch
  BR5 ....38 C2
Ramsden La TN17 ....180 F4
Ramsden Rd Erith DA8 ....8 D7
  Orpington BR5,BR6 ....38 B1
Ramsgate Cl E16 ....1 C1
Ramslye Cotts TN3 ....162 D8
Ramslye Rd TN4 ....162 E8
Ramus Wood Ave BR6 ....51 E5
Rance Ho **15** SE18 ....1 E2
Rancliffe Gdns SE9 ....5 E3
Randall Cl DA8 ....8 C8
Randall Hill Rd TN15 ....71 F3
Randall Rd ME4 ....47 E1
Randall Row ME15 ....106 F5
Randle's La TN14 ....67 D5
Randolph App E16 ....1 C7
Randolph Cl DA7 ....8 C4
Randolph Cotts ME2 ....33 B1
Randolph Ho **17** DA11 .....48 C5
Randolph Rd
  Gillingham ME7 ....48 C5
  Orpington BR5 ....38 F1
Rangefield Rd BR1 ....22 A3
Rangeworth Rd DA15 ....6 E1
Rankine Rd TN2 ....149 D7
Ranleigh Gdns DA7 ....7 F7
Ranmore Path BR5 ....38 A5
Ranscombe Ct ME2 ....46 D5
Ranscombe Farm Cotts
  ME2 ....46 C4
Ransom Rd **1** SE7 ....1 C1
Ranters La TN17 ....167 C7
Ranters Oak TN17 ....181 B4
Ranworth Cl DA7,DA8 ....8 E5
Raphael Ct TN11 ....116 E7
Raphael Rd DA12 ....30 D8
Rashleigh Way DA4 ....41 C5
Ratcliffe Cl SE12 ....22 A8
Ratcliffe Highway
  High Halstow ME3 ....18 D5
  Hoo St Werburgh ME3 ....34 C7
Rathmore Rd
  Gravesend DA11 ....30 B8
  Greenwich SE7 ....1 B1
Raven Cl ME20 ....75 A1
Raven Ho **2** SE18 ....24 A3
Ravens Dane Cl ME15 ....93 A1
Ravens Knowle ME1 ....60 D4
Ravens Way SE12 ....5 A2
Ravens Wood Sch for Boys
  BR2 ....50 D7
Ravensbourne Coll of
  Design & Communication
  BR7 ....22 F3
Ravensbourne Rd
  Bromley BR1 ....36 A6
  Crayford DA1 ....9 A4
Ravensbourne Sch BR2 ....36 B4
Ravensbury Rd BR5 ....38 A5
Ravenscourt Rd BR5 ....38 B7
Ravenscroft Cl **1** E16 .....1 A8
Ravenscroft Cres SE9 ....22 F5
Ravenscroft Rd E16 ....1 A8
Ravenshill SE7 ....38 A8
Ravensleigh Gdns BR1 ....22 B3
Ravensquay Bsns Ctr BR5 ....38 A4
Ravenswood ME2 ....24 C7
Ravenswood Ave
  Rochester ME2 ....33 B1
  Royal Tunbridge Wells TN2 .149 D6
Ravensworth Rd SE9 ....22 F4
Ravine Gr SE18 ....6 E8
Rawdon Rd ME15 ....92 A1
Rawlings Cl **8** BR6 ....51 F5
Rawsthorne Cl E16 ....1 F5
Ray Lamb Way DA8 ....9 B7
Rayfield Cl Bromley BR2 ......36 E3
  Snodland ME2 ....60 A1
Rayford Cl DA1 ....9 C2
Rayleigh Cl ME15 ....108 E6
Rayleigh Rd E16 ....1 B5
Raymer Rd ME14 ....92 B8
Raymere Gdns SE18 ....6 E7
Raymond Postgate Ct **5**
  SE7 ....1 B6
Rayneham Jun & Inf Sch
  DA2 ....27 D5
Rayners Ct DA11 ....12 B1
Raynham Villas TN12 ....122 A4
Rays Hill DA4 ....41 C4

Read Way DA12 ....30 E3
Reader's Bridge Rd TN30 .....172 E4
Reading House **4** ME15 ...107 F5
Readscroft Rd ME8 ....63 D5
Rebecca Ct DA14 ....24 B4
Recreation Ave ME6 ....75 A8
Recreation Cl ME14 ....92 B6
Recreation Ground Rd
  TN30 ....183 B7
Rectory Bsns Ctr **2** DA14 ...24 B4
Rectory Cl Crayford DA1 ....8 E3
  Sidcup DA14 ....24 B4
  Snodland ME6 ....75 A8
  Wouldham ME1 ....60 C5
Rectory Dr TN3 ....132 D3
Rectory Field Cres SE7 ....1 C7
Rectory Fields TN17 ....169 D5
Rectory Grange ME1 ....47 B2
Rectory La Brasted TN16 ......82 C3
  Harrietsham ME17 ....110 E5
  Ightham TN15 ....86 C5
  Maidstone ME16 ....91 A1
  Sevenoaks TN13 ....84 C1
  Sidcup DA14 ....24 C4
  Sutton Valence ME17 ....124 C6
  Sutton Valence ME17 ....124 F7
Rectory La N ME19 ....74 E2
Rectory La S ME19 ....74 E1
Rectory Meadow DA13 ....29 A2
Rectory Paddock Sch BR5 ....38 C7
Rectory Park Rd TN12 ....153 A2
Rectory Pl SE18 ....2 A2
  3 Grays RM17 ....12 D8
  New Ash Green TN15 ....57 D5
  Orpington BR2 ....50 D3
  Swanscombe DA10 ....28 E8
  Tilbury RM18 ....13 D8
Reculver Wlk ME15 ....107 F7
Red Barracks Rd **4** SE18 ...1 F2
Red Cedars Rd BR6 ....37 E2
Red Hill Chislehurst BR7 ......23 B3
  Denton ME3 ....32 A2
Red Hill Hlth Ctr BR7 ....23 B3
Red House Gdns ME18 ....104 C7
Red House La DA6 ....7 E3
Red Lion Cl BR5 ....38 C3
Red Lion La SE18 ....6 A8
Red Lion Pl SE18 ....6 A6
Red Lodge Cres DA5 ....25 E5
Red Lodge Rd DA5 ....25 D5
Red Oak TN18 ....184 E8
Red Oak Cl BR6 ....51 B8
Red Oast Cotts TN5 ....177 C3
Red Robin Cotts ME9 ....65 B6
Red St DA13 ....29 B2
Redbank ME19 ....74 D2
Redbridge Cl ME5 ....62 C4
Redcliffe La ME14 ....92 B7
Redding Cl DA2 ....27 C6
Redding Ho SE18 ....1 E3
Reddy Rd DA8 ....8 F8
Rede Court Rd ME2 ....46 E8
Rede House SE18 ....90 F3
Redfern Ave ME7 ....48 E5
Redfern Rd ME12 ....22 A7
Redgate Dr BR2 ....50 B8
Redhill Rd DA5 ....56 F6
Redhill Wood DA3 ....57 A7
Redland Shaw ME4 ....47 E1
Redlands Rd TN13 ....83 F1
Redleaf Cl Erith DA17 ....8 A8
  Royal Tunbridge Wells TN2 .149 D6
Redmans La BR5,TN14 ....53 E4
Redpoll Wlk SE2 ....3 C6
Redpoll Wlk TN12 ....136 A5
Redruth Manor **3** ME7 .....48 C6
Redsells Cl ME15 ....93 A1
Redshank Rd ME4 ....34 B1
Redstart Cl E6 ....1 E8
Redvers Rd ME7 ....48 A2
Redwall La ME15, ME17 .....122 C6
Redwell La TN15 ....86 B4
Redwing Cl ME20 ....75 A2
Redwing Path SE28 ....2 D4
Redwing Rd ME5 ....62 B7
Redwings La TN2 ....134 E2
Redwood Cl Chatham ME5 ....62 B2
  Sidcup DA15 ....24 A7
Redwood Ct SE1 ....10 A3
Redwood Pk TN12 ....135 A5
Reed Ave BR6 ....51 E7
Reed Cl Eltham SE12 ....5 A2
  Newham E16 ....1 A8
Reed Court Cotts TN12 ......122 A5
Reed Court Farm Trail*
  TN17 ....122 A5
Reed St TN16 ....16 B6
Reedham Cres ME3 ....33 C7
Reeds Cotts TN17 ....170 A8
Reeds La TN11 ....101 E5
Reeves Cl TN12 ....139 E4
Reeves Cres DA8 ....39 D6
Reeves Ct Ditton ME19 ....75 A1
  Fordcombe TN3 ....147 B5
Reeves Rd SE18 ....6 B8
Reeves Terr TN5 ....176 E1
Reform Rd ME4 ....48 A4
Regal Ho SE2 ....3 C6
Regency Cl Gillingham ME8 ...63 C3
  West Kingsdown TN15 ....55 E4
Regency Hall **10** TN2 ....149 A2
Regency Ho TN2 ....149 B2
Regency Way DA7 ....7 E4
Regent Cl DA14 ....24 B4
Regent Pl TN2 ....149 D3
Regent Rd ME7 ....107 A8
Regent St ME14 ....92 A4
Regent Sq DA17 ....4 B2

Regent St TN17 ....181 E4
Regent's Pl SE3 ....5 A5
Regents Ct **2** DA11 ....13 B1
Regents Dr BR2 ....50 D5
Regina Ct TN4 ....148 F4
Reginald Ave ME2 ....46 C3
Reginald Rd ME16 ....91 E3
Reidhaven Rd SE18 ....2 F1
Reigate Rd BR1,SE12 ....22 A5
Reinden Gr ME15 ....92 F1
Rembrandt Ct TN10 ....117 E6
Rembrandt Dr DA11 ....29 E5
Remington Rd E6 ....1 E7
Rendlebury Ho **15** SE18 ....1 F7
Renfrew Cl E6 ....2 A6
Rennets Cl SE9 ....6 E3
Rennets Wood Ho SE9 ....6 D2
Rennets Wood Rd SE9 ....6 D2
Renown Rd ME5 ....62 C2
Renshaw Cl **7** DA17 ....7 F8
Renton Dr BR5 ....38 D2
Repository Rd SE18 ....1 F1
Repton Rd BR5 ....52 A6
Repton Way ME5 ....61 F4
Resolution Cl ME5 ....61 E5
Resolution Wlk SE18 ....11 F3
Resthaven Rd ME14 ....92 E4
Restharrow Way ME4 ....34 C1
Restons Cres SE9 ....6 E1
Retreat The Grays RM17 ......12 B8
  Orpington BR6 ....52 B4
Revell Rise SE18 ....6 F8
Revenge Rd ME5 ....77 C8
Reventlow Rd SE9 ....23 C7
Reynard Cl BR1 ....37 A6
Reynolds Cl TN12 ....117 E6
Reynolds Fields ME8 ....32 C6
Reynolds La TN4 ....148 F6
Reynolds Pl SE3 ....5 B7
Rhode St ME4 ....48 A4
Rhodes Ho **5** ME5 ....48 C2
Rhodewood Cl ME15 ....93 A1
Rhododendron Ave DA13 ....158 A2
Ribblesdale Rd DA2 ....27 C7
Ribston Cl BR2 ....36 F1
Ribston Gdns TN12 ....135 F7
Ricardo Path **8** SE28 ....3 C5
Rice Par BR5 ....37 D4
Richard Cl SE18 ....1 E2
Richard House Dr E16 ....1 F7
Richard St Chatham ME4 ......47 F4
  Rochester ME1 ....47 C3
Richard's Cl TN11 ....114 F2
Richardson Cl DA9 ....11 A2
Richardson Rd TN4 ....149 A5
Richborough Cl BR5 ....38 D5
Richborough Drive ME2 ....33 A1
Richings House BR5 ....38 A8
Richmer Rd DA8 ....9 A2
Richmond Cl Chatham ME5 ...62 B4
  Upper Upnor ME2 ....33 F1
Richmond Ct Lewisham BR1 ...22 B1
  Sevenoaks TN13 ....84 D4
Richmond City Inf Sch
  ME7 ....48 C6
Richmond Pl
  Royal Tunbridge Wells TN2 ..149 B1
  SE18 ....2 C2
Richmond Rd
  Gillingham ME7 ....48 C7
  2 Grays RM17 ....12 C8
Richmond Way ME15 ....107 A8
Richmount Gdns SE3 ....5 A4
Rickyard Path SE9 ....5 E3
Riddlesdale Ave TN4 ....149 A6
Riddons Rd SE12 ....22 C1
Rideout St SE18 ....1 F2
Rider Cl DA15 ....6 E1
Ridge Ave DA1 ....10 A3
Ridge Cl SE28 ....2 D4
Ridge La La DA3 ....58 A2
Ridge Meadow
  Cty Prim Sch ME5 ....61 F6
Ridge The
  Groombridge TN3 ....161 A6
  Orpington BR6 ....51 D8
  Sidcup DA15 ....24 F8
Ridge View SE18 ....117 D5
Ridge Way Crayford DA1 ....8 F1
  Marlpit Hill TN8 ....112 D4
Ridgebrook Rd SE3 ....5 C3
Ridgecroft Cl DA5 ....25 C7
Ridgelands DA3 ....132 C4
Ridgeway Dartford DA2 ....27 E3
  Gillingham ME8 ....50 A8
  Hurst Green TN19 ....184 A3
  Pembury TN2 ....150 D7
  The Moor TN18 ....184 E8
Ridgeway Ave DA12 ....30 B5
Ridgeway Bglws DA12 ....31 F1
Ridgeway Cres
  Orpington BR6 ....51 E7
  Tonbridge TN10 ....117 D4
Ridgeway The TN4 ....131 A4
Ridgewood DA3 ....43 C7
Ridgway ME16 ....91 B2
Ridgwell Rd E16 ....1 C8
Ridgy Field Cl TN15 ....72 A2

Riding La TN11 ....100 D2
Riding Pk TN11 ....116 D7
Ridings The
  Paddock Wood TN12 ....136 A7
  Royal Tunbridge Wells TN2 .149 F6
Ridley Ct BR6 ....51 C6
Ridley Rd Bexley DA16 ....7 B6
  Bromley BR2 ....36 A6
  Rochester ME1 ....47 B4
Riefield Rd SE9 ....6 C2
Riggs Way TN15 ....71 F3
Ring Cl BR1 ....22 B1
Ringden Ave TN12 ....135 F6
Ringer's Ct BR1 ....36 A6
Ringer's Rd BR1 ....36 A6
Ringle Gn TN18 ....186 C5
Ringlestone Cres ME14 ....91 F8
Ringlestone Rd ME17 ....95 D6
Ringlet Cl E16 ....1 B8
Ringlett Rd ME4 ....34 C2
Ringmer Way BR1 ....36 F4
Rings Hill TN11 ....116 B4
Ringshall Rd BR5 ....38 A6
Ringwood Ave BR6 ....52 C1
Ringwood Cl ME8 ....63 D8
Ringwood Rd ME15 ....107 C8
Ripley Cl BR1 ....36 F4
Ripley Rd Erith DA17 ....4 A2
  Newham E16 ....1 C1
Ripon Cl ME8 ....49 D3
Ripon Rd SE18 ....6 B8
Rippersley Rd DA16 ....7 A6
Rippolson Rd SE18 ....2 F1
Risden La TN18 ....185 D7
Rise The Crayford DA1 ....8 F3
  Gillingham ME4 ....47 A3
  Gillingham, Hempstead ME7 ..63 A3
  Gravesend DA12 ....30 E4
  Rochester ME1 ....47 D3
  Sevenoaks TN13 ....99 C7
  Sidcup DA5 ....24 C8
Risedale Rd DA7 ....8 C4
Riseden Rd TN5 ....174 C1
Ritch Rd ME6 ....74 E8
Ritter St SE18 ....6 A8
River Bank Cl **8** ME15 .....92 B4
River Cl ME15 ....106 A7
River Cotts BR5 ....38 C7
River Ct TN13 ....83 E5
River Dr ME2 ....46 F7
River Lawn Rd TN9 ....117 B1
River Park View BR5 ....38 B8
River Rd IG11 ....3 A8
River St ME7 ....48 A6
River View **1** Dartford DA1 ..10 A3
  Gillingham ME8 ....49 D3
  Greenwich SE7 ....1 C7
River View Cl **6** ME4 ....47 F2
River Way DA12 ....75 B4
River Wlk TN9 ....117 B1
Riverbank Rd BR1 ....22 A5
Riverdale Est TN9 ....133 D8
Riverdale Rd Erith DA8 ....4 C1
  Sidcup DA5 ....23 F2
  Woolwich SE18 ....2 F3
Riverhead Cl ME16 ....91 D6
Riverhead Cty Prim Sch
  TN13 ....83 F5
Riverhead Mews TN13 ....83 E4
Riverhill TN15 ....99 F6
Riverhill Cotts TN15 ....99 E5
Riverhill House Gdns*
  TN15 ....99 E5
Riverhope Mans SE18 ....19 E5
Rivers Cl ME18 ....104 E7
Rivers Wlk ME17 ....111 C5
Riversdale DA11 ....29 E5
Riverside Edenbridge TN8 ...112 C1
  Eynsford DA4 ....54 B8
  Greenwich SE7 ....1 B3
Riverside Cl BR5 ....38 C7
Riverside Cotts TN14 ....53 F1
Riverside Ct
  2 Orpington BR5 ....38 C4
  Tonbridge TN9 ....117 C1
Riverside Cty Pk* ME7 ....49 D5
Riverside East Rd ME4 ....34 C1
Riverside Ind Est DA1 ....9 F2
Riverside Rd DA14 ....24 E6
Riverside Rest TN14 ....84 C8
Riverside Way DA1 ....9 E2
Riverston Sch SE12 ....5 A2
Riverview Mts SE18 ....6 B7
Riverview Inf Sch DA12 ....30 E4
Riverview Jun Sch DA12 ......30 E4
Riverwood La BR7 ....37 D8
Rixon Ho SE18 ....6 B8
Roach St ME7 ....47 A7
Roan Ct ME2 ....46 F8
Robert Napier Sch The
  ME7 ....48 E3
Robert St Newham E16 ....2 B3
  Woolwich SE18 ....2 D2
Roberton Dr BR1 ....36 C8
Roberts Cl Eltham SE9 ....23 D7
  3 Orpington BR5 ....38 C4
Roberts Ho SE18 ....6 B8
Roberts Mews BR6 ....38 A1
Roberts Orchard Rd ME16 ....90 F3
Roberts Rd Erith DA17 ....63 E8
  Gillingham ME8 ....63 E8
  Snodland ME6 ....74 F8
Robertson House SE18 ....1 F6
Robin Cres E6 ....1 E8
Robin Ct ME1 ....47 D4
Robin Hill Dr BR7 ....22 E2

obin Hood Gn BR5 ....38 A4
obin Hood La Bexley DA6 ....7 E2
Chatham ME5 ....61 D1
obin Hood Lane (Lower)
ME5 ....61 F2
obin Hood Lane (Upper)
ME5 ....61 E1
obin Rd ❺ ME16 ....91 E4
obin Way BR5 ....38 B6
obina Cl DA8 ....7 D3
obina Ct BR8 ....40 A5
obina Ave DA11 ....29 D8
obins Ave ME17 ....111 C5
obins Cl ME17 ....111 C4
obins Ct Lewisham SE12 ....22 C5
Maidstone ME14 ....92 B7
obins Gr BR4 ....50 A7
obson Dr TN15 ....84 F8
obson Cl E6 ....1 E7
obson Dr Aylesford ME20 ...75 D2
Hoo St Werburgh ME3 ......34 D6
obson Ho SE18 ....6 A7
obyns Croft ❺ DA11 ....29 E5
obyns Way
Edenbridge TN8 ....128 D8
Sevenoaks TN13 ....83 F5
ocfort Rd ME5 ....75 A8
ochdale Ho TN11 ....149 C5
ochdale Rd
Royal Tunbridge Wells TN1 .149 C6
Woolwich SE2 ....3 B2
ochester Airport
ME1,ME5 ....61 C6
ochester Ave Bromley BR1 .36 B7
Rochester ME1 ....47 C4
ochester Castle* ME1 ......47 C6
ochester Cath* ME1 ....47 C6
ochester Cl ❶ DA16 ....7 B1
ochester Cres ME5 ....34 D6
ochester Ct ME2 ....47 E8
ochester Dr DA5 ....8 A1
ochester Dr ME14 ....93 D2
ochester Gate ME1 ....47 D5
ochester Gram Sch
for Girls ME1 ....47 C2
ochester Ho ❶ ME15 ......107 D7
ochester Mathematical
Sch The ME1 ....47 C1
ochester Rd Burham ME1 ...60 E2
Chalk DA12 ....31 B6
Dartford DA1 ....27 A8
Gillingham ME7,ME8 ....63 D1
Gravesend DA11 ....30 D8
Halling ME2 ....60 C5
Horton Kirby DA4 ....27 E2
Matfield TN12 ....135 F7
ochester Way
Dartford DA1 ....25 F8
Eltham SE9 ....6 B4
Eltham,Kidbrooke SE3,SE9 ...5 D4
ock Ave ME7 ....48 C3
ock Cotts TN3 ....163 B1
ock Farm Oasthouse
ME18 ....104 C6
ock Hill BN6 ....53 B4
ock Rd TN27 ....127 E2
ock Rd
Borough Green TN15 ....86 F7
Maidstone ME14 ....92 A6
ock Villa Rd TN1 ....149 A4
ockdale TN13 ....84 B2
ockdale Rd TN13 ....84 C2
ockliffe Manor Prim Sch
SE18 ....6 F8
ockmount Rd SE18 ....2 F1
ocks Cl ME14 ....90 A6
ocks Hill TN17 ....156 A4
ocks Rd The ME19 ....90 B6
ocky Hill ME16 ....91 E4
ocky Hill Terr ❷ ME16 .....91 E4
odeo Cl DA8 ....9 B6
oding Rd E6 ....2 B8
odmell Rd TN2 ....149 A2
odney Ave TN10 ....117 E4
odney Gdns BR4 ....50 A6
odway Rd BR1 ....36 B8
odwell Way E16 ....2 A5
oebuck Rd ME1 ....47 C5
oedean Cl BR6 ....52 B6
oedean Rd TN2 ....149 A1
oehampton Cl DA12 ....30 E8
oehampton Dr BR7 ....23 C2
ogersmead TN30 ....183 B8
offen Rd ME1 ....47 C2
ogers Ct BR8 ....40 A5
ogers Rough Rd TN17 ....167 B2
ogues Wood La DA3 ....56 B6
ogley Hill TN27 ....171 B6
ogues Hill TN11 ....131 C3
okesby Cl TN16 ....6 D5
olinsden Way BR2 ....50 D6
ollesby Way SE28 ....3 D7
olleston Ave BR5 ....37 B3
olleston Cl BR5 ....37 B2
ollo Rd BR8 ....25 F1
olvenden Ave ME9 ....49 C3
olvenden Gdns BR1 ....22 D1
olvenden Rd TN17 ....182 C5
olvenden Prim Sch
TN17 ....181 E3
olvenden Rd
ochester ME2 ....33 C2
enterden TN30 ....182 E7
olvenden Sta TN30 ....182 D6
oman Cl DA11 ....61 D1
oman Hts ME14 ....92 C6

Roman Rd Edenbridge TN8 .128 D5
Northfleet DA11 ....29 C5
Snodland ME6 ....74 F8
Roman Sq SE28 ....3 A5
Roman Villa Rd DA2,DA4 ....27 C2
Roman Way Crayford DA1 ....8 E2
Rochester ME2 ....46 F4
Romany Ct ME5 ....61 F4
Romany Rd ME8 ....49 C2
Romany Rise BR5 ....37 C1
Romden Rd
Biddenden Green TN27 .....143 D1
Haffenden Quarter TN27 ...159 B8
Rome Terr ME4 ....47 F4
Romero Sq SE3 ....5 C3
Romford Rd TN2,TN12 .....150 F7
Romney Cl DA11 ....30 E7
Romney Dr BR1 ....22 D1
Romney Gdns DA7 ....7 F6
Romney Pl ME15 ....92 A4
Romney Rd Chatham ME5 ...62 B5
Northfleet DA11 ....29 C5
Woolwich SE18 ....2 C1
Romney Way TN10 ....117 C5
Romsey Cl Orpington BR6 ...51 C6
Rochester ME2 ....46 C4
Ron Green Ct DA8 ....8 D8
Ronald House SE3 ....5 C3
Ronalds Rd BR1 ....36 A8
Ronaldstone Rd DA15 ....6 E1
Ronfearn Ave BR5 ....38 D4
Ronver Rd SE12 ....22 A7
Roodlands La TN8 ....113 D6
Rook La ME9 ....65 A6
Rookdean TN13 ....83 C5
Rookery Cres ME13 ....16 B6
Rookery Ct RM20 ....11 A8
Rookery Dr BR7 ....37 A8
Rookery Gdns BR5 ....38 C4
Rookery Hill ME6 ....74 F8
Rookery La BR2 ....36 D3
Rookery Lodge ME3 ....16 C5
Rookery Rd BR6 ....51 A1
Rookery The RM20 ....11 A8
Rookery View ❹ RM17 .....12 D8
Rooksley Cl TN2 ....149 D2
Rooks Hill TN15 ....100 D6
Roopers TN3 ....148 A7
Roosevelt Ave ME5 ....62 A8
Rope Wlk ME4 ....47 F5
Rope Wlk The TN18 ....186 B5
Rope Yard Rails SE18 ....2 B3
Ropemakers Ct ME4 ....48 A1
Roper Cl ME8 ....63 C3
Roper St ❶ SE9 ....6 A1
Roper's Gate TN2 ....148 E1
Roper's Green La ME3 ....18 B2
Ropers WIk ❶ BR3 ....34 F8
Ropery Bsns Pk SE7 ....1 C2
Ropewalk TN17 ....169 C5
Rose Ave DA12 ....30 E7
Rose Bruford Coll DA15 ....24 B7
Rose Cotts ME7 ....46 B8
Rose Ct ME17 ....106 D1
Rose Dale BR6 ....51 B8
Rose Hill Ho TN1 ....149 A3
Rose Hill Sch TN4 ....148 E5
Rose St Northfleet DA11 ....12 B1
Rochester ME1 ....47 D3
Tonbridge TN9 ....133 C8
Rose Terr ME19 ....88 D7
Rose Way SE12 ....5 A2
Rose Yd ME14 ....92 A4
Roseacre Gdns ME14 ....93 A3
Roseacre La ME14 ....93 A4
Roseacre Rd DA16 ....7 B4
Rosebank Gdns DA11 ....29 E7
Rosebank Wlk ❺ SE18 ....1 E2
Roseberry Gdns
Dartford DA1 ....26 C8
Orpington BR6 ....51 E7
Rosebery Ave DA15 ....23 E8
Rosebery Ct DA11 ....29 E7
Rosebery Rd Chatham ME4 ..47 E2
Gillingham ME7 ....48 D7
Grays RM17 ....11 E8
Rosecroft Cl BR5 ....38 C3
Rosedale Cl Dartford DA2 ...27 B8
Woolwich SE2 ....3 B3
Rosedene Cl DA6 ....26 C8
Rosefield Sevenoaks TN13 ...84 A3
Rosehill Wlk TN1 ....149 A3
Roseholme ME16 ....91 D2
Roselare Cl TN16 ....81 D1
Roseleigh Ave ME16 ....91 C5
Rosemary Cl ME15 ....61 F4
Rosemary Ct ME1 ....47 D4
Rosemary La
Culverstone Green TN15 ....57 D3
Lindbum TN5 ....177 A5
Rosemary Rd Bexley DA16 ...6 F6
East Malling ME19 ....74 F1
Rosemount Cl ME15 ....104 F4
Rosemount Dr BR1 ....36 F5
Rosenheath Cl BR6 ....52 C3
Rosetta Prim Sch E16 ....1 B8
Roseveare Rd SE12 ....22 C4
Rosewood DA2 ....25 E4
Rosewood Cl DA14 ....24 C5
Rosewood Ct BR1 ....36 D8
Rosher Ho DA11 ....12 F1

Rosherville CE Prim Sch
DA11 ....12 E1
Rosherville Way DA11 ....12 E1
Roslin Way BR1 ....22 A3
Ross Ct BR7 ....22 F1
Ross House SE18 ....5 E6
Ross Rd DA1 ....9 A1
Ross St ME1 ....47 D4
Ross Way SE9 ....5 E6
Rossdale TN7 ....149 D5
Rosse Mews SE3 ....5 B6
Rossell Rd RM18 ....12 F5
Rossland Cl DA6 ....8 B3
Rosslyn Gn ME16 ....91 B5
Rossmore DA14 ....24 A3
Rother Ct ❷❹ BR5 ....38 D1
Rother Rd TN10 ....117 C5
Rother Vale ME5 ....62 C3
Rothermere Cl TN17 ....180 E6
Rothesay Ct ❷ SE12 ....22 B5
Rothley Cl TN30 ....183 B8
Rouge La DA12 ....30 B7
Roughetts Rd ME19 ....73 F3
Roughway La TN11 ....102 C7
Round Ash Way DA3 ....42 E3
Round Green Cotts TN17 ...154 F4
Round St DA12,DA13 ....42 A1
Round Wood Cl ME5 ....62 A1
Roundel Way TN12 ....138 D5
Roundhill Cl TN2 ....149 D1
Roundhill Rd TN2 ....149 D1
Roundlyn Gdns BR5 ....38 B5
Roundtable Rd BR1 ....22 A5
Roundwell ME14 ....93 D3
Roundwood BR7 ....37 B7
Rouvray Cl SE9 ....5 F1
Rover Rd ME5 ....62 B2
Row The DA3 ....56 F8
Rowan Cl Aylesford ME20 ...76 C7
Longfield DA3 ....42 D7
Meopham Sta DA13 ....44 B3
Paddock Wood TN12 ....135 F5
Rowan Cres DA1 ....26 C7
Rowan Ct ❷ SE12 ....22 A8
Rowan Ho ❸ Chatham ME5 .61 F5
Sidcup DA14 ....23 F5
Rowan Lea ME5 ....48 B1
Rowan Rd Bexley DA7 ....7 E4
Swanley BR8 ....39 D6
Rowan Shaw TN10 ....117 D6
Rowan Tree Rd TN2 ....148 E1
Rowan Wlk Chatham ME4 ...47 E3
Orpington BR2 ....50 F7
Rowanwood Ave DA15 ......24 A7
Rowbrocke Cl ME8 ....63 D3
Rowdow La TN14,TN15 .....69 E5
Rowe Pl ME20 ....75 F6
Rowenden Vineyard*
TN17 ....181 B2
Rowfield ❻ TN5 ....112 D3
Rowhill Cotts DA2 ....25 E2
Rowhill Rd DA2 ....26 A3
Rowhill Sch DA2 ....26 A3
Rowland Ave ME7 ....48 E2
Rowland Ct ME7 ....48 E1
Rowlatt Cl DA2 ....26 C4
Rowlatt Rd DA2 ....26 C5
Rowley Ave DA15 ....24 B8
Rowley Hill TN2 ....134 D1
Rowmarsh Cl DA11 ....29 D4
Rowntree Path ❶ SE28 ......3 B5
Rowton Rd SE18 ....6 C2
Royal ❻ RM8 ....25 F2
Royal Albert Way
Newham E16 ....1 E6
Newham,Cyprus E6 ....2 A6
Royal Ave TN9 ....133 D8
Royal Chase TN4,TN1 ......148 F4
Royal Cl BR6 ....51 B6
Royal Docks Com Sch E16 ...1 C7
Royal Docks Rd E6 ....2 B7
Royal Eagle Cl ME2 ....47 B2
Royal Engineers Mus* ME7 .48 B6
Royal Engineers' Rd ME14 ..91 F7
Royal Oak Rd DA6 ....8 A3
Royal Par BR7 ....23 C1
Royal Parade Mews BR7 ....23 C1
Royal Park Prim Sch DA14 ..23 C1
Royal Pier Rd DA12 ....13 C1
Royal Rd Hawley DA2 ....27 A3
Newham E16 ....1 D7
Sidcup DA14 ....24 D5
Royal Sovereign Ave ME4 ...48 B7
Royal Star Arc ❶ ME14 .....91 F4
Royal Tunbridge Wells
Bsns Pk TN1 ....133 D1
Royal Victoria Place
Sh Ctr TN1 ....149 B4
Royal Victoria Sta E16 ....1 A6
Royal West Kent Ave
TN11 ....117 D4
Roycraft Ave IG11 ....4 A8
Roydon Hall Rd TN12 ......103 F4
Roydon Rd Crayford DA1 .....8 F1
Maidstone ME15 ....93 A3
Royston Rd Crayford DA1 .....8 F1
Rubin Pl ME19 ....89 B3
Ruck La TN12 ....152 E3
Ruckinge Way ME8 ....49 C3
Ruddstreet Cl SE18 ....2 C2
Rudge ❶ ME5 ....62 D2
Rudland Rd DA7 ....8 B4
Ruegg House ❺ SE18 ....6 A8
Ruffet Ct TN4 ....148 E1

Ruffets Wood DA12 ....30 C2
Rugby Cl ME5 ....61 F4
Ruggles Cl ME23 ....17 E3
Rumania Wlk DA12 ....30 F5
Rumstead La ME17,ME9 ....79 D4
Rumstead Rd ME9 ....79 E4
Rumwood Ct ME17 ....108 B5
Runciman Cl DA9 ....52 C1
Runham La ME17 ....110 E3
Running Horse Rndbt The
ME14 ....76 E1
Runnymede Ct DA2 ....27 C7
Runnymede Gdns ME15 ....107 A8
Rural Vale DA11 ....29 E8
Ruscombe Cl TN4 ....132 F2
Rush Cl ME5 ....62 A3
Rushbrook Rd SE9 ....23 C6
Rushdean Rd ME2 ....46 C6
Rushdene SE2 ....3 D3
Rushet Rd BR5 ....38 A7
Rushetts Rd TN15 ....55 E3
Rushetts ❶ SE18 ....2 F1
Rushford Cl TN27 ....141 D5
Rushgrove St SE18 ....1 F2
Rushley Cl BR2 ....50 E6
Rushlye Cl TN3 ....163 F5
Rushmead Dr ME15 ....107 A7
Rushmere Cl TN15 ....86 D7
Rushmore Cl BR1 ....36 E6
Rushmore Hill BR6,TN14 ...67 D6
Rushymead TN15 ....70 B6
Ruskin Ave DA16 ....7 A5
Ruskin Cl TN4 ....149 B6
Ruskin Dr Bexley DA16 ......6 F4
Orpington BR6 ....51 E7
Ruskin Gr Bexley DA16 ......7 A5
Russant Cl DA10 ....10 A2
Ruskin Rd DA17 ....4 A2
Ruskin Wlk BR2 ....36 F3
Rusland Ave BR6 ....51 D7
Russell Cl Bexley DA7 ....8 A3
Crayford DA1 ....9 A3
Greenwich SE7 ....1 C7
Russell Ct ME4 ....48 A3
Russell House Sch TN14 ....69 C3
Russell Pl DA4 ....41 A8
Russell Rd Gravesend DA12 .13 D7
Kit's Coty ME20 ....76 D7
Newham E16 ....1 B7
Tilbury RM18 ....12 F6
Russell Sq DA3 ....42 D6
Russell Terr DA4 ....41 C5
Russells Ave ME8 ....44 A6
Russells Yd TN17 ....169 D4
Russet Ave DA12 ....30 F6
Russet Cl ME7 ....46 E8
Russet Ho SE9 ....6 C3
Russet House ME17 ....107 C2
Russet Way ME19 ....88 F2
Russets The
Maidstone ME16 ....91 B5
Orpington BR5 ....38 C3
Russett Rd DA12 ....119 F6
Russett Way BR8 ....39 D8
Rusthall Grange TN4 ....148 D4
Rusthall High St TN4 ......148 C4
Rusthall Pk TN4 ....148 D4
Rusthall Rd TN4 ....148 D4
Ruston Rd SE18 ....1 F3
Rustwick TN4 ....148 D4
Ruth House ME16 ....91 D2
Rutherford Way TN10 ......117 D7
Rutherglen Rd SE2 ....7 A8
Ruthin Rd SE3 ....5 A8
Rutland Ave DA15 ....24 A1
Rutland Cl Dartford DA1 ....26 D8
Sidcup DA5 ....24 D7
St Paul's Cray BR5 ....38 B6
Rutland Ct Chislehurst BR7 ..37 A8
Sidcup SE9 ....23 D8
Rutland Gate ❷ 4 B1
Rutland Ho ❶ SE18 ....1 F2
Rutland Pl ME8 ....63 C3
Rutland Way
Maidstone ME15 ....107 E8
Orpington BR5 ....38 C3
Ruxley Cl DA14 ....24 E2
Ruxley Cnr DA14 ....24 E2
Ruxley Corner Ind Est
DA14 ....24 E2
Ruxley Ct ❶ BR1 ....36 C7
Ruxley Manor Prim Sch
SE9 ....23 A4
Ruxton Cl BR5 ....39 E6
Ruxton Ct ❺ BR8 ....39 E6
Ryan Cl SE3 ....5 C3
Ryan Dr ME15 ....93 A2
Ryarsh Cres BR6 ....51 E6
Ryarsh Prim Sch ME19 .....74 A4
Ryarsh Rd ME19 ....74 B5
Rycaut Cl ME8 ....63 D3
Rycroft La TN14 ....84 B4
Rydal Cl TN4 ....148 E5
Rydal Dr Bexley DA7 ....8 B6
Royal Tunbridge Wells TN4 .148 E5
Ryde Cl ME5 ....62 B8
Rydens Ho SE9 ....22 C5
Ryder Cl BR1 ....22 B3
Ryders TN3 ....148 A3
Rydons Cl SE9 ....5 E4
Rye Cres BR5 ....38 D1
Rye Field ❷❺ BR5 ....38 D1
Rye La Otford TN14 ....69 A2
Sevenoaks TN13,TN14 ......83 F7

Rye Rd Four Throws TN14 ..185 D8
TN18 ....179 B1
Rye Wood Cotts TN14 ......83 F7
Ryeca ult Cl ❹ ME16 ....91 E3
Ryecroft Gravesend DA12 ...30 E3
New Barn DA3 ....42 A3
Ryecroft Rd Orpington BR5 .37 D3
Otford TN14 ....69 A2
Ryedale Ct TN13 ....83 E6
Ryegrass Cl ME5 ....62 C6
Ryelands Cres SE12 ....5 C1
Rymers Cl TN2 ....149 D7
Rymill St E6 ....2 A5
Rysted La TN16 ....81 D1

S

Sabre Ct ME7 ....49 A1
Sackville Ave BR2 ....36 A1
Sackville Cl TN13 ....84 B5
Sackville Rd DA2 ....26 E6
Sackville Sch TN11 ....116 C6
Sacred Heart Sch TN3 .....174 D5
Saddington St DA12 ....30 C8
Saddler's Pk DA4 ....54 D7
Saddlers Cl ME14 ....92 E5
Sadlers Cl ME5 ....61 D2
Saffron Way ❶ ME5 ....61 F5
Sage Cl ❷ E6 ....1 E8
Sage Rd ME1 ....47 B3
Saigasso Cl E16 ....1 D7
Sailfield Ct ME4 ....47 F7
Sailmakers Ct ❷ ME4 ....48 B2
Saints Hill TN11 ....147 A8
SS Peter & Paul
RC Prim Sch BR5 ....37 E7
St Aidan's Way DA12 ....30 E5
St Alban's Cl DA12 ....30 D5
St Alban's Gdns DA12 ....30 D5
St Alban's Rd DA1 ....9 E1
St Alban's Rd Inf Sch DA1 ...9 F1
St Albans Cl ME7 ....49 A1
St Albans Ct ME7 ....49 A1
St Albans Rd ME8 ....46 D6
St Alfege Rd SE7 ....5 D8
St Andrew Rd ME7 ....48 D7
St Andrew's Cl ME16 ....91 A2
St Andrew's Ct ❹ BR8 ......39 E6
St Andrew's Ho
❶ Gravesend DA12 ....30 B8
Maidstone ME16 ....91 A3
Tilbury RM18 ....12 E5
St Andrews Cl TN12 ....136 A6
St Andrew's Pl
❷ Gravesend DA12 ....13 B1
Royal Tunbridge Wells TN4 .133 A1
St Andrews Dr BR5 ....38 B2
St Andrews Mews SE3 ....5 A7
St Andrews Park Rd TN4 ...133 A1
St Andrews Rd
Paddock Wood TN12 ....136 A6
Sidcup DA14 ....24 E4
St Ann's Green La TN12 ....138 F8
St Anne Ct ME14 ....91 E4
St Anselm's RC Prim Sch
DA1 ....10 A2
St Anthony's Ct DA6 ....51 B8
St Aubyns Ct BR6 ....38 A5
St Aubyns Gdns BR6 ....51 F8
St Audrey Ave DA7 ....8 A5
St Augustine Ho ❶ TN9 ...133 B8
St Augustine of Canterbury
RC Prim Sch
ME8 ....63 D3
St Augustine's Ave BR2 .....36 E4
St Augustine's
Jun & Inf Schs DA17 ....3 F2
St Augustine's
RC Prim Sch TN4 ....149 A7
St Barnabas CE Prim Sch
TN1 ....149 B5
St Barnabas Cl
Gillingham ME7 ....48 D3
Maidstone ME16 ....91 C8
St Barnabas' CI TN1 ....149 B5
St Bartholomew's Hospl
ME1 ....47 E4
St Bartholomew's La ❶
ME1 ....47 E4
St Bartholomew's Terr ❶
ME1 ....47 E4
St Bartholomews
RC Prim Sch BR8 ....39 E6
St Benedict Rd ME6 ....74 E8
St Benedict's Ave DA12 .....30 E5
St Benedict's RC Prim Sch
ME5 ....62 C8
St Benets Rd TN30 ....183 B8
St Benets Way TN30 ....183 B8
St Benjamins Dr BR6 ....52 C2
St Bernards Rd IG11 ....4 A1
St Blaise Ave BR1 ....36 B7
St Boltophs Ct TN13 ....84 B3
St Botolph's Ave TN13 ....84 A3
St Botolph's CE Prim Sch
DA11 ....29 D8
St Botolph's Rd TN13 ....84 B3
St Bredale's Ct TN4 ....112 A3
St Brides Cl DA18 ....3 D1
St Catherine's Hospl 47 D4
St Catherine's RC Sch
for Girls 8 B2

St Chad's Dr DA12 ....30 E5
St Chad's Rd RM18 ......13 A7
St Chad's Sch RM18 ......13 A6
St Christopher's (Trng Coll,
Dr Barnardo's Home)
TN2 ......149 D4
St Clement's Ave RM20 ...11 B8
St Clement's Ho ME1 ......47 D5
St Clement's Rd RM20 ....11 C7
St Clements Cl DA11 ......29 F5
St Clements Ct RM17 ......11 F8
St Clere Hill Rd TN15 ......70 F7
St Columba's Cl DA12 .....30 E5
St Columba's RC Prim Sch
DA6 ......8 B2
St David's Bridge TN17 ...169 D4
St David's Cres DA12 ......30 D4
St David's Rd
Allhallows ME3 ......19 D8
Hextable BR8 ......25 F1
Royal Tunbridge Wells TN4 ..149 B6
St Domingo Ho SE18 ......1 F3
St Dunstan's Dr DA12 ......30 E5
St Dunstan's Rd TN15 .....30 E5
St Edith's Rd TN15 ......70 A2
St Edmund's Cotts TN15 ..56 A2
St Edmund's Ct TN15 ......56 A2
St Edmunds Cl DA18 ......3 D4
St Edmunds Rd DA1 ......10 A3
St Faith's La ME14 ......93 B4
St Faith's St ME14 ......91 F4
St Fidelis RC Prim Sch DA8 ..8 C8
St Fidelis' Rd DA8 ......4 D1
St Francis Ave DA12 ......30 E4
St Francis Cl
Maidstone ME14 ......92 B7
Orpington BR6 ......37 E3
St Francis RC Prim Sch
ME14 ......92 A5
Maidstone, Penenden
Heath ME14 ......92 B7
St Francis Rd DA13 ......58 B3
St Francis Sch ME14 ......92 B7
St Francis' Rd DA8 ......4 D2
St George's Bickley
CE Prim Sch BR1 ......36 C7
St George's CE Prim Sch
TN15 ......71 F3
St George's CE Sch DA11 ..30 A6
St George's Cres DA12 ....30 D4
St George's Ct TN15 ......71 F3
St George's Inf Sch DA11 ..13 B1
St George's Pk TN2 ......162 F8
St George's Rd
Gillingham ME7 ......48 C6
Sevenoaks TN13 ......84 B5
Sidcup DA14 ......24 D2
St George's Sch TN2 .....150 A5
St George's Sq ME16 ......91 E3
St George's Wlk ME3 ......19 D8
St Georges Cl SE28 ......3 B6
St Georges Mews 🔢 TN9 ..133 B8
St Georges Rd Bromley BR1 ..36 F6
Orpington BR5 ......37 D3
Swanley BR8 ......39 F5
St Georges Rd W BR1 ......36 E7
St Georges Sq DA3 ......42 E6
St German's Pl SE3 ......5 A6
St Giles Cl SE25 ......51 D5
St Gregory's
Catholic Comp Sch TN4 ..149 A7
St Gregory's Cres DA12 ..30 E6
St Gregory's Rd DA12 ....30 E6
St Helens CE Prim Sch
ME16 ......16 B5
St Helens Cotts ME15 ....105 E8
St Helens La ME15 ......105 E8
St Helens Rd Cliffe ME3 ..16 B5
🔢 Erith DA18 ......3 D4
St Helier's Cl ME16 ......91 B2
St Hilda's Way DA12 ......30 E5
St Hildas TN15 ......101 F8
St James Cl
East Malling ME19 ......89 F8
Grain ME3 ......21 B6
St James Ct SE3 ......5 B6
St James Oaks DA11 ......30 A8
St James Pl ME1 ......9 D1
St James RC Prim Sch
BR5 ......37 B4
St James Rd ME3 ......21 B5
St James Sq DA3 ......42 E6
St James Terr ME6 ......52 C2
St James Way DA14 ......24 E3
St James' CE Inf Sch
TN2 ......149 C4
St James' CE Jun Sch
TN2 ......149 C4
St James' Inf Sch ME19 ..89 F8
St James' La DA9 ......27 E8
St James' Pk TN1 ......149 C5
St James' Prim Sch ME3 ....1 B5
St James' Rd TN1 ......149 C5
St James's Ave DA11 ......30 A8
St James's Cl SE18 ......2 C1
St James's Ct TN1 ......149 B4
St James's Rd
Gravesend DA11 ......13 A1
Sevenoaks TN13 ......84 B5
St James's St DA11 ......13 A1
St Joachim's RC Sch E16 ..1 C7
St John Fisher
Catholic Sch ME4 ......47 E3
St John Fisher
RC Lower Sch ME4 ......47 F2

St John Fisher RC Prim Sch
DA18 ......3 E3
St John's CE Inf Sch ME4 ..47 E3
St John's CE Prim Sch
Maidstone ME14 ......92 E4
Royal Tunbridge Wells TN4 ..149 A5
Sevenoaks TN13 ......84 D4
St John's Cl ME3 ......32 C4
St John's Ct TN13 ......84 C5
St John's Hill TN13, TN14 ..84 C5
St John's La DA3 ......42 F3
St John's Par DA14 ......24 B4
St John's Pk Greenwich SE3 ..5 A7
Royal Tunbridge Wells TN4 ..149 A8
St John's RC Comp Sch
DA12 ......30 D7
St John's RC Prim Sch
St John's Rd Bexley DA16 ..7 B4
Dartford DA2 ......27 C8
Erith DA8 ......4 D1
Gillingham ME7 ......48 C3
Gravesend DA12 ......30 D8
Higham ME3 ......32 C4
Newham E16 ......1 A7
Orpington BR5 ......37 E3
Royal Tunbridge Wells TN4 ..149 A6
Sevenoaks TN13 ......84 C5
Sidcup DA14 ......24 B4
St John's Terr SE18 ......6 D8
St Johns CE Prim Sch
TN8 ......149 B7
St Johns Cl DA8 ......4 D1
St Johns Rd ME3 ......34 D6
St Johns Way ME1 ......47 A2
St Joseph's RC Inf Sch
Bromley BR1 ......22 B1
Crayford DA1 ......8 E3
Northfleet DA11 ......29 D8
St Josephs Cl BR6 ......51 F6
St Josephs Ct 🔢 SE12 ....22 B5
St Josephs Prep Sch
DA12 ......30 C6
St Justin Cl BR5 ......38 D6
St Katherine's La ME6 ......74 F7
St Katherine's Prim Sch
ME6 ......74 F7
St Katherines Cotts DA12 ..31 E3
St Katherines Rd DA18 ......3 D4
St Keverne Rd SE9 ......22 E4
St Kilda Rd BR6 ......37 F1
St Laurence Ave ME16 ......91 C8
St Laurence Cl BR5 ......38 D6
St Lawrence Ave TN4 .....132 D3
St Lawrence CE Prim Sch
TN15 ......71 F3
St Leonard's St ME19 ......89 B7
St Leonards Ave ME4 ......47 F2
St Leonards Cl
🔢 Bexley DA16 ......7 A4
Grays RM17 ......11 F8
St Leonards Rd ME16 ......91 C8
St Leonards Rise BR6 ......51 E6
St Luke's Ave ME14 ......92 B5
St Luke's CE Prim Sch
ME14 ......149 C7
St Luke's Rd
Maidstone ME14 ......92 B5
Royal Tunbridge Wells TN4 ..149 B6
St Luke's Way ME3 ......19 D8
St Lukes Cl Dartford DA2 ..27 E3
Swanley BR8 ......39 D7
St Lukes Cotts BR8 ......39 D7
St Margaret Clitherow
RC Prim Sch
Tonbridge TN10 ......117 B6
Woolwich SE28 ......2 D7
St Margaret's at Troy Town
CE Prim Sch ME1 ......47 C4
St Margaret's Banks ME1 ..47 D5
St Margaret's CE Prim Sch
ME8 ......63 E8
St Margaret's Cl ME1 ......47 C6
SE18 ......2 C1
St Margaret's Cl DA2 ......27 D6
St Margaret's Cres DA12 ..30 E5
St Margaret's Ct ME17 ......97 A1
St Margaret's Gr SE18 ......6 C8
St Margaret's Inf Sch ME8 ..63 E8
St Margaret's Mews ME1 ..47 C5
St Margaret's Rd
Northfleet DA11 ......29 E7
Sutton at Hone DA2,DA4 ..27 E2
St Margaret's Terr SE18 ......2 C1
St Margarets Ave DA15 ....23 D5
St Margarets CE Prim Sch
TN12 ......121 D1
St Margarets Cl
Maidstone ME16 ......91 B2
Orpington BR6 ......52 A8
St Margarets Dr ME8 ......63 C5
St Margarets Villas TN12 ..137 D8
St Mark's Ave DA11 ......29 F8
St Mark's CE Prim Sch
Bromley BR2 ......36 A6
Royal Tunbridge Wells TN4 ..148 D1
St Mark's Rd Bromley BR2 ..162 F7
St Marks CE Prim Sch
ME20 ......75 F6
St Marks Rd ME20 ......75 F6
St Marks Ho ME7 ......48 C5
St Marks Ind Est E16 ......1 D5
St Martin's Cl ME14 ......48 B7
St Martin's Dr DA4 ......54 D7
St Martin's Rd DA1 ......9 F1
St Martins Cl Erith DA18 ....3 D4
Newington ME9 ......65 C7

St Martins Mdw TN16 ......82 C4
St Mary & St Joseph's
RC Sch DA14 ......24 A3
St Mary Cray Prim Sch
BR5 ......38 C3
St Mary Cray Sta BR5 ......38 B5
St Mary St SE18 ......2 A2
St Mary's ME3 ......18 D5
St Mary's Abbey ME19 ......89 C8
St Mary's
CE (VA) Prim Sch BR8 ..39 C5
St Mary's Church Rd TN14 ..82 F2
St Mary's Cl
Gravesend DA12 ......30 C6
Grays RM17 ......12 D8
Laddingford ME18 ......120 C4
Platt TN15 ......87 C7
St Paul's Cray BR5 ......38 C7
Ticehurst TN5 ......176 D1
St Mary's Ct
🔢 Westerham TN16 ......81 D1
Woolwich DA17 ......3 D2
St Mary's Cty Prim Sch
Sch ME7 ......47 B7
St Mary's Dr TN13 ......83 E4
St Mary's Gdns ME4 ......48 B7
St Mary's Island
CE Prim Sch ME4 ......34 B2
St Mary's La
Speldhurst TN3 ......148 A8
Ticehurst TN5 ......176 D1
St Mary's Pl Eltham SE9 ....6 A1
Newington ME9 ......65 C7
St Mary's RC Prim Sch
Eltham SE9 ......6 A2
Gillingham ME7 ......48 A8
Tilbury RM18 ......12 F5
St Mary's Rd Coldblow DA5 ..25 C7
Gillingham ME7 ......48 C6
Rochester ME2 ......47 B7
Stone DA9 ......10 E2
Swanley BR8 ......39 E5
Tonbridge TN9 ......133 B7
Wrotham TN15 ......72 A2
St Mary's View ME5 ......65 C7
St Mary's Wlk ME1 ......60 F1
St Marys Way DA14 ......42 E6
St Matthew's CE Inf Sch
ME1 ......47 A2
St Matthew's Cl ME9 ......65 C7
St Matthew's High Brooms
CE Prim Sch
TN4 ......149 C4
St Matthew's Way ME3 ....19 D8
St Matthews Dr
Bromley BR1 ......36 F6
Rochester ME1 ......47 A2
St Merryn Cl SE18 ......6 D7
St Michael's CE Jun Sch
ME16 ......91 E3
St Michael's CE Prim Sch
Maidstone ME16 ......91 D3
Tenterden TN30 ......173 A3
St Michael's Cl
Chatham ME4 ......47 E3
Erith DA8 ......3 D4
St Michael's Cl 🔢 ME2 ....47 B8
St Michael's Cty Prim Sch
TN7 ......160 B5
St Michael's East Wickham
CE Prim Sch
ME4 ......7 C6
St Michael's RC Prim Sch
ME4 ......47 F3
St Michael's Rd Bexley DA16 ..7 B4
Maidstone ME16 ......91 D3
St Michaels Rise DA16 ......7 B4
St Michaels Ct 🔢 TN30 ..173 A3
St Mildreds Rd 🔢 SE12 ....22 A8
St Nicholas CE Cty Inf Sch
ME2 ......47 A7
St Nicholas Ct SE18 ......2 A2
St Nicholas Dr TN13 ......84 C1
St Nicholas Gdns ME8 ......46 F8
St Nicholas Rd SE18 ......2 C1
St Nicolas La BR7 ......36 E8
St Olave's Sch BR7 ......58 E7
St Olaves Prep Sch SE9 ....23 A6
St Patrick's Gdns DA12 ....30 C5
St Patrick's RC Prim Sch
SE18 ......2 D2
St Paul's Cl
Greenwich SE7 ......1 D1
Rochester ME2 ......47 B8
Swanscombe DA10 ......28 E8
St Paul's Cray Rd BR5,BR7 ..37 D6
St Paul's Ct TN4 ......148 C4
St Paul's RC Sch SE2 ......7 A8
St Paul's Sq BR2 ......36 A7
St Paul's St TN4 ......148 C4
St Paul's Wood Hill BR5 ....37 F7
St Paulinus CE Prim Sch
DA1 ......8 E3
St Paulinus Ct DA1 ......8 E3
St Pauls CE Inf Sch TN4 ..148 B4
St Pauls CE Jun Sch TN4 ..148 B4
St Pauls Cl TN10 ......117 D5

St Pauls Cray CE Prim Sch
BR5 ......38 D6
St Pauls Inf Sch ME14 ......92 A7
St Peter Chanel
RC Prim Sch DA14 ......24 C3
St Peter St ME1 ......47 D4
St Peter's Bridge ME14 ......91 F4
St Peter's CE Prim Sch
Aylesford ME20 ......76 A3
Royal Tunbridge Wells TN2 ..149 C3
St Peter's Cl DA10 ......28 F8
St Peter's Ct ME20 ......75 C1
St Peter's Cty Inf Sch ME17 ..97 A1
St Peter's Path ME1 ......47 D5
St Peter's RC Prim Sch
SE18 ......2 B2
St Peter's St TN2 ......149 C3
St Peters Cl
Chislehurst BR7 ......23 D1
Ditton ME20 ......75 B1
St Peters La BR5 ......38 A7
St Peters Path ME20 ......75 F6
St Peters Rd ME20 ......75 B1
St Peters Row SE3 ......147 A5
St Peters St ME16 ......91 F4
St Philips Ct ME15 ......92 B2
St Philips Cl TN2 ......149 D6
St Philomena's
RC Prim Sch BR5 ......38 C2
St Quentin Rd DA16 ......6 F4
St Ronan's Cl ME15 ......107 C7
St Ronan's Sch TN18 ......179 D2
St Saviours Rd ME15 ......107 D6
St Simon Stock Sch ME16 ..91 C4
St Stephen's Cl ME7 ......48 C8
St Stephen's Cty Prim Sch
TN9 ......133 D8
St Stephen's RC Prim Sch
DA16 ......7 A5
St Stephen's Sq ME15 ......91 E2
St Stephen's St TN9 ......133 B8
St Stephens Ct TN1 ......149 B5
St Stephens Mews ME1 ....61 E8
St Thomas Cl DA5 ......25 A8
St Thomas More
RC Prim Sch Bexley DA7 ....7 F5
Eltham SE9 ......5 E4
ME8 ......62 A5
St Thomas More
RC Sec Sch SE9 ......6 A1
St Thomas of Canterbury
Prim Sch ME8 ......49 B2
St Thomas' Prim Sch
TN13 ......84 B2
St Thomas Rd Erith DA17 ....4 A4
Newham E16 ......1 A7
Northfleet DA11 ......29 E6
St Thomas' Dr BR5 ......37 C1
St Thomas' RC Prim Sch
RM17 ......12 C8
St Thomas's Ave DA11 ......30 B7
St Thomas's Pl 🔢 RM17 ..12 C8
St Thomas-a-Becket
RC Prim Sch SE2 ......3 A3
St Timothy's Mews 🔢 BR1 ..36 B8
St Vincents Ave DA1 ......10 A2
St Vincents La ME19 ......73 A2
St Vincents Rd DA1 ......10 A2
St Vincents Rd DA1 ......10 A3
St Welcume's Way ME17 ..110 E6
St Werburgh Cres ME3 ....34 D5
St Werburgh Ct ME3 ......34 D5
St William of Perth
RC Prim Sch ME1 ......47 D2
St William's Way ME1 ......47 D2
Sala House SE3 ......5 B3
Salamons Way RM13 ......4 E7
Salcote Rd DA12 ......30 E3
Salem Pl DA11 ......29 D8
Salem St ME15 ......92 A3
Salisbury Ave
Gillingham ME8 ......63 D8
Swanley BR8 ......40 A5
Salisbury Cl TN10 ......117 D7
Salisbury Ho 🔢 ME15 ....107 D7
Salisbury Mews BR2 ......36 E4
Salisbury Rd Bromley BR2 ..36 E4
Chatham ME4 ......48 A3
Dartford DA2 ......29 F7
Gravesend DA11 ......29 F7
🔢 Grays RM17 ......12 C8
Kit's Coty ME20 ......76 D7
Maidstone ME14 ......92 A6
Royal Tunbridge Wells,
High Brooms TN4 ......149 C8
Royal Tunbridge Wells,
Langton Green TN3 ......147 F3
Sidcup DA15 ......25 A7
Tonbridge TN10 ......117 D4
Salix Rd RM17 ......12 D8
Sallows Shaw DA13 ......44 C4
Sally Port ME7 ......48 B6
Sally Port Gdns ME7 ......48 B6
Salmon Rd Dartford DA1 ....9 F4
Erith DA17 ......4 A1
Salomons Rd Newham E13 ..1 C8
Royal Tunbridge Wells TN4 ..148 C4
Salt La ME1 ......9 C8
Salter Cl ME15 ......106 F3
Saltash Rd DA16 ......7 C6
Salter's Cross ME18 ......105 A1
Saltford Cl DA8 ......4 B8
Saltings Rd ME6 ......75 A7

Saltley Cl E6 ......1 E7
Salts La ME15 ......107 A4
Saltwood Ct BR6 ......52 C6
Saltwood Rd ME15 ......91 F1
Sam Bartram Cl SE7 ......1 C1
Samara Cl ME5 ......62 A1
Samphire Cl ME14 ......92 D6
Samphire Ct RM17 ......12 E8
Samphire Way ME4 ......34 A2
Sampson Cl DA17 ......3 D3
Samson Ho SE18 ......1 E7
Samuel Palmer Ct BR6 ....38 A2
Samuel St SE18 ......1 E7
Sanctuary Cl DA1 ......9 D1
Sanctuary Rd ME8 ......49 B4
Sanctuary The ME5 ......7 D1
Sand La TN17 ......156 F4
Sand Rd TN3 ......166 A4
Sandalwood House DA15 ..23 F5
Sandbach Pl SE18 ......2 C2
Sandbanks Hill DA2 ......28 B2
Sandbourne Dr ME14 ......76 F3
Sandby Gn SE9 ......5 E4
Sandcliff Rd DA8 ......4 D1
Sanderling Ct SE28 ......3 C6
Sanderson Way TN9 ......117 E3
Sandersons Ave TN14 ......53 B3
Sanderstead Ave BR5 ......38 B3
Sandfield Rd TN11 ......147 A2
Sandford Rd Bexley DA7,DA6 ..7 E3
Bromley BR2 ......36 A5
Sandgate Ct ME8 ......63 F4
Sandgate Rd DA16 ......7 C6
Sandham Point SE18 ......2 B2
Sandhill La ME17 ......109 D3
Sandhurst Ave TN2 ......150 E6
Sandhurst Cl
Royal Tunbridge Wells TN2 ..149 C5
Sandhurst TN18 ......186 A4
Sandhurst Cross TN12 ......140 F7
Sandhurst Cty Prim Sch
TN18 ......186 C5
Sandhurst Ho TN2 ......149 D5
Sandhurst La TN17 ......181 B2
Sandhurst Pk TN2 ......149 C6
Sandhurst Rd Bexley DA5 ....7 D2
Orpington BR5 ......52 A6
Royal Tunbridge Wells TN2 ..149 D6
Sidcup DA15 ......24 A5
Tilbury RM18 ......13 C5
Sandhurst Vineyards*
TN18 ......186 E5
Sandilands TN13 ......83 D5
Sandling Cl ME14 ......92 B7
Sandling La ME14 ......92 B8
Sandling Prim Sch ME14 ..92 B8
Sandling Rd
Maidstone ME14 ......91 F6
Maidstone,Ringlestone ME14 ..91 F7
Sandling Rise SE9 ......23 A5
Sandling Way ME4 ......34 B3
Sandown Cl TN2 ......149 F6
Sandown Court Com Coll
TN2 ......149 F5
Sandown Dr ME8 ......63 D7
Sandown Gr TN2 ......149 F6
Sandown Pk TN2 ......149 F6
Sandown Rd
Gravesend DA12 ......30 C2
New Town ME19 ......89 B8
Sandpiper Dr DA8 ......9 B7
Sandpiper Rd ME5 ......62 D2
Sandpiper Way BR5 ......38 D5
Sandpipers The DA12 ......30 D6
Sandpit Pl SE7 ......1 E3
Sandpit Rd DA1 ......9 A3
Sandringham Ct ME19 ......89 A3
Sandringham Dr DA16 ......6 E3
Sandringham Ho ME1 ......47 D2
Sandringham Rd
Bromley BR1 ......22 A3
Gillingham ME8 ......63 E7
Sandrock Ho TN2 ......149 D4
Sandrock Rd TN2 ......149 C4
Sandrook Villas TN18 ......178 F3
Sandstone Rd SE12 ......22 B6
Sandstone Rise ME5 ......77 C8
Sandtoft Rd SE7 ......5 B8
Sandway Path 🔢 BR5 ......38 C5
Sandway Rd
Lenham ME17 ......110 F4
🔢 ME17 ......110 F4
Sandy Bank Rd DA12 ......30 B5
Sandy Bury BR6 ......51 D7
Sandy Dell ME7 ......63 A2
Sandy Hill Ave SE18 ......2 A1
Sandy Hill La SE18 ......2 B1
Sandy Hill Rd SE18 ......2 B1
Sandy La Bean DA13,DA2 ..28 D5
Ightham TN15 ......86 B2
Maidstone,Harbourland
ME14 ......92 C6
Maidstone,Ware Street ME14 ..93 B5
New Town ME19 ......73 A1
Orpington BR6 ......52 A3
Sevenoaks TN13 ......84 C4
Snodland ME6,ME19 ......74 E6
St Paul's Cray BR5 ......38 D8
Tenterden TN30 ......183 B8
Tilbury RM16 ......11 E8
West Thurrock RM20 ......11 B8
Westerham TN16 ......81 A1
Wrotham Heath TN15,ME19 ..72 F7
Sandy Mount ME14 ......93 B5

Sandy Ridge
Borough Green TN15 .....87 A7
Chislehurst BR7 ....23 A2
Sandycroft SE2 ....7 A8
Sandycroft Rd ME2 ....32 F1
Santana House SE18 ......6 B7
Santer Ho TN18 ....184 E8
Sapho Pk DA12 ....39 A7
Saphora Cl BR6 ....51 D5
Sappers Wlk ME7 ....48 C5
Sapphire Cl E6 ....2 A7
Sara Cres DA9 ....11 B3
Sara Pk **1** DA8 ....9 F7
Sara Pk DA12 ....30 E4
Sara Turnbull Ho **3** SE18 ..1 F7
Saracen Cl ME7 ....49 A1
Saracen Fields ME5 ......77 C8
Sarafand Ho ME1 ....47 B7
Sark Wlk E16 ....1 B7
Sarsen Hts 61 F1
Sarsens Cl DA12 ....44 F6
Sassoon Cl ME20 ....75 A4
Satanita Cl E16 ....1 F6
Saunder's Cross TN14 .....53 B2
Saunders Cl DA11 ....29 E6
Saunders Rd
  Royal Tunbridge Wells TN4 .148 E1
  Woolwich SE18 ....2 F1
Saunders St **3** Gillingham ME7 .48 C6
  4 Rochester ME4 ....47 F3
Saunders Way Dartford DA1 .26 F6
  Woolwich SE18 ....3 B6
Savage Gdns E6 ....1 F7
Savage Rd ME5 ....62 B3
Savill Ho E16 ....1 E5
Saville Rd E16 ....1 E5
Savoy Rd DA1 ....9 D2
Sawyers Ct ME4 ....48 B2
Saxby Wood TN11 ....115 F1
Saxbys Rd TN15 ....85 D5
Saxon Cl Kings Hill ME19 ..88 F2
  Northfleet DA11 ....29 C5
  Otford TN14 ....69 E2
  Rochester ME2 ....32 F1
Saxon Pl Horton Kirby DA4 ..41 C4
  Rochester ME2 ....46 F5
Saxon Rd Bromley BR1 .....22 A1
  Hawley DA2 ....26 C4
Saxon St ME14 ....94 D2
Saxons Dr ME14 ....92 B7
Saxton St ME7 ....48 C5
Saxville Rd BR5 ....38 B6
Sayer Cl DA9 ....11 A2
Sayers La TN30 ....183 A7
Sayes Court Rd BR5 ......38 B5
Scabharbour Rd TN14 .....99 C1
Scadbury Gdns BR5 ......38 A7
Scadbury Park
  Nature Reserve* BR7 ....23 E2
Scads Hill Cl BR6 ....37 F3
Scarborough La ME1 ......60 D2
Scarlet Cl BR5 ....38 B5
Scarlett Cl ME5 ....62 C5
Scarsbrook Rd SE3 ....5 C4
Schofield Wlk SE3 ....5 A7
Scholars Rise ME2 ....46 D7
Scholey Cl ME2 ....60 B4
School App TN15 ....86 F7
School Ave ME7 ....48 C4
School Cl DA13 ....44 A2
School Cotts
  Crockenhill BR8 ....39 D2
  Sidcup DA14 ....24 C3
School Cres DA1 ....8 F3
School Field TN8 ....112 C2
School Hill TN15 ....166 B6
School House La TN12 ....153 F7
School La Bean DA2 ......28 C5
  Bexley DA5 ....7 B4
  Chestnut Street ME9 .....65 F4
  Hadlow TN11 ....118 E8
  Hextable BR8 ....26 B1
  Higham ME3 ....32 C5
  Horton Kirby DA3,DA4 ....41 E4
  Knockmill TN15 ....70 F8
  Maidstone ME15 ....92 E1
  Newington ME9 ....65 B7
  Platt's Heath ME17 ......110 F2
  Plaxtol TN11,TN15 ......101 E6
  Seal TN15 ....84 D5
  Sutton Valence ME17 ....124 E7
  Trottiscliffe ME19 ......73 A5
  Vigo Village DA13 ......58 A2
  Wouldham ME1 ....60 D5
School Rd Chislehurst BR7 ..23 C1
  Gravesend DA12 ....30 C5
  Hoo St Werburgh ME3 ...34 E5
School Rise TN2 ....148 F1
School Terr **11** TN18 .....178 F2
School Villas ME18 ......104 D5
Schoolfield Rd RM20 .....11 A8
Schooner Ct DA2 ....10 C3
Schrieber Mews ME1 ......4 B8
Scilla Ct **11** RM17 ......12 D8
Scimitar Cl ME7 ....49 A1
Scords La TN16 ....97 C4
Scotby Ave ME5 ....62 B4
Scotland La DA12 ....44 F6
Scotney Castle* TN3 .....166 D3
Scotney Castle Gdns*
  TN3 ....166 D3
Scotney Cl BR6 ....51 A6
Scotney Ho ME2 ....33 C1
Scotsdale Cl BR5 ....37 F5
Scotsdale Rd SE12 ....5 B2
Scott Ave ME8 ....64 A8
Scott Cl ME20 ....90 C8
Scott Cres DA8 ....8 F6
Scott Ho **4** DA17 ....3 F1

Scott Rd Gravesend DA12 ..30 D3
  Tonbridge TN9 ....132 F8
Scott St ME14 ....91 F6
Scott Wilkie Prim Sch E16 .1 C7
Scott's Terr ME4 ....47 F3
Scotteswood Ave ME4 ....47 F2
Scotts Ho ME4 ....47 F4
Scotts Park Prim Sch BR1 .36 C8
Scotts Pas **11** SE18 ......2 B2
Scotts Rd BR1 ....22 A1
Scotts Way
  Royal Tunbridge Wells TN2 .162 E8
  Sevenoaks TN13 ....83 E5
Scoulding Rd E16 ....1 A7
Scragged Oak Rd
  Detling ME14 ....78 C5
  Hucking ME17 ....79 C1
Scratchers La DA3 ....55 E7
Scratton Fields DA12 .....44 D4
Scrubbs La ME16 ....91 D4
Scudders Hill DA3 ....42 C3
Seabrook Rd TN10 ......117 A3
Seabrooke Rise RM17 ....12 A8
Seacourt Rd SE2 ....3 D4
Seaford Ct ME1 ....47 B5
Seaford Rd ME4 ....46 D6
Seal CE Prim Sch TN15 ...84 F7
Seal Dr TN15 ....84 F6
Seal Hollow Rd TN13 .....84 F5
Seal Rd TN13,TN14,TN15 ..84 C6
Sealand Ct ME1 ....47 B5
Seamew Ct ME7 ....46 C7
Searles Dr E6 ....2 B8
Seaton Rd Bexley DA6 ....7 C7
  Dartford DA1 ....26 A8
  Gillingham ME7 ....48 E3
Seaview ME7 ....21 B5
Seaview Rd ME7 ....48 C4
Second Ave Chatham ME4 ..48 C1
  Gillingham ME7 ....48 E5
  West Thurrock RM20 .....11 A8
Secretan Rd ME1 ....47 B1
Sedcombe Cl DA14 ......24 C4
Sedge Cres ME5 ....61 E4
Sedgebrook Rd SE3 ......5 D4
Sedgemere Rd SE2 ......3 C3
Sedley Cl DA13 ....29 A2
Sedley Cl Aylesford ME20 ..75 F4
  Cliffe Woods ME3 ....33 C7
  Gillingham ME8 ....63 C3
Sedley's CE Prim Sch
  DA13 ....29 A3
Sefton Cl BR5 ....37 F5
Sefton Rd BR5 ....37 F5
Sejant House **4** RM17 ....12 B8
Selah Dr BR8 ....39 C8
Selborne Ave ME5 ......24 E7
Selborne Rd DA14 ....24 B4
Selbourne Cl DA3 ....43 D6
Selbourne Rd ME7 ......48 D7
Selbourne Wlk ME15 .....107 F6
Selby Cl Chislehurst BR7 ..23 A1
  5 Newham E6 ....1 E7
Selby Rd Maidstone ME15 ..107 F4
  Newham E13 ....1 B8
Selkirk Dr DA8 ....8 E6
Sellbourne Pk TN3 ......163 C4
Sellinge Gn ME8 ....49 C3
Sellwood Ct ME1 ....47 B5
Selsey Cres DA16 ....7 D6
Selstead Ct ME14 ....49 C2
Selwyn Cres DA16 ....7 B3
Selwyn Pl **1** BR5 ....38 B6
Selwyn Rd RM18 ....12 F5
Semple Gdns ME4 ....47 E3
Senacre La ME15 ....107 E5
Senacre Sq ME15 ....107 F7
Senacre Tech Coll ME15 ..107 D6
Senacre Wood Prim Sch
  ME15 ....107 F7
Senator Wlk SE28 ......8 C8
Sencler Ho SE2 ....3 D1
Sencler House SE2 ......7 D8
Senlac Pl ME1 ....161 C7
Senlac Rd SE12 ....22 A8
Sennen Wlk SE9 ....22 E7
Sennocke Ct TN13 ....84 B2
Sequoia Gdns BR6 ......37 F2
Serman Dr BR8 ....39 C6
Serpentine Ct TN13 ......84 D5
Serpentine Rd TN13 .....84 D4
Serviden Dr BR1 ....36 D8
Sessions House Sq ME14 ..91 F5
Setford Rd ME5 ....62 C6
Settington Ave ME5 .....48 C1
Seven Acres
  Crockenhill BR8 ....39 D3
  New Ash Green DA3 .....56 E7
Seven Mile La
  Kings Hill TN15,ME18 ....88 A3
  Mereworth TN11,TN12 ...103 E3
  Wrotham Heath TN15 ....87 F7
Seven Wents TN15 ......86 A4
Sevenoaks Bsns Ctr TN14 ..84 C6
Sevenoaks By-Pass
  TN13,TN14 ....98 F7
Sevenoaks Hospl
  Sevenoaks TN13 ....84 B2
  Sevenoaks, St John's TN13 .84 C6
Sevenoaks Prep Sch TN15 ..85 A1
Sevenoaks Rd
  Borough Green TN15 ....86 F7
  Ightham TN15 ....86 B4
  Orpington BR6 ....51 F6
  Otford TN14 ....69 B3
  Pratt's Bottom BR6,TN14 ..52 C2

Sevenoaks Sch TN13 .....84 C1
Sevenoaks Sta TN13 ....84 A3
Sevenoaks Way BR5 .....38 C7
Sevenoaks
  Wildfowl Reserve* TN14 ..111 C5
Severn Cl TN10 ....117 C5
Severn Rd ME5 ....62 C5
Sevington Pk ME15 ......106 F6
Sewell Rd SE28 ....3 F6
Sextant Pk ME2 ....47 E6
Sexton Rd RM18 ....12 F6
Seymour Dr BR2 ....36 F1
Seymour Rd
  11 Chatham ME5 ....48 B3
  Gillingham ME8 ....64 C8
  Northfleet DA11 ....12 B4
  Tilbury RM18 ....12 F6
Seymour St SE18 ....2 C3
Seymour Wlk DA10 .....28 E8
Shacklands Rd TN14 .....53 D1
Shackleton Cl ME5 ......62 B6
Shades The ME2 ....46 C7
Shaftesbury Cl ME19 .....74 F1
Shaftesbury Ct **3** SE28 ...3 F5
Shaftesbury Ho ME16 ....91 C4
Shaftesbury La DA1 .....10 B3
Shaftesbury Rd TN4 .....149 A5
Shaftesbury Ct E6 ....2 A7
Shakespeare Ave RM18 ..13 B6
Shakespeare Farm Rd
  ME4 ....18 F7
Shakespeare Ho **11** DA7 ..3 F1
Shakespeare Rd Bexley DA7 .7 F6
  Dartford DA1 ....10 B3
  Gillingham ME7 ....48 E7
  Tonbridge TN9 ....132 F8
Shalder Ho ME7 ....48 D7
Shalford Cl BR6 ....51 C6
Shallons Rd SE9 ....23 B4
Shambles The TN13 .....84 C2
Shamel Bsns Ctr ME2 ....47 C7
Shamley Rd ME5 ....62 D2
Shamrock Cl DA12 ......30 F8
Shandon Cl TN2 ....149 C4
Shankin Cl ME5 ....62 B6
Shannon Ct ME5 ....38 A2
Sharfleet Dr ME2 ....46 B7
Sharland Rd DA12 ......30 C4
Sharman Ct DA14 ....24 A4
Sharnal La ME6 ....75 A7
Sharnal St ME3 ....18 A2
Sharnbrooke Cl DA16 ....7 D4
Sharon Cres ME5 ....61 E4
Sharon Rd ME7 ....48 E4
Sharp Way DA1 ....9 F5
Sharp's Field TN27 ......141 E5
Sharps Gn ME8 ....49 D5
Sharsted Way
  Gillingham ME7 ....63 A3
  Maidstone ME14 ....92 D7
Shaw Cl Cliffe Woods ME3 ..33 B8
  Woolwich SE28 ....3 B5
Shaw Cres ME18 ....13 B6
Shaw Ho **8** Erith DA17 ....3 F1
  5 Newham E16 ....2 A2
Shaw The TN2 ....149 C2
Shawbrooke Rd SE9 .....5 D3
Shawcroft Sch ME5 .....62 C6
Shawfield Pk BR1 ....36 D7
Shaws Way ME1 ....47 C3
Shawstead Rd ME7,ME4 ..62 D5
Sheal's Cres ME15 ......92 A2
Sheal's Ct ME15 ....92 A2
Shears Cl DA2 ....26 C6
Shears Green Inf Sch DA11 .29 C5
Shears Green Jun Sch
  DA11 ....29 C5
Shearwater
  Maidstone ME16 ....91 B5
  New Barn DA3 ....43 B6
Shearwater Cl ME2 ......47 C7
Shearwood Cres DA1 ....9 A4
Shee Rd BR5 ....37 F5
Sheepcote La BR5,BR8 ...38 F4
Sheephurst La TN12 ....137 E5
Sheerness Harbour Est
  ME12 ....21 F3
Sheerwater Rd E16 ......1 D6
Sheet Hill TN15 ....86 D2
Sheffield Rd **4** TN4 ......132 F2
Sheilings The TN5 ....84 F7
Shelbury Cl DA14 ......24 A4
Sheldon Dr ME15 ......107 A6
Sheldon Bsns Ctr ME2 ....47 C7
Sheldon Cl SE12 ....5 B2
Sheldon Rd DA7 ....7 F6
Sheldon Way ME20 .....75 B3
Sheldrake Cl E16 ....1 F5
Sheldwich Terr BR7 .....37 E8
Shell Cl BR2 ....36 E3
Shellbank La DA2 ....28 B6
Shellbrake Cl ME14 ......21 B5
Shelley Cl BR6 ....51 E7
Shelley Dr DA16 ....6 E6
Shelley Pl RM18 ....13 B6
Shelley Rd ME16 ....91 C2
Shelleys La TN14 ....67 A3
Shelvin Cl DA13 ....57 C6
Shenden Cl TN13 ....99 C6
Shenden Way TN13 .....99 C7
Shenfield Ho SE18 ......5 E7
Shenley Gr ME14 ....76 F2
Shenley Rd DA1 ....27 A8

Shenstone Sch DA1 ......8 D3
Shepherd St DA11 ....29 D8
Shepherds Cl BR6 ....51 F7
Shepherds Gate ME7 .....62 F5
Shepherds Gate Dr ME14 ..92 E6
Shepherds Gn BR7 ......23 D1
Shepherds La DA1 ....26 E6
Shepherds Leas SE9 .....6 D3
Shepherds Way
  Langley Heath ME17 ....108 E4
  Lower Stoke ME3 ....19 C4
Shepherds Wlk BR2 .....149 D6
Shepherdsgrove La
  RH19 ....144 A4
Shepperton Cl BR5 ......62 C4
Shepperton Rd BR5 .....37 C3
Sheppey Cl DA8 ....9 B7
Sheppey Rd ME15 ....107 A7
Sheppey Way ME8 ......28 E8
Sheppy Ho **1** BR1 ......22 B1
Sheppy Pl DA12 ....30 B8
Shepway Inf Sch ME15 ...107 E8
Shepway Jun Sch ME15 ..107 E8
Sherard Mans SE9 ......5 F2
Sherard Rd SE9 ....5 E2
Sheraton Ct ME5 ....61 F1
Sherborne Rd BR5 ......37 F4
Sherbourne Cl
  Royal Tunbridge Wells TN2 .149 D2
  West Kingsdown TN15 ...55 E4
Sherbourne Dr
  Maidstone ME16 ....91 B2
  Rochester ME2 ....33 A1
Sherbrooke Cl DA7 ......8 A3
Sherenden La TN12 .....154 D8
Sherenden Pk TN11 .....119 A5
Sherenden Rd TN11 .....134 D7
Sherfield Rd RM17 ......12 B8
Sheridan Cl Chatham ME5 ..62 C7
  Maidstone ME14 ....91 E8
  Swanley BR8 ....39 E6
Sheridan Cres BR7 ......37 E2
Sheridan Ct DA1 ....10 A3
Sheridan Lodge **2** BR7 ....36 C5
Sheridan Rd Bexley DA7 ..7 E4
  Erith DA7 ....4 A2
Sheriff Dr ME5 ....62 A2
Sheringham Cl ME16 ....91 D7
Sheringham Ho **6** ME16 ..107 D8
Sheringham Prim Sch SE7 ..5 B8
Sherington Rd SE7 ......5 B8
Sherlies Ave BR6 ....51 F8
Sherman Cl ME4 ....49 B1
Sherman Ct **4** BR1 ......36 B8
Sherman Rd BR1 ....36 B8
Shernden La TN8 ....128 C4
Shernold Sch ME16 .....91 D5
Sherway Ct TN27 ....141 E5
Sherway Rd TN27 ....142 D6
Sherwin Knight
  Jun & Inf Sch ME2 .....46 E5
Sherwood Ave ME5 .....62 A2
Sherwood Cl DA5 ....7 C2
Sherwood Ho DA8 ......8 B8
Sherwood Park Ave DA15 ..7 B1
Sherwood Park
  Cty Prim Sch TN2 ....149 D6
Sherwood Park Prim Sch
  DA15 ....7 A1
Sherwood Pl TN3 ....147 E3
Sherwood Rd Bexley DA16 ..6 F4
  Royal Tunbridge Wells TN2 .149 E1
Sherwood Way TN2 .....149 D6
Shieldhall St SE2 ....3 C2
Shieling The DA13 ....57 F1
Shillingheld Cl ME14 ....92 F5
Shinecroft TN14 ....69 A3
Shingle Barn La ME15 ...106 B5
Shinglewell Rd DA8 ......8 A7
Ship La Chatham ME1 ...47 E4
  Sutton at Hone BR8,DA4 ..40 E8
Shipbourne Prim Sch
  TN11 ....101 C4

Shipbourne Rd
  Shipbourne TN11 ....101 D2
  Tonbridge TN10,TN11 ...117 C5
Shipley Cl ME14 ....92 A4
Shipley Hills Rd DA13 ....43 E1
Shipman Rd E16 ....1 C7
Shipwrights Ave ME4 ....48 B2
Shire Ct SE12 ....22 B8
Shire La Farthing Street BR6 ..51 C2
  Orpington BR6 ....51 E5
Shirebrook Rd SE3 ....5 D4
Shirehall Rd DA2 ....26 E4
Shires The TN12 ....136 A7
Shirley Ave Chatham ME5 ..61 D5
  Sidcup DA14 ....24 D7
Shirley Cl Chalk DA12 ....31 B6
  Dartford DA1 ....9 F2
Shirley Ct ME15 ....107 E5
Shirley Gdns TN4 ....148 C5
Shirley Gr ME14 ....148 C5
Shirley House Dr SE7 ....5 C7
Shirley Rd DA15 ....23 E6
Shirley Way ME15 ......93 A3
Sholden Gdns BR5 ......38 C4
Sholden Rd ME2 ....33 C1
Shooters Hill SE18 ....6 A6
Shooters Hill Rd SE18,SE3 ..5 C6
Shore The Northfleet DA11 ..12 C2
  Northfleet, Rosherville DA11 ..12 B2
Shoreham Aircraft Mus*
  TN14 ....68 F8
Shoreham Cl DA5 ......24 D7
Shoreham Cty Prim Sch
  TN14 ....68 F8

Shoreham Ho TN14 ......69 A8
Shoreham La
  Badgers Mount TN14 .....68 A7
  Chelsfield BR6 ....53 A3
  Sevenoaks TN13 ....83 F4
  Tenterden TN30 ....173 A3
Shoreham Pl TN14 ......69 A7
Shoreham Rd Otford TN14 ..69 B5
  St Paul's Cray BR5 ......38 B7
Shoreham Sta TN14 .....69 B8
Shoreham Wlk BR2 ......36 A3
Shoreham Way BR2 .....107 F7
Shorehill La TN15 ....69 F4
Shoreland Ct ME1 ....47 B5
Shorne CE Prim Sch DA12 .31 E3
Shorne Cl Orpington BR5 ..38 D5
  3 Sidcup DA15 ....7 B1
Shorne Ifield Rd DA12 ....31 C2
Shoreham Sta TN14 .....69 B8
Shornefield Cl BR1 ......37 A6
Short Path SE18 ....6 B8
Short St **3** ME4 ....48 B3
Shortlands Cl DA17 ......3 F3
Shortlands Gn ME15 ....107 F5
Shorts Way ME1 ....47 A3
Shortway SE9 ....23 C5
Shottenden Rd ME7 .....48 D7
Shottery Cl SE9 ....22 E5
Showfields Rd TN2 .....148 F1
Shrapnel Cl SE18 ....5 F4
Shrapnel Rd SE12 ......5 F4
Shrewsbury La SE18 .....6 B6
Shrewsbury Rd DA11 ....29 B7
Shropshire Terr **1** ME7 ..107 E7
Shrubbery Rd
  Gravesend DA12 ....30 C7
  Sutton at Hone DA4 ....41 D8
Shrubcote TN30 ....183 C7
Shrublands Ct
  Royal Tunbridge Wells TN2 .149 C4
  4 Tonbridge TN9 ....117 C2
Shrubsall Cl SE9 ....22 E7
Shrubsole Dr ME14 .....76 F3
Shurlock Ave BR8 ......39 D7
Shurlock Dr BR6 ....51 C6
Shuttle Cl Biddenden TN27 ..187 E8
  Sidcup DA15 ....23 F8
Shuttle Rd DA1 ....9 A4
Shuttlemead DA5 ....24 F8
Sibley Cl DA6 ....7 E2
Sibthorpe Rd SE12 .....22 C8
Sidcup By Pass Rd
  Sidcup DA14 ....23 F3
  St Paul's Cray BR5,BR7,DA14 ..24 B1
Sidcup Hill DA14 ....24 B3
Sidcup Hill Gdns DA14 ...24 C3
Sidcup Hill Prim Sch
  DA14 ....24 A3
Sidcup Pl DA14 ....24 A3
Sidcup Rd SE12 ....5 D5
Sidcup Sta DA15 ....24 A6
Sidewood Rd SE9 ......23 D7
Sidmouth Ct DA1 ....27 B7
Sidmouth Rd Bexley DA16 ..7 C7
  Orpington BR5 ....38 B5
Sidney Ct TN2 ....162 F8
Sidney Gdns TN14 ......69 C2
Sidney House SE18 ......5 F6
Sidney Rd Gillingham ME7 ..47 A2
  Rochester ME1 ....47 A2
Sidney St ME16 ....91 C2
Siebert Rd SE3 ....5 A8
Siedle House SE18 ......6 A8
Siemens Rd SE18 ....1 D3
Silchester Ct ME14 ......92 C7
Silecroft Rd DA7 ....8 A6
Silk Cl SE12 ....5 A1
Silk Mills Cl TN13 ......84 C6
Silver Bank ME5 ....62 A6
Silver Birch Ave ME4 ....62 A6
Silver Birch Cl
  Dartford DA2 ....25 E4
  Woolwich SE28 ....3 B5
Silver Birches ME5 ......62 A3
Silver Cl TN9 ....133 B6
Silver Hill Chatham ME4 ..47 F3
  Hurst Green TN19 ......184 B1
  Rochester ME1 ....47 F3
  Tenterden TN30 ....173 B1
Silver Hill Gdns ME4 ....47 F3
Silver Rd DA12 ....30 E6
Silver Spring Cl DA8 ....8 B8
Silver St ME9 ....80 E5
Silver Tree ME5 ....62 B1
Silverdale Hartley DA3 ...42 F5
  Maidstone ME16 ....91 A2
Silverdale Dr
  Chislehurst SE9 ....22 E6
  Gillingham ME8 ....63 F7
Silverdale La
  Royal Tunbridge Wells TN4 .149 B6
  Sandhurst TN18 ....185 F5
Silverdale Rd Bexley DA7 ..8 B5
  Orpington BR5 ....38 B7
  Royal Tunbridge Wells TN4 .149 B6
  St Paul's Cray BR5 .....38 A6
Silverden Cotts TN18 ....185 F4
Silverhurst Dr TN10 .....117 C7
Silverland St E16 ....1 F5
Silverlocke Rd RM17 ....12 D8
Silverspot Cl ME8 ....63 F7
Silverstead La TN16 ....81 D6
Silverstone Ct **3** BR1 ....36 C7
Silvertown Sta E16 ......1 E5

Stanley Rd continued
Orpington BR6 . . . . .37 F1
Royal Tunbridge Wells TN1 . .149 B5
Sidcup DA14 . . . . .24 A5
Swanscombe DA10 . . . . .11 F1
Stanley Ways BR5 . . . . .38 B4
Stanmore Rd DA17 . . . . .4 C2
Stanning Ct TN10 . . . . .117 C4
Cansfield Rd E16 . . . . .1 D7
ansted CE Prim Sch
  TN15 . . . . .56 F1
ansted Cl ME16 . . . . .91 D7
ansted Cres DA5 . . . . .24 D7
ansted Hill TN15 . . . . .57 A3
ansted La TN15 . . . . .56 C1
anton Cl BR5 . . . . .38 C2
anton Ct 8 Bromley BR1 . . . .36 C7
8 Sidcup DA15 . . . . .24 A5
aple Cl DA5 . . . . .25 D5
aple Dr TN12 . . . . .139 F4
apleford Ct TN11 . . . . .83 F4
aplehurst House BR5 . . . . . .38 C4
aplehurst Rd
  Bogden TN12 . . . . .123 C2
  rittenden TN12,TN17 . . . . . . .140 D1
  illingham ME8 . . . . .49 B3
  aplehurst Sta TN12 . . . . .139 E3
  aplehurst Sta TN12 . . . . .139 E5
aplers Cl ME14 . . . . .92 B8
aples Ho E6 . . . . .2 A7
aples The BR8 . . . . .40 B8
apleton Rd Erith DA7 . . . . . . .7 F8
  rpington BR6 . . . . .51 F7
apley Rd DA17 . . . . .4 A1
  ar Bsns Ctr RM9 . . . . .4 D8
  ar Hill Crayford DA1 . . . . .8 D2
    Rochester ME1 . . . . .47 D5
  ar Hill Rd TN14 . . . . .68 A2
  ar La Gillingham ME7 . . . . . . .63 A7
  ar Mill Cl BR5,BR8 . . . . .38 E5
  ar Mill Ct ME5 . . . . .62 A7
  ar Mill La ME5 . . . . .48 D2
arboard Ave DA9 . . . . .11 B1
arling Cl DA3 . . . . .43 B6
arnes Ct 8 ME14 . . . . .92 A5
arr Cotts TN12 . . . . .121 C2
arts Cl BR6 . . . . .51 A7
arts Hill Ave BR6 . . . . .51 B6
arts Hill Rd BR6 . . . . .51 B6
arvecrow Cl TN11 . . . . .117 D8
  ate Farm Ave BR6 . . . . .51 C6
ation App
  exley,Barnehurst DA7 . . . . . . .8 C5
  exley,Bexleyheath DA7 . . . . . .7 E5
  exley,Welling DA16 . . . . .7 A5
  brough Green TN15 . . . . .86 F7
  hislehurst BR7 . . . . .37 A7
  hislehurst,Elmstead BR7 . . . . .22 C2
  artford DA1 . . . . .9 E1
  denbridge TN8 . . . . .112 C2
  rays RM17 . . . . .12 A8
  reenwich SE3 . . . . .5 B4
  ayes BR2 . . . . .36 A1
  aidstone ME15 . . . . .91 F3
  rpington BR6 . . . . .51 F8
  rpington,Chelsfield BR6 . . . . .52 B5
  tford TN14 . . . . .69 C3
  addock Wood TN12 . . . . .136 A7
  t Paul's Cray BR5 . . . . .38 B5
  aplehurst TN12 . . . . .139 E5
  wanley BR8 . . . . .39 E5
ation Approach Rd
  M18 . . . . .13 A3
ation Cotts
  ill's Green TN18 . . . . .178 F5
  artley TN17 . . . . .168 E2
  orsmonden TN12 . . . . .153 B5
ation Cres SE3 . . . . .1 A1
ation Ct TN15 . . . . .86 F7
ation Hill Chiddingstone
  Causeway TN11 . . . . .131 A8
  ayes BR2 . . . . .50 A8
ation Mews 3 TN30 . . . . . . .183 A7
ation Par DA15 . . . . .24 A6
ation Rd Aylesford ME20 . . . .75 E2
  etsham DA13 . . . . .29 A4
  Bexley DA7 . . . . .7 E4
  Borough Green TN15 . . . . .86 F7
  Brasted TN16 . . . . .82 B4
  Bromley BR1 . . . . .36 A8
  Cliffe ME3 . . . . .16 B3
  Crayford DA1 . . . . .9 A1
  East Farleigh ME15 . . . . .106 A7
  East Tilbury RM18 . . . . .14 B7
  Edenbridge TN8 . . . . .112 C2
  Erith DA17 . . . . .4 A1
  Eynsford DA4 . . . . .54 D7
  Gillingham ME8 . . . . .49 F1
  Goudhurst TN17 . . . . .167 C7
  Groombridge TN3 . . . . .161 C7
  Halstead TN14 . . . . .67 B8
  Harrietsham ME17 . . . . .110 D6
  Headcorn TN27 . . . . .141 D5
  Hurst Green TN19 . . . . .184 A3
  Longfield DA3 . . . . .42 E6
  Maidstone ME14 . . . . .91 F5
  Meopham Sta DA13 . . . . .44 A4
  Nettlestead Green ME18 . . . .104 C1
  Newington ME9 . . . . .65 B6
  Northfleet DA11 . . . . .12 B1
  Northiam TN31 . . . . .187 C1
  Orpington BR6 . . . . .51 F8
  Otford TN14 . . . . .69 C3
  Paddock Wood TN12 . . . . . . .135 F7
  Rochester ME2 . . . . .47 C7
  Sevenoaks TN13 . . . . .83 E7

Station Rd continued
  Shoreham TN14 . . . . .69 A7
  Sidcup DA14,DA15 . . . . .24 A5
  St Paul's Cray BR5 . . . . .38 C5
  Staplehurst TN12 . . . . .139 F5
  Stone TN15 . . . . .11 A2
  Sutton at Hone DA4 . . . . .41 B7
  Swanley BR8 . . . . .39 E5
  Tenterden TN30 . . . . .183 A7
  Wadhurst TN5 . . . . .174 E3
  Withyham TN7 . . . . .160 B5
Station Rd N DA17 . . . . .4 B3
Station Sq BR5 . . . . .37 C4
Station St E16 . . . . .1 E6
Steadman ME8 . . . . .63 A5
Steadman Cl DA5 . . . . .32 C6
Stede Hill ME17 . . . . .95 F3
Stedley 17 DA14 . . . . .24 A4
Stedman Cl DA5 . . . . .25 C5
Steele Ave DA9 . . . . .11 A2
Steele St ME2 . . . . .47 A8
Steele Wlk DA8 . . . . .8 B7
Steele's La DA13 . . . . .58 A6
Steellands Rise TN5 . . . . . . .176 F1
Steep Cl BR6 . . . . .51 A4
Steerforth Cl ME1 . . . . .47 C2
Steers Pl TN11 . . . . .102 E2
Stella Cl TN12 . . . . .138 D5
Stelling Rd DA8 . . . . .8 D7
Stephen Cl BR6 . . . . .51 F7
Stephen Rd DA7 . . . . .8 C4
Stephen's Rd TN4 . . . . .149 B6
Stephenson Ave RM18 . . . . . .13 A6
Stephenson Ho S2 . . . . .3 D1
Stephenson's Way TN11 . . . .117 C7
Steps Hill Rd TN14 . . . . .181 C7
Sterling Ave ME16 . . . . .91 C5
Sterling House SE3 . . . . .5 B3
Sterndale Rd DA1 . . . . .26 F8
Stevanne Ct 1 DA1 . . . . .4 A1
Stevedale Rd DA16 . . . . .7 C5
Stevens Cl
  Dartford, Joydens End DA5 . . .25 D4
  Dartford, Lane End DA2 . . . . .27 E3
  Egerton TN27 . . . . .127 F3
Stevens Rd ME20 . . . . .75 F6
Stevenson Cl Dartford DA8 . . .9 B7
  Maidstone ME15 . . . . .91 F3
Stevenson Way ME20 . . . . . .74 F4
Stewart Cl BR7 . . . . .23 B4
Stewart Ho ME3 . . . . .33 F6
Stewart Rd TN4 . . . . .149 C2
Steynton Ave DA5 . . . . .24 D6
Stickens La ME19 . . . . .89 E7
Stickfast La TN27 . . . . .125 D3
Stickland Rd DA17 . . . . .4 A2
Stilebridge La
  Underling Green ME17 . . . . . .123 A5
  Underling Green TN12 . . . . . .122 E3
Stiles Cl Bromley BR2 . . . . . . .36 F3
  Erith DA8 . . . . .4 B1
Still La TN4 . . . . .148 D7
Stirling Cl Gillingham ME8 . . .63 E4
  Rochester ME1 . . . . .47 A3
Stirling Dr BR6 . . . . .52 B5
Stirling Rd 8 SE18 . . . . .2 B1
Stirling Rd ME19 . . . . .89 F3
Stisted Way TN27 . . . . .127 F3
Stock La DA2 . . . . .27 E1
Stockbury Dr ME16 . . . . .91 D7
Stockbury House 7 BR5 . . . . .38 D1
Stockenbury TN12 . . . . .119 F6
Stockett La ME15 . . . . .106 D6
Stockfield 11 TN8 . . . . .112 D3
Stockland Green Rd TN3 . . . .148 B8
Stocks Green Cotts
  TN11 . . . . .116 C5
Stocks Green Rd TN11 . . . . .116 C5
Stocks Rd TN30 . . . . .189 F3
Stockwell Cl ME14 . . . . .92 B8
Stockwell Ct BR1 . . . . .36 B7
Stofield Gdns SE9 . . . . .22 D5
Stoke Com Sch TN14 . . . . . . .19 C5
Stoke Rd Allhallows ME3 . . . . .19 C7
  Hoo St Werburgh ME3 . . . . . . .34 F6
  Kingsnorth ME3 . . . . .35 C8
  Lower Stoke ME3 . . . . .18 E1
Stokesay Ct 10 DA2 . . . . .10 B1
Stone Cotts TN3 . . . . .165 F4
Stone Court La TN2 . . . . .150 E8
Stone Cross Rd TN5 . . . . . . .175 A4
  Stone Crossing Sta DA9 . . . . .10 F2
Stone Ct DA8 . . . . .4 F1
Stone Hill Rd TN27 . . . . .127 F2
  Stone House Hospl DA2 . . . . .10 F1
  Stone Lake Ind Pk SE7 . . . . . . .1 C2
  Stone Lake Ret Pk SE7 . . . . . . .1 C2
  Stone Lodge Farm
    Park* DA1 . . . . .10 D1
Stone Pit La TN18 . . . . .186 E5
Stone Place Rd DA9 . . . . .10 E2
Stone Row DA1 . . . . .9 C3
Stone Row TN3 . . . . .147 B5
Stone Row Cotts TN3 . . . . . .147 D1
Stone St Cranbrook TN17 . . . .169 D5
  Gravesend DA11 . . . . .13 A1
  Royal Tunbridge Wells TN1 . .149 B4
Stone Street Rd TN15 . . . . . .85 E2
Stone Wood DA3 . . . . .28 C5
  Stone, St Mary's
    CE Prim Sch DA9 . . . . .27 E8
Stonebridge Cl ME8 . . . . .63 D5
Stoneacre Cl ME15 . . . . .92 A1
Stoneacre La ME15 . . . . .108 B7
Stonebridge Green Rd
  TN27 . . . . .127 F4

Stonebridge Rd DA11 . . . . . .12 B2
Stonechat Sq 6 E6 . . . . .1 E8
Stonecroft DA11 . . . . .73 A8
Stonecroft Rd DA8 . . . . .8 C7
Stonecrop Cl ME4 . . . . .34 C1
Stonecross Lea ME5 . . . . .48 C1
Stonefield Cl DA7 . . . . .8 A4
Stonefield Way SE7 . . . . .5 D7
Stonegate BR7 . . . . .38 C6
Stonegate Rd TN5 . . . . .175 C1
Stonehorse Cl ME3 . . . . .33 A3
Stonehorse La ME2 . . . . .33 A2
Stonehouse Cnr RM19 . . . . . .10 E8
Stonehouse La
  Pratt's Bottom TN14 . . . . .52 E1
  Purfleet RM19 . . . . .10 E8
Stonehouse Rd BR6,TN14 . . . .52 D1
Stoneings La TN14 . . . . .81 F8
Stoneness Rd RM20 . . . . .11 C7
Stones Cross Rd BR8 . . . . . . .39 C4
Stonestile Rd TN27 . . . . .141 A7
Stonewall E6 . . . . .2 A8
Stonewall Park Rd TN3 . . . . .147 E3
Stonewood DA1 . . . . .10 A1
Stonewood Rd DA8 . . . . .4 F1
Stoney Alley SE18 . . . . .6 A5
Stoney Bank ME7 . . . . .48 B8
Stony Cnr DA13 . . . . .43 E6
Stony La ME1 . . . . .61 C5
Stonyfield TN8 . . . . .112 D3
Stopford Rd ME7 . . . . .48 B6
Store Rd E16 . . . . .2 A5
Storehouse Wharf ME12 . . . . .21 F3
  Storey Prim Sch E16 . . . . .2 B5
Storey St E16 . . . . .2 B5
Stornaway Strand DA12 . . . . .30 F4
Stour Cl Orpington BR2 . . . . . .50 C6
  Rochester ME2 . . . . .46 F7
  Tonbridge TN10 . . . . .117 B5
Stour Ct 22 BR5 . . . . .38 D1
Stour Rd DA1 . . . . .9 F4
Stove Rd BR6 . . . . .52 B6
Stowting Rd BR6 . . . . .51 E6
Strait Rd E6 . . . . .1 E6
Strand Approach Rd ME7 . . . .48 E7
Strand Cl DA13 . . . . .44 A3
Strand Rdbt The ME7 . . . . . . .48 E7
Strandfield Cl SE18 . . . . .2 E1
Stratfield Ho SE12 . . . . .22 A6
Stratford Ave ME8 . . . . .63 D4
Stratford House Ave BR1 . . . .36 E5
Stratford La 2 ME8 . . . . .63 F8
Stratford Rd ME19 . . . . .89 A8
Strathaven Rd SE12 . . . . .22 B8
Strathden Par SE3 . . . . .5 B1
Strathden Rd SE3 . . . . .5 B1
Stratton Cl DA7 . . . . .7 E4
Stratton Rd DA7 . . . . .7 E4
Stratton Terr TN16 . . . . .96 C8
Straw Mill Hill ME15 . . . . . . .91 E1
Strawberry Cl TN2 . . . . .162 E7
Strawberry Fields BR8 . . . . . .39 D7
Strawberry Vale TN9 . . . . . . .117 C1
Stream La TN18 . . . . .186 A5
Stream Lane Cotts TN18 . . . .185 A4
Stream Side TN10 . . . . .117 D6
Stream The ME20 . . . . .75 C1
Stream Way DA17 . . . . .8 A8
Streamdale SE2 . . . . .7 B8
Streamside ME20 . . . . .75 B1
Streamside Cl BR2 . . . . .36 A5
Streatfield TN8 . . . . .112 D1
Streatfield Ho TN16 . . . . .81 C1
Street End Rd ME5 . . . . .48 B1
Street Farm Cotts ME3 . . . . .34 F6
Street The Ash TN15 . . . . .56 E5
  Benenden TN17 . . . . .180 D6
  Boxley ME14 . . . . .77 C3
  Bredhurst ME7 . . . . .63 B1
  Cobham DA12 . . . . .44 F6
  Detling ME14 . . . . .78 A1
  Egerton TN27 . . . . .127 F3
  Fenn Street ME3 . . . . .18 A8
  Frittenden TN17 . . . . .156 E7
  Hartlip ME9 . . . . .64 D5
  High Halstow ME23 . . . . .17 E3
  Horton Kirby DA4 . . . . .41 B5
  Ightham TN15 . . . . .86 D6
  Maidstone ME14 . . . . .93 C4
  Meopham DA13 . . . . .44 A1
  Mereworth ME18 . . . . .103 D8
  Plaxtol TN15 . . . . .101 F7
  Ryarsh ME19 . . . . .89 C6
  Shorne DA12 . . . . .31 E3
  Silver Street ME9 . . . . .80 F5
  Sissinghurst TN17 . . . . .170 B8
  Teston ME18 . . . . .90 F3
  Trottscliffe ME19 . . . . .73 A5
  Ulcombe ME17 . . . . .125 F7
  Upper Halling ME2 . . . . .59 E5
  Wateringbury ME18 . . . . .90 F5
  Wormshill ME9 . . . . .95 F7
Streetfield ME17 . . . . .125 F7
Streetfield Mews SE3 . . . . .5 A4
Strettit Gdns TN12 . . . . .136 A8
Strickland Ave DA1 . . . . .9 F5
Strickland Way 4 BR6 . . . . . . .51 F6
Strongbow Cres SE9 . . . . .5 F2
Strongbow Rd SE9 . . . . .5 F2
Strood Sta ME2 . . . . .47 C7
Strover St ME7 . . . . .48 A7
Struttons Ave DA11 . . . . .29 F6
Stuart Br BR2 . . . . .36 A1
Stuart Cl Hextable BR8 . . . . . .26 A1
  Maidstone ME14 . . . . .92 C6

Stuart Cl continued
  Royal Tunbridge Wells TN2 . .162 F8
Stuart Evans Cl DA11 . . . . .7 C4
Stuart Mantle Way DA8 . . . . .8 E7
Stuart Rd Bexley DA16 . . . . . . .7 B6
  Gillingham ME7 . . . . .48 D3
  Gravesend DA11 . . . . .13 A1
  Royal Tunbridge Wells TN4 . .149 A8
Stubbs Hill BR6,TN14 . . . . . . .67 C6
Stubbygrove Cotts TN3 . . . . .163 E4
Studland Cl DA15 . . . . .23 F5
Studley Cres DA3 . . . . .43 C7
Studley Ct DA14 . . . . .24 B3
Stumble Hill TN11 . . . . .101 C5
Sturdee Ave ME7 . . . . .48 E4
Sturdee Cotts ME3 . . . . .35 A6
Sturges Field BR7 . . . . .23 D2
Sturla Rd ME4 . . . . .48 A3
Sturmer Ct ME19 . . . . .89 A2
Sturry Way ME8 . . . . .49 C2
Styants Bottom Rd TN15 . . . .85 F5
Style Cl ME8 . . . . .63 E4
Styles Cl TN18 . . . . .113 B5
Styles Cotts TN8 . . . . .113 B5
Sudbury E6 . . . . .2 A7
Sudbury Cres BR1 . . . . .22 A3
Suffolk Ave ME8 . . . . .49 F1
Suffolk Rd Dartford DA1 . . . . . .9 F1
  Gravesend DA12 . . . . .13 D1
  Maidstone ME15 . . . . .107 D8
  Sidcup DA14 . . . . .24 C2
Suffolk Way TN13 . . . . .84 C2
Sullivan Ave E16 . . . . .1 D8
Sullivan Cl DA1 . . . . .26 C8
Sullivan Rd Tilbury RM18 . . . .13 A6
  Tonbridge TN10 . . . . .117 E5
Sultan Rd ME5 . . . . .62 C2
Summer Ct TN30 . . . . .173 C1
Summer Hill BR7 . . . . .37 A7
Summerfield
  7 Bromley BR1 . . . . .36 B8
  Marden TN12 . . . . .154 B6
Summerfield St 9 SE12 . . . . .22 A8
Summerhill La TN4 . . . . .141 A6
Summerhill Ave TN4 . . . . . . .132 F1
Summerhill Rd DA1 . . . . .51 E7
Summerhill Rd
  Bogden TN12 . . . . .123 C1
  Dartford DA1 . . . . .26 D8
Summerlands Lodge BR6 . . . .51 A6
Summerton Way SE28 . . . . . . .3 D7
Summervale Rd TN2,TN4 . . . .148 E1
Sumner Cl Orpington BR6 . . . .51 C5
  Rolvenden TN17 . . . . .181 F3
Sun Ct DA8 . . . . .8 F5
Sun Hill DA3 . . . . .56 A8
Sun La Gravesend DA12 . . . . . .30 C6
  Greenwich SE3 . . . . .5 B7
Sun Rd DA10 . . . . .11 F1
Sunbright Cl TN4 . . . . .149 B6
Sunburst St SE18 . . . . .1 F3
Sunderland Cl ME1 . . . . .47 A3
Sunderland Dr ME8 . . . . .64 A8
Sunderland Ho 3 ME7 . . . . . . .48 C7
Sundew Ct 8 RM17 . . . . .12 D8
Sundorne Rd SE7 . . . . .1 C1
  Sundridge & Brasted
    CE Prim Sch TN14 . . . . .82 E2
Sundridge Ave Bexley DA16 . . .6 D4
  Bromley BR1 . . . . .36 D8
Sundridge Cl DA1 . . . . .10 A1
Sundridge Dr ME5 . . . . .62 A4
Sundridge Hill Cuxton ME2 . . .46 B3
Sundridge La TN14 . . . . .67 C2
  Sundridge Park Sta BR1 . . . . .22 A1
Sundridge Rd TN14 . . . . .83 B8
Sunfields Pl SE3 . . . . .5 B7
Sunhill Ct TN2 . . . . .150 C6
Sunland Ave DA6 . . . . .7 E3
Sunningdale Cl
  Woolwich SE28 . . . . .3 B7
Sunningdale Ct ME15 . . . . . . .92 B4
Sunningdale Dr ME8 . . . . .63 D6
Sunningdale Rd BR1,BR2 . . . .36 E4
Sunninghill DA11 . . . . .29 F5
Sunnybank TN15 . . . . .177 E3
Sunnydale BR6 . . . . .52 B5
Sunnydale Rd SE12 . . . . .5 B2
Sunnyfield Rd BR7 . . . . .38 A6
Sunnyfields Cl ME8 . . . . .63 B8
Sunnymead Ave ME7 . . . . . . .48 E5
Sunnyside TN4 . . . . .112 B3
Sunnyside Rd TN4 . . . . .148 C4
Sunray Ave BR2 . . . . .36 F3
Sunset Cl DA8 . . . . .9 B7
Sunset Rd SE28 . . . . .3 A5
Sunshine Ct 1 ME8 . . . . .63 F8
  Superabbey Est ME20 . . . . . . .76 B2
Superior Dr 3 BR6 . . . . .51 F4
Surlingham Cl SE28 . . . . .3 D6
Surrenden Rd TN12 . . . . .139 E3
Surrey Cl TN2 . . . . .162 F8
Surrey Rd ME15 . . . . .107 D8
Susan Rd SE3 . . . . .5 B5
Susan Wood BR7 . . . . .37 A8
Sussex Cl TN2 . . . . .149 C1
Sussex Dr ME5 . . . . .62 A4
Sussex Mews 18 DA10 . . . . . .11 E1
Sussex Rd Dartford DA1 . . . . .27 A8
  Erith DA8 . . . . .8 F5
  Maidstone ME15 . . . . .107 D8
  Orpington BR5 . . . . .38 A3
  Sidcup DA14 . . . . .24 B3
  Tonbridge TN9 . . . . .133 A8

Sussex Road Cty Prim Sch
  TN9 . . . . .133 A8
Sutcliffe Rd Bexley DA16 . . . . .7 C5
  Woolwich SE18 . . . . .6 E8
Sutherland Ave Bexley DA16 . .6 E3
  Orpington BR5 . . . . .37 F4
Sutherland Cl DA11 . . . . .11 B6
Sutherland Gdns ME8 . . . . . .63 E6
Sutherland House SE18 . . . . . .5 F6
Sutherland Rd Erith DA17 . . . .4 A3
  Royal Tunbridge Wells TN1 . .149 B3
Sutlej Rd SE7 . . . . .5 C7
  Sutton at Hone
    CE Prim Sch DA4 . . . . .27 A1
Sutton Cl ME8 . . . . .64 A8
Sutton Ct TN12 . . . . .138 C5
Sutton Forge TN12 . . . . .138 C5
  Sutton Rd
    Langley Heath ME17 . . . . . .108 C5
    Maidstone ME15 . . . . .107 D6
    Sutton St ME14 . . . . .93 D4
  Sutton Valence Prim Sch
    ME17 . . . . .124 E7
  Sutton Valence Sch
    ME17 . . . . .124 E7
Swadelands Cl ME17 . . . . . . .111 C5
Swadelands Sch ME17 . . . . . .111 C5
Swaffield Rd TN13 . . . . .84 C5
Swain Cl ME2 . . . . .46 F8
Swain Rd Gillingham ME8 . . . .63 B6
  Tenterden TN30 . . . . .173 D3
Swaisland Rd DA1 . . . . .9 B1
Swaislands Dr DA1 . . . . .8 F2
Swale Rd Crayford DA1 . . . . . . .9 A3
  Rochester ME2 . . . . .46 C7
Swaledale Rd DA2 . . . . .27 C7
Swallow Cl Erith DA8 . . . . .8 E6
  Greenhithe DA9 . . . . .11 A2
Swallow Ct 3 SE12 . . . . .22 A8
Swallow Dr TN12 . . . . .149 F6
Swallow House 4 ME16 . . . . .91 E4
Swallow Rd ME7 . . . . .48 B8
Swallow Rise ME5 . . . . .62 A5
Swallow St E6 . . . . .1 E8
Swallowfield 8 DA11 . . . . . . .29 E5
Swallowtail Cl DA15 . . . . .38 D5
Swan Apartments 17
  ME15 . . . . .107 E5
Swan App E6 . . . . .1 E8
Swan Bsns Pk DA1 . . . . .9 C5
Swan Cl BR5 . . . . .38 A4
Swan Cotts TN30 . . . . .189 D3
  Swan Marsh La DA11 . . . . . . .112 C4
Swan Rd SE18 . . . . .1 D3
Swan Ridge TN8 . . . . .112 D4
Swan St West Malling ME19 . .89 C8
  Wittersham TN30 . . . . .189 C3
  Swan Valley Com Sch
    DA10 . . . . .28 F8
Swanbridge Rd DA8 . . . . .8 B6
Swanland Dr TN9 . . . . .132 F7
  Swanley Ctr BR8 . . . . .39 E6
Swanley La BR8 . . . . .39 F6
  Swanley New Barn Rly*
    BR8 . . . . .39 E8
Swanley Rd DA16 . . . . .7 B6
  Swanley Sta BR8 . . . . .39 E6
Swanley Village Rd BR8 . . . .40 B8
Swanmead Way TN9 . . . . . . .117 D2
  Swanscombe Bsns Ctr
    DA10 . . . . .11 E2
  Swanscombe House 1
    BR5 . . . . .38 B7
  Swanscombe Inf Sch
    DA10 . . . . .11 F1
Swanscombe Sta DA10 . . . . . .11 F2
Swansea Ct E16 . . . . .2 B4
Swanton Rd Erith DA8 . . . . . .103 A8
  Mereworth ME18 . . . . .25 A8
Swanzy Rd TN14 . . . . .84 C7
Sward Rd BR5 . . . . .38 A4
Swattenden La TN17 . . . . . . .169 B1
Swaylands Rd DA17 . . . . .8 A8
Sweeps Hill Cl TN2 . . . . .150 D7
Sweeps La BR5 . . . . .38 D5
Sweetings La TN3,TN5 . . . . .165 D1
Sweetlands La TN12 . . . . . . .140 A5
Sweets La ME19 . . . . .90 A4
Swetenham Wlk SE18 . . . . . . .2 C1
Sweyne Jun Sch The
  DA10 . . . . .28 F8
Sweyne Rd DA10 . . . . .11 E1
Swift Cl ME20 . . . . .75 A6
Swift Cres ME5 . . . . .62 A6
Swift House 8 ME16 . . . . .91 E4
Swift's Ct TN15 . . . . .85 A6
Swifts View TN17 . . . . .169 D6
Swinburne Gdns RM18 . . . . . .13 B5
Swinburne Rd ME5 . . . . .16 B6
Swingate Cl ME5 . . . . .62 C1
Swingate La SE18 . . . . .6 E7
Swingfield Ct BR2 . . . . .36 C4
Swinton Ave BR3 . . . . .33 F5
Swires Shaw BR2 . . . . .50 D6
Swinland Gdns SE9 . . . . .23 A4
Syamore Mews DA9 . . . . .4 D1
Sycamor Ct DA8 . . . . .4 D1

Sycamore Ave DA15 .....6 F1
Sycamore Cl Eltham SE9 ...22 E6
  Gravesend DA12 ....30 D8
  Tilbury RM18 ....13 A5
Sycamore Cotts TN2 ...150 C6
Sycamore Cres ME16 ....91 C5
Sycamore Gr Swale 27 E8
Sycamore Dr
  Aylesford ME20 ....75 E1
  Swanley BR8 ....39 E7
Sycamore Lodge TN12 ..135 F5
Sycamore Gdns BR6 .....52 A8
Sycamore Rd Dartford DA1 ..26 D7
  Rochester ME2 ....46 E5
Sychem La TN12 ....135 A6
Sychem Pl TN12 ....135 A7
Sydenham Cotts SE12 ...22 C6
Sydney Rd Bexley DA6 .....7 D3
  Chatham ME4 ....48 A3
  Erith SE2 ....3 D3
  Sidcup DA14 ....23 E4
  Tilbury RM18 ....13 A5
Sydney St SE18 ....2 C3
Sydney Terr TN18 ......178 F3
Sylewood Cl ME1 ....61 B8
Sylvan Glade ME5 ....77 A8
Sylvan Rd ME8 ....63 C8
Sylvan Wlk BR1 ....36 F6
Sylvester Ave BR7 ....22 F2
Sylvestre Cl ME2 ....60 A4
Sylvestres TN13 ....83 E6
Symonds Cl TN15 ....55 E5
Symonds La ME18 ......120 F6
Symonds Rd ME3 ....16 A4
Symons Ave ME4 ....48 A3
Syon Lodge **1** SE12 ....22 A8
Syringa Ct **9** RM17 ....12 D8

T

Tabor Ct TN12 ....153 A6
Tadburn Gn ME5 ....62 B4
Taddington Wood La ME5 ..61 E2
Tadley Ct Chatham ME1 ...61 C8
  Gillingham ME7 ....48 A6
Tail Race The ME15 .....91 E2
Tainter Rd TN11 ....102 E1
Talbot Pk TN2 ....149 D5
Talbot Rd Maidstone ME16 ..91 C6
  The Moor TN18 ....184 F8
Tall Trees Cl ME17 ....109 D2
Tallents Cl DA4 ....27 E8
Tallis Cl DA1 ....1 B7
Tallis Gr SE7 ....5 B8
Tamar Dr ME2 ....46 F7
Tamar Rd TN10 ....117 B5
Tamar St SE7 ....1 E2
Tamarind Cl ME7 ....63 A4
Tamesis Strand DA12 ...30 E3
Tan Yard La DA5 ....25 A8
Tandridge Dr BR6 ......37 D1
Tandridge Pl **2** BR6 ...37 C1
Tangier La TN3 ....163 B6
Tangleberry Cl BR1 .....36 F5
Tanglewood Cl ME8 ....63 C6
Tanglewood Ct BR5 ....38 C6
Tangmere Cl ME7 ......48 F5
Tanker Hill ME8 ....63 D6
Tanners Mead TN8 ....112 C1
Tannery Rd TN9 ....117 C1
Tansy Cl E6 ....1 E8
Tanyard Rolvenden TN17 ..181 E4
  Sandhurst TN18 ....186 B5
Tanyard Cotts DA12 ....31 E1
Tanyard Hill DA12 .....31 E2
Tanyard La TN4 ....132 F1
Tanyard The TN17 .....169 D4
Tapsell's La TN5 ......174 D5
Tarbutts TN17 ....169 A4
Target Bsns Ctr ME15 ..107 F4
Tarland Ho TN2 ....149 D3
Tarling Cl DA14 ....24 B5
Tarnwood Pk SE9 ......22 F7
Tarragon Rd ME16 .....91 B3
Tasker Cl ME15 ....93 B3
Tasman Wlk E16 ....1 D7
Tasmania House RM18 ..13 A6
Tassell Cl ME19 ....75 A1
Tate Rd E16 ....1 F5
Tates TN18 ....179 A1
Tates Orch DA3 ....42 F3
Tatler Cl ME5 ....62 D2
Tatsfield Cl ME8 ....49 A2
Tatsfield La TN16 ......81 A6
Tattersall Cl SE9 ......5 E2
Tattershall Ct **2** DA2 ..10 B1
Tattlebury La TN17 ....153 F1
Tattlebury Rd TN27 ...141 C8
Taunton Cl Bexley DA7 ..8 D5
  Maidstone ME15 ......107 F6
Taunton Rd DA11 ......12 A2
Taunton Vale DA12 ....30 D5
Tavern Cl TN15 ....86 F7
Tavern Cotts TN15 .....85 A3
Taverners Rd ME8 .....63 E7
Tavistock Cl Chatham ME5 ..61 F1
  Maidstone ME15 ......93 B3
Tavistock Rd Bexley DA16 ..7 C6
  2 Bromley BR2 ....36 A5
Tavy Bridge SE2 ....3 C4
Tawney Rd SE28 ....3 B6
Tay Cl ME5 ....62 A5
Taylor Cl
  Harrietsham ME17 ....110 D6

Taylor Cl continued
  3 Orpington BR6 ......51 F6
Taylor Ct TN2 ....149 C7
Taylor Rd ME6 ....74 F8
Taylor Row DA2 ....26 C5
Taylor St TN4 ....149 A8
Taylor's Bldgs SE18 .....2 B2
Taylor's La Higham ME3 ..32 B5
  Rochester ME2 ....42 F7
Taylors Cl DA14 ....23 F4
Taylors La ME19 ....72 F6
Tea Garden La TN3, TN4 ..148 C2
Teal Ave BR5 ....38 D5
Teal Cl Grain ME3 ......21 B5
  Newham E16 ....1 D8
Teapot La ME20 ....75 E1
Teasaucer Hill ME15 ..106 F8
Teasel Cl ME14 ....92 F4
Teasel Rd ME5 ....61 F4
Teasels TN27 ....158 A1
Teasley Mead TN3 ....146 F4
Tebbs Way TN15 ....86 C3
Tedder Ave ME5 ....62 A7
Tedman Rd ME4 ......149 B7
Teesdale Rd DA2 ....27 C7
Teeswater Ct SE2 ......3 D3
Teignmouth Rd DA16 ...7 C5
Teise Cl TN2 ....149 D2
Telegraph Hill ME3 ....32 C3
Telemann Sq SE3 ......5 B4
Telford Ho **2** Erith DA17 ..4 A3
  1 Maidstone ME14 ...92 A6
Telford Rd SE9 ....23 D6
Tellson Ave SE18 ....5 E6
Telscombe Cl BR6 .....51 E8
Telston La TN14 ....68 F2
Temeraire Manor **2** ME7 ..48 A6
Tempest Rd ME19 ......88 F3
Templar Dr Erith SE28 ..3 D7
Templars Cl **1** TN8 ...112 D3
Temple Cl SE28 ....2 C3
Temple Gdns ME2 ......47 A6
Temple Hill DA1 ....9 F2
Temple Hill Cty Prim Sch
  DA1 ....10 A2
Temple Hill Sq DA1 .....9 F2
Temple Manor* ME2 ...47 A6
Temple Way ME19 ......74 F1
Templemore DA14 ......24 B3
Tenney House RM17 ...12 B7
Tennyson Ave **2** DA7 ..3 F1
Tennyson Cl DA16 ......6 F6
Tennyson Ho **2** DA17 ..3 B7
Tennyson Rd Dartford DA1 ..10 A2
  Maidstone ME14 ......48 C3
Tennyson Wlk
  Northfleet DA11 ....29 D5
  Tilbury RM18 ....13 B5
Tensing Ave DA11 ......29 E5
Tent Peg La BR5 ....37 C4
Tenterden & District Mus*
  TN30 ....183 A7
Tenterden CE Jun Sch
  TN30 ....183 B7
Tenterden Cl SE9 ....22 F4
Tenterden Inf Sch TN30 ..183 B7
Tenterden Rd
  Biddenden TN27 ......172 B7
  Tenterden TN18 ....62 B5
  Fosten Green TN27 ....171 F4
  Tenterden TN17 ......182 A5
Tenterden Sta*
  TN30 ....183 A8
Tenterden Vineyard*
  TN30 ....183 C1
Tenzing Ct SE9 ....22 E6
Terence Ct **6** DA17 ....7 A2
Terminus Rd ME16 .....91 A2
Tern Cres ME2 ....46 C6
Terrace Rd ME16 ....91 E3
Terrace St DA12 ....13 B1
Terrace The
  2 Gravesend DA12 ...13 B1
  Rochester ME1 ....47 C3
  Sevenoaks TN13 ....83 D5
Terraces The DA2 ......27 C8
Terry Wlk ME16 ....74 E2
Terry's Lodge Rd TN15 ..71 C6
Teston House ME18 ...105 A7
Teston La ME15,ME18 ..105 C7
Teston Rd Kings Hill ME19 ..89 B5
  Offham ME19 ....88 C7
  Red Hill ME18 ....89 C2
  West Malling ME19 ....89 A6
Tetty Way BR1,BR2 .....36 A7
Teviot Cl DA16 ....7 B6
Tewson Rd SE18 ....2 E1
Teynham Gn
  Gillingham ME8 ....49 A4
  Hayes BR2 ....36 A4
Teynham House SE9 ....6 D1
Thackeray Ave RM18 ...13 B6
Thackeray Rd ME10 ....74 F3
Thames Ave Gillingham ME8 ..63 E8
  High Halstow ME23 ...17 E4
Thames Barrier Visitor Ctr*
  SE18 ....1 B3
Thames Gate DA1 ......10 A3
Thames Rd Crayford DA1 ..9 A4
  Grays RM17 ....12 B7
  Newham E16 ....1 D5
  Tonbridge TN10 ......117 C5
Thames Road Ind Est E16 ..1 D4

Thames Terr ME3 ....16 B6
Thames View ME3 ......33 C7
Thames View Cotts ME3 ..32 D3
Thames View Inf Sch ME8 ..49 D2
Thames View Jun Sch
  ME8 ....49 D2
Thames Way
  Gravesend DA11 ....13 A1
  Northfleet DA11 ....29 E7
Thamesbank Pl SE28 ....3 C7
Thameside
  Cty Inf & Jun Schs RM17 ..12 C8
Thameside Ind Est E16 ..1 D4
Thamesmead Com Coll
  DA18 ....3 E4
Thamesmere Dr SE28 ...3 A6
Thamesview Sch DA12 ..30 F5
Thanet Dr BR2 ....50 D7
Thanet Ho **8** DA11 ....29 F7
Thanet House **7** ME15 ..107 F5
Thanet Rd Erith DA8 ....8 E7
  Sidcup DA5 ....25 A8
Thanington Ct SE9 ......6 F1
Thatch Barn Rd TN27 ..141 D6
Thatcher Cl DA1 ....26 D8
Thatcher Rd TN12 .....139 E4
Thatchers La ME3 ......16 A5
Thatchers The ME16 ...91 B5
Thaxted Rd SE9 ....23 C6
Theatre Sq **7** TN30 ...183 A7
Theatre St TN4 ....149 B8
Thelma Gdns SE3 ....5 E6
Theobalds TN18 ....178 F2
Theobalds Cl TN15 .....70 A1
Theodore Cl TN12 .....149 E7
Theodore Pl ME7 ....48 C5
Thicketts TN13 ....84 C4
Third Ave Chatham ME5 ..48 C1
  Gillingham ME7 ....48 F4
  West Thurrock RM20 ..11 E8
Third St TN3 ....147 F3
Thirlemere Cl ME16 ....91 D8
Thirlmere Cl
  Gillingham ME7 ....49 A5
  Rochester ME2 ....33 C1
Thirlmere Rd Bexley DA7 ..8 C6
  Royal Tunbridge Wells TN4 ..148 E5
Thirsk House **6** ME15 ..107 F6
Thirza Rd DA1 ....9 F1
Thistle Ct DA2 ....27 B7
Thistle Rd DA12 ....30 E8
Thistlebank ME5 ....62 A3
Thistlebrook SE2 ....3 C4
Thistledown
  Gravesend DA12 ....30 D2
  Maidstone ME14 ......92 F4
Thistledown Cl ME7 ....63 A4
Thistlemead BR7 ....37 B7
Thomas Aveling Sch The
  ME1 ....61 C8
Thomas Cotts DA13 ....29 B1
Thomas Cribb Mews E6 ..2 A7
Thomas Dinwiddy Rd
  SE12 ....22 B6
Thomas Dr DA12 ....30 D6
Thomas Dunk
  Almshouses **8** TN18 ..179 A2
Thomas St Rochester ME1 ..47 C3
  Royal Tunbridge Wells TN4 ..149 A5
  Woolwich SE18 ....2 B2
Thomas Tallis Sch SE3 ..5 B4
Thomas Wyatt Way TN15 ..71 F3
Thompson Cl ME8 ......64 A8
Thomson Cl ME6 ....60 A1
Thong La Basted TN15 ..86 F5
  Maidstone DA12 ....30 B2
Thornton Cl Bromley BR2 ..37 A3
  Chatham ME5 ....61 D1
Thorn Rd TN12 ....138 E4
Thorn's Mdw TN16 ....82 C2
Thorndale BR7 ....22 F1
Thorndale Cl ME5 ......61 D4
Thornden Cl TN17 .....188 A8
Thornden La TN14 .....61 F8
Thorndon Cl BR5 ....37 F7
Thorndon Rd BR5 ......37 F7
Thorndyke Way TN15 ..71 F3
Thorne Cl Erith DA8 ....8 B8
  Newham E16 ....1 A7
Thornet Wood Rd BR1 ..37 A6
Thorney Croft Cl ME17 ..109 D2
Thornfield Gdns TN2 ..149 F5
Thornham Rd ME8 .....49 C3
Thornhill Ave SE18 .....6 E7
Thornhill Pl ME14 ......92 A6
Thornton Dene DA14 ...24 A3
Thornton Rd Bromley BR1 ..22 B1
  Erith DA17 ....4 B2
Thorntree Rd SE7 ......1 D1
Thorntree Sch SE7 .....1 D1
Thorold Rd ME5 ....48 A3
Thorpe Ave TN10 .....117 C5
Thorpe Cl BR6 ....51 E8
Thorpe Wlk ME8 ....63 D3
Thorpe Works TN4 ....148 F8
Thrale Way ME8 ....63 A4
Three Corners DA7 .....8 B5
Three Elm La TN11 ....118 D5
Three Gates Rd DA3 ...42 A2
Three Oaks La TN5 ....174 C7
Thresher Field TN8 ....130 A6
Threshers Dr ME14 ....92 E5
Thrift The DA2 ....26 D5
Throckmorten Rd E16 ..1 B7
Throwley Cl SE2 ....3 C3
Thrush Cl ME5 ....62 B7
Thunderer Rd RM9 ....1 D8

Thurnham CE Inf Sch
  ME14 ....93 A4
Thurnham House **5** BR5 ..38 C6
Thurnham La ME14 ....93 C7
Thurrock Bsns Ctr RM20 ..10 F8
Thurrock Ent Ctr RM17 ..12 C7
Thurrock Park Way RM17 ..12 D7
Thursland Rd DA14 ....24 E3
Thursley Rd SE9 ....22 F5
Thurston Rd ME2 ......46 D7
Thurstone Ct ME14 ....91 F6
Thwaite Cl DA8 ....8 C8
Thyer Cl BR6 ....51 C6
Tibbs Court La TN12 ..152 A6
Ticehurst Cl BR5 ....24 A1
Tichborne Cl ME16 ....91 C6
Tickford Cl SE2 ....3 C4
Tidal Basin Rd E16 .....1 A6
Tidebrook Cl **4** BR5 ...38 C5
Tideside Cl SE18 ....1 E3
Tideway The ME1 ......61 C8
Tidford Rd DA16 ....6 F5
Tiger La BR2 ....36 B5
Tilbrook Rd SE3 ....5 D4
Tilbury Cl BR5 ....38 B7
Tilbury Fort* RM18 ....13 E4
Tilbury Manor Cty Inf Sch
  RM18 ....13 B7
Tilbury Town Sta RM18 ..12 F5
Tilden Cl TN26 ....173 D7
Tilden Gill Rd TN30 ...183 C7
Tilden La TN12 ....122 C3
Tilden Rd ME17,TN27 ..125 E2
Tile Farm Rd BR6 ......51 D7
Tile Fields ME17 ....94 D2
Tile Kiln La Coldblow DA5 ..25 C6
  Maidstone ME15 ......107 E7
Tilehurst Dr TN3 ......117 C4
Tilehurst Point **2** SE2 ..3 C4
Tilghman Way ME6 ....60 B1
Till Ave DA4 ....40 F2
Tillinghourne Gn BR5 ..38 A5
Tillmans TN15 ....87 A7
Tilmans Mead DA4 ....41 A2
Tilsden La TN17 ....169 E3
Tilt Yard App SE9 ......5 F1
Tilton Rd TN15 ....86 F7
Timber Bank DA13 .....72 F8
Timber Cl BR7 ....37 A7
Timber Ct RM17 ....12 A8
Timber Tops ME5 ......77 D8
Timberbank ME5 ......62 A6
Timbercroft Jun Sch SE18 ..6 C7
Timbercroft La SE18 ...6 C7
Timothy Cl DA6 ....7 E3
Timothy Ho DA18 ....3 E4
Tinker Pot La TN15 ....70 D6
Tinker's Alley ME4 .....47 F7
Tintagel Gdns ME2 .....46 F7
Tintagel Manor **6** ME7 ..48 C6
Tintagel Rd BR5 ....38 C1
Tinton Rd ME16 ....91 D7
Tippens Cl TN17 ......169 D4
Titan Rd RM17 ....12 B8
Titchfield Cl **5** ME15 ..107 F6
Titchfield Rd ME15 ...107 F6
Tithe Yd ME17 ....111 D5
Titmuss Ave SE28 ......3 B6
Tiverton Dr SE9 ....23 C7
Tivoli Gdns Gravesend DA12 ..30 B7
  Woolwich SE18 ....1 B2
Tobruk Way ME15 .....61 F6
Toby Gdns TN11 ....118 E8
Tockwith Ct TN13 .....84 C4
Toddington Cres ME5 ..61 D1
Tolcairn Ct **2** DA17 ...4 A2
Tolgate La ME2 ....47 B7
Tolgate Way ME14 .....76 E4
Tolhurst Rd TN12 .....135 F4
Tollgate Mews TN15 ...87 A8
Tollgate Pk TN27 .....141 E5
Tollgate Rd Dartford DA2 ..27 D8
  Newham E6 ....1 F8
Tolsey Mead TN15 .....87 A8
Tom Coombs Cl SE9 ....5 E3
Tom Cribb Rd SE28 .....2 D3
Tom Jenkinson Rd E16 ..1 A5
Tom Joyce Cl ME6 .....74 F7
Tomlin Cl Snodland ME6 ..75 A8
  Staplehurst TN12 ....139 E4
Tonbridge By-Pass
  Tonbridge
  TN11,TN9,TN4,TN14,TN15 ..116 B5
  Tonbridge TN4,TN9,TN11 ..133 C6
Tonbridge Chambers
  TN9 ....117 C8
Tonbridge Cottage Hospl
  TN11 ....133 C6
Tonbridge Cl SE16 .....91 D3
Tonbridge Gram Sch
  for Girls TN9 ....133 C8
Tonbridge Ho ME2 .....33 C1
Tonbridge Rd
  Hadlow TN11 ....118 C7
  Ightham TN15 ....86 C3
  Little Mill TN11,TN12 ..119 D4
  Maidstone ME16 ......91 E3
  Pembury TN2,TN11 ..150 E8
  Sevenoaks TN13,TN15 ..99 D7
  Tonbridge TN11 ......116 E5
  Wateringbury ME18 ..104 E8
  Tonbridge TN9 ....117 D5

Tong La TN12 ....152 B2
Tong Rd TN12,TN3 ...152 A4
Tongswood Dr TN18 ..179 C2
Topley St DA11 ....29 D6
Top Dartford Rd BR8,DA2 ..26 A2
Topcliffe Dr BR6 ....51 D6
Topley Dr ME23 ....17 E1
Topley St SE9 ....5 D1
Tor Rd DA16 ....7 C6
Torbay Rd TN12 ....120 B5
Torbrook Cl DA5 ....7 E1
Tormount Rd SE18 ......6 F8
Toronto Rd Gillingham ME7 ..48 E5
  Tilbury RM18 ....13 B6
Torrens Wlk DA12 .....30 E1
Torrington Ct ME18 ...103 D8
Torver Way BR6 ....51 D7
Totnes Rd DA16 ....7 C7
Tovil Gn ME15 ....91 E1
Tovil Green Bsns Pk ME15 ..91 E1
Tovil Hill ME15 ....91 E1
Tovil Rd ME15 ....91 F1
Tovil, St Stephen's
  CE Inf Sch ME15 ......91 E1
Tower Cl Gravesend DA12 ..30 E2
  Orpington BR6 ....54 E7
Tower Croft DA4 ....54 E7
Tower Gdns ME14 ......93 B6
Tower Hill ME17 ....88 D6
Tower Ind Est TN15 ...71 D7
Tower La ME14 ....93 A8
Tower Park Rd DA1 .....8 F4
Tower Rd Bexley DA7 ...8 A3
  Dartford DA1 ....9 C3
  Erith DA17 ....4 C2
  Orpington BR6 ....51 F7
Tower Ret Pk DA1 ......9 B3
Tower View ME19 ......89 B6
Towerfields BR2 ....50 E
Towers Wood DA4 .....41 D
Town Acres TN10 .....117 C
Town Hill
  Lamberhurst TN3 .....166 A
  West Malling ME19 ....74 C
Town Hill Cl ME19 .....74 C
Town Lock Ho **3** TN9 ..117 C
Town Meadow TN17 ..169 D
Town Pier **4** DA11 .....13 B
Town Rd ME3 ....33 A
Town Sq DA8 ....8 E
Town Square Cres BR6 ..27 F
Town Station Cotts TN8 ..112 D
Towncourt Cres BR5 ...37 D
Towncourt La BR5 .....37 D
Townfield Cnr DA12 ....30 D
Townland Cl TN27 ....158 A
Townlands Rd TN5 ....174 F
Townley Gram Sch
  for Girls DA6 ....7 F
Townley Rd DA6 ....7 F
Townsend
  Snodland ME6 ....74 F
  Woolwich SE18 ....6 E
Townsend Sq ME19 ....89 A
Townshend Cl DA14 ....24 C
Townshend Ho **4** SE18 ..1 F
Townshend Rd BR7 ....23 B
Toy's Hill TN14,TN8 ...97 C
Toynbec Cl BR7 ....23 B
Tracies The ME9 ....65 C
Trader Rd E6 ....2 B
Tradescant Dr DA13 ...44 E
Trafalgar Rd Dartford DA1 ..26 E
  Gravesend DA11 ....30 A
  Wouldham ME1 ....60 A
Trafalgar St ME7 ....48 C
Tramways ME5 ....48 C
Tranquil Rise DA8 ......4 D
Transfesa Rd TN12 ...136 A
Transmere Cl BR5 .....37 C
Transmere Rd BR5 ....37 C
Transom Ho **3** ME1 ...47 C
Trapfield Cl ME14 .....93 C
Trapfield La ME14 .....93 C
Trapham Rd ME16 .....91 C
Travers Gdns ME9 .....65 A
Travertine Rd ME5 .....62 B
Trebble Rd DA10 ......11 F
Trebilco Cl TN2 ....162 C
Tredegar Rd DA2 ......26 A
Tredwell Cl BR2 ....36 E
Tree La TN15 ....101 E
Tree Rd E16 ....1 C
Treetops Gravesend DA12 ..30 E
  Kemsing TN15 ....70 A
  Tonbridge TN9 ....133 E
Treetops Cl SE2 ....4 B
Treeval Gdns BR1 ......22 E
Trefoil Ho Erith DA18 ...3 E
  Grays RM17 ....12 E
Tregony Rd BR6 ....51 F
Trelawn Cres ME5 .....62 B
Trellyn Cl ME16 ....90 F
Trench Rd TN10 ....117 C
Trenear Cl BR6 ....52 A
Trent Rd ME5 ....62 B
Trentham Dr BR5 ......38 A
Trenton Cl ME16 ......91 E
Trevale Rd ME1 ....47 E
Trevelyan Cl DA1 ......10 A
Trevereux Hill RH8 ....96 A
Trevino Dr ME5 ....62 A
Trevithick Dr DA1 .....9 B
Trevor Cl BR2 ....36 A
Trevor Dr ME16 ....91 C
Trevor St **3** ME15 .....91 F
Trewsbury Ho **2** SE2 ..3 E
Triangle Ct E16 ....1 F

Triangle The DA15 ...24 A8
Trident Cl ME2 ...47 E7
Trinity Cl Orpington BR2 ...36 E5
  Royal Tunbridge Wells TN2 ...149 D4
Trinity Ct Aylesford ME20 ...76 A3
  Dartford DA1 ...27 B1
  Eltham SE9 ...6 B1
Trinity Gdns DA1 ...9 D1
Trinity Pl DA6 ...7 F3
Trinity Rd Gillingham ME7 ...48 C6
  Gravesend DA12 ...30 C8
Trinity Sch, Belvedere
  DA17 ...4 C2
Trinity St [1] E16 ...1 A8
Tristan Gdns TN4 ...148 D4
Triumph Rd E6 ...1 F7
Trivett Cl DA9 ...11 A2
Trolling Down Hill DA2 ...27 C6
Troodos Hill ME14 ...91 F8
Troon Cl SE28 ...3 D7
Trosley Ave DA11 ...30 B6
Trosley Ctry Pk Visitor Ctr*
  DA13 ...72 E7
Trosley Ctry Pk* ME19,DA13 ...73 A7
Trosley Rd DA17 ...8 A8
Trottiscliffe CE Prim Sch
  ME19 ...73 A5
Trottiscliffe Rd ME19 ...73 D3
Trotts La TN16 ...96 C8
Trotwood Cl ME5 ...77 A8
Troughton Rd SE7 ...1 B1
Troutbeck Ho ME20 ...75 C1
Troy Cl [1] SE18 ...2 B2
Troys Mead ME17 ...94 D2
Trubridge Rd ME3 ...34 E5
Truro Cl ME8 ...49 D3
Truro Rd DA12 ...30 D5
Truro Wlk TN10 ...117 D5
Trusedale Rd E6 ...1 F7
Trycenwell La TN15 ...86 D6
Tuam Rd SE18 ...2 D8
Tubbenden Cl BR6 ...51 E7
Tubbenden Dr BR6 ...51 D6
Tubbenden Inf & Jun Sch
  BR6 ...51 E7
Tubbenden La BR6 ...51 E7
Tubbenden La S BR6 ...51 D5
Tubs Hill TN13 ...84 B3
Tubs Hill Par TN13 ...84 A3
Tudeley La Tonbridge TN9 ...133 D7
  Tonbridge,
  Tudeley TN11,TN9 ...134 B8
Tudor Ave ME14 ...92 B6
Tudor Cl Bromley BR7 ...36 F8
  Dartford DA1 ...9 B2
  Northfleet DA11 ...29 E7
Tudor Cres TN14 ...69 D3
Tudor Ct Crockenhill BR8 ...39 C2
  Royal Tunbridge Wells TN2 ...148 E1
  Sidcup DA14 ...24 A5
Tudor Dr TN14 ...69 C3
Tudor Gr Chattenden ME3 ...33 F4
  Gillingham ME8 ...63 F8
Tudor Par SE9 ...5 E2
Tudor Way DA5 ...37 D3
Tudor Wlk DA5 ...7 E1
Tufa Cl ME5 ...62 B1
Tuff Cotts ME13 ...69 C3
Tufnail Rd DA1 ...9 F1
Tufton Rd ME8 ...49 F1
Tufton St ME14 ...92 A4
Tugboat St SE28 ...2 E4
Tugmutton Cl BR6 ...51 B6
Tulip Cl [5] E6 ...1 F8
Tulip Tree Cl TN9 ...133 B8
Tumblefield Rd TN15 ...71 F8
Tumblefield Rd TN15 ...71 E7
Tumblers Hill ME17 ...124 F7
Tunbridge Wells Gram Sch
  for Boys TN4 ...149 A7
Tunbridge Wells Gram Sch
  for Girls TN4 ...149 A6
Tunbridge Wells Ind Hospl
  The TN3 ...147 B3
Tunbridge Wells Mus*
  TN1 ...149 B2
Tunbridge Wells Trade Pk
  TN2 ...149 D8
Tunbridge Wells West Sta*
  TN3 ...148 F1
Tunbury Ave ME5 ...61 F1
Tunbury Ave S ME5 ...61 F1
Tunbury Cty Prim Sch
  ME5 ...61 F1
Tunnan Leys E6 ...2 A7
Tunnel Ave [1] SE10 ...1 A1
Tunnel Cotts RM20 ...11 A8
Tunnel Est RM20 ...10 F8
Tunnel Rd TN1 ...149 B4
Tunstall Cl BR6 ...51 E6
Tunstock Way DA17 ...3 E3
Tupman Cl ME1 ...47 B4
Turgis Cl ME17 ...108 E4
Turks Hall Pl ME2 ...59 E5
Turley Cotts TN14 ...84 A8
Turnberry Way BR6 ...37 D1
Turnbull Cl DA9 ...27 E8
Turnbury Cl SE28 ...3 D7
Turnden Rd TN17 ...169 A3
Turner Ave TN17 ...169 E3
Turner Ct DA1 ...9 C2
Turner Ho Gravesend DA12 ...30 C8
  [5] Greenwich SE7 ...5 B8
Turner Rd Bean DA2 ...28 B5
  Tonbridge TN10 ...117 E5
Turner St ME3 ...16 B5
Turners Ave TN30 ...183 B8

Turners Gdns TN13 ...99 C7
Turners Green La TN5 ...174 F6
Turners Green Rd TN5 ...174 F6
Turners Pl DA4 ...41 C8
Turnpike Ct DA4 ...7 D3
Turnpike Dr BR6 ...52 D2
Turnpike La RM18 ...13 D8
Turnstone Dr ...43 A7
Turnstone Rd ME5 ...62 C1
Turnstones The DA12 ...30 D6
Turpin La DA8 ...4 F1
Turpington Cl BR2 ...36 E2
Turpington La BR2 ...36 E3
Turton House [5] SE18 ...2 B2
Tuscan Dr ME5 ...77 F4
Tuscan Rd SE18 ...2 D1
Tutsham Way TN12 ...135 F6
Tuxford Rd TN4 ...148 B5
Tweed Rd TN10 ...117 C5
Tweedy Rd BR1 ...36 A8
Twigg Cl DA8 ...8 F7
Twisden Rd ME19 ...89 F8
Twiss Ho [6] SE18 ...2 B1
Twistleton Ct DA1 ...9 D1
Twitton La TN14 ...68 E3
Twitton Meadows TN14 ...68 E3
Two Gates Hill ME3 ...32 F5
Twydall Ent Ctr ...49 A2
Twydall Grn ME8 ...49 B3
Twydall Inf Sch ME8 ...49 A2
Twydall Jun Sch ME8 ...49 B2
Twydall La ME8 ...49 B2
Twyford Cl ME14 ...92 D6
Twyford Rd TN11 ...102 E1
Twysden Cotts TN18 ...186 A4
Tydeman Rd ME15 ...92 F2
Tye La BR6 ...51 C5
Tyeshurst Cl SE2 ...3 E1
Tyland Barn Wildlife
  Conservation Ctr* ME14 ...76 E3
Tyland La ME14 ...76 F3
Tyler Cl ME19 ...89 F8
Tyler Dr ME8 ...63 E4
Tyler Gr DA1 ...9 F1
Tylers Green Rd BR8 ...39 C2
Tylney Rd BR1 ...36 D7
Tyndall Rd DA16 ...6 F4
Tyne Cl ME5 ...62 C5
Tyne Rd TN10 ...117 B5
Tynedale Cl DA2 ...27 D7
Tynemouth Cl E6 ...2 B7
Typhoon Rd ME19 ...88 F3
Tyron Way DA14 ...23 F3
Tyrrell Ave DA16 ...7 B2
Tyrrells Hall Cl RM17 ...12 D8
Tyrwhitt-Drake
  Mus of Carriages* ME15 ...92 A3

U

Uckfield La TN8 ...129 D4
Udall Cotts DA15 ...23 E5
Ufton Cl ME15 ...92 E1
Ulcombe CE Prim Sch
  ME17 ...125 F6
Ulcombe Hill ME17 ...109 F1
Ulcombe Rd
  Headcorn TN27 ...141 C6
  Langley Heath ME17 ...108 E3
Ullswater Ho [5] ME15 ...107 E7
Underdown Ave ME4 ...47 F1
Underhill Jun Sch
  to Sutton Valence ME17 ...124 C7
Underlyn Ind Est TN12 ...122 F2
Underlyn La TN12 ...122 D1
Underriver House Rd
  TN15 ...100 D5
Underwood ME19 ...88 D7
Underwood Cl ME15 ...91 F2
Underwood The SE9 ...22 F6
Unicorn Wlk DA9 ...10 F2
Unicumes La ME15 ...91 C2
Union Ph ME15 ...107 F4
Union Pl ME4 ...48 A4
Union Rd BR2 ...36 D4
Union Sq St Chatham ME4 ...48 A3
  Flimwell TN5 ...177 B3
Unity Way SE18 ...1 D3
Univ of East London E16 ...2 A6
Univ of Greenwich
  Gillingham ME4 ...48 B8
  Woolwich SE18 ...2 A2
Univ of Greenwich
  (Dartford Campus) DA1 ...26 C6
Univ of Greenwich
  (Riverside Ho Annexe)
  SE18 ...2 A3
Univ of Greenwich
  (Southwood Site) SE9 ...6 C2
Univ of Greenwich
  Avery Hill Campus SE9 ...6 C1
Univ of Greenwich
  Avery Hill Campus
  Southwood Site SE9 ...23 D8
University Gdns DA5 ...24 F8
University Pl DA8 ...8 C7
University Way Dartford DA1 ...9 F3
  Woolwich E16 ...2 B6
Unwin Cl SE20 ...2 B6
Upbury Manor High Sch
  ME7 ...48 B4
Upbury Way ME4 ...48 A4
Upchat Rd ME3 ...33 F3
Updale Rd DA14 ...23 F4

Upland Inf Sch DA7 ...7 F4
Upland Jun Sch DA7 ...7 F4
Upland Rd DA7 ...7 F4
Uplands Cl Rochester ME2 ...46 D6
Uplands Com Coll TN5 ...175 A4
Uplands Rd BR6 ...38 B1
Uplands Way TN13 ...83 E7
Upnor Castle* ME2 ...33 F7
Upnor Rd
  Hoo St Werburgh ME3 ...33 E6
  Upnor ME2 ...33 E6
Upnor Rd Rochester ME2 ...47 D8
  Upper Upnor ME2 ...33 E2
Upper Abbey Rd DA17 ...4 A2
Upper Austin Lodge Rd
  DA4 ...54 D4
Upper Ave DA13 ...43 E8
Upper Barn Hill ME15 ...105 E3
Upper Britton Pl ME7 ...48 B5
Upper Bush Rd ME2 ...45 E5
Upper Church Hill DA9 ...10 E2
Upper Cumberland Wlk
  TN1 ...149 B1
Upper Dunstan Rd TN4 ...149 B6
Upper East Rd ME4 ...48 B8
Upper Fant Rd ME16 ...91 D2
Upper Green La TN11 ...101 D5
Upper Green Rd TN11 ...101 D5
Upper Grosvenor Rd
  TN1,TN4 ...149 B6
Upper Grove Rd DA17 ...7 F4
Upper Haysden La
  TN11,TN9 ...132 E6
Upper Holly Hill Rd DA17 ...4 B1
Upper Hunton Hill ME15 ...106 B2
Upper Luton Rd ME5 ...48 C2
Upper Mill ME18 ...104 D8
Upper Nellington TN3 ...148 B4
Upper Park Rd
  Bromley BR1 ...36 C8
  Erith DA17 ...4 B2
Upper Platts TN5 ...176 F1
Upper Profit TN3 ...148 A3
Upper Rd ME15 ...92 B2
Upper Sheridan Rd DA17 ...4 B1
Upper Spring La TN15 ...86 B5
Upper St
  Hollingbourne ME17 ...94 E3
  Leeds ME17 ...108 F5
  Royal Tunbridge Wells TN4 ...148 D4
Upper Stephens TN3 ...148 B3
Upper Stone St ME15 ...92 A3
Upper Street N ME6 ...74 F8
Upper Street S ME6 ...56 F8
Upper Walderslade ME16 ...7 B6
Upperton Rd DA14 ...23 F3
Upton Cl DA5 ...7 F1
Upton Day Hospl DA6 ...7 E3
Upton Dr DA5 ...7 F2
Upton Quarry TN3 ...147 F3
Upton Rd Bexley DA6 ...7 E2
  Woolwich SE18 ...6 D8
Upton Rd S DA5 ...7 F1
Upton Villas [4] DA6 ...7 E3
Uptons TN27 ...141 C6
Uridge Cres TN10 ...117 C4
Uridge Rd TN10 ...117 C4
Urquhart Cl ME5 ...62 A5
Ursula Lodges DA14 ...24 B3
Usborne Cl TN12 ...139 E3

V

Vale Ave
  Royal Tunbridge Wells TN1 ...149 A3
  Tunbridge
  Wells,Southborough TN4 ...132 F1
Vale Cl BR6 ...51 A6
Vale Cotts ME9 ...80 A8
Vale Ct TN4 ...133 A2
Vale Dr ME15 ...107 A8
Vale Rd Bromley BR1 ...37 A7
  Dartford DA1 ...26 B7
  Hawkhurst TN18 ...178 F3
  Maidstone ME15 ...106 E4
  Northfleet DA11 ...29 F7
  Royal Tunbridge Wells TN1 ...149 A3
  Tonbridge TN9 ...117 C1
Vale Rise TN9 ...133 E8
Valence Ho ME15 ...107 C7
Valence Rd DA8 ...8 D7
Valence Sch TN16 ...82 E3
Valence View TN17 ...156 E7
Valentine Ave DA5 ...24 E6
Valentine Cl ME7 ...49 A1
Valentine Dr ME23 ...17 E4
Valentine Rd ME15 ...107 E7
Valerian Cl ME4 ...61 E4
Valetta Way ME1 ...47 B4
Valiant Ho [5] SE7 ...1 C1
Valiant Rd ME5 ...62 C2
Valiant Way E6 ...1 F8
Valley (Charlton Athletic FC)
  The SE7 ...1 C1
Valley Cl DA1 ...8 F1
Valley Dr
  Gravesend,Riverview Park
  DA12 ...30 D4
  Gravesend,Singlewell DA12 ...30 D2
  Maidstone ME15 ...106 F6
  Sevenoaks TN13 ...84 B1
Valley Forge Cl TN10 ...117 F4
Valley Gdns DA9 ...11 B1
Valley Gr SE7 ...1 C1
Valley L Ctr SE9 ...23 C8

Valley La DA13 ...58 B2
Valley Park Com Sch
  ME14 ...92 C4
Valley Rd Crayford DA1 ...8 F1
  Erith DA8 ...4 D2
  Fawkham Green DA3 ...42 E2
  Gillingham ME7 ...48 E4
  Royal Tunbridge Wells TN4 ...148 D4
  St Paul's Cray BR5 ...38 B8
Valley Rise ME5 ...61 F1
Valley The ME17 ...106 D3
Valley View
  Royal Tunbridge Wells TN4 ...133 A2
  Swanscombe DA9 ...11 B1
Valley View Rd ME1 ...47 B1
Valley View Terr DA4 ...40 F1
Valleyside SE7 ...1 D1
Valliers Wood Rd DA15 ...23 E7
Vambery Rd SE18 ...6 C8
Vanbrugh Pk SE3 ...5 A7
Vanburgh Cl [1] Newham E16 ...1 D8
  Orpington BR6 ...37 E1
Vancouver Cl BR6 ...52 A6
Vancouver Dr ME8 ...49 C1
Vandome Cl E16 ...1 B7
Vandyke Cross SE9 ...5 E2
Vanessa Cl DA17 ...4 A1
Vanessa Dr DA12 ...30 D3
Vanessa Way DA5 ...25 D1
Vanessa Wlk DA12 ...30 D3
Vange Cottage Mews ME1 ...47 B4
Vanguard Cl E16 ...1 A8
Vanity La ME17 ...106 D1
Vanoc Gdns BR1 ...22 A4
Vanquisher Wlk DA12 ...30 F5
Varley Rd E16 ...1 B7
Varnes St ME20 ...75 F6
Vaughan Ave TN10 ...117 E6
Vaughan Rd DA16 ...6 F5
Vauxhall Cl DA11 ...29 F8
Vauxhall Cres ME6 ...75 A6
Vauxhall La TN4,TN9 ...133 C7
Vauxhall
  Bidborough TN11,TN4 ...133 B4
  Tonbridge TN11 ...133 D6
Vauxhall Pl DA1 ...26 E8
Veitchil Barn RM18 ...39 F8
Veles Rd ME5 ...74 F8
Venmead Ct [4] DA17 ...4 A2
Venners Cl DA7 ...8 E5
Ventnor Cl ME5 ...62 C8
Venture Cl DA5 ...24 E8
Venture Ct ME15 ...22 A8
Venus Rd SE18 ...1 F3
Verdun Rd SE18,SE2 ...7 A8
Vernham Rd SE18 ...6 C8
Vernham Rd SE18 ...6 C8
Vernon Cl
  St Paul's Cray BR5 ...38 B6
  West Kingsdown TN15 ...55 F2
Vernon Rd
  Royal Tunbridge Wells TN1 ...149 C6
  Swanscombe DA10 ...11 F1
Veroan Rd DA7 ...7 E5
Verona Gdns DA12 ...30 F4
Verona House DA8 ...8 F7
Vert House MN17 ...12 C7
Veryan Cl BR5 ...38 C5
Vesper Ct TN27 ...143 A1
Vestry Cotts New Barn DA3 ...43 C5
  Sevenoaks TN14 ...84 C8
Vestry Rd TN14 ...84 C8
Via Romana DA12 ...31 B7
Viaduct Terr DA4 ...41 C7
Vicarage Ave SE3 ...5 A7
Vicarage Cl Aylesford ME20 ...75 F3
  Erith DA8 ...8 C8
  Halling ME2 ...60 A5
  Lower Stoke ME3 ...19 A3
Vicarage Ct Chalk DA12 ...31 A6
  Newington ME9 ...65 B7
Vicarage Dr DA12 ...12 C1
Vicarage Hill TN16 ...81 D1
Vicarage La Chalk DA12 ...31 A6
  East Farleigh ME15 ...106 B6
  Hoo St Werburgh ME3 ...34 E4
  Sevenoaks TN13 ...83 D8
Vicarage Pk SE18 ...2 C1
Vicarage Rd Coldblow DA5 ...25 B7
  Gillingham ME7 ...48 C5
  Halling ME2 ...59 F5
  Rochester ME2 ...47 B8
  Royal Tunbridge Wells TN4 ...132 F2
  Yalding ME18 ...105 A1
Vicarage Row ME3 ...32 C4
Vicarage Sq RM17 ...12 A8
Vicarage Way TN19 ...184 A3
Vicary Way ME16 ...91 D5
Vickers Rd DA8 ...4 D1
Victor Mills Cotts DA14 ...25 A1
Victoria Ave [3] DA12 ...30 B8
Victoria Bglws DA14 ...24 F5
Victoria Cl BR8 ...39 F6
Victoria Cotts
  Cranbrook TN17 ...169 D5
  Kings Hill ME19 ...128 C8
Victoria Ct [6] ME16 ...91 E3
Victoria Dock Rd E16 ...1 B6
Victoria Dr Kings Hill ME19 ...128 B7
  Sutton at Hone DA4 ...41 D7
Victoria Ind Pk DA1 ...9 E2
Victoria Ind Est BR8 ...40 A8
Victoria Rd Bexley DA6 ...8 A3
  Bromley BR2 ...36 D4
  Chatham,Luton ME4 ...48 B2
  Chatham,Walderslade ME5 ...61 E3

Victoria Rd continued
  Chislehurst BR7 ...23 A3
  Dartford DA1 ...27 B2
  Edenbridge TN8 ...128 C8
  Erith DA8 ...8 E8
  Golden Green TN11 ...118 F6
  Gravesend DA11 ...29 F7
  Royal Tunbridge Wells TN1 ...149 B4
  Royal Tunbridge
  Wells,Modest Corner TN4 ...132 E1
  Sevenoaks TN13 ...84 B2
  Sidcup DA15 ...24 A5
Victoria St Eccles ME20 ...75 F6
  Erith DA17 ...3 F1
  Gillingham ME4 ...48 D6
  Maidstone ME16 ...91 E3
  Rochester ME2 ...47 B7
  Rochester,Troy Town ME1 ...47 D5
Victoria Terr ME1 ...47 A2
Victoria Wharf DA1 ...9 E2
Victory Cotts TN14 ...99 C2
Victory Manor [1] ME7 ...48 A6
  DA7 ...47 E7
Victory Terr ME17 ...124 E8
Victory Way DA2 ...10 C3
Vidal Manor ME7 ...48 C5
Videon Ave ME3 ...34 D6
View The SE3 ...3 E1
Viewfield Rd DA5 ...24 C7
Viewland Rd SE18 ...2 F1
Viewlands ME5 ...48 C3
Viewlands Ave TN16 ...81 F7
Viewpoint Ct DA3 ...42 F5
Vigilant Way DA12 ...30 F3
Vigo Rd TN15 ...72 C7
Vigo Village Sch DA13 ...73 A8
Viking Cl ME2 ...46 F4
Viking Gdns E6 ...1 F8
Viking Ho [3] SE18 ...1 E2
Viking Rd DA11 ...29 C5
Viking Way Erith DA8,DA17 ...4 C3
  West Kingsdown TN15 ...55 E5
Villa Cl DA12 ...31 B6
Villa Ct DA1 ...26 E6
Villa Rd ME3 ...32 B3
Village Cl SE18,SE2 ...7 A8
Village Green Rd DA1 ...9 A3
Village The SE7 ...5 D8
Village View ME5 ...48 C2
Villas Rd SE18 ...2 C2
Vincent Cl Bromley BR2 ...36 B5
  Sidcup DA15 ...23 E7
Vincent Rd Kit's Coty ME20 ...76 C7
  Woolwich SE18 ...2 C2
Vincent St [1] E16 ...1 A8
Vine Ave TN13 ...84 B3
Vine Court Rd TN13 ...84 C4
Vine Ct Staplehurst TN12 ...139 F3
  Wateringbury ME18 ...104 D8
Vine Lodge Ct TN13 ...84 B3
Vine Rd BR6 ...51 F4
Vine The TN13 ...84 C3
Vine Wlk TN12 ...139 E3
Vineries The ME7 ...48 E5
Vines La
  Hildenborough TN11 ...100 C1
  Rochester ME1 ...47 C5
Viney's Gdns TN30 ...173 C1
Vineyard La TN5 ...174 C5
Vinson Cl BR6 ...38 A1
Vinters Rd DA15 ...24 A6
Vinters Rd ME14 ...92 E4
Vintners Way ME14 ...92 E4
Viola Ave SE2 ...3 B2
Violet Cl ME5 ...77 A8
Violets The TN12 ...136 A5
VIP Trad Est SE7 ...1 C2
Virginia Rd ME7 ...48 C7
Virginia Wlk DA12 ...30 E4
Viscount Dr E6 ...2 A8
Vista The SE9 ...22 E8
Vixen Cl ME5 ...62 C6
Voce Rd SE18 ...6 E8
Vogue Ct [8] BR1 ...36 B8
Volante Way DA12 ...30 E4
Voyagers Cl SE28 ...3 C7
Vulcan Cl Chatham ME5 ...62 B7
  New Barn DA3 ...43 B7
Vyne The DA7 ...8 B4
Vyvyan Cotts TN17 ...180 C3
Vyvyan House SE18 ...6 A6

W

Wadard Terr BR8 ...40 C5
Wade Ave BR5 ...38 C2
Wadeville Cl DA17 ...4 A1
Wadhurst Bsns Pk TN5 ...174 B7
Wadhurst CE Prim Sch
  TN5 ...174 F5
Wadhurst Par TN5 ...174 F4
Wadhurst Sta TN5 ...174 C6
Wadlands Rd ME16 ...18 E5
Waghorn Rd ME6 ...75 A8
Waghorn St ME4 ...48 A2
Wagon La TN12 ...120 C1
Wagoners Cl ME14 ...92 E4
Wagtail Way BR6 ...38 D5
Waid Cl DA1 ...9 F1
Wainhouse Cl TN8 ...112 D3
Wainscott Prim Sch ME2 ...33 D2
Wainscott Rd ME2 ...33 D2

Wainscott Wlk ME2 . . . . .33 D3
Waite Davies Rd **6** SE12 . .22 A8
Wake Rd DA1 . . . . .61 C8
Wakefield Cl ME2 . . . . .46 D6
Wakefield Rd DA9 . . . . .11 C2
Wakehurst Cl ME17 . . . . . . .106 B3
Wakeleys Cotts ME8 . . . . . . .64 B8
Wakerly Cl **6** E6 . . . . .1 E7
Waldair Ct E16 . . . . .2 B4
Waldeck Rd DA1 . . . . .10 A1
Waldegrave Rd BR1 . . . . .36 F5
Walden Ave BR7 . . . . .22 F4
Walden Cl DA17 . . . . .3 F1
Walden Par BR7 . . . . .22 F2
Walden Rd BR7 . . . . .22 F2
Waldenhurst Rd BR5 . . . . . . .38 D2
Waldens Cl BR5 . . . . .38 D2
Waldens Rd BR5 . . . . .38 E3
Waldens The ME17 . . . . .109 E2
Walderslade Ctr ME5 . . . . . . .62 A3

Walderslade Girls Sch
ME5 . . . . .61 F5

Walderslade Prim Sch
ME5 . . . . .62 A3

Walderslade Rd ME5 . . . . . . .61 F6
Walderslade Woods ME5 . .61 E2
Waldo Ind Est BR1 . . . . .36 D6
Waldo Rd BR1 . . . . .36 D6
Waldrist Way DA18 . . . . .3 F4
Waldron Dr ME15 . . . . .106 F6
Waldstock Rd SE28 . . . . .3 A6
Walk The ME17 . . . . .109 E2
Walkden Rd BR7 . . . . .23 A3
Walker Cl Crayford DA1 . . . . . .8 F4
Woolwich SE18 . . . . .2 C2
Walker Pl TN15 . . . . .86 D6
Walkhurst Cotts TN17 . . . .180 F7
Walkhurst Rd TN17 . . . . . . .180 F7
Walkley Rd DA1 . . . . .9 F2
Walks The TN3 . . . . .161 C8
Wall Cl ME3 . . . . .34 D7
Wallace Cl Erith SE28 . . . . . . .3 D6
Royal Tunbridge Wells TN2 . .163 A8
Wallace Gdns DA10 . . . . .11 E1
Wallace Rd ME1 . . . . .61 E8
Wallace Terr TN15 . . . . .56 E4
Waller Hill TN17 . . . . .156 B5
Wallers TN3 . . . . .148 A8
Wallhouse Rd DA8 . . . . .9 C7
Wallis Ave ME15 . . . . .107 E5
Wallis Cl DA2 . . . . .25 F5
Wallis Field TN3 . . . . .161 B6
Wallis Pk TN11 . . . . .116 C7
Walmer Cl BR6 . . . . .51 D6
Walmer Ct **5** ME14 . . . . .92 A5
Walmer Ho ME2 . . . . .33 C1
Walmer Terr SE18 . . . . .2 D2
Walmers Ave ME3 . . . . .32 A4
Walnut Cl Chatham ME5 . . . . .62 B8
Eynsford DA4 . . . . .54 D7
Paddock Wood TN12 . . . . . . .136 A6
Yalding ME18 . . . . .104 F1
Walnut Hill Rd DA13 . . . . . . .43 E6
Walnut Tree Ave
Dartford DA1 . . . . .26 E6
Maidstone ME15 . . . . .107 A5
Walnut Tree Cl BR7 . . . . .37 C8
Walnut Tree Cl ME20 . . . . . . .75 B1
Walnut Tree La TN15 . . . . . . .107 A5
Walnut Tree Rd DA8 . . . . .4 E1
Walnut Tree Way DA13 . . . . .44 B3
Walnut Way
Royal Tunbridge Wells TN4 . .133 D1
Swanley BR8 . . . . .39 D7
Walnuts Rd BR6 . . . . .38 B1
Walnuts The BR6 . . . . .38 B1
Walpole Cl ME19 . . . . .74 F1
Walpole Pl SE18 . . . . .2 B2
Walpole Rd BR2 . . . . .36 D4
Walsham Cl ME5 . . . . .3 D6
Walsham Cl SE28 . . . . .3 D6
Walsham House **2** ME14 . .92 A6
Walsingham Ho ME8 . . . . . . .63 D3

Walsingham House **3**
ME14 . . . . .92 A6

Walsingham Pk BR7 . . . . .37 D7
Walsingham Rd BR5 . . . . .38 B8
Walsingham Wlk DA17 . . . . . .8 A8
Walter Burke Ave ME1 . . . . . .60 C5
Walter's Farm Rd TN9 . . . . .117 C1
Walters Green Rd TN11 . . . .146 F6
Walters Ho SE18 . . . . .6 A7
Walters Rd ME3 . . . . .34 E6
Walters Yd BR1 . . . . .36 A7
Waltham Cl Dartford DA1 . . . .9 A1
Orpington BR5 . . . . .38 D1
Waltham Rd ME8 . . . . .49 C3

Walthamstow Hall Inf Sch
TN13 . . . . .84 C4

Walthamstow Hall Jun Sch
TN13 . . . . .84 B5

Walton Rd Sidcup DA14 . . . . .24 C5
Tonbridge TN10 . . . . .117 C6
Walwyn Ave BR1 . . . . .36 D6
Wanden La TN27 . . . . .143 C8
Wansbury Way BR8 . . . . .40 A5
Wanstead Cl BR1 . . . . .36 C7
Wanstead Rd BR1 . . . . .36 C7
Wanstead Rd DA5 . . . . .25 C7
Warblers Cl **13** ME2 . . . . .47 A7
Ward Cl Erith DA8 . . . . .8 D8
Wadhurst TN5 . . . . .174 E5
Ward's La TN5 . . . . .175 E4
Warde's ME18 . . . . .104 F2
Warden Cl ME16 . . . . .91 C4

Warden Mill Cl ME18 . . . . . .104 E7
Warden Rd ME1 . . . . .47 C2
Wardens Field Cl **2** BR6 . .51 F4
Wardona Ct DA10 . . . . .11 F1
Wardwell La ME4 . . . . .65 C8
Ware St ME14 . . . . .93 A5
Warepoint Dr SE28 . . . . .2 D4
Warham Rd TN14 . . . . .69 B3
Waring Cl BR6 . . . . .52 A4
Waring Dr BR6 . . . . .52 A4
Waring Rd DA14 . . . . .24 C2
Warland Rd
West Kingsdown TN15 . . . . . . .55 F2
Woolwich SE18 . . . . .6 E7
Warmlake ME17 . . . . .108 F1
Warmlake Est ME17 . . . . . . .108 E1
Warmlake Rd ME17 . . . . . . .108 C1
Warne Pl **4** DA15 . . . . .7 B1
Warner St ME4 . . . . .47 F3
Warnett Ct ME2 . . . . .46 C6
Warnford Gdns ME15 . . . . .107 A8
Warnford Rd BR6 . . . . .51 F5
Warren Ave BR6 . . . . .51 F5
Warren Cl DA6 . . . . .8 A2
Warren Cotts TN11 . . . . .131 A3
Warren Ct TN15 . . . . .84 C3
Warren Dr BR6 . . . . .52 B5
Warren Farm La TN3 . . . . . . .162 B4
Warren Gdns BR6 . . . . .52 A5
Warren La Hartlip ME9 . . . . . .64 C3
Warren Rd Bexley DA6 . . . . . . .8 A2
Dartford DA1 . . . . .26 E5
Hayes BR2 . . . . .50 A8
Kit's Coty ME5 . . . . .76 D7
Luddesdown ME2 . . . . .45 D3
Northfleet DA13 . . . . .29 B3
Orpington BR6 . . . . .52 B5
Sidcup DA14 . . . . .24 C5
Warren Ridge TN3 . . . . .163 C3

Warren Road Prim Sch
BR6 . . . . .51 F6

Warren The
Gravesend DA12 . . . . .30 D4
Penshurst TN11 . . . . .131 A4
Ticehurst TN5 . . . . .176 E1
Warren View DA12 . . . . .31 E2
Warren Wlk **8** SE7 . . . . .5 C8
Warren Wood Cl BR2 . . . . . . .50 A8

Warren Wood
Cty Prim Sch
& Language Unit ME1 . . . . . .61 C8

Warren Wood Rd ME1 . . . . . .61 C7
Warrens The DA3 . . . . .42 F3
Warrington Rd TN12 . . . . . . .136 A6
Warrior Ave DA12 . . . . .30 C4
Warspite Rd SE18 . . . . .1 E3
Warwall E6 . . . . .2 B7
Warwick Cl Orpington BR6 . .52 A7
Sidcup DA5 . . . . .24 F8
Warwick Cres ME1 . . . . .46 F2
Warwick Gdns DA13 . . . . .58 A8
Warwick Pk TN2 . . . . .149 B1
Warwick Pl
Maidstone ME16 . . . . .91 E3
Northfleet DA11 . . . . .12 B2
Warwick Rd Bexley DA6 . . . . . .7 C4
4 Royal Tunbridge
Wells TN1 . . . . .149 A2
Warwick Terr SE18 . . . . .6 D8
Washneys Rd BR6 . . . . .67 B6
Washwell La TN5 . . . . .174 F3
Wassall La TN17 . . . . .186 A3
Wat Tyler Way ME15 . . . . . . .92 A4
Watchgate DA2 . . . . .27 E3
Watchmans Terr **6** ME5 . .48 C2
Water La
Biddenden Green TN27 . . . . .142 F2
Four Wents TN18 . . . . .179 B4
Harrietsham ME17 . . . . .110 B5
Headcorn TN17,TN27 . . . . . .141 A4
Hunton ME15 . . . . .121 D6
Kingswood ME17 . . . . .109 F3
11 Maidstone ME15 . . . . . .92 A4
Maidstone,Bearsted ME14 . . .93 E6
Shoreham TN14 . . . . .68 F6
Sidcup DA14 . . . . .24 E6
Smarden TN27 . . . . .89 C8
Water Mill Way DA4 . . . . .41 B7
Water Slippe TN11 . . . . .102 D1
Watercress Cl TN14 . . . . .84 C7
Watercress Dr TN14 . . . . .84 C7
Watercroft Rd TN14 . . . . .52 F1
Waterdale Rd SE2 . . . . .7 A8
Waterdales DA11 . . . . .29 D7
Waterdown Rd TN4 . . . . .148 E1
Waterfield TN2 . . . . .163 A2
Waterfield Cl Erith DA17 . . . . .4 A3
Woolwich SE18 . . . . .3 B5
Waterfrets Cotts TN3 . . . . . .147 F5
Watergate Ho **2** SE18 . . . . . . .2 A2
Waterglade Ind Pk RM20 . . . .10 F8
Waterhead Cl DA8 . . . . .8 E7
Waterhouse Cl E16 . . . . .1 D8

Wateringbury CE Prim Sch
ME18 .104 E6

Wateringbury Rd ME15 . . . . .88 B7
Wateringbury Rd ME19 . . . . .89 F3
Wateringbury Sta ME18 . . .104 E6
Waterlakes TN8 . . . . .128 C8
Waterloo Pl
Cranbrook TN17 . . . . .169 D5
Tonbridge TN9 . . . . .133 B8
Waterloo Rd
Cranbrook TN17 . . . . .169 D6
Gillingham ME7 . . . . .48 C4

Waterloo St
1 Gravesend DA12 . . . . . . .30 C8
Maidstone ME15 . . . . .92 A3
Waterlow Rd
Maidstone ME14 . . . . .92 A6
Vigo Village DA13 . . . . .58 F2
Watermeadow La TN12 . . . .136 B3
Watermeadow Cl Erith DA8 . . .9 B6
Gillingham ME7 . . . . .62 F6
Watermill Cl
Maidstone ME8 . . . . .91 B5
Rochester ME2 . . . . .47 C8
Watermint Cl BR5 . . . . .38 D5
Waters Cotts TN5 . . . . .175 A4
Waters Edge ME15 . . . . .91 F2
Watery Rd ME7 . . . . .63 A6
Waterside LA 8 F2
Waterside Ct
Leybourne ME19 . . . . .74 E2
Rochester ME2 . . . . .47 C6
Waterside La ME7 . . . . .48 F7
Waterside Mews ME18 . . . .104 D6
Watersmeet Way SE28 . . . . . .3 D7
Waterton BR8 . . . . .39 D6
Waterton Ave DA12 . . . . .30 E8
Watery La Heaversham TN15 .85 D7
Sidcup BR5,DA4 . . . . .24 B2
Watford Rd E16 . . . . .1 A8
Watkins Ave ME3 . . . . .33 F4
Watling Ave ME5 . . . . .48 D2
Watling House **10** SE18 . . . . . .6 B8
Watling St Bexley DA6,DA7 . . .8 C3
Chatham ME5 . . . . .48 D2
Dartford DA1,DA2 . . . . .27 C8
Gravesend DA11,DA12 . . . . . .30 C2
Northfleet DA11,DA13 . . . . . .29 C5
Rochester ME2 . . . . .46 D7
Watson Ave ME5 . . . . .61 D5
Watson Cl RM20 . . . . .11 A6
Watt Ho SE2 . . . . .3 C1
Watt's Cross Rd TN11 . . . . .116 B6
Watt's La BR7 . . . . .37 C8
Watts Cl Snodland ME6 . . . . .75 B8
Wadhurst TN5 . . . . .174 F4
Watts' Ave ME1 . . . . .47 C4
Watts' St ME4 . . . . .47 E3
Watts Cl DA15 . . . . .6 E1
Waveney Rd TN10 . . . . .117 B5
Waverley Cl Bromley BR2 . . .36 D4
Chatham ME5 . . . . .62 D2
Dartford DA1 . . . . .9 F1
Waverley Cres SE18 . . . . .2 D1
Waverley Dr TN2 . . . . .149 F6
Waverley Gdns E6 . . . . .1 E8
Waverley Rd SE18 . . . . .2 D1
Wayfield Cty Prim Sch
ME5 . . . . .62 A7
Wayfield Link SE9 . . . . .6 D1
Wayfield Rd ME5 . . . . .62 A7
Waylands BR8 . . . . .39 F5
Waylands Cl TN14 . . . . .67 C4
Wayne Cl BR6 . . . . .51 F7
Wayne Ct ME2 . . . . .33 D2
Wayside ME9 . . . . .173 B2
Wayside Ave TN30 . . . . .173 B3
Wayside Dr TN8 . . . . .112 D3
Wayside Flats TN30 . . . . . . .173 B2
Wayside Gr SE9 . . . . .22 F4
Wayville Rd DA1 . . . . .27 B8
Weald Cl Istead Rise DA13 . .29 E1
Maidstone ME15 . . . . .107 C6
Orpington BR2 . . . . .50 E8
Sevenoaks Weald TN14 . . . . . .99 C2

Weald Com Prim Sch
TN14 . . . . .99 B2

Weald Cl TN11 . . . . .116 D6

Weald of Kent Gram Sch
for Girls TN9 . . . . .133 C7

Weald The BR7 . . . . .22 F2
Weald View
Frittenden TN12 . . . . .156 E6
Paddock Wood TN12 . . . . . . .136 A1
Wadhurst TN5 . . . . .174 F6
Weald View Rd TN9 . . . . . . .133 B7
Wealden Ave TN30 . . . . .173 B1
Wealden Cl TN11 . . . . .116 E5
Wealden Ct **8** ME5 . . . . .48 B6
Wealden Pl TN13 . . . . .84 D6
Wealden Way ME20 . . . . .90 E7
Wealdon View TN17 . . . . . . .167 E8
Weardale Ave DA2 . . . . .27 C7
Weare Rd TN4 . . . . .149 C8
Weatherly Cl ME1 . . . . .47 C4
Weathersfield Ct SE9 . . . . .5 F1
Weaver Cl E6 . . . . .2 B6
Weaver's Orch DA13 . . . . .29 A2
Weavers Cl **3** ME5 . . . . .48 C6
Weavering Cotts ME14 . . . . . .92 E3
Weavering St ME14 . . . . .92 F4
Weavers Cl Gravesend DA11 . .30 A7
Staplehurst TN12 . . . . .139 F4
Weavers Cotts TN17 . . . . . . .167 E8
Weavers La TN14 . . . . .84 C6
Weavers The
Biddenden TN27 . . . . .158 A1
Maidstone ME15 . . . . .91 E5
Webb Cl ME3 . . . . .34 D6
Webb Ct **8** SE28 . . . . .3 B6
Webb's Mdw TN15 . . . . .84 C2
Webber Cl DA8 . . . . .9 B7
Webster Rd ME8 . . . . .49 F1
Wedgewood Cl ME16 . . . . . . .91 B5
Wedgewood Ct BR2 . . . . .36 A6
Wedgewood Dr ME5 . . . . .62 A7
Weeds Wood Rd ME5 . . . . . . .62 A4
Week St ME14 . . . . .92 A4
Weeks La TN27 . . . . .158 A5

Weigall Rd SE12,SE3 . . . . .5 A3
Weir Rd DA5 . . . . .25 B8
Weird Wood DA3 . . . . .43 C6
Welbeck Ave Bromley BR1 . . .22 A4
Royal Tunbridge Wells TN4 . .149 C8
Sidcup DA15 . . . . .24 A7
Welcombe Ct ME8 . . . . .63 D8
Weld Cl TN12 . . . . .139 F4
Weldstock Ho SE28 . . . . .2 D3
Well Cl TN11 . . . . .115 F1
Well Field DA3 . . . . .42 E5
Well Hall* SE9 . . . . .5 E3
Well Hall Par SE9 . . . . .5 F5
Well Hall Rd SE18,SE9 . . . . . . .5 F5
Well Hill BR6 . . . . .53 B5
Well Hill La BR6 . . . . .53 B4
Well Penn Rd ME3 . . . . .16 C3
Well Rd Maidstone ME14 . . . .92 A5
Otford TN14 . . . . .69 C3
West St Mailing ME19 . . . . . . .89 E6
Maidstone ME15,ME17 . . . . .106 E4
Wellan Cl DA16 . . . . .7 B2
Welland Rd TN10 . . . . .117 B4
Wellands Cl BR1 . . . . .36 F7
Wellbrook Rd BR6 . . . . .51 A6
Wellcome Ave DA1 . . . . .9 E3
Weller Ave ME1 . . . . .47 D2
Weller Pl BR6 . . . . .66 A8
Weller Rd TN4 . . . . .148 C4
Wellers Cl TN16 . . . . .96 C8
Wellesley Cl **7** SE7 . . . . .1 C1
Welling High St DA16 . . . . .7 B4
Welling Sch DA16 . . . . .7 B6
Welling Sta DA16 . . . . .7 B5
Welling Way DA16 . . . . .6 D4
Wellingfield Cl TN16 . . . . .7 A4
Wellington Ave Sidcup DA15 . .7 A1
Welling Way DA16 . . . . .6 D4
Wellington Cotts
Gill's Green TN18 . . . . .178 E4
Meopham DA13 . . . . .58 A7
Wellington House **6**
ME15 .107 E5
Wellington Par DA15 . . . . .7 A1
Wellington Pl
Maidstone ME14 . . . . .91 F6
Wadhurst TN5 . . . . .174 F5
Wellington Rd Bexley DA5 . . . .7 B2
Bromley BR2 . . . . .36 C5
Dartford DA1 . . . . .9 F1
Gillingham ME7 . . . . .48 C4
Orpington BR5 . . . . .38 C3
Tilbury RM18 . . . . .13 A5
Wells Cl
Royal Tunbridge Wells TN1 . .149 A3
Tenterden TN30 . . . . .183 B8
Tonbridge TN10 . . . . .117 D4
Westerham TN16 . . . . .96 C8
Wells Cotts ME18 . . . . .104 C2
Wells Ct ME2 . . . . .46 D5
Wells Ho Bromley BR1 . . . . . .22 B3
Royal Tunbridge Wells TN4 . .148 F4
Wells Rd Bromley BR1 . . . . . .36 F6
Rochester ME2 . . . . .46 D5
Wellsmoor Gdns BR1 . . . . . . .37 A6
Welton Cl TN6 . . . . .132 F7
Welton Rd SE18 . . . . .2 E2
Wemmick Cl ME1 . . . . .61 D7
Wendover Cl ME7 . . . . .63 A4
Wendover Ct BR2 . . . . .36 B6
Wendover Rd
Bromley BR1,BR2 . . . . .36 B6
Eltham SE9 . . . . .5 D4
Wendover Way Bexley DA16 . .7 A3
Orpington BR6 . . . . .38 A3
Wensley Ct SE9 . . . . .5 F1
Wents Wood ME14 . . . . .92 F5
Wentworth Cl
Gravesend DA11 . . . . .30 A3
Hayes BR2 . . . . .50 A8
Orpington BR6 . . . . .51 E5
Woolwich SE28 . . . . .3 D7
Wentworth Dr
Cliffe Woods ME3 . . . . .33 B8
Dartford DA1 . . . . .9 A4
Gillingham ME8 . . . . .63 E7
Wentworth Prim Sch DA1 . .26 A8
Wenvoe Ave DA7 . . . . .8 B5
Wernbrook St SE18 . . . . .6 C1
Wesley Ave E16 . . . . .1 E5
Wesley Cl Maidstone ME16 . . .90 F3
St Paul's Cray BR5 . . . . .38 C6
Wessex Dr DA8 . . . . .8 E6
West App BR5 . . . . .37 C4
West Borough Prim Sch
ME16 . . . . .91 B3
West Brow ME5 . . . . .61 E3
West Common Rd BR2 . . . . . .50 B7
West Crescent Rd DA12 . . . . .13 C1
West Cross TN30 . . . . .182 F7
West Cross Gdns TN30 . . . . .182 F7
West Ct SE18 . . . . .5 A1
West Dr
Chartway Street ME17 . . . . . .125 B7
Chatham ME5 . . . . .61 D5
West End Brasted TN16 . . . . .82 B2
Kemsing TN15 . . . . .70 A2
Marden TN12 . . . . .138 C6
West Hallowes SE9 . . . . .22 E7
West Heath Cl DA1 . . . . .8 F1

West Heath La TN13 . . . . .99 B7
West Heath Rd Crayford DA1 . .8 F1
Erith SE2 . . . . .7 D8
West Hill DA1 . . . . .9 D1
West Hill Dr DA1 . . . . .9 C1
West Hill Dr DA1 . . . . .9 C1
West Hill Rise DA1 . . . . .9 D1
West Holme DA8 . . . . .8 D2
West Kent Ave DA11 . . . . .12 C1
West Kent Coll TN9 . . . . .133 A7
West Kingsdown Ind Est
TN15 . . . . .55 F2
West Kingsdown
St Edmund's CE Prim Sch
TN15 . . . . .56 A2
West La ME3 . . . . .21 A6
West Lodge Prep Sch
DA14 . . . . .24 A5
West Malling CE Prim Sch
ME19 . . . . .89 B8
West Malling Ind Pk ME19 . .73 E2
West Malling Sta ME19 . . . . .89 D8
West Mersea Cl E16 . . . . .1 B5
West Mill Rd ME20 . . . . .75 C4
West Park Ave TN4 . . . . .132 F1
West Park Rd ME15 . . . . .92 B2
West Pk ME9 . . . . .22 E7
West Rd Gillingham ME4 . . . . .48 A7
Goudhurst TN17 . . . . .167 E8
Kilndown TN17 . . . . .166 F3
West Shaw DA3 . . . . .42 D7
West St Bexley DA7 . . . . .7 F4
Bromley BR1 . . . . .36 A7
Erith DA8 . . . . .4 E1
Gillingham ME7 . . . . .48 D6
Gravesend DA11 . . . . .13 B1
Grays RM17 . . . . .12 A8
Harrietsham ME17 . . . . .110 C6
Hunton ME15 . . . . .121 D7
Lenham ME17 . . . . .111 E8
Rochester ME2 . . . . .33 B1
West Malling ME19 . . . . .89 B8
Wrotham TN15 . . . . .71 F3
West Terr DA15 . . . . .23 E7
West Thurrock Prim Sch
RM20 . . . . .11 A8
West Thurrock Way RM20 . . .11 B8
West View Hospl TN30 . . . . .182 E6
West View Rd
Crockenhill BR8 . . . . .39 D3
Dartford DA1 . . . . .9 E2
Swanley BR8 . . . . .40 A5
West Way BR5 . . . . .37 D4
West Wlk ME16 . . . . .91 A3
West Woodside DA5 . . . . .24 F7
West Wood Rd ME3 . . . . .79 B8
Westbere Ho BR5 . . . . .38 C4
Westbourne Rd DA7 . . . . .7 E7
Westbrook Cl SE3 . . . . .5 B6
Westbrook Dr BR5 . . . . .38 D1
Westbrook Terr TN2 . . . . . . .149 D1
Westbrooke Cl ME4 . . . . .48 A2
Westbrooke Cres DA16 . . . . . .7 C4
Westbrooke Rd Bexley DA16 . .7 C4
Sidcup DA15 . . . . .23 D6
Westbrooke Sch DA16 . . . . . . .7 C4
Westbury Ct **5** DA14 . . . . . . .24 A4
Westbury Rd BR1 . . . . .36 D8
Westbury Terr TN16 . . . . .96 C8
Westcombe Hill SE3 . . . . .5 A8
Westcombe Park Rd SE3 . . . . .5 A7
Westcombe Park Sta SE3 . . . . .1 A1
Westcott Ave DA11 . . . . .30 A5
Westcott Cl BR1 . . . . .36 D4
Westcott Ave ME7 . . . . .48 A6
Westcourt Sch DA12 . . . . .30 F7
Westdale Rd SE18 . . . . .6 B8
Westdean Ave SE12 . . . . .22 C7
Wested La BR8 . . . . .40 A3
Westerdale Rd **2** SE10 . . . . .1 A1
Westergate Rd Erith SE2 . . . . . .7 E8
Rochester ME2 . . . . .32 F1
Westerham Cl ME8 . . . . .49 B3
Westerham Dr DA15 . . . . .7 B2
Westerham Hill TN16 . . . . . . .81 B5
Westerham Rd
Brasted TN16 . . . . .82 A2
Orpington BR2 . . . . .50 D4
Sevenoaks TN13 . . . . .83 C4
Westerham TN16 . . . . .96 A8
Westerhill Rd ME17 . . . . .106 C1
Westerham BR7 . . . . .23 C2
Western Ave
Gillingham ME4 . . . . .48 A8
2 TN18 . . . . .178 F2
Western Cross Cl **6** DA9 . . .11 C1
Western Rd
Borough Green TN15 . . . . .86 F7
Hawkhurst TN18 . . . . .178 F2
Maidstone ME15 . . . . .106 B8
Royal Tunbridge Wells TN1 . .149 C5
Royal Tunbridge
Wells,Southborough TN4 . .133 A1
Wadhurst TN5 . . . . .174 F6
Western Way SE28 . . . . .2 E4
Westfield
New Ash Green DA3 . . . . .56 F6
1 Orpington BR6 . . . . .51 F5
Westfield Bsns Ctr ME2 . . . . .33 C1
Westfield Cl DA12 . . . . .30 C2
Westfield Cotts
Cudham TN14 . . . . .81 A1
West Kingsdown TN15 . . . . . . .55 F4
Westfield House TN30 . . . . . .182 F7

Westfield Rd DA7 . . . . .8 C4
Westfield Sole Rd
  ME5,ME15 . . . . .77 D8
Westfield St SE18 . . . . .1 D3
Westfield Terr TN17 . . . . .168 F1
Westgate Ct SE12 . . . . .22 A7
Westgate Prim Sch DA1 . . .26 D6
Westgate Rd DA1 . . . . .9 D1
Westhall BR8 . . . . .39 D6
Westhill Cl DA12 . . . . .30 B7
Westholme BR6 . . . . .37 F2
Westhorne Ave SE12,SE9 . . .5 C2
Westhurst Dr BR7 . . . . .23 B5
Westland Ho **1** E16 . . . . . . .2 A5
Westland Lodge **2** BR1 . . .36 C7
Westleigh Dr BR1 . . . . .36 E7
Westmarsh Cl ME15 . . . . . .107 F7
Westmead ME20 . . . . .75 C4
Westminster Ind Est SE18 . .1 D3
Westmoor St SE7 . . . . .1 D3
Westmoreland Ave ME14 . . .6 E3
Westmoreland Pl **5** BR1 . . .36 A6
Westmoreland Rd BR2 . . . . .36 A5
Westmorland Ave ME15 . . .107 E7
Westmorland Cl ME15 . . . . .107 E7
Westmorland Rd ME15 . . . .107 E7
Westmount Ave ME4 . . . . . .47 F3
Westmount Rd SE9 . . . . .6 A3
Weston Ave RM20 . . . . .10 F8
Weston Rd ME2 . . . . .47 A8
Westree Ct **7** ME16 . . . . . .91 E3
Westree Rd ME16 . . . . .91 E3
Westrise TN9 . . . . .133 A7
Westway Coxheath ME17 . . .106 C2
  Pembury TN2 . . . . .150 D7
Westways Marplit Hill TN8 . .112 C2
  Wateringham TN16 . . . . . .81 C1
Westwell Cl BR5 . . . . .38 D1
Westwell Ct TN30 . . . . .182 E7
Westwell House TN30 . . . . .182 F7
Westwood Cl BR1 . . . . .36 D6
Westwood Jnr Sch DA16 . . .6 E3
Westwood La DA16 . . . . .6 F4
Westwood Rd
  Betsham DA13 . . . . .28 E2
  East Peckham TN12 . . . . .119 E6
  Maidstone ME15 . . . . .107 A7
  Newham E16 . . . . .1 B5
  Royal Tunbridge Wells TN4 . .148 C5
Westwood Tech Coll DA16 . .6 E3
Westwood Way TN13 . . . . . .83 C5
Wetheral Dr BR1 . . . . .62 B4
Wey Cl ME5 . . . . .62 C5
Weybridge Cl ME5 . . . . .62 C4
Weyhill Cl ME14 . . . . .92 C6
Weyman Rd SE3 . . . . .5 C6
Weymouth Cl E6 . . . . .2 B7
Wharf La ME5 . . . . .62 B8
Wharf Rd Gillingham ME7 . .48 C7
  Gravesend DA12 . . . . .13 E1
  Grays RM17 . . . . .11 F8
  Maidstone ME15 . . . . .91 E2
Wharf Rd S RM17 . . . . .11 F8
Wharfedale Rd DA2 . . . . . . .27 C7
Wharnecliffe DA1 . . . . .11 B1
Wharton Rd BR1 . . . . .36 B8
Whatcote Cotts TN15 . . . . .87 C7
Whatman Cl ME14 . . . . .92 C6
Wheatcroft Gn ME8 . . . . . . .63 F7
Wheatear Way ME5 . . . . . . .62 B7
Wheatfield ME19 . . . . .74 E1
Wheatfield Cl TN17 . . . . . .169 C5
Wheatfield Rise TN2 . . . . . .169 C5
Wheatfield Lea TN17 . . . . . .169 C5
Wheatfield Way TN17 . . . . .169 C5
Wheatfields Chatham ME5 . .62 D2
  Maidstone ME14 . . . . .92 D4
  Newham E6 . . . . .2 B8
Wheatley Cl DA9 . . . . .11 A2
Wheatley Terrace Rd DA8 . .8 F8
Wheatsheaf Cl ME15 . . . . .107 B8
Wheatsheaf Hill
  Chelsfield TN14 . . . . .52 F2
  Idle Hill TN14 . . . . .97 A4
Wheatsheaf Way TN10 . . .117 D6
Wheelbarrow Park Est
  . . . . .138 B7
Wheeler St
  Headcorn TN27 . . . . .141 E5
  Maidstone ME14 . . . . .92 A5
Wheeler's La ME17 . . . . . .122 E7
Wheelers The ME8 . . . . .63 B6
Wheelock Cl DA8 . . . . .8 B7
Wheelwrights The ME17 . .110 D6
Whenman Ave DA5 . . . . . . .25 C5
Whernside Cl SE28 . . . . .3 C6
Whetsted Rd
  Five Oak Green TN12 . . . .135 C8
  Whetsted TN12 . . . . .119 F1
Whetstone Rd SE3 . . . . .5 D6
Whiffen Wlk ME10 . . . . .75 B1
Whiffen's Ave ME4 . . . . . . .47 F5
Whiffen's Ave W ME4 . . . . .47 F5
Whimbrel Cl SE28 . . . . .3 C6
Whimbrel Gn ME20 . . . . . . .74 F2
Whimbrel Wlk ME5 . . . . . . .62 C1
Whimbrels The ME4 . . . . . . .34 B1
Whinchat Rd SE28 . . . . .3 C4
Whinfell Way DA12 . . . . . . .30 F4
Whinyates Rd SE9 . . . . .5 E4
Whippendell Cl BR5 . . . . . . .38 B8
Whippendell Way BR5 . . . . .38 B7
Whistler Rd TN10 . . . . .117 D6
Whitby Cl DA9 . . . . .11 A2
Whitby Rd SE18 . . . . .1 F2
Whitchurch Cl ME16 . . . . . .91 E4
Whitcombe Cl ME5 . . . . . . .62 C3

White Ave DA11 . . . . .29 F5
White Bear Pas **3** TN1 . . .149 A2
White Cottage Rd TN10 . .117 D6
White Gates DA14 . . . . .24 A3
White Hart SE18 . . . . .1 D3
White Hart Par TN13 . . . . . .83 E5
White Hart Rd
  Orpington BR6 . . . . .38 A2
  Woolwich SE18 . . . . .2 E2
White Hart Wood TN13 . . .99 C6
White Hart Yd **4** DA11 . . .13 B1
White Hill Rd ME9,ME14 . .63 D1
White Horse Hill BR7,SE9 . .6 A4
White Horse La
  Harvel DA13 . . . . .58 C2
  Otham Hole ME15 . . . . . .108 A6
White Horse Rd DA13 . . . .58 E1
White House La TN14 . . . . .98 F5
White House Rd TN14 . . . .98 F5
White Lodge TN1 . . . . .149 C4
White Lodge Cl TN13 . . . . .84 B4
White Oak Cl **15** TN9 . . . .133 B8
White Oak Prim Sch BR8 . .39 E7
White Oak Sq **16** BR8 . . . .25 F8
White Post Four Elms TN8 . .113 A6
  Hollingbourne ME17 . . . . .95 B5
White Post Corr TN11 . . . .101 F5
White Post Hill DA4 . . . . . .41 A2
White Post La
  Culverstone Green DA13 . .57 F2
  Sole Street DA13 . . . . .57 F4
White Rd ME4 . . . . .48 A2
White Rock Cl ME16 . . . . . .91 E3
White Rock Pl **5** ME16 . . .91 E3
White's La TN18 . . . . .179 B2
White's Mdw BR1 . . . . .37 A5
Whitebeam Ave BR2 . . . . . . .37 A3
Whitebeam Dr ME17 . . . . .106 B8
Whitebine Gdns TN12 . . . .120 A6
Whitebread La TN31 . . . . .187 C1
Whitecroft BR8 . . . . .39 E7
Whitefield Cl BR5 . . . . .38 C6
Whitefield Rd TN4 . . . . . . .149 A6
Whitefriars TN13 . . . . .99 A8
Whitegate Cl TN4 . . . . .149 A8
Whitegate Ct ME8 . . . . .63 D5
Whitegates Ave TN15 . . . . .55 C4
Whitehall La
  Beltham DA13 . . . . .85 A8
  Grays RM17 . . . . .12 C8
Whitehall Dr ME17 . . . . . . .109 D3
Whitehall La Erith DA8 . . . .8 F5
  Grays RM17 . . . . .12 C8
Whitehall Rd
  Broad Street ME14 . . . . . .94 A6
  Bromley BR2 . . . . .36 A4
Whitehaven Cl BR2 . . . . . . .36 A5
Whitehead Cl DA2 . . . . .26 C5
Whiteheads La ME14 . . . . . .93 B4
Whitehill Inf Sch
  . . . . .72 B3
Whitehill Cty Inf Sch
  DA12 . . . . .30 C5
Whitehill Cty Jun Sch
  DA12 . . . . .30 C5
Whitehill La DA12 . . . . .30 D5
Whitehill Par DA12 . . . . . . .30 C5
Whitehill Rd Crayford DA1 . .9 A2
  Gravesend DA12 . . . . .30 C6
  Longfield,Whitehill DA13 . .42 D8
  Meopham DA13 . . . . .58 B7
Whitehorse Hill ME5 . . . . . .48 B3
Whitehouse Cl ME3 . . . . . . .34 E4
Whitehouse Cres ME1 . . . .76 A8
Whitelake Rise ME2 . . . . . .46 B3
Whiteleaves Rise ME2 . . . .46 B3
Whitelimes TN18 . . . . .178 D8
Whiteoak Ct **1** BR8 . . . . . .39 E6
Whitepost La DA13 . . . . . . .73 A8
Whites Cl DA9 . . . . .11 A2
Whitewall Rd ME2 . . . . .47 D7
Whitewall Way ME2 . . . . . .47 D7
Whitewebbs Way BR5 . . . . .37 F8
Whitfield Rd DA7 . . . . .7 F7
Whitings Way E6 . . . . .2 A8
Whitmore St ME16 . . . . .91 D2
Whitney Wlk DA14 . . . . . . .24 E2
Whittaker St ME14 . . . . . . .48 A4
Whitworth Rd SE18 . . . . . . .6 A7
Whybourne Crest TN2 . . .149 D1
Whyman Ave ME4 . . . . .47 F2
Wichling Cl BR5 . . . . .38 D1
Wicken House ME14 . . . . . .91 E4
Wickenden Rd TN13 . . . . . .84 C1
Wickens Pl ME19 . . . . .89 C8
Wickets The TN12 . . . . .99 C2
Wickham Cl ME9 . . . . .65 B6
Wickham Common
  Prim Sch BR4 . . . . .50 A6
Wickham Ct La 6 E5
Wickham Field TN14 . . . . .68 F3
Wickham Gdns TN14 . . . .148 D5
Wickham La SE18,SE2 . . . .7 B8
Wickham Pl ME17 . . . . . . .111 D5
Wickham St Bexley DA16 . .7 A6
  Rochester ME1 . . . . .47 A2
Wickhams Way DA3 . . . . . . .42 F4
Wickhurst Rd TN14 . . . . . .98 F5
Wicks Cl SE9 . . . . .22 D4
Wicksteed Cl DA5 . . . . .25 D5
Widbury TN3 . . . . .147 F2
Widecombe Rd SE9 . . . . . . .22 F5
Widgeon Cl E16 . . . . .1 B7
Widgeon Path SE28 . . . . . . .2 D3
Widgeon Rd Erith DA8 . . . .9 B7
  Rochester ME2 . . . . .46 D6
Widmore Ctr, The BR1 . . .36 C6
Widmore Rd BR1 . . . . .36 C7

Wierton Hill ME17 . . . . . .123 D7
Wierton La ME17 . . . . .107 E1
Wierton Rd ME17 . . . . . . .123 E8
Wigmore Rd ME8 . . . . .63 B4
Wilberforce Ct **2** SE28 . . .3 C5
Wilberforce Rd ME17 . . . .106 D3
Wilberforce Way DA12 . . . .30 D3
Wilde Cl RM18 . . . . .13 C5
Wilde Rd DA8 . . . . .8 B7
Wilderness Ave BR5 . . . . . .38 C3
Wilderness La ME15 . . . . .106 B3
Wilderness Ave TN15 . . . . .84 E5
Wilderness Mount SE9 . . . .84 D5
Wilderness Sch The
  TN13 . . . . .84 E6
Wildfell Cl ME5 . . . . .77 C8
Wildfell Rd ME17 . . . . .63 D3
Wildwood Cl
  Kingswood ME17 . . . . . . .109 E2
  1 Lewisham SE12 . . . . . .22 A8
Wildwood Glade ME7 . . . . .63 B4
Wilford Ho **3** SE16 . . . . . . .2 B1
Wilfred St **21** DA12 . . . . . .13 B1
Wilkinson Cl **1** DA1 . . . . .10 A3
Wilkinson Rd E16 . . . . .1 C7
Wilks Ave DA1 . . . . .26 F6
Will Adams Ct **6** ME7 . . . .48 C6
Will Adams Rdbt ME8 . . . .48 F2
Will Adams Way ME8 . . . . .48 F1
Will Crooks Gdns SE9 . . . .5 D3
Will Thorne Par The E16 . .1 E7
Willenhall Rd SE18 . . . . .2 B1
Willersley Ave
  Orpington BR6 . . . . .51 D7
  Sidcup DA15 . . . . .23 F7
Willersley Cl DA15 . . . . . . .23 F7
Willesley Gdns TN17 . . . . .169 D6
Willett Way BR5,BR6 . . . . .37 E3
Willetts Cotts TN3 . . . . . .146 C4
Willetts La TN3 . . . . .146 C4
William Baker Ho ME20 . .90 F8
William Barefoot Dr SE9 .23 A5
William Judge Cl TN30 . .183 D7
William Luck Cl TN12 . . .119 E6
William Rd ME5 . . . . .62 A2
William Smith Ho **10** DA17 . .4 A3
William St Gravesend DA12 . .30 B8
  Grays RM17 . . . . .12 C8
  Royal Tunbridge Wells TN4 . .149 A5
Willicombe Pk TN2 . . . . . .149 D4
Willicombe Pl ME15 . . . . . .107 E7
Willington St ME15 . . . . . . .92 F2
Willis Ho ME1 . . . . .47 C4
Willis Rd DA8 . . . . .4 D2
Willoughby Ho SE18 . . . . . .1 E7
Willow Ave
  Hoo St Werburgh ME3 . . .34 E3
  Sidcup DA15 . . . . .7 A1
  Swanley BR8 . . . . .39 D6
Willow Cl Bromley BR2 . . .36 F4
  Orpington BR5 . . . . .38 B2
  Sidcup DA5 . . . . .7 F1
Willow Cres
  Five Oak Green TN12 . . . .135 B7
  Stapleshurst TN12 . . . . . .139 F5
Willow Ct ME15 . . . . .107 A6
Willow Ct BR7 . . . . .23 B2
Willow House **2** ME15 . . .61 F5
Willow La
  Paddock Wood TN2 . . . . .136 E6
  Woolwich SE18 . . . . .2 A2
Willow Lea TN10 . . . . .117 C7
Willow Pk TN14 . . . . .68 C2
Willow Rd Dartford DA1 . .26 C7
  Erith DA8 . . . . .9 A6
  Larkfield ME20 . . . . .74 F3
  Rochester ME2 . . . . .46 C6
Willow Rise ME15 . . . . . . .107 A6
Willow Terr ME4 . . . . .54 E8
Willow Tree Cl DA14 . . . . .23 F3
Willow Tree Rd TN2 . . . . .148 F1
Willow Tree Wlk BR1 . . . .36 B8
Willow Vale BR7 . . . . .23 B2
Willow Way ME18 . . . . .92 B3
Willow Wents ME18 . . . . . .88 D1
Willow Wlk
  Culverstone Green DA13 . .57 F3
  Royal Tunbridge Wells TN2 . .149 E8
Willow Wood DA13 . . . . . . .57 F2
Willowbank Ct **3** ME15 . . .92 B4
Willowbank Dr ME23 . . . .17 F4
Willowby Gdns ME8 . . . . . .63 E4
Willowfields Cl **1** SE18 . . .2 E1
Willowherb Cl ME4 . . . . . .34 C1
Willowmead ME19 . . . . . . .74 E2
Willows The Gillingham ME8 . .49 E2
  Grays RM17 . . . . .12 D8
  Newington ME9 . . . . .65 B6
Willside ME6 . . . . .60 A1
Willrose Cres SE2 . . . . .3 B1
Willys Cotts TN8 . . . . .96 C2
Wilman Rd TN4 . . . . .149 B7
Wilmar Way TN15 . . . . .84 F7
Wilmecote Cl ME8 . . . . . . .63 D8
Wilmington Ct ME15 . . . . .92 B4
Wilmington Gram Sch
  for Boys DA2 . . . . .26 B5
Wilmington Hall Sch DA2 . .26 B5
Wilmington Prim Sch DA2 . .26 B5
Wilmington Way ME8 . . . . .49 B2
Wilmot Rd DA1 . . . . .9 B2
Wilmount St SE18 . . . . .2 B2
Wilson Ave ME1 . . . . .47 C2
Wilson Cl Maidstone ME15 . .107 E7
  Tonbridge TN11 . . . . .116 E5

Wilson Ho **5** SE7 . . . . .5 C8
Wilson La DA4 . . . . .41 F7
Wilson Rd TN10 . . . . .117 C5
Wilsons La ME15 . . . . .106 A5
Wilsons Way DA13 . . . . . . .57 F3
Wilton Dr ME20 . . . . .90 B8
Wilton Rd SE2 . . . . .3 C2
Wiltshire Cl Chatham ME5 . .62 C8
  Dartford DA2 . . . . .27 D8
Wiltshire Rd BR6 . . . . .38 A2
Wiltshire Way
  4 Maidstone ME15 . . . .107 E8
  Royal Tunbridge Wells TN2 . .149 D7
Wimborne **6** DA14 . . . . . . .24 B4
Wimborne Ave BR7 . . . . . . .23 A7
Wimborne Dr ME8 . . . . . . .63 D6
Wimpole Ct BR2 . . . . .36 C5
Win'freds Cl TN17 . . . . . .181 E3
Winch Cl TN17 . . . . .169 D3
Winch's Garth TN12 . . . .139 F5
Winchcomb Gdns SE9 . . . . .5 D4
Winchelsea Ave ME2 . . . . . .7 F7
Winchelsea Rd ME5 . . . . . .62 B5
Winchester Ave ME5 . . . . . .61 F4
Winchester Cl **1** E6 . . . . . .1 F7
Winchester Cres DA12 . . . .30 D5
Winchester Gr TN13 . . . . . .84 B4
Winchester Ho
  1 Maidstone ME15 . . . .107 D7
  Woolwich SE18 . . . . .5 D7
Winchester Pl **9** ME14 . . .92 A5
Winchester Rd Bexley DA7 . .7 D5
  Harold Wood TN18 . . . . .179 A8
  Orpington BR6 . . . . .52 C6
  Tonbridge TN10 . . . . .117 D5
Winchester Way ME8 . . . . .64 A8
Wincliff Rd TN9 . . . . .133 B8
Wincrofts Dr SE9 . . . . .6 D3
Windermere Cl
  Dartford DA1 . . . . .26 B7
  Orpington BR6 . . . . .51 A7
Windermere Dr ME8 . . . . . .63 D7
Windermere Ho **4** ME17 . .107 E7
Windermere Rd DA7 . . . . . .8 C5
Windhover Way DA12 . . . . .30 E4
Windmill Cl ME2 . . . . .33 B1
Windmill Cotts
  Cranbrook TN17 . . . . . . .169 D6
  Lower Stoke ME3 . . . . . . .19 C5
Windmill Ct
  Cranbrook TN17 . . . . . . .169 D6
  Royal Tunbridge Wells TN2 . .149 C3
Windmill Dr BR2 . . . . .50 C6
Windmill Hill
  Hill Top TN12 . . . . .136 B1
  Platt TN15 . . . . .87 D7
  Pye Corner ME17 . . . . . .126 B7
Windmill Hts ME14 . . . . . .93 B4
Windmill La
  Wadhurst TN5 . . . . .174 E4
  Woodchurch,Coursley Wood
  TN5 . . . . .175 C8
  Wrotham Heath TN15 . . .87 E8
Windmill La E ME19 . . . . .89 C6
Windmill Manor ME17 . . .48 C4
Windmill Pk TN15 . . . . .87 E7
Windmill Rd
  Gillingham ME7 . . . . .48 C4
  Sevenoaks TN13 . . . . .99 B6
  Sevenoaks Weald TN14 . .99 B2
Windmill Row ME17 . . . .108 D2
Windmill St
  Gravesend DA12 . . . . .30 B7
  Rochester ME2 . . . . .33 B1
  Royal Tunbridge Wells TN2 . .149 C3
Windrush Prim Sch SE28 . .3 B5
Windsor Ave ME4 . . . . .47 E7
Windsor Cl Chislehurst BR7 . .23 B3
  Maidstone ME14 . . . . .92 B6
Windsor Ct **1** ME15 . . . . .36 E6
Windsor Dr Dartford DA1 . .9 A1
  Orpington BR6 . . . . .52 A4
Windsor Hall E16 . . . . .1 B1
Windsor Rd Bexley DA6 . . . .7 E3
  Gillingham ME7 . . . . .48 D5
  Gravesend DA12 . . . . .30 B4
Windward Rd ME1 . . . . .47 C2
Windy Ridge BR1 . . . . .36 E8
Windyridge ME7 . . . . .48 E1
Winfield La TN15 . . . . .86 E3
Winford Mews ME1 . . . . . .47 A2
Wingate Rd DA14 . . . . . . .24 C2
Wingfield Prim Sch SE3 . . .5 B4
Wingfield Rd DA12 . . . . . . .30 B8
Wingham Cl
  Gillingham ME8 . . . . .49 C3
  Maidstone ME15 . . . . .107 F7
Wingrove Dr
  Maidstone ME2 . . . . .92 E5
  Rochester ME2 . . . . .47 C2
Winifred Rd Dartford DA1 . .9 D7
  Erith DA8 . . . . .4 E1
  Maidstone ME15 . . . . .92 F3
Winifred St E16 . . . . .1 E5
Winn Common Rd SE18 . . . .6 D8
Winn Rd SE12,SE9 . . . . .22 B7
Winnipeg Dr **3** BR6 . . . . . .51 F4
Winser Rd TN17 . . . . .182 A1
Winsor Prim Sch E6 . . . . . . .2 A7
Winsor Terr E6 . . . . .2 A7
Winston Cl DA9 . . . . .10 F1
Winston Cl **1** BR1 . . . . . . .36 B8
Winston Dr ME2 . . . . .33 D2
Winston Rd ME2 . . . . .46 A5
Winstone Scott Ave TN3 . .147 E4
Winterborne Ave BR6 . . . .51 D7
Winterfield La ME19 . . . . .89 E8

Wintergarden Cres DA9 . . .28 A8
Wintergreen Cl
  2 Newham E16 . . . . .1 E8
  St Mary's Island ME4 . . . .34 C1
Winters Croft DA12 . . . . . .30 D2
Winterton St **3** TN16 . . . .81 D1
Winton Ct BR8 . . . . .39 E5
Winton Rd BR6 . . . . .51 B6
Wirral Wood Cl BR7 . . . . . .2 A2
Wirrals The ME5 . . . . .62 A4
Wise Ho SE18 . . . . .6 A7
Wise's La TN15 . . . . .56 E2
Wiseacre TN3 . . . . .166 A3
Wishart Rd SE3 . . . . .5 D5
Wisley Rd BR5 . . . . .24 B1
Wistaria Cl BR6 . . . . .51 B8
Wisteria Gdns BR8 . . . . . . .39 D7
Wisteria Ho **1** ME15 . . . .107 E7
Witches La TN13 . . . . .83 D4
Witham Way ME2 . . . . .46 F7
Withens Cl BR5 . . . . .38 C5
Witherston Way SE9 . . . . .23 A5
Withyham Rd TN3 . . . . . . .161 B7
Wittersham CE Prim Sch
  TN30 . . . . .189 D2
Wittersham Cl ME5 . . . . . .62 B5
Wittersham House **2** BR5 . .38 D1
Wittersham Rd Potman's
  Heath TN17,TN30 . . . . . .188 D4
  Wittersham TN30 . . . . . .189 C5
Wittersham Road Sta
  TN17 . . . . .188 D6
Wixom House SE3 . . . . .5 C3
Woburn Cl SE28 . . . . .3 D7
Woburn Ct **1** DA6 . . . . . . .7 E3
Wodehouse Cl ME20 . . . . .74 F4
Wodehouse Rd DA1 . . . . . .10 A3
Woldham Pl BR2 . . . . .36 C5
Woldham Rd BR2 . . . . .36 C5
Wolds Dr BR6 . . . . .51 A6
Wolfe Cl BR2 . . . . .36 A3
Wolfe Cres SE7 . . . . .1 D1
Wolfe Rd ME16 . . . . .91 B2
Wollaston Cl ME8 . . . . .63 D3
Wolseley Rd TN4 . . . . .149 C7
Wolsey Ct SE9 . . . . .5 F1
Wolsey Mews BR6 . . . . .51 F5
Wolsley Cl DA1 . . . . .8 F2
Wolvercote Rd SE2 . . . . .3 D4
Wombwell Gdns DA11 . . . .29 E6
Wood Cl Dartford DA5 . . . .25 F5
  Ditton ME20 . . . . .90 E8
Wood Dr Chislehurst BR7 . .22 E2
  Sevenoaks TN13 . . . . .83 F1
Wood End BR8 . . . . .39 C5
Wood La Dartford DA2 . . . .27 F4
  East End TN17 . . . . .171 C3
Wood Lodge Gdns BR1 . . .22 E1
Wood Lodge Grange TN13 . .84 C1
Wood Pl DA1 . . . . .24 A3
Wood Point **1** E16 . . . . .1 A8
Wood Retreat SE18 . . . . . . .6 D7
Wood Ride BR5 . . . . .37 E5
Wood Side Sch DA17 . . . . . .4 B2
Wood St Cuxton ME2 . . . . .46 B2
  12 Grays RM17 . . . . .12 C8
  Newham E16 . . . . .1 B6
  Royal Tunbridge Wells TN1 .149 B4
  Swanley Village BR8 . . . . .40 D8
Wood View Ct TN15 . . . . . .55 E3
Wood Way BR6 . . . . .51 A8
Woodberry Gr DA5 . . . . . . .25 D5
Woodbine Rd DA15 . . . . . . .23 E7
Woodbridge Dr ME15 . . . .91 F1
Woodbrook Rd SE2 . . . . . . .7 B8
Woodbury Cl TN4 . . . . . . .149 A5
Woodbury La TN30 . . . . . .183 A7
Woodbury Park Gdns
  TN4 . . . . .149 B5
Woodbury Park Rd TN4 . .149 B5
Woodbury Rd Chatham ME5 . .61 F1
  Hawkhurst TN18 . . . . . . .179 A2
Woodchurch Cl
  Chatham ME5 . . . . .62 B5
  Sidcup DA14 . . . . .23 D5
Woodchurch Cres ME8 . . .49 C2
Woodchurch Dr BR1 . . . . .22 D1
Woodchurch House BR5 . . .38 D1
Woodchurch Rd TN30 . . .183 D8
Woodclyffe Dr BR7 . . . . . . .37 A7
Woodcock La
  Benenden TN17 . . . . .180 E3
  Grafty Green ME17 . . . . .126 E5
Woodcocks
  Headcorn TN27 . . . . .141 D5
  Newham E16 . . . . .1 D8
Woodcot Dr BR6 . . . . .37 D2
Woodcroft SE9 . . . . .22 F5
Woodcut ME14 . . . . .92 A8
Woodfall Dr DA1 . . . . .8 F3
Woodfalls Ind Est ME18 . .120 D6
Woodfield Rd TN9 . . . . . . .133 B8
Woodfield Way ME3 . . . . . .33 E4
Woodfields TN13 . . . . .83 D3
Woodford House **3** SE18 . .6 B8
Woodford Rd ME16 . . . . . . .91 B2
Woodgate Cl ME19 . . . . . .73 A6
Woodgate La ME19 . . . . . .65 C2
Woodgate Rd DA1 . . . . . . .25 D3
Woodgate Way TN9,TN11 .133 C2
Woodgers Gr BR8 . . . . .39 F7

Woodget Cl E6 . . . . .1 E7
Woodhatch Cl E6 . . . . .1 E8
Woodhayes BR7 . . . . .23 B2
Woodhead Dr BR6 . . . . .51 E8
Woodhill SE18 . . . . .1 E2
Woodhill Pk TN2 . . . . .150 C6
Woodhill Prim Sch SE18 . . . . . . .1 E2
Woodhurst ME5 . . . . .61 D4
Woodhurst Ave BR5 . . . . .37 C3
Woodhurst Cl ME2 . . . . .46 B2
Woodhurst Rd SE2 . . . . .3 A2
Woodington Cl SE9 . . . . .6 A1
Woodknoll Dr BR7 . . . . .36 F8
Woodland Ave DA3 . . . . .42 F5
Woodland Cl New Barn DA3 .43 C6
New Town ME19 . . . . .89 A8
Royal Tunbridge Wells TN4 . .149 C7
Woodland Dr TN8 . . . . .112 D3
Woodland Rd TN4 . . . . .149 C7
Woodland Rise TN15 . . . . .84 E4
Woodland Terr SE7 . . . . .1 E2
Woodland View TN30 . . . . . .189 E4
Woodland Way
Bidborough TN4 . . . . .132 D3
Erith SE2 . . . . .3 D2
Maidstone ME14 . . . . .92 B7
Orpington BR5 . . . . .37 C4
Swanscombe DA9 . . . . .11 A3
Woodlands Bexley DA6 . . . . . . .8 B2
Chatham ME5 . . . . .62 A2
Coxheath ME17 . . . . .106 B3
Cranbrook TN17 . . . . .169 D6
Paddock Wood TN12 . . . . . . .135 F7
Pembury TN2 . . . . .150 F7
Royal Tunbridge Wells TN4 . .133 A2
Swanley BR8 . . . . .39 E6
Woodlands Ave
Sidcup DA15 . . . . .23 E7
Snodland ME6 . . . . .74 F8
Woodlands Cl Bromley BR1 . .36 F7
Maidstone ME14 . . . . .92 B7
Swanley BR8 . . . . .39 F7
Tonbridge TN9 . . . . .133 A7
Woodlands Inf & Jun Schs
TN10 .117 E6
Woodlands La DA12 . . . . .31 E1
Woodlands Par ME20 . . . . . . .90 D8
Woodlands Pk DA5 . . . . .25 D4
Woodlands Prim Sch ME7 . .48 F4
Woodlands Rd Bexley DA7 . . .7 E4
Bromley BR1 . . . . .36 F7
Ditton ME20 . . . . .90 D8
Gillingham ME7 . . . . .48 F4
Orpington BR6 . . . . .52 A4
Tonbridge TN9 . . . . .133 A7
Woodlands Rise BR8 . . . . .39 F7
Woodlands Terr BR8 . . . . .39 B3
Woodlands The BR6 . . . . .52 B4
Woodlands View TN14 . . . . . . .53 A1
Woodlark Rd ME4 . . . . .34 B1
New Barn DA3 . . . . .43 C6
Woodlea Larkfield ME19 . . . . .74 F2
Woodley Rd BR6 . . . . .52 C8
Woodman Par ME4 . . . . .2 A5
Woodman St E16 . . . . .2 A5
Woodmere SE9 . . . . .22 F7
Woodmount BR8 . . . . .39 D2
Woodpecker Cl ME2 TN8 . . . .112 D3
Woodpecker Glade
ME8 . . . . .63 D6

Woodpecker Rd
Larkfield ME20 . . . . .74 F1
Woolwich SE28 . . . . .3 C6
Woodrow SE18 . . . . .1 F2
Woodrush Pl ME4 . . . . .34 B1
Woods Green Cotts TN5 . . . .174 F7
Woodsgate Way TN2 . . . . . . .150 B6
Woodside Gillingham ME8 . . . .63 C6
Kilndown TN17 . . . . .166 F2
Orpington BR6 . . . . .52 B5
Vigo Village DA13 . . . . .72 F8
Woodside Ave BR7 . . . . .23 C3
Woodside Cl Crayford DA7 . . . .8 D3
Pembury TN2 . . . . .150 E6
Woodside Cres DA15 . . . . . . .23 E5
Woodside Dr DA2 . . . . .25 E4
Woodside Gn ME3 . . . . .33 B7
Woodside La DA15 . . . . .7 D1
Woodside Par DA15 . . . . .23 E5
Woodside Rd Bromley BR1 . . .36 E4
Crayford DA7 . . . . .8 D3
Maidstone ME15 . . . . .107 C7
Pembury TN2 . . . . .150 E6
Sidcup DA15 . . . . .23 E5
Sundridge TN14 . . . . .82 E3
Tonbridge TN9 . . . . .133 B7
Woodside Sch DA7 . . . . .8 D3
Woodstock Cl DA5 . . . . .24 F7
Woodstock Ct SE12 . . . . .5 A1
Woodstock Rd ME2 . . . . .47 A7
Woodvale Ct BR1 . . . . .36 B7
Woodview Cl BR6 . . . . .51 C8
Woodview Cres TN11 . . . . . .116 F5
Woodview Rd BR8 . . . . .39 D7
Woodview Rise ME2 . . . . .32 F1
Woodville SE3 . . . . .5 B6
Woodville Cl SE12 . . . . .5 A2
Woodville Gr 2 DA16 . . . . .7 A4
Woodville Pl DA12 . . . . .30 B8
Woodville Rd ME15 . . . . .92 A2
Woodville St 18 SE18 . . . . .1 E2
Woodward Terr DA9 . . . . .10 E1
Woodyates Rd
Lewisham SE12 . . . . .22 B8
Lewisham SE12 . . . . .5 A1
Woolacombe Rd SE3 . . . . .5 C6
Woolaston Cl ME15 . . . . .91 F1
Wooldeys Rd ME8 . . . . .49 F2
Woolf Cl SE28 . . . . .3 B5
Woolf Wlk RM18 . . . . .13 C5
Woollett Cl TN4 . . . . .9 A3
Woollett St ME14 . . . . .92 A5
Woolley Cl TN4 . . . . .132 F1
Woolley Rd
Maidstone ME15 . . . . .107 F7
Royal Tunbridge Wells TN4 . .132 F1
Woolpack Cnr TN27 . . . . . . .172 A7
Woolpack Cotts TN27 . . . . . .172 A7
Woolwich Arsenal Sta SE18 . .2 B2
Woolwich Church St SE18 . . .1 E3
Woolwich Cl ME5 . . . . .62 A7
Woolwich Coll SE18 . . . . .2 C2
Woolwich Coll
(Charlton) SE7 . . . . .1 D3
Woolwich Comm SE18 . . . . . .6 A8
Woolwich Dockyard Ind Est
SE18 . . . . .1 F2
Woolwich Dockyard Sta
SE18 . . . . .1 F2
Woolwich High St SE18 . . . . . .2 A3
Woolwich Manor Way E6 . . . .2 A7
Woolwich Manorway E16 . . . .2 B4

Woolwich Poly Sch
(Lower) SE18 . . . . .2 B3
Woolwich Poly Sch
(Upper) SE18 . . . . .2 B1
Woolwich Rd Bexley DA7 . . . .8 A4
Erith SE2 . . . . .3 E1
Greenwich SE10,SE7 . . . . .1 C2
Wootton Gn ME8 . . . . .49 D3
Wootton House SE9 . . . . .6 D1
Wopsle Cl ME1 . . . . .61 D7
Worcester Ave ME19 . . . . . . .89 A2
Worcester Cl
Istead Rise DA13 . . . . .29 F1
Rochester ME2 . . . . .46 E8
Swanscombe DA9 . . . . .11 B3
Worcester Rd ME15 . . . . .107 D7
Wordsworth Way
Dartford DA1 . . . . .10 A3
New Hythe ME20 . . . . .75 A4
Workhouse La ME15 . . . . . . .106 C4
Workhouse Rd
Chartway Street ME17 . . . . . .125 A8
Ryarsh ME19 . . . . .73 F4
World of Silk* DA1 . . . . .8 E2
Worlds End La BR6 . . . . .52 B3
Wormdale Hill ME9 . . . . .65 B3
Wormdale Rd ME9 . . . . .65 B4
Worsenden TN27 . . . . .157 E1
Worsfold Ct ME15 . . . . .92 A1
Worships Hill TN13 . . . . .83 E4
Worth Cl BR6 . . . . .51 E6
Wotton Cl ME15 . . . . .107 E5
Wotton Gn BR5 . . . . .38 D5
Wouldham CE Prim Sch
ME1 . . . . .60 C5
Wouldham Rd
Grays RM17,RM20 . . . . .11 E8
Rochester ME1 . . . . .46 E1
Wouldham Terr 9 BR5 . . . . . .38 B6
Wrangleden Cl ME15 . . . . . . .107 E5
Wrangleden Rd ME15 . . . . . .107 E5
Wrangling La DA13 . . . . .58 F3
Wrekin Rd SE18 . . . . .6 C7
Wren Cl Larkfield ME20 . . . . .74 F1
St Paul's Cray BR5 . . . . .38 D6
Wren Rd ME8 . . . . .107 F4
Wren Path SE28 . . . . .2 D4
Wren Rd DA14 . . . . .24 C5
Wren Way ME5 . . . . .62 B6
Wren Wlk RM18 . . . . .13 B7
Wrens Croft DA11 . . . . .29 E4
Wrens Rd ME9 . . . . .80 F6
Wricklemarsh Rd
Greenwich SE3 . . . . .5 B6
Greenwich SE3 . . . . .5 D6
Wright Cl Gillingham ME8 . . .49 C2
Swanscombe DA10 . . . . .11 D1
Wrights Cl TN30 . . . . .183 A8
Wrot & Hill Ct DA4 . . . . .41 B8
Wrotham Hill Rd TN15 . . . . .72 A6
Wrotham Rd Bexley DA16 . . . .7 C6
Borough Green TN15 . . . . .87 A8
Culverstone Green DA13 . . . . .57 E2
Gravesend DA11,DA13 . . . . . . .30 A4
Meopham Sta DA13 . . . . .44 A3
Wrotham Road Prim Sch
DA11 . . . . .30 B8
Wrotham Sch TN15 . . . . .72 A1

Wrotham Water La
ME19,TN15 . . . . .72 E5
Wrotham Water Rd
TN15,ME19 . . . . .72 E4
Wrottesley Rd SE18 . . . . .6 C8
Wrotham Rd SE28 . . . . .3 D6
Wulfred Way TN15 . . . . .70 B1
Wyatt Cl TN15 . . . . .86 F7
Wyatt Ho 1 ME2 . . . . .47 A7
Wyatt Pl ME2 . . . . .47 A7
Wyatt Rd DA1 . . . . .8 F4
Wyatt St ME14 . . . . .92 A4
Wyborne Prim Sch SE9 . . . . .23 B7
Wyborne Rise TN2 . . . . .163 B8
Wybournes La ME23 . . . . .17 C3
Wycliffe Cl DA16 . . . . .6 F6
Wycliffe Ho 5 DA11 . . . . .29 F7
Wycliffe Row DA11 . . . . .29 F7
Wycombe St SE3 . . . . .5 A7
Wydeville Manor Rd SE12 . .22 B4
Wye Rd BR6 . . . . .37 F2
Wye Rd Borough Green TN15 .87 A8
Gravesend DA12 . . . . .30 D6
Tonbridge TN10 . . . . .117 C5
Wyfold Ho 10 SE2 . . . . .3 D4
Wyke Manor Rd ME14 . . . . . .92 A4
Wykeham Cl DA12 . . . . .30 E2
Wykeham Cotts ME17 . . . . .106 F2
Wykeham Ct BR7 . . . . .23 E2
Wykeham Gr ME17 . . . . .109 A7
Wykeham St ME2 . . . . .47 B8
Wyles Rd ME4 . . . . .47 E2
Wyles St ME7 . . . . .48 C7
Wylie Ho ME3 . . . . .33 B6
Wylie Rd ME3 . . . . .34 D6
Wyncham Ave DA15 . . . . .23 E7
Wyncroft Cl BR1 . . . . .36 F6
Wyndam Rd ME4 . . . . .47 E2
Wyndcliff Rd SE3,SE7 . . . . .5 B8
Wyndham Ave TN11 . . . . . . .115 F1
Wyndham Cl Leigh TN11 . . .115 F1
Orpington BR6 . . . . .37 C1
Wynford Gr BR5 . . . . .38 B6
Wynford Pl DA17 . . . . .8 A8
Wynford Way SE9 . . . . .22 F5
Wynn's Ave DA15 . . . . .7 A2
Wytchlings The ME17 . . . . . .109 D2
Wythens Wlk SE9 . . . . .6 B1
Wytherling Cl ME14 . . . . .92 F5
Wythes Cl BR1 . . . . .36 F7
Wythes Rd E16 . . . . .1 E5
Wythfield Rd SE9 . . . . .5 F1
Wyvern Cl Dartford DA1 . . . .26 C8
Orpington BR6 . . . . .52 B7
Snodland ME6 . . . . .75 A7
Wyvern House 3 RM17 . . . . .12 B8
Wyvill Cl ME8 . . . . .63 E5

Y

Yalding Cl ME2 . . . . .33 B1
Yalding Gr BR5 . . . . .38 D5
Yalding Hill ME18 . . . . .105 A3
Yalding Organic Gdns*
ME18 .120 F8
Yalding St Peter
& St Paul CE Prim Sch
ME18 .105 A1
Yalding Sta ME18 . . . . .104 D1
Yantlet Dr ME2 . . . . .46 C7
Yardley Cl TN9 . . . . .117 D3
Yardley Park Rd TN9 . . . . . . .117 D3
Yarnton Way DA17,DA18 . . . . .3 E4

Yarrow Cres E6 . . . . .1 E8
Yarrow Ct ME14 . . . . .92 F5
Yarrow Rd ME5 . . . . .61 F4
Yateley St SE18 . . . . .1 D3
Yaugher La ME9 . . . . .64 C3
Ye Olde Tudor Ct BR7 . . . . . . .23 B3
Yelsted La Chatham ME14 . . .77 D7
Yelsted ME5 . . . . .64 A1
Yelsted Rd ME9 . . . . .79 A4
Yeoman Cl E6 . . . . .2 B6
Yeoman Ct ME14 . . . . .93 B3
Yeoman Dr ME7 . . . . .48 F1
Yeoman Gdns TN12 . . . . . . .135 F6
Yeoman Ho ME1 . . . . .47 D4
Yeoman La ME14 . . . . .93 B4
Yeoman Pk ME15 . . . . .93 A2
Yeoman Way ME15 . . . . .93 A3
Yeoman's Mdws TN13 . . . . . .84 A1
Yeovil Ct BR5 . . . . .51 D8
Yester Dr BR7 . . . . .22 E1
Yester Pk BR7 . . . . .22 F2
Yester Rd BR7 . . . . .22 F1
Yew Rd ME3 . . . . .34 E3
Yew Tree Cl Aylesford ME20 . .75 E1
Bexley DA16 . . . . .7 A6
Chatham ME5 . . . . .62 D1
New Barn DA3 . . . . .43 D7
Sevenoaks TN13 . . . . .83 D4
Yew Tree Cotts
Groombridge TN3 . . . . .161 F8
Halstead TN14 . . . . .67 F7
Maidstone,Sandling ME14 . . .76 F1
Yew Tree Green Rd
TN12 .137 A1
Yew Tree Pl ME7 . . . . .63 B1
Yew Tree Rd TN4 . . . . .149 B8
Yews The DA12 . . . . .30 D7
Yewtree Ind Est ME20 . . . . . . .75 D2
Yoke Cl ME2 . . . . .47 B8
Yolande Gdns SE9 . . . . .5 E2
Yopps Gn TN15 . . . . .86 E1
York Ave Chatham ME5 . . . . .61 F3
Gillingham ME7 . . . . .48 C4
Sidcup DA15 . . . . .23 F6
York Cl E6 . . . . .1 F7
York Hill ME5 . . . . .48 C2
York Par TN10 . . . . .117 C6
York Pl RM17 . . . . .12 A8
York Rd Dartford DA1 . . . . . . .26 F8
Gravesend DA12 . . . . .30 C5
Maidstone ME15 . . . . .92 C2
Northfleet DA11 . . . . .29 D8
Rochester ME1 . . . . .47 C3
Royal Tunbridge Wells TN1 . .149 A4
Tonbridge TN10 . . . . .117 C6
York Rise BR6 . . . . .51 E8
York Road Jun Sch DA1 . . . .26 F8
York Terr DA8 . . . . .8 C8
Yorkland Ave DA16 . . . . .6 F3
Youens Pl ME3 . . . . .32 B3
Young Rd E16 . . . . .1 C7

Z

Zambra Way TN15 . . . . .84 F7
Zangwill Rd SE18,SE3 . . . . .5 D6
Zealand Ho SE18 . . . . .1 E2
Zelah Rd BR5 . . . . .38 C8
Zetland Ave ME7 . . . . .48 E2
Zillah Gdns ME8 . . . . .63 C6
Zion Pl DA12 . . . . .30 B8
Zion St TN15 . . . . .84 F6

Any feature in this atlas can be given a unique reference to help you find the same feature on other Ordnance Survey maps of the area, or to help someone else locate you if they do not have a Street Atlas.

The grid squares in this atlas match the Ordnance Survey National Grid and are at 500 metre intervals. The small figures at the bottom and sides of every other grid line are the National Grid kilometre values (**00** to **99** km) and are repeated across the country every 100 km (see left).

To give a unique National Grid reference you need to locate where in the country you are. The country is divided into 100 km squares with each square given a unique two-letter reference. Use the administrative map to determine in which 100 km square a particular page of this atlas falls.

The bold letters and numbers between each grid line (**A** to **F**, **1** to **8**) are for use within a specific Street Atlas only, and when used with the page number, are a convenient way of referencing these grid squares.

Example   The railway bridge over DARLEY GREEN RD in grid square B1

Step 1: Identify the two-letter reference, in this example the page is in **SP**

Step 2: Identify the 1 km square in which the railway bridge falls. Use the figures in the southwest corner of this square: Eastings **17**, Northings **74**. This gives a unique reference: **SP 17 74**, accurate to 1 km.

Step 3: To give a more precise reference accurate to 100 m you need to estimate how many tenths along and how many tenths up this 1 km square the feature is (to help with this the 1 km square is divided into four 500 m squares). This makes the bridge about **8** tenths along and about **1** tenth up from the southwest corner.

This gives a unique reference: **SP 178 741**, accurate to 100 m.

Eastings (read from left to right along the bottom) come before Northings (read from bottom to top). If you have trouble remembering say to yourself "Along the hall, THEN up the stairs"!

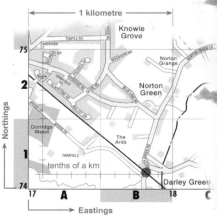

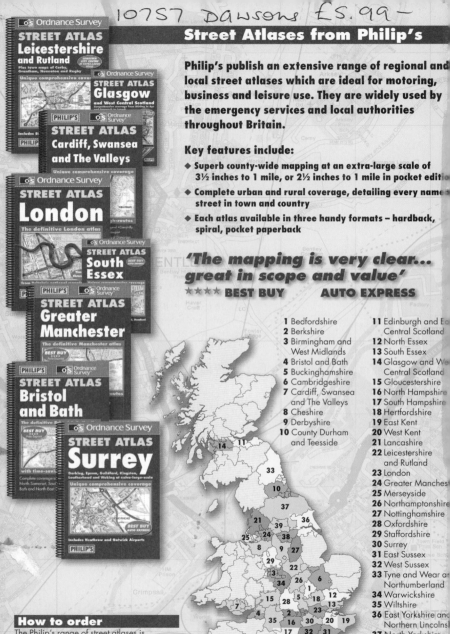

Street Atlases from Philip's

Philip's publish an extensive range of regional and local street atlases which are ideal for motoring, business and leisure use. They are widely used by the emergency services and local authorities throughout Britain.

Key features include:

◆ Superb county-wide mapping at an extra-large scale of 3½ inches to 1 mile, or 2½ inches to 1 mile in pocket edition

◆ Complete urban and rural coverage, detailing every named street in town and country

◆ Each atlas available in three handy formats – hardback, spiral, pocket paperback

'The mapping is very clear... great in scope and value'
★★★★ BEST BUY   AUTO EXPRESS

1 Bedfordshire
2 Berkshire
3 Birmingham and West Midlands
4 Bristol and Bath
5 Buckinghamshire
6 Cambridgeshire
7 Cardiff, Swansea and The Valleys
8 Cheshire
9 Derbyshire
10 County Durham and Teesside
11 Edinburgh and East Central Scotland
12 North Essex
13 South Essex
14 Glasgow and West Central Scotland
15 Gloucestershire
16 North Hampshire
17 South Hampshire
18 Hertfordshire
19 East Kent
20 West Kent
21 Lancashire
22 Leicestershire and Rutland
23 London
24 Greater Manchester
25 Merseyside
26 Northamptonshire
27 Nottinghamshire
28 Oxfordshire
29 Staffordshire
30 Surrey
31 East Sussex
32 West Sussex
33 Tyne and Wear and Northumberland
34 Warwickshire
35 Wiltshire
36 East Yorkshire and Northern Lincolnshire
37 North Yorkshire
38 South Yorkshire
39 West Yorkshire

How to order

The Philip's range of street atlases is available from good retailers or directly from the publisher by phoning 01933 443863

STREET ATLAS
West Kent

First published in 1994

Philip's, a division of
Octopus Publishing Group Ltd
2–4 Heron Quays, London E14 4JP

Second colour edition 2002
First impression 2002

ISBN 0-540-07982-0

© Philip's 2002

Ordnance Survey®

This product includes mapping data licensed
from Ordnance Survey® with the permission
of the Controller of Her Majesty's Stationery
Office. © Crown copyright 2002. All rights
reserved. Licence number 100011710

Contents

III **Key to map symbols**

IV **Key to map pages**

VI **Route planning**

VIII **Administrative and Postcode boundaries**

1 **Street maps** at 2½ inches to 1 mile

190 **Town maps** of Ashford, Canterbury, Dover
and Folkestone

192 **Index** of towns and villages

193 **Index** of streets, hospitals, industrial estates, railway
stations, schools, shopping centres and universities

Digital Data

The exceptionally high-quality mapping found in this atlas is available as digital data
in TIFF format, which is easily convertible to other bit mapped (raster) image formats.

The index is also available in digital form as a standard database table. It contains
all the details found in the printed index together with the National Grid reference
for the map square in which each entry is named and feature codes for places of
interest in eight categories such as education and health.

For fu... ...ease contact
Philip'... ...uk

C45796